PABLO
PICASSO

HIS LIFE AND TIMES

PABLO PICASSO

HIS LIFE AND TIMES

by PIERRE CABANNE

Translated from the French by Harold J. Salemson

WILLIAM MORROW AND COMPANY, INC. / NEW YORK / 1977

FIRST MORROW QUILL PAPERBACK EDITION 1979

Printed in the United States of America.

1   2   3   4   5   6   7   8   9   10

Library of Congress Cataloging in Publication Data

Cabanne, Pierre.
    Pablo Picasso.

    Translation of Le siècle de Picasso.
    Bibliography: p.
    Includes index.
    1. Picasso, Pablo, 1881-1973.   2. Painters—France-
Biography.
ND553.P5C2613   759.4 [B]   77-4984
ISBN 0-688-03232-X
ISBN 0-688-08232-7 pbk.
BOOK DESIGN   CARL WEISS

CONTENTS

CONTENTS

INTRODUCTION

IN A COLORFUL FARMHOUSE AT MOUGINS ON THE RIVIERA, POETICALLY named Notre-Dame-de-Vie (Our Lady of Life), behind high cypress-shaded walls, an old artist each day goes through the same motions. In over seventy-five years they have given birth to one of the most diversified and amazing, as well as controversial, bodies of work in the history of art.

This man, soon to die at ninety-two, hardly shows his great age; his features scarcely reveal the hard imprint of time beneath the patina of the smooth flat cheeks. Vanity demands, when he has a caller—or even more rarely, these days, when he allows himself to be photographed—that he present only the "good" profile, the right one, which is not marked by an unseemly brown patch. And, as best he can, he hides the fact that he is hard of hearing. These slight inconveniences aside, he is robust, active, and each day devotes long hours to his work, for, knowing that his days now are numbered, he thinks of neither amusement nor rest. He is Pablo Picasso.

Work is his whole existence on this superb estate, his last refuge after so many changes of location, from the first studio in Barcelona, on Calle de la Plata, to the hyperbaroque Cannes villa called La Californie. His life is shared with Jacqueline, the wife he married late in life, the silent but active vestal whose sacred beauty has been seen, in the most diverse of disguises, in so many paintings, and with just a few servants and intimates. There are very few visitors, mainly his dealers, or their agents. The telephone connects Don Pablo, as his Spanish friends call him, to the outside world, by way of Jacqueline or his secretary; they tell those who call, his son, nieces and nephews, or some of his friends, he is at work. That means he is well.

In his studios of Our Lady of Life, where he seems to fill all the rooms at once, from top to bottom, outbuildings and garage included, Don Pablo hardly leaves room to sit down, read, eat, or sleep. You have to clear piles of drawings, papers, letters, and catalogs from armchair or sofa; the table can be set only when the mess on it has been shifted elsewhere. No luxury or comfort; just Jacqueline's constant watchfulness. "She is the only woman who ever was able to lead him around by the nose," according to Totote Manolo, the sculptor's widow.

Picasso never felt any need to "settle"; all his life the gypsy part of him led him to maintain an unbelievable retinue of courtiers and hangers-on, now disbanded by Jacqueline, which he seemed to require. Those who never saw Don Pablo at a bullfight in southern France, in the 1950s, surrounded by women, children, nephews, Spaniards, followers and toadies, from the local Communist cell to the traditional gang of autograph hounds, by way of the pack of newsmen and photographers—jostled by the crowd, laughing, embracing one, joshing another in Catalan, scratching a drawing on a notebook held out by some anonymous arm, crushed, shoved, hailed, in a shower of cries, laughs, calls, all beneath the torrid sun—those who missed those mad days cannot picture Picasso, showman extraordinary. Now he is alone—and working.

He, who so deeply feared the shipwreck of old age, the progressive loss of faculties, died serenely, on April 8, 1973, at 11:40 A.M., with his wife close by. Grippe, for the past weeks, had kept him from his walks with Jacqueline in the garden of the estate . . .

Picasso witnessed, and often participated in, over seventy-five years of modern art. Symbolism, Modernism, Fauvism, Cubism, Dadaism, Surrealism, Abstract Expressionism came and went. He borrowed from this trend or that—except for Cubism, which he created—whatever he felt he could use. Starting from his compatriot Isidro Nonell, and the French Steinlen and Toulouse-Lautrec (the only artist he would have liked to know, he used to say), and ending up with Cézanne, all of his painterly existence paralleled that of Matisse, his friendly enemy (the only man he never stopped being worried about as long as he lived). When this rival's death eliminated that concern, Pablo took over from him: his constant identification with others was not the least of his behavioral paradoxes. The Spanish sculptor Fenosa several times heard him say, "I am God."

He worked every day. Creating? Innovating? No matter. In truth, he never much worried about being creative. "It is not what the artist does that counts, but what he is," he said.

That statement might have endeared him to the younger generation, if Picasso had not so long seemed to them to belong to the recent past of our cultural history: he was somebody in history books and dictionaries. Yet the fascination with him remained, as evidenced by the Picassos revised and corrected "technically" by the American pop artist Lichtenstein, or the *Funeral of the Anarchist Pinelli,* which Baj based on *Guernica.*

Articles about Picasso appear constantly in papers and magazines the world over, people come to see his works on the walls of the greatest museums, collectors and dealers keep a sharp eye out for the occasional item up for sale. Picasso shows are held everywhere, and his retrospectives in Paris, New York, London, and Zurich have displayed the breadth and multiplicity of an output any one of whose "periods" might be a lifetime's work for another artist. The 1967 retrospective at Paris' Grand and Petit Palais was seen by over a million and a half people, a figure unparalleled in Europe.

Death and Spain: these were the old man's two constant obsessions. Amazing how, through the centuries, in the whole pathetic history of the peninsula, these two themes have always been linked. Picasso thought of death as he thought of Spain, but the latter was permanently estranged from him, while each day brought death that much closer. Because a rebellious general had spelled death to his country by a merciless war won only through the aid of foreign fascism, Picasso decided never to return; ever since he lived in exile. His farewell to Spain, more than just an artistic masterpiece, is a cry of wrath and pity: *Guernica*. For in midafternoon of Sunday, April 26, 1937, Franco's Nazi allies for three hours bombed and strafed that peaceful little Basque city, sowing death . . .

Spain, Picasso's Spain, was the Calle de Montcada museum in Barcelona, to which he continually gave his works, many of them dedicated to the master's confidant, witness, buffer, and scapegoat, that man full of resignation and pride, Jaime Sabartés, one of Don Pablo's oldest friends, until his death in 1968. Spain was friends, exiles like himself, such as Manuel Pallarés, who, past ninety, still came to Mougins each year to see his schoolmate from Barcelona's School of Fine Arts, his companion of the long months spent in the Horta Mountains, painting and dreaming. He it was who had been asked by Don José Ruiz Blasco, Pablo's father, to get his son "back on the straight and narrow," when he first discovered that son's resistance to academic painterly training, and divined the revolts to come.

Spain was memories, the country of memory. Looking for Spain, Picasso had long frequented the bullfights throughout the French Midi and been a fan of Manitas de Plata's guitar.

But his Spain was also the Madrid art critic, José Maria Moreno Galvan, thrown into jail because, on October 25, 1971, the day Picasso turned ninety, he publicly paid tribute to the greatest living Spanish painter, even though it was officially forbidden. As the police were clubbing him, students shouted, "Picasso! Liberty!"—the same words with which Catalan students had hailed Paul Éluard when, a few months before the outbreak of the Civil War, he came to Barcelona to speak about his friend Pablo's painting.

In his final years the Minotaur was to be nothing but an old tomcat, though still knowing how to use the phallus-shaped dagger the man-bull had sported on the cover of the first issue of *Minotaure* magazine. And, with unfailing mastery, he continued to spring his surprises, to such a degree that in the breathtaking abundance of his production none would note the growing lack of inventiveness, the dryness, the mechanization. While young artists were turning away from picture painting, Don Pablo continued the somewhat empty comedy of using brush and colors on canvas or paper to present musketeers, clowns, maternities, or erotic scenes. But the amazing thing was that, without any new vein or any constraint either, as naturally as could be, all these paintings, gouaches, watercolors, drawings, etchings constituted a celebration—a paean of love and liberty, an irresistible hymn to life.

And, thus, a defiance of death.

Just as there were various periods in his work, Pablo put on different masks; there was not one Picasso but several, and that is what most clearly emerges from the testimony of those who knew, heard, and studied him. His early companions are all dead, except for Manuel Pallarés, whom I met several times in Barcelona: his memory, for certain facts, remains amazing. Sabartés lived until 1968, but it was scarcely possible to accept the veracity of his statements, since so often he had been in on the very creation of the Picasso legend, which Pablo himself had fostered—both out of love for storytelling and because of a turn of his mind, so profoundly Spanish with its imagination based on rejection of or flight from reality, preferring the arbitrary. Sabartés, faithful to a fault, went right along.

Jean Cassou sees two notions making up this arbitrariness: *gana* and *capricho*. The former, he says, means a desire to do, or more often not to do, something; and as reference he cites Angel Ganivet's *Idearium español,* of 1897, which defines the "juridical ideal" of his countrymen as:

> All Spaniards will carry in their pockets an identification card with a single clause couched in these short, clear, and peremptory terms: The above-mentioned Spaniard is hereby authorized to do whatever pops into his head (*todo lo que de la gana*).

Picasso, Spanish to his very marrow: Cassou wanted to call him a "caricature of the Spaniard." He not only carried the virtues and faults of his people to their extremes, but also the differences between them and the virtues and faults of other men belonging to different peoples. His genius lies not only in his work, but also in his manner of being the most *castizo* of Spaniards: at every instant he determines to overcome what he is, his blood boiling with the irresistible *furia* for every struggle, an eminently *castiza* tendency sublimated by the heroic sense of existence. To live is to act; to multiply one's acts, even if incomprehensible or bizarre; *to do,* to go as far and as high as possible in what Don Quixote calls *hazaña:* feat and exploit, derring-do.

There is no common measure between Picasso and such eminently moralistic and disciplined creators as Kandinsky, Duchamp, Mondrian, or Malevitch; as the last great painter of the nineteenth century, whose longevity carried him almost to the threshold of the twenty-first, he is at opposite poles from these twentieth-century inventors whom he passed near while hardly noticing them. No one ever knew what he thought of them, and perhaps he did not think of them at all: Pablo did not have to compare his message with theirs, to confront it, or effect a give-and-take as he did with Braque, Léger, the Surrealists, and most especially Matisse. His painting resolves itself only into itself; it influenced no one and did not carry within it the slightest share of the future. It was a sort of ideal prison in which the artist, closeted alone with his works, was convinced he was sufficient unto himself.

Was he wrong? No matter.

Only one thing could he do nothing about: time.

Any who tried to get an explanation or comment from him about his work or behavior met a blank wall; in over seventy years as a painter there are only three or four interviews or statements of his worth taking seriously, all the rest being jokes, paradoxes, pirouettes, or contradictions, from the famous "Negro art? Never heard of it!" of 1920 to the final confidences made to his barber or his physician.

It is rare for well-known artists to avoid conversational exchanges: from Matisse to Kandinsky, Léger to Duchamp, Mondrian to Pollock, all agreed to them, sometimes even sought them out. Picasso left a blank. After talking to Christian Zervos at Boisgeloup in 1935, he refused to check the proofs of the text to be published in *Cahiers d'Art,* saying that what mattered most was the enthusiasm, anyway.

"How many people," Picasso asked, "read Homer? Yet everybody talks about him. This is how the Homeric superstition was created."

And, abetted by Sabartés and a few others, he went about creating the Picassian superstition. Which is why he was totally indifferent to everything written about him, every statement attributed to him. . . . Just another way of being free.

Not wishing to yield his inner self, it often happened that, when approached, he substituted something colorful: so we have pictures of him without a shirt, going swimming, playing with his children, pushing their carriages, aping a religious procession as he shields Françoise Gilot with a huge beach umbrella, wearing a mask with Jacques Prévert, or playing cowboys with Gary Cooper. After Henri-Georges Clouzot and his camera, no one ever saw him at work again; that film was the only public confession Picasso ever agreed to make. Once and for all. But, the way it was done, you could not understand much about his way of painting; audiences saw nothing but finger exercises, and believed once again that he was putting them on. Perhaps not entirely untrue . . .

Besides, the moving picture was called *Le Mystère Picasso* (The Picasso Mystery).

Over a thousand works have been written, around the world, about Don Pablo; some are remarkable, almost all hail the genius of the artist who first broke with classic tradition and opened modern art to new conquests. Very few analyze the slowing down of the creative process after World War II, although this happened to be the period of his widest acceptance and his worldwide glory. True, it was also the period of his most unbelievable metamorphoses, his most unexpected paradoxes, imaginings, and caprices. The very last act of the show, before the final asbestos curtain. All the comings and goings of Don Pablo were known, recorded, hailed; the least of his wisecracks repeated, admired; any bit of a sketchlet acclaimed a masterpiece; his paintings fetched astronomical prices . . .

But is the old master of Mougins better "known" for that—he whose final decision was the humble submission of vassal to lord: that he be buried at the foot of Ste.-Victoire Mountain? For it was there that modern painting was born, in the pictures that scene inspired in Paul Cézanne, of whom Picasso said, "To us, he was like a mother protecting her children."

PABLO PICASSO

HIS LIFE AND TIMES

I

THE CHILDHOOD
OF A
PAINTER
(1881–1895)

ONE EVENING IN OCTOBER 1881, DR. SALVADOR RUIZ BLASCO WAS
rushing through Málaga's Plaza de la Merced toward one of the huge
Cases de Campos apartment buildings, in which his sister-in-law María,
the wife of the painter, was about to be delivered. As usual in Spain, the
whole family was there, chattering and carrying on. Her husband, Don José Ruiz
Blasco, familiarly nicknamed Pepe, a tall thin man with a fine face sporting a
blond beard, could not hold still. But things calmed down when the doctor arrived and took charge. The child, born with great difficulty at 11:15 P.M., October
25, was a boy, their firstborn after a year of marriage.

Three days later he was registered at the city hall under the names of Pablo
Diego José Francisco de Paula Juan Nepomuceno Cipriano de la Santissima Trini-
dad, son of José Ruiz Blasco, painter, teacher at the San Telmo School of Arts
and Crafts, age thirty-one, and Doña María Picasso y Lopez, his spouse, age
twenty-six, "concerned with preoccupations proper to her sex." The boy would
make his mother's name famous the world over, as the most important and controversial painter of the twentieth century: Pablo Picasso.

He was always amused by the details of his birth: for a few minutes, he was
thought to be stillborn. Uncle Salvador was desperate—until suddenly the baby
began to move.

"Doctors in those days," Picasso would say, "smoked fat cigars. My uncle did
too. And he blew his smoke in my face. I puckered up and started to cry."

Pablo was baptized on November 10 at the parish church of Santiago el Mayor.
The Christian names already recorded were increased with that of his godmother,
Doña María de los Remedios Alarcon y Herrera. The godfather was a lawyer,
Juan Nepomuceno Blasco y Barroso; the baby already had his name.

The name of Picasso was not foreign to Málaga, for during one of the *pro-*

nunciamientos earlier in the century, General José Lachambre had bombed his native city so recklessly that homes were hit, including theirs, as recorded in a local satirical ditty. His mother must often have told Pablo how the terrified family took refuge in the kitchen, where they saw a piece of flaming shrapnel come down the chimney—to die in the hearth without doing any harm.

As dark as her husband was blond, and typically Andalusian, Doña María had the strangely mobile sharp black eye that her son inherited, and she had a great influence on him, for as mother and son they were very close, whereas Don José, given to melancholy, unstable, neurotic, and disappointed by life (he died at age seventy-three in 1913), always remained somewhat aloof, and, for all that they denied it, the two looked upon him with a bit of pity. Indeed, in many ways, even to his son Don José was always to remain an enigmatic figure.

One day at Antibes in 1923, Picasso's mother was introduced to Gertrude Stein; despite the language barrier, since Doña María spoke only Spanish, they understood each other well enough to drown the painter in the most excessive compliments. Miss Stein extolled his handsomeness when she first met him in 1905, only to be told, "it was nothing compared to his looks when he was a boy. He was an angel and a devil in beauty; no one could cease looking at him!"

This is indeed borne out by his childhood photos, so striking in the regularity of features and the wild yet tender depth of his almost wide-eyed stare already seeming to want to go beyond appearances. One shows him in his Sunday best, hair well combed and plastered down over the right eye, wearing a vermilion suit with gold buttons, bronze-colored shoes, and a white collar and bow.

Three years after him, on an evening in December 1884, his sister Lola was born, in circumstances that would be hard to forget. Don José was chatting with friends in the rear of a pharmacist's shop, when a sudden temblor sent the shelves of medicine bottles to the floor. The startled men ran out, to find the people in panic, shouting, "Earthquake!" The painter, his wife in the ninth month, rushed home.

"My mother was wearing a kerchief on her head," Pablo would later tell his friend Sabartés. "I had never seen her like that. My father grabbed his cape from the rack, threw it over himself, picked me up in his arms, and wound me in its folds, leaving only my head exposed." *

The family, including the maternal grandmother and two aunts who lived with them, was fortunately able to take refuge in the better-protected home of a close friend, painter Antonio Muñoz Degrain, then away in Rome. They were less concerned, then, with earth movements than with the condition of Doña María, who gave birth on Christmas night to a little girl named Dolores, after her godmother, the painter's wife, Doña María de los Dolores de Muñoz Degrain, later nicknamed Lola or Lolita.

The Ruiz Blasco family goes back to the fourteenth century, descended from one Juan de León. He and his progeny, who settled in Córdoba, were gentlemen of means who owned much land; their lineage continued till the appearance of

* Jaime Sabartés, *Picasso: An Intimate Portrait*, translated from the Spanish by Angel Flores (New York: Prentice-Hall, Inc., 1948).

Picasso, four years old

the name of Ruiz, then Ruiz Blasco, although we have no explanation of how one of the branches of the de Leóns acquired this name.

Beginning with Don Gaspár Ruiz, in 1720, Picasso's ancestry is clear. Don Gaspár's grandson, José Ruiz y de Fuentes, married María Josefa de Almoguera y Gonzalez, who gave birth to eight children, bearing, as was customary, the matronym after the patronym. Don José Ruiz was the first to settle in Málaga, where the family continued to prosper; one of the eight children, Diego Ruiz y Almoguera, married María de la Paz Blasco y Echeverria, who in turn bore eleven Ruiz Blascos. These were Pablo's grandparents, whom he never knew.

Don Diego Ruiz y de Almoguera owned a factory in Málaga producing gloves and other leather goods, in addition to handling the finances of several wealthy families of the city; he also got paid for playing double bass in the city theater's orchestra.

Picasso's grandfather was also given to drawing, but there seems no reason to see in that a basis for the choice of a career by one of his eleven children, José, ninth in line, who was to father the painter of *Guernica.* The eldest of the family, Diego, a career diplomat, won some little note as a portraitist. The fourth child, Pablo, a doctor of theology and canon of the cathedral of Málaga, did his best, when the father died, to take care of two unmarried sisters, Josefa and Matilda, as well as younger brother José. In addition to emotional instability and day-dreaming, the latter's tendency toward dilettantism considerably worried the canon.

Don José, as Picasso was to tell Gertrude Stein, looked "like an Englishman," and was known as "The Englishman" to his friends in Málaga, for like a Briton he was distinguished, reserved, had a somewhat cool humor and almost feminine grace. Mentally as well as physically, Don José was truly an "artist," in the fullest sense of the term; he liked to spend time at the Café Chinitas with local Bohemians, and listen to the aesthetic discussions at the country home of his painter friend Ferrandiz at Barcenillas.

The good canon felt better when his brother expressed his love for a wellborn young lady of the city, and did his best to see the marriage to conclusion, but just before it was to take place he died suddenly, at age forty-seven, in October 1878, leaving Don José to take care of the two spinster sisters. This was a terrible blow to the young man, in no way equipped for such adversity. His brother, his staunch guide and support, had encouraged him through all his doubts to go on with his painting, certainly a laudable attitude on his part, since in those days conservative and clerical circles saw all artists as anarchists or rakes.

Now having to feed two more mouths, would Don José be able to support a family on his teaching salary and the occasional sale of a few pictures? Would he not be forced to give up painting, in which he had shown a faith, a determination, and a passion that had warranted the approval and encouragement of the late canon? Pepe had to break with the girl he loved and wanted to marry. All his life he would regret this. Forsaking the Bohemian life, he would turn somber of nature and feel sure he had failed as a painter, transferring all his dreams and ambitions to his son.

Two years after these tragic events, Pepe met a young cousin, María Picasso y Lopez and forthwith asked for her hand in marriage. Small, dark, and plumpish, María was twenty-five. Her vivacious nature was very good for her husband, restoring some of his mirth and self-confidence. Pablo was to inherit her strong body and her decisiveness and generosity, as well as her temper and sudden changes of mood.

Matteo Picasso, a Genoese portrait painter, born at Recco in 1794, seems significant to those who, because of the double *s* in the name, claim Italian origin for the mother's family. It has never been proved, but Pablo was interested in this hypothetical relative, since his mother's father had also been born near Recco. He owned a small portrait of a man by Matteo Picasso who, in his later years, turned to painting flowers, birds, and mythological or historical scenes, and died two years before Pablo was born.

Sabartés, wildly against any idea of Italian extraction, discovered in the seventeenth-century *Chronicle of King Don Pedro of Castille* a Moorish prince named Picasso, thus opening new suggestions of African ancestry.

The fact is, both sides of the family were Spanish, New Castilian in one line, Andalusian in the other, which predominated. He was Spanish to his marrow, bound to the land of shadow and fire from which his people had sprung, to its anguish, its passion, and its doubts. From his half-peasant, half-bourgeois stock, he got their virtues, their love of the land which never faltered despite a voluntary exile that death alone would end, marked by three years of civil war, confirmed by his choice of Barcelona as the location for his museum which he never ceased enriching with his donations. He spent twenty-three years in his native land, till 1904, when he settled in Paris; from 1904 to 1936, a number of visits, notably to Barcelona; and after the establishment of the Franco régime, exile to the end of his days.

Life in Málaga at the end of the century in which Spain had seen so many upheavals—wars, riots, military uprisings, coups, and even eleven months as a republic—was uneventful. The big provincial capital seemed happy. The sky was admirably clear; the unusually mild weather attracted many winter tourists, mainly British. Thanks to the commercialization of its famous wine, huge fortunes had sprung up, gorgeous villas been built surrounded by gardens full of magnificent trees and tropical flowers, completely transforming the residential quarters—in contrast to the sordid slums, especially the one known as *Chupa y Tira* (Suck and Throw), hard by the citadel.

"The people there were so poor," Picasso explained, "that all they had to eat was cockle soup. The field behind them was full of empty shells that the people sucked [*chupa*] clean and then threw [*tira*] out the windows."

Plaza de la Merced was at the center of the old city; it was full of people and animation, with pigeons constantly flying through. Pensioners dozed beneath the plane trees, children played around the statue commemorating General Torrijos and his men who, in 1831, raised the banner of liberal revolt, and were shot. For Málaga, beneath its calm exterior, was a rebellious city, whose inhabitants traditionally had "advanced ideas." Eleven years before Torrijos, another general named Riego had risen against royal absolutism, and been hanged. The Malagueños had not forgotten.

Picasso always liked talking about his childhood and life in Málaga. He spoke most fondly of Don José, even though his mother was much closer to him. But his father had been a painter and, despite his academicism, had a great influence on him. "Every time I draw a man," he would say, "I think of my father. To me, man is Don José, and will be all my life . . ."

With the family growing, after Lola's birth, household costs increased. Fortunately, in addition to teaching at San Telmo, Don José also became curator of the municipal museum, meaning it was his job to restore deteriorated paintings. He also sold a picture of his own from time to time. These various incomes were rounded out with the home handiwork of the spinster aunts, Elodia and Heliodora, who produced gilt chevrons and braid for caps and tunics of railway and municipal uniforms.

Don José had set up a studio in the museum, "a room," his son would recall, "like any other, nothing special; and perhaps a little dirtier than the one he had at home. But he was undisturbed there."

The wind from the sea gave impetus to daydreams: over there, beyond the Mediterranean, was Africa, the desert, adventure. The port was equally alive with singsong Arab music and gypsy flamenco—and everywhere, like a haunting breath, there was the *cante jondo,* that cry turned song that the Andalusian Federico García Lorca turned into the very rhythm of the people's life, for "it comes from faraway races beyond the graveyards of years and the withered leaves of the winds." Picasso once told Cocteau of seeing "a streetcar conductor singing and reducing or increasing the speed of the tram as the rhythm of the song slowed or sped up, while ringing his bell in cadence."

The seashore at the end of the century was still wild; grapevines ran right down to the edge, and everywhere there were gardens with exotic scents and the buzz of fountains and birds; a real paradise for the privileged of the earth. There it was that, as an adolescent, he was first kissed by glory.

Apart from Antonio Muñoz Degrain and Bernardo Ferrandiz, both come from Valencia to decorate the Cervantes Theatre and now settled in Málaga, Don José's friends were mainly young local painters, Moreno Carbonero and José Denis Belgrano, noisy and idealistic like him, but hardly rebellious in their conventionally academic work; adventurous only in lighting, color, matter. The Impressionist revolution had not yet touched these faraway provincials.

The School of Málaga (as they were somewhat pretentiously known) would have been no-different from other pictorial movements of backward late-nineteenth-century Spain, had not a naturalized Belgian, Carlos de Haës, who had lived in the city since childhood, created modern Spanish landscape painting. He was, indeed, the first to paint directly "from nature," and when he exhibited his Málaga landscapes in Madrid in 1856, their sensitive renderings of the open air made such an impression that he was immediately hired to teach at the San Fernando Academy. He carried great weight with the Malagueño painters, who imitated his study of nature. The leader in this was Muñoz Degrain, who was

Don José Ruiz' closest friend and greatly influenced him. The families saw a lot of each other, and his father often took young Pablo to the master's studio.

Don José's friends exhibited in Madrid with some success, but he plodded on with his meticulous still lifes, precisely realistic, showing wild game, birds, or flowers, usually lilacs. These were his specialty, with a certain preference for pigeons. "Father painted dining-room pictures, with partridges and pigeons, hares and rabbits. Every hair and every feather," Pablo would later say.

One huge oil that he especially remembered was a pigeon coop, "with hundreds of pigeons. Thousands of pigeons. Millions of pigeons. Thousands and millions." In retrospect, Pablo often liked to exaggerate, to adduce figures that grew in his fertile mind. "They were lined up in the coop—this enormous coop. It's in the Málaga Museum; I've never seen it again" (there are nine birds in all).

Picasso remembered the sudden flights of pigeons from the leafy trees of Plaza de la Merced, their cooings, and the endless droppings they scattered about. He also remembered the fierce and often unexpected tempers of his fellow Malagueños, despite their addiction to daydreaming, and their noisy passionate love of the bullfights to which his father took him at the bullring just outside the Gibralfaro citadel, facing the sea. Don José was a true aficionado, and he passed his love of the arena on to his son.

Don José fitted in well here, and his son would watch him work, or go to the museum with him. Doña María said the first syllables Pablo uttered were *piz, piz,* immediately translated as *lapiz* (pencil). He himself was more prosaic about it: "I learned to walk by pushing a tin of crackers around, because I knew what was in it"—adding that it was at least a foot and a half high.

Don José's son, from the beginning, was inventive, stubborn, and highly independent; he seems also to have had very good practical sense. Hours on end he drew arabesques that, he said, suggested a sugar cake called *torruela.* He often talked about this time of his life, as some object, event, or word triggered memory. Picasso actually "saw" his childhood when he talked about it: he unreeled the film of his life the same way he painted; his creative impulses grew out of a shock, an idea, a memory. He told a story just the way he started a picture, from any point in it; then he would drop it, start another, yet another, and come back to the first. The amazing tales his grandmother told him, the bullfights his father took him to, the latter's painter friends and his pictures with the countless pigeons, the night processions of Holy Week, and the midsummer *feria* with its songs, dances, and flags flapping in the wind, the ladies' elegant dresses, walks with Uncle Antonio Suarez and his girl cousins whom he amazed one day by producing a sparrow from beneath his jacket, all of this and more mingled with the memory of Uncle Perico, as Brother Pedro de Cristo was familiarly known, and the mystery surrounding his mother's father. Don Francisco Picasso Guardeno had died in Cuba, where he was customs administrator in Havana, but his family learned of his death only some fifteen years later. This grandfather he never knew was a legendary character of Pablo's childhood. The baggage he had sent to Málaga before sailing away and disappearing was in the attic and no one dared open it.

However, his father's pictures were what left the deepest impression. He could still describe them, after all those years, albeit embroidering or multiplying the number of pigeons. He was wide awake, and recorded whatever he heard or saw, storing up shapes, colors, and images. Imagination took over from there.

Pablo did not like school. After a few months in the public school, his father enrolled him at the private Colegio San Rafaelo, the best in the city, whose principal was a friend. Despite the level of teaching and the principal's special interest, the painter-to-be would not study. He fought every morning against going to school; a sturdy servant, Carmen Mendoza, was entrusted with the job, and often had to resort to force. Pablo refused to go, unless he was allowed to take along one of the pigeons his father used as models; in school, the teacher let him raise the lid of his desk and set the bird up behind it, to draw peacefully, shielded from the others. But even this was not enough to keep him quiet: he would go over to the window and knock on it to attract the attention of passersby.

Picasso liked to exaggerate this misbehavior later. Since in the public school he had caught a "kidney disease" (probably intestinal flu), he was wrongly considered "sickly," when in fact he was the picture of health, and made the most of it. He pretended to be indisposed, or demanded his father take him to school personally. Besides the pigeon, he begged him to let him take along his cane or his paintbrushes.

"I was sure that if he left the cane, he would come back for it," he later told Sabartés. "But the pigeon or brushes were even better, because he couldn't get along without them."

Sometimes he left the classroom without permission to go into the principal's living quarters. His wife was especially attractive—"I followed her around like a puppy," he laughed later.

And, of course, he learned next to nothing.

Like all children, he drew and painted. But his father was an artist, and he saw painters every day, people who, in dress, behavior, and tone, were different from others, spoke loudly and violently, denouncing, name-calling, prophesying. As for their pictures . . . It was mainly his father's which, from the first, made an impression. Pigeons and lilacs. But their visits to Ferrandiz' studio, too, and watching Carbonero paint among the bullfighters right in the ring . . .

He could draw for hours on end, if not disturbed. If his cousins were there, he would show off for them, drawing what they wanted, starting where they said—and the line would take off and go to its conclusion, as if by miracle, before the little girls' wonder-filled eyes. This gift of starting at a point and carrying the line around to the end, without hesitation or return for correction, was peculiar to Don José's son. "As if he were going over something traced earlier," as Sabartés put it.

From the Málaga period there is a Picasso *Toreador on Horseback* in gleaming yellow, caracoling in the bullring. It was the future painter's first oil painting, at age eight, and he kept it. The quality of the warm tones is surprising, the gift of observation no less amazing, and, despite childish awkwardness, there is a very lively spontaneity of line, stroke, rhythm, and harmony. The eyes of the three characters, one woman and two men, have holes in them. "My sister made them with a nail," Picasso explained. "How old could she have been at the time? Five or six?"

At nine, he drew the pigeons and the bullfight scene—with a row of doves up above—now in the Picasso Museum at Barcelona. The drawing of a plaster cast, from November 1890, is amazing in its decisiveness, a statue of Hercules with his club that was in his father's studio . . . "It was not a child's drawing," Picasso said. "It was really a drawing of Hercules with his club. Strange—I never did children's drawings. Never."

But this happy period was about to end. The city of Málaga decided to review its payroll and did away with the job of museum curator. Don José lost both the extra income and the studio. He complained, but to no avail. Then he offered to carry on the work at the museum without pay until after the next election, hoping that the new city council might reestablish the position and even pay him the arrears. The offer was turned down; Don José, offended, requested a transfer. On April 4, 1891, he was named professor of figure and ornamental drawing at the Provincial Fine Arts School of La Coruña, at the other end of Spain. He accepted without a thought for the psychological consequences of this change in status; he took his wife and three children along, but the grandmother and aunts stayed on in Málaga. That many fewer mouths to feed.

Thereby, Don José made a break with a city, a world he loved, a milieu of friends and established habits. His wife, too, was very attached to Málaga, where she had always lived, had been married, and where her children had been born, and life, despite financial problems, offered no grave difficulties. She and her husband had brothers and sisters, and relatives there; Uncle Salvador came running as soon as a child coughed or ran a fever; and Don José occasionally found a customer for a painting.

La Coruña was in Galicia, a city not without charm, what with its active port, picturesque old neighborhoods overlooking the sea, and fine gardens, but the Ruizes knew no one there. Besides, the Galician character, calculating and secretive, was the opposite from the Andalusian, exuberant, generous, with a backdrop of melancholy expressed in popular songs and music. The climate was humid and foggy, and the vegetation too was different from that on the Andalusian coast. Fortunately, Don José was able to find an apartment near where he taught, at 14 Calle Payo Gomez; they moved in in a dull mood, following a sea voyage so stormy that they had to land at Vigo and finish the trip by train.

September 1891: As soon as they arrived, Don José enrolled his son at the Instituto da Guarda, of which the School of Fine Arts occupied the ground floor. Pablo's total lack of interest in study persisted.

To cap the misfortune, little Conchita—María de la Concepción—barely four years old, contracted diphtheria and died on January 5, 1895. This loss in a strange city was a terrible blow to the whole family. Don José felt it the more because of all the children she was the only one who looked like him.

Pablo was now ten. He also felt displaced, the climate in La Coruña weighed heavily on him, he closed in on himself; he went on drawing and painting, but his father no longer encouraged him, and his father's depression only incited him, too, to lose interest. Don José was scarcely working. Mostly, Pablo recalled, "he just watched the rain outside the window."

Yet he was concerned about Pablo's education; he and Doña María, back in Málaga, had worried over the child's lag in his studies, had tried to get a professor they knew to take special charge of him. But it had not done much good.

In October 1892, he was enrolled in the drawing and decoration class of the School of Fine Arts, while continuing to go to the Institute. In 1893–1894, he was in the figure drawing class, and in 1894–1895 in what was then called "plaster, copy of ancient," meaning drawing from antique statues. His report-card marks for these courses were respectively *sobresaliente con accessit* and twice *sobresaliente,* or excellent, the first with additional honorable mention. For the last course in figures from the antique, he took the examination on March 29, 1895, because his father had been named to a position at the School of Fine Arts in Barcelona; but, despite Don José's departure, the Ruiz family stayed on at La Coruña till the summer vacation. Since March 1, Pablo had been enrolled in the studio for painting and copying from nature.

The plasters drawn in school—faun's head, bust, arm and hand holding a stick, bas-relief of cupids, and so on—were done diligently according to the institutional academic method that so-called teaching of the fine arts has made interchangeable. No personality, no plastic research, but studied perfection according to imposed principles. By contrast, outside of school, Pablo gave free rein to his inventiveness, his fantasy, and his great variety of inspiration. A drawing of two pigeons near a nest and rabbits with a tuft of flowers shows that these animals still fascinated him; they had come over from Don José's conventional pictures to the nervous drawings of his son, who would make turtledoves, pigeons, and doves his lifelong companions and models.

There are some more casual pencil sketches of bullfights, dated 1892, as well as a monkey attacking some dogs, perhaps based on some story or news item. Already, in these drawings, Pablo was keeping his diary.

But mainly there is one small painting signed P. Ruiz, dated 1893, of a little yellow-and-pink house, in white light, against a sky with heavy running clouds. It is an "on-the-spot" thing full of the same freshness and charm as in the *Group of Children, Little Girl Sitting,* or landscapes painted at the same period around La Coruña. They show the adolescent's bent for the direct study of reality.

There are many lively, happy drawings from the same time; Pablo drew on either detached sheets or pads; the Barcelona Picasso Museum has seventeen such sketchbooks, all from La Coruña, with extremely varied subjects, including many portraits of those close to him. One of them includes two heads of little Conchita probably done in October or November 1894, two or three months before she died. His father, his mother, Lola were often sketched, then drawn more carefully, more seriously, and the psychological expression of these portraits is often amazing. Scribblings and brief notations made as the pen dashed on are evidence not only of Pablo's amazing curiosity, but his quickness to satisfy it; he was always ready, pen in hand, as others at the same age would later keep their cameras ready to catch candid shots of life.

Predominant concerns in his drawings were old people, hands, and women. The first was to occasion an oil study, probably of 1894, *Two Old People* (now in the Málaga Museum)—an old man leaning on his cane whispering to an old blind woman—in which we already find humanity's haunting fear: fear of old age, or decay and death. A *Bearded Man wih Cap, Man in a Béret,* and studies of heads of old people (now in the Picasso Museum, Barcelona) were also done in 1894–1895; his taste for old and humble people, his sort of *misérabilisme* (accent on the poor) recurs in several other works of that period. Two interior paintings at the home of Dr. Ramón Perez Costales, the family friend who took care of little Conchita during her illness, show how attentive Pablo was to the slightest detail of the well-to-do overfurnished apartment, catching its heavily "bourgeois" character with heavy applications of ochers and browns set off with vermilion or garnet. The unctuous whites are not without their spice.

Soberly and robustly realistic, these Galician works contrast sharply with the academicism practiced in Spain at the end of the century; they are reminiscent of what Van Gogh painted at Nuenen when he was starting.

The pigeons recurred once or twice. "My father cut off the feet of a dead pigeon. He pinned them to a board in proper position, and I copied them in detail until he was satisfied." And the studies of hands also seem to have been guided by paternal advice. "In the hands is where you see the [artist's] hand, my father used to say," as he later told Sabartés.

After Conchita's death, Don José was ready to leave La Coruña; his wife, despite her deep sorrow, could cope with the tragedy, but not he. He applied for a transfer in February and, on March 17, 1895, was given royal consent to trade places with a colleague in Barcelona who wanted to return to his hometown of La Coruña. At the Barcelona School of Fine Arts his salary was to be three thousand pesetas.

This move did not satisfy Don José, who requested another transfer, to Palma de Mallorca, but without success. He was very disappointed, for while the great Catalonian capital represented a considerable promotion, the overpopulated, noisy port city, where he knew no one, scared him. Mallorca seemed a kind of quiet retreat with a provincial ambience reminiscent of Málaga.

Don José did not wait until school reopened in October 1895, when his family moved to Barcelona, to take over the new job; he began it six months earlier, on April 16. But he became sick as soon as he got there and forthwith got a leave, during which he again tried to engineer a move, again without success, and reported for work in June. At the end of the school year, a few weeks later, he returned to La Coruña, and the whole family went to spend their vacation at Málaga, delighted to be shed of the Galician port with its ugly memories.

Picasso's La Coruña production is not only remarkable for its abundance and the variety of his inspiration; as during his whole life, he worked in all techniques, pencil, pen, watercolor, oil, at unbelievable speed, at times filling a whole

Picasso at fifteen, in 1896

(HOLMES-LEBEL)

sketch pad in a few days. His hand never failed the extraordinary mobility of his eye. But it was at La Coruña that one day Don José turned his brushes over to his son. With this dramatic, and not unimpressive, gesture, he was accepting Pablo's mastery. As his son later several times said, "He then gave me his paints and brushes, and never painted again."

Was Pablo conscious of the responsibility he now had: to use his father's brushes for a body of work that in size and quality would vindicate his father's life through his own? The father, who had had many students and learned how to judge them, to tell real promise when he saw it, knew he was making no mistake. And to prove the point, he would never paint again; he was the melancholy man of whom, with unconscious cruelty but an unerring sense of observation, his son was to make such atrocious portraits, and who through him would have the most bitter of disillusionments.

For Don José did make a mistake. Pablo was to renounce his teaching and his example. The brushes he gave him would be used to contradict everything that, in the father's eyes, had spelled nobility and greatness in his life as painter and professor. Pablo's would be a different ambition; his success would owe nothing to academic teaching. And it was just because he turned his back on him that Picasso was original and became what Don José had never been able to be: a creator.

The younger man seems to have had an amazing premonition of how his father was going to suffer, in silence, over his own choice; the portraits show a wounded man, painfully resigned to his fate, a fallen man, in whose look there is still an ardent flame, but whose body seems emptied of strength, of any ardor for life. From year to year, as Pablo went from conquest to conquest, beginning in 1897–1898, Don José was to sink into a silent reproof that would create an unbridgeable gulf between his son and himself. And if he had ever expected Pablo to make the name Ruiz famous and respected as he had been unable to, his disappointment would be no less bitter: it was his mother's name, Picasso, not the father's that his son would emblazon around the world.

Where did Pablo get the facility, the curiosity, the sense of observation so evident in his huge La Coruña output? Not from his father or the latter's very academic friends. Dr. Juan Ainaud de Lasarte, Director of Barcelona Museums, showed me a notebook of sketches by a Galician painter, Isidoro Brocas Gomez, one of Picasso's teachers at La Coruña; leafing through it, one cannot miss the similarity of line, observation, and subject—so great that one might mistake the master's drawings for the pupil's.

Did Brocas Gomez give this sketchbook, done in Paris in 1856, or others like it, to Picasso? With his extraordinary facility of adaptation, did Pablo take over his teacher's style and subjects? Perhaps, and if so, it would be the first evidence of the "science of legitimate larceny," as Goethe called it, he was to practice with such virtuosity and audacity all his life.

When not drawing, he wrote. Writing and drawing all his life long would be the same to him. Not liking to write letters, he found a way to tell Uncle Salvador and the family back in Málaga about life in La Coruña: a newspaper. A popular journal of the day was called *Blanco y Negro;* he called his, a single sheet of paper folded over, first *La Coruña,* then *Azul y Blanco.* The masthead announced publication every Sunday. Articles and drawings, signed "P. Ruiz, *el director,"* or "Pin Pan Pun," were as always under his alert pen full of imagination and caricatural bite. The rain, fog, and grayness of La Coruña were among his favorite subjects. Showing heavily bundled-up women dipping their feet cautiously in the water, Pablo captioned: "How people bathe at Betanzos" (a small nearby beach); or elsewhere: "The rain has begun. It will go on till summer." He was to have a lifelong aversion to that kind of weather, and even for the people of such hostile climates. "The wind is blowing and will go on blowing till La Coruña blows away" was yet another caption.

Back in Málaga he especially liked the Tower of Hercules, the only Roman lighthouse left on the Iberian coast. Restored and still operating, it was a favorite joke of the Ruizes; Don José, because of its color, called it the Caramel Tower. So Pablo drew it in his paper, on a tray, titled "Sketch for a Caramel Tower."

Sabartés once said to Ainaud de Lasarte: "Picasso keeps everything; some day his first-communion outfit may turn up in one of his studios." The Barcelona director, visiting Mougins, repeated that to the painter, who replied: "No, not the first-communion outfit. The diocese of La Coruña insisted we dress as cardinals or bishops, and rented us the costumes. I made mine as a bishop!"

Vacationing at Málaga, Pablo took his paintings and drawings to show the family. Uncle Salvador loved them, and was sure his nephew would soon be famous; he not only awarded him a stipend of five pesetas a day as long as he was in town, but also allowed him to use as a studio one of the rooms at the port's Health Inspection Bureau, which he directed. He even got him a model, an old sailor named Saramon, whose portrait he knocked off in quick time, to the amazement and mild dismay of his benefactor-uncle.

Remembering the sea trip to La Coruña, the Ruizes came back to Andalusia by train. Don José decided to stop off in Madrid and show his son the Prado Museum. And with commentaries from his father, Pablo saw the Goyas, Grecos, Zurbaráns, Velázquezes, all the masters of Spain's realistic and epic tradition. He was fourteen; he had grown, put on weight, become somewhat stocky; his features were still as regular as ever beneath the crewcut hair, and the dark eye even more intense, with something both dreamy and hard about it.

In Málaga, Uncle Salvador asked him to do a portrait of Aunt Pepa, nickname of Josefa Ruiz Blasco, his sister and Don José's, an eccentric old maid whose sudden manias amused her family. After living with her brother the canon, since his death she had a small lodging at Don Salvador's, full of religious objects and images from the late cleric's oratory. She kept his memory faithfully alive, spending long hours in prayer at home or at the cathedral; nor did she ever miss any of the ceremonies which in earlier days it had been her great pleasure to watch her brother perform.

Naturally, Aunt Pepa would not hear of posing for Pablo; she always said no to everything asked of her. The boy himself insisted, but it did no good. Yet, one day during the following summer (1896), while in the courtyard of Uncle

Salvador's house with his sister and cousins, Pablo heard Aunt Pepa calling him; looking up, he saw her at the window, fitted out to the nines, with a mantilla over her hair, her black dress adorned with every jewel she owned and, the heat notwithstanding, in her fur coat. She was ready to pose for him now!

Pablo had no canvas at hand but, not one to let the chance slip by, he did her portrait on a simple cardboard. He scarcely flattered her, but the hard ascetic face, with its sad, slightly wild look, is painted vigorously, shadows emphasizing the features that are highlighted. The hair beneath the black mantilla, and the dark dress, contrast with the powerfully etched, almost tragic mask. The portrait was done in an hour. Whether or not she liked it, no one knows. The superb work long remained in the home of her niece Lola, Señora Vilato; today the Picasso Museum has it, in Barcelona.

There are several portraits of Don José from the year 1895, drawings and oil studies of his face, strongly constructed, done in large part in Barcelona. Two watercolors are especially remarkable: one (now in Barcelona) was doubtless painted at La Coruña before the summer, the other in December. How implacably lucidly the fourteen-year-old adolescent saw his father! In one, under the guise of a failure, romantic style, as if crushed by fate, his head on his left hand, ruminating terrible thoughts; in the other, as a sick man, stocking cap on his head, warding off the cold with a plaid shawl. The second portrait (now in the Museum at Málaga), signed "P. Ruiz Picasso. 12.95," is inscribed (in Spanish) "To my dear Antonio Muñoz Degrain, I send this Christmas present with my affection."

Don José looked at these portraits with emotion. Tears came to his eyes. For it was to a well-known, respected, "successful" master, his old friend from Málaga, Muñoz Degrain, that Pablo inscribed and gave the pitiless evidence of his decay: the effigy of a ridiculous old man in stocking cap and blanket, when he was scarcely forty-five years old! The adolescent did not know how cruel his eye could be as it sought out the truth. A few months before, he had done a drawing of his father that showed him standing, looking youthful, dressed in a large overcoat, with his fine blond beard framing his long hidalgo's face. Had he changed? Or had his son discovered, beneath the appearances, the deeper man, the one whose distress he had summed up in that awful phrase, "No Málaga, no bulls, no friends, no nothing"—whose brushes had been put into other hands?

Pablo painted that nothing: Goya's tragic *nada*.

September 1895: toward the end of the month, the Ruizes left Málaga for Barcelona. The trip was not long, so they went by boat, at the special rate afforded Uncle Salvador as director of the Health Inspection Bureau. They went up the uniformly blue Mediterranean coast, making short stops at Almería, Cartagena, Alicante, Valencia, Castellón de la Plana, Tarragona, finally ending in the capital of Catalonia.

II

THE
APPRENTICE
YEARS
(1895–1901)

"**M**ODERNISM" WAS THE KEY WORD IN TURN-OF-THE-CENTURY Barcelona. At the tip end of backward Spain, the city was trying to wrest the secrets of the future from Europe, and "modernists" was its name for the lusty bravos, the wide-felt-hatted intellectuals or artists, with defiant Ascot ties and waving canes. With half a million inhabitants, three-quarters of them workers exploited by quasi-feudal bosses supported by the Church, and subjected to anarchist propaganda, Barcelona held the peninsula's record for *pronunciamientos,* with just a handful of young men of goodwill trying to get to know the people and take them into the modern ideas of the new century.

In cafés and bars, these "modernists" proclaimed their wrath in lyrical tones that the bourgeoisie alternately scoffed at or feared. There were symbolist, pantheist, and "decadent" poets, writers who read Nietzsche and Dostoyevsky, philosophers imbued with the fire of Bakunin or Kropotkin, the arch-anarchists. Their painting confrères did "social" subjects, or else expressed their revolutionary ideas in explosions of Impressionist light.

"Better to be symbolists and unbalanced, even crazy and decadent, than vile and cowardly. Common sense is choking us; prudence, here, is overdone . . ." Thus Santiago Rusiñol, who, with his large mop of hair, beard, wide cape floating in the wind, and ardent speech, resembled a prophet. The purest Catalan blood imbued him with this florid lyricism, rich with the age-old accents of the race; he was the leader of the young Barcelona intellectuals who met at his superb neo-Gothic château of Cau Ferrat, at Sitges.

For three years, 1892, 1893, and 1894, Sitges was the scene of noisy "modernist events" characteristic of the Catalan state of mind: tributes to César Franck, to the local composer Morera, to Maurice Maeterlinck, whose *L'Intruse* (The

Intruder) was staged there in 1893, and a solemn El Greco procession, in which two of his paintings owned by Rusiñol were paraded through the streets as Italian cities once had paraded the *Maestà*. These demonstrations, disapproved by the conservative bourgeoisie and authorities, expressed the divergent attitude of the intellectuals, their protest; literary liberalism, as understood at the time, was not far from anarchism, and Spanish traditionalists felt the same fear of all such movements. In a few years, Picasso would be reacting to Rusiñol's 1893 call to Catalan artists

> to live on the abnormal and unheard-of, relate the terrors of reason peering into the abyss, the crushing of catastrophes, and the thrill of the imminent, tell the anguish of supreme suffering and discover the calvaries of earth, attain the tragic by way of the mysterious, divine the unknown . . .

For the moment he knew nothing of the huge city he and his family were landing at in this fall of 1895, when he was fourteen. From the deck of the ship, a grayish fog appeared as a huge protective sheet between sky and city. Barcelona was Spain's first industrial and commercial city; its fantastic mass of low dark houses, spiked with towers, domes, and belfries, led down to the sea like an angry wave dominated by the citadel of Montjuich.

The Ruizes at first stayed in a port *pensión,* perhaps the one Don José had boarded at on his earlier visit; then had an apartment on Calle Cristina before settling at 4 Calle de Llauder, hard by the wharves where Pablo would often loiter. His father enrolled him at the School of Fine Arts known as La Lonja (The Stock Market, because it was in the same building), at which he taught. It was close to home, Don José always having tried to arrange to be within walking distance of his job.

Catalonia was more hospitable than Galicia, its climate mild, the winters sunny if sometimes very cold; but Catalans are not reputed to be easy to get on with. The new province and new climate did not cheer Don José up; Barcelona seemed no better than La Coruña.

The Junta de Comerç, established in 1758, had created the School of Fine Arts in its building. And La Lonja had the same academic curriculum as at La Coruña. The admission examination was in three stages: copy of a print, copy of a casting, and studies from live models.

"I finished the whole thing the first day," Picasso would one day proudly say, "and took a good look at the model, to see what I could add. But there was nothing, really nothing."

The examination was to last a month; his two surviving drawings are dated respectively September 25 and 30, 1895. They show the same model, in nude front view, and then draped in a broad material in profile. So, he did not remember it accurately—a frequent occurrence when he wanted to give the impression of an impulsive youngster, thumbing his nose at rules and disdainful of scholarly obligations. He likewise liked to be seen as a creator without culture or masters, a sort of conscious primitive—as against the unconscious primitivism of a Douanier Rousseau he was so to admire.

The Picasso legend, which he created with the support of Sabartés, who would have called day night at Pablo's behest, began at La Lonja. The painter several times stated he had been a woolgathering disruptive student, uninterested in studying, as he found this unnecessary, since he was so far ahead of his fellows, though they were all older than he. He also liked to portray his art as growing out of instinct alone, as in that fabled one-day examination yarn. The fact was, he fitted effortlessly into the constricting curriculum of the school, because he knew how to outwit it with what his fellows most lacked: imagination and curiosity.

Having passed the examination, he became No. 108, alphabetically, on the roll for 1895–1896, as Pablo Ruiz Picano (*sic*).

As at La Coruña, he went on painting and drawing with extraordinary rapidity, facility, and variety of subject matter. Expressing himself by pen or brush had already become an organic function for him. He kept on with landscapes and street scenes on little wood panels. Like his drawings, these picturelets served as "diaries" through which he discovered Barcelona and its people, catching the characteristics of both.

Picasso's bent for portraits was most naturally encouraged by Antonio Caba, head of the school and professor of painting; a locally well-established portraitist, he was struck by the gifts of his colleague José Ruiz' son. Pablo's *Self-Portrait with Wig* (Picasso Museum, Barcelona), done in 1896, confirmed the vigor of his touch, his handling of material, and a psychological understanding amazing for his age.

Like the rest of the family, Pablo did not know a word of Catalan. Yet, by listening and observing, and talking with his schoolmates, unlike his father, who remained cloistered in hostility, he plunged into the new life, the city, the country, its spirit and its manners, which were so profoundly to influence him. Loitering in the old port area, he would often draw in the Ciudadela Park: one such pen-and-ink drawing is of a lady beneath a parasol on a terrace, watching the swans in the tree-shaded lake. There is bite in the stroke, the shadows are intensely revealing, and the little scene is as sharp as an etching; on the reverse side, three or four years later, Pablo did crayon-and-wash caricatures of two characters, himself and a friend.

At La Lonja, a boy five years older than he, Manuel Pallarés y Grau, became his best friend. A native of Horta, a picturesque little village of the *comarca* of Terra Alta, in Tarragona province, he lived alone in Barcelona and was often a guest at the Ruizes', where he was treated as one of the family. Other chums of Pablo's were the brothers Joaquim and Josep Bas, Josep and Juan Cardona, who were not related to each other, and the Andalusian Josep Garnelo.

Manuel Pallarés, now ninety-six, lives with his son René, a dentist, and a housekeeper in a large house on Via Layetana in downtown Barcelona. His dark old-fashioned apartment almost seems uninhabited, its shutters closed most of the time to keep out the sounds of the street. The walls are covered with huge paintings by Pallarés, who taught painting at La Lonja, where he had studied, and scarcely got beyond the academic sense inculcated in him there. Among the outdated landscapes, bouquets of flowers, and portraits, there are a few realistic paintings, typically Iberian in tone: one in particular, *The Sick Woman,* which Pallarés says Picasso was fond of for its naturalistic power, its dark and solid sculptural masses—not unlike the paintings Pablo was to do under the influence of Nonell.

Within this last-century apartment there is a small room, always locked; Pallarés never lets the key off his person—it is the sanctuary of friendship. Its pictures, prints, drawings, photographs, framed newspaper clippings, and books reflect with charming disorder eighty years of admiration and devotion. For Pablo and Pallarés never lost touch after La Lonja: despite his great age, the old painter each year went with his son to spend a fortnight visiting his younger friend. They stayed at a hotel in Cannes and each morning Pablo sent a car to take them to Mougins, and return them in the evening.

Above Don Manuel's desk in Barcelona is a portrait of him that Picasso did at Horta in 1908, in the "Cézannish" manner he used between *Les Demoiselles d'Avignon* and Cubism; also a drawing of Pallarés standing and painting, when they first met, and another profile pencil portrait of him. Done at the same time, it was signed and inscribed by the author almost forty years later, on August 21, 1933, in memory of their joint boyhood. Sitting beneath his self-portrait with palette, in the contrasty bituminous style of turn-of-the-century academicism, Pallarés recalls his first meeting with Picasso in the pictorial anatomy and perspective class, and how the school year of 1895–1896 saw their friendship start. The Ruizes were not unhappy to see a lad a few years older (Pallarés was born on March 6, 1876) as their son's friend; his more mature nature could not but have the best effect on Pablo's thoughtless rashness.

"He had a very strong personality," says the old man, whose waxen face comes alive in two sharp eyes. "He was appealing, and way ahead of the others, who were all five or six years older . . . he grasped everything very quickly; paid no apparent attention to what the professors were saying. Picasso had no artistic culture, but had extraordinary curiosity . . . took things in in the blink of an eye, and remembered them months later. . . .

"In everything, he was different. . . .

"Sometimes very excited, at other times he could go for hours without saying a word. . . . He could get angry quickly, but calm down just as fast. He was aware of his superiority over us, but never showed it. He often seemed melancholy, as if he had just thought of some sad things. His face would cloud over, his eyes become dark. . . .

"At fifteen, he neither seemed nor acted like a boy his age. He was very mature. . . ."

Pallarés staunchly denies that the episode of Don José turning over his palette and brushes ever took place. He thinks it was made up out of whole cloth. When told that Picasso himself had recounted it, he did not comment, but he did accuse Sarbartés, whom he did not like—the feeling was mutual—of being largely responsible for the Picasso legends.

Unlike his father, and despite Catalan prejudices against Andalusians, says

Pallarés, Picasso had no trouble in getting accepted and making friends in Barcelona. And he never wearied of doing pictures of his family and friends—sometimes even unknown to them. His first portrait of Pallarés, oil on cardboard, was probably done at the end of 1895; the face, in bright colors laid on with authority, stands out against a green-blue background done in semi-relief; the desire for a good likeness is evident.

The Flight into Egypt dates from the same period. It is in a "bold" style, with the classical scene rendered in quick sharp strokes; Joseph, Mary, and the Child Jesus sit huddled together at the foot of a tree, before a Palestinian landscape; the setting sun fills the sky with golden tints. More logically titled a *Holy Family* or *Nativity*, this work greatly intrigued the American photographer David Douglas Duncan when, with Picasso, he discovered it in a pile of paintings at La Californie in 1956. Duncan, who had spent several years in the Near East, asked his host where he had seen houses such as those in the background, which did not exist in Spain. Picasso just shrugged—but when the photographer asked whether the strange shape above the trio represented the Holy Spirit, Picasso burst out:

"Holy Spirit! Those are dates! That's a palm tree—with dates! They had to eat *something*!" *

The Alms (1895–1896) is painted somewhat differently, in flat surfaces and scumbling, in bright gay colors; it has an intimistic note reminiscent of the contemporary style of the Nabis: a black-clad couple of old people in high hat and mantilla giving alms to a girl with a kerchief, who nods her thanks.

"See how properly they are dressed, and how graciously he gives the girl the peseta, though it may be his last" was Picasso's comment.

In his second school year, 1896–1897, Pablo was aware that the school work meant even less to him; he had already outgrown it. Director Caba almost shared this view, but was afraid to set the young man off on his own too soon. Picasso's precocious mastery, his skill and speed of execution scared him, as they did Don José. On a sheet of paper on which his son had drawn a portrait of him seated, his hands in his pockets, and sketched several quick impressions at random, Don José marked four times *suspenso* (F for failure) and six times *sobresaliente* (E for excellent): the teacher took precedence over the father.

Pablo now decided to carry off a big coup: he would paint three large compositions in what is known as "Salon style" and submit them to the various big group shows. This was amazingly ambitious, sensationally daring, for a sixteen-year-old still at the School of Fine Arts. But was it beyond him?

The public liked uplifting or inspirational subjects, that gave food for thought, preached serenity, or taught a moral, so, after consultation with his father, he selected three such: *The Choir Boy, First Communion,* and especially *Science and Charity,* which most appealed to Don José. All three were owned by the Vilatos before being given to the Picasso Museum in Barcelona; in them, the mastery of the supremely gifted prize academic student stands cheek by jowl with adolescent naïvetés.

* David Douglas Duncan, *Picasso's Picassos* (New York: Harper & Row, 1961), p. 40.

Science and Charity reflects many influences of the era: the search for a luminous effect inherited from Impressionism, but tempered by provincial timidity, joins with the social-humanitarian intentions of the "modernists." The academic palette of ochers, browns, and earths opens out to turn-of-the-century tones, mauve, lilac, white, and pale-yellowish green. The execution, somewhat dry but enlivened with delightful impasto, clashes with the free hand of the preparatory sketches. One of the latter, now at the Picasso Museum in Barcelona, highly colored and contrasting, suggests remarkably daring textural effects—but what a scandal if Antonio Caba's pupil had presumed to paint the little girl in a pure vermilion dress, as she was in the sketch!

Don José appears in the painting, the theme of which he had suggested to his son: he is the doctor taking the pulse of the poor woman in bed. On the other side, a nun holds the sick woman's baby as she offers her a cup of soup. A beggarwoman of the neighborhood and her child were models for the mother and baby, while a friend of Pablo's became the nursing sister, dressed in a habit lent by a Malagueña nun who was a friend of the Ruiz family, Sister Josefa Gonzalez, of the Order of St. Vincent de Paul, at the Convent of La Granja, Barcelona.

First Communion was exhibited at the Third Municipal Exposition of Fine Arts in Barcelona, April 1896, where most of the well-known Catalan painters were represented: Mas y Fontdevila, who was one of the first to take an interest in young Picasso, Juan Brull, Santiago Rusiñol, Ramón Casas, Lluis Graner, Isidro Nonell, and so on. It was No. 80 in Room I, with a price tag of fifteen hundred pesetas, and moved a local critic, Miguel y Badia, in the *Diario de Barcelona* of May 15, to say it showed "sensitivity in the characters and firmness in the sketching of certain parts."

There was no "modernism" in the proper picture: neither idea, symbol, dream, nor anger. Picasso was not unaware of the concerns of Catalan artists, but for now he mainly followed their gray or mauve luminosity, with the ochers tinted purple or pale green. The Impressionism influencing the Barcelonese was less that of Monet or Renoir than the more reassuringly elegant style of a Whistler; their dramatic scenes were straight out of Munch.

The city was going through parlous times, with often violent demonstrations provoked by anarchists in the streets. The "black terror" was rampant in Europe, but it was at Barcelona that, on November 8, 1893, two months after Marshal Martinez Campo was assassinated by the anarchist Pallas, the worst outrage took place. Two bombs thrown during a performance at the Liceo Theatre, by another anarchist, Santiago Salvador, resulted in six executions, and the prisons were jammed. On June 7, 1896, a bomb thrown at a passing procession killed seven.

Shortly before the summer vacation, the Ruizes moved, but not far; they took the second floor at 3 Calle de la Merced, and Don José got his son a studio at 4 Calle de la Plata, halfway between home and La Lonja. This certainly indicates that the father felt his son had taken over; after the matter of the brushes, the studio completed it.

To Pablo it was an event, to his friends confirmation of a superiority they could no longer deny in view of his brilliant successes. At fifteen, he was now free. He may have visited museums and studied contemporary painting, but it is less certain, as some have alleged, that Gaudí's architecture and the challenge it represented had any great effect on him. The builder of the Sagrada Familia was less a "modernist" than the last of the Gothic architects: he used their plastic vocabulary and structures, adapting them to his surprising visionary genius. "Originality," he said, "means returning to the origins." Picasso might well have said as much, but once, when asked about it, he replied: "I was not impressed. Gaudí did not influence me at all." Then, as an afterthought, after apparently peering back into the past, "In fact, maybe just the opposite."

Science and Charity got an honorable mention at the Madrid General Fine Arts Exhibition of 1897, and a gold medal at the Provincial Exhibition at Málaga—but this did not keep a critic (quoted by Sabartés but not identified) from satirizing it in doggerel as a picture of a "doctor taking the pulse of a glove."

Pablo gave the painting to his Uncle Salvador, who kept it for many years on the main landing of his Málaga home at 49 Calle de la Alameda, alongside one by his brother-in law, Don Francisco Morales. It may be that in suggesting this subject Don José had meant a tribute to the brother who, by virtue of his profession, fortune, and authority, had been the "protector" and even benefactor of the family.

Picasso always considered *Science and Charity* of great significance. To begin with, it was his first large work and the one that won him his first success; then, it was part of a period of his life he could never think of without being moved, however he might minimize his paintings of the time. From Uncle Salvador's, it went on to the Vilatos', where it was hung in a dark, almost invisible, spot; it required considerable cleaning up when taken into the museum on Calle Montcada in 1970.

Sabartés tells how, one day around 1935 in the studio on Rue des Grands-Augustins in Paris, Picasso came across the name of Joaquim Martinez de la Vega in a newspaper, and exclaimed: "Didn't I ever tell you about him? I must have. You'll remember I did . . ." and recounted how in the summer of 1897 the Ruiz family came across this painter friend of Don José's from Málaga, when Pablo had just gotten the honorable mention at Madrid.

"One day, when my father had taken me to the club that he and his friends went to, there was talk of what I was doing. At the mention of my award in Madrid, Don Joaquim was the one who proposed I be christened a painter by pouring some champagne over my head. . . ."

After the transfer of the brushes and the rental of the studio, this third eloquent symbolic ceremony solemnly set Pablo up as a full-fledged painter. This time it was his peers anointing him, a fact that must have carried weight in convincing the family to take Uncle Salvador's advice and send him to Madrid to go on with his studies.

His early successes do not seem to have gone to Pablo's head. Photos and

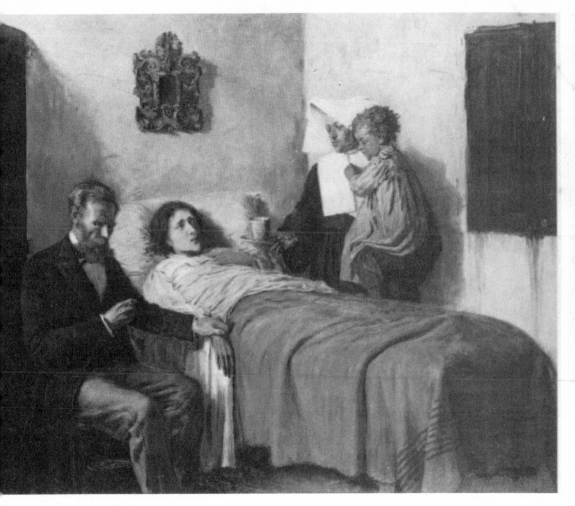

"Science and Charity"   *Barcelona 1897 (Museo Picasso—Barcelona)*

(CIRI)

portraits of him at that time, notably one by a fellow student named Rius or Riu, show a serious, even almost sad-looking adolescent, although he was never reluctant to join in noisy activities of his fellows nor the customary *novatada:* the series of hoaxes or hazing inflicted on new matriculants.

Pallarés recalled that even then Picasso loved weird disguises and false faces; every year he dressed up for the pre-Lenten carnival as well as other street festivities.

His landscapes now became much more fluid; the colors melted into a sort of highly diluted Impressionism. The *Modernist Landscape* (Barcelona), 1897, in which we see a man in a cape dreaming alongside a pool in a park bathed in the mauve and orange shades of sunset, owed a great deal to Rusiñol, whose influence Pablo was later to reflect. Highly versatile, as usual, Don José's son was also painting religious scenes, although now of a neoclassical bent, and self-portraying himself in the most varied guises, as a dandy with flourishing mane parted in the center, small mustache, and high stiff collar, or as an hidalgo with masculine but slightly emaciated face, somber of eye. Here and elsewhere, Picasso tried to make himself look older, to give a more virile picture of himself at sixteen or seventeen. His touch, also, was maturing apace.

Toward the end of 1898, he was to stop signing "Ruiz," though sometimes including its initial in "P. R. Picasso." Adopting his mother's name rather than his father's was not the expression of any favoritism. He was merely bowing to his Catalan friends who found it more colorful to call him Picasso instead of Ruiz. Jaime Sabartés recalled that the very first time he was introduced to him, as Ruiz Picasso, he spontaneously addressed him as Picasso, because it had so outlandish a sound for Catalonia.

As Picasso was to tell Brassaï in 1943,

I'm sure [what attracted me to it] was the double *s*, which is very rare in Spain. . . . Can you imagine me being called Ruiz? Pablo Ruiz? Diego-José Ruiz? Or Juan-Nepomuceno Ruiz? . . . Have you ever noticed that there's a double *s* in Matisse, in Poussin, in Rousseau?

He piled sketchbook on sketchbook, two in 1895, two in 1896, two more in 1896–1897—that we know of; many may have been lost—with his naturalism giving way to a freer style. Then Pablo started on a trend toward geometric construction, especially notable in sketches for which Lola posed. His paintings, some significant notations of landscapes, sunsets, views of Barcelona, groups of passersby, interiors, or sun-drenched impressions of the Málaga countryside done during the 1897 vacation, evidence the young man's insatiable curiosity, his ever lively sense of "life in the raw," as well as the delight in sun and light common to the Catalan painters tagging along after the Impressionists.

He must certainly have known of the movements of art in Europe, for on November 3, 1897, he wrote Joaquim Bas, his schoolmate at La Lonja, "If I had a son who wanted to be a painter, I would not leave him an instant in Spain, but don't think I would send him to Paris (where I myself would delight to be), but to Munich . . . There people seriously study painting, without worrying about fads like Pointillism and all the others . . .''

When he wrote this, Pablo had been in Madrid a month already; there, as in Barcelona, the main influence was that of the German intellectuals, although Schopenhauer, Nietzsche, and Wagner had been brought in by way of Catalonia. The Catalan poet Maragall had introduced Nietzsche, as he would also Goethe and Novalis. These Nordic ideas seem to harmonize with the Symbolism of Maeterlinck, whom Rusiñol was heralding, and the social naturalism of Ibsen and Munch, as well as the Scandinavian Expressionists, English Pre-Raphaelites, Aubrey Beardsley, Steinlen, and Toulouse-Lautrec. Humanitarian compassion as seen in *Science and Charity* made its bed alongside Nietzsche's cult of the self. Nor should one overlook El Greco, the great revelation of the period, in which his "modernism" seemed especially inspiring. Miguel Utrillo, editor of the magazine *Pel i Ploma* (Brush and Pen) in Barcelona, was to be his first exegeticist; his book did not appear until 1906, but long before that he had been telling the world about the then-unknown work of the great Cretan. Utrillo's influence on young Picasso was to be great; getting him to appreciate both Greco and the medieval frescoes of the Catalan churches, he would provoke a decisive turn in his oeuvre.

It was Miguel Utrillo,* "the man of great ideas and great initiatives in our country," who had the idea of opening a Parisian-type cabaret in which artists, intellectuals, dilettantes, and other like-minded people might forgather, says Josep Palau y Fabre, Picasso's Catalan historian, who knows all about the Malagueño's love story with Catalonia. Pere Romeu, who had worked for Rodolphe Salis at the Chat Noir in Paris, was the first to be told about it. He was delighted, but when their friends heard about it, they replied with *"Només son quatre gats,"* a local idiom, "There will only be us four cats," meaning "We'll never draw a crowd." The allusion to the name of the Chat Noir prompted them to dub it Els Quatre Gats.

It had a very brilliant opening on June 12, 1897. The obvious attempt to create "artistic" disorder accounted for somewhat fanciful takeoffs on the Chat Noir and other Montmartre night spots in the decor, along with Teutonic heaviness intended to represent "modernism" with Wagnerian overtones. A large painting by Ramón Casas of himself and Romeu on a tandem dominated the main room, which had Valencian porcelain tiling halfway up; the ceiling, with its huge chandelier, had visible beams, intended to underline the "period" character of the overall clutter of pictures, drawings, plates, ironwork, posters, and sundry objects. In the back there was a smaller room in which Utrillo staged puppet shows and shadow plays such as Salis put on in Paris.

Its opening poster was addressed to "Persons of good taste, citizens who, from river to river, inhabit our city, those who, beyond their bodies, wish to nourish their minds . . ." A month later, there was a painting show there, which Picasso visited before leaving for his vacation at Málaga. Casas, Rusiñol,

* This was the man who allowed the use of his name to "legitimize" the son of Suzanne Valadon, now world-famous as Maurice Utrillo. (TR. NOTE)

Miguel Utrillo, Nonell, Joaquim Mir, Torent, and others were in it. So Els Quatre Gats became the true home of modern art in Barcelona, as was to be confirmed by the later shows of the "modernist" Frances Xavier Gosé, Ricardo Opisso, and Casagemas, among others.

Back in Andalusia, Pablo worked hard. Word of his "baptism" by Don Joaquim had gotten around and, what with his earlier success in the capital, he was now a local celebrity. He spent many an evening beneath the plane trees with his cousin Carmen Blasco, and did give her a tambourine decorated with flowers. But he later pooh-poohed this "affair" with "My mother would have liked me to settle in Málaga where I was already considered a painter."

Don José felt that his son should be sent to Madrid, to study at the San Fernando Academy, where his best Malagueño friend, Muñoz Degrain, whom Pablo knew from earliest childhood, was teaching, as was Carbonero, another intimate. Don Salvador agreed fully, especially since—to hear him tell it—it was his idea in the first place; a useful fact, since the doctor was the rich uncle. A widower, he had just remarried, and his young wife who loved art, especially music, was as convinced as he was of Pablo's precocious promise.

One of Don José's brothers-in-law, Don Bartoloméo Chiara, who had been married to his wife's eldest sister, also pitched in. So all he needed was to make up the small difference for his son's support—in what he considered a natural family mutual-aid project for the one whose talent honored them all.

Once when Sabartés was telling what a fine allowance Pablo had gotten from his father and his two uncles, the painter interrupted: "Bah! A pittance! A few pesetas. Barely enough to keep from starving; no more." Actually, he had a very adequate stipend. This tale of near-starvation was one of his favorite fables, accommodatingly spread by Sabartés.

He got to Madrid in the fall, alone for the first time. He boarded on Calle San Pedro Martín, but when his landlords moved he went with them to Calle Jesus y María and then to Calle de Lavapies, all very close to the Plaza del Progreso, a main intersection of the picturesquely "Goyaesque" working-class neighborhood leading down to the Manzanares River in the southeast. It was so rainy and cold that long afterward Picasso would still shiver thinking of this early Madrid winter.

He entered the Academy as a "disciple of Muñoz Degrain," another juvenile attempt to disassociate himself from his father, but right off they failed to get along. Muñoz Degrain expected to see the little boy who did sketching at the port in Málaga, but instead found a young man confident of himself, his personality, and his talent. No way to establish rapport. The gap between them was the first sign of Pablo's independence. Degrain liked his friend's son, appreciated his talent, and was wise enough to ascribe the gap to Andalusian pride. Later, he would wistfully say, "Had I been able to help him, he would have turned into a good naturalist painter like me."

Pablo told Sabartés he never set foot in the Academy. But he did go regularly for several weeks: the studio was well heated. With the teachers he never got along: he knew what he wanted, and how he wanted to do it, and they, pillars of academic tradition, surrounded by commissions and titles that set them apart from life, could not accept that.

In the letter Pablo wrote Bas on November 3, telling of his introduction to San Fernando, he is furious: the professor found the figure he was working on well proportioned and drawn, but poorly positioned on the sheet. Picasso rebels, and writes:

That means I am supposed to create a case to pack the figure in! I can't believe that people can be so stupid. And yet there is no doubt that, however far he may be from our way of thinking, he does not draw badly. He is probably one of those who draw the best because he attended several Parisian academies. But make no mistake: in Spain we are not so stupid as we have always pretended. The trouble is we are poorly taught.

Returning several times to the painting halls of the Prado, which he had first visited with his father, Pablo informs Joaquim Bas:

. . . Velázquez is first rate. There are some magnificent Grecos. Murillo is not always convincing. Titian's *Dolorosa* is good, and there are some fine portraits by Van Dyck. Rubens has serpents of fire for his prodigy. Teniers some good little pictures of drunks, and everywhere *Madrileñitas* so beautiful that no Turkish woman can compare.

He also studied the paintings at the Academy he attended; its galleries had Zurbaráns, Murillos, Goyas, and many German canvases, but the whole thing struck Pablo as repellent.

These were the judgments of a sixteen-year-old, a prize student who knew the teaching he got was deplorable. But they were free judgments as well, uninfluenced by anyone, and growing out of no culture. He looked. His eye was already pitiless. He also judged the city, its people, and its manners; he was not from here, and one may well wonder whether the Prado masterpieces even existed for him. Had he not already opted, not for the masters, but for life?

He now also split away from his family, for he realized that, in paying for his education, they were laying out his path for him: honors, scholarships, Prix de Rome, teaching appointments, painting commissions, official glory—a nice safe painterly reputation.

The fact that he went with his whole class to Toledo under the guidance of Moreno Carbonero shows he did stay a while at the Academy. The students admired the paintings in the churches, especially El Greco's *Burial of Count Orgaz,* which Carbonero had them copy. Pablo, with his usual skill, began with the upper part, then he got the strange notion of replacing the faces of the real characters of the count's burial, in the lower register, with those of his classmates and even his teachers! Carbonero, outraged at the joke, became violently angry, and Pablo decided never to set foot in the studio again.

"Naturally," Picasso recalled the event for Sabartés, "they cut me off . . . but all's well that ends well. My father, who was putting up the lion's share, continued, poor fellow, to send what he could"—even though it was just his type of teaching that Pablo was turning his back on. So, as the young man wrote Bas:

> I am going to do a drawing for you to take to *Barcelona Cómica.* We'll see whether or not they buy it. It has to be modernistic for a paper like that. Neither Nonell, the young mystic, nor anyone else has gone so far as I do in this. . . .

The winter in Madrid was harsh. Picasso regularly copied Velázquezes and El Grecos at the Prado; the portrait of Philip IV, and some drawings after the Cretan, still remain. Weather permitting, he would paint out of doors: the views of the Retiro Park, the Salón del Prado dripping with rain, under a hazy sky, as the passersby scamper past beneath their umbrellas, evidence his experiments with atmosphere caught on the spot. The five Madrid sketchbooks—two in one month, March 1898—contain many street scenes, with fights, sidewalk musicians, women arguing, animals, drawings of chimneys with strange ghostly outlines—and a pencil copy of one of Goya's *Caprichos.*

Picasso tried the most varied styles, going with disconcerting ease from naturalistic drawing with clear outline to a free stroke with so light an arabesque that it suggests rather than shows. He liked flashbacks, syncopated narration, mixtures of chronology and forms. What mattered to him was the visual impression: he used paper, board, or canvas as others did film.

Probably in March or April, he contracted scarlet fever, which his parents found out about when he returned to Barcelona, looking drawn and depressed, apparently sometime after June 13, for Pablo remembered having been at the San Antonio *verbena,* one of the main Madrid street fetes, on that date.

It was the time of the Spanish-American War. Spain was quickly and shamefully overwhelmed. Pablo returned to a shattered Barcelona. The anarchists were riding high, and the young intellectuals seeking causes for so ignominious a defeat knew nothing of political or sociological realities: all their café discussions ran up blind alleys or turned into jokes.

The "1898 generation" would try to react and see things more clearly, pay more attention to Spanish "personality," tradition, culture, and attitudes toward life; it would seek better human understanding. To the "modernists," the disaster gave one more reason for defending "Catalaneity," that easy out against adversity. They went on talking and dreaming, sometimes with talent, their "modernism" now turning more humanitarian, more realistic.

For the sake of his health, after a few days at home, Pablo at the end of June left with Pallarés to stay with the latter's family at Horta. They got to Tortosa by train, and there Manuel's older brother José was awaiting them with two mules: one for the luggage; they took turns riding the other.

There were three Pallarés brothers and one sister, José, Manuel, Salvador, known as Salvadoret, and Carmen. It was picturesque mountainous country, and after a few days of rest, there were strenuous outings and hikes. Manuel and Pablo often painted from nature, Salvadoret going along to lead the necessary mule carrying their painting supplies—Picasso did a small painting of him— and stores of food.

The two friends discovered that the entrances to the caves in the hillside, ports as they were called, had nice protected flat areas where they could paint undisturbed. They would make a blanket of lavender and straw, and there were days when the wind was so strong they had to build a rock wall, Pallarés recalls, for protection. The summer of 1898 was especially hot, but up in their ports they were quite comfortable. They sometimes remained up there for several weeks, with only brief interludes down at Horta, talking, dreaming, painting, or walking through the wild hills, whose untamed grandeur appealed so to Picasso, city-born and -bred, to whom this outdoor life was something new.

He inhaled the fragrance of the earth, filled his lungs with fresh air; this rough, austere Spain, borderline Catalonia and Aragón, was to stay with him. At night, by starlight, after a meager meal cooked over their campfire, Manuel and he talked on and on. Salvadoret and the mule brought foodstuffs up to the nearby Mas del Quiquet, a half-ruined farmhouse where they stored their materials and took shelter if it got too stormy. The youngest Pallarés boy also acted as mailman and newsboy, bringing them the news of August 13, 1898: with the help of Filipino rebels Manila had fallen to the Americans, an armistice was signed, and that part of Spain's empire was ended.

Picasso and Pallarés accomplished a lot. Pablo did many very adroit sketches of donkeys, horses, bulls, and goats. He was to remember them, some thirty-five years later, when, without models, he did a set of illustrations for Buffon's *Histoire naturelle*. Toward the end of September, they came down from the hills, and Pablo used the rest of his time at Horta to perfect his Catalan.

"He learned to take care of a horse and chickens, to draw water from the well, talk to people, milk cows, cook rice, take fire from the hearth," was Sabartés' straight-faced version of it—making Picasso roar with laughter and Pallarés deny it completely, for, while his guest took part in village life, he never played at being a peasant.

His realism now turned more sober, vigorous, and also more tactile in its intimate knowledge of its subject. So Pablo would say, "Whatever I know I learned in Pallarés' village." It was at Horta that he came to appreciate manual labor, and also freedom: the men struggling with the earth, and against the elements, were free men, despite poverty and solitude. They left an indelible mark on the seventeen-year-old "artist," the "bourgeois," who would stand beside them when the Spanish people had to defend themselves against the aggression of "nationalist" forces supported by foreign fascism. He would know these were the true "nationalists," who had made Spain.

While Don José always remained an Andalusian far from home, Pablo took to Catalonia; it was there that he wanted to see his museum, in its capital, and not at Málaga, as Sabartés suggested. He would return to Horta, at the start of Cubism, to measure his painting against the countryside which, like it, was austere, grave, making no concessions to the easy way or to sentimentality.

José-María Bertosa was a Madrid lawyer before turning to film making. In 1970 he made a *Brouillon d'un reportage sur Picasso* (Draft Report on Picasso), shown on French TV April 11, 1971. The camera slowly pans over the old buildings of Horta and weatherbeaten faces of peasants who had known the painter during his second visit in 1908. In their gravelly voices they speak of the past, the planned Picasso Museum, the unlikely prospect of a return of the famous old man to whom Pallarés is their ambassador. Then the camera stops on the street sign with the name of the exiled painter.

Hundreds of miles away the latter was silently watching the scene on his TV set, his forefinger against his right cheek in his familiar position. When the peasant said his name would be added to Horta's when liberty came back, he nodded approval. Was he not the one who had dubbed the village Horta de Ebro in the old days, to avoid confusion with the Barcelonese neighborhood of Horta? It has been called Horta de San Juan only since 1919.

That first time, Picasso was struck by an adolescent girl, Josefa Sebastia Membrado, whose portrait he did in November 1898. He put her name and the date with his signature on the picture of the sad, frightened-looking face and the shawl-draped shoulders. Always the same feeling for the humble, the anxiety or resignation of the wretched of the earth, the same sensitivity singling out scenes or people devoid of joy.

The young man who returned to his family in Barcelona in February 1899, after an eight-months absence, was a changed person. With his new roots in the Iberian soil, he had taken a definitive stand against academic teaching. He had established ties with his gens, their strength, their traditions that time would not alter: from now on, he was of Spain, and nowhere else.

Barcelona too had changed: with defeat and the signing of the Treaty of Paris, December 10, 1899, proud Spain gave up her last colonial possessions, in the very area where she first had brought Western civilization.

Picasso was eighteen. He refused to enroll for the new school year at La Lonja, even after his father in vain begged Pallarés to get him to change his mind. Instead, Pablo was now obliged to share the studio of one of his schoolmates' brothers, Josep Cardona Santiago, a painter set up at the Calle des Escudillers Blancs. This was on a mezzanine, a tiny room at the end of long corridors in the apartment where their friends' mother, Señora Cardona, had her corset shop.

Mateo Fernández de Soto and his brother Angel belonged to the Bohemian youth of Barcelona following the "modernists." Mateo was a sculptor, who worked in Fucha's studio. At mealtimes, he was joined by a friend, a long-haired bespectacled young writer and poet, Jaime Sabartés. One day Soto told him about an Andalusian with terrific painting and drawing skill, and very nice to boot. His brother had been amazed at the sketches he saw this Pablo Ruiz make at a cabaret. Besides, he was a friend of friends of theirs, the Reventos brothers, Carlos Casagemas, the Vidal Ventosas, and others. His being Andalusian did not sit well with Sabartés, a self-conscious Catalan of ancient lineage. However, the man sounded truly interesting—and a real artist did not come along every day!

At Pablo's studio, he was doing a picture that de Soto had on occasion posed for. After the introductions, Sabartés explained that he had hoped to be a sculptor, but had had to give it up because of serious eye trouble that made any taxing work out of the question. The host said little, but let his guest look through his paintings and drawings. Not much conversation was exchanged, and when it came time to leave, at noon, Sabartés voiced only some banal compliments: the fact was, he was amazed, overwhelmed indeed, by the extraordinary mastery of the young Andalusian, not yet twenty. His behavior was surprising too. If the arrival of the two friends disturbed him, he did not show it; he asked Sabartés nothing about himself. As they left the studio, Picasso was standing at the corner of the hall leading to the door, looking at his new acquaintance with his dark gaze. It got to Sabartés. Some forty years later, he would say, "As I stepped in front of him to say good-bye, I was ready to bow, in surprise at the power emanating from his whole being."

As soon as he returned to Barcelona, Don José's son had become part of the Els Quatre Gats gang. In addition to the founders, Rusiñol, Utrillo, and Romeu, the group now included the painters Ramón Casas and Isidro Nonell, Sebastián Junyent, Rafael Moragas, Ramón Pichot, Joaquim and Josep Bas, Josep Cardona Santiago, the de Sotos, Ramón and Jacinto (nicknamed Cinto) Reventos, Joseph and Emilio Fontbana, Carles and Sebastián Junyer-Vidal, Jaime Brossa, Eugenio d'Ors, Manuel Martinez Hugué, who would later be famous as Manolo, and Carlos Casagemas. All of them, the youngest being Pablo's age, claimed to be painters, sculptors, poets, journalists, critics, or writers. Except for the already-established Rusiñol, Casas, and Nonell, few of the artists had shown any of their work, the opportunities for a beginner being virtually nonexistent in Barcelona at the time, while the writers and poets found outlets for their prose or verse in many little magazines, some abroad, especially in France or Germany. For all of them, Els Quatre Gats was a meeting hall, a gallery, and a tribune.

Pablo was no aspiring adolescent, but a full-fledged painter. His friends realized this, not foreseeing his future genius, but admiring the strength of character reflected in his eyes, in which Fernande Olivier would later say one sensed "an inner fire." He worked like a madman, with terrific energy; Pallarés says he was indefatigable, but that never kept him from being in on all the discussions in the smoke-filled room of Els Quatre Gats or in his friends' studios. At Casagemas', on Calle San Ramón, on Sunday afternoons, they drank *cremat* (coffee laced with flaming rum) through straws, recited poems, made speeches, and sang "Els Segadors," the oft-prohibited Catalan marching song.

He also visited Sala Parés, the only local art gallery; the lessons of Impressionism were no less effective for being delayed, and Catalan painters were beginning to let light in. Sebastián Junyer-Vidal, who was only to become a close friend of Pablo's in 1903–1904, had come back from Mallorca with sun-drenched landscapes; Ramón, one of the Pichot brothers, known as Ramonet, had built a house at Cadaqués where he painted landscapes and outdoor scenes intended to be shown in Paris.

Don José had little use for the Bohemian life or the Els Quatre Gats atmosphere; the gap between father and son grew deeper. The family tried to get the more reasonable Pallarés to talk to Pablo, but it did no good; even his mother, usually on his side, was helpless. He moved out. But there was never to be a total break with the family; in 1901, briefly back in Barcelona after his second stay in Madrid, Pablo visited them at Calle de la Merced several times. And, returning from Paris in January 1902, he stayed with them. Father and son made up.

The movement known in Paris, Brussels, or London variously as Art Nouveau, Modern'style, Liberty, and as *Jugendstil* in Munich and *Sezession* in Vienna—the actual first step of modern art—in Barcelona, far from the great centers and currents of exchange, took on a somewhat provincial aspect, burdened with rather maudlin sensitivity, complications, and overtones.

Symbolism's bastard, "decadent" poetry, was fashionable. Sabartés, one of its practitioners, later termed it "stupefying." Picasso portrayed him wearing a long black coat, crowned with roses, walking in a cemetery with a rose in his hand, a true *poeta decadente*. The painter, too, for a time adopted the corkscrew style of Art Nouveau, as evidenced by the posters he did for Els Quatre Gats, with their Toulouse-Lautrec influence. Romeu tried to start a magazine called *Els Quatre Gats,* but it did not catch on. In June 1899 Miguel Utrillo published the first issue of *Pel i Ploma.*

Picasso was not a major figure in this, rather just a bystander. To be sure, most of the habitués of Els Quatre Gats, some of whom he portrayed "modernistically," and others more naturalistically, were his elders, but in general, despite the interest he had, or appeared to have, in their doings, he did not take them very seriously. His colored drawing of the "decadent poet" Sabartés shows it.

Pablo acted in the turbulent declamatory Barcelona circles as he would later in Montmartre and the meetings at which Cubism was born—attentive but distant. Watching and analyzing, he would not jump headlong into this or that aesthetic trend, but stand back, singling out only the essential, convinced that the rest would come in good time. If it was to come at all.

"Gothic Barcelona" at this time was a city of contrasts, drunkenly turning toward the northern breezes wafting in fragrances of Nietzsche and Novalis, delighting in César Franck. Alongside its anarchist troublemakers and its aesthetes, its staid bourgeois and pious industrialists, it had a horribly poverty-stricken population, living in sordid filth; thousands of wretches were penned in to the notorious *barrio chino,* where a dubious fauna of whores, killers, deserters, footpads, and street urchins permeated the huge mass of workers exploited by their bosses. And now there were super-added the sick and wounded repatriated from forever-lost Cuba, forgotten and made to order for the fomenters of rebellion.

How could so curious a boy, so passionately interested in the ideas, forms, and movements of his day as Picasso, remain untouched in his youthful ardor by the irresistible urge to protest, the anarchist parades with their black flags, the mingled faces of apostles and assassins, the chorus of cries of hate, revolt, and love? What made him a painter was not an irresistible vocation, but a mixture of social rebellion and observation of reality—the dramatic, often atrocious, unbearable reality about him. From here on, Picasso's fate was to look tragedy in the eye.

Where his precociousness had surprised his friends, his maturity troubled them. "He could see further than we," said Pallarés; adding with the hindsight of old age, "he fascinated us." Sabartés once said to me, "When he wasn't there, we spoke of him as of a legendary hero."

Yet, among his peers, Pablo did not seem an exceptional being; he did not dominate them, was not the leader or standard-bearer. At meetings in Els Quatre Gats, at the bullfights, the Eden Concert cabaret, or the cafés on the Paralelo, in the whorehouses, Don José's son was just a hungry young wolf, wildly independent, more sensitive perhaps than some, but closed off, secretive, as well as spontaneous and violent, a hodgepodge of pessimism and exuberance, gravity, and a humor both satirical and sarcastic. Drawn irresistibly to humanitarian anarchism and, like all those of the "generation of '98," humiliated by the end of the far-flung empire, he obviously had something of the romantic about him.

He was well acquainted with the bawdry. Old and young whores swarmed in Barcelona, where the clergy could in no way restrain them. Picasso's sexuality was demanding and, from his fourteenth year on, he was introduced to lovemaking in its more direct and uncomplicated form. On several occasions, he was to boast to friends of his precociousness.

"I was still just a little fellow," he would say, holding his hand at little-boy height, as he laughed with a glint in his eye. "I started well before the age of reason. If we didn't, well, reason might well keep us from . . ." But he would stop, titillated by the memories that returned and delighted him—for never did any affair leave him with bitterness.

Not only was he a regular customer of the brothels; he once lived in one for several weeks, and decorated the walls of his room there. Whores, the city's nocturnal revelries, its underside, were subjects of drawings and paintings for him.

Looking at *Girls of the Streets,* which he had kept, almost sixty years later, he asked his wife, Jacqueline, "How could I ever have painted that?"

His loves always triggered creative periods in Picasso; the greater the sexual pleasure, the more fruitful his work. It was that way all his life long, so that in a given series of canvases, drawings, or engravings, we can chart the course of his lust: onset, paroxysm, decline. A new woman meant a new form for his art, too, another language. An unexpected mode of expression. Sabartés was right when he said most of his "periods" might be named after a woman instead of being given the aesthetic or symbolic designations they have—"the woman to him was not an end in herself, but just one essential element of his thought and work."

Between the spring of 1899 and October 1900 (when he left for Paris with Casagemas and Pallarés), he did such things as *Redemption* (or *The End of the Road*). This sad procession of old people, bent women and children, staggering on toward the end of the way where death awaits them, shows the complexity of feelings and impetuses in the painter. The taste of death, decadence, illness, was common to the Catalonian intelligentsia, influenced by Munch, Nietzsche, and the German/Scandinavian Expressionists. His macabre and religious scenes were many.

In 1952, being shown an 1896 landscape, Picasso was to tell Kahnweiler, "I hate that period of my studies in Barcelona. What I did before that was much better."

There were now several dramatic portraits, lighter and airier: the *Greco-like Face,* with its fluid tones lightly scumbled vertically and its waxen flesh rising from an immaculate white collar in the opaque blackness of the background, is especially striking. As is *Greco's Fiancée,* that greenish mask of Ophelia with closed eyes, "modernist" as can be on its ivory-white tablecloth sprinkled with mauve petals, and the "modernist" *Young Girl in White near a Window*—none other than his sister Lola—the ghostly chiaroscuro silhouette against the brilliant golden-lighted background. How can one believe the same artist painted the *Interior Scene* influenced by Munch in the final farewell of the couple in the room pervaded with tragic light, and the sprightly *Courtyard in Andalusia* or the *Window,* reminiscent of Manet?

Barcelona had a well-regarded portrait painter: Ramón Casas. He and Rusiñol were the ones who had introduced modern art, especially Impressionism, into Catalonia, revolutionizing the highly academic local artistic circles. As art director of *Pel i Ploma,* Casas was also one of those who led Utrillo to the rediscovery of El Greco. His painting was not without character, and his portraits had a tone, as shown by the one of Picasso he did in 1901 for the magazine. But comparing those he did of their Barcelona friends, now in that city's Museum of Modern Art, with the same viewed by Pablo, we see what differentiated the two men, and what gave the originality and power to the latter. The personality of each model is expressed by one essential, with a sense of character sometimes carried to satire, while Picasso shows more, often to excess, in order to say more. But Barcelonese society was not ready to accept such outspokenness from him: Casas would remain their favorite portraitist because he showed them as they saw themselves.

Pastel, which Pablo used frequently at this time, led to fluid technique, with diluted forms, contrasts of muzzy tones; the arabesque, with its satiny suppleness, does not underline the shape so much as stroke its outline, sometimes with a bit of mannerism. The portrait of Lola "in the big shawl," known as *L'Espagnole,* formerly in a Barcelonese collection, *The Meeting, The Woman in a Shawl,* and several other works of 1898–1900 or later show that the young painter could work as well in a soft blending style as in the hatchmarked manner of turpentine painting or charcoal.

What if Picasso invented nothing? What if these accented portraits, these dramatic scenes, the judiciously selected lighting effects, and robust, well-constructed figures were but an intelligent and highly skillful assimilation of a complex heritage combining all the currents that, by way of magazines and young Catalan artists who had worked in Paris, were in the air in Barcelona?

He never denied these contributions, though he did not much like the pictures of the period; and it took a shrewd person to get him even to mention Nonell, to whom he owed so much. Isidro Nonell is not, or hardly at all, known outside Catalonia, which is too bad. That fact made young Picasso a "creator," whereas, with his extraordinary skill, he had purely and simply followed in the footsteps of his compatriot, eight years older than he, who had worked in Paris and been there often since 1897. There was real friendship between the two men, and Nonell held Pablo to be an exceptionally gifted painter; he lent him his studio in the Rue Gabrielle when the latter got to Paris in 1901.

Isidro Nonell Monturiol came from a family of Barcelonese bourgeois, well-to-do merchants of Calle Baix de Sant-Pere. Headstrong and having also come under anarchist influence, Nonell proclaimed social ideas that his people considered revolutionary. But his affirmation that the slum wretches, gypsies, prostitutes, and outcasts of the *barrio chino* were the equals of the bourgeois who condemned them to their ghettos won him the empathy of the Els Quatre Gats crowd.

Picasso made no mystery of his admiration for the man he held to be the least provincial of the city's painters; he had been deeply impressed by his paintings and drawings shown at the cabaret in 1898, a veritable inventory of the *desdichados* of eternal Spain: wretched starvelings, beggars, whores, penniless mutilated soldiers, gypsies, alcoholics, café flotsam, cripples, and others. There was something of Steinlen and Lautrec, whom Nonell had known in Paris, in them, but also of Daumier and of the Spanish naturalistic tradition, from Murillo and Ribera to Velázquez. Pablo was truly influenced by him, adopting not only his themes, but also his kind of almost too-heavy impasto way of painting them. He took for his own the great sculptural nudes that looked like poorly squared stone blocks, squatting women coiled in on themselves, often shown in rear view, in earthy colorations, ocher or reddish, as if seen in half-light. This emphasis on poverty became his because it fitted with his own feelings: Nonell became the first painter Picasso swallowed into his universe.

Nonell did not consider his art only a vehicle for his own ideas; it was his weapon for the defense of the poor and oppressed. He was the first to introduce—with such strength and authority!—true life, that of the masses, into Catalonian painting of his day. Ahead of all others, he showed the men and women of his country in their true light: destitution. Revealing this to Pablo, he led him to forsake the blandness of Art Nouveau and Symbolist Mannerism for a more human art, rooted in life.

What Pablo continued to do till he left for Paris does not seem unusual. His biographers (too often hagiographers) wax ecstatic over these naturalistic portraits and slices of life, which indeed reflect the young man's skill and mastery. Yet—would they so glow over them, if they were not aware of what the man and his work were to become?

There is a sheet on view at the Picasso Museum, dated 1897–1898, on which he wrote: "This is what you are like, never wanting to do like others." Whether this is a sentence read somewhere, or overheard, or his own personal thought, the words are significant.

Carlos Casagemas, a year older than he, was one of Pablo's closest friends at this time. His father, who was consul-general of the United States in Barcelona, originally intended for him to have a naval career, but the war put a stop to that and he happily forswore the uniform to go to work with Urgellers, a theatrical designer. Casagemas, good-looking and good company, though unstable and passionate, had an excessive interest in firearms. Picasso did a caricature of himself, dragging along with his head as usual down into his coat collar, a sketch pad under one arm and a cane under the other, alongside this friend whose elongated aristocratic profile was set atop a high stiff collar, his especially pronounced nasal appendage sticking out above a receding chin.

Pablo was also close to the Pichot brothers, Josep (Pepito), Ramón (Ramonet), Lluis, and Ricard. They and their parents and two sisters, Mercedes and María, lived right in the *barrio gótico,* at 21 Calle de Montcada, not far from today's Picasso Museum.

In the Pichots' Bohemian home, art was always the subject of conversation, whether painting, music, or poetry. Pablo especially liked Ramón the painter, and they were to meet again in Paris, and remain friends all their lives. In 1910, Pablo and his mistress Fernande Olivier stayed with the Pichot brothers and sisters at their little house near the port of Cadaqués, where friends were always welcome.

The painter Ricardo Canals initiated Pablo into engraving, and probably at his urging in 1899 he made his first etching, *The Left-Hander,* an experiment unrepeated for the moment.

Early in 1900, Pablo left the Escudillers Blancs studio for a larger one at 17 Calle Riera de San Juan, which until September he shared with Casagemas, now his intimate, "perhaps," Sabartés has suggested, "because better than any others of the chums he was ready to help him with his plans, or listen to the endless ideas he kept dreaming up."

The former naval student seems to have become a painter more by contagion than vocation. Rich, without financial problems, he was also interested in literature, and on Sunday afternoons, in his parents' huge apartment, held huge get-togethers where he and his friends acted out ideas selected by chance; the main participants were the Reventos and the de Soto brothers, Vidal Ventosa, Pallarés, and of course Picasso. They also indulged in doing "fried drawings": their art work was dipped in a pan of boiling oil and "fried," often with strange results. Sometimes they met at Vidal Ventosa's ground-floor place on Plaza del Pino, in summer setting their chairs out on the sidewalk for greater comfort.

Manuel Martinez Hugué (Manolo), nine years older than Pablo, on rare occasions joined them; the two became real friends only later in Paris. Manolo had painted before becoming a sculptor, and later was to work in decorative Cubism, all solid compact masses, mainly anecdotally interesting. He remained Picasso's lifelong friend.

Casagemas paid the rent at Calle Riera de San Juan, but Picasso made most use of the unfurnished, broad-windowed studio on the top floor of an old house, high above the city. Casagemas served especially as Picasso's companion in going to cabarets and night spots in the *barrio chino* and the port, and whoring—although the onetime midshipman usually ducked away before Picasso got inside these resorts, giving varied excuses.

They had "furnished" the studio by painting closets, a safe, a sofa, chairs, and a pantry on the walls. They had a manservant and an attractive maid to serve them, doubtless paid by Casagemas, for Pablo, since the break with his family, was quite penniless, earning very little from any commissions he got.

After several of his friends exhibited at Els Quatre Gats, Pablo in turn had a show, in the magic-lantern room: his drawings of his cronies and one painting of a priest, breviary in hand, at the bedside of a dying woman. The opening took place February 1, 1900, in an atmosphere both grave and happy. It may be that not Picasso but his friends organized the show, for it was good publicity for the young painters and writers.

"We wanted the public to know that there was someone other than Casas, that he was not the only portrait painter and his art not the whole extent of Barcelona's talent," Sabartés was later to say.

The show was announced on the day of the opening in the evening paper, *La Veu de Catalunya,* but *La Vanguardia* of February 3 carried the first critique, unfortunately misspelling his name.

The un-bylined reporter may well have been a teacher at La Lonja, and one of Don José's colleagues, Rodriguez Codola. While faulting "Picazzo" (*sic*) for certain things "excusable because of his age" and "hesitancies about what path to follow," he does allow that "many of the portraits have character . . . that some are sketched with laudable sobriety and in all one must note . . . the ease of handling of the pencil. . . ."

As for the only painting in the show,

> In this canvas painted with assurance there are conditions not to be sneered at, and one must hope that these conditions will reach their maturity when Mr. Ruiz Picazzo, without any sort of prejudice and with a wealth of experience and study greater than he now possesses, reaches the stage at which one aims at the highest, and tries to make typically personal works.

Can we assume that this somewhat contorted sermon is in fact a doctoral warning by a teacher voicing Don José Ruiz' regrets and reproaches? On this special occasion, *La Vanguardia*'s regular critic, who covered all art shows however insignificant, Alfredo Opisso, father of Ricardo who was a friend of Pablo's, had let someone replace him. Was he perhaps worried about offending the famous Casas by speaking about a possible rival?

A large number of people came, and some collectors bought a few of the drawings for a peseta or two. Even if these buyers were mainly Pablo's models acquiring their own pictures, it constituted a sizable commercial success. The unusual length of the *Vanguardia* piece, about a totally unknown beginner, was a subject of much comment.

To try to make a little money, Pablo decided to give some lessons, but finally gave up for want of pupils; we know of only one, the "professor" having done his portrait, one Fita i Fita.

On February 24, 1900, *La Vanguardia* published a final list of the artists entering the official competition for inclusion of works in the Spanish section of the Universal Exposition to open in Paris in May. Several paintings by Picasso, under his real name of Pablo Ruiz, are listed. A few days later he was to learn that one of them, *Last Moments,* had been selected. Several well-known Spanish painters, such as Zuloága, were left out, provoking loud protests.

Most biographers have failed to note Pablo's participation at the Paris Exposition of 1900, but the catalog clearly shows it. So we know why the young artist made his trip to Paris: to see his work in the Grand Palais in this ten-year survey of contemporary painting.

On July 12, *Joventut,* one of the avant-garde magazines of Catalonian intellectuals, printed a drawing ordered from Picasso as illustration for a poem by Juan Oliva Bridgman, "El Clam de les verges" (The Clamor of the Virgins), a declamatory lyrical call to free love. Conforming to the Symbolistic tone of the poem, Pablo showed a naked woman, asleep, half reclining, in profile, her body with its flabby breasts covered by a shroud she was trying to throw off. Her dream is of a phantom male whose head and torso are rising out of a broadly hatch-marked background. They must have liked it, for the magazine's issue of August 16 had another Picasso drawing illustrating another of the same poet's works, "Ser o no ser" (To Be or Not to Be). The Picassos are in keeping with the other "modernist" art work printed, by Boecklin, Burne-Jones, Aubrey Beardsley, and so on.

In September *Catalunya Artistica* called on him to draw a portrait of the poet Anton Busquets Punset, who had won the Catalan Floral Games; it was published in No. 6, October 4. But Pablo also had some failures, with some magazines turning down his work: two of them, *L'Esquella de la Torratza* and *La Campaña de Gracia,* did not even return his originals! When a new owner, Alberto Maluquer, took over *L'Esquella,* he found in a batch of unpublished drawings an envelope with a self-portrait of Picasso and two illustrations he had done, marked: "Do not publish. Too poor."

Picasso's friends appear to have been taken by surprise by his decision to go to Paris. Yet, how could they not have known the real reason for his trip! In addition to seeing his own canvas hung at the Exposition, he wanted to see all the contemporary art of which the black-and-white magazine reproductions had given him only approximations. In addition, there would be the unparalleled chance to see the hundred-year survey of French painting and movements of the nineteenth century, from David and Ingres to Cézanne.

Despite Germanic influences, Paris and French painting held a strong attraction for Catalan artists; the returnees from Paris were favorites at Els Quatre Gats. So Casagemas and Pallarés decided to go with Picasso, the former accompanying him, the latter to follow when he finished decorating a chapel at Horta. Before leaving Barcelona, Picasso did a self-portrait with the Catalan words *Yo el rey* (I the King) three times, circling his head. Presumably stolen from Junyer-Vidal's home, it is lost.

A series of paintings Pablo did before leaving reveal a turning point in his career; breaking out of the constricting Els Quatre Gats mode, he seemed to want to inventory Barcelona's teeming, warm, animated street life, and its bullfights.

He made wide use of pastels, often mixed with gouache or oil. High in color, these works are typical of the Mediterranean port, and may have been intended for sale in Paris, where Picasso probably thought they would seem exotic, with action, brilliance, and originality. Bullfights were indeed not too common in France. *In the Arena, Bullfights,* and *Entrance to the Plaza* all fit this description.

Manolo, Ramón Pichot, Sebastián Junyent, and Nonell were among the fellow Catalans awaiting Picasso and Casagemas in Paris. (In 1950, Picasso would tell Roland Penrose that Paris was to have been only a way station for him, that he had wanted to live and work in London, and was very fond of pre-Raphaelite painting.) He planned to live in Montparnasse, namely in the Rue Campagne-Première, with its many studios, but Nonell, who was going back to Barcelona, suggested he take his, at 49 Rue Gabrielle in Montmartre. With that offer, Pablo's fate took shape.

Montmartre in those days was really the country. The hillsides above Rue Caulaincourt (built up on only one side) were covered with the wild rickety shacks of the *maquis.* Dance halls, cabarets, and other pleasure pits, usually of ill repute, hid behind the decaying facades of the steep streets leading up to the old village with its church, cemetery, calvary, and small square surrounded by cheap cafés, all dwarfed by the frightful cream cheese known as the Sacré-Coeur. Badly paved alleys slipped between old buildings that in springtime had hawthorn and lilac in their hedges. Through a clearing one could see Paris with its bluish haze, but Picasso had none of the opportunistic ambitions of Balzac's Rastignac.

He dawdled in the streets, watching shops, monuments, and people with a curious but cautious eye. The tarts of Montmartre quickly noted his solid shoulders and darkling glance; from them, he would learn his first words of French— at first, just enough to get him what he wanted.

In museums, at the Louvre, and in the hundred-year survey at the Exposition, he now saw the originals of Manet, the Impressionists, Cézanne. *Last Moments* was well hung in the Spanish section of the ten-year survey, listed as No. 79 in the catalog, under: *Ruiz Picasso (Pablo), Barcelona, 3 rue de la Merced.* The selections had created as much brouhaha on the French side as in Spain, and the curator of the Luxembourg Museum, Léonce Benedite, hardly an avant-gardist, wrote in *La Gazette des Beaux-Arts* that "the spirit of the Inquisition came to life again in the jury of academicians." There were 106 Spanish paintings by sixty painters, and Picasso hung on the walls of the Grand Palais alongside Moreno Carbonero, and two of his Els Quatre Gats companions, Santiago Rusiñol and Ramón Casas.

Pablo had been in Paris only a few days when by chance he bumped into a compatriot who immediately announced he was a dealer and asked to see his work: Pedro Manach. Strange turn of events!

Manach was a sturdy fellow, very self-confident, with abundant enterprise and contacts, who had set out to establish young Catalan painters on the Parisian market. He had turned his back on his family, wealthy Barcelonese industrialists, to come to Paris a few years earlier. And he had done all right; through him

Nonell, Junyent, Canals, Pichot, Torent, Manolo, and a few others had sold quite a number of canvases; this Pablo Ruiz Picasso, selected for showing in the *décennale*, might prove a real find.

At the Rue Gabrielle studio, he saw the Barcelona paintings, full of movement and light, displayed on easels or against the wall. Their originality struck Manach: they showed a temperament, a new vision of the people and things of the Catalonia he knew so well, and brilliance of color. He offered Pablo 150 francs * per month, for a given number of paintings to be supplied on demand. No great fortune, but the average French worker at the time earned seven francs a day, so Picasso agreed to it forthwith. Who could have thought he would get such a deal just a few days after reaching Paris?

He wrote home. Don José could only sigh—obviously Pablo would go on amazing and shocking him. After all, was it not quite immoral for a boy of twenty to get that much money? Had he himself not spent years slowly climbing the ladder of their profession?

Manach was neither philanthropist nor gifted with second sight. He merely thought the young fellow's work showed early mastery and, with such picturesque colorful subjects, was sure to sell.

Pablo took to Paris much better than to Madrid. With his friends from home, he was often out in night spots, low-down as well as more respectable. (He had hoped to meet up with Lautrec, but by the fall of 1900, the latter, felled by alcoholism and other excesses, had gone back to his family's château at Malromé.) Sometimes they went to the classy Moulin Rouge, with its cancan, or the Moulin de la Galette: Pablo liked the overheated, lust-laden muskiness of these pleasure palaces where formally dressed society people rubbed elbows and things with footpads and bareheaded girls.

The first painting that, by his own say-so, he painted in Paris was in fact *Le Moulin de la Galette.* Was this, as has been said, a tribute to Toulouse-Lautrec? The latter's *Moulin Rouge,* 1892, might have inspired this curious composition, with its aquarium greenness to capture the atmosphere. That picture of Montmartre night life is a "period piece," while *Cancan* and *Stiff Shirts* more fully show the Lautrec influence and justify Picasso's statement, "It was in Paris I learned what a great painter Lautrec had been."

Now in November, his work done, Pallarés got to Paris, and immediately fell in with Picasso, Casagemas, and the rest of the Spaniards. Thanks to Manach's stipend, Pablo could often entertain on Rue Gabrielle; the artists brought pretty girls, and many models, among whom Odette and Germaine, with her sister Antoinette, were favorites. Casagemas fell violently and demandingly in love with Germaine (real name: Laure Gargallo), but she returned the feeling only moderately.

In a drawing intended for mailing back to Barcelona, probably to the Reventos brothers, Pablo showed himself at the Universal Exposition, in company with Ramón Casas, Pichot, Miguel Utrillo, Casagemas, and Germaine. Naturally, he

* Thirty dollars at the time. (Estimated by the author to be equivalent to approximately one hundred dollars per month today.) [TR. NOTE]

immediately dragged Pallarés over to see his paintings, as if, the old man now recalls, "he were going there for the first time." This was often Pablo's way; he was loath to reveal a price, or the interest he felt for a given work or artist; he always preferred secrecy. But he wrote the Reventoses that with Casagemas and Pallarés he saw a good deal of Alexander Cortada, the ardent Catalan separatist who would later organize the first Impressionist show in Barcelona, as well as the collector Alexander Riera, and Jaime Brossa, one of the anarchist leaders.

Paris the city was what fascinated him, streets, cafés, pleasure places, circus, fairs, and slums, outlying avenues, clip joints, one-eyed bars, dance halls on the outskirts. To him, that was where painting was, on the faces of tarts, poor tramps, underfed children, the leprous facades of buildings, the tawdry of dance halls and the bawdry of bals-musettes on a Saturday night, the side streets with couples slipping away into them, the comings and goings of streetwalkers, the unwholesome curiosity of "fancy people," coming slumming and gazing at this outcast fauna, isolated like a running sore far from the residential neighborhoods, and titillating to their jaded senses. Nobody was painting that at the time.

Renoir had seen the Moulin de la Galette as sprightly entertainment, and even Van Gogh showed Montmartre's gardens happy in winter. Lautrec, pitiless chronicler though he was, had, as a cripple, been too well treated by the tarts and their johns to display their social taints; only at the gateway to his own decay did he turn cruel (that is, true). No artist had shown Montmartre as it was beneath the playtime mask.

Picasso probably was imbued with Nietzscheism; and he also doubtless realized the Belle Époque was a false front, that the enjoyment in Montmartre hid the awful existence of an odiously exploited working class, ravaged by prostitution and alcohol. His Nietzscheism was also coupled with the "socialism" he had picked up in Barcelona, but beyond that he painted the suffering and wretchedness of Montmartre along with its lowlife, because he was in it, living it, just as in Barcelona he had painted his friends, the bullfights, and the local cafés. At nineteen, he might have said of the daily record of his surroundings what he told his publisher Tériade thirty years later: "The work we do is a way of keeping a diary."

Picasso always based his art on his own vision alone, so that that of others, even when he used it, did not interest him much. He quickly forgot what he had digested; he painted what was before him, what had to be seen, and gave an essential image of it. Cubism would be the logical outcome of that.

There are street and café scenes, dancing girls, artists, cabaret turns, twisty hillside streets and gray houses. Coming out of a cabaret at night, Pablo would see the sidewalk pleasure purveyors, go up to their rooms, and paint the girls in chemises, making up again after turning their tricks. Behind a theater flat, in one quick nimble stroke, he caught a cancan dancer or Sada Yacco, the exciting Japanese girl who was that season's big hit. A woman went by, wearing· a large hat, and in a pen stroke enhanced by color crayons, there she was.

Pablo's letters to his friends were always sown with sketches. His eye was a recording machine that missed nothing. His hand, no less quick, set up the inventory of what his avid, lucid, and acute eye saw. Drawn or written, the two narrations corresponded. The girls were precisely portrayed, thin faces with pinched lips, coal-black eyes, "dog collar" around the neck, high chignon, long skirt, and the disillusioned but promising air of the professionals of love for sale. Cutthroats and pickpockets under Pablo's pen flanked society ladies or the Eiffel Tower with a bottle of sparkling wine, symbol of Paris by night.

Manach was as good as his word. Thanks to him, the young painter was without financial pressures; he was privileged among his neighbor artists, who were on starvation diets. And he could show his family he could make it living on his art—something his father had never accomplished.

Among Manach's business contacts was a small, intelligent, passionate, curiosity-prone young woman who had worked for an antiquarian picture dealer named Mayer, and when the latter died set up on her own. Berthe Weill by name, in the advent of modern art she did not really play the part she claimed and some devotees have attributed to her. She was never one of the real pioneers, and all her undertakings were commercial. However, she is due credit for having been interested mainly in young artists and trying to do the impossible to help them, finding collectors, showing their works in her gallery at 25 Rue Victor-Massé, and boosting their prices.

Manach had consigned to her some of the works of Nonell, Sunyer, and several others of the innumerable young Spaniards now working in Montmartre. She bought the first three Picassos sold in Paris, three pastels for a flat hundred francs, turned over the next day at a fifty-franc profit to Adolphe Brisson, publisher of the prestigious *Annales politiques et littéraires*. They were scenes of bullfights.

In her memoirs Weill tells how Manach made an appointment for her at the Rue Gabrielle studio, but there was no answer when she rang the doorbell. Returning a bit later with a surprised Manach at her side, they found two characters hiding in bed, Pablo and Manolo having a joke at her expense! But there were "piles of paintings," and "little Old Lady Weill," as she was known to the artists, found a selection she thought she could use.

Manach was deeply impressed by the dynamic young woman's interest in Picasso. At nineteen, could he really mean something commercially? Either alone or through Weill, Manach did apparently sell several of his discovery's Spanish paintings. In contrast to the legend, he had no trouble finding takers: "Nobody wanted anything but Picassos!" Weill would detail in her memoirs.

One small pastel, *Spanish Women,* sold for 50 francs; four paintings, 225 francs; two painted heads, 110 francs; "enchanting painting of a child in a symphony in white," bought for 60 francs by Olivier Sainsère; while a Mr. Huc, who happened to be publisher of *La Dépêche de Toulouse* and an experienced collector, took the *Moulin de la Galette* for 250 francs.

This Arthur Huc played a big role in Picasso's early success, though the latter never knew who he was. A former lawyer and a lover of modern art, as early as 1894 he had allowed the Paris offices of his newspaper to be used for exhibiting the works of young painters including Bonnard, Maufra, Sérusier,

Lautrec, Vallotton, and Vuillard. The posters for his advertising were done by Toulouse-Lautrec and Maurice Denis, and his parlor, at his home on Rue Matabiau in Toulouse (France's "Athens of the South"), had doors decorated by Denis and walls hung with the works of "innovators" who horrified the local bourgeoisie, in thrall to the academicism of Salon and Institute. He hung the *Moulin de la Galette* alongside his other favorites.

Though ignored by Picasso's biographers, Huc, along with Maurice Fabre of Narbonne, was Picasso's first provincial French collector, and the *Moulin de la Galette* in 1900 was the painer's first work to grace a French home. By now the signature "P. Ruiz Picasso" had become "P. R. Picasso."

In mid-December, Pablo decided to take a trip back to Barcelona, but did not have the fare (relatively much higher then than in recent years, according to Picasso), despite Manach's stipend, and he had to borrow it. Casagemas, jilted by Germaine, was drinking and talking of suicide, so Pablo and Pallarés thought it would be a good idea to take him down to Málaga, where the milder climate and pretty Andalusian girls might make him forget his troubles.

Picasso, who always hated the cold, knew that Barcelona would be uncomfortable (and poorly heated) in January. In his native city, family and friends could now see he had not let them down; Uncle Salvador would find out that, even without his allowance, he had made out all right.

Besides, he wanted to use this occasion to break off his affair with a girl, a Spanish prostitute in Paris whose existence never came to light until Pierre Daix showed Picasso the reproduction of a pen-and-ink drawing of two men and a small, chubby young lady greeting them at the door, which had been entitled *Picasso, Casagemas, and the Concierge.*

"That was no concierge!" Picasso exclaimed. "That was a girl friend named Rosita!"

But he was much less emotionally involved with her than Casagemas with Germaine. Pallarés and Pablo tried to convince Casa that the latter was a fickle trollop, and he finally agreed to go with them. They left for Barcelona on December 20, and a few days later Casa and Pablo went on to Málaga. But Casagemas, unable to live without Germaine, was soon on his way back to Paris.

On reaching Málaga on December 30, they had tried to register at Hotel Tres Naciones, on Calle de las Casas Quemadas, but they were so unconventionally attired that the innkeeper turned them away. But Aunt María de la Paz Ruiz lived right next door, which her nephew well knew, and Pablo called on his cousin Antonio to vouch for him at the Tres Naciones. They got the room, and Pablo created the small scandal he intended.

He was not unhappy to shock Málaga, knowing how his long hair and Bohemian getup would strike his family and fellow citizens. Uncle Salvador was completely taken aback: his nephew was not only one of those "artists," but probably an anarchist to boot! And he was not slow to express disapproval.

Pablo now could see the depth of conventions that separated him from his kin whom he adored, but he also knew that his youthful defiances would not weaken his deep attachment to these provincial bourgeois from whom he had sprung.

He was provoking them only to get to know them better, and have them see him differently. (A few years later, when Don Salvador was gravely ill, he would dash off a note to his cousins Concha and María, "Let me know the news every day, for I cannot be quiet for a single instant!")

Alone after Casagemas left, Pablo dragged from brothel to bar, for two weeks drawing the dancing girls in cabarets and cheap waterfront joints, and befeathered ladies in a box at the theater. But neither women nor entertainment ever took his mind off his work and his art. His main concern was to remain master of himself. So Casagemas' conduct was incomprehensible to him; to him, a man could not be the slave of his emotions, however great his passion for a woman. Pablo always avoided emotional entanglements, and could not understand how others deferred to them.

He suddenly decided to go back to Madrid, though he had not liked it three years earlier: he wanted to get its smell and its feel again, proving perhaps that he had not yet decided to settle in Paris. Remember, he had thought of going to London.

He first took a room in a boardinghouse on Calle Caballero de Gracia, then in early February moved to Calle Zurbano to a loft that had only a table, a camp bed, and a chair in it. He was not flush, for he had sent no work to Manach and the latter had sent him no money. So he was on a diet of "fried eggs and all like that," as he cryptically told Sabartés. But of course all his life he was to plead poverty, say he was a beggar, that there was never enough to eat, no one loved or cared about him!

Alone in Madrid, he entertained himself by doing drawings in cabarets, and visited whorehouses for purposes of hygiene. In his loft, he froze, "no fire or light, never was I so cold," as he was to tell Sabartés. Especially since he liked to work at night.

But he did hop to Toledo for a day or so to see the Grecos. And he met a young Catalan writer, Francisco de Assis Soler, whom he had known in Barcelona. The latter was in Madrid as sales representative for his father, inventor of an "electric belt to cure all illnesses," its advertisement said—but mainly he concerned himself with literature.

Pablo and Soler decided to start a little magazine. The profits from the electric belt paid the costs of *Arte Joven* (Young Art), in which the two friends proposed to bring the Catalan intellectuals' "modernism" to Madrid. Francisco Soler was editor, with Picasso, who illustrated almost all of the first issue, called art editor. It appeared on March 10, 1901, with the bold promise, "*Arte Joven* will be a sincere publication."

The contents were not very revolutionary: their eclectic anarchism embraced Spanish-style *Jugendstil* with a Parisian flavor. Picasso's drawings were much like the Montmartre sketches done in the vein of Steinlen, Lautrec, and Nonell. The two portraits of Pío Baroja and Santiago Rusiñol were more accented: the latter was caught in incisive pen strokes, slightly bent of back beneath his long topcoat, his fine face, heavy beard, and flowing hair, against the background of a garden with a fountain. Neither Pablo nor the literary contributors left the beaten paths, and Soler's "decadent" aestheticism mixed with the protesting anarchism that trumpeted its café noisiness throughout the five issues, echoing the tone of talk at Els Quatre Gats.

Pablo and Soler had sounded a call for young artists and writers to join them, and these were delighted to have an uncensored forum; one of the drawings shows the two editors with Cornuti and Alberto Lozano, Madrid poets. Naturally, the magazine ran into financial difficulties, and Picasso sent a copy to Uncle Salvador, with a request for a subscription. He got a furious answer in insulting terms. So they went after advertisements: the ones for Els Quatre Gats and the electric belt were on the house—and no others appeared. The final issue, out in June, announced the coming of a new magazine, *Madrid. Notas d'Arte* (Madrid: Art Notes), run by the same editors, drawn by Picasso in a flattering frontispiece that showed them in flowing romantic capes, looking thoughtful. But it never did appear.

Picasso did not await the downfall of *Arte Joven* to make tracks to Barcelona, and thence to Paris. He had heard in a letter from Ramón Reventos of the death of Casagemas, but did not know just how what he knew must be a suicide had taken place. Casagemas was quietly buried in Barcelona, attended only by intimate friends who, at the request of the family, made no public comments. On February 28, an obituary notice appeared in *Catalunya Artistica,* with Picasso's portrait of the deceased.

Casagemas dead stayed with Pablo, almost like an obsession, and he was terribly moved on visiting his Paris studio and the café where, before the very eyes of Pallarés, who even today remembers every last detail of the pitiful affair, he killed himself. In his own way, Picasso would pay tribute to this, his earliest companion in his life as an artist. Why the sudden departure for Barcelona? Perhaps just for money reasons. But also no doubt because Manach had sent word of a possibility of being exhibited by Vollard, Cézanne and Gauguin's dealer. Miguel Utrillo was also at the same time preparing a show of Pablo's pastels at the Sala Parés, probably in the hope of keeping him in Barcelona.

In Madrid, Picasso had done several portraits of women, bedecked courtesans or theater performers, alive with feathers and boas, in gaudy dresses and lurid makeup. Their cruel objectivity takes nothing away from the pictorial qualities; quite the opposite. As Degas did, he saw woman as an animal, and portrayed her as the companion in debauchery, the libidinous partner on the night prowl, the sex object; without exaggeration, he was showing these girls as they were, with all their artifices. Nude, they would be nothing but hunks of painting, and Pablo did not possess Degas's plastic genius; but dressed in their sumptuous shimmering allurements they symbolized the lechery of big cities, Madrid or Paris, the depravity of nightlifers squandering a fortune for an embrace, the whole of the *Belle Époque.*

Picasso's mastery was accompanied by his progress on the technical level. The authority of oil was matched by the fluidity of pastel handled in discrete touches in the Impressionist manner; and sometimes the painter lent his oil the lightness and transparency of pastel, to the point that the two have been indistinguishable in reproductions. Thus, some works, such as the *Spanish Woman,* for instance, with its high-colored, divisionist, and hammered-out stroke, forecast pictures to come to be seen in the first Vollard exhibit, for example, *Woman with Feathered Hat* and *Woman in Blue.*

This time, in Barcelona, Pablo did not seek out his friends, but rather worked, promenaded up and down the Ramblas, talked, and made plans, described by Sabartés as "a fireworks illuminating imaginary constructs, opening new perspectives for our anticipation." But the memorialist's shortcoming is that he insists on seeing in the early Picasso the fascinating, peremptory famous man whom he was to get back together with in 1935, after years and years of separation, whose every word, gesture, and work to him are so many flashes of genius.

In point of fact, Don José's son was concerned about the exhibition of his works Manach was setting up with Vollard, and he spent long hours at his easel, disregarding, indeed avoiding, what was being prepared locally at the Sala Parés. Had he already said a mental good-bye to Barcelona? Cities, to Picasso, were like women; one did not break things off roughly, for that created complications, tears, and shouting, but progressively drifted away from them when they had nothing more to give and you nothing more to get from them.

When he found out that Utrillo planned to hang Ramón Casas' works at the Sala Parés along with his, he took this as patronizing, threw a fit of anger, and refused to attend the opening. Although Utrillo said he meant to honor his friend by including Barcelona's principal exponent of modern painting, Pablo stuck to his guns: Andalusian pride was no misnomer.

And so to Paris. Not because he felt insulted, but only because he had heard from Manach: Gustave Coquiot, a fashionable art and theater columnist, liked his work and wanted to do the Vollard introduction. The sooner he got back with his Spanish paintings the better. Manach had gotten him a studio in his own building, 130 *ter* Boulevard de Clichy—Casagemas' old studio.

This time, Pablo's traveling companion was another friend from Els Quatre Gats, Jaime Andreu Bonsoms, where eight months earlier it had been Casagemas. On returning to Paris in January, Casagemas had resumed his courtship of Germaine, despite her rebuff. He was staying with Pallarés, until, he said, he could find a place to move into with her. On February 17, Casagemas, Pallarés, Manolo, and Alexander Riera were dining out on Boulevard de Clichy, with Germaine and her friend Odette. Casagemas got into a quarrel with Germaine, and shouted, "Then, let this be farewell!" Germaine, surprised and upset, pulled a packet of letters out of his pocket: the one on top was addressed to the Police Commissioner. Thereupon, Casagemas whipped out a revolver, aimed at the young woman trying to get away, and fired, shouting, "So much for you!" Pallarés had the presence of mind to deflect his arm, but Casagemas thought he had hit Germaine and, turning the weapon on himself, shouted, "And so much for me!" as he put a bullet through his head. Casagemas died a short time later at Bichat Hospital; Germaine was not hurt.

Because it appeared so late, Pablo, already in Paris, did not see the June issue of *Pel i Ploma* with Miguel Utrillo's article on him, signed "Pincell." It had five reproductions of his work, including his portrait of Casas—no irony intended.

> Picasso's art is enormously young [it said]. Out of a pitiless observation of the foibles of our day, it sees beauty even in the horrible. He notes what he sees, acutely, soberly, concerned only for the truth, not with showing he knows how to draw a nose from memory. The pastels in the exhibit . . . are but one aspect of his talent, a talent which will be widely debated, but none the less appreciated by those who, forsaking ready-made molds, look for art in its different aspects. Picasso, not yet twenty, has acquired a nickname in Paris; because of his big *pavero* * hat faded in Montmartre's inclement weather, his lively eyes of a self-controlled Southerner, his neck ringed with the legendary post-Impressionist cravats, his French friends have dubbed him "Little Goya." We hope his appearance will not be misleading, and our heart tells us we will turn out to be right.

This was the first time that Picasso's name was actually written by a critic in print, as it was to be so many thousands of times thereafter, throughout the world, and by now "Picasso," all by itself, was the way his signature appeared.

The paintings done in the less than two months in Barcelona again show the climate he lived in and the people he saw. He worked prodigiously in this period, and color, whether oil or pastel, became very intense in his work. There was a share of Impressionism in it, especially in the *tachiste* technique he used; but instead of a divisionist touch, he preferred a flaking of tones, the spots of color subtly diluted in relation to each other. In the gleaming reddish *Bullfight* in the Niarchos Collection, Picasso appears once more as precursor of the Fauves: the same experimenting, flaking or stick strokes, subtle relationships among figure, light, and surrounding in the "character figures" in which the young painter expresses his interest in strange, albeit repulsive, personages. What matter that, as some have been at pains to point out, these ugly, deformed creatures suggest Velázquez' or Goya's buffoons and cripples, Degas's greaseballs, or Lautrec's fallen women? The search for the truth is what is basic.

In *La Nana* (The Dwarf Dancer) or the *Woman with Jewels,* his attempts at contrasts of colors and shapes through the pointillist handling show how the twenty-year-old, in his drive to go beyond realism, was delving more and more into the pictorial. He knew, having proved it to himself, that daring led to arbitrariness, which in turn ceases to be a game if the mastery is rooted in a solid technique: the picture is a whole based on free reconstruction of the real. But color also would henceforth be a determinant with Picasso, no longer just the clothing of shape, but an autonomous plastic element. No doubt that he had to go through such a stage in order to reach the monochromes of the Blue Period.

Perhaps it was at this time in Barcelona (April–May 1901) that Picasso met the sculptor Julio Gonzalez, and did the watercolor-and-ink portrait of him that his daughter Roberta has. All he could remember was where it had been done: Tibidabo Hill. Gonzalez, with chiseled face, drooping mustache, ascot tie, and "artist's" hat, is seated in front of a panorama of the distant city. The son and

---

* A turkey dealer or raiser.

"La Nana (The Dwarf Dancer)" Barcelona 1901
(Museo Picasso—Barcelona)

grandson of respected Catalan goldsmiths, and a goldsmith himself, his skill had earned him and his brother Joan the Gold Medal of the Exposition of Applied Art in 1892, when he was only sixteen. As Picasso had, he had "gone up" to Paris in 1900, but, despite his success in gold, aiming to be a painter. They had known each other at Els Quatre Gats, which both Julio and Joan attended, but Pablo and Julio would become great friends mainly after 1904, when Pablo often went to dinner at the Gonzalezes' on Avenue du Maine, in Montparnasse.

III

LIFE
IN
BLUE
(1901–1904)

JUNE 1901, JUST A FEW DAYS BEFORE THE OPENING OF THE SHOW AT Vollard's, set for the twenty-fourth, Picasso got to Paris and settled in on Boulevard de Clichy. The studio that had been Casagemas' was on the top floor, right next to Manach's room. So Pablo was back in Montmartre, but not in the village on the hill: this was the lower-middle-class storekeeping Montmartre of the boulevards, with their habitué-haunted cafés and nightclubs. Several "established" artists lived in the neighborhood.

As self-chronicler, the painter sketched himself arriving in Paris with Jaime Andreu Bonsoms, in an ink-and-crayons caricature perhaps sent to the Junyer-Vidals in Barcelona. Despite the late season, Pablo was dressed against the cold and carried a display case of drawings, while his less warmly dressed companion had only a small valise: to the left, the Seine, a bridge, and the Eiffel Tower; to the right, a pert-looking Parisienne.

The number of paintings and drawings he had with him were enough to scare Manach. All the Madrid and Barcelona work now piled up on top of the earlier Paris things the young dealer had. Enough for a huge show, bigger than Vollard's could hold.

Vollard in his memoirs tells how a young Spaniard he knew, "named something like Manache," brought in to him

> the painter Pablo Picasso who, only nineteen or twenty years old, had done no less than a hundred-odd canvases he was bringing for possible showing. The show was not at all successful and, for a long time, Picasso was to find no better reception with the public . . .

Vollard often wrote as vaguely as this. In fact, Manach had been to see him before Picasso came back to Paris, introduced by Gustave Coquiot, who had been won over by the originality of Pablo's work. The show had been decided on without Picasso being consulted, as in the case of Miguel Utrillo and the Sala Parés. Fate, again . . .

Ambroise Vollard was no ordinary man. He was said to doze most of the time, between naps turning away potential customers, for each time he awoke the requested paintings had gone up in price. No one knew exactly what he had stashed away in his little treasure-house on the Rue Laffitte, where he crawled, virtually on all fours, among stacked Cézannes, Renoirs, and Gauguins.

Born in Réunion Island, he had come to Paris to study as a *notaire,* so as to take over his father's practice; but art appealed to him more than the law. Highly cautious and a born digger-out, despite his apparent colonial nonchalance, Vollard began by peddling prints by Rops, Steinlen, John Lewis-Brown, Willette, Forain, and bought a Renoir nude that, after many unsuccessful attempts, he finally sold for 450 francs, a real feat at the time. After several years "of working out of his home," he set up first at 39, then 41, Rue Laffitte, at the time an art gallery area. It was at No. 41 that he first attracted scandalous attention by exhibiting the Cézanne "daubings" that made the general public rage or laugh. The Bernheim Brothers and Durand-Ruel, principal dealers in "innovators" on the market, had turned them down.

Making much in his memoirs of his flair concerning Cézanne, he rather dismisses his "discovery" of Picasso, whose show, he says, flopped—which is just not true.

Having now moved to 6 Rue Laffitte, he had just had a Nonell show, and he probably found similar appeal in Picasso's work: the same kind of dramatic subjects reminiscent of Steinlen, scenes of poverty, nightlife, street types, with a very vivid sense of color added. To make the show that Coquiot suggested more "Spanish," Vollard split his gallery between Picasso and Iturrino, a Bilbao Basque, who had not the slightest artistic link with him.

Coquiot knew why he had liked Picasso's work, and said that this "passionate lover of modern life" reflected the circles and people he himself frequented. A friend of Huysmans and Jean Lorrain, and admirer of Bonnard and Rodin, Coquiot was no fool. He wrote interestingly, though often relating gossip or tales of doubtful credibility, doing books on Lautrec, Cézanne, Van Gogh, Rodin, and Degas, whom he detested so much that in his 1924 *Des gloires déboulonnées* (Some Debunked Reputations) he included him with such academic has-beens as Meissonier, Henner, Carolus Duran, Bonnat, or Félicien Rops. He was more original in his books about Parisian life and felt that the "types" he met in his off-the-beaten-path or tenderloin wanderings were what he found in this gifted follower of Steinlen and Toulouse-Lautrec. He never understood Picasso's later work, and wrote venomous stupidities about him. However, the many fine Cézannes Pablo was to see at Vollard's would be of greater importance to his future.

Picasso had sixty-five works listed in the show's catalog, No. 65 being "Drawings" (not identified). Among the "Spanish" works several bullfight scenes, *The Matador, The Victims, Bullring, Village Bullfight,* and some landscapes, were hung alongside nightlife scenes done earlier in Paris, or in Madrid or Barcelona. The nightlife scenes (like the bullfights) were an imposing body of work, done with robust frankness and high in color; wherever they were painted, all had an original style, new at the time, also to be found in the portraits (of the artist, his fellow exhibitor Iturrino, and Manach).

Several scenes were observations of Paris, *Public Square, Kids, Brasserie,* and especially *Races,* all hard to identify, especially the last, which might be any of four known works. They had been painted a few days before the Vollard show, in all likelihood at the Auteuil racetrack, and reflect a refinement in the color flaking that does not interfere with realistic observation, the search for the truth through a remarkable sensitivity for the showmanship, the movement of the figures—elegant women in the paddock—and open air.

His early kinship to Bonnard, as his later to Matisse, shows that certain problems, namely those of color, were in the air. Pablo's Fauvism before the Fauves— and, as the future would prove, even against the Fauves—explained his recent conquest: color's energy content makes it an autonomous mode of expression that affects both the senses, through immediacy of vision, and the mind.

This was 1901, Cézanne and Gauguin were still known and appreciated by only a few. In March, a Van Gogh show at Bernheim-Jeune's made a stir, but only among the young.

Picasso was still interested in café and cabaret scenes, his most frequent field of experimental research. The *Café de la Rotonde* (the place where Casagemas committed suicide) appears as a sort of synthesis, with daring composition, construction out of colors laid in plaques or sticks with bold forthrightness, a harmony of dark greens and blacks lightened by solid reds and yellows, underlined by silvery whites. The influence of the Cézannes he had seen at Vollard's was undeniable; from him he had gotten the colored structuring, already latent in the earlier canvases, but now asserting itself fully in conjunction with a most recherché baroqueness of form. And there were other contemporary influences, Gauguin, Van Gogh (that year's big revelation for the young), soon to lead to the asceticism of the Blue Period.

At Vollard's, the portrait of Manach stood out from all the others. The character, standing with right hand on hip, is vigorously silhouetted in black. Its simplification speaks volumes; the face is painted in a few authoritative vertical brushstrokes, while shirt, trousers, and background are made of violently colored broad flats; no superfluous detail, tie and hands barely suggested. The color harmony is also of the simplest: white, black, and bright yellow, with the loud red spot of the necktie.

Also during that summer of 1901 he did several death portraits of Casagemas, in his coffin, from the right or suicide side, and two based on the incident: *Death* and *Evocation* (or *Burial of Casagemas*). The last-named, originally Vollard's and now in the City of Paris' Museum of Modern Art—it might well, like Courbet's famous *Atelier,* be titled *True Allegory*—has proved intriguing to many who wish to analyze Picasso. He probably was trying, in line with current Symbolist thought, pictorially to pose the problem of man's fate and the hereafter.

Casagemas, a victim of love, might well, Picasso thought, achieve in the beyond what had eluded him here on earth. That is shown in the splitting of the composition into two levels, earth and heaven, as in the *Burial of Count Orgaz.*

When Picasso had a show in Zurich in 1932, Dr. C. G. Jung in a "psychological study of Picasso" in the *Neue Zürcher Zeitung* was to interpret the start of the Blue Period as the very signal of schizophrenia, the blue there as in earlier paintings expressing a "moral tearing apart," a basic pessimism increased by the artist's attraction to the underworld, especially prostitutes, thus proving his unwholesome concern with the ugly and evil! Jung also felt that the painter periodically became reincarnated "in the infernal shape of the tragic Harlequin," reminiscent of the successive incarnations of Dr. Faust, like him "implicated in a murder."

Picasso was deeply traumatized by Casagemas' suicide, less the act itself than its cause, that mad, limitless, irresistible love, annihilating the individual in its violence, making him the plaything of fate—and it was to remain a lesson he would never forget: all his life long, he would beware of women and of love.

After that tragedy of February 17, 1901, his work acquired a new tone: now, he was facing the unbearable. He could not understand, could not *tolerate* this death, and it gave him a new attitude toward life; on top of the revolt born of the social injustices and miseries of Barcelona, a new malaise of bitterness and wrath now drove his work toward a tragic expressionism. The obsession with Casagemas' absurd suicide colored the entire Blue Period; gone were his youthful virtuosity and brilliant eclecticism. Pablo now came to grips with man's fate; thirty-five years later, faced with a shock as dramatic as his friend's fatal act, the Spanish Civil War, he would assume as his own the fate of his country.

At Vollard's, he had exhibited nudes, impossible at the time in Spain. Not pink, smooth, languorous nudes, of some doubtful titillating quality, as might be hung in the Salon or belong to society collectors, but worn-out bodies painted with a cruelty brutal enough to horrify admirers of modish beauty and to allow Jung to make his sweeping diagnosis. Pablo went beyond Degas and Toulouse-Lautrec, not even invoking the "functional" pretexts of intimate grooming or mercenary love; his women, with their flesh of molded mud, their flabby breasts and thighs, carrying all the stigmata of decay, were not far removed from the repulsive or questionable creatures that symbolized sin in the Middle Ages. Yet the nude of recumbent Jeanneton, one of the few professional models he ever employed, shows a tenderness far from being devoid of sensuality.

Pablo at twenty was without illusions about women. Society belles at the races, cabaret performers, wretched alcoholic larvae, fallen whores—he showed them all as they were, without cheating or flattery. "No work of art can be made without the cooperation of the demon," André Gide would say.

But Picasso also did charming children's portraits, especially little girls. So he was not, as some have claimed, obsessed by decay and ugliness. Children, beginning with his own, were one of the joys of his life, and he painted and repainted them.

Despite what the dealer said, Vollard's show was a hit.

"Things were going very well. People liked them a lot," as Picasso recounted it. "Only later, when I started doing the blue paintings, they didn't take at all. It's always been that way for me. Very good, and then all of a sudden, very bad. . . ."

A number of the pictures, as noted by Vollard, were sold to collectors, although some already had been bought before the show. *Public Square,* two *Flowers,* and *Boulevard de Clichy* belonged to Mme. Besnard, wife of Pablo's canvas and color supplier, at 68 Rue de La Rochefoucauld. A Mr. Fabre was listed as owning the otherwise unidentified *Sun King* (perhaps Maurice Fabre, of Gasparet, in the department of Aude, who built up a remarkable collection). It was probably also he who on his own authority entered one of his Picassos in the Salon of the Fine Arts Society of Béziers, April–May 1901, while the artist was in Barcelona.

Fabre wrote the preface for that exhibition, which, thanks to him and his friend Gustave Fayet, a landed gentleman of the Béziers area with a fine contemporary collection including Van Goghs and Gauguins, boasted the latter, Degas, Renoir, Cézanne, Pissarro, Odilon Redon, Rodin—and "M. Picasso. Spain (*Woman at the Seashore*)." Also represented was Jacques Villon—and this was in backwater Béziers in 1901!

Messrs. Ackerman, Coll, and Personnas listed by Vollard are forgotten, even by Picasso, although the last-named might be Personnaz, a Bayonne banker, who collected Impressionists. The M. Virenca in the catalog was a misspelling for Virenque, owner of the *Japanese Divan,* one of the Vollard pieces that remain unknown. He was an early Picasso collector, as was Mr. Blot, a dealer, who acquired *Chanteuse* and *Amoureuse,* also not convincingly identified.

One canvas unidentifiable as any we know of, *The Beast,* has never been heard of again. It was bought by Käthe Kollwitz, the young German painter-engraver who often visited Paris, where she did work at the Académie Jullian until 1904. She was to die in 1945 in Berlin, a few months after her home was destroyed in an air raid.

The Paris press, almost exclusively interested in the academic, largely ignored the Iturrino-Picasso show. One critic, Félicien Fagus of the Natanson brothers' *Revue Blanche,* did cover it. A dreamy Symbolist poet, too absentminded to see the truck that was to run him over at sixty-one in 1933, Fagus was the Brussels-born son of a Frenchman exiled after the Paris Commune. An anarchist sympathizer (later reverting to Catholicism and monarchism), Fagus remains interesting because he so well reflected the criteria of the day in his exegesis of Picasso (whom he would later not understand at all).

Under the heading of "Spanish Invasion: Picasso," he wrote:

> He is a painter, an absolute painter, beautifully; his divination of his "matter" shows it; like all pure painters, he adores color per se, and each matter has its own coloration.
>
> . . . Any subject can captivate him . . . the wild surge of flowers out of a vase and toward the light, and the luminous air dancing around them . . . the multi-

colored teeming of crowds on the greenswards of racetracks or the sun-drenched sand of a bullring; the nudity of women's bodies, any of them. . . .

His urgency has not yet left him time to develop a style of his own; but his personality lies in that very urgency, that impetuously juvenile spontaneity (. . . he is said to do three canvases a day). . . . This could lead him to facile virtuosity. . . . Prolific and fruitful are two different things, as are violent and energetic. And that would be most regrettable, given his brilliant virility.

Another critic, François Charles, that September in *L'Ermitage,* noted the brilliance of his debut, and warned the young man "for his own good no longer to do a painting each day."

The Vollard show ended July 14. Manach was satisfied, as was Picasso, who had made some Parisian contacts as a result. It also gave birth to a friendship that, despite ups and downs, was to be ended only by death. A young poet born at Quimper (Brittany) in 1876 of a Jewish family that came from Alsace, Max Jacob, visited the exhibit and asked who did the paintings. He was a small, hypersensitive, curious, perspicacious man, trying his hand at everything, unable to settle down, jack of all trades, terrified of women, and living in poverty. Perhaps these paintings by an unknown echoed his own torments, his inner obsessions.

The next day, referred by Manach, he went to the Boulevard de Clichy.

> Picasso knew no more French than I did Spanish [he was to recall], but we looked at each other and shook hands enthusiastically. It was a big studio . . . with Spaniards sitting all over the floor, eating and conversing happily. . . . The next day they came to my place and, on a huge canvas since lost or painted over, Picasso did a portrait of me sitting on the floor among my books before a huge fire. I remember giving him a Dürer woodcut that he still has. . . . Picasso and I talked sign language all through the night.*

Among his Barcelona friends, Mateo de Soto had been the first to come to join Pablo in Paris, in October, followed by Sabartés. Pablo and Soto met him at the station, early in the morning, despite Picasso's distaste for early rising.

They took him to Montmartre to a room they had rented for him in a small hotel on Rue Bréda (now known as Rue Henri-Monnier), and Soto, forsaking Pablo's studio, moved in with him. It was Picasso who wanted them near him, though not too close for comfort and privacy.

Pablo had gone to work hard after the Vollard show, boiling with creativity ("the beginning of the Blue Period," said Sabartés). Technical experiments now replaced the search for truth: reality was to be not in the subject but in the picture itself that constituted an independent whole: expression, shapes, rhythms, and colors.

While Barcelona had nurtured it, Paris allowed the daemon to bloom. That would have been impossible in the quasi-feudal Spain of the turn of the century. As Pablo told Maurice Raynal, "Had Cézanne worked in my country, he would have been burned at the stake."

* *Cahiers d'Art,* Paris, No. 6, 1927.

The Dwarf Dancer, Races, Bullfights, Nude with Stockings, Portrait of Ma-nach, Absinthe-Drinking Woman, Round of Little Girls were not only all different from each other, but also from the 1901 summer paintings with the "playing-card shades" that had so impressed Sabartés. He was not prepared for what he now saw.

"Well?" Picasso asked, and Jaime replied, "I'll get used to it."

Picasso always said he could never understand why people talked about *research* in modern painting. "To search means nothing. . . . To find, is the thing," he felt, and:

> The several manners I have used in my art must not be considered as an evolution, or as steps toward an unknown ideal of painting. All I have ever made was made for the present and with the hope that it will always remain in the present. . . . When I have found something to express, I have done it without thinking of the past or the future. . . . I have never made trials nor experiments. Whenever I had something to say, I have said it in the manner in which I felt it ought to be said. Different motives inevitably require different methods of expression. This does not imply either evolution or progress, but an adaptation of the idea one wants to express and the means to express that idea.

Death, inscribed to Casagemas, was done in that autumn of 1901; it is a prelude to the tender *Child with Pigeon* recently acquired by Courtauld, the great English collector, recalling one of Picasso's childhood memories, and *The Tub* (or *Blue Room*) in the Phillips Collection in Washington. The young nude woman, at her boudoir à la Degas, introduces us to Picasso's studio; over the undone bed there is a reproduction of Lautrec's May Milton poster hung near a little seascape, a bouquet of flowers on the table. One day, around 1905, a young German collector, Wilhelm Uhde, strolling in Montmartre, was to see the painting in a secondhand shop and buy it for ten francs.

The group of Spaniards around him had improved considerably with the arrival of Soto and Sabartés. One evening, as they were dawdling in the Latin Quarter, Sabartés decided he liked the carefree atmosphere there, and took a room at the Hôtel des Écoles, on Rue Champollion, near the Café La Lorraine, where henceforth each evening Picasso, Soto, Manach, Pallarés, Manolo, and Max Jacob would join him. Sometimes at noon, when he got up, Pablo would cross Paris to have lunch with Jaime in a Turkish restaurant on Place de la Sorbonne. Otherwise, he would go down with the others, at day's end, for the long talks, discussions, and walks far into the night. Usually, Picasso said, they all ended up in a whorehouse—except Max Jacob.

This was the time of *The Glass of Beer.* Sabartés explained to me how it came about:

> Coming into the café, he saw me sadly waiting for him—for he was often late—my nearsighted eyes half closed; in a flash, before I had even seen him arrive, he took it all in, then shook my hand and sat down, and we talked. A few days later, at his studio, I was surprised to see myself as I had been when he came in, as if snapped on the wing by his amazingly quick eye. I asked him why he hadn't told me about it.
> "Why should I have?" Picasso asked. "Isn't it you?"

*"Portrait of Sabartés (The Glass of Beer)"   Paris
1901 (Pushkin Museum—Moscow)*

(GIRAUDON)

Sabartés did not completely understand the paintings of his friend that he saw at Boulevard de Clichy, for Pablo never let himself be fully grasped; when you thought you had him, he slipped away. Jaime gazed at those great poignant figures of poverty, distress, and abandonment that replaced the vivid motley of the months gone by. In place of the fireworks, a blue light, a kind of twilight illumination, bathed things and people expressing weariness with living, self-disgust, irreparable downfall.

And, in this winter of 1901, along with the tragic alcoholic females with desperate eyes, the Saltimbanques, and the amazing naked *Gommeuse,* turned in on herself like a plucked bird shivering with cold, there came the first Maternities.

A pessimist obsessed by Casagemas' suicide and, like any Spaniard, haunted by death, at twenty Pablo loved life, friendship, and women. He had a big square head, thick black hair, and a new fringe of beard biting into his hollow cheeks; his eyes reflected unplumbable sadness; in his 1901 self-portrait they are lost as in a daydream. In Sabartés' words,

> He asserted that the authentic artist must remain unaware of anything, that culture kept one from seeing, put a brake on spontaneity, while the artist must be able to project directly on to the canvas what he wants to say. The Primitives did not saddle themselves with knowledge, their innocence was not bridled by theories; Picasso was sure that a painter found his deepest sincerity in suffering.

While recent works showed that Pablo had missed nothing in the development and techniques of painting since Impressionism, even to such fads as Art Nouveau, these inspirations or influences were only a pretext, a springboard to him. He alone knew their value and intensity. Who else, as the century came in, understood the importance of the Impressionists' divided touch, Cézanne's construction through color, Gauguin's syntheticism? As for the young painters following in the footsteps of these masters, Pablo ignored them; he lived alone, seeing only his Spanish artist friends.

He never paid attention to what Sabartés or others wrote or said. One evening, during the Cubist period, Sabartés came to Montmartre to show him something he had written about his work. Some British journalists from *The Studio* were visiting, looking at his new paintings and asking a lot of questions, which in his usual manner he answered only with vague rumblings.

Suddenly it occurred to Pablo to suggest that Sabartés read them his piece.

"But it's written in Castilian," the writer answered.

"So what?" said Picasso. "That's not your fault. You'll see whether or not they understand." -

Sabartés started, but it was a long article, and he was reading slowly. "Read faster," Pablo nervously whispered.

Sabartés speeded up, and the Englishman seemed to enjoy the pace. At the end, they congratulated Jaime; they might not have gotten the literal meaning, they said, but the intonation showed them many hidden things! And they bowed out with thanks.

"See," said a delighted Picasso. "Otherwise, we never would have got rid of them. And you said they wouldn't understand!"

The maternities piled up: progressively, mother and child became one unit, sometimes merged through the movement of drapes, in their solitude and tenderness. Anecdote turned into symbol: Picasso was erecting a monument to motherhood, a blue monument; the two largest in the series, the *Maternity* belonging to the late William Goetz in Los Angeles, and *Woman Squatting and Child*, in Harvard University's Fogg Art Museum, are two of the key works of the period.

"I saw that *blue* style appear little by little and melted into it; it began to take hold of me," said Sabartés, who had long talks with Pablo on his favorite subjects, the importance of the idea, the place of knowledge in a work of art, the share of impulse, instinct. Pablo did most of the talking, and his friend was often embarrassed by his verbiage, the twists and turns of his mind, the tough questions he asked. Picasso hated discussions about art, and when Sabartés started to get analytical he would often cut him short with a joke or a wisecrack.

At twenty, in 1901, Pablo should have doing his compulsory military service, but he got out of it, gaining three years that were of considerable importance to his work at the time. None of his biographers has ever questioned why, though short but strong and perfectly healthy, he had been exempted. Nor did Picasso ever clear it up.

Manuel Pallarés later explained to me that his friend had drawn a *número alto* (high number) in the annual draft, only the lower numbers being called up. While this was doubtless true, we may certainly assume that his well-connected Uncle Salvador "greased the way" for this high number. At the time, in Spain, well-to-do conscripts could buy their way out, with or without furnishing a substitute. His brother Don José, on the other hand, was sorry to see this; he thought military service would have been very good for his son, strengthening his character while giving him time for salutary thought. He wore a uniform only once— long enough to be photographed dressed as Sergeant Braque, who was on leave during a reserve period in 1909.

While doing the Sabartés portrait signed and dated shortly before his return to Barcelona in mid-January 1902, he was also painting Mateo de Soto, another pale physiognomy emerging from a blue penumbra, and a self-portrait. Manach was upset by his protégé's turn, as dismayed by the blue monochromes as he had been elated by the stormy high-color style displayed at Vollard's. And Pablo's behavior did not help: he entertained at night, in his studio next door to Manach's, keeping him awake with the endless discussions interspersed with guitar chords, and songs, and asking for ever greater financial advances. When Manach said no, he would threaten to leave Paris with all his paintings . . .

Late of an afternoon when Sabartés realized Pablo was not coming down to the Latin Quarter to see him, he would walk up, alone or with Soto, to Montmartre, when the *Burial of Casagemas* stood in the center of the studio—not only out of affection or symbolism, but also because it was big enough to act as a screen. There was unbelievable disorder in the room, the same disorder Pablo would unconsciously "organize" around him throughout his life. With nightfall,

"Evocation (Burial of Casagemas)" Paris 1901
(Musée d'Art moderne de la Ville de Paris)

(GIRAUDON)

the Spanish friends would come in, and then Max Jacob, who, when there was a silence, would recite poems—usually Verlaine's. He did them dramatically, and especially liked the effects of a poem called *Sleep:*

> A cradle, I,
>   Rocked in a grave:
> Speak low, pass by,

then going to a bare whisper:

> Silence I crave! *

as he lay motionless on the floor.

At times, the gang of them prowled the Montmartre night spots, the no-longer-fashionable Chat Noir, the Moulin Rouge with its cancan, or a new discovery, the Zut, on Rue Ravignan, in so low-down an area that rumor had it "someone was scalped there . . . with a pointed knife" (by the local apaches).

Pablo was never very brave, and Sabartés was blind as a mole, but they blundered in through the door with BIÈRE in black lettering: three barrels in front of banquettes were all there was, no tables or chairs, and then a second room, a sort of hangar nicknamed "Stalactite Hall," because of the paper streamers stuck to its ceiling, and yet another little room off to the side, likewise with an earthen floor. The owner was called Frédé. He and his shop were quickly adopted by Pablo, Jaime, Manolo, Soto, the sculptor Paco Durio, Ramón and Germaine Pichot, and other Montmartre Bohemians.

Frédé would set glasses out on a barrel in the middle of the room and serve beer all around. "That's all we have," he would tell those who wanted wine or spirits. Sometimes he would sing, accompanying himself on the guitar, or local performers would volunteer their services. The Spaniards were entranced by the heartrending sobs of a violin, the raggy rhythm of the guitar, or the stanzas of a poem—in the almost unreal Montmartre of our century's first year . . .

The gang decided to clean up their crummy headquarters at the Zut: Frédé had the walls whitewashed, and the lamps cleaned, and on one of the wall panels with the tip of a brush Picasso did several blue nudes, in a long thin arabesquelike stroke. Then a hermit in a niche he had left open, only to drop it when someone dubbed it *The Temptation of St. Anthony.*

On another piece of wall, there was a group of nudes, then a picture of Sabartés declaiming, manuscript in hand, perhaps a recall of his Barcelonese figure as a "decadent poet." A bat was flying over his head. Facing this, Ramón Pichot more modestly did a brush drawing of the Eiffel Tower and Santos-Dumont's dirigible in the Paris sky.

Little by little they deserted La Lorraine in the Latin Quarter, and *"la bande à Pablo"* (Pablo's gang) forgathered on the Butte, even Sabartés moving there. Largely for financial reasons, Pablo had drifted away from Manach, and he now

---

* Translated by Gertrude Hall in *Baudelaire Rimbaud Verlaine,* edited by Joseph M. Bernstein (New York: Citadel, 1947).

wanted to start a new life elsewhere: he wrote Don José asking for fare to return
to Barcelona.

Max Jacob and Pablo saw each other almost daily. The poet was fascinated
by the painter's studio as by a cave in the *Thousand and One Nights*. He described Picasso as "perfectly handsome, a face like ivory, without a wrinkle, in
which eyes shone, much larger than they are today, while the crow's wing of
hair was like a caress on his low forehead." Pablo sometimes visited Max's hovel
on the Quai des Fleurs, where he would read him the poetry of Baudelaire or
Verlaine or his own witty verses, and sometimes give him one of the prints
that decorated the walls. An evening with Pablo left Max "encouraged about
life. . . . I believed in him more than in myself."

One evening Pablo and Sabartés called on Paco Durio, who lived right near
the Zut, at 13 Rue Ravignan, in a strange stone, glass, and wood building nicknamed the Bateau-Lavoir (the "Laundry Boat" or "Wash Boat"). They talked
sculpture with the Basque until dawn—mainly about Gauguin, his newly published book, *Noa Noa,* and the great Polynesian totems that impressed them
with their wild roughness.

While Picasso had several times been inspired by the style (*cloisonnisme*)
of Gauguin, who that August had left Tahiti for Atuona on Hiva Oa Island
(Marquesas), he was also deeply impressed by his personality. Gauguin's rejection of civilization, the distance he put bewteen himself and his fellowmen
by living as a primitive in the Pacific islands, his haughty pride, his taste for
the symbol, the Idea, based on rather confused philosophies but linked to respect for nature, mankind, and the love of freedom, were destined to appeal
to him.

But without Manach's stipend, and his father still not having sent the fare,
Pablo had to admit defeat. His pride was hurt, but the cold and hunger in Paris
were just too much for him.

The year 1902 was beginning: Picasso looked at the self-portrait he had
done, a picture of a matured, bitter man, scarred by life, almost overwhelmed,
and when he finally did leave took it with him, along with those of Sabartés and
Soto, witnesses to the dawn of the blue world, friendly but solitary figures,
homesick as himself. Manach still retained a number of his paintings, left from
the Vollard show, to be shown again in April at Berthe Weill's; and Vollard
also had some stashed away.

More than thirty years later, Pablo and Sabartés were taking a walk in Montmartre, their first together since that night with Durio in the Bateau-Lavoir.
Pablo had spent a good part of the afternoon engraving at Lacourière's, beneath
the Sacré-Coeur. What used to be Rue Ravignan since 1911 had been named
after a Montmartre poet, Place Émile-Goudeau. They saw where the Zut had
once stood, now the site of ugly new buildings, and went on down toward Rue
Gabrielle, where Picasso pointed to a bakery and said, "That was where I bought
my first bread." Near the Bateau-Lavoir, he added, "Look. Nothing's changed.
The trees and benches, just like they used to be . . ."

"But older, maybe," said the skeptical Sabartés.

"You think so? . . . I always saw them just like this . . ."

His friends knew he had just been waiting for the money from home to go back to Barcelona; he had even told Paco Durio about it during that long night in December 1901. But Sabartés, as they headed home in the morning, wanted to know why he had stopped supplying Manach. No answer. They went to see whether the mailman had brought the money order yet. Upstairs, they found the letter had arrived—but Manach, fully dressed, was lying on his stomach on his bed, repeating, as if delirious, "The letter . . . the letter . . ."

A strange scene, indeed, as told by Sabartés, and maybe it did not actually take place the day after the night at Paco Durio's, since Soto seemed to be along, too. But why the haughty disdain with which Picasso looked down on Manach?

The dealer probably did not want him to leave, but his behavior was still strange. He claimed to have more Picassos than there was a demand for, and he criticized his latest manner. But perhaps in fact Manach was doing much better with the Picassos than he admitted, and Pablo felt he was being short-changed. That would explain Manach's despair at his leaving. At any rate, it was a serious break, and they were not to see each other again for fifteen years, until Barcelona, 1917.

Back with family and friends, Pablo would not feel Paris had been total failure, but it had not given him too much assurance. As usual, he said little, which worried his mother. No, he was not ill, but he needed time for thought, for self-examination. He gazed long at the canvases brought from Paris: distress, solitude, poverty, abandonment were characteristic of these people disinherited by life. The blue figures, the blue world must be seen beyond anecdote and beyond the more or less likely-seeming theories advanced by Sabartés. For Picasso to have returned, after the Montmartre nightlife, to the sufferings and miseries of the street seems all the more natural since he was always close to them and, through Steinlen, Lautrec, and Nonell, had grown even closer to such painful humanity.

But, to understand his behavior, his reactions to Manach, Paris, painting, his influences, his friends, he must first be seen as a man alone. Pablo's revolt against his father, as was to appear later, left him rudderless; the art of his day nurtured him, but without really enriching him, and he went from one technique, one style to another, with extraordinary facility, letting all influences converge on him and working out his own range of vocabulary. As Pierre Guéguen would say, "his stomach forewent nothing."

At twenty, he was looking for himself, and for Man, whom only one painter of the time was really concerned with, Gauguin.

The Blue Period took shape during his stay in Barcelona until October 1902, then in Paris; it would not be without its artifices or cop-outs. It displayed a slightly conventional sentimental picturesqueness and was crossed by many influences: medieval painting, Symbolism, Pre-Raphaelism, El Greco, Puvis de Chavannes, Carrière, Art Nouveau . . .

Picasso told me that it was in that year that he discovered and admired the masterpieces of Romanesque Catalan painting. These frescoes, still to be seen in small mountain churches, were not well known. Santa María and St. Clement of Tahull, over fifteen hundred meters (about a mile) high in the Valley of Bohi, had the most beautiful examples of it, notably a Virgin Mary and a majestic Christ of striking linear simplicity. But other country chapels had equally powerful works which, at the beginning of the century, seemed very "modern." They were akin to Gauguin's *cloisonnisme* and German/Scandinavian syntheticism with its rough-hewn hieratic figures, its sturdy dramaticism. While the Barcelona intellectuals appreciated these works for their "Catalanism," Picasso was one of the first to understand their deep ties, across the centuries, with contemporary experiments.

Barcelona's artistic life still centered around Els Quatre Gats. Picasso did his work in a studio rented by Angel de Soto, at 6 Calle Nueva, called "la Nou" (today named Calle Conde de Asalto), hard by the Eden Concert, where he often spent his evenings drawing the singing girls. He shared it with another artist, Josep Roquerol i Faura, who paid part of the rent, and they often entertained their friends there.

Thus began a new phase in the young Andalusian's life, to last about two years, until his final settling in Paris in April 1904 (though he visited the Parisian capital briefly from October 1902 to January 1903). Legend has it— Sabartés in support—that before returning to Barcelona in January 1903, Picasso kept warm by burning many of his paper or cardboard works in his Paris digs. Actually, he stored them with Pichot, and got some back, but most disappeared.

The Barcelona Blues show us social outcasts, lonely, miserable people, women alone or with a child, old people, Bohemians. The facade of the *Blue House* has rows of blue windows above a blue street, with equally blue roofs merging into a blue sky.

Nonell's influence remains apparent, but in Picasso the climate was now timeless, as if men and women belonged to some immemorial age, outside any known geography. The varied shades of sky have symbolic uses, and blue hunger is not blue poverty, or blue distress. "The dagger of blues so graceful to use," as Pablo was to formulate it in a very meaningful poem, could also be a scalpel.

His blue women serve as analyses and deepening of the possibilities of monochrome as shape, color, space, an inventory of his means. This "wet painting, blue as the humid depths of the abyss and pitiful," to quote Guillaume Apollinaire, became for him a painterly vocabulary, an autonomous medium of expression that was also a process of psychological, sociological, and spiritual investigation—a way of knowing himself.

Come spring, Sabartés also returned to Barcelona, and first thing on the morning of his arrival had his great head of hair cut short so as not to be taken for an anarchist. Then he went to the Ruizes', to surprise a sleeping Pablo—but the latter was already up and over at his studio. Jaime rushed over there, to find both him and Roquerol working.

The "Well, how are you?" that Pablo greeted him with, as he went right on working, might as well have been "What the hell are you disturbing me for?"

Finally, interrupting his drawing, Pablo introduced Sabartés to Roquerol, and asked what he intended to do. He seemed quite moved at the idea that Jaime had rushed to his parents' house to try to surprise him. And now Sabartés got a chance to inspect the recent works, namely a rooftop view, one of the few landscapes without people done in this blue spring.

Each day, after lunch, they would meet at Els Quatre Gats, after which Pablo worked at the studio. Jaime going along only when invited. They planned what their evenings would be like, for our Malagueño hated the unexpected. They talked a lot, the painter throwing out ideas that his poet friend elaborated on. They visited friends, went to Els Quatre Gats or other cafés, or looked at art at the Sala Parés, still the city's only haven for contemporary painting. With their bunch, they might go to eat mussels and drink local wine in sailors' dives at Barceloneta, and at times they took in the big new attraction, the movies at the Cinematógrafo Napoleón. If they were really feeling low, they ended up at the whores'.

Picasso went to bed and got up late. It was an orderly life in that each day's routine was the same. With trousers tight around the ankles, big broad hat, and ascot tie, he really looked the "artist," but the fringe of beard was gone, and now he had only a rather full drooping mustache. At times, he wore a beret or a cap, reflecting his feelings of the moment, Sabartés said, as aspects of his art in different periods expressed his pictorial concerns.

Having met the tailor Soler, whom he painted surrounded by his family, Pablo traded him paintings for suits, and got his first taste of vestimentary elegance: affecting garish vests often adorned with refinements of his own, he carried a cane that he twirled in conversation as if challenging an imaginary opponent.

Always reluctant to turn in at night, he would walk his friends home, loiter on the Rambla or pace the Plaza de Cataluña. Sometimes he played the slot machines in cafés, having very crafty systems and usually winning. Before going to sleep, he read voluminously, anything that was at hand; if a book bored him, he dropped it. To his father, this was the useless life of a do-nothing.

He started going to a sort of private club that some avant-garde young people had created in the studio that Juan Vidal Ventosa and his bosom pal Joaquim (nicknamed Quim) Borraleres had taken in January 1902 at 4 Plaza de l'Oli. A model had strangely dubbed the place El Guayaba (an unintentional mispronunciation of Valhalla). Artists and writers from Els Quatre Gats gathered there to drink and talk, in the company of models or other available girls, those who were flush picking up the tab for their strapped friends. Picasso was among the latter.

He often ate lunch at the home of the Junyer-Vidals, whose family had a haberdashery in Calle de la Platería. They ate well. After the meal, he would draw all afternoon in the room behind the store, as he talked the while, covering with unbelievable speed the backs of bills, advertisements, and other commercial documents with bright light sketches, dramatic, imaginative, erotic, or inspired by the day's news.

Sebastián Junyer-Vidal, the painter, appealed especially to Pablo with his good old round head crowned with a huge curly mane, his enormous forehead, staring, slightly haggard eyes, and bushy mustache hiding his full lips. He appears in many a Picasso drawing, naked, alongside an equally bare Pablo, in a parody of Manet's *Olympia,* in a tavern, accompanied by a horrible one-eyed brothel woman from the *barrio chino* whose portrait (*La Celestina*) Pablo did at the same time. He also showed him standing on a cliff, dressed in a peplum as he declaimed verses while holding a lyre. And as a bullfighter, or, with the title *Painter Junyer and His Vision of Mallorca,* dreaming before the paradisiac landscape of the island, one of his favorite pictorial subjects. Sebastián had never set foot on Mallorca, which he spoke of as an unattainable Eden, much to his friends' amusement.

It was he who accompanied Pablo to Paris on his third trip. Manach was showing what Picassos he had left at Berthe Weill's, April 1–15, 1902. The walls were shared by one Louis Bernard-Lemaire. "No sale," Berthe noted; adding, "Still, Picasso is holding up." Later, she was to write,

> I did sell a few Picassos, drawings or paintings, here and there, but was not able to give him all the money he needed, and this upset me badly, for he held it against me; his eyes scared me, and he took advantage of it! To stay in business, I have to buy a little from all of them; with only one I could never make it, but how to get him to understand that?

In May or June, he wrote Max Jacob that he was planning a big canvas to show "a whore at St. Lazare [women's prison] and a sister," and appended an illustrative sketch. In half-Spanish, half-French jargon he told his friend that the Barcelona *artistes* (underlined) felt there was too much soul in his pictures, and not enough form. "You know how to talk to guys like that; but they write very bad books and paint idiotic pictures. *C'est la vie.*"

The rest of the letter, as usual, was also illustrated. One quick sketch showed a bullfight movement, the *arrastre,* when the mules drag the dead horses out of the arena. At the top right, another sketch, "the head of the horse being taken away," he specified, also showing himself leaning on his cane between a bullring and a church: "Picasso in Spain."

The Barcelona Blues reflect a troubled spirit, but not a pessimistic one; their spirituality has little in common with the behavior of Pablo, whose Catholicism, like that of many Spaniards, was superstition linked to tradition rather than any deep faith. At this point already, we must separate the pictorial and the mental in his work; his reactions were purely epidermic, rarely conscious.

In the spring of 1902, La Chelito was packing them in at any cabaret she appeared at. One of her sketches, called *La Pulga* (The Flea), during which she stripped as she tried to locate the biting insect, brought the house down.

All of Barcelona was talking about Chelito and her *Pulga.* Picasso was a great fan and went to see her any number of times at the different music halls. One morning when Sabartés came for him, his mother showed him in to the bedroom, but Pablo was still asleep, while table, chairs, and floor were covered with a hundred drawings of the girl in every position. Forty years later, in the mess in his friend's studio, Sabartés was to come upon two faded snapshots. "Yes, there she is!" Pablo commented. "What do you think of that!"

By April 15, Berthe Weill had not sold one of the paintings she was showing. Fortunately, Manach still had quite a few Picasso drawings that, being cheaper, Berthe could sell more readily. She held a group show, June 2–15, set up by Manach: Picasso was represented along with compatriots including Zuloaga, Nonell, Losada, and Iturrino. The Picassos all dated back to 1900 and 1901.

Picasso in Barcelona was growing impatient, and wanted to get back to Paris. He could not stop Manach from exhibiting the works he controlled, but they belonged to a past period, now over. And he lived then as he always would in the present.

His father agreed once more to pay his fare, but Pablo, unwilling or unable to go alone (no analyst has yet probed this need for a companion in his assaults on the French capital), got Sebastián Junyer to go with him. Since the latter was well fixed, it helped, for Pablo was without a peseta. But Pablo stayed in Paris only to mid-December or early January.

They left about mid-October, not long after the traditional celebration of La Merced, for which a newspaper, El Liberal, asked Picasso to illustrate its front page for October 5. He turned a simple drawing into a manifesto. It was, indeed, a good chance to contrast the poverty of the masses with the brilliant procession and the crowd of smug bourgeois watching with little concern for their fellows' hunger or cold. Picasso used a figure from one of his blue paintings: a poor woman in a kerchief holding a baby in her arms and the hand of a little girl who happily wants to get closer to the parade and its floats. But the crowd ignores the pitiful figure, who perhaps had not seen a crust of bread all day.

Junyer and Picasso moved into a room at the very Hôtel des Écoles, in the Latin Quarter, where Sabartés had lived. Pablo memorialized their trip to Paris in five drawings: 1) in the train from Barcelona, Pablo naturally feeling cold; 2) crossing the border; 3) a stop at Montauban during the night; 4) Paris, 9:00 A.M. (symbolized by the Eiffel Tower and Notre Dame), with Junyer carrying a trunk under his arm; and 5) he is holding a painting in his hand and getting a bagful of gold from a little bald-headed man; all captioned in Spanish in Picasso's hand, the last one reading: "I call Durand-Ruel [misspelled in Spanish phonetics: Duran-Rouel] who gives him a lot of money!"

Pablo called these his Hallelujahs, the name Spaniards give to religious images full of skulls, caskets, and other symbols that recall man's tragic fate. But this was an optimistic, if utopian, view of Junyer's rapid rise to fame and fortune in Paris. Pablo was too superstitious to show himself in that vein.

He could not afford to stay at the Hôtel des Écoles, so he left Junyer there and moved to the Hôtel du Maroc, at 57 Rue de Seine, sharing a miserable loft, messy even for him, with a sculptor-compatriot, a penniless Bohemian named Sisket.

Max Jacob, alerted to his arrival, called on him with a young man he was tutoring, who was even more shocked at the sight than he. Said Max later: "I trust the young gentleman will never forget having seen poverty coupled with genius." And promptly went out to fetch some fried potatoes.

Sisket and Picasso had only one bed, in which they took turns sleeping; the rest of the time it was loaded down with the drawings Pablo had brought from Barcelona. None of the Spaniards in the neighborhood offered to help them. So, Max Jacob thought it was up to him: dropping his tutoring, he took a job with the Paris-France department store that an uncle of his named Gimpel owned on Boulevard Voltaire. (This same Gimpel, as Picasso told it, came to see him once at Max's request, bought a couple of his drawings for a few francs, and then, amazed at the pile of work strewn all over, said, "But that's a fortune that you have there!")

With his first pay, Max Jacob took a room near his work, at 137 Boulevard Voltaire, and invited Pablo to move in with him. They hired a horse and buggy to move his baggage and paintings. All they had was a rather large room, well lighted, and Max provided an oil lamp and a tub. They had only one bed and only one high hat between them; the latter each wore according to his needs. As for the bed, since Pablo painted all night, he retired to it in the morning after Max had left for work.

Poverty-stricken though they were, Pablo would write his friend, after he returned to Barcelona: "Good old Max, I remember the room on Boulevard Voltaire and the omelets, the string beans, the Brie, and the fried potatoes, and also the hungry days, and I am sad . . ." The letter was illustrated with sketches of the parts of the cathedral he could see from his studio in Calle Riere de San Juan, and the outline of the roofs of a nearby church.

It was not quite so idyllic. Max Jacob hated his work, as he did any obligations. Pablo was not selling, scarcely went out, saw no one, and worked a great deal; he could not afford to set foot in Montmartre. The day Max got fired for total incompetence, they hit bottom. Max was to say they contemplated suicide, and write: "Picasso may remember the day we looked down from the high balcony toward the ground . . ." But Picasso did not.

All we know of this period comes from Max's recollections and what Pablo off and on told Sabartés—nothing dependable. In fact, Max was not fired from Paris-France (which he called the "Voltaire Warehouse") while Picasso was in Paris, but later, probably in 1903, and from there he went into journalism. Their life together seems to have been much less poverty-stricken than poet and painter made out, but for want of witnesses or documents, we cannot say. There is only that letter quoted above, which Picasso wrote to Max in French.

Nor can we be sure they moved together from Boulevard Voltaire to Boulevard Barbès, as Max described, dragging all their belongings on a handcart. Max Jacob would seem to have moved to 35 Boulevard Barbès after Pablo left for Barcelona.

The painter, no longer apparently in touch with his Spanish friends in Montmartre, hoped to turn a small profit from a new show he was to share with Girieud, Launay, and Ramón Pichot at Berthe Weill's. It ran from November 15 to December 13, but was a disappointment. The catalog was prefaced by one

Harlor, who vaunted Picasso's "indefatigable ardor to see and show everything" and the "wild light" around his characters. But it made no more impression than did a big article by Gauguin's friend Charles Morice in the prestigious *Mercure de France* in December 1902. Morice wrote of Picasso:

> He seems a young god trying to remake the world. But a dark god . . . His world is no more inhabitable than old leprous houses. And his painting itself is sick. Incurably? I do not know. But, surely, it shows a strength, a gift, a talent . . .
>
> In the final analysis, should one wish to see this painting cured? Is this frighteningly precocious child not fated to bestow the consecration of a masterpiece to the negative sense of living, the illness from which he more than anyone else seems to be suffering?

This floored Pablo. That so renowned a poet and writer, a onetime friend of Verlaine, twenty years older than he, should have written it, made him overlook his reverses. He called on Morice, who told him about Gauguin, how he had prevailed on him to write his life story, published as *Noa Noa,* the account of his stay in Tahiti unfortunately overrevised by his friend Morice. It had come out just a few months before, and he gave Pablo a copy, which soon had his sketches in all the margins. Some of the Blue Period figures suggest Gauguin's Art Nouveau-ish decorative mannerism.

Depressed by the failure of the Weill show and his lack of funds, Pablo did not produce much, but did do some paintings in the winter of 1902 close to the Barcelona Blues, the characters of which, including the famous *Holly Seller,* expressed his mood. Max Jacob's friendship alone comforted him.

But he refused to sell out. He might have knocked out scenes of Montmartre or colorful "Spanishisms" that would have been easily sold, for genre work was much sought after at the time, especially if somewhat exotic. He would neither earn his bread through a "second trade" nor make money in artistic media other than his own, as, for instance, the cartoons that Jacques Villon, Van Dongen, Marcoussis, or Juan Gris did.

Once, in a confiding mood, he recounted, "One time I tried to do something for money. I'm a little ashamed to admit it, but it's a fact; and I did this pastel."

The scene, quite tender despite the somewhat angular and stiff character of the figures, was of two women and two children, one a newborn babe, in a brightly lighted setting.

"I went out in the snow to give it to Berthe Weill, carrying it under my arm. Unfortunately, she did not have any cash, so I left it and went away . . ."

Weill was to display it in her Picasso one-man show in October 1904. Called *Home Scene,* or *Intimacy,* it was very soon bought by André Level.

Anxious to return to Barcelona, Pablo had no money for his fare. Meantime, on January 13, 1903, he drew *The Clear and Simple Story of Max Jacob,* which showed the poet writing his verses, and taking them to a hoary old publisher, who reads them. He emerges triumphantly waving bank notes and shouting, *"Olé! Olé!"* To celebrate, he consumes a huge meal that distends his belly hugely, to the amazement of a girl he has picked up; then, having been driven in a chariot to the Arc de Triomphe, he is greeted by the gods in the Elysian Fields with a crown and a sack of gold. Betoga-ed Max has now lost his belly but once again has the umbrella he carried earlier.

A few days later, the sale of a pastel to the wife of his paint supplier Besnard, who already owned several of his works, gave Picasso the fare money. This pastel was probably the *Maternity at the Seaside* shown in the November Weill show.

The man who returned to Barcelona had matured during the recent long hard months of eating catch-as-catch-can and suffering from the cold, but he was neither overwhelmed nor despairing. The main thing had been not to let others know what he had been through. He deliberately had only Max Jacob as a companion in this period, and he was the only one he wrote to from home. Later he was to resent Max's harping on the setbacks and deprivations of that Parisian winter.

He was again working in the Calle Riera de San Juan studio that he had once shared with Casagemas and now shared with Angel F. de Soto, who earned his keep with a small clerkship at the Ayuntamiento. Of an evening, their friends would come to the studio before going to Els Quatre Gats, to Juan Vidal Ventosa's El Guayaba, or one of the Paralelo cafés, usually the Trianon, of which they were habitués. Sometimes, they all ate at the studio; the meal, supplied by a nearby restaurant, was hauled up in a well bucket, with a bill attached, made out to the "Gentlemen Painters."

Blue was still dominant. Through the studio windows, Pablo did a number of views of Barcelona roofs, but today it is hard to identify the streets and houses, since the whole neighborhood was rebuilt between 1907 and 1913. On one, in the Bührle Collection, the roof and gable of the baroque church of Santa María are recognizable, and on another the Palace of Fine Arts, which came down in 1940 as a result of the Civil War bombings.

But personalization increased: instead of symbolic figures, Picasso now painted clearly recognizable people among the street poor. Several themes predominated, relations between the sexes, maternity, old age, all linked to loneliness. *Poor People at the Seashore, Old Guitar Player, Old Jew, The Ascetic,* and *Poor People's Household* are so true to life as to be upsetting. The woman in *Mother and Child with Kerchief,* also called *Desemparats,* looks hunted; the painter was in even greater empathy than before with the troubles of these unemployed, penniless, unloved unfortunates, especially the old.

The previously quoted letter to Max Jacob ended, "I expect to spend next winter here so as to get something done." Max being out of a job, and having had—most amazing for him!—an ill-starred affair with a married woman, Pablo sent him a roll of paintings and drawings to turn into cash; which might indicate he was not the drug on the market that has been alleged.

Sabartés had a small apartment in an old house with a spiral staircase on Calle del Consulado: two whitewashed rooms and a badly tiled kitchen. Each room had a window and the partition between had a porthole. Picasso could not see white walls without wanting to paint them; with the tip of a brush dipped in blue he traced large figures in lithe dancing arabesques. Sabartés described it:

> As always when involved in creations that obsessed him, he seemed to become isolated from everything around him, to take over the surrounding space, and drink in the air as if ideas were floating around in it that he was afraid would get away. . . .
> The brush never left the wall and the line it made there seemed not deliberate, but as if part of the wall itself. . . .

Facing the blue-outlined figures around the window, Pablo painted a half-clad Moor, hanged from a tree, in a state of erection, a babouche dangling from one foot. Unmoved by this sight, or perhaps turned on by it, a naked couple were passionately making love. Then Picasso put down the brush and told Sabartés, "I'll come back another day and go on . . ."

The porthole or bull's-eye in the partition he turned into a huge wide eye staring at the strange scene, and beneath it wrote in all capitals one of his favorite sayings: "The hairs of my beard, albeit separated from me, are gods as much as I." Eventually, Sabartés moved; new tenants came in—and the startling decorations disappeared.

Sabartés and Picasso saw each other daily. Pablo preferred being alone when he worked, any presence bothering him, but in the evening he liked to talk, have fun, or take walks with his friends. Though worried by his Parisian setbacks, he never mentioned them. But Don José, as Pallarés told it, kept reminding his son that his painting was hardly likely to earn him a living or a reputation. Meals at home now were rather an ordeal.

Sometimes, Sabartés remembered, Pablo would turn to him suddenly in a café and whisper, "Come on along." They would walk silently through one dark street after another. When they got to his studio in Calle Riera, or the one he had in Calle del Comercio from January 1904 on, Sabartés wondered whether he should go up, or rather leave him alone. "Come up a minute," Pablo would say. "I don't feel like working. We can talk."

This was often the way when he was in his dark moods. They sat on the floor or a sofa, talking or keeping quiet. Sometimes one or the other opened a window, and the sound of the city came in, girls laughing, a passerby calling, the keys of a *sereno* tinkling. A cool breath of air come into the studio, warmer with springtime, that mild Catalan spring with its scent of the sea. And over all the city, the blue fabric of the night.

He was beginning to be bored beyond words by the so-called night life of Barcelona, and its habitués, "those imbeciles!" as he characterized them to Sabartés. The friends from Els Quatre Gats had begun to go each his own way, and he heard nothing from those in Montmartre, not even Pichot, with whom he had left a whole bunch of paintings. Max Jacob alone kept in touch.

Symbolist painters and poets such as Munch, Klimt, and others, had often used the theme of the embrace. The most heavily symbolic picture of the Blue Period, *La Vie*, bathes in a climate of longing portrayed by an admirable sym-

"The Embrace" Barcelona 1903 (Photograph from the Réunion des musées nationaux, Walter-Guillaume Collection)

phony of blues heightened in spots by more colorful shades, flesh tones for the nude couple, flat white for the maternity. But it is yet not so convincing as some other works of the same era. It was done in the studio on Calle del Comercio, in the first weeks of 1904, but earlier drawings show he had been thinking about it for a long time. Don José himself prepared the huge canvas (197 by 127.3 centimeters or approximately 77 by 50 inches) that the spread of the composition called for; he was doubtless moved by his son's ambitious project, approving of the allegorical and moralizing character of the subject. He also recalled the success of *Science and Charity,* which he had suggested to Pablo. In *La Vie* there were none of his customary distortions or plastic excesses, only exemplary pictorial behavior.

Along with the new studio, Pablo rented a room on the same street and ceased living at home.

The blue paintings done in Paris and Barcelona are among the most "Spanish" of his entire oeuvre. Most are scenes from life, their types plucked from among the denizens of the Catalan capital's populous quarters. Allowing for the conventional picturesqueness of the *Old Guitar Player, Holly Seller,* or *La Celestina,* the poor forlorn characters are an image of the fate that Pablo at the moment was sharing. What thoughts these *desdichados* suggest to him are hard to pin down; the theme of blindness occurs often, associated as in the watercolor of *The Old Man and the Child* with maternity. In the India-ink drawing entitled *Old Man and Little Girl* (1904), an old blind man stretches his hesitant hands toward the face of the little girl looking tenderly up at him. Several drawings and watercolors, a sculpture, *The Mask of a Blind Singer,* evidence the persistence of the blindness theme until his departure for Paris. And beyond.

As time went by and a new urge to try his luck in Paris set in, Pablo's blue canvases changed style, the influences or borrowings also changing. He drew a great deal in this period, people in the street, women, passersby seen from his window, Angel de Soto in a café with a girl displaying her naked breasts, maternities, old women, nudes, what have you.

The Poor Man's Meal and *The Tramp's Meal,* on an identical theme, are contemporaneous (1903–1904), but *El Loco* (The Madman) was done early in 1904. It is a monochrome figure done in blue wash on two sheets of paper pasted together in the middle, one of the last done in Barcelona. He was now completing his gallery of the types of this city he was about to leave—the same ones found from time immemorial in Spanish painting and theater: Celestina, the whore, the blind man, the idiot, the beggar, the old Jew, the poor woman, the guitar player, the ascetic, the madman, and so on. He had become "recharged."

Now, back to Paris; by March of 1904, he was packing, the previous years' setbacks having left no apparent bitterness. He left Barcelona with Sebastián Junyer in April, and since Paco Durio was vacating his Bateau-Lavoir studio, Pablo moved in. That was where he had his paintings sent. He knew the place well and, despite age and condition, liked its low rental. He was now twenty-three.

But for his tremendous creative outlet, Picasso's extreme character might have

*"Life" Barcelona 1904 (The Cleveland Museum of
Art, Gift of Hanna Fund)*

led him to all kinds of excesses. He had some successes, but also setbacks: on the inventive level, his work did not seem to show so exceptional a personality, it was not—at this point—so much in conflict with or opposition to the vision of his time as that of a Van Gogh, Cézanne, or Seurat had been in theirs. Having sold a few canvases, then found relative financial security through Manach and Berthe Weill, having aroused the interest of Vollard, one of the great dealers in "innovators," he was still to experience rejections and poverty. His work did not have the kind of aggressive newness that called forth the insults or sarcasms heaped on so many other creators. For all that the Blue Period might shock or dismay, it did not arouse hostility, and critics were far from being negative toward him; in which he was rather lucky.

It was true that Pablo did not exhibit much. He was taking his time. No more than Van Gogh, Seurat, or Cézanne, who also met with lack of understanding, painful setbacks, sarcasm, and poverty, did he attempt to gain attention through conventional, not to say pandering, forms. But Van Gogh, Seurat, or Cézanne would have been unable to appreciate their commercial value; he was not.

From the beginning, his sex life was active and demanding. It mattered little to him whether his enjoyment was shared; his glands functioned healthily. Sex was no riddle to be solved, and whoring was better because it was easy and gleeful.

No deep liaisons; Casagemas' example taught him that lesson. Until 1905, when he set up housekeeping with Fernande Olivier at the Bateau-Lavoir, he is known to have had only one other involvement, with a Montmartre woman, whose name he let slip sixty years later when showing an old portrait to a friend: "You never knew Madeleine, did you?"

He had few creative problems—and was not really interested in their solutions. Even if he had some technical difficulties in developing his medium, it was not a major worry; one thing was worth another. As he told Tériade in 1932: "How many times, going for blue, I found I didn't have any. So I used red instead . . ." This was the kind of statement that led detractors to claim he was "making fun of the world."

Picasso ignored such criticisms, or dismissed them with a joke. Can we tell today what courage it took for the twenty-year-old Andalusian to bring his blue world to that Paris of the *Belle Époque,* refusing to bend to the norms and conventions of fashionable painting, to compromise, to concede a thing? He maintained his vocabulary, his vision against all and sundry.

Spain always remained present for him; present-day Spain with its Barcelonese Bohemia, and that of the Middle Ages with its altarpieces and frescoes, from which he took the wild character, raw tones, distortions, and expression.

IV

MONTMARTRE
AND THE
BATEAU-LAVOIR
(1904–1907)

THE STUDIO IN THE BATEAU-LAVOIR WAS ANYTHING BUT COMFORTABLE, scorching in summer, freezing in winter. The building had only one floor fronting Rue Ravignan. In the rear, its fantastic underpinning of glass-enclosed constructs looked out over the lots on Rue d'Orchampt that were beginning to build up. All around, shacks, food stands, and drinking gardens nestled in the greenery at the foot of tall gingerbread tenements, erected in the last years of the century, that towered over the trees like the masts of ships, the laundry hanging from the windows as their sails. At night the gas of the streetlights cast a pale glow over deteriorating facades and dilapidated pavements.

The place Pablo took over from Paco Durio was a far cry from the studios he had had in Barcelona: a box mattress on four legs, a cane chair, some easels, an old trunk, and a table were its total furniture. A yellow earthen bowl on a little rusted potbellied stove served as washstand—a towel and bit of soap lying on the table. Of course, no running water. But everywhere, the blue paintings of paupers, gaunt sad streetgirls of Barcelona, blind men, old people in rags, hungry children . . .

Many artists, all down on their luck, lived in the Bateau-Lavoir, also referred to as The Trapper's House. The concierge who superintended it lived next door, so tenants moved in and out at will; she never knew who lived where. The neighbors were not the kind to tell. There were two other Spaniards in the building when Pablo moved in, Joaquim Sunyer and Ricardo Canals. The latter was married to a statuesque Roman beauty, Benedetta Bianco Coletta, who had posed for Degas and been the model for Bartholomé's monument to the dead in Père-Lachaise cemetery. Her beautiful body being reserved for her husband, friends had to be satisfied with enjoying her cooking. Picasso did a superb portrait of her in 1905, as a señora wearing a huge lace mantilla (now in the Picasso Museum in Barcelona).

Also nearby, however, were Manolo, Ramón Pichot, and Paco Durio, who had set up his ceramist's kiln in one of the shacks of the *maquis*. That was where Pablo was to learn that art.

One critic later remembered Pablo as looking at the time like "an acrobat from the Médrano Circus hiding his working tights under too long a raincoat."

One midnight, Manolo barged in on him with a long, lean, pipe-smoking poet who stayed far into the small hours, André Salmon, who was to become the period's most ardent chronicler. Pablo, dressed in blue mechanic's coveralls, a candle in one hand, paintbrush in the other, was doing one of his blue pictures by the meager additional light of a small oil lamp.

"Come for lunch tomorrow," Picasso insisted. "You have to meet Max Jacob." A week earlier, Pablo had met Guillaume Apollinaire, through one of his good friends, Jean Mollet, who did not yet style himself Baron. They had met at Austin Fox's Bar, in Rue d'Amsterdam, one of the little cafés around the Gare St. Lazare frequented by tarts and trainers and jockeys from the Maisons-Laffitte racetrack. Since Apollinaire lived in a nearby suburb with his mother, he often stopped here or in the Criterion, next door. That day, he had with him a red-headed Englishman and two black girls whose huge feathered picture hats in garish colors seemed sensational to Picasso. He thought right off that Guillaume ought to meet Max, and invited him to lunch along with Salmon. But Apollinaire was busy all day writing advice to small investors for the paper he worked on, so they met him instead after work in Austin Fox's.

"He did not break off his speech about the Roman emperors," Max Jacob later said, "nor look at me, as he held out his short strong hand for me to shake. Then suddenly he got up and led us out into the night with great bursts of laughter; this was the beginning of the endless walks that for years were to be a daily occurrence. . . ."

"This," as Picasso was to put it with melancholy, "was at the time when painters and poets had an influence on each other."

Eight years later, Apollinaire would write of his first visit to Picasso in the Bateau-Lavoir in 1904:

> His blue electrician's outfit, his sometimes cruel humor, the strangeness of his art, were known throughout Montmartre. His studio, crammed with canvases of mystical harlequins, and drawings underfoot everywhere that anyone had a right to carry off, was the rendezvous for all the young artists, all the young poets.

Ricardo Canals took a photograph of Picasso in his studio on Rue Girardon, to which he moved after leaving the Bateau-Lavoir. It was inscribed a few months later to Suzanne and Henri Bloch (and again half a century afterward to Elsa and Louis Aragon). "A thin pale young man who dominated through the strange depth of his eyes" was how Max Jacob described him, but in this photo Pablo had a round regular face, strong nose and lips, a tenderness in the eyes that, as Gertrude Stein said, had "a strange faculty of opening wide and drinking in what he wished to see." His jet-black hair was disheveled; he had on a velvet jacket and ascot tie.

The tenants of the Bateau-Lavoir were like the characters in his paintings, their horizons limited by their poverty, the flea-bitten cabarets of the area, tarts prowling and lifting their skirts for a few pennies, with an occasional fling at the Moulin de la Galette or the Lapin Agile, havens of forgetfulness, with their music, laughter, and drinks. Alcohol was the principal escape for the jetsam of Montmartre, less Bohemian than poverty-stricken, of which Pablo bore the weight on his shoulders. "Up here" was not like "down there," in the Montmartre he had lived in earlier; like his neighbors he was low on funds and did not eat every day. Once, Paco Durio surprised him by leaving a can of sardines, a loaf of bread, and a bottle of wine outside his door, but most often you got drunk to forget your hunger.

As she was getting water from the single faucet in the basement, Picasso had noticed a fine-looking girl who lived in the Bateau-Lavoir. She thought he was "rather curious," but his black eyes with their piercing pupils did something to her. They often met in the corridors, and he spoke to her. She could hardly face up to the fire in his eye, which more than fifty years later, when she was a semi-invalid old lady, still stirred her when she talked of it. "But I think he went for my eyes, too," she said. He also went for her hats, for she dressed elegantly, and Pablo was captivated by the attractiveness of this Parisienne incarnate, who looked just like the ones Lautrec and others had immortalized. Indeed, she was the embodiment of the inimitable chic he himself had detailed in some of his earlier paintings.

So Picasso "fell." Who was this tenant of the Bateau-Lavoir, who was neither artist nor tart? She was born Fernande Bellevallée * in Paris, June 6, 1881, to a family of Jewish craftsmen, "modest manufacturers of artificial flowers, feathers, and bushes," as she herself once put it.

She claimed to be the ex-wife of an obscure sculptor named Olivier, but in fact her husband was a shop clerk named Paul-Émile Percheron, who married her on August 8, 1889, five months after the birth of their son, never again heard of. Dead? Put out for nursing? We do not know. Percheron himself disappeared just as completely.

. Friendly with many artists through her sister, who was the mistress of Othon Friesz, Fernande Olivier—as she now styled herself—lived alone in the Bateau-Lavoir, "already a little disillusioned with life." According to one later version, she was the mistress of a painter who turned her out to whore and lived off her take, while he spent his days sleeping. With Picasso, it would be just the opposite.

Picasso intrigued her, and one rainy afternoon, when they bumped into each other in the hallway, he asked her if she wanted a kitten he had just brought in from the storm, and invited her in to his studio. After that, things did not go quite so quickly as has been alleged (even by Fernande herself).

They first met in the fall of 1904, but did not start living together until the beginning of the next year. At the outset, their affair was purely physical; he

* An obvious Gallicization of "Schoenfeld." (TR. NOTE)

Fernande Olivier (Collection of Sir Roland Penrose)

liked her ample charms no less than her nonchalant sensuality. To the hot-blooded Spaniard, she personified sex uncomplicated and ever available as he had always liked it.

She wrote, in her memoirs:

> I was, or so people said, the very essence of health and youth: tall, full of life, optimistic, cheerful and confident: with my head in the clouds, in fact. A perfect contrast to him! It is said that people are attracted to their opposites; it certainly seems to be so. . . .*

Impressive and elegant enough so he was proud to be seen with her, to the penniless little émigré she was the perfect sex object, without the least inhibition or hang-up. He worked a great deal as her presence regularized his indispensable sex life. They virtually had a bourgeois marriage: no more Spaniards dropping in at all hours, no more drunken toots, no more whorehouses. Max Jacob, for all her cordiality to him, was terrified of Fernande and came around less often—though always available if Pablo called. In down periods, Max was still to act as his intermediary with dealers or collectors.

Apollinaire and Salmon were at the Bateau-Lavoir regularly. The former, eventually to write the first history of Cubism, in 1904 knew few painters. He had met Derain at Chatou the previous year, and through him Vlaminck, who did Apollinaire's portrait shortly before he met Picasso.

Pablo's passion for Fernande took the form of numerous portraits. She appeared, perhaps for the first time, in two pencil sketches of heads on a study for *The Actor,* a large rose-blue and gray canvas with a broad brick-red flat area in the foreground. Since his return to Paris, Picasso had continued his blue figures, but in a new spirit that had been foreshadowed in Barcelona in *The Madman.* The characters were almost stringy, their skeletal limbs breaking at acute angles, their heads bent, as if overwhelmed with despair and abandonment.

A curious mannerism that Pablo was to make use of all his life marked this series of works interesting mainly for their expression: *The Couple, Woman Ironing,* repeating a theme done three years earlier, *Two Women Friends,* and *Woman with the Crow* (now in the Toledo Museum of Art). This last canvas, one of the earliest of the Rose Period, has impressive dramatic intensity. The woman, modeled by Marguerite Luc, or Margot, daughter-in-law of Frédé, now owner of the Lapin Agile, who had tamed a crow, bends her bloodless emaciated face toward the bird, which she is petting with her unwontedly lengthened fingers. The head scrunched down into the shoulders, the arms as if squeezed in, form one angular block of faded old rose striking against an azure blue background.

He painted these in solitude, and would do the same a few months later after Fernande was living with him. She was not indifferent to his work, as has been claimed, and wrote, "The morbid side of it certainly perturbed me somewhat, but it delighted me too." He did not care; all he wanted was for Fernande to let

---

* *Picasso et ses amis* (Paris: Stock, 1933); translated only in 1964, by Jane Miller, as *Picasso and His Friends* (London, Heinemann; New York: Appleton, 1965).

him work in peace and not get in his way. He could not have put up with a bluestocking, or one of those nice accommodating girls that went from one artist's bed to another, peppering their conversations with "art criticism." He was proud that he had a beautiful mistress, a desirable female who attracted all eyes and awakened lust when they went into the Lapin Agile, or Chez Axon on Rue Ravignan or Chez Vernin on Rue Cavalotti, the restaurants at which they and their peers usually ate. Being shorter, next to her he looked like a student having an affair with one of his mother's friends.

But Fernande's statuesque walk, her proud bosom, and huge flowered picture hats in no way inhibited him. Since she was four months older than he, he would joke, "She is very beautiful—but old." He amused her, took her mind off her past "misfortunes," and fulfilled her with his assiduous lovemaking.

Ever obliging, Max Jacob acted as their errand boy, always available, peddling his friend's drawings to dealers, mainly secondhand types, since Vollard rejected the Blue Period canvases, telling Max, "Your friend has lost his mind!"

One such, Père Soulier, on Rue des Martyrs, a hoary old man handling wares of every description in an unbelievable shop where pictures stood alongside mattresses, washstands, bootleg tobacco, after haggling, bought drawings at fifty centimes (ten cents) apiece. When Max got rid of several, he would rush back to the Bateau-Lavoir, his arms loaded with victuals, and friends were invited in to feast and celebrate until it was time for Pablo to start his night's work. Having no money to go to shows, they staged their own, and Max Jacob often wrote about them later:

> We did the Burial of Sarah Bernhardt, although she was still very much alive. There was also a tragedy about The Prompter and the Prima Donna. Picasso laughed, and making him laugh was our goal. . . . We did Pirandello long before Pirandello, and made solemn speeches.

One afternoon in 1944 or 1945 Picasso took Françoise Gilot up to see the Bateau-Lavoir. It was customary for the painter to make such pilgrimages with each new woman, setting up a confrontation between past and present. "It hasn't changed much in forty years," said Picasso, but she noted that "the floorboards . . . wobbled under our steps."

"All we need do," said Pablo, "is open this door and we'll be back in the Blue Period." But there was no answer when he knocked, so the Blue Period remained locked behind the door.

Françoise wrote, in *Life with Picasso* (coauthored with Carlton Lake):

> When we went out into the square again, it was still deserted. We walked over to the fountain in the center. "The first time I saw Fernande Olivier was here at this fountain," he said. . . .
>
> "When I lived here there was a little girl, the concierge's daughter, who used to play hopscotch and jump rope outside my windows all day long. She was so sweet I would have liked to have her never grow up. After I moved away and came back to visit, I saw that she had become a serious young woman. . . . Years later I saw her here again and she looked quite old and it depressed me. In my mind's eye I had

kept on seeing that little girl with her jump rope and I realized how fast time was flowing and how far away I was from the Rue Ravignan."

What, at the end of 1904, made him switch from blue to rose? From him, we would never find out. All we know is that Fernande Olivier, after several months' courtship, became his companion, and with that the rose of happiness appeared in his work.

From October 24 to November 20, Pablo was part of a group show at Berthe Weill's with six others: Charbonnier, Clary-Baroux, Raoul Dufy, Girieud, Picabia, and Tiesson. Maurice Le Sieutre wrote the preface to the catalog.

All the Picassos exhibited predated his return to Paris, mostly street scenes already familiar to us, some Montmartre subjects, the *Burial of Casagemas,* and so on. *The Madman* and a few blue watercolors showed his development since then, included at his insistence so visitors might see what he was now doing and compare it to the older work. Several belonged to Manach.

Now in his portraits he was much less mannered than in his poverty-stricken figures, his women ironing, or his couples. Gaby, Harry Baur's mate, was done in a serene style with nobly rhythmic lines, the beautiful serious face of the black-veiled young woman and her long delicate hands painted with application and acuity. No concession to flattery in the one of Suzanne Bloch, whose Semitic features, with the large nose, sensuous lips, determined chin, and thick neck, were clearly shown; a magnificent mane of bluish hair crowned the girl who was to become the famous Wagnerian diva. Suzanne was the sister of the violinist Henri Bloch, a friend of Max Jacob's, who had introduced them to Picasso. Pablo never hesitated to take advantage of such contacts: he frequently dropped notes to the musician, who was well connected, asking him to put in a good word with some possible collector.

Pablo once again portrayed Sebastián Junyer, his high forehead, curly hair, and bristling mustache; and he drew his friend Manolo, Max Jacob on a sheet of letterhead of the Faurena Café, 75 *bis* Boulevard de Clichy, friends or young women randomly met, as well as himself in varied attitudes, costumes, and circumstances. In the watercolor called *Contemplation,* the man with his head resting on his hand and looking at a young woman (without doubt, Fernande), asleep in charming abandon, has his own features. There is a striking contrast between the half-undressed sleeping woman's face, exuding happiness, and the worried look of the meditative man.

He did many lesbians, naked women embracing each other, petting, or lovingly watching each other sleep. There were many feminine "couples" in Montmartre, and he remembered Courbet's famous pictures on the same theme.

He did try to earn a little money by executing various orders, but only in a pinch, and without taste for it. He never begged dealers for advances, or did commercial illustration. Roland Dorgelès relates that he once turned down seven hundred francs—a veritable fortune—offered him by fellow Bateau-Lavoir tenant Van Dongen to illustrate a humor magazine in his stead. When really pinched, he asked a friend to sell a few of his drawings.

Fernande often did the cooking—for a group, since friends frequently dropped in unannounced—on a franc or two a day. When there was some money, Pablo would run out to buy her a bottle of the cologne she loved, while she in turn spent it on dime novels at a nearby bookshop. Since she was so beautiful that she was often propositioned quite overtly, the Spaniard had violent fits of anger; sometimes he forbade her to go out for several days at a time.

Pablo did do two posters for plays by Gustave Coquiot and Jean Lorrain, but with so little luck that he decided this was not for him; no toadying; let them come to him when they were ready.

The Actor, in his faded tights, painted at the beginning of 1905, opened the Rose Period. It was done just before the magnificent *Seated Nude* that Gertrude Stein was to acquire, in which the gradations of roses and vinous reds enrich a drawing of fine firmness. The young woman who posed for it is doubtless the one in *Woman Ironing, Woman in Chemise* of the Tate Gallery, and several others. Unless her type was one that Picasso deliberately affected.

A blue and rose gouache, *Maternity,* shows highly subtle refinements, but unlike the preceding period in this one the painter is not committed to monochrome; he sometimes softens it with gray or heightens it with brighter colors. Often, it rises up to red, or else the red contrasts with gray, and blue reappears. His palette has a new shimmer.

The firmness and authority of the Blue Period gave way to a sort of instability, fragility; his circus world was inhabited by aging adolescents with drawn features, and their multicolored outfits barely covered their skinny limbs, hollow chests, and narrow hips. The slightly sad gracefulness of the *Harlequin Family, Acrobat's Family with Monkey, Seated Harlequin Against Red Backing,* or *Death of Harlequin* harmonizes with a delicacy of shape and touch that softens the animal aspect of the people. Rilke, celebrating Picasso's Saltimbanques in the fifth of the *Duino Elegies,* was to compare the awkward movements of the young acrobats to the leaps of young animals,* and Jean Starobinski wrote in 1970 that in some of the drawings, the lank adolescents embodied, "before the artist expressly decided to portray minotaur and centaur . . . , the strange symbiosis of saltimbanque and beast."

The Blue Period had been revolt and despair; the Rose Period now was solitude and melancholy.

Picasso had always loved circuses and often went to the Médrano, only a few hundred yards from the Bateau-Lavoir. But in 1905 his interest in saltimbanques

---

* But tell me, who *are,* these acrobats, even a little
  more fleeting than we ourselves,—so urgently, ever since childhood,
  wrung by an (oh, for the sake of whom?)
  never-contented will? . . .
                          . . . as though from an oily
  smoother air, they come down on the threadbare
  carpet, thinned by their everlasting
  upspringing, this carpet forlornly
  lost in the cosmos.
            (RAINER MARIA RILKE, *Duino Elegies,*
            translated by J. B. Leishman and Stephen
            Spender [New York: W. W. Norton & Co.,
            Inc., 1939], p. 47)

*"Saltimbanque Family with Monkey"   Paris 1905
(Göteborgs Konstmuseum)*

was symbolic: to him, these wandering, often hungry adventurers were close to the poets and painters of the Bohème of Montmartre in similar straits. Painting them, Picasso was portraying his own youth. He shows his own face as one of them in the canvas called *At the Lapin Agile,* or *Harlequin with Glass,* in which the bright reds and oranges stand out in lozenges of light on the equally red dress of the hooker's feathered hat, while in the background Frédé plays his guitar. For years it hung in the main room of the Lapin, Pablo having given it to Frédé, who sold it shortly before 1914.

From February 25 to March 6, 1905, Picasso was in a three-man show at the Galerie Serrurier, 37 Boulevard Haussmann, with Albert Trachsel and Auguste Gérardin. This time he seems to have made his own selection to exhibit: over thirty oils, some etchings and drawings, ranging from 1902 to the latest Harlequins. Only one older, *Montjuich Landscape,* probably from 1901–1902.

Charles Morice prefaced it, lauding Pablo's precociousness as "a miracle that nothing explains," though regretting his "disenchantment." Apollinaire took exception to the term, and in the *Revue immoraliste* for April replied:

> It has been said of Picasso that his works reflect a precocious disenchantment.
> I believe the opposite.
> Everything enchants him, and his incontestable talent seems to me to be in the service of a fantasy that indeed combines the delightful and the horrible, the abject and the delicate.
> His naturalism addicted to precision is accompanied by the mysticism that, in Spain, is present deep in even the least religious souls . . .
> Beneath the brilliant trappings of his lithe saltimbanques, one feels real young members of the masses, adaptable, sly, clever, poor, and deceitful.
> His mothers clench delicate hands such as one often finds among young mothers of the populous class, and his nude women proudly display the fleece that traditional painters disdain, the shield of Western modesty.

In another article, in *La Plume,* May 15, Guillaume waxed his most poetically ecstatic over "The Young: Picasso, Painter." Despite the friendly warmth of his verbiage and the effort to render a poetic equivalent of Picasso's painting, Apollinaire's knowledge of painting, its content, its spirit, was too vague, too superficial, for him to succeed. His language was still dated, with its Symbolist decadence and Art Nouveau pathos; later, when he "talked painting," it would be with a deeper understanding of his friend's plastic motivations. Habitué of the Bateau-Lavoir though he was, and a member of the *bande à Picasso,* Apollinaire did not really share the Bohemian and slightly disreputable life-style of the artists on Montmartre's Butte. He worked for a living and lived with his mother.

In the Bateau, the March 15 issue of *Le Mercure de France* evoked warm interest. Charles Morice, quoting from his own preface to the Serrurier show, wrote of the "luminous transformation of [Picasso's] talent," congratulating him on having dropped "his earlier somber vision." Gauguin's friend, who three years earlier in the same publication had bemoaned such "sick" painting, now stated:

The dawn of pity is upon us. . . . What was especially sad in Picasso's first works was that he seemed to wallow in sadness without compassion. His sensitivity has deepened. . . .

The Serrurier show was no commercial hit, but it confirmed Pablo's choice of direction. It deepened his friendship with Guillaume, not because he really liked the poet's outpourings, but because he felt his enthusiasm and empathy. He would know how to use him, too.

From saltimbanques, he went on to *bateleurs;* frail Harlequins were superseded by sturdy types who looked like the portly Apollinaire; jesters appeared with pointed hats adorned with bells in place of the old bearded kings. Humor and mockery took the place of the sadness of Harlequin's tale. Buskers and carnival folk introduced a new idea in his work: wandering and exile.

He knew he would not make a name with this kind of picture: the lack of composition or links among the characters, the "dissolute" drawing, the lusterless harmony and incompletion of certain parts were not made to appeal to the public. In this, as in all his work, everything went counter to contemporary taste, which could be judged by what was hung in the Salon. The scandal provoked by the "Fauves' cage" in the 1905 Salon d'Automne proved that any novelty gave rise to sarcasm and insults. There was nothing to expect from critics who, with rare exceptions, kowtowed to the dullest academicism nor from dealers, and even less from officials.

Fortunately, there were a few who took an interest in the nonconformists, the outlaws of art, usually picturesque secondhand dealers such as Père Soulier or Clovis Sagot, the onetime Médrano clown who shamelessly exploited his hungry suppliers. Pablo bitterly remembered, "He was a hard man, Clovis Sagot, very hard—almost a usurer." Yet, he was to be the starting point for Picasso's fortune, for it was in his shop that Gertrude Stein's brother got his first glimpse of the Spaniard's work.

When money was not in too short supply, the "gang" might take in the Médrano Circus, but more often they went to Frédé's new Lapin Agile, so named not for any agile rabbit, but because its sign with the rabbit had been painted by one A. Gill. But the future lay "down there," in Paris proper, that enormous teeming mass below, from which Montmartre, "the hill of martyrs," seemed cut off by its green flanks with their gaping quarries, its *maquis,* its gardens, deteriorating tenements, grogshops, clip joints, and quarriers' and drivers' cafés. Paris seemed so far, so different from this little village nestled away from the world, outside civilization, that some, as they went down toward the boulevards, called it "going into town."

Picasso was often ill-tempered, at times not opening his mouth for hours, at others lashing out in brief cutting phrases that somehow seemed less cruel in his hybrid Spanish-French lingo. In a few words, he could pillory as he did with his pen dealers, critics, and collectors. Nor was he any less cruel to those who "sold out," with commercial art or more "accessible" painting, or who prostituted themselves to get into the Salon. As for his painting, let them wait until they deserved it.

His friends listened, without fully believing, but that was because they did not realize who he was. Even in his darkest hours, Picasso never compromised.

A young German collector, Wilhelm Uhde, had bought *The Tub* from Soulier, and wanted to meet the man who had signed "Picasso" at the bottom left. He was told he might find him at the Lapin Agile, and went there, starting a conversation with people at the next table. He did not quite seem to fit in, but he had money, and he was treating. So he had soon made "friends," whom he asked, "Do you know a Mr. Picasso?"

One of them turned his dark eye on him, took a good look, and introduced himself as the painter. A delight, both for the collector and for the artist who had found a fan.

"Ever since," Uhde later said, "I lived for years in Picasso's blue kingdom."

Pablo was finishing *Death of Harlequin,* one of his most moving 1906 paintings, which Uhde was also to buy, and later lend to Rilke, before it ended in Somerset Maugham's collection.* This gouache, of an intensity akin to that of medieval Pietàs, was a fine example of painting, the sobriety of its colors no less impressive than the lack of artifice, the absolute purity. Even as the Fauves were unleashing their wild orgy of colors, Pablo sought rigor in monochrome, monumentality in simplicity.

A young American woman of twenty-nine, from a well-to-do Jewish family, sloppily dressed but passionately interested in literature and art, Gertrude Stein arrived in Paris in 1903, fresh from graduation in medicine from Johns Hopkins; she wanted to see France and go forward with her study of psychology. Living at 27 Rue de Fleurus, she looked like a Roman senator (and later more like a Buddha), with nothing feminine about her except a true tenderness in the eyes that lit up her smooth fat face. She had two brothers, Michael, the family financial genius, and Leo. The former had a wife named Sarah, intelligent and strong-willed, while Leo was a bachelor. A lean bearded giant of a man, and somewhat eccentric, while living at Bernard Berenson's in Florence, Leo had accidentally discovered Cézanne. From then on, he had to know all there was to know about his work.

When he came to Paris, he went to see Vollard, who he had been told had the best Cézannes available. His sister went to the Rue Laffitte shop with him, and they bought "a wonderful small green landscape," then, later, other inexpensive Cézanne oils and watercolors. At the appearance of the Fauves in the 1905 Salon d'Automne, Leo discovered the unknown Henri Matisse, and bought his *Woman with Hat* for 150 francs. Gertrude and he became friendly with the painter, who was married and lived in modest circumstances on the Quai St. Michel. Little by little, Gertrude was assimilating modern art, of which she had known little, and, guided by Leo, entering a new world that was soon to be her fief. These Cézannes and Matisses were the first steps toward one of the finest collections of contemporary paintings in our time.

* After Maugham's death, it was sold in 1962 for eighty thousand pounds sterling (about two hundred thousand dollars). On the other side, *Woman Seated in a Garden* had been painted and dated 1905.

One day Leo discovered Sagot's shop, close to Vollard's. He went in and saw some work by two men the dealer said were Spaniards, as yet unknown. One, a café scene, he bought readily, but he haggled over the other, signed Picasso, a name that meant nothing to him. Too high-priced, he thought; "almost as expensive as Cézanne," said Gertrude, who went there with her brother the next time. Sagot showed them a big one, "the now well known painting of a nude girl with a basket of red flowers," for which he wanted 150 francs.

"Gertrude did not like the picture, she found something rather appalling in the drawing of the legs and feet, something that repelled and shocked her," as she was to write in *The Autobiography of Alice B. Toklas.* Sagot was quite amenable to cutting off the feet and leaving just the head, if that was what they wanted, but of course they did not agree. She finally bought the painting of the skinny girl with the big feet; on its back were the simple words, "Picasso/13 rue Ravignan/1905."

At their request, a short time later, Sagot arranged for them to meet Picasso in his shop. Again fate was taking a hand, and the event was as historically memorable as Pablo's encounter with Apollinaire. Among paintings, old furniture, mattresses, water jugs, sundry secondhand goods, the three came together in the half-twilight of the shop. It contained several of the most beautiful Picassos in the world, that the owner could not even give away. Bearded Leo with his candid look, matronly Gertrude, hair coiled up, in flowing sack-robe and babouches on her feet, and the stocky bashful Spaniard, Pablo, hardly knew what to do or say. Yet, they got along, and decided to meet again. The words they spoke were banal. But the writer, with amazing intuition, divined the rare strength of character, the ferocious willpower in that painter whose black eye expressed as much curiosity as passion.

What was more extraordinary, Gertrude liked Fernande Olivier, and the Picassos started coming to Rue de Fleurus, where they met the Matisses. The Steins also called on them at the Bateau-Lavoir studio with "its general smell of dog and paint," as Gertrude put it. They became friendly with Max Jacob, Van Dongen, the Pichots, and all of Pablo's Montmartre friends, including Apollinaire.

With an authority hard to contradict, Gertrude Stein decreed that she alone had discovered Picasso; later, she would claim, equally peremptorily, to have had a decisive influence on him. This led to stormy confrontations with Leo, and he, with Michael and Sarah, decided to concentrate on Matisse, Gertrude having made ôff with Picasso.*

"The one who finds something, no matter what it might be, even if his intentions were not to search for it, at least arouses our curiosity, if not our

---

* The correspondence between Picasso and Leo and Gertrude Stein (69 letters, 37 postcards, 8 notes, and 2 telegrams from him to them) was all turned over by Miss Stein to the Yale University Library, which also has 55 letters and 11 postcards from Fernande Olivier to them, 8 letters and 19 postcards from Eva, and 9 notes from Olga addressed to Gertrude Stein and Alice Toklas, as well as a postcard from Paulo. Picasso's letters cover 1906–1930, Fernande's 1907–1946 (?), Eva's 1912–1914, and Olga's 1918–1932.

admiration," he would say later. And in those dark years he was already sure of that.

For the moment, he had to carry on with the means at his disposal, the principal one of which was his stubbornness in affirming his personality which, thanks to friendships, was now no longer lost in loneliness. Yet without ceasing to be the distant being who had to be sought out in his Bateau-Lavoir den, and whose first steps in the Parisian world of dealers, critics, and collectors would be only in response to their appeals.

In 1905, he was to do several key works, as far from the conventional naturalism of the day as from the harshly vivid language of the Fauves, and several sculptures. The first of these, *Head of a Jester*, has a pointed hat such as worn by jesters or buffoons in his paintings; the bust is also sometimes known as *Smiling Buffoon*.

Picasso shaped it one night after coming back from the circus with Max Jacob; the "Impressionist" technique was intended to accentuate its luminous vibrations, but the influence of Rodin can also be felt in it. The deep eye sockets contrast the power of their shadowy holes, symbolic of the look inward, with the shiver of matter, and give the character its timelessness. Max is supposed to have posed for it, but it does not look like him.

Working tremendously hard, he, who a few years before had not known a word of French, was now becoming amazingly familiar with French literature, as reflected in his letters to Spain.

Among his friends in Montmartre was a young Dutch writer named Tom Schilperoort, who invited him to spend a few days with him in the summer of 1905, in his native village of Schoorl, near Alkmaar. This was a chance to see some new country, but he did not have the fare. Ever obliging, Max Jacob borrowed twenty francs from his own concierge to help out!

As Pablo told it, "I had a bag that I put my colors in; the brushes wouldn't fit, so I broke off the handles and left. I had turned my studio over to Salmon and my friends, and before leaving I had drawn a man of the law, pointing warningly, à la Daumier, and signed it, 'H. Daumier.' When I got back from Holland, I found they had sold it for a Daumier—and now when I go into a museum, I'm always a little afraid I'll come across it."

He stayed at Schoorl with Schilperoort and his wife, Nelly; a photograph taken by the writer's brother shows the three of them inside the light, airy abode. This "flat country" was completely new to Pablo, who was without Fernande, probably mostly for financial reasons. The blond Dutch girls appealed to him, and completely changed his concept of the nude, as subsequent paintings and drawings would show. Bursting with health, their flesh white and firm, faces round and smooth, and very placid, they seem to have nothing to do but pose for artists. He did several nudes, and as a tribute to the country whose boundless horizons, vast skies, and windmills he so admired, he painted three Graces in native dress and headgear, in a stark landscape before a single little house: *Three Dutch Girls*. It is more just a somewhat local-colorish travel memento than a thought-out and completed picture; it was done at Schoorl in gouache on paper.

Returning from Holland, perhaps to calm Fernande's doubts about his behavior, he told her, "It was ridiculous to see those parades on the streets of young schoolgirls built like cavalrymen!" He gave the *Dutch Girl in Coif "a mi querido amigo/Paco Durio."* This was when he also said, "The most beautiful women's breasts are the ones that give the most milk."

In the fall of 1905, he painted one of his slim adolescents, whose athletic deportment he liked, dressed in the washed-out blue overalls he sometimes wore, completing the costume's originality with a cap or top hat. Then he put it aside until that night of palavering in a café when he had a sudden inspiration to paint, as so often happened; back at the studio, he completed the *Boy with Pipe* by crowning him with roses. "By that sublime whim," said André Salmon, "he turned it into a masterpiece."

Gertrude Stein had bought *Woman with a Fan.* Around 1930, wanting to bring out a book but finding no publisher, she decided to publish it on her own, and to sell a painting to finance it. Very much upset at the idea, she called together a "family council" that included no one from her family, but friends, mainly Alice B. Toklas and Picasso. The latter brutally decided, "The *Woman with a Fan* has been hanging on your walls long enough. You can get rid of it!"

Relieved at not having to make a decision herself, Gertrude did as he advised, although regretfully; she was so anxious to have her writings published that she would not let Alice B. Toklas change her mind.

"Miss Stein thought *Woman with a Fan* was a charm and would bring her luck," the latter wrote. This came true.

Historians, who like cataloging and labeling, tend to prolong the Rose Period up to the portrait of Gertrude Stein completed in the fall of 1906. That year, Picasso was still painting rose or reddish canvases, but no longer in the same spirit as the saltimbanques of 1905, pre-Holland. Anatomical research now became more important than the romanticism of the image, figures became more personalized, scenes shed any trace of anecdote; mass replaced outline, a new conception of the human body appearing. Pablo's incubation years were ending; he was headed for analysis of form in itself, which was to be the main contribution of this first turn in 1905–1906. Pictures such as *Horses at the Bath, The Coiffure,* for all its "genre scene" character, or *The Harem,* also known as *Rose Nudes,* are symptomatic of what his concerns then were. Although the color may remain, the Rose Period was over for him because he had gone beyond it through different researches in a domain no longer that of color harmony or climate. However, he liked rose, and used it throughout his life.

Now Ambroise Vollard, who had not liked the Blue Period and refused to buy or show the works in it, returned to see Picasso and bought several recent things. The dark years were ending for the painter; he, who had believed or pretended to believe that suffering was the source of art, was changing his outlook: the poverty-stricken jetsam of society, the skinny sad women and lanky adolescents were being eclipsed by a kind of serenity. Could this have been under the influence of Matisse, whom he often met at Gertrude Stein's, and with whom he was on good terms despite their fundamentally different natures?

At about this time, spring of 1906, Picasso did the portrait of Leo Stein in the style of the Rose Period which his subject had liked. He also did Allan, son of Michael and Sarah. The portrait of Gertrude, already under way, was giving him a lot of trouble.

Physically, from the first, the American woman had seemed interesting to him. Her massive body that displayed none of the natural feminine charms, her powerful energetic face not without a kind of nobility of feature, struck him, and at Sagot's, without awaiting further acquaintance, he had already suggested doing her portrait; as she wrote, "Gertrude Stein and Pablo Picasso immediately understood each other."

The work on the portrait began at the Bateau-Lavoir:

> She took her pose, Picasso sat very tight on his chair and very close to his canvas and on a very small palette which was of a uniform brown grey colour, mixed some more brown grey and the painting began. This was the first of some eighty or ninety sittings.
> Toward the end of the afternoon Gertrude Stein's two brothers and her sister-in-law and Andrew Green came to see. They were all excited at the beauty of the sketch and Andrew Green begged and begged that it should be left as it was. But Picasso shook his head and said, non.

Pablo sometimes took Gertrude and her American friends, including Andrew Green, who was silently in love with Fernande, to the Médrano Circus. Gertrude was delighted to see her painter, usually rather dispirited, laugh with childish glee at the clowns and acrobats. Etta Cone, who was to be one of the great American collectors of contemporary art, often went with them. Her fine collection, which was given to the Baltimore Museum of Art, started with several Picassos, even though she found his work "appalling but romantic."

With spring, Gertrude Stein's "sittings were coming to an end. All of a sudden one day Picasso painted out the whole head. I can't see you any longer when I look, he said irritably. And so the picture was left like that."

The Steins were planning their annual trip to Florence, and Pablo felt a profound need to return to Spain. This was always to be one of the beneficent recourses for him, spiritually and artistically, allowing him to analyze himself, take a good look at the present, and consider the future.

In the spring of 1906 the dead end of the Stein portrait, the mutations or evolutions occurring in his art, and those he felt to be coming, led him to turn inward and think deeply on matters also related to the change in his social condition. Now that Vollard had just bought two thousand francs' worth of his work, and Gertrude Stein was continuing to buy while also talking up his reputation all about her, he no longer had any financial problem about a trip to Barcelona and back. So he decided to take Fernande along.

He was not in the best of health. He had worked hard and, while poverty and privations were a thing of the past, he still had bitter memories of them. He had tried smoking opium, more out of curiosity than desire, first at friends' and then

*Portrait of Gertrude Stein Paris, autumn 1906 (The
Metropolitan Museum of Art, New York)*

at the Bateau-Lavoir. Fernande Olivier, in her memoirs, says that "for several months, two or three times a week, there was the admirable forgetfulness of time and self," but it never became a habit with Pablo.

The lovers left for Spain in mid-May.

Pablo was delighted to show off his beautiful Parisian mistress, and Fernande could meet his family and see where he had spent his youth. They went to Els Quatre Gats, to other cabarets, and to El Guayaba, where Juan Vidal Ventosa took a photograph of them with Ramón Reventos—Fernande wearing one of those outsize hats that she adored.

Don José had decided not to question his son about his work or the direction it had taken. He made no issue of the presence of Fernande, although she could not fail to feel his disapproval, whereas Pablo's mother was all attention to her: if Pablo had chosen her, she had to be the model of all perfections!

After a few days in Barcelona, they went to Gosol, a village of the *comarca* of Upper Urgel, in Lerida province, very beautiful and picturesque country.

They had been told about Gosol by a sculptor named Casanova, and a friend of his, the son of the Greek prime minister, Venizelos. Casanova had gone there to work in peace and quiet, at the suggestion of Dr. Cinto Reventos, who sent all his depressed patients there for a rest cure. This was just what Pablo needed. They took the newly opened rail line that went from Barcelona to La Pobla de Lillet, but to reach Gosol they had to get off at Guardiola de Berga and do the last thirty kilometers on burros.

Just below the abandoned medieval village, the gray rocks of which stood out against the sky, was the present town in an imposing half-circle of mountains. Like Horta, Gosol was far from everything; the nine hundred-odd people who lived off its soil were unaware of modern civilization.

Pablo's arrival, and especially Fernande's, caused a bit of a sensation. They lodged in the only local inn still in operation, the Can Tempenada, whose only two rooms looked out on the street. Pablo randomly sketched the excellent view of old Gosol on the pages of a pad in which he also penned notations that fill us in on their stay there.* The drawings are more sculptural and denser in form, their color inspired by the red-ocher earth of Gosol.

There are a number of nudes, too, of classical line and heft; less lush than the Dutch ones, they are closer to the luscious but harmonious build of Fernande, his only nude model at the time. Sexually and emotionally, Pablo was still deeply attached to her. As she wrote, "in that vast, empty, magnificent countryside, or in those mountains with their paths bordered by cypress trees, he no longer seemed, as he did in Paris, to be outside society . . ."

For the first time, Picasso was painting without second thoughts, without artifice; his concerns were purely formal and plastic, but they went beyond form, line, and mass, to the very essence of being. There was the first suggestion of a new conception of the figure to come in those *Catalan Notebook* sketches, as well as this sentence that he wrote: "A tenor who hits a note higher than the one in the score. Me!"

* Published in facsimile in 1958, as *Carnet catalan,* with notes by Douglas Cooper.

Hellenism certainly was present in this move of his to establish his plastic imagination on "historical" bases, but this was just another stage in the integration of the arts of the past to his own, a lifetime preoccupation with him. He saw himself not as a revolutionary, but rather as an inheritor.

In Paris, Pablo often went to the Trocadéro's Museum of Ethnography and the Louvre, where the primitive-art department was in an embryonic stage. He did not forget that at La Coruña he had been in classes devoted to fragments of molds of antique Greek sculpture. But his museum visits belonged to Pablo's secret life: he never told anyone about them.

In Gosol, they had little social life; he was delighted to be back in his homeland; Fernande, untouched by her lover's concerns, was studying English. They did see the sculptor Casanova and the pianist Vidella and through them learned that the artistic life of Pablo's Barcelonese friends was following a development similar to his own, beyond Art Nouveau to a more rigorous concern with form, a new classicism.

One dog day, as Fernande lay lazily nude on the bed, Pablo took a sheet of paper and did a gouache painting of her beautiful supine figure, arms behind her head, surrounded by cushions (now in the Cleveland Museum of Art). A few days later, he replaced the face by a vigorously realistic mask. Bound in a scarf, it contrasts with the Impressionist technique of the body; without trying to link the two disparate parts, he left the nude as it was. However unintentional, this experimental gesture must be seen as an indication of things to come.

For the past twenty years and more there had been several important books on Spanish archaeology and the Iberian bronzes of the fourth and fifth centuries unearthed at Osuna. Now, in the spring of 1906, the Louvre was exhibiting them. These bronzes, with others found at Cerro de los Santos near Albacete, illustrated a part of the Spanish past that fascinated Picasso. Their barbaric power and plastic efficiency contributed to the synthetic spareness of forms in his works of that autumn and winter. As he was to tell Christian Zervos thirty years later, "If the *Demoiselles d'Avignon* was conceived before I knew of Negro sculpture, it was certainly inspired by the Louvre's Iberian sculptures."

There was a great movement afoot to bring to light the past sources of the peninsula through these new finds; Picasso was doing the same thing, for his own personal benefit.

At the beginning of August, the Gosol innkeeper's daughter contracted typhoid, and Pablo, terrified of disease, left with Fernande immediately for Paris, bypassing Barcelona. As soon as he was back in the sultry heat at the Bateau-Lavoir, he began to paint *The Peasants*.

In a single session, he redid Gertrude Stein's face. Peremptory brushstrokes formed its lines and outlined its planes; as with the supine nude of Fernande, he was placing a mask over the face without retouching the rest: a rough mask, terribly rigid, with uneven eyes that give it a look of extraordinarily intense attentiveness. No halftones or shadows, just impressively authoritative geometrical schematization.

Miss Stein always claimed to be perfectly satisfied with the portrait, though not all of those around her were. Later, when she had her hair cut, Pablo "caught sight of her" and called out,

> Gertrude, what is it, what is it. What is what, Pablo, she said. Let me see, he said. She let him see. And my portrait, said he sternly. Then his face softening he added, mais, quand même, tout y est, all the same it is all there.

Picasso's circle grew larger, but Gertrude was a tough judge of the friends of her "little Napoleon," accepting or rejecting them, often on Alice B. Toklas' say-so, especially where women were concerned. Gertrude liked but thought little of André Salmon; he reciprocated by writing that she never discovered any painter, especially Picasso. Leo, who had exceptional flair, deserved the credit: his sister merely followed in his wake, before laying claim to the fine Rue de Fleurus collection, which but for him would probably not have existed. On the other hand, she thought that "Apollinaire was very attractive and very interesting." Unfortunately, his great friend Marie Laurencin struck her as a little bourgeoise whose painting was depressingly ordinary. In 1907, after much resistance, Marie became his mistress; and Apollinaire, who lived on Rue Léonie (today called Rue Henner) at the foot of Montmartre, was a close enough neighbor to be almost constantly around. Pablo fervently admired his poetic gifts, and said so, although mistrusting his aesthetic strictures.

Picasso had dubbed his studio, in blue chalk, *Au rendezvous des Poètes,* but there were few poets apart from Salmon, Apollinaire, and Max Jacob. More commonly met in the Bateau-Lavoir had been Derain, Modigliani, Van Dongen, Vlaminck, the actor Harry Baur, the future "Baron" Mollet, and a few Spaniards. But in 1906, a year of work and thought, Picasso kept apart from the public displays of the Fauves, the young Cézannians, the disciples of Gauguin or heirs of Neo-Impressionism. The only ones he occasionally saw socially were Derain and Matisse, at Gertrude Stein's, though never on their own.

Paul Signac, who considered himself the repository of Seurat's theories, tried to convert Matisse to Divisionism. Matisse tried to use it in such works as *Luxe, calme et volupté.* But when his *Bonheur de vivre,* which adapted the Divisionist theories to his own free manner, was exhibited in the 1906 Salon des Indépendants, Signac was furious. He accused Matisse of treason. Picasso saw the painting: its linear figures with pronounced rhythms, conforming more to the inner organization of the composition than to anatomical correctness, were just what he was thinking about. Matisse, of course, had not avoided mannerism or heaviness; his flamboyant Fauve colors were applied in flat surfaces sometimes heightened with baroque accents. Therein, he parted company from Picasso, who at the time had not yet resolved his color problem.

Pablo many times stated that at that time he knew nothing of African sculpture, but it seems unlikely. He had certainly seen some of the masks or statuettes belonging to Braque, Derain, Vlaminck, and Matisse. Several bric-a-brac dealers had some on display, notably Heyman, on Rue de Rennes, from whom Matisse bought most of his. The art of Blacks was not of interest only to French painters; as early as 1904, Kirchner had noticed the fetishes in the Dresden Ethnographic

Museum, and two years later the members of Die Brücke showed how deeply they had been affected by the simplified expression of African masks.

In 1928, Max Jacob told how one evening Salmon, Apollinaire, Picasso, and he had had dinner at the Matisses', on Quai St. Michel.

> Matisse took a black wooden statuette off a table and showed it to Picasso. This was the first Negro wood. Picasso held it in his hands all evening. The next morning, when I came to his studio, the floor was covered with sheets of drawing paper. Each sheet had virtually the same drawing on it, a big woman's face with a single eye, a nose too long that merged into the mouth, a lock of hair on the shoulder. Cubism was born.

But that was oversimplification. The year before, in the "Recollections" he wrote for *Cahiers d'Art,* he had said:

> Picasso never confided in me anything about the invention of Cubism, so that I am reduced to hypotheses, and there is nothing to keep me from enunciating this one: Cubism was born of Negro statuary.

And that was oversimplification, too. "Matisse . . . introduced Picasso to negro sculpture," wrote Gertrude Stein in *The Autobiography of Alice B. Toklas,* as he himself had discovered it in the shop of "a curio-dealer of the rue de Rennes."

Matisse told it this way:

> On Rue de Rennes, I often passed the shop of Père Sauvage [nickname for Heyman]. There were Negro statuettes in his window. I was struck by their character, their purity of line. It was as fine as Egyptian art. So I bought one and showed it to Gertrude Stein whom I was visiting that day. And then Picasso arrived. He took to it immediately. Everybody then started looking for Negro statuettes. They were plentiful in those days . . .

Finally, when asked about it in April 1920, Pablo told the magazine *Action,* "Negro art? Never heard of it!"

In the winter of 1906–1907, his figures became heavier, powerfully built on solid foundations, mainly made up of geometrical shapes whose juxtaposition gave them an intense hieratic power. The faces, clearly inspired by pre-Iberian sculpture, also show the influence of Romanesque frescoes. While the poses may be those of the bronzes from Osuna or Cerro de los Santos, they are also definitely out of Cézanne.

The red ocher of Gosol continued to dominate for a while, with palish pastel colors now appearing, but color, as well as form, no longer is as important as before. Hatchmarks replace flat surfaces, angular masses supplant curved rhythms. A key work of the pre-mutation period, *Two Nudes* (sometimes known as *The Two Sisters,* now in the New York Museum of Modern Art), painted in the fall of 1906, was preceded by a series of studies in which Picasso played on every potential variation: he used oil, gouache, watercolor, ink, pencil, and charcoal, and mixed his styles, from Ingresque linear naturalism to Impressionism, while running the gamut of color harmonies.

The end result of all this experimenting is two gigantic matrons with brownish, greenish flesh against a curious "tobacco juice" background, with powerful thighs and breasts, wrestlers' forearms and pectoral muscles, bulls' necks, and part-Iberian, part-Negroid faces. Facing each other, the two forms seem to be seen in a combination front and three-quarters view.

Following this canvas, Picasso painted several monstrously distorted female nudes, in which there is no colored charm to attenuate the expressionism, as in the case of the Fauves. His deliberate ugliness was wildly aggressive; not only was he breaking with the millenary concept of beauty, but he was brutally savaging the human body, the reputedly admirable result of divine creation. What was he painting? Women or things that looked like women, in which certain parts of the body, as among the primitives, were exaggerated outrageously to give them a symbolic character? This "objectivity" led him to the re-creation that was to be one of the foundations of Cubism.

When his great retrospective took place at the Zurich Kunsthaus in 1932, he did not hesitate to say of *La Vie,* being shown there: "That picture is awful. The rest can be said to be not too bad . . ."

During this fall/winter of 1906, he did several figures, of women mainly, as well as a self-portrait, in which the illustrative or sentimental values more and more gave way to plastic energy alone. It was mainly on this level that Negro or primitive arts would exert their influence. All visual delight was thenceforth set aside, all subjectiveness detached from meaningful fact was rejected, an objective vocabulary taking shape in a total break with the past. Yet the Bateau-Lavoir studio, despite his improved financial condition, had no new comforts and remained as sordid and messy as ever.

An adventure was starting which Picasso, from the moment he got into it, conducted toward its paroxysm. When Pierre Daix asked him whether these female figures had been done from life, he replied:

> No, I did them in the Rue de Ravignan atelier, just like that, without a model, working till they worked out . . . I did not use models again after Gosol. Because just then I was working apart from any model. What I was looking for was something else . . .

He was later to tell Gertrude Stein, as she related it,

> when you make a thing, it is so complicated making it that it is bound to be ugly, but those that do it after you they don't have to worry about making it and they can make it pretty, and so everybody can like it when the others make it.

This was when Apollinaire, who had met Braque at Kahnweiler's, introduced him to Picasso. *Two Nudes* was done at the same time as Pablo's self-portrait now in the Gallatin Collection of the Philadelphia Museum of Art. He is wearing a white shirt, slightly open at the collar on his powerful torso, holding a palette in his hand; his head, rather small in relation to the rest of the body, is schematized like a mask, but in a spirit nearer to the Gosol paintings than his current work. There is something Romanesque in the body and the serene face, as if anticipative, whereas the muscles seem to be tensing so as to be in top shape for struggles to come.

Violently disjointed, broken down into a juxtaposition of planes sharply outlined and fitted into one another, *La Danseuse,* kept by Picasso as the incontrovertible evidence of the plastic adventure he was entering upon, indeed marks a capital stage in his process of decomposition of form. Antonina Vallentin discovered it in a pile of pictures behind the stove in the studio on the Rue des Grands-Augustins. Picasso dragged it out, stuck in a strange white frame, which was what the painter wanted to point out to his visitor. "It's one of Degas's frames that I was able to get hold of," he explained proudly. "He had them made to order for him." And his hand caressed the old-fashioned moldings of the wood selected by Degas for his *danseuses* "on the wing" in their spangled tutus. Picasso, Antonina Vallentin commented, was looking at the frame as if its connection with the repulsive monster it framed seemed absolutely normal to him. Why in the world should it have seemed abnormal?

V

"TALKING TO THE PILOT IS FORBIDDEN"
(1907–1909)

IT IS THE SPRING OF 1907. IN THE BATEAU-LAVOIR STUDIO, PICASSO PAINTS. Around him his monsters, women with unhealthy flesh, Negroid heads with broadly striated cheeks, masks shaped as by scythe strokes with empty sockets, pink and gray nudes strong as tree trunks, and his self-portrait with the staring eye, open collar, palette in hand, stand like totems of some barbaric cult of which he is the high priest. Fernande, nonchalantly sprawled on the couch, looks on.

It was a fantastic spectacle: the stocky little man in front of the picture, a huge canvas he had been fighting with for months, in which disjointed women were carrying on. In reality, they were geometrical constructs, with unbelievable faces and erratic arms, a tohubohu of shapes going every which way, looking like nothing, reminiscent of nothing known, unless perhaps the targets in carnival games of skill. The bodies with their broad flesh-pink planes were not shaded by either light or chiaroscuro, but chiseled with frigid violence, unrestrained fury. Here and there, on each disjointed torso, a terrifying mask with madwoman's eyes.

At the beginning he had planned an allegorical composition like *La Vie*, in a different spirit and more or less representing a synthesis of the previous months' operations of destruction in which geometry occupied an ever-greater placé, but on an instinctual, not a descriptive or impressionistic, level. He had a title for the composition: *The Wages of Sin*. It was to be set in a brothel.

A few years later, he was to tell Kahnweiler,

> In my first plan, there were to be men in it; you saw those sketches. There was a student holding a skull. And a sailor. The women were eating, and the basket of fruit remains from that. Then it changed, and became what it is now.

In the first sketch, now in the Basel Museum, there is one character seated among the nude women in their very free postures, the student with the skull in his lap. To the left, a man is coming in with a package under his arm, and in the center are two still lifes, flowers and fruit. The composition is enclosed by curtains, as if it were a theatrical stage. The characters are sketchily indicated, the nudes rough, their faces featureless. In a second version, a nude woman replaces the man with the package, and the fruit has disappeared.

The theme developed. A watercolor in the Gallatin Collection, Philadelphia, reduces the figures to five women, with the same rhythmic relationship as in the final work. Throughout his research for it, Picasso seems to have been influenced by Cézanne's large *Women Bathers,* and another smaller Cézanne, painted in 1879–1882, also of women bathers, which he had seen at Matisse's. As he changed the figures and varied their places and positions, he also modified the composition, simplified the drop curtains, eliminated the customers, and brought back the fruit. Through a series of studies as schematic as they were expressive, he succeeded in replacing the subject by a plastic idea, as he had done in the fall of 1906 with his nudes.

This canvas, for which Picasso did several studies, mainly of heads, is almost unbearably violent; as he built up the bodies of the gesticulating women and the composition took shape, with the presence and disappearance of other characters, the student and the man with the package, the whorehouse idea became more precise. Memories of the Carrer d'Avinyo, a Barcelona street in which he used to buy his watercolors and paper, that also boasted a whorehouse, slid in alongside the original allegory.

"It was called the *Avignon Brothel* at first," he was to tell Kahnweiler. "Know why? Because Avignon was a name I had always known, linked to my life. I lived just off the Carrer d'Avinyo . . .

"Today they call it the *Demoiselles d'Avignon.* How that name irritates me!" he sighed.

Little by little, the curvaceous rhythms of the sketch gave way to angular planes, sharply detached, without the painter succeeding in fixing a general type of woman. Each of the figures is different from the others; there is the manner of the nudes or heads with large outlined eyes of the fall of 1906, but also an asymmetrical aspect derived from the Iberian sculptures; whereas the Negro masks, from which he was later to take inspiration, are on the contrary quite symmetrical. Several women's heads of this spring of 1907 have almond-shaped empty eye sockets, long noses, mouths that are merely indicated, ovoid noses. It was probably then, in March, that Picasso bought from Apollinaire's friend and sometime secretary, the Belgian adventurer Géry-Piéret, the two Iberian heads he had stolen from the Louvre, which were to cause such troubles later.

The shadow cast by the nose in hatchmarks on either side of the bridge gave him the idea, first tested in a small plaster sculpture, of flattening the vertical plane onto the face by heavy striations. After a few isolated heads, this became the character of the studies for the *demoiselles'* faces on the right side of the picture, notably the *Demoiselle d'Avignon* in the Paris Museum of Modern Art,

"Les Demoiselles d'Avignon" Paris 1907 (Collection, The Museum of Modern Art, New York. Acquired through the Lillie P. Bliss Bequest)

formerly in the Lefèvre Collection, the *Head* in the Kiruna Museum, Sweden, and those in the Berggruen and Penrose collections. They show how Picasso experimented with what has been called the *"quart-de-Brie"* (or cheese-wedge) nose, marked by strong hatchmarks to stress its volume. There is no influence of African masks in these faces, and the 1907–1908 works have erroneously been classed under the label of "Negro Period."

Is there any such in the *Demoiselles d'Avignon*? This controversy has been going on for a long time, despite the fact that Picasso himself was quite definite about it; but we know that he often asserted things that were contrary to the most elementary truth. That is probably why the question of whether there are African influences in the picture continues to arouse polemics.

"The artist formally certified to me that at the time he painted *Les Demoiselles d'Avignon* he was ignorant of Black African art. It was revealed to him only some time later," wrote Christian Zervos, relating what Picasso had told not only him but other persons. However, the French verb *ignorer* can mean "to ignore" as well as "to be ignorant of," and we may draw the conclusion that, while Picasso had already seen many examples of this work, he meant he had ignored it, not yet made its characteristics part of the current experimenting. Zervos again:

> One day, coming out of the Museum of Comparative Sculpture, then in the left wing of the Palace of the Trocadéro, out of curiosity he opened the doors across the hall that led into the rooms of the old Ethnographical Museum. Even today, Picasso speaks with deepest emotion of the shock he received that day on seeing the African sculptures.

This very likely took place before the summer break of 1907, perhaps at the end of June or the beginning of July, as other points of reference allow us to conclude. Picasso already had seen a number of examples of African art and knew it well. If he really got a deeper revelation of it at this date, it is easy to conclude that the part of the *Demoiselles* he was then working on was transformed by his replacing the faces on the right by "African masks." This is the belief of experts as distinguished as Alfred Barr, Jr., John Golding, Jean Laude, and André Fermigier, the last of whom has asserted: "The faces of the two charming creatures [on the right] are almost literal copies of African masks." Jean Laude sees as undeniable "the appearance of African masks in the right hand part of the *Demoiselles d'Avignon*," and John Richardson boldly writes that Picasso redid the two right-hand figures of the *Demoiselles* in a style that cannot be anything but that of "Negro" art.*

Now, Picasso never did say he redid the two right-hand faces of the picture basing them on Negro masks.

After visiting the Bateau-Lavoir, Kahnweiler had occasion to get an overall view of all the canvases preparatory to *Les Demoiselles d'Avignon,* and he wrote in his *Juan Gris* (1946):

> The 1907–1909 period has been called "Picasso's Negro Period," a most regrettable name since it suggests an imitation of African sculpture, when in reality there was a

---

* Cf. André Fermigier, Jean Laude, and John Richardson, in Bibliography.

similarity of tendencies between the sculpture of the Blacks and what in Picasso as well as in Braque was one phase of an autonomous development.

African sculptors base their work on simplification and abstraction; they show not only what they see, but also what they know; indeed, knowledge often over-shadows appearance. The path to Cubism was thus slowly taking shape; most of the young artists who admired Negro art would espouse Cubism, except for Vlaminck, who loathed it.

Pablo had already felt a need for a mask, as shown in the portrait of Gertrude Stein. A similar plastic necessity seems to have determined the painting of the two right-hand heads in the *Demoiselles*. Various studies show the researches which, along with those cited earlier, led to the changes that strike us so in the women's faces, especially the hatchmarks, a way of trying to impart relief that was nothing new in Picasso's work.

A drawing he did on a piece of the newspaper *Le Vieux Marcheur*, dated August 23, 1907, shows a lozenge-shaped face the relief of which is almost entirely built on sets of parallel streaks; setting it beside the upper-right-hand face in the *Demoiselles*, one is struck by the similarity of construction. So it would seem clear that the changes in the features of the two Avinyo whores date from that summer.

Picasso's poring over the sculpture of the Blacks thus opened a new path to him; it could not yet be called a "Negro Period," but a different field of shapes was available. There are several examples of this in the canvases the painter kept that Douglas Duncan photographed for the first time in 1957–1960 at La Californie. They are studies of heads obviously inspired by Black masks with all the characteristics of the latter; and they are dated in the last months of 1907 and in 1908. By 1909, they show Picasso's evolution toward a schematic roughness that is deliberately "barbaric," with a clearly Cézannian construction technique different from the heads of the preceding months.

In between, he had done the *Nude with Drapery*.

The heads that led up to the *Demoiselles d'Avignon* were marked by a new, capital element: the affirmation of color. We must turn to Cézanne for their source: his example and lessons were ever present with Picasso in his develop-ment.

When a friend mentioned to him the decisive influences of El Greco and Cézanne in the pre-Cubist years, Picasso replied, "Of course, a painter always has a father and a mother."

The nudes of the Carrer d'Avinyo, standing in the Bateau-Lavoir studio, were as enigmatic and magical as the man who made them. Their composition, based on an oblique axis, was without depth and the geometricization of solid masses was accompanied by the imbrication of cold and hot colors, light rose and brown-ish ocher. One of the whores on the left is raising the heavy drop curtain to let us in on the terrifying spectacle which Fernande alone had been watching unfold for months. As Picasso told Zervos in 1935:

How can you expect a spectator to live my picture as I lived it? A picture comes to me from far away. Who can say how far away? I have guessed it, seen it, done it, and yet, the next day, I myself cannot see what I've done. How can one get into my dreams, my instincts, my desires, my thoughts that have taken so long to shape up and come to light especially so as to grasp what I may have put in in spite of my own will.

I had finished half the picture. I felt: this is not it! I did the other half. I wondered whether I ought to redo the whole thing. Then, I thought, "No, they'll understand what I wanted to do."

André Salmon, in 1912, in his *Histoire anecdotique du cubisme,* wrote:

The artist was already fascinated by the Negroes whom he placed above the Egyptians. His enthusiasm was not supported by any empty taste for the picturesque. Dahomean and Polynesian figures struck him as being "reasonable." The large canvas with its severe figures and without lighting did not long remain in its original state. Picasso would go after the faces, the noses of which were mostly placed head-on in the shape of isosceles triangles. The sorcerer's apprentice kept quizzing the Oceanic and African witch doctors.

When Salmon wrote this, he had not seen the figures painted during and after the stay at Gosol, or he would not have failed to add to what he took for the Negro influences (identified by him as "anything that does not conform to our acquired vision") those of Catalan Romanesque painting, Iberian heads, El Greco, and especially Cézanne. He mentions Egyptians. When Uhde spoke to Kahnweiler of Picasso, before the latter knew him, he said he was painting "a very strange picture, with something Assyrian in it."

Derain's influence on Pablo has generally been sloughed off. But it seems significant, for the ex-Fauve had done a number of geometrically inclined paintings before 1907 that were inspired by Cézanne; moreover, his male nudes painted at Collioure in 1904–1905, his *After Gauguin* (1904) and *Bathers* (1907), were certainly known and remembered by Picasso. Period mimesis? Undoubtedly. But Derain was an admirer of Negro art and thought that "barbarism" could be a salutary tonic for the efforts of young painters caught between the naturalism of Manet, whose importance at the time was as great as that of Cézanne, and the Divisionism of Seurat. From Derain's *Bathers* to Picasso's *Demoiselles d'Avignon* the distance is as short as the link is tenuous. Derain stopped along the way, yet he was the first to have introduced what was to become Cubism. Picasso and Braque easily left him behind when it came to realizing it.

Whether out of regret or bitterness, Derain wrote to Vlaminck from the trenches in 1917, "Cubism is a truly idiotic thing that I find more and more revolting."

Pablo had let no one in the studio while he was painting the *Demoiselles;* the months of intense work exhausted him. Then, he finally invited Leo and Gertrude Stein to come and see what he was working on, along with several friends; what they saw overwhelmed them. Salmon and then Apollinaire, both so voluble, were speechless.

Apollinaire, with his poet's intuition, knew very well that scandalizing was necessary to break down the gateway to adventures, and that no new vocabulary could be imposed without deliberately raping the past; but before his friend's painting, he lost countenance, and could only mention the word "revolution," which he knew to be handy and not too compromising. But he regretted the absence of the poetic sentiment Pablo had achieved in his Maternities and Saltimbanques, in which, as Guillaume wrote, his inspiration "bloomed into wonderful works." His poetic paraphrases now no longer obtained, and the whole critical vocabulary called for renovation. Apollinaire the poet did not "understand" *Les Demoiselles d'Avignon* because his poesy did not "talk" that kind of painting.

He brought Félix Fénéon to see the *Demoiselles* at the studio, and Seurat's friend, the critic of *La Revue Blanche,* could only tell Picasso paternally, "Very interesting, my boy. You should try your hand at caricature."

When the Steins saw it, like Vollard, they thought Picasso was "finished." Gertrude did not mention the *Demoiselles* in her various books about him; Leo thought that, betraying his extraordinary promise, he had engaged on a destructive path and "let down" his sister and him.

Pablo one day overheard a conversation at the Steins' between Leo and Matisse, who claimed Picasso was ridiculing modern painting and swore he would make him sorry for what he had done. It was not his first attempt to discredit Pablo in their eyes; he was jealous of Gertrude's growing interest in him, and hoped to find an ally in Leo.

For all that she did not understand the *Demoiselles,* Gertrude Stein did not drop her "little Napoleon." He and Matisse, until then good friends who swapped paintings with each other, now became implacable rivals. They still met at Rue de Fleurus, but virtually never spoke to each other again. Then, one day Matisse had words with Gertrude; he accused her of no longer caring for painting— meaning his, of course. And he stopped going to see her.

For years, the two painters were to be friendly enemies, watching each other, sniffing critically, spitting sarcasms or double entendres, and both actually rather enjoyed the fun of it. With age, they found serenity, but not forgetfulness. The general reaction of Picasso's admirers to *Les Demoiselles d'Avignon* was condensed in one phrase—erroneously attributed by many to the Russian collector Serge Shchukine, who did not yet know him—"What a loss for French art!"

In his turn, Braque came to see the picture, and was overwhelmed. Himself so thoughtful and methodical, he could not understand painting like this, with uncontrolled fury, with limitless passion. Why should his Spanish friend have distorted the human body so violently? Why such monstrous figures, and especially that coign smack in the middle of the face in the place of a nose? *By what right?*

"Yes, Braque," Picasso insisted to him. "That's what noses are like."

But Braque suddenly grabbed him and burst out, "No matter what you saw, it's as if you were making us eat cotton waste or swallow gasoline so we can spit fire!"

Derain's judgment was more pessimistic: "It is a desperate undertaking. One day they'll find Picasso hanged behind it."

As Pablo later told Kahnweiler, "Even at that time they claimed my noses were cockeyed. I had to make them cockeyed so they'd know they were noses."

Word spread around Montmartre: "You know, it seems Picasso has gone mad!" Shopkeepers looked at Fernande pityingly. But Leo Stein, after his first surprise, came back to Pablo to say, "Now I know what you were trying to do. You were trying to paint the fourth dimension! How funny it is!"

Braque, overcome by it, had shut himself up in his own studio, which set tongues wagging. Some said he was out to paint an even more "scandalous" picture than Picasso's, others said a landscape based on studies he had done in the south; it turned out to be a simple nude done during the winter of 1907–1908, a monumental isolated figure, with curved rhythms stressed by thick outlines cutting off the solid masses streaked with colored hatchings. The austere blue-gray, green, and rose-brown harmony, drawn without shadings or chiaroscuro, set off the ruggedness of the angular planes. All of it, deliberately schematized, bespoke laborious stylization.

The scandal at the Bateau-Lavoir was known to only a very small group; Paris and its official "artistic circles" did not even hear of it, and painting was in no way affected. But the unattached émigré in Montmartre with one stroke of his wand had returned to its place the magic universe of forms, suspended by the illusionism of the Renaissance. The *Demoiselles d'Avignon*'s shout of insurrection and rage was a call to adventure: a new art was being born that once again would question, once again upset; here again was anxiety and fervor, balance and violence, truth and duration. What today was a break, tomorrow would be creation. "That was when questioning, sometimes serene and almost always distressed, took precedence over annexation," André Malraux was to write, "when Picasso replaced Cézanne."

A twenty-eight-year-old young German, a few months before, had run out on the financial business his family wanted him to work at, and started a picture gallery in Rue Vignon, near the Madeleine, in Paris. His name was Daniel-Henry Kahnweiler. He did not know many painters, but he knew what he liked: Cézanne and Gauguin. In his new profession, he emulated two masters: Paul Durand-Ruel and Vollard. At the March 1907 Salon des Indépendants, showing all the young adventurers of art, with the sole exception of Picasso, he bought Derains and Vlamincks, as well as Braques and Van Dongens, Fauves one and all.

"One day a young man came into my shop on Rue Vignon. His looks surprised me, but then at the time very few people ventured into my gallery. He was rather small, stocky, poorly dressed, with dirty, down-at-the-heel shoes, but he had eyes that struck me as superb. He went around the gallery, not very big then, about four meters by four, and left. The next day, he came back in a carriage with an older man, very heavy and with a beard; they also toured the shop and left without a word . . ."

Thus, Kahnweiler, seated in the office of the gallery that bears the name of his sister-in-law Louise Leiris, but which is truly his, on Rue Monceau in Paris, thinking back on the start, his first encounters, his first artistic loves. Three years younger than Picasso, he is now an old half-deaf man, reading with difficulty

D.-H. Kahnweiler at his home in Boulogne (Louise Leiris Gallery)

through a magnifying glass, walking painfully. Yet his memory is amazing, his clear-mindedness and critical faculties intact. We had several talks between 1961 and 1971.

"I had met a truly extraordinary man, whom I remember most fondly," he said, "Wilhelm Uhde. He was the first to speak to me about a strange painting done by a Spanish painter whose name I had seen on some drawings at Sagot's, Picasso. A picture that he said looked Assyrian. Being curious, I went up to the Bateau-Lavoir in Montmartre, and knocked at the door of the painter Uhde had talked to me about. He opened the door in his shirt sleeves—it was early in the morning—and I recognized my visitor of the other day; the man with him had been Vollard.

"The poverty he lived in was just terrifying." Mr. Kahnweiler stressed that last word. "It took unbelievable heroism to live in such poverty and so very alone. Picasso shared the studio with Fernande Olivier, who was a very beautiful woman, and their dog Frika.

"I did not find the painting 'Assyrian,' but I could not put a label on it. It was something mad and monstrous at the same time. I was deeply and violently moved, and immediately thought this was an important work. It was *Les Demoiselles d'Avignon*."

"What made you immediately feel it was important?" I asked.

"I don't know. I might say that it was because of its absolute novelty, but that's not exactly it. I could not define just where and how the novelty showed itself, yet I could feel it bursting out."

"It was an intuition, not an analyzed aesthetic feeling?"

"Exactly. I think it's something one might call aesthetic conscience. There is an ethical, moral conscience that determines what is good and what bad; I think such a conscience exists for the fine arts as well. It said to me, 'This is fine. This is important.'"

Kahnweiler bought the studies and sketches preparatory to the *Demoiselles*. He would have liked to take the painting with him, too, but the painter kept insisting that it was not yet completed. Kahnweiler came back to see him several times, but with his habitual mistrust Picasso was on his guard with the young German he hardly knew. However, since Vollard was horrified by the *Demoiselles*, and the Steins, lectured by Matisse, were less than interested, he decided to sell him some things. Kahnweiler did not hide his admiration for everything Pablo showed him; what he said about the big work seemed sincere, and this attitude which was so rare profoundly touched the painter in his loneliness and general rejection.

Picasso, having made such an enormous effort in doing the *Demoiselles*, stopped working the better part of each night as had been his custom. Often, of an evening, his friends now met as they had used to in the studio, to talk, smoke, and drink. Sometimes they went to see people such as the critic Maurice Raynal, whom they had known since 1905. Fernande was to say that he had just inherited a small fortune from his father and was wasting it royally on carousing. Actually, he was being very generous with it. When he did his military service at Toul, he invited all of his friends to come and sample the pleasures of that provincial town, from the local Madame Bovarys to the houses of joy. Manolo recalled spending several days as his guest there, mainly in whorehouses and cafés.

On Mondays, Max Jacob, who now lived at 7 Rue Ravignan, practically across the street from the Bateau-Lavoir, was "at home" in his sordid room, so dark that a railway-station kerosene lamp was needed to light it even during the day. On Wednesday evenings, Apollinaire had open house. His place was ugly, but as neat as Picasso's studio and Max's room were messy. To Fernande it reeked of "a mixture of smoke, kerosene and incense, old furniture and ether." Guillaume had recently become Marie Laurencin's lover. Picasso had introduced her to him, saying, "Here's a fiancée for you," for she acted like a real Goody-Two-Shoes. And he was not wrong; their love affair would never get beyond the engagement stage.

Since the time of the *Demoiselles* Picasso had ceased his regular attendance at Gertrude Stein's Saturday evenings, but he met a new generation of painters and poets at the Lapin Agile.

One day Picasso and Fernande got the strange idea of adopting a little girl. Named Léontine, she came from an orphanage on Rue Caulaincourt. At the beginning, it was fun for her at the Bateau-Lavoir; Fernande and their friends spoiled her rotten; but then they found she was in the way. The studio was not large, and their life anything but well organized. After the spoiling came the whacks. They obviously had to return the child, but the nuns were no longer willing to take her. Fortunately, a neighboring concierge felt sorry for her and took her in. Max, always available for such chores, handled her moving; when he took the kid over to her new family, her valise contained candy and a doll he had bought for her.

There was a good deal of talk in Montmartre about this event, which did no credit to the Picassos; some said the painter had left the little girl on a Boulevard de Clichy bench on a winter's night. Léontine was to be immortalized (in somewhat altered form) in André Salmon's *La Négresse du Sacré-Coeur* alongside Sorgue (Picasso) and Septime Fébur (Max Jacob).

The figures Pablo painted in late summer and at the end of 1907 led him into a new plastic vocabulary. His final break with naturalism was under way; from canvas to canvas, he was reinventing human anatomy and space; he took bodies, decomposed them, and then reassembled them, and did the same for objects as in *Still Life with Skull* (Fall 1907), which reflects Picasso's desire to restructure the entire picture, making each part relate to its neighbor in a coherent whole conceived as a pictorial and mental totality. Cézanne had had no other aim; but Picasso, for a few months, was going to have to let this go by the board.

Previously considered only food for thought, Negro art was now to become an element in structuring, and then in knowing; the experiments Picasso was to try were first on a formal plane, then on a mental one. The right-hand figures of the *Demoiselles d'Avignon* were the axis around which his new vocabulary could be developed: starting with his tests on these masks, he embarked on a transformation of faces based on the specific characteristics of African art he had seen

"Nude with Drapery" Paris 1907 (The Hermitage
—Leningrad)

(GIRAUDON)

at the Trocadéro Museum. So, it is not proper to speak of Negro art's intrusion into his painting, but rather its penetration, which occurred rather rapidly and can be seen in the various preparatory studies for the *Nude with Drapery* (now in the Hermitage, Leningrad) that were revealed mainly through the Gertrude Stein Collection. The penetration was not limited to faces alone; Picasso's plastic vocabulary took off from the mask but covered the whole of the painting, in which it was conductor, reference point, and authentication.

Picture space in a few months had undergone profound modifications: in the *Demoiselles* it was strictly limited, closed, a theatrical stage on which five characters acted out a play and "performed" virtually facing the audience—except for those on the right, the experimental area of the canvas. They alone began to move during the painting of the picture as their heads were being transformed. The women painted during the succeeding months also started to move, and their movements seemed freer and freer before reaching the frenetic dynamism of *Nude with Drapery* and its plastic earthquake.

Was *The Offering* a sketch for a major work never completed? That may be. It belongs to a series of canvases done at the start of 1908, in which the very first drawing has an inscription in Spanish written by Picasso that says, "She is lying on a bed and he discovers her by raising the sheets. Behind them are the curtains of the bed and the room. He is holding a bouquet of flowers." Is this not the theme of Cézanne's *Afternoon in Naples* or *A Modern Olympia?* It was to be elaborated in several preparatory works in which the "Negro" influence progressively gave way to that of the master of Aix.

The scandal here, as with Cubism, lay mainly in Pablo's insult and injury to the human figure. And those who voiced their disapproval were far from being backward bourgeois or academic artists: they belonged to the tumultuous Montmartre youth of studio and press, painters, poets, writers, ready to upset everything. But suddenly the master upsetter terrified them! And kept on doing it! All of 1908 was devoted to a series of challenges violently repeating that the break Picasso had made was no accident.

Pablo was twenty-seven and alone facing an awe-inspiring world in which he was the master of wizardry. "Success is the result of rejected discoveries. Otherwise, you merely become a collector of yourself," he said. "I don't sell myself anything."

Cézanne had advised to "treat nature by the cylinder, the sphere, the cone, all in perspective." The problem, however, was to get into two dimensions things that had three, without trickery or *trompe-l'oeil,* without the illusionist effects of classical perspective—to succeed in making the two-dimensional figures retain their depth, and space its fullness.

The return to Cézanne was also a return to order after the tumult of the "Negro" canvases. In looking for the essential structure of the being, as Kahnweiler put it, Picasso went after "all the problems at once." In the heart of this profusion, Cézanne suggested to him an experiment parallel to those he was trying on the geometrical decomposition of bodies, its denominator being the substitution of architectonic rhythm and volume for the frenetic iconoclastic destruction of the previous months. Now he had to put the pieces together again.

While painting his amazing ocher, earth-colored, or sometimes reddish nudes, against their nocturnal backgrounds, hewn from the material of sensuality as idols might be from a tree or clay, Picasso had the delight of getting back to Cézanne's luminous lessons of the ordinary table on which he set a bowl of apples, a loaf of bread, and a napkin in front of a drape. His *Landscape with Breads* (now in the Basel Kunstmuseum) is an act of grace addressed to the man without whom neither the painting of the early part of our century nor indeed Pablo Picasso himself would have been what they are.

A regional Salon at Toulouse, unveiled on March 15, 1908, had two Picassos, *Poverty* and *Portrait,* and these two, plus *The Ball* and *Cabinet particulier,* were shown again three months later, June 7–20, in the same southern city. *The Ball* and perhaps some of the others belonged to the organizer of the latter show, a local critic and collector named Charles Malpel.

But that summer, while Braque was painting down south at L'Estaque, where Cézanne had once worked, Pablo and Fernande went to La Rue-des-Bois, a small village in the Oise, to the north of Paris. He painted wooded landscapes there with deep dense broad green masses. As at the Bateau-Lavoir, their lodgings were the most rudimentary, an outbuilding of a farm, with two bedrooms, a kitchen, and a huge hangar to serve as studio; no more of a housekeeper here than in the city, Fernande did nothing to fix it up. "We ate in a room that smelled of the stable," she wrote, "and were rocked to sleep by the indistinct murmurings of the forest."

But Pablo was happy. He was painting, and had with him Frika, his beloved bitch, his gravid cat, and the frequent visits of friends—Max Jacob, Braque, Apollinaire, and the critic Vanderpyl and his wife, who, according to Fernande, raised the devil with her husband the first night because he would not perform his conjugal duty.

Landscapes and figures are witness to the fact that the studio painter Picasso was borrowing from nature to prove Cézanne's lessons of architecture and order. He was setting foot in reality again. Comparing the canvases he brought back from La Rue-des-Bois with the virtually unchanged topography of the area, we can see that Picasso was trying to apply to nature the experiments undertaken at Gosol and after his return. Or, rather, to enclose them within an already existing natural organization, articulated, constructed, marked by persistency. Paradoxically, Picasso was inserting reality into his picture after completion.

Back home, for more privacy, Pablo rented a studio at the rear of a small garden entirely ringed by tumbledown old buildings, on Rue Cortot, and locked himself in it days on end, sometimes returning to the Bateau-Lavoir in the middle of the night. Fernande made scenes, accusing him of neglecting her, and on occasion she was unfaithful to him, mainly "out of curiosity," as she was to explain it.

It seems unlikely that Matisse said to Picasso about Serge Shchukine, "If you get a chance, offer him something. He buys," although this legend has been widely repeated. It does not sound like Matisse, nor was he disposed to help

Pablo in that way. Kahnweiler introduced the rich Moscow draper to the Spaniard.

He owned the exuberantly rococo Trubetzkoi Palace, in Moscow, which his unbounded passion for French painting had filled with the largest and most daring canvases around. He was so taken with the Fauves that he bought their works by the score; in 1909, he was to commission Matisse's double masterpiece, *Dance* and *Music,* for its monumental staircase.*

He immediately started buying Picassos and bought more through Kahnweiler on each of his succeeding visits to Paris. He carried off, up to the outbreak of war in 1914, the most important works of the Blue and Rose periods and of Cubism—or those that were to become so. Kahnweiler and other dealers and collectors, such as Vollard and Shchukine's fellow Russian Ivan Morosov, followed his lead.†

Picasso's works, smaller in size, never struck him as being as "decorative" as Matisse's, but that did not inhibit his acquisitions. An intuition for artistic value plus a rare intelligence and incomparable culture made him the first great Picasso collector after the Steins. He obviously enjoyed scandalizing Russian high society with these purchases. His Muscovite friends were astounded and wondered who were the bigger suckers, they for playing up to him by lauding his cockeyed paintings out of politeness, or he for being taken in by the Parisian fakers. As what Kahnweiler called "the only great collector of avant-garde painting" of the period, Shchukine kept Picasso financially afloat in 1908–1909.

Braque sent six canvases to the 1908 Salon d'Automne, and the lot were rejected. Matisse, Marquet, and Rouault, on the jury, got the decision reversed at the last minute for two of them, but Braque refused the compromise. In November, Kahnweiler held a Braque show for which Apollinaire wrote a preface: young painters came curiously to look at it, but not the public. So, who was first to apply the term "cubes" to Braque's geometric constructions?

Uhde said it was Max Jacob. Kahnweiler attributed it to Matisse, as did Apollinaire, but Matisse denied he was responsible for the "burlesque word, Cubism," even when Cocteau said he had spawned it. It was first written by Louis Vauxcelles, the critic who had also unintentionally given their name to the Fauves.

No friend of innovations, he was walking through the Salon d'Automne with Matisse when the latter mentioned to him a Braque "picture made of little cubes," a landscape from L'Estaque that had been rejected. The better to make him understand, Matisse made a sketch of it.

Vauxcelles remembered, and when in *Gil Blas* for November 14, 1908, he reviewed Kahnweiler's Braque exhibition, he wrote that he "constructs distorted, metallic little people, awfully simplified. He scorns form, reducing everything— sites, figures, houses—to geometrical diagrams, to cubes. . . ." And when the

* He also paid good prices, twenty-seven thousand francs for them (about $5,500), fifteen and twelve thousand respectively, extremely high at the time.

† Nationalized after the Revolution, in 1948 the Shchukine collection was split between Moscow's Pushkin Museum and the Leningrad Hermitage; it is the world's greatest assemblage of early Picassos, prior to 1914; twenty-five of the canvases were lent to the Paris Museum of Modern Art for the painter's ninetieth birthday, but at the request of the Soviet government Shchukine's name was not mentioned in the catalog or publicity.

Salon des Indépendants came along the following spring, he spoke of "Georges Braque's cubic oddities."

Also in that Salon was Henri Rousseau. The retired local toll collector, a strange man whose true personality is very hard to pin down, had been exhibiting here since 1886, with his work usually laughed at. Undaunted, with his unshakable self-confidence, Rousseau went right on dishing up the pictures, called "naïve," that revealed his extraordinary intuitive knowledge. Self-educated, he had only the vaguest idea of what his contemporaries were painting; Impressionism, Divisionism, Fauvism scarcely had any effect on him. If he was seen at the Indépendants, it was exclusively because he was rejected everywhere else, including "M. Bouguereau's Salon," which to him, as to Cézanne, was the great goal. He did not especially admire the famous academic painter's gelatinous nudes, but he did envy his success—his name and art symbolizing Salon and Academy.

Such singularity and the constant state of revolt against comfortable culture and art in which Rousseau stood could not but attract the dissidents who saw in his paintings the opposite of all current work. Alfred Jarry, Rémy de Gourmont, Vallotton, and the *Mercure de France* critic Louis Roy were to be among his first admirers. Apollinaire did not immediately fall in line, feeling that "Rousseau should have been nothing but a craftsman"—a statement he would find hard to live down. On the other hand, Robert Delaunay considered him a fine artist and got his mother to commission a picture from him, *La Charmeuse de serpents* (The Snake Charmer), today in the Louvre.

Picasso, from his first encounter with Rousseau, was an enthusiast; a few days later he bought a portrait of the painter's wife from Père Soulier for five francs. "Not expensive," the bric-a-bracster told him, "and you can paint over it!" With a few other Rousseaus, it remained in Pablo's own collection.

In view of his friends' reactions, Apollinaire changed his mind and began to extol the so-called Douanier (customs-man). Uhde organized a small one-man show—the only one held during his lifetime—and Delaunay, Braque, Picasso, and Apollinaire were in the forefront of the painters and poets who attended the musicales in his Rue Perrel studio. Pablo wondered whether the old man was a sly fox hiding behind pretended innocence, or a foolish, ill-developed fool. The pictures intrigued him, their mixture of fastidious realism and popular poesy allowing him to reinvent for his own use a kind of painting that had not been done for centuries. In 1907–1910, when painting was opening its eyes to the super-real, was not his métier, so starkly nude, the best confirmation available for the avant-gardists who flocked to Rousseau as admirers?

Picasso was especially struck by a thing the Douanier had said to him: "We're the two great painters of our day, you in the Egyptian genre, and I in the modern." And it was more than a joke: Rousseau, whose art education was not as nonexistent as some pretended, with his extraordinary intuition had realized that Picasso found his sources in museum art, whereas he himself followed no one's traces.

It was not Rousseau who was the "barbarian" or "savage," but rather the

Spaniard, who was nurtured on some complex obscure past whose idols he was reviving, and who felt that the poor Douanier represented the most dangerous of rivalries, that of an art without forerunners or artifice, a raw, noncultural art, at the opposite pole from Cubism's intellectual experimentations.

But Picasso remained stoutly uncompromising; he entered no Salon, refused to let Kahnweiler exhibit *Les Demoiselles d'Avignon,* which, had it been hung in his gallery, would doubtless have created furore and controversy, been as it were a manifesto. But that was not what Pablo wanted; scandal was a stench in his nostrils.

Usually reserved, he could quickly turn irritable or violent. Being totally wrapped up in his work, he could not tolerate being distracted from it. Above all, despite his physical resistance and the absence of any alarm in this area, he was afraid of sickness or incapacity. As all heavy smokers do, he had a rough cough, and he thought his lungs might be affected, despite the reassurances of a friendly physician.

Matisse found fame much more quickly and easily than he, not only in France, but also abroad. He had many collectors and dealers, and had just opened a school which had many students. To many, he was the symbol of new French painting.

Not so Picasso: known only to a few initiates, he did not readily participate and few of his canvases were shown. Already a bit notorious, he now became known as "hard to handle," not without reason; admired, he was also feared. He was a "character."

"I was never aware of Cubism," Braque told Dora Vallier, "for if I had been I would have exploited it. I was always on the lookout. What could Cubism give me? As far as I was concerned, it had to be created. . . ." And Picasso to Zervos: "When we were doing Cubism, we were not trying to do Cubism, but just to express what was inside us."

Summer of 1909: Picasso felt a need to go back to Spain. This urge for return to his sources coincided with his periods of thoughtfulness and mutation. He decided that for a few weeks he and Fernande would go to the village where ten years before he had spent with Pallarés some of the happiest and most fruitful moments of his life. On the way, they stopped in Barcelona, staying at a hotel, but lunching frequently at his family's; dinner and the evening were for friends.

El Guayaba had moved from Plaza de l'Oli to 17 Calle Riera de San Juan, to the studio that Pablo had once shared with Casagemas and then with Soto, but Els Quatre Gats was still in the same old place, though the habitués were new. Most of Picasso's old Bohemian friends were now married and settled. He and they discussed the past, Paris, and painting. What of the Cubism that papers talk so much but know so little about? Picasso's answers, as usual, were quips and evasions.

He was anxious to get to Horta. Pallarés' brother-in-law was mayor of the village, and was to find proper lodgings for Picasso, who meantime spent several fine evenings in Barcelona with his oldest chum, now in an apartment on Calle de Pelayo, with a studio above it. For all his ease with Pallarés, he never let himself go, as reluctant to confide as to take public stands. While awaiting the brother-in-law's reply he did a very Cézannian portrait of Manuel, in blue-gray, old rose, and mauve tones. He inscribed it and gave it to him; it is still in the latter's "Picasso corner" in his apartment on Via Layetana.

The first "Cubist" painting seen in Barcelona was this very un-Cubist portrait of Pallarés (the very one whom Don José had implored, as a classical painter, to show his son the error of his ways!). Yet, in its geometrical shaping as in its colored harmony, it seemed terribly revolutionary to the local artists, Pallarés included. When I asked him what he had thought of it at the time, he said:

"I was surprised, but not shocked because I knew Picasso could do anything. I thought he was trying everything out and would not continue in that vein."

But not a word was exchanged between Picasso and his father about painting, or between Pablo and his local friends, who knew his ability, admired his earlier work, and thought Cubism might be his way of having his fun at the expense of the Parisians. "At Horta, he never mentioned Cubism," said Pallarés. They probably went there at the beginning of July.

After a stay in two rooms lent by one Tobias Membrado, they moved into the only inn of the place, Hostal del Trompet, as soon as it had a vacancy. As usual, in his native land, Pablo was more relaxed than in Paris. He laughed at every little thing, chattered in Catalan with the peasants, asked about their work. Evenings were spent in a café where Fernande and he played endless games of dominoes with friends, while the owner, Joaquim Antonio Vives, played the guitar, the way Frédé did at the Lapin Agile.

When it was learned that Fernande and Pablo were not legally married, some of the village prudes raised a storm. One day, two of them stoned the windows of the inn, and a furious Picasso ran out waving a revolver. His weapon, however, impressed the villagers much less than the thousand-peseta notes he took out to settle any bill, however small. As soon as he used those all up, they headed back for Paris.

Gertrude Stein has told how "very much struck" she was, the first time she crossed the Pyrenees in 1910, "to see how naturally Cubism was made in Spain." This grew out of a comparison between the canvases Picasso had brought back from Horta, *Houses on the Hill, The Reservoir,* and *The Factory,* and the little Spanish villages, their cubic houses placed one atop another. Such landscapes, she said, were the birth of Cubism. But there was nothing to link the Horta paintings and those that followed them with *Les Demoiselles d'Avignon,* no logical continuity; that imposing work remained an isolated phenomenon in the Picasso oeuvre.

Miss Stein, for whom he had just painted a *Homage to Gertrude,* with nude women and angels sounding the trumpets of Fame as in busy Renaissance ceilings, saw Cubism everywhere, even

In the shops in Barcelona [where] instead of post cards they had square little frames and inside it was placed a cigar, a real one, a pipe, a bit of handkerchief etcetera, all absolutely the arrangement of many a cubist picture and helped out by cut paper representing other objects.

In the Horta landscapes, the fixed light of Catalonia models in space the architectonic layering that reveals the analytical process of Cubism, the bursting and crystallization of volumes by a system of articulated facets allowing one to see and study an object from all angles, in near monochrome. As in his figures, evidenced by the portrait of Fernande done at Horta (*Head,* now in the New York Museum of Modern Art), in the landscapes, too, Picasso was now concerned with the essential, primitive, raw form. The village roofs, factory chimney, the reservoir break down into parallelepipeds, pyramids, polyhedrons, and arcs of circles. Only the palm trees are imaginary; the mountain above the *Houses on the Hill* is actually a homage to Cézanne's Montagne Ste. Victoire.

To show that he was not, as some claimed, an enemy of reality, Pablo brought back from Horta photographs taken by Fernande, and displayed them at the Steins' Saturday soirées, where Gertrude told detractors, "if you had objected to these landscapes as being too realistic, there would be some point to your objection . . . [they] might be declared to be too photographic a copy of nature."

For several months, Braque had been seeing Picasso daily. They were both engaged in research, parallel yet different, for they did not have the same character or motivations. Against the Spaniard's anarchic outbursts, Braque tried to set up an order based on the sensitive values that Picasso, after having made use of them so long, was sacrificing to exclusively plastic needs. Braque's paintings at La Roche-Guyon and Carrières-St.-Denis, while Pablo was at Horta, were fat, fresh landscapes, with a flavorful earthy sensuality, as opposed to his friend's diagrammatic constructions as lush Normandy was to the rough, austere, thankless countryside, with its sharply delineated planes, in which Pablo had chosen to "verify" his work.

While Braque's work might have turned out differently had there been no Picasso, it remained purely his own. Pablo was tough on him, sometimes verbally cruel, and gossips were only too happy to spread his witticisms. Sonia Delaunay claimed "Picasso ran Braque down abominably," but the latter had great dignity, and never admitted this. "Picasso and I," he said, "from 1909 on, worked in perfect understanding. What people say does not matter."

Their rivalry was to be as valuable as their friendship, each getting from the other what he himself needed. Quoting Braque:

> Picasso and I said things to each other that no one will ever say again, that no one could say, no one could understand any more. . . . Until the war, we were very intimate, and if we drifted apart afterwards it was perhaps because we no longer needed one another. What critics have written is one thing; their business is writing, analyzing, defining. . . . Painters don't have to justify themselves in words.

One day Pablo decided Braque ought to be married, and he selected as bride the daughter of the owner of a Montmartre nightclub, Le Néant, who happened to be Max Jacob's cousin. Pablo and Max rented dress suits for Braque and themselves, and made a formal call on the club owner and his blushing daughter, immediately responsive to their fine manners. Unfortunately, the discussions ran on and on and after a sufficient number of drinks ended in a row when the matchmakers tried to take other customers' clothes from the checkroom and had to be bounced. No wedding, of course, but Pablo did not take no for an answer. He introduced his friend to a young girl named Marcelle Lapré, whose charms and merits he knew more directly. Her marriage to Braque proved to be an especially happy one.

Pablo also played some strange part in Derain's relations with Alice Princet. She was married to a minor clerk who as a joke was referred to as "the mathematician of Cubism," a favorite topic of banter for a brief time (and later treated seriously by some uninformed authors). Alice, after deceiving him with Derain, got divorced and married the painter. Picasso liked bringing about such unexpected couplings, creating delicate if not dangerous situations, mixing things up, as when he introduced Apollinaire and Marie Laurencin.

He was more and more Gertrude Stein's great man, and she brimmed with praise of him; Leo, with brother Michael and sister-in-law Sarah, concentrated now on Matisse. He had left his discovery completely to his bothersome (and estranged) sister, rather than dispute her claim to have recognized his genius first. This did not make Matisse and Pablo any friendlier.

Gertrude Stein and her friend Alice B. Toklas, as small, thin, and delicate as Gertrude was imposing, round, and large, were a strange couple whom Pablo often disparaged. Fernande and he dined almost every Saturday at Rue de Fleurus in the picture-filled apartment where friends gathered around 10:00 P.M. Gertrude sat at the head of the table under her 1906 portrait, which she grew more and more to look like, but this friendship was never to keep Pablo from criticizing her, attacking her for not knowing a thing about art, among other compliments. She reacted with great dignity, the more laudable since she had in fact been the one to save him from his early poverty.

In September 1909 he left the Bateau-Lavoir after five years, and moved to a building at 11 Boulevard de Clichy, right near Place Pigalle, that belonged to Théophile Delcassé, the sometime Minister of Foreign Affairs who had engineered the Entente Cordiale: this was progress up the social ladder.

Fernande now had a respectable apartment and he a large studio with high bay windows looking out on the boulevard. She bought furniture, and had a maid who could cook Picasso's favorite dishes, but the new existence seemed foreboding to her, even though their way of life had hardly changed, except for the more luxurious surroundings. Pablo was delighted; this material "success" meant taking root in "society," which flattered his pride. He had "arrived": Fernande's "at home" was on Sunday afternoons, and her maid wore a white apron. Some of his friends thought this meant the end of creativity and adventurousness for him: they were wrong. The next five years were to be among the most important in the history of modern painting, with Picasso at the heart of it.

A young financier, André Level, one of the first to collect African art back in 1904, got the idea of bringing together a few wealthy friends in a joint collection, to be known as La Peau de l'Ours (literally, The Bear Skin).* For a period of ten years, they would jointly invest in works by young painters, to be

* From the French proverb, "One must never sell the skin of the bear before it is brought down," the equivalent of our "Never count your chickens before they are hatched." (TR. NOTE)

sold at auction at the end of that time. Each man put in 250 francs (or about fifty dollars) per year as his share, purchases being made on the recommendation of Level, as approved by a small committee; the ownership of individual paint-ings was determined by drawing lots. At the suggestion of one member, Robert Ellissen, the artists were given a percentage of eventual profits; the arrangement lasted until after the start of World War I. This group bought several Picassos, as well as works by Matisse, Derain, Othon Friesz, Van Gogh, Marie Laurencin, Manguin, Marquet, Bonnard, Jean Puy, Sérusier, Utrillo, Vlaminck, plus some others that did not prove so profitable.

By now, apart from Wilhelm Uhde, the Steins, Shchukine, and Olivier Sainsère, there were other Picasso collectors: Kahnweiler's Swiss friend Hermann Rupf (who probably was the first to make a purchase in the Rue Vignon gallery), a northern industrialist named Roger Dutilleul, and Shchukine's Russian asso-ciate, Ivan Morosov. There were few avant-garde galleries at the time (there are even fewer today), and they did not advertise or hold fancy openings; word of mouth was their sole source of support. Picasso understood the uselessness of mass appeal, since all it brought was sarcasm or attack, and, like Kahnweiler himself, he "did nothing" to help matters along, knowing that his work would catch on only if one collector whetted the enthusiasm of another.

Apollinaire, who had already written on art in various newspapers and maga-zines, in 1910 joined the staff of *L'Intransigeant,* the mass-circulation evening paper, on which for four years he reviewed art shows and Salons, as successor to André Salmon, courageously presenting and defending his Cubist friends. Salmon was now doing the same at *Paris-Journal,* under the pen name of "La Palette," and in 1912 he was to join the weekly *Gil Blas,* where he tried to undo the malign influence of Louis Vauxcelles. At the height of the Cubist struggle, then, three leading Parisian publications were printing Apollinaire and Salmon, the most ardent champions of a movement that "respectable" people considered an outrageous piece of fakery, that was officially called to account in speeches in the Chamber of Deputies and the City Council.

As it turned out, the provinces were more "advanced" than Paris in this case; the Lyons magazine *L'Art Libre* (Free Art), in November 1910, published one of the first analyses of Cubism, by Roger Allard—although never calling it by name. And in 1912 Olivier Hourcade founded the *Revue de France et des Pays français* (Magazine of France and French[-Speaking] Countries) in Bordeaux; it also vigorously defended contemporary art.

Picasso remained indifferent to the antagonisms, the stands taken, and the discussions and polemics surrounding them. His slogan remained the one he had swiped from the *bateaux-mouches* that plied up and down the Seine: "Talking to the pilot is forbidden." This was truer than ever, with him.

VI

"LOOK AT ME
CHANGING . . ."
(1909–1912)

L
es Demoiselles d'Avignon, ROLLED UP IN THE BOULEVARD DE CLICHY
studio, remained unseen for over fifteen years. Rarely was there a revolution of which so few were concerned with the pretext. The pretext,
though not the cause—for that 1907 work had little to do with Cubism
in its motivations or development. Cubism's influence on contemporary painting
owed nothing to the tour de force that picture was: however important historically,
the isolated work had only limited relevance at the time. Braque alone may be
said to have been shaken by its pictorial impact, and changed as a result.

Picasso and he went on developing what, because labels come so easily, is
called Cubism; they eschewed the word, and even more its content and overtones.
They were of course aware of setting out on a new path, but did not know where
it would lead; the geometric discipline of their canvases corresponded to no system, but rather to research on form, volume, and space, for the time being based
on a Cézannian gospel. This was not anarchy, or deliberate differentness, but on
the contrary an attempt to find a new and autonomous poetics of creation without
breaking away from reality.

As André Breton was to express it later,

> There will be passionate investigation into what may have animated Picasso toward
> the end of 1909. Where was he? How was he living? Yet, can the silly word Cubism
> disguise the prodigious sense of the discovery that, to me, came between the *Factory*
> *at Horta de Ebro* and the portrait of Mr. Kahnweiler?

Cubism did not grow out of scientifically presented speculations, nor was there
a single Cubism. At the beginning, as Picasso told Penrose, it was all experiment,
like squaring the circle; the pictures themselves less important than what the
painters discovered through them.

The summer before there had been violent uprisings in Barcelona, followed
by savage repression. The riots having had no leader, Francisco Ferrer, an anar-

chist theoretician, had been made the scapegoat, condemned, and executed. There were demonstrations throughout the world against this miscarriage of justice, and in Paris there was even one casualty. Pablo and other Spaniards were afraid of being deported; if he avoided public demonstrations despite his sympathies, it was for that reason, and because he was worried that, if returned to Spain under such circumstances, he would have to do his military service.

After *Woman Seated,* one of the first paintings done in his new studio, he did some portraits, of Vollard, Uhde, Braque, and Kahnweiler. Space was now decomposed into superimposed geometrical planes, the figure, environment, and background all merging into one another. In monochromatic harmony. And amazing likeness. Vollard claimed that a child of three, seeing his portrait, had said, "That's Vollard!" And Penrose relates that, seeing Wilhelm Uhde by accident for the first time in his life twenty-five years later, he recognized him immediately.

These portraits, especially the Kahnweiler, required innumerable sittings, even though that of the dealer was the least a "likeness," that is, the one in which Picasso least sought to capture the actual expression. Occasional reminders of the model jump out of the chaotic yet orderly scaffolding, the thousand pieces of broken mirror.

"There is no such thing as abstract art," he told Zervos in 1935, and

> "You must always start from something. After that, any trace of reality can be eliminated; no danger to it, for the idea of the thing has left an indelible imprint. It is what provoked the artist, stimulated his thinking, got his emotions going. Ideas and emotions then remain permanently imprisoned in the work; do what they may, they cannot get out of it; they are an integral part of it, even when their presence is no longer discernible."

Picasso delighted in the idea of "settling in" at Boulevard de Clichy, a new experience for him. To the north he could look out on the Sacré-Coeur, which he painted in the cubic Horta manner, to the south Avenue Frochot with private houses and studios, one of which Lautrec once had. He bought all kinds of disparate furniture secondhand, mainly heavy cumbersome things, often truly ugly, contrasting with a charming Italian marquetry cabinet given to him by Don José. He especially liked what Fernande referred to as "Louis XIV style," as it represented respectability and comfort to him, through its noble rhythms and majestic massiveness.

Fernande never entered the studio without his permission; a late riser, Pablo would lock himself in there shortly after noon and not emerge till nightfall, amid the Bateau-Lavoir mess quickly reconstituted, subject to no straightening out. The maid was not allowed in. There were African sculptures on the wall, Pablo buying more and more of them, not by way of making a collection, but because he was taken with their expressive simplicity.

Beside the African pieces hung every which way, there was a charming Corot portrait that he had picked up at the flea market, and of course many works by such friends as Douanier Rousseau, Matisse, Vlaminck, Derain, Braque, and

Portrait of Wilhelm Uhde Paris, spring 1910 (Collection of Sir Roland Penrose)

(GIRAUDON)

others. These gifts, or exchanges, were to make him one of the biggest of collectors of contemporary art—though also one of the most secretive. In her *Picasso and His Friends,* Fernande wrote:

> He loved old pieces of tapestry: verdure, Aubusson or Beauvais, which were often in such bad condition that it was impossible to make out their subject. He collected musical instrument cases and old, chipped gilt frames. Pale prints, with frames made of straw, hung on the dining-room wall. They would not have been out of place in the concierge's office, and that was part of their charm for him. . . .
>
> He prided himself on seeing charm in things which would have seemed ridiculous to most people.

Picasso always remained unconcerned with interior decoration, harmonizing of objects and pictures, or color schemes. Unlike most of his friends who, once "established," wanted a life of luxurious ostentation, he never set up such a "home," and his successive women learned to respect his disregard for taste and comfort, as well as his positive allergy to anything durable, organized, or planned. These were the same characteristics as were found in his constantly changing, evolving work.

Sometimes, of an afternoon, he would go to the Louvre. Alone. To look at the rather skimpy Spanish paintings, some primitives, and, among moderns, Ingres. Evenings, he went out much less, but he still attended Gertrude's Saturday nights, at which he was a generally frowning and uncommunicative star attraction. If the conversation turned to someone else, especially Matisse, he fumed. Any little thing could irritate him, most particularly questions about his painting, which he considered pointless or out of place.

Once, when he found that two of his works belonging to Gertrude Stein had been varnished without his consent, he had a violent fit of anger, and it was all they could do to keep him from carrying them off. She soothed him by saying it had just been an experiment that would not be repeated, and the varnish would soon disappear of itself.

Ever since adolescence, he had been a demon for work, and now he went at it with gusto. Whatever was not his painting left him rather indifferent, and if it interfered made him hostile. However, he allowed exceptions for some social gatherings, because of the useful contacts they might provide. There were also many pretty women at such parties, who, by way of confirming his acceptance in "society," created stormy scenes in his various legal or extralegal households, right up to the peaceful twilight marriage.

Picasso's dog, Frika, and his three Siamese cats, moving with him from the Bateau-Lavoir, were the only creatures allowed in the studio, along with Monina, a newly acquired she-monkey. As 1910 progressed, there appeared, starting with the portraits done that winter, a kind of internal explosion of the picture, as if, once completed, a violent punch had destroyed the positioning of the masses without disrupting the overall organic unity. That is why the works of this period have often been compared to cracked mirrors. Each facet represents the most meaningful aspect of its particular mass, the painter thus urging the viewer to adopt as his own his creative visual mechanism. Whence, the "analytical Cubism" of both Picasso and Braque.

Where previously Picasso had been reconstituting forms on a geometrical basis, the cubes were now giving way to all kinds of different shapes, overlapping, juxtaposing, or fitting into one another. They filled the whole picture, not leaving a single blank spot; they were the framework of reality, or else the ledger of its various angles, as if the painter were circling around it, arresting its simultaneous fixed aspects. In Cézanne's words, grasping not the appearance but the inside of things. For so perilous an enterprise, one had to sacrifice the entire illusionist apparatus of painting, that is, everything the public was used to, everything it judged a picture by: perspective, lighting, shading, values, to say nothing of the subject, which remained the stumbling block of taste.

In view of that, the public's panic, anger, and sarcasm against Cubist paintings are understandable. How could such works not be taken for madness or hoaxes?

In the name of the Surrealists, Breton was to write about Picasso in 1928:

> By what miracle did this man . . . happen to have what it took to give shape to what up to then had remained in the domain of wildest fantasy? What revolution had to take place in him for him to hang on to it? . . . So great an awareness of the betrayal of tangible things is needed for one to dare an open break with them, especially in the easy approach their customary aspect offers us, that one cannot fail to recognize Picasso's immense responsibility. Had the will of this man faltered even once, our present endeavors would at least have been postponed, if not lost.

In 1910, Fernand Léger met Braque and Picasso at Kahnweiler's gallery. He had already exhibited at the Salons d'Automne of 1908 and 1909, and was working on a very large painting, *Nudes in the Forest,* which was to be one of the revelations of the 1911 Salon des Indépendants. He was in touch with a group of young avant-gardists, Brancusi, Marcel Duchamp, Metzinger, La Fresnaye, Gleizes, Le Fauconnier, who in their various ways were to subscribe to a sort of tangible Cubism closer to Cézanne's heritage than to Picasso's and Braque's researches. All of them exhibited in the two antiacademic Salons, the Autumn and the Independents', along with Picabia, Kupka, Delaunay, Herbin, and the sculptors Duchamp-Villon and Archipenko, while the champions of what was called "orthodox Cubism," Braque and Picasso, showed their works only at Kahnweiler's.

"We held no more one-man shows after the Braque in 1908," Kahnweiler told me. "I just hung the paintings. The painters worked quietly, and I advanced them money to live on. They brought the works in, collected what was owed them, we hung the pictures, and those who wanted to came to see them. Not too many, but we knew we could depend on them. Artists came, too, and people who didn't like this sort of thing but wanted to keep informed, to know about this Cubism the papers were making fun of.

"Try to picture the period, entirely different from today. There were very few galleries, infrequent exhibits, no advertising. The Salons were all the general public saw."

"Was it not an unusual gesture of contempt for critics and public for Braque and Picasso not to enter them?"

"Yes, but mainly it was contempt for the sarcasms and insults. You can't imagine how Cubism was hated in some circles. And even worse, there were people who went to the Indépendants or the Salon d'Automne just to laugh. Or to start trouble . . ."

Since Braque and Picasso did not join these public exhibits, Cubism was represented there by people like Gleizes, Metzinger, or Delaunay, with their paintings based on geometrical stylization. The first large showing of "Cubism" at the Indépendants of 1911 was only to compound confusion through the arrival of new recruits. When Kahnweiler today says that "it happened all by itself," and that Picasso's success was due exclusively to his genius "for joy and enthusiasm," this is not really the whole story. He does not mention that, sale of paintings aside, his painters, Picasso most of all, owed everything to him. Mistrustful at first, Pablo became quickly and totally sure of his young and ingenious dealer, an unusually faithful friend, a daring art lover, and a wily businessman. He once said to someone, "What would have become of us if Kahnweiler had not had good business sense?" And that was true.

In the summer of 1910, Braque went to L'Estaque again, this time for figure work and still lifes rather than landscapes. Picasso returned to Spain. Ramón Pichot had told him of a little port on the Costa Brava, Cadaqués, and how his sister could get her friends down there without paying any fare. A singer in Parisian cabarets, she had group tickets for her supposed "troupe" to travel to Barcelona as a road show. And that was how Pablo and Fernande got from Paris to Figueras, the border station where the train line ended at the time. They took a hotel room, while awaiting Alice and André Derain, who were to spend the vacation with them. They arrived shortly thereafter, and all four went to Barcelona, to see Pablo's family and old friends before going on to Cadaqués.

Pablo and Fernande took a little house on the quay not far from the Pichots' (perhaps with the Derains, since there was no hotel in town). While Picasso worked on the etchings he had promised Max Jacob to illustrate his *Saint Matorel,* that Kahnweiler was to publish in the fall, Derain painted local landscapes, with a kind of volumetric structuring that was new in his work. Despite all their differences, Pablo and Derain got along well; Pablo never having based his friendships on aesthetic affinities, they more often discussed the fine food and drink in the fishermen's inns than artistic matters. And their ladies got along together, too.

Taking time out from his analytical constructions, Pablo did a few landscape sketches with fishing boats; also some drawings of musical instruments—especially the guitar—and fruit, glasses, and bottles in Pichot's studio. Some of these drawings show the transpositions, from object to female body, to be found in the paintings of the following autumn; they evidence a kind of geometrical abstraction, appreciable in one of the etchings for Max's book, known as *Mademoiselle Léonie on a Chaise Longue.*

Max asked Kahnweiler to show him the etchings when they arrived, not, he said, because he was interested in art, but because he wanted "to know what Homunculus inspired in Faust. Homunculus is Matorel." Faust, then, of course was Picasso.

He was doing nudes and several versions of the *Port of Cadaqués* in a familiar monochrome construction whose angular planes juxtaposed or fitted together caught the rhythms of keels, spars, and sails.

In the same year of 1910, a young Russian, Wassili Kandinsky, in Munich to study painting, having gone successively through Impressionism, Fauvism, and Expressionism, did a highly dynamic composition of shapes and colors, to be known as *First Abstract Watercolor*. The Dutch Piet Mondrian and Russian Marc Chagall arrived in Paris. Paul Klee, deep in trying to figure out how to find an Impressionist translation of nature, had his first show in Bern. Matisse, having finished Shchukine's commissioned *Dance,* was at work on the *Music* counterpart.

The Guitar Player confirmed Picasso's move toward hermeticism. The brownish, reddish composition, built with diagrammatic sparseness, allowed only the slightest relation to reality: the size of a man, the bare suggestion of a guitar, both impossible to recognize if not for the title.

Looking back on this work five years later, Kahnweiler would write:

> The following fall he returned to Paris dissatisfied, with unfinished canvases despite his long weeks of hard work. But the great step had been taken. Picasso had freed himself from the closed form, a new tool had been forged to serve new ends.

A willing if confused spokesman, Apollinaire took the occasion of the Salon d'Automne (in which Pablo, of course, did not participate) to decree the absolute mastery of the painter of the *Demoiselles* and say where the truth lay. But not in the mass-circulation *L'Intransigeant,* for which he reviewed exhibits; he defended his friend in the very limited-circulation magazine *Poésie.* He called the "strange exhibition of Cubism" at the Salon d'Automne a pale imitation of the really important works of a "great artist . . . Pablo Picasso. The Salon d'Automne Cubism is but a jackdaw in peacock's feathers." This was the first time he used the term "Cubism." Apollinaire was aiming mainly at Gleizes and Metzinger. He had not mentioned the former in his review for *L'Intransigeant,* but severely slated the latter, "who has undertaken to try out every process of contemporary painting."

A new collector took up Picasso in 1910, Dr. Vincenc Kramář, an Austrian physician who until 1913 lived in Paris and was a friend of Kahnweiler, Vollard, Braque, Léger, and others. Instrumental in bringing French painting to Prague, he long cherished an old dried-out apple that Picasso had once used for a still life.

Kramář bought from Vollard Pablo's *Self-Portrait* of 1907, and from Sagot a small 1905 piece showing a girl's head. He was to acquire the 1909 gouache *Harlequin* at an auction, but most of his collection came from Kahnweiler's; one of Europe's biggest for Cubism, it is now in the National Gallery at Prague and covers mainly the period 1906–1914. In 1921, Kramář published one of the first studies of Cubism in the capital of Czechoslovakia, recently independent.

"Guitar Player" (Musée national d'Art moderne—Paris)

(GIRAUDON)

Cubism was now growing more and more Jansenist. Picasso and Braque were like two ivory-tower scientists in their respective laboratories, doing experiments that they alone understood and whispering their results to each other. Their paintings of the winter of 1910–1911 were more and more incomprehensible, seeming like the uncompromising and decisive expression of a new pictorial religion, as austere as it was enigmatic, intended only for a chosen few. Which was not what they wanted. They were leery of being dubbed "intellectual" artists and losing any public at all. Kahnweiler was afraid collectors might drop them. Yet Braque and Picasso were sure that, for the development of their medium, they had to do these severe colorless constructions, making a concession to reality only in their titles. The juxtaposition of volumes, linked by verticals inserted into space, was devoid of any sensorial attraction. It was not the object or the figure that Picasso addressed himself to, but their decomposition and recomposition in terms of relationships of rhythms and volumes expressing a reality deeper than that apparent to the eye. This flopping of planes so they could work against each other, as the Impressionists similarly had done with colors, was one of the most frequent experiments for achieving the expression they sought.

Maurice Raynal told of attending a session at Picasso's, where he demonstrated the method to several "disciples." On a painted figure "the nose thus grew out of a series of planes in no way imitative," while the artist asserted, as he had once before, "But that's what a nose is like."

Aviation fascinated both Braque and Picasso, and they tried their hands at building aeroplanes, applying to their Cubist work the things they were learning about aerodynamics. For a while, they assiduously attended the pioneer flying meets at Issy-les-Moulineaux. Because of his physique, the fledgling aviators nicknamed Braque Wilbur Wright, and Pablo often later so referred to him.

Max Jacob had become a Catholic convert. *Saint Matorel,* published in February 1911 with the Picasso etchings, was the first of four volumes devoted to his revelation. When Derain was first approached to illustrate it, he had turned Kahnweiler down, because he doubted the sincerity of Max's conversion. Pablo agreed to do them, but Max wondered what they would turn out to be, and was taken aback by the hermetic constructions that eventuated. *Mademoiselle Léonie* left him literally speechless. But not witless. And he inscribed a copy,

> To Picasso
> for what I know he knows
> for what he knows I know.

They were no longer so close as they had been in their poverty-stricken beginnings. Pablo did not like having Max constantly about to remind him of the short rations of those days, which the poet liked to blow out of proportion. He was irritated beyond words by the poet's irresponsible gossiping, his homosexual exhibitionism, his fantasying, his conversion and apparitions, much as he appreciated his talent.

In one photograph of this period Picasso is posing in Braque's military reservist's uniform: he is heavier but just as tense as back at the Bateau-Lavoir, his eye now alive with authority rather than worry. In another he is lying on a couch in his studio with one of his Siamese cats. Gone were the old lean days.

But Picasso never let up on those who, in Braque's term, went about "Cubifying." He attacked these imitators once again when the Salon des Indépendants opened on April 21, 1911, on the Quai d'Orsay near Place de l'Alma.

The "Cubist Room" had three Parisian landscapes, including a superb *Eiffel Tower* by Robert Delaunay; Le Fauconnier's *Abundance* and four other works; *Landscape, Woman's Head, Still Life,* and a *Nude* by Metzinger; landscapes and powerful figures by Gleizes, including the *Woman with Phlox;* and Léger's *Nudes in the Forest,* which caused so much comment. In nearby rooms were such Cubists, or would-be ones, as Marcel Duchamp, Archipenko, Marie Laurencin, André Lhote, Picabia, La Fresnaye, and Alfred Reth.

There was in Room 41 a retrospective for Douanier Rousseau, dead only a few months, of whom, one enlightened aristarch averred, "soon no more will be heard." But of course Picasso and Braque were not there. In place of the originators, there were followers, "Cubistors," among whom Metzinger seemed the standard-bearer of what was only a caricature of Cubism.

Apollinaire, disoriented by the absence of Picasso and the variety of things shown, seemed at a loss, and compounded confusion in his review, saying:

> Metzinger is the only true follower of Cubism here, and the attractiveness of his work shows us that this discipline is not incompatible with reality. . . . Later on will be seen what influence the works of a Picasso had on the development of so new an art!

On April 20 André Salmon had written in *Paris-Journal:*

> Let us just remind these "innovating" young masters that Cubism was invented five years ago by a Spanish painter after long aesthetic digressions, along with philosophers, poets, and mathematicians. It seemed at first inoffensive mental juggling. But Picasso laid the first stone, the first cube of the temple, which was not the most laudable thing he has done. . . .

A few months later, he elaborated:

> While it is true that Cubism was born of Picasso's speculations, he himself was never a Cubist. The first evidences of Cubism, still very hesitant . . . came from Georges Braque. . . . Much more intellectual, Jean Metzinger brought together the diffuse elements of Cubism, outlined a discipline, or at least a theory; so that while Cubism really does come from Picasso, Metzinger is justified in calling himself its leader.

Which, of course, pleased no one, and solved nothing.

While the exegetists were splitting hairs, Picasso had a one-man show in May at Alfred Stieglitz' Photo Secession Gallery in New York, his first in the United States, introduced by the writer-painter Marius de Zayas. This introduction was printed in issue No. 35–36 of *Camera Work* three months later, and de Zayas did a longer piece in Spanish on Picasso, published in *America* for May 1911, illustrated with reproductions of Cubist paintings and a portrait of Pablo by the author. This was Picasso's second foreign show, after the one in Munich at the Thannhauser Gallery in 1909.

In November 1910, Roger Fry organized a "Manet and the Post-Impressionists" show at the Grafton Gallery in London, in which Picasso's work appeared alongside paintings of Cézanne, Derain, Matisse, Rouault, Vlaminck, Friesz, and others, only to have an outraged press wonder how such horrors had ever gotten across the Channel. Yet Pablo found a defender in England, the young poet John Middleton Murry, later to marry Katherine Mansfield. He wrote two laudatory articles about him, in his own magazine, *Rhythm,* in August 1911, and in November and December in *The New Age.* He saw Picasso as greater than the great, because he was trying to do something more. The Picasso drawing he used in *Rhythm* was the first printed in Great Britain.

For the summer of 1911, Pablo, Fernande, and the Braques spent several weeks of vacation in what was then the tiny village of Bas-Vallespir, outside Céret, in the French Pyrenees. Manolo and his colorful wife, Totote, were also there, as well as Frank Burty Haviland, a French industrialist of American descent, who had an imposing collection of Negro art.

Everything in this Catalan village reminded Manolo and Pablo of their native Spain, which the sculptor had fled to avoid military service, thus being technically a deserter. The Delcros house, in which Picasso stayed, was large and surrounded by broad grounds; Pablo had several big rooms in it, so he could work at ease, with the sole company of his monkey (he came down in July, Fernande joining him only the next month).

They loved the place, although the locals were not too happy to be invaded by these strange characters and their questionable women. They were even rumored to be German spies!

From Collioure, they heard a funny (if perhaps apocryphal) story from Apollinaire: Matisse, looking out his window, had seen on a wall across the way the inscription KUB. He thought it was a prank pulled by his Cubist enemies—until he found out it was the advertisement for a bouillon cube of that name.

What Picasso painted at Céret, while still "hermetic Cubism," seemed to indicate a lessening of the abstract tendencies. In *Man with the Pipe,* the smoker's head and his pipe are clearly recognizable at the top of a cascade of intermingled geometrical forms, while some printed letters just begin to make an appearance. For the first time, he used an oval canvas, an unusual shape revived the year before by Braque, that he was to use several times again.

Yet, while he had become less hermetic, we can hardly fault the collector who bought *The Accordionist* and, seeing the place-name "Céret" on the back of the canvas, took it to be a landscape!

Picasso was headed for serious troubles in Paris, having to do with those two Iberian heads he had bought from Géry-Piéret a few years before. This man, after dropping out of sight, had returned to France in 1911 and, knowing Apollinaire from their newspapering days, stayed with him and left another head at his place.

On August 21, the *Mona Lisa* disappeared from the Louvre. Sensational news!

On August 28, Géry-Piéret came to *Paris-Journal,* where Salmon worked, with the head hidden at Apollinaire's, asking for cash for it: the paper immediately headlined a story on how easy it was to rob the Louvre. After displaying the Iberian head for a few hours in its show window, it returned it to the Louvre.

Apollinaire, now apparently in the position of an unwitting fence, worried about the two heads belonging to Picasso, who was at Céret at the time. He went to ask Kahnweiler to warn him, but Pablo, having had wind of the affair through *Paris-Journal,* rushed back by train. Guillaume met him at the station and they went straight to his studio. They decided to get rid of the incriminating evidence by dropping the heads in the Seine, but then decided they might be seen, so they thought it would be better to take them to *Paris-Journal* and let the newspaper discreetly return them to the museum as it had done with the other.

Unfortunately, someone talked. And Géry-Piéret, now working in Belgium under the name of Baron Ignace d'Ormessan, wrote to the Louvre to confess the theft of the *Mona Lisa,* which he had had nothing to do with! On the morning of September 7, the police came to Apollinaire's on Rue Gros, searched the place, and arrested him: he was accused not only of complicity in stealing the Iberian heads, but of heading a gang of robbers specializing in art thefts. From that, it was easy to jump to the conclusion that he had also stolen the *Mona Lisa.* Two days later, Picasso in turn was awakened at break of day with a summons to appear before an investigating magistrate.

Was he telling the truth when he said he did not know where the heads he bought from Géry-Piéret had come from? In view of their quality and rarity, we may doubt it. The more so since he was very familiar with the pieces at the Louvre. If Apollinaire appears amazingly to have been taken in, Picasso must have known the seller was a thief and the Louvre his field of operation. He had once heard him say to Marie Laurencin, "I'm on my way to the Louvre. Anything I can get you?"

The meeting between Apollinaire and Pablo before the authorities was a disaster; both got confused and contradicted themselves and each other—for, both being foreigners, their main object was to avoid being deported. The tearful poet and panicky painter made the magistrate understand they had been victimized. Apollinaire was given a final interrogation, with his two lawyers present, and released on September 12; Pablo was never indicted, though told not to leave the jurisdiction. The charges against Apollinaire were dismissed in January 1912.

This made a deep impression on Picasso. Fernande said that for months he would not take the bus that passed the Palais de Justice, and he jumped at the slightest early-morning noise, as if the cops were coming for him again. Apollinaire's friends had filed a petition urging the poet's release, and Pablo wondered whether his would do as much if he had actually been under arrest. His health was impaired, and many of his friends were calling him a coward for having tried to shift the blame to Guillaume. It took months for him to get back to normal.

There was a flowering of Cubism in the Salon d'Automne that opened on October 1, and it met with hostile criticism. Gabriel Mourey wrote in *Excelsior:*

Allow me to say I do not see any future for Cubism. Neither the Cubism of its inventor, M. Picasso, nor that of Messrs. Metzinger, Gleizes, Le Fauconnier, etc., his imitators. Cubism, integral or not, has already had its say; this is the swan song of pretentious impotence and self-satisfied ignorance.

But it found defenders in Apollinaire, Salmon, Roger Allard, Maurice Raynal, and others such as André Warnod, Olivier Hourcade, Jules Granié, the judge who had finally cleared the two friends, Gustave Kahn, and others.

"Cubists Dominate the Paris Salon d'Automne" was the headline in the (London) *Times* for October 8, which ran a photograph of Picasso and a geometric drawing titled *Meditation*. Similar views were expressed by *The Outlook* (London), Amsterdam's *De Amsterdammer,* which printed three Picassos, one of which was actually a Braque, New York's *Literary Digest,* running two Picassos but attributing one to Herbin, and John Middleton Murry in *The New Age*. G. K. Chesterton commented in *The Daily News* (London), and the Madrid *Heraldo* ran a glorifying essay by Ramiro de Maetzu, "La Idea Platon-Picasso." And for all the death knell that traditional critics were sounding, Cubism was also being enthusiastically hailed in Milan, St. Petersburg, Prague, and elsewhere.

La Voce of Florence published two articles by Ardengo Soffici, an Italian writer-painter who was often in Paris. A friend of Picasso, Max Jacob, and Apollinaire, he was to form a link between the Cubists, who had greatly influenced him, and the Italian Futurists.

The latter had contributed something new, and the Cubists, who were not crazy about them, were somewhat upset by the affirmation of the plastic value of motion they espoused. "A profile is never motionless before our eyes," their 1910 Technical Manifesto had stated, "but it constantly appears and disappears. On account of the persistence of vision, moving objects constantly multiply themselves; their form changes like rapid vibrations, in their mad career. . . ."

Kahnweiler says that in 1910 Picasso had been thinking of "sculptures that would have moved mechanically, and paintings that would have 'gone off' like targets at a carnival, on the release of a trigger." Not unrelated to later Calder mobiles. But he never followed through, and perhaps never really intended to. Pablo's concern with the varied aspects of a figure was purely pictorial; he believed a picture could be dynamic without actually "moving," through mere decomposition of motion.

Just what Marcel Duchamp was to prove with the epochal *Nude Descending a Staircase.*

Relations between Picasso and the Futurists never got very close. On September 1, 1911, Boccioni, writing to Apollinaire, asked him somewhat tongue-in-cheek to remember him to "M. Picasso, in a most special way, for I have the most charming memory of this great artist! He is truly a delightful person and an admirable painter whose work interests me in a truly strange way!"

In that fall of 1911, Picasso had his second show at the Thannhauser Gallery in Munich.

The "old gang" was no longer held together at the Lapin Agile, and when they met it was largely at L'Ermitage, a café of shady reputation. "Young men like characters from a [Francis] Carco novel [about pimping] waited there for their women," Fernande wrote in her book, "who for their part would occasionally allow themselves to be seduced by an artist. This earned them some pretty brutal reprimands from their men."

They mainly came in there after attending the Médrano Circus: Picasso and Fernande, Derain, Braque, Kahnweiler, Max Jacob, Salmon, Apollinaire and Marie Laurencin, the Futurists Severini and Boccioni, Metzinger, the poet Jean Pellerin, Juan Gris, the Russian painter Serge Férat with his amazing sister (or so-called sister) known as Baroness d'Oettingen, Mario Meunier, the tragedian Roger Karl, the poet Édouard Gazanion, and Harry Baur, of whom Salmon said no one knew his real name. Pablo had painted a portrait of his wife, Gaby, in 1904, and in his strange Franco-Spanish jargon referred to him as *el Cabot* (or: "el Ham").

Wives, mistresses, models, and pickups tagged along, creating all kinds of emotional and similar complications. One week Apollinaire and the Baroness d'Oettingen stayed together in a hotel on Boulevard Berthier; Fernande made attempts to forget Pablo's difficult character in the arms of Mario Meunier and Roger Karl (in what exact order is now forgotten); Gazanion's wife consoled herself with Pellerin; and later there was to be the Picasso-Marcoussis dispute.

One time, Pablo even gained brief local celebrity such as his pictures were not achieving by knocking out one of the pimps who had tried to push him around. But the movement toward Montparnasse was already under way: Juan Gris was living in the Bateau-Lavoir, and Braque on Rue Caulaincourt, but Pablo's digs on Boulevard de Clichy were no longer considered "really Montmartre." And a number of their contemporaries had had, at least temporarily, to abandon fine art for something more lucrative. One of these was a young Polish painter named Louis Markus (or Markous), who supported himself by doing cartoons. Apollinaire had renamed him Marcoussis, to make things easier, since there was a town by that name just outside Paris.

For three years, he had been living with a frail young woman, of delicate beauty, Éva Gouel, or Marcelle Humbert, as she was called. Pablo was struck by her beauty and, since she was the very opposite of Fernande and therefore not disliked by her, the two couples took to going out together, to Médrano, and to the Steins'. Gertrude, an expert in such matters, found Éva "a little French Evelyn Thaw, small and perfect"; Pablo concurred.

"I kiss you and love you as ever," Pablo had written Fernande the previous August 8, when arranging for her to join him at Céret, but since the move to Boulevard de Clichy things had not been so harmonious. Pablo, still bothered by that statue business, wanted a change, so as to forget himself; it was a dull winter, and he worked less enthusiastically than usual. Fernande went out without him frequently, and he made no effort to stop her, even when she was seen at L'Ermitage with every Tom, Dick, and Harry. And one day, probably in the early spring of 1912, quite simply, she just moved out and Éva moved in.

Marcoussis, the jilted one, was not terribly upset. His family had been urging him to marry Éva, but he wanted to quit cartooning and go back to serious

Éva Gouel, known as Marcelle Humbert, 1912

painting; married responsibility was the last thing he needed. Éva, preferring security, did not encourage his artistic aspirations, so her leaving was the answer.

"His sense of humour triumphed over his sorrows," wrote Fernande, summing up the incident a couple of decades later, "when he exploited them in a drawing for *La Vie Parisienne;* and I can still see that picture of a happy gambolling Markous watching as Picasso drags himself away in heavy chains."

"Fernande left yesterday with a Futurist painter. What will I do about the dog?" Picasso wrote to Braque. If Severini can be believed, she went off with one Ubaldo Oppi, but she was soon to regret it. Despite her boredom, and Picasso's sullenness and jealousy, he was still to her the fascinating young Bohemian of the Bateau-Lavoir, with his piercing eyes and broken Franish. He was also the man who lorded it over all youthful painting through his authority, the inventor of Cubism, almost always absent but ever present, for he held a place not even his worst enemies would try to deny him.

Pablo's switch to Éva caused no commotion; only his closest friends were even aware of it. One day Gertrude Stein and Alice B. Toklas dropped in on him unannounced at the studio he had rented on a lower floor of the Bateau-Lavoir; he was not in, and Gertrude left her visiting card. Not hearing from him, they came back a few days later and found him working on a picture that bore the legend "Ma Jolie" (My Pretty One), with Gertrude's card reproduced down in the corner. When they left, Gertrude said to Alice, "Fernande is certainly not ma jolie, I wonder who it is."

Except for visiting his family while he was at Cadaqués or Céret, Picasso had not returned to Barcelona since 1909, and no one there had seen his work since the Sala Parés show in 1901. But a painter and former habitué of Els Quatre Gats, Josep Dalmau, now an antique dealer, art dealer, and picture restorer, was interested in the new painting. He had made several buying trips to Paris, and in his shop in Calle Portaferrissa he displayed several pre-Cubist Picassos he had gotten at Pablo's Montmartre studio. The interest in them made him decide to hold a Picasso show, for which he acquired several of the Blue and Rose period works. Hanging Cubist paintings in his gallery was out of the question, and might have ruined his reputation.

The Picasso show opened its doors in February 1912 and immediately made a wide impression. On March 2, the art magazine *Picarol* hailed this "truly admirable man" who had made his name in Paris and promised "to eclipse most of the important personalities in painting." In the next issue, the editor-in-chief, Josep Aragay, spoke up to laud "the intrepid artist who, having begun at Els Quatre Gats with enthusiastic verve, made a triumph in Paris after reducing Nature to cubes!"

Coincidentally, José Junoy published *Arte y Artistas,* a study of contemporary Catalan art, which asserted, "Wherever Picasso touches he leaves the imprint of his temperament of genius." But he added, among other reservations, "Picasso understands things without loving them and interprets them cruelly. His love is a domination."

While these reservations reflected the general view, they upset Pablo's unconditional admirers, and Miguel Utrillo in *La Publicidad* replied to Junoy.

Since the show did not represent his current phase, Picasso had nothing to do with it and did not attend. Dalmau saw his own mistake and went to Paris to try to organize a Cubist exhibition. Unfortunately, he did not go to see Kahnweiler, but concentrated on the Cubists appearing in the Salons. So Pablo was not included in his new Barcelona show, entitled "Cubistas." Prefaced by Jacques Nayral and running April 26–May 10, 1912, it had works by Juan Gris, Metzinger, Léger, Gleizes, Marie Laurencin, Le Fauconnier, and Marcel Duchamp. But Picasso bore no grudge against Dalmau and invited him in November to his new place on Boulevard Raspail.

As impenetrable, paradoxical, and puzzling as four years before, the painter went his way. Now, as always, *Les Demoiselles d'Avignon* lay unseen in a corner at the Bateau-Lavoir; Picasso said it was too big to hang, and besides he always claimed the picture was unfinished. And now, with Apollinaire, Salmon, Raynal, and a few others writing about Cubism, Kahnweiler selling it, and more and more painters "cubifying," it was spreading increasingly.

Éva Gouel, now living with Picasso on Boulevard de Clichy, was four years younger than he. Born at Vincennes, outside Paris, the daughter of Adrien Gouel and Marie-Louise Ghérouze, she was a petite-bourgeoise who detested the Bohemian life. Very practical-minded, she aimed at security, comfort, and respectability. Not only was she Fernande's physical opposite; she was even more so temperamentally, and as fine a family budget-planner as her predecessor had been a spendthrift. Picasso, now possessor of a bank account, had been forced to hold to a minimum the household allowance he gave Fernande, and she, having no means of her own, eked this out with French lessons she gave to young Americans referred by Gertrude Stein. Several times, when she ran short, she had pawned her earrings.

All of Montmartre knew Éva as Marcelle Humbert, which she alleged, not quite truthfully, to be the name of a divorced husband. So Pablo restored her real first name and thereafter believed he had created it. Imaginative and ill-informed, Sabartés wrote that Pablo called his friend Éva "by way of compliment, as if to show he considered her the first woman." Jaime made frequent errors of this sort, which later biographers perpetuated as gospel.

Pablo was happy as a schoolboy, completely changed, to the amazement of his friends. With Éva, he felt he was starting a new life and wanted absolutely nothing to be as it had been. First of all, he had to move; he left all details of that to Kahnweiler, and while it was going on, he would take Éva to Céret.

But his love for her did not alter his aesthetic approach; at most, he superimposed a realistic reminder of matters that affected him on his current experiments. Not by using Éva's face or anything that might be taken for her, but by using her as a symbol. In inscribing "Ma Jolie" on that canvas that Gertrude saw, he was incorporating the sentimentalism of a currently popular song, "O Manon, ma jolie. Mon coeur te dit bonjour!" (O Manon, my pretty one. My heart greets you!)

During these years, no female figure appears in Picasso's paintings. He never did a portrait of Éva. Kahnweiler has said that "considering what he was trying to do at the time, he could not do a portrait." But Pablo wrote to his dealer on June 12, 1912, "I love [Éva] very much and will write it on my pictures."

"Writing his love on his pictures was all he ever did," according to Kahnweiler. Writing was also a conquest to Pablo: he *wrote,* literally, "Ma Jolie" or "Jolie Éva" as he would later write *J'aime Éva* (I love Eva) on a heart-shaped gingerbread in another picture. The last was a reminder of a mutual remembrance: he had bought her one at a fair on Boulevard de Clichy.

For the first time he introduced a note of frivolity into the rigorous Cubist Jansenism; not only must he have loved Éva deeply, but also felt that he had to tell the world. The dozen-odd canvases dedicated to Ma Jolie are his happiness announcement.

Another innovation of Spring 1912 bespoke new experiments: in *Still Life with Chair Caning,* an oval picture neither signed nor dated, he used a piece of oilcloth to simulate the chair's canework. This was his first use of a "real" object, his first collage. It was preceded, as Picasso himself confirmed, by the first free-form sculpture he did: an assembly of sheet metal and wire, called *Guitar.* That work holds a key place in the development of his inquiry into discontinuous three-dimensional shape in space. The sculpture-construction assemblages thus came before the picture-collages, rather than being, as supposed, their three-dimensional extension.

Guitar, shown publicly for the first time in 1966, had long been known to the Museum of Modern Art of New York, which wanted it and in 1971 offered Picasso a Cézanne in exchange. Two days later, he presented it to the great American museum. (This gives an idea of what Picasso might have done in France if the government and national museums had exhibited at least a minimum of interest in him.)

Picasso's painting was in constant mutation. He was putting into practice the famous line of the sixth stanza of Paul Valéry's *Le Cimetière marin,* "Look at me changing. . . ."

Of all those around him, Apollinaire was the most deeply taken by the mobility, the ceaseless search for novelty marked by challenges that he did not always understand, but followed as best he could. His friend's example moved him to try to do likewise in his own poetic medium, but Guillaume was really tradition-bound, and in attempting to explain Picasso tended to throw him back into the past while imagining in all sincerity that he was making good the future.

Entirely engrossed in his new love, Picasso had been seeing little of his old friends, avoiding the haunts where one might ask what happened to Fernande or who the new girl was. So it was for privacy as much as for a change of scenery that he took Éva to Céret. He missed the light and the things of Catalonia. Just recently he had painted the *Scallops,* about which he would tell Jean Cassou, "All of a sudden I could smell the port of Barcelona."

Before getting to the Catalan village, Pablo and Éva made a brief stopover at Avignon, but found it disappointing and went right on to Céret, May 18. To his chagrin, Fernande was there with the Pichots, who were vacationing here on

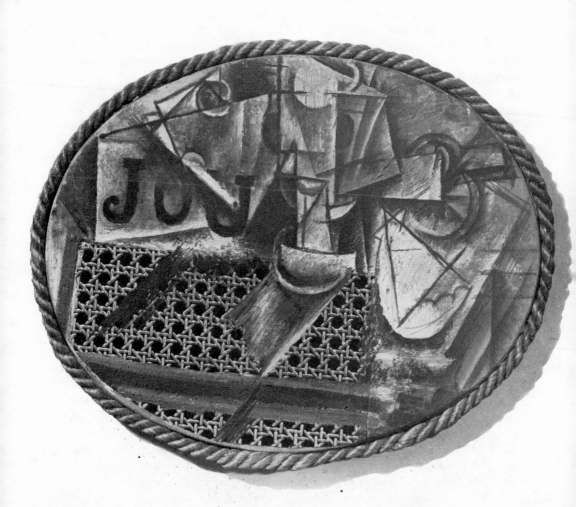

"Still Life with Chair Caning" Paris 1912, *artist's collection*
(GIRAUDON)

Manolo's recommendation. The Pichots lectured Pablo about having dropped Fernande without providing for her, and the arguments got so violent that Éva threatened to leave. On June 12, Pablo had had enough; they returned to Sorgues-sur-l'Ouvèze, outside Avignon, to join the Braques.

He rented two bedrooms and a studio in the villa Les Clochettes, a very ordinary house that is still there. It belonged to an old lady whose nephew, one M. Couturier, was supposed to collect the eighty francs' monthly rent for her. After decorating the whitewashed wall of one room with a still life, Picasso asked Couturier whether he could have it removed, packed, and sent to Kahnweiler. The landlord got a mason, François Perrin, to do the job, and it was done with the greatest of skill. The two men, both now dead, remembered having recognized on the wall a mandolin, a sheet of music with the title "Ma Jolie," and a bottle of Pernod. When I related this to Braque, he laughingly replied, "Why, then, they understood Cubism!"

Pablo worked hard at Sorgues, stimulated by the presence of Braque at the nearby Villa Bel-Air. The Braques and Picassos saw virtually no one but each other. A happy Pablo was very attentive to Éva, whose health was not good, and she, according to Marcelle Braque, wanted to know all about how he had met Fernande and how their liaison had started.

During this time, painters and critics were flocking to Céret, where Cubism was in blossom; strangely, *after the fact,* Picasso's presence was always an irresistible magnet. When the imitators and followers appeared, he had long since changed his manner and locale. Céret was an earlier version of Vallauris.

The Sorgues canvases have the architectonic nobility of synthetic Cubism. They either celebrated Jolie Éva, Ma Jolie, or Pablo-Éva in lettering, or in their titles proclaimed his new love. Pieces of real things reappeared after having been absent during the hermetic period, but for the moment newsprint, wrapping paper, imitation wood, or imitation marble were used to imitate imitation.

Picasso spent the first two weeks of September in Paris, to see how Kahnweiler was getting him moved, then returned to Sorgues on September 13, as we know from a note sent to Gertrude Stein.

Meantime, Braque, walking around Avignon, had noticed at a color shop some wallpaper in imitation-wood texture. Having started as a house painter and decorator, he always remained interested in the procedures of those crafts, and he was the first to suggest use of such *trompe-l'oeil* in pictures. "Ever trying to get closer to a reality," said Braque, "from 1911 on I started using letters in my canvases." Note that "*a* reality," for reality itself is something else again. Picasso believed he had gone further, indeed solved the problem, with the oilcloth he had used a bit earlier in *Still Life with Chair Caning.*

Typical of him, Braque waited until Picasso came back from Paris, before he bought that wallpaper; then he did the *Compote Bowl and Glass,* made by using three bands of imitation-wood paper connected by charcoal lines. At the top right, the word BAR, and bottom left ALE, also in charcoal. Pablo looked at it, said nothing, but then, using his friend's method, without mentioning it to Braque did several "collages." He knew he was more of an "artist" than the "artisan" Braque: he did not conduct experiments; he made pictures.

He was later to say that they tried to achieve reality (no "*a* reality" for him) by using materials they did not know how to handle, but which they liked just because they were not indispensable, neither the best nor the most suitable. Braque and Picasso in their collages used all kinds and forms of paper, then sand, fabrics, even pieces of mirror. Their assemblages were often held together by charcoal, gouache, or ink lines. The materials were deliberately poor, the colors dull or washed out; color was not one of their major concerns.

What was painting? "To see is one thing, to paint is another," said Picasso. And Aragon was to write, in 1930, in *La Peinture au défi* (The Challenge to Painting):

> One can foresee a time when painters, who already do not mix their own colors, will consider it childish and beneath them to spread the paint themselves, and feel that the personal touch which today gives the value to their works has no more than the documentary interest of a manuscript or an autograph. . . .
> One can foresee the time when painters will no longer even have others lay on the color, nor do any drawing. Collage gives us a foretaste of that time.

That time came less than thirty years later.

The Sorgues period for both of them was very profitable; their studios formed a double laboratory for the most varied kind of experiments. They did not always know where these would lead, but they sensed they were invaluable to the development of their métier. Picasso's genius lay in understanding that the introduction of collage into canvases did not replace either drawing or painting, but was merely something else, a foreign element with its own design and color that created a space different from that of the traditional picture. To prove it, Picasso had the bits of paper or fake wood flutter against the basic drawing, thus creating dialogues based on substitution processes.

When they returned to Paris at the end of September, Pablo had made a clean break, moving out of Montmartre across the river to Montparnasse. His and Éva's address was 242 Boulevard Raspail. In November he went to visit Braque's family at Le Havre, and brought back the curious *Memory of Le Havre:* its vertical structure, inside an upright oval, combines numerous visual elements he had seen in the port, notably hawsers and seashells.

Cubism waxed ever greater. Beyond Braque and Picasso, that is. In 1912, Figuière published the first exegetical work, *Du cubisme* (On Cubism), by Gleizes and Metzinger. The Salon des Indépendants shaped up as the greatest of all Cubist shows: Delaunay, Gleizes, Juan Gris with his *Homage to Picasso,* Kupka, La Fresnaye, Le Fauconnier, Léger, Lhote, Metzinger, Mondrian, Picabia, Alfred Reth, Archipenko, Brancusi, Diego Rivera from Mexico, and more.

They were all present and accounted for again on October 1 in the Salon d'Automne, joined by Marcoussis and the sculptor Duchamp-Villon, whose brother Jacques Villon was founding the Salon de la Section d'Or, with the statement: "Where Cubism uproots, the Golden Section takes root. One rethinks perspective, while the other tries to penetrate its secrets." This new Salon opened its doors on October 10 at the Galerie La Boétie: the Cubists from the Salons des Indépendants and d'Automne were represented, alongside realistic painters such as Luc-Albert Moreau and Dunoyer de Segonzac.

VII

SELLING
THE "CHICKENS
BEFORE THEY HATCHED"
(1912–1914)

THE YEAR 1912 WAS THE TURNING POINT FOR MODERN PAINTING. ON February 5, the Galerie Bernheim-Jeune opened its first Futurist show; Delaunay was painting his *Windows* series, *Simultaneous Disc,* and *The Punch,* in which he tried to express motion through simultaneous color contrasts. Marcel Duchamp contributed his *Nude Descending a Staircase* to the Salon des Indépendants, but the Cubists, worried by this dynamism that did not coincide with their views and fearsome of new givens in painting different from their own conceptions, delegated Gleizes and Duchamp's brother Villon to ask him to withdraw it.

Matisse was at work on the *Still Life with Oranges* that Pablo was to acquire several years later and the *Capucines à la danse,* the background of which is the big *Dance* composition he had done for Shchukine two years earlier. In the same year, Picasso was exhibiting at Der Sturm in Berlin and Sonderbund in Cologne, as well as having some of his graphics and drawings in the Blaue Reiter show in Munich. The first London one-man Picasso show opened at the Stafford Gallery in April, but the management prudently restricted it to drawings and watercolors of the Blue and Rose periods. In October, he was to be represented in the Post-Impressionist show at the Grafton Gallery, as well as the Jack of Diamonds in Moscow. However, there was a difference between the shows Picasso was personally invited to participate in and the ones to which Kahnweiler submitted entries.

The latter's activity was untiring, and covered most of Western Europe. One of his main contacts was Alfred Flechtheim, a leading European dealer before 1914. His two principal galleries, in Berlin and Düsseldorf, were extraordinarily effective centers of living art (he also had showplaces in Frankfurt, Cologne, and for a time Vienna). In 1912, while still trading in grain, in which he had made his fortune, he organized the Sonderbund show in Cologne with a few local artists and museums, then in 1913 he quit his business to devote himself entirely to the art field. His first gallery, at Düsseldorf, displayed local Rhineland painters plus some "Dômiers," his punning name for the French painters he had found at the Café du Dôme—mainly, Picasso.

The London *Morning Post* in January 1912 was typical of British reaction to Picasso's work in the first show organized by Roger Fry: the work of an impostor and charlatan, an "atrophied, perverted talent."

The Grafton's second show, organized by Fry and Clive Bell, concentrated on the Van Gogh-Cézanne inheritance by way of Matisse, Herbin, Lhote, Vlaminck, Derain, Picasso, Braque, Jean Marchand, Bonnard, and Othon Friesz. Fry felt Rouault was the great revelation of the day, and did not especially care for Cubism; yet Picasso, along with Matisse, was the most heavily represented in the show, with thirteen paintings and some drawings of both realistic and Cubist periods.

In Paris, he remained aloof from the Salons, and all public controversies. His Olympian detachment was the more intriguing because while disciples and followers hailed him as their forerunner, he invariably withdrew or fled, whenever he felt he was being dubbed a leader.

Apollinaire thought he ought to enter the arena and straighten things out, enjoying the friendship of Picasso, Braque, and Kahnweiler. But he did not have their trust, for they recognized his gaucheries and flightiness, despite the real courage he showed in defending new art. Such daring positions not only brought him no fortune, but got him into a lot of trouble.

Friendly with Picabia, Léger, and Delaunay, he lauded the meritorious efforts of Metzinger, whose painting, he said, "always contains its own explanation." He appreciated the "majesty" of Gleizes, and of course had nothing but praise for Marie Laurencin. These opinions of his, and others, alarmed Kahnweiler and his stable of artists. The idea that he was planning a book on Cubism scared them to death.

On December 18, 1912, following their discussions of a business relationship, Picasso wrote Kahnweiler a letter that was to be the only contract ever made between them. He agreed for three years to sell nothing to anyone other than Kahnweiler, except old pictures and drawings; all new production was to go exclusively to Rue Vignon. Picasso reserved the right only to keep for himself a maximum of five pictures per year and whatever drawings he felt were needed for his further work. And specified, "You will accept my decision as to when a picture is completed." Portraits and mural decorations did not enter into the agreement. And during these three years, Picasso agreed not to sell any of the works he was keeping for himself.

Kahnweiler for his part agreed to buy "a minimum of twenty drawings per year," plus all the Picasso paintings and gouaches, at predetermined prices. This was the scale: drawings, 100 francs apiece; gouaches, 200 francs; paintings, up to six points, 250 francs; eight, ten, eleven, fifteen, or twenty points, 500 francs; twenty-five points, 1000; thirty, forty, fifty points, 1500; sixty points and above,

Apollinaire circa 1913 at the time when he wrote
Les Peintres cubistes

(ROGER-VIOLLET)

3000 francs. (A franc at the time was worth about twenty cents, or five to the dollar.) Prices of sculptures and engravings were left open.*

This formalized what had existed since the first time Kahnweiler visited him at the Bateau-Lavoir; except for works already sold, no new Picassos would be seen anywhere but on Rue Vignon. Clovis Sagot was to die two months later (February 1913); Vollard, unable to understand Cubism, had dropped Pablo after 1910; and Berthe Weill and Père Soulier were not buying anymore. Uhde continued to collect until 1914, when his holdings as well as Kahnweiler's were seized as alien property: at the time he had sixteen Picassos, thirteen oils among them.

Prices were rising; yet the contract terms above were exceptionally high for a thirty-one-year-old artist with little mass following, identified with the notoriety of Cubism. But his name and work were continuing to be recognized.

Gertrude Stein (Leo having switched entirely to Matisse), Roger Dutilleul, Serge Shchukine, Vincenc Kramář, Hermann Rupf, André Level, Robert Ellissen and his friends in the *Peau de l'Ours* were to remain the principal buyers of Picassos until 1914. From 1912–1913 on, there were also the Catalan Luis Plandiura, whose large collection was eventually to go into the Barcelona Museum of Modern Art, and Alphonse Kann and André Lefèvre in Paris. They would all come back after World War I.

Now, what about Apollinaire's book? An excellent poet, he had understood that, in this era of mutation, poetry as well as painting needed renewing, and that the latter might assist the former. He wanted to conjugate them, associate colors and words, pictorial visuals with poetical musicals, but unfortunately in this he turned out to be more of a genius of juggling than a true creator. What to the painters was a means of knowing became for him only a verbal game. His lyrical paraphrasing was only atmospheric, impressionistic criticism. In a sense, he was simply carrying on with Symbolism, which at one time had also found expression in Picasso's Harlequins and Maternities of the Blue and Rose periods. But with Cubism, Apollinaire lost his footing, seeking in vain the way to verbalize this plastic revolution. He tried using technical terms in place of the suggestive images of his 1905–1907 writings, and attempted to deepen his descriptiveness and analysis. In his efforts to interiorize Cubist painting his critical vocabulary too often, for want of being able to "talk" aesthetics that were also poetics, fell into approximations and clichés. His statements came out with a hollow ring.

His hagiographers to the contrary notwithstanding, his critical sense fluctuated along with his friendships, as well as with the internal rivalries of cliques. While not belonging to any one coterie or doctrine, Apollinaire had his own short-comings. However, we can only bow to his unwavering devotion to and ad-miration of Picasso. In February 1912, the first issue of *Les Soirées de Paris,* of which he was one of the founders, proved at last a worthy tribune from which

* The "points" referred to are the standard French commercial method of measuring the size of canvases. Six points mean approximately 16½ inches by 13 inches; twenty points, 29 inches by 24 inches; fifty points, 46½ inches by 39½ inches; and so on. (TR. NOTE)

to proclaim, "The subject no longer counts, or barely counts. . . . A Picasso studies an object the way a surgeon dissects a cadaver." A very correct and excellent formulation.

Now, Guillaume had a real problem: how could he reconcile his admiration for Picasso, who was developing in a way that dismayed him, with his growing taste for Delaunay (the least Cubist among the group)?

Les Peintres cubistes, méditations esthétiques (Cubist Painters: Aesthetic Meditations), Apollinaire's collection of his articles from 1905 on, was supposed to appear in October 1912, but his publisher brought out the Gleizes-Metzinger book in that month, and his did not come out until March 1913. Between those two dates, many things occurred.

Apollinaire had grown close to Picabia and, in July 1912, visited England and then the Jura Mountains with him. One of the few well-do-do among the painters, Picabia, in exchange for a chapter on him in the book, covered the publishing costs of *Les Peintres cubistes*.

Beyond that, Guillaume had become a bosom buddy of the Delaunays, who hated Picasso and never stopped defaming him and the whole of Kahnweiler's Rue Vignon "Cubist cathedral." On October 11, he gave a lecture at the Salon of the Golden Section, in which he credited Delaunay's Orphism (a term invented for the occasion) with "drawing and quartering Cubism."

In January 1913, with Delaunay, he went to Berlin to give a lecture on modern painting at the Der Sturm Gallery. Between the speed of artistic developments and the trauma of his break with Marie Laurencin, he was struggling to keep a footing. His book was a paste-up job. He had simply added a few pieces on selected artists to his old articles and, under Delaunay's influence, posited four separate categories of Cubism. In no way a glorification of Picasso, it made no mention of Delaunay, either in relation to him or to Braque, Metzinger, Juan Gris, Marie Laurencin, Léger, Picabia, Marcel Duchamp, or even in the appendix alongside Duchamp-Villon. Apollinaire had promised Delaunay a separate book on him; without Marie Laurencin, he was now truly dependent on the Delaunays, especially willful Sonia, who dominated both her husband and him.

A typescript found in Apollinaire's papers, "Propos de Pablo Picasso" (Statements of Pablo Picasso), gave evidence that he intended to do another book on Pablo. He had a deal with a publisher to be general editor of a collection on all the arts, in which it was to appear. His typescript said, in part:

> Probably no living painter has had so great an influence on young French artists as Pablo Picasso.
> The most recent school of painting, Cubism, stems from him. . . .
> With me, who am, I believe, his closest friend, Picasso . . . never spoke at length about art, though the Lord knows we mentioned it often enough. . . . He never formulated his views in precise terms, never claimed to have any system. . . .

There followed some "statements by the artist" that were certainly never spoken by him, for, beyond their pretentiousness, they are filled with arrant misstatements of fact: "I experienced my purest emotions in a great Spanish forest where I had taken refuge in order to paint at the age of sixteen." Or, "Above all, I love light. . . . Colors are but symbols, and reality is in light alone."

The same thoughts, in virtually identical words, appeared in several places at the time under Delaunay's signature.

Kahnweiler, furious at seeing Apollinaire go over to the detested Delaunay, wanted to make him come out fully and frankly about Cubism. But Picasso and Braque thought neither Kahnweiler nor they should get into such public disputes. On hearing of the dealer's stand, Apollinaire wrote a stinging letter to Kahnweiler, claiming that he was the first to defend, "alone among writers, painters whom you espoused after me," adding that this was "the simple warning of a poet who knows what must be said." Yet he must have thought better of it, for a few days later, he wrote him that "you are my friend, and when you say anything against me it hurts me."

Kahnweiler claimed that Picasso could not care less what Apollinaire wrote about him; that was incorrect. Pablo did pay attention to what his friend wrote, for he knew he had a very special poetic intuition, even though he was aware of his lack of artistic knowledge, his shortcomings and shiftings, to say nothing of the influence of the Delaunays. But neither his closeness to the Delaunays nor the appearance of the book and the controversies that followed affected Picasso's friendship for Apollinaire. Frequent notes and cards reflect the always warm, sometimes humorous, relationship. Pablo peppered the cloudless friendship with caricatures of the poet pictured in all sorts of guises, as pope (*His Holiness Apollinaire*), Hercules, academician, tough guy, sailor, toreador, and even, because of his broad face, as a teapot or pear.

Shchukine went on regularly buying Pablo's Cubist paintings, while Morosov cared only for the earlier works. In 1913, Picasso was exhibited at the Moderne Galerie, Munich, the Neue Galerie, Berlin, and in the Salon of the Rhine at Cologne. With Braque, he also participated in the Sezession in Berlin. Kahnweiler handled all details: through his foreign representatives, he selected and shipped the canvases, whether as consignments or as shows. His painters trusted him, and there was never a shadow in their relationships.

Kahnweiler was also responsible for sending several Picassos to the 1913 New York Armory Show, and to Prague, through the Manes Artistic Circle, along with those of Derain, Braque, and Juan Gris. In August 1912, Alfred Stieglitz' *Camera Work* had published a special issue with two articles by Gertrude Stein on Matisse and Picasso, illustrated with reproductions of their works.

In the spring of 1913, Pablo and Éva moved from Boulevard Raspail to a large studio-apartment nearby, at 5 *bis* Rue Schoelcher. Another move up the social ladder, in a thoroughly uneventful existence: life in Montparnasse followed a new pattern. Pablo went to the cafés around the Vavin intersection, the Dôme and the Rotonde, where artists mixed with local petits-bourgeois. He went out less frequently of an evening and no longer regularly attended Gertrude Stein's Saturday nights. The color and lightness of his paintings reflected his passionate love for Éva.

*Picasso in his studio at Rue Schoelcher 1914–1915
(Collection of Sir Roland Penrose)*

It is easy to date his first paper collages from the bits of newspaper in them: November–December 1912; then again in Céret, beginning mid-March 1913, though now the paper collages proper were replaced by linear nonfigurative architectures the pictorial result of which can be assimilated to synthetic Cubism. A third period was to come between spring of 1914 and the start of that summer. The earliest collage is very likely the *Guitar, Score, and Glass,* since the scrap of the newspaper *Le Journal* is dated November 10, 1912: its purely plastic elements, tapestry, imitation wood, colored papers confront linear elements, printer's type, charcoal drawing, and musical staffs. The silhouettes of objects are distributed in a shallow space within which they seem to float; free, moving, colored space the role of which would prove increasingly important in the Picasso and Braque pictures of the months ahead.

No less important for Picasso's experiments of the moment was the collage called *Violin* (part of the 1969 Cuttoli-Laugier Gift to the Paris National Museum of Modern Art, which erroneously dated it 1914): the newspapers in it are from November 20, 1912. For the first time, he was using symmetrical clippings as elements of form and value in the structure of the drawing, some parts being shaded with black spots. Those shadows were not long to remain: in the later collages, of which *Violin* might be termed an "incunabulum," the space was to be created solely by the effect of contrast between pasted object and drawing. Such is the case of *Coup de théâtre,* in the same Cuttoli-Laugier Gift, its title coming from the bit of newspaper reporting the First Balkan War with Turkey, December 4, 1912.

The Céret collages are intimately connected with the oils of the same period, the two media often interconnecting in their verbalism, but, while sometimes a painting "reproduces" a collage effect, the latter when used gives a raw tactile element, the texture, thickness, value, and so on, of it, creating different lighting effects. The new chapter that the Catalan collages opened in his work was characterized by the search for a figuration reduced to its own analytical content in which the idea, replacing the image, gave a purely conceptual view of the object.

In 1913, he drew a Cubist portrait of Apollinaire as frontispiece for the poet's *Alcools* (Paris: Mercure de France). This "undecipherable trigonometric masterpiece" (as it was called by Henri Ghéon) was originally printed in blue ink, but Pablo, advised of the fact by Max Jacob, wrote Guillaume to demand "that it be printed in black and no other way."

Picasso had deliberately made this construction geometric without any suggestion of reality, for he well knew that Guillaume had never become resigned to the disappearance of the "tangible" communicating image, and therefore had turned to Delaunay, whose Orphism still retained in its movements some of the sensuality of Fauvism. But *Alcools* thus became forever identified with Cubism, with which its poems had nothing in common.

At the end of April, Picasso was called to Barcelona, his father having just died. With Don José, the most adventurous part of Pablo's youth was gone, the time of far-reaching choices and challenges. Following to the cemetery the body

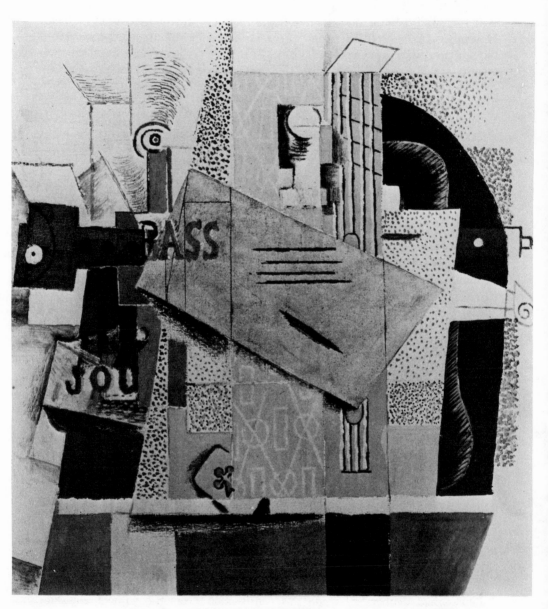

"Violin" Paris 1914 *(Musée national d'Art moderne—Paris)*

(GIRAUDON)

of the father he had involuntarily killed, Pablo felt isolated—from family, friends, everything. With his deep Spanish sense of belonging, this isolation, this lack of communication was the most terrible of ordeals. Chained to his vocation, he carried it like a cross. As Apollinaire aptly wrote, "Artists above all are men trying to become inhuman."

He returned to Paris more concerned over Éva's health than grieving for his father. His adoring mother, now alone, would live with his married sister, Lola. She would keep the Calle de la Merced apartment as long as possible so as to welcome Pablo whenever he came to Barcelona. Shortly after the return to Paris, he and Éva left for Céret.

Kahnweiler was about to publish Max Jacob's *Le Siège de Jérusalem,* the follow-up to *Saint Matorel,* again illustrated by Picasso. Pablo invited the still-penniless Max to join them on vacation. Max was delighted, both because of this proof of friendship and the chance to spend a few weeks in the beautiful Catalan country his friends had raved to him about. He got along much better with Éva than with Fernande: she had been so big and beautiful she scared him, and she made fun of the crushes he got on any bemustached uniform he saw.

Max was happy as a baby in the country, so different from his native Brittany. Daytimes, if not busy working, they went to the café, to see the Manolos, Frank Haviland, and other local friends, as well as the Braques and Juan Gris, who arrived shortly.

But it rained; Éva had trouble getting rid of a sore throat, and her harsh cough worried Pablo. Once, they went to Figueras to a bullfight. Picasso worked prodigiously, amazing his friends with his productivity as well as the way in several collages he was able to master his imagination as well as the matter and the form. In the one called *Glass and Bottle of Bass,* sawdust was mixed into the oil as well as papers being pasted on. On the other hand, in *Musical Instruments,* ash, sand, and plaster created contrasts between the smooth surfaces and the gritty planes that made variations of intensity in both the matter and the light. *The Blue Violin* used the same technique, with imitation wood added; as in *The Bottle of Suze,* the color harmony was sprightly, contrasting with the austerity of the earlier collages.

Pablo and Éva returned to Paris on June 20. His main companion at this time was Juan Gris, a new entry in Kahnweiler's "stable." The two Spaniards had grown very close at Céret. Gris, six years younger, had great admiration for Picasso and by way of tribute had exhibited a portrait of him at the 1912 Salon des Indépendants. Now he was working on collage. The industrious atmosphere around Pablo at Céret had helped Juan, who also felt at ease so close to Spain: it was his first time away from Paris since coming there in 1906.

But the two men were not long to remain on such good terms: in place of the ever-devoted disciple Pablo had anticipated, he found a painter with his own style who loomed as a rival at Kahnweiler's. So he changed; he did not mind his dealer having other painters beside him, but another Spaniard was too much. Henceforth, Pablo became pitiless toward the modest, retiring Gris; he never missed a chance to run him down; but for Kahnweiler, he might have made a beggar of him.

Pablo was soon to discover his own importance: taking sick in early July after going back to Céret with Éva, he found his health commented upon in weeklies, dailies, and even financial sheets. His illness proved he had "arrived"; he just had to stay up there. They returned finally to Paris around August 15.

The ninth Salon d'Automne, opened in November, was termed "clearly Cubist" by Salmon, though, of course, Braque and Picasso were among those missing. Apollinaire was now editor-in-chief of a reorganized *Soirées de Paris,* which he dubbed the "official" organ of Cubism. Located at 278 Boulevard Raspail, it was Picasso's close neighbor, and he was the main topic of the first issue in the new format, published November 15, the very day the Salon opened. Reproduction of five of his paintings along with much other material on Cubism brought in floods of cancellations, but this did not discourage Apollinaire from his campaign.

A seventeen-year-old medical student who read the magazine commented forty-eight years later:

> I have the eyes of youth again when I think of first coming across the work of Picasso in Apollinaire's *Soirées de Paris,* reproducing—rather murkily—five recent still lifes (this was 1913). . . . After the shock of the *jamais-vu,* there was a feeling of the sovereign balance of work accomplished, promoted—willy-nilly—to organic life and thereby justifying its own necessity.

Thus, André Bréton writing in *Combat* on November 6, 1961. And the old Surrealist master added:

> Nearly half a century has gone by. From what Picasso once told me, those faraway constructions have been dismantled, but the image recalled is enough to show how much they foreshadowed the forms of expression considered the most daring today. Indeed, how much they so often outdid them.

At soirées held at the *Soirées,* neighbor Picasso might run into Fernand Léger, Kisling, Archipenko, Maurice Raynal, Blaise Cendrars, Modigliani, Derain, Picabia, André Salmon, Brancusi, André Level, Henri-Pierre Roche, Kahnweiler, or Vollard. Serge Férat and his sister the Baroness d'Oettingen, the new owners and Apollinaire's patrons, always had their doors open to this Who's Who of the avant-garde. Braque and Max Jacob dropped down from Montmartre, the Villon brothers came in from the suburb of Puteaux, and Gleizes from Courbevoie. The Futurists Severini and Boccioni never missed a chance to attend, bringing with them other Italians, including Chirico and his brother Savinio, known as "the piano smasher," Magnelli, Giovanni Papini, and others.

They forgathered at the Rotonde, the Dôme, Chez Papa, or the Café des Vigourelles, named after the pretty daughters of its owner, M. Vigoureux, as well as Restaurant Baty, and sometimes the Closerie des Lilas, the hangout of the more traditional poets. Montparnasse, still somewhat countrified, had its share of "wine and coal shops," where one might always find a pal to bend an elbow. "The painters are no longer in their element in modern Montmartre, hard to climb up to, with its phony artists, fast-talking businessmen, and assorted opium smokers," as Apollinaire chronicled it.

In January, studios and cafés were electrified: The Bear Skin was going to auction off its holdings! At last, there would be proof of whether modern painting had made it; most were sure that Cubism would collapse pitifully and "true" values come back to the fore. Many artists were worried, for this first commercial test might decide the whole future of the new art.

The auction was set for March 2, 1914, at the Hôtel Drouot, Paris' traditional auction gallery. Rooms 7 and 8 were filled to capacity for the historic event, half the crowd curious, the other mocking. Me Henri Beaudouin, licensed auctioneer, wielded the ivory gavel, flanked by the dealers, the Bernheim brothers and Eugène Druet, appointed as experts. On the block were works by Bonnard, Maurice Denis, Derain, Gauguin, Van Gogh, Matisse, Laprade, Utrillo, Valadon, Manguin, Sérusier, Vlaminck, Vuillard, but especially Picasso (no less than twelve items), La Fresnaye, Herbin, Metzinger, Marie Laurencin—and that was what all the excitement was about.

At auction, how would the notorious Cubists stack up? Not only were the artists' reputations at stake; there was the added fact that The Bear Skin had assigned 20 percent of the take to each of them. So several were present who might not otherwise have come at all.

The enemies of Cubism were there, too, to be in at the kill. But in fact only two actual Cubist paintings were up for sale, a Metzinger landscape and La Fresnaye's *Still Life with Handles.* All the Picassos predated the *Demoiselles d'Avignon.* A lot of dealers attended, to see what prices would be like: Ambroise Vollard, Kahnweiler, Heinrich Thannhauser of Munich, Alfred Flechtheim of Düsseldorf, Gaspari of Milan, Gutbier of Dresden. Heading the pro-Cubists was Max Jacob in a red greatcoat (*Man in the Greatcoat* was one of the Picassos on sale), along with Prince Bibesco, the poet Joachim Gasquet, La Fresnaye, Maurice Raynal, André Billy, Baroness d'Oettingen with Serge Férat, "Baron" Mollet, and André Salmon.

The first canvas knocked down was Bonnard's *Aquarium:* 720 francs. Derain's *The Bedroom:* 210 francs. Metzinger's Cubist landscape brought a mere 100 francs (about $20). The foes of Cubism were beginning to snicker, but they looked up when the La Fresnaye fetched 300 francs. Until then, the highest earner had been Matisse, whose *Compote Dish with Apples and Oranges* went for 5000 francs, a thousand more than Gauguin and Van Gogh!

Hold your breath: here come the Picassos!

But these were no geometrical figures, no polyhedrons, rectangles, or cylinders, but lanky adolescents, saltimbanques, heartwarming maternities, bums, and clowns. Blue and Rose nostalgia!

Sales: *Woman and Children,* 1100 francs (just under what was paid for Maurice Denis and Manguin), and *The Man in the Greatcoat,* 1350. Vuillard's *Lady in Blue* had brought 2400, and Laprade's *Girl Singing* 2100, but 1350 for a

Picasso seemed extraordinary! Yet the applause drowned out the protests and hisses when *Three Dutch Girls,* in gouache on cardboard, was knocked down to André Level's brother Émile for 5200 francs.

"And now, still by the same artist, *The Tumblers,*" announced the auctioneer, "a canvas measuring two meters twenty-five by two meters thirty-five . . ." (approximately 89 by 93 inches). This superb 1905 composition, with its poignant emotivity, both sculptural and phantomatic in its orange ochers, bluish grays, violets, and azure blues, bought by Level for The Bear Skin, had, according to the rules, gone by lot to one of the members, Robert Ellissen, who, finding it too cumbersome to hang, had kept it in storage until now.

"Asking price eight thousand francs," the auctioneer continued. "Do I hear nine thousand . . . ten thousand . . . on the left . . . a bid on the right? . . . eleven thousand . . . any more? . . . Eleven five . . . going . . . going . . . gone!"

His gavel rapped. Picasso's friends exploded into a leap of delight. The foes of modern painting tried to explain it away by saying this was no triumph for Cubism because *The Tumblers* antedated the geometrical lucubrations by three years—but no one was listening. On their feet, Salmon, Raynal, Max, the critic Basler, Billy, Jean Mollet, Baroness d'Oettingen, Férat, André Warnod, Allard were clapping their hands off. Kahnweiler forced his way through the wild crowd to go and bring the good news to Pablo, who, as usual, had not bothered to come.

The Tumblers brought the highest price of all at this historic sale. Ellissen could not get over the fact that he had shunted aside something of such value. But what struck him—and André Salmon—most was the panic of the traditionalists who had expected to see modern painting given its comeuppance. "All we can do now is turn out Picassos," one of them lamented.

The picture, bought by Thannhauser of Munich, later became the property of Herta von Koenig before going on to the Chester Dale Collection. The sale infuriated the conservative press, and one Maurice Delcourt wrote an article headed "Before the Invasion" in *Paris-Midi,* to say:

"Big prices" were paid for grotesque and unspeakable works by undesirable foreigners, and it was Germans who bid them up to those levels!

We can now see their plan. Naïve young painters will . . . imitate Picasso the imitator who, . . . having run out of things to imitate, sank into the fakery of Cubism.

That winter, as Leo Stein moved permanently to Florence, he and Gertrude split their joint collection, she keeping the Cézannes and Picassos, he taking "the Matisses and Renoirs, with the exception of the original Femme au Chapeau." She now had many more American guests, including the writer Mildred Aldrich, who asked Alice B. Toklas whether the paintings on the walls were "really alright, I know Gertrude thinks so, and Gertrude knows, but really is it not all a fumisterie, is it not all false." The huge sale price made others who were asking the same thing wonder whether Picasso had not been wrong to depart from that earlier manner. "He draws so well," they commented. "Why does he have to make fun of people?"

But, as he told Gertrude Stein: "They say I draw better than Raphael, and they're probably right; maybe I do. But if I just draw as well as he did, I ought to have the right at least to decide what I will do, and they should recognize it. Instead, they don't, and they just say no."

When she questioned the durability of the papers in the collages, she reported his saying, "Paper lasts as long as paint, and if it all gets old together, why not?" And, "Later no one will see the picture. They'll see the legend, the legend the picture created; so what matter whether the picture lasts or not. It'll be restored. But a picture lives only through its legend, not through anything else; the pasted paper can just as well be part of the legend."

On May 25, Apollinaire complained in *Paris-Journal* that "the Luxembourg [Museum—devoted to living artists] does not have a single sketch by Matisse or Picasso whose reputations, nevertheless, are worldwide." The Italian Futurists were now adopting Pablo, and one of them, Ardengo Soffici, referred to him as "one of us," "one from my ground." Pablo returned the compliment by including the title of the Futurist magazine *Lacerba* in a still life.

Max Jacob now had a new vocation: explaining Cubism to tourists on the terraces of the Flore and Deux-Magots. He invented apocryphal stories to explain Picasso's cubes, as did many others, and all of these stories only increased the feeling that the whole thing had been a hoax, with Pablo the hoax master. Nor was such mistrust relieved by Apollinaire's excesses, as when he enthused in the magazine *Marches de Provence* for February 1912:

> Picasso is one of those of whom Michelangelo said they should be known as eagles because they surpass all others and find their way through the clouds right up to the light of the sun. . . .
> Goethe's last words, "More light!" rise from the sublime and mysterious of a Picasso as they still rise from the work of Rembrandt!

Picasso was turning back to sculpture. It may seem surprising that, after the few works done in 1905, he had abandoned it just when he was trying to make his painting three-dimensional. The Cubist constructions of 1913–1914 were not far removed from the collages, but painted sheet iron and wood had greater strength and solidity.

More than that: he imparted a magical power to it. With simple debris found anywhere, thrown-away objects, mere "things," he made barbaric-looking totems with gaudy colors endowed with sur-real virtues. As African or Polynesian sculptors did, he turned the rawest bareness into the sacred. Here were the divinities of a new religion whose high priestesses were the whores of the Carrer d'Avinyo. Beyond the need for concretization that Picasso felt before tactile objects there was his awareness of a new phenomenon: all creation is metamorphosis when it is also language. With sculpture, painting could come closer to the raw reality *itself,* which his pictures merely projected through a vehicle and procedures that were illusionistic—that is to say, *one* of the forms of reality. Half a century ahead of time, he was paving the way for Objectism.

In July 1914, Pablo and Éva went south to Tarascon, and then Avignon, for the summer, not far from the Derains and Braques, who were at Sorgues. War was in the air, and while Pablo as a Spaniard was not involved, almost all his friends were on the alert for a first-day call-up.

Picasso did a series of drawings leading to *Seated Man with Glass,* one of his most baroque plastic innovations, reminiscent of the pasted papers. A jade-green background slightly dotted with white sets off the large, very sober black jacket of the seated man, while a stripe of tender color runs across the picture. A violet-festooned poster announces the Avignon Festival in capital letters. Was this ornamental lyricism, apparently disregardful of Cubist advances, a sign for the future? Braque was marking time and Gris was undecided, but Pablo wanted to feel freer than ever; he had made his turn toward the "figurative."

On August 2, 1914, the war broke out, and M. Frantz Jourdain, president of the Salon d'Automne, rang the death knell of Cubism. The same day, Pablo saw Derain and Braque off at the Avignon station, amid the patriotic crowd. "We never saw each other again," he sadly told Kahnweiler. They did meet again, of course, but never on the same friendly terms, as he had foreseen.

Apollinaire, on a story at Deauville, rushed back to Paris to enlist, just in time to be filmed in a newsreel among the crowd already shouting victory. He was not called up for three months, and in the interim Picasso sent him a card from Avignon showing the apotheosis of the poet Frédéric Mistral, who had just died. He wrote on it, "I will do the apotheosis of you."

Only in November did Pablo and Éva return to Paris. Montparnasse was deserted. Much as he sought solitude for working, he hated it; war, to him, was death even if he was not directly involved. Looking out on the tombstones of the Montparnasse cemetery from his studio window did nothing to cheer him up. Gertrude Stein and Alice B. Toklas, Max Jacob, Foujita, and Juan Gris, who got back from Céret on November 6, were the only friends around in this sad, worrisome period. Kahnweiler, German and a fugitve from military service to boot, was in Rome, having thought of joining the Foreign Legion but deciding not to. What Derain called his Rue Vignon "Cubist shop" was locked up. In December, the dealer went to Bern, at the urging of his friend Rupf, and there he learned that the alien-property custodian in Paris had taken charge of his pictures and worldly goods.

Max Jacob's letters of the period give us a log of Pablo's pictorial work, and his relations to Cubism. He wrote Maurice Raynal on November 30, 1914: "Picasso's return is that of a new art in which pure lines follow the vulgar lines of nature." And "Was Cubism, as some felt, just a new School intended to replace the School?" And a little later, "Picasso is partly giving up Cubism."

One evening, walking up Boulevard Raspail with Gertrude Stein, Picasso saw a convoy of camouflaged artillery go by. "C'est nous qui avons fait ça, he said— it is we that have created that . . ." He was delighted to see Cubist forms and colors, so recently mocked by the public, taken up by the military. As he was to tell Cocteau, "If they want to make an army invisible, they have only to dress their men as Harlequins."

Sometimes of an evening he and Éva joined Serge Férat and the Baroness d'Oettingen in a Montparnasse restaurant, as the latter tried desperately to keep together some of the friends from their late *Soirées de Paris*. To pass the time, Pablo asked them to teach him Russian, and the Baroness spent the whole winter at it, sometimes far into the night—which set tongues wagging. Some of those in uniform or about to be felt that Pablo, a power of a man, who owed his entire reputation to France, ought to enlist. This bothered him considerably, although, as Jacques Villon was to tell me, "We never dreamt of holding against him that he did not go to war. We knew he was worth much more than that. And besides, it was not his country that needed defending."

Among the canvases Gertrude Stein had had to relinquish when she and her brother split them up, there was an *Apple* by Cézanne that she deeply regretted losing. As she complained of it one day, Picasso retorted, "Don't let it worry you. I'll do your Cézanne over for you." And on Christmas Day 1914 he brought her an *Apple* (today the property of Mr. and Mrs. David Rockefeller) that was the exact duplicate of the one she had lost, with an inscription in French, "Souvenir for Gertrude and Alice."

The two women were as much overwhelmed by Picasso's extraordinary skill in duplicating it as they were charmed by his thoughtfulness.

"Any work more or less grows out of another," he told them simply.

VIII

THEATER
AND LOVE
(1915–1917)

OR SEVERAL YEARS, MAX JACOB HAD BEEN HAVING VISIONS THAT inclined him toward Catholicism. But his tales of conversations with Christ and the Holy Virgin, spiced freely with his witticisms, made many doubt the sincerity of his conversion. He dutifully took instruction, but the date for his baptism was delayed several times—as when his vision of Christ right in the middle of the Paul Féval film *La Bande des Habits noirs* (The Black-Suit Gang) in a movie theater on December 17, 1914, disconcerted his spiritual advisors: the Saviour, in a long white robe, with long wavy black hair, was shielding the children of Max's concierge, whom the poet had just recently reconciled with their mother!

Despite all that, on January 7, he was able to write Apollinaire, in artillery training at Nîmes: "On January 20, Pablo will be my godfather and Sylvette Filacier of the Théâtre des Variétés my godmother, God willing."

Picasso wanted his godson to add the new name of Fiacre but, this saint being the patron of French cabdrivers, it upset Max, who thought Pablo was not taking his baptism seriously. They compromised on Cyprien, also one of Pablo's Christian names, and the oft-postponed christening finally took place February 18, 1915, at the chapel in Notre-Dame-de-Sion monastery, on Rue Notre-Dame-des-Champs. The Fathers of Zion, whose house this was, were an order founded by the brothers Ratisbonne, converts who hoped to lead other Jews to Christ.

Picasso inscribed a copy of *The Imitation of Jesus Christ,* "To my brother Cyprien Max Jacob. Souvenir of his baptism, Thursday, February 18, 1915."

His new faith did not change Max's habits: scarcely purified by the baptismal waters, he was back to his usual tricks in Montmartre, then climbing to the Sacré-Coeur in the middle of the night to ask pardon for his sins.

Picasso was going through a period of bitter solitude. Éva, who was tubercular, thought her lover was not aware of her condition, and made up to hide her pallor, for she knew how he detested illness, and was afraid he might leave her.

In fact, he may have actually considered doing so—in order to join the Foreign Legion, but his aversion to uniforms and his deep-rooted pacifism finally won out.

In the fog of that first winter of the war, the thousand stone crosses and small chapels of Cimetière Montparnasse obsessed the lovers. They tried to avoid looking out, spent evenings in cafés; but the uniformed men, often just back from the front, stared disagreeably at the sturdy "slacker" with the pretty woman. Pablo was embarrassed and preferred to stay home for weeks on end, painting.

Derain, Braque, Léger were in the service, and Matisse, not subject to draft, was trying to get some collectors together to help Gris, without resources since Kahnweiler left. Apollinaire, still in the rear at Nîmes, was teaching modern art to his barracks mates, and writing poetry. In January 1915 Max Jacob wrote him that Pablo was doing a pencil portrait that looked like "my grandfather, an old Catalan peasant, and my mother, all at the same time."

A young Russian writer, Ilya Ehrenburg, who met Picasso at this time was invited to his studio. The mess in the huge room amazed him, "everywhere canvases, sheets of cardboard, tin, wires, and pieces of wood." Heaps of tubes of color were in one corner, and as Ehrenburg wondered at so lavish an abundance, his host told him that having once been short of money for supplies he now made it a habit to stock up "for life."

The collection of tin intrigued the visitor: Picasso was fascinated by the material, but had not figured out how to use it. On the walls, the young Russian saw Negro sculptures, and a Douanier Rousseau painting bought from Vollard, showing *Delegates of the Foreign Powers Coming to Salute the Republic as a Sign of Peace.*

"If Black sculptors changed the proportions of bodies, heads, and arms," Picasso told him, "it was not because they didn't see them right, nor because they didn't know their craft, but because they had a different concept of proportions, just as the Japanese had a different notion of perspective." And he added, "Do you think Rousseau never saw the classics? He often went to the Louvre, but he was trying to do something else."

They would go to the Rotonde together, and Picasso's changes of mood sometimes irritated his friends; he could be silent or garrulous, worried or boastful, all in a kind of Franco-Castilian hodgepodge, which he peppered with Catalan if anyone present was from there or understood the tongue of his youth and his first painting years.

He cared about the war only insofar as it affected his friends, he said. In the papers, he read only the funnies and gossip, until the outbreak of the Russian Revolution, when he suddenly grew passionately—unexpectedly—interested in the people overthrowing the Czarist régime. He was thinking of the anarchist riots, the bombs in Barcelona, and the *pronunciamientos;* to celebrate the victory over oppression he gave Ehrenburg a painting when the latter headed back to Moscow.

On May 11, 1915, Braque was seriously wounded at Carency on the Artois front; he went from hospital to hospital for skull surgery and never, Salmon said, heard a word from Pablo. They met again only two years later when Braque was invalided out. At their first meeting, Picasso could not contain his joy at seeing Braque: such displays occurred only when he could directly impart his warmth and spontaneity to their object.

Pablo took up with a fellow Spaniard, the sculptor Pablo Gargallo, whom he often visited in his studio to talk about Barcelona and old times. A photo taken there shows the painter in unusual garb, dignified dark suit, starched collar, and black tie, while his eye magnetizes the viewer with almost unbearable intensity. In other photos of the period, usually taken at Rue Schoelcher, Pablo is always informal in the extreme—unpressed clothing, cap, pants stained with paint, or shorts.

Seated Character, redone several times in watercolor or gouache, *Harlequin, Still Life in a Landscape, Man with the Pipe* go back to Cubist formulations but with new procedures. Perhaps by way of reaction against the awful events of 1915, war, weariness, Eva's worrisome illness, Picasso headed more and more toward a decorative style, the colorful attractiveness of which was related to the prewar pictures only by the geometrical structuring. He seemed to be doing pastiches of himself. But it is mainly in small watercolors or gouaches that he gets away from his worries. Working less nowadays, doing no more of the experimenting of the early fertile years, without the sounding board of Braque, he seemed to have lost some of his creative vitality. In a few months he was to find a new outlet—in the theater.

That summer he did not leave Paris, less because of the war than because Éva was seriously ill. Terrified of catching her disease, he nevertheless could not bear to send her to the hospital, so he spent as much time out as he could. Salmon believes he went up to the Bateau-Lavoir and worked in the studio he kept there as a storeroom. This was one of his most dramatically difficult periods.

The pencil portrait he did in August of Ambroise Vollard seated contrasted with the geometrical decompositions of other figures of the period by its fine-honed realism. Such works as this make the admirers of his naturalistic mastery deplore his affair with Cubism; to him, it was another problem entirely, one of language, not style: the method employed mattered much less than what it said.

Éva got worse and finally had to be hospitalized. Pablo had hoped to get her in somewhere in the neighborhood, where he might see her often, but finally had to have her admitted to a clinic across town in Auteuil, 57 Avenue de Montmorency. There was no longer any question about the outcome; Picasso was heartbroken, but her departure from home reduced the danger of contagion.

In December 1915, the composer Edgar Varèse, who, on the eighteenth, was to sail for America, brought a voluble, bubbly young man to the studio. At twenty-six he already knew "everyone who was anyone" in Paris, was an intimate of Edmond Rostand and André Gide, Maurice Barrès and Erik Satie, Jacques-Émile Blanche and Picabia, Empress Eugénie and Misia Sert, and was named Jean Cocteau. He had long been anxious to meet the painter whose Cubism got to him with its uncompromising authority. A young woman painter, Valentine Grosz, acting as his mentor in avant-garde art, had introduced him on various occasions at the Dôme or Rotonde to Derain, André Lhote, Gleizes, Roger de

Jean Cocteau, sleepwalking, at the villa of his friends
Charles and Marie-Laure de Noailles in Hyères

La Fresnaye, Kisling, and Juan Gris, but since 1912 he had been associating mainly with several of those represented in the Salon of the Golden Section, where he made his real discovery of the new painting.

Not without surprise, as he went up the stairs, Jean noted the huge molding on the wall of a Parthenon frieze; the severe Cubist constructions were a different mythology, temples of new deities called rigor and harmony. Over forty years later, he was to tell me (December 1960):

"I have never forgotten Picasso's studio because the whole height of its prow-like bay window looked out on the Montparnasse cemetery. . . .

"Picasso and I eyed each other for quite a while. I admired his intelligence, and clung to everything he said, for he spoke little; I kept still so as not to miss a word. There were long silences and Varèse could not understand why we stared wordlessly at each other. In talking, Picasso used a visual syntax, and you could immediately *see* what he was saying. He liked formulas and summed himself up in his statements as he summed himself up and sculpted himself in objects that he immediately made tangible.

"He told us he was very much in love with a young woman who was about to die."

Cocteau, usually so talkative, listened almost silently to the little man "with charming hands and feet, terrific eyes that bored out and in." Later he would write that "intelligence squirts from him as water from the nozzle of a hose." His accent made some words and sentence endings sing, while he stumbled over others and slurred them. To the accompaniment of this verbal music Jean looked from the Andalusian to his paintings, from the paintings out to the tombstones— a disorderly mob of crosses, columns, chapels, statues. The constant nearness of death under the eye of one so horrified by it, because like any Spaniard he was haunted by it, had something obsessive, almost unreal about it. Cocteau noted that the work in progress was a Harlequin.

Two or three months later, disguised as Harlequin under his tired trench coat, he returned to see Picasso, in the hope that the flattered painter would do a portrait of him. He also figured that the sittings would let him get to know Pablo better. He once told me, off the cuff, "Picasso was more than a prodigy, he was a miracle, giving life to everything he touched. Picasso and Braque were the great males of the painting of that fabulous period. Cubism to painting was what Stravinsky was to music . . . coming after a feminine era whose charm had to be undone."

"And what did you get from meeting Picasso?" I asked.

"A discharge of electricity . . ."

The painter, however, did not do that portrait, although he accepted the harlequin costume as a gift, and used it later.

Jean understood the prodigious contained power within this fascinating Malagueño. With his own sense of the present, though he took only a superficial interest in Cubism, he divined that here was the language of the future. He was wrong, for Cubism by the end of 1915 had already passed its peak; but he was to aid Picasso in transforming the intellectual vocabulary of his paintings into a more readable style, more readily accessible to taste and fashion, so as to go from the public of laborious though friendly exegeticists to that of snobs, from Bohemians to society women. From Kahnweiler's narrow shop to the international stage.

Pablo had reached what he set out to do, and was now ready and willing to have the know-how of his new promoter make the most of him—joining in his cartwheels, illustrating his puns, and deliberately going in for brilliance, virtuosity, and facility. What he would not have done for anyone five years earlier, he now would do for this "frivolous prince" who, with his quick intelligence, seemed the one who could open the doors that the uncompromising austerity of Cubism had maintained shut against him; Cocteau was the bridge over seven years of asceticism, to a new shore to conquer.

Loneliness contributed greatly to this new turn of Picasso's. From 1907 to 1914, Cubism had been teamwork; with the members of the team scattered, he was at a loss. When he did his first realistic drawings in Spring 1914, Pablo had said to Kahnweiler, "Say, that's better than before, isn't it?" Meaning better than before the Cubist period, of course, for, whatever he might say, he was always nostalgic about "sentiment."

Until war broke out, Jean Cocteau had been the spoiled child of a social-homosexual clique who, from Maurice Rostand to Reynaldo Hahn, from Anna de Noailles to Misia Sert, Robert de Montesquiou to Stravinsky, contributed to one of the great star attractions of the era: Serge Diaghilev's Ballets Russes. Their première of Stravinsky's *Rite of Spring* on May 29, 1913, had been a huge sensation, comparable to the Cubist rooms at the Salon des Indépendants two months before. Yet the protesters were not the same. How come, Cocteau wondered, those who damned the *Rite* were not the enemies of Cubism, and vice versa? In both cases, after all, the challenge was the same: modernity. There must then be two audiences, quite unaware of each other, although there was only a single scandal!

Cocteau was to write:

> A dictatorship existed in Montmartre and Montparnasse. Those objects that could fit on a table top, such as a Spanish guitar, were the only allowable pleasures. To paint a setting, especially for the Ballets Russes (this devout younger generation knew nothing of Stravinsky), was simply a crime.

To bring the two avant-gardes, musical and pictorial, together, to combine Bakst's Oriental ostentations, his symbolic effects, his "Fauve" luxuriances with Cubist austerity, to mix the two opposite audiences in one single front of scandal and modernity—there was a program for you!

Already a link between Left Bank and Right Bank, Jean Cocteau, if he could pull that off, would emerge triumphant: the mentor of modern art. And to get Picasso from the Bateau-Lavoir to the spectacular stage of the Théâtre du Châtelet, what a coup!

Éva's death on December 14, 1915, interfered for a time. But the amazing thing (or could he have been awaiting this chance?) was that Cocteau got to Picasso while Apollinaire, Salmon, and Blaise Cendrars, champions of modern art all, were away from Paris, as were Braque, Léger, and Derain. "The city was almost empty, ripe for taking, and we took it," he would later write. A confession worth remembering.

Once Cocteau had finally grabbed off Picasso, he also needed the goodwill of his friends and defenders, so he assiduously frequented the Flore with Apollinaire (seriously wounded in March 1916 and ostentatiously wearing a leather bandage around his head), or the Rotonde in Montparnasse with Salmon, Cendrars, Pierre Reverdy, or Max Jacob. How could any of them resist this devoted, faithful, and ever-obliging friend? Even if he did help himself to their output. For they were unknowns who needed a socially acceptable impresario to move them outside the limited world of cafés, city rooms, and studios.

Maurice Sachs was to write, in *Le Sabbat*:

> Neither Apollinaire, Max Jacob, nor Picasso was pleased by the arrival of this society poet. But the interests that at first had seemed opposed were not deeply so. . . . Cocteau was offered the key to a new vocabulary, . . . introduced to the secret of these tough, fortuneless men, greater and more poetic actually than he, and he was permitted to make use of their common fund, provided he popularized it and made the public he so wonderfully knew how to speak to aware of this unknown treasure, which someone, after all, had to capitalize on so that their community might live. . . .

Picasso's entry into the theater had other reasons than Cocteau's persuasive charm; beyond his own desire for a change, there was his curiosity about a new milieu and his taste for teamwork. He had no dealer since Kahnweiler's departure and, with his obsessional fear of being without money and falling back into the penniless state of his beginnings, accepted, albeit not without great hesitations, a work he thought would be remunerative.

There was in fact a new dealer interested in the Cubists, Léonce Rosenberg, who had taken over after Kahnweiler and allowed them to have a respectable existence in a Paris where war made artistic concerns rather secondary. But he had neither the intuitive intelligence nor the sharp business sense of the Rue Vignon diviner. However, we must admit he had real courage—for the time was not propitious, and Cubism, which many considered to be "Boche," was in rather bad odor. Léonce Rosenberg had the assistance of his brother Paul, who, in 1918, was to become Pablo's principal dealer, and, after Kahnweiler's return in 1920, remain so, in conjunction with the latter, from 1923 to 1940.

All of Picasso's friends then in Paris came to Éva's funeral, despite his own horror of burials and the whole business. Her family were stupefied at the appearance of these "artists" they did not even know, whose behavior and attire were scarcely suited to the occasion. "There were seven or eight friends at the burial," Juan Gris wrote to Maurice Raynal in the trenches, "a sad affair, and Max's jokes added immeasurably to the horror of it." According to Maurice Sachs, Max Jacob took a liking to the coachman of the hearse and invited him to pray at Éva's grave before taking off with him.

In fact, however, it was only that the trip from hospital to cemetery was very long and cold, and Max had warmed himself with a few libations along the way.

Portrait of Erik Satie   Paris 1920, artist's collection
(GIRAUDON)

When he acted indecorously, Picasso called him on it, and that was as far as it went. Pablo, who had had several months to get used to the idea of Éva's dying, was still terribly upset by it. With her he had left the Montmartre of his Bohemian youth; without her, he would leave Montparnasse, and, to the amazement of his friends, decide to move to the sad and drab southern suburb of Montrouge, where in February or March of 1916 he rented a small house with a garden in front at 22 Rue Victor-Hugo. That was to be the banal setting for this obscure period of his life.

Cocteau called the portrait Pablo was doing of him on May 1, 1916, an "Ingres" head, and Max Jacob also posed for him again in Montrouge. Often after an evening spent in a café in Montparnasse, he would walk home with Erik Satie, who lived in nearby Arcueil. They crossed endless empty suburban avenues south of the city limits and then, at their parting spot, doffed their hats, with a "Good night, Mr. Picasso," "Good night, Mr. Satie."

Gertrude Stein and Alice, recently returned from Palma de Mallorca, visited Pablo and were full of admiration for a superb pink silk counterpane. In response to Gertrude's question, Picasso said he had gotten it from a lady.

The donor, in fact, was a rather widely known Chilean lady, Eugenia Errazuriz, a beautiful eccentric who was to sponsor Pablo in "society" after his marriage. Gertrude Stein never again spoke her name, accusing her of having "stolen" Pablo from her, one of the ultimate causes of the break between Miss Stein and her "little Napoleon."

But Pablo now was again a regular at Gertrude's Saturday evenings, bringing pretty girls, as well as introducing three newcomers, Erik Satie, the Princess de Polignac, and Blaise Cendrars, who had lost his right arm to the elbow in combat on September 25, 1915.

Life went on and Pablo had resumed a fairly normal schedule, painting Cubist compositions as well as realistic figures.

Apollinaire, on leave, was cracking out of his too-tight uniform; in October 1916 he did the preface for a Derain show at Paul Guillaume's. Cocteau, after a brief stint in the marines, had been discharged; his war was over. But he was now organizing an exhibit in the studio of a Swiss painter, Émile Lejeune, on Rue Huyghens, and Pablo reluctantly agreed to be hung there.

Actually, Cendrars was the one who had discovered the huge studio and thought it would be a good place to show paintings, or give concerts and lectures; but Cocteau was the one who made it one of the haunts of Tout-Paris, his own Tout-Paris set of society-cum-culture figures. The painting show, called "Lyre and Palette," ran from November 19 to December 5, 1916, and included works by Kisling, Matisse, Modigliani, and Ortiz de Zarate, as well as Picasso. Cocteau brought society together with the Bohemian world of "sensational" painting: Anna de Noailles and Princess Murat tingled at rubbing elbows with "artists."

Then, a startling rumor in Montparnasse: Picasso was working for the Ballets Russes! Unbelievable! On a furlough in April 1915, Cocteau had heard Erik Satie give a four-handed performance with Ricardo Vinès of his *Morceaux en forme de poire* (Pear-Shaped Pieces), and got the idea of turning it into a

Gertrude Stein, friend, patron, and collector of Picasso, her "little Napoleon"

(ROGER-VIOLLET)

ballet. On leaving to report to duty, he gave the composer a whole sheaf of notes about it. Getting Pablo involved was a more delicate matter, and Jean used all his diplomacy and charm to that end. Pablo liked the idea but was reluctant to commit himself. Diaghilev came up from Rome to Paris in May to meet him; they had lunch with Cocteau and Satie. Pablo, meticulous and careful as ever, inquired about every detail of his involvement, in relation not only to the poet and composer but also to the choreographer and dancers.

At Jean's request, Pablo took Diaghilev up to see his studio and the theater-oriented Harlequins—but when the impresario saw the view of Montparnasse cemetery he was literally terrified. Being highly superstitious, he was all for calling it off, but Cocteau talked that down. Picasso wanted to remain in control of his end, without Diaghilev or anyone else interfering. During his long night walks home with Satie, he questioned him about his music; the answers led to his final acceptance. On August 24, Satie and Cocteau wired Valentine Grosz, "PICASSO DOING PARADE WITH US."

On December 31, a committee made up of Picasso, Cendrars, Reverdy, Max Jacob, Juan Gris, and Paul Dermée gave a banquet at the Palais d'Orléans, Avenue du Maine, in honor of Apollinaire and the publication of his *Poet Assassinated*. The menu listed, among other delights, "Cubist, Orphist, and Futurist hors d'oeuvres." The first appearance of modern art in the potboiling department.

Cubism took Pablo away from the representation of stage folk, but he was still fascinated by all kinds of shows: in April 1913, he and his friends often went from Céret to catch the bullfights, and Max Jacob wrote Kahnweiler about a carnival circus they had attended, with "equestriennes who don't get familiar because they are respectable married mothers and mustachioed clowns who seem to be made up for Cubist studio farce."

Cocteau would later write, "My responsibility was Picasso as theatrical designer. Those around him could not believe he would follow my lead. . . . My dream, in music, would be to hear Picasso's guitars."

He was the more fascinated by Picasso, because he found him hard to encompass. Pablo full well realized the poet was using him as a springboard toward the avant-garde he wanted to be part of. "One day I was walking in Rome with Picasso," Cocteau told me, "and I dared speak to him about Cubism. 'You understand,' he said, 'a painter walks around with a tape measure. He measures objects, transfers them to canvas, and then does the best he can with them.' That's all he ever told me on the subject."

Picasso distrusted Cocteau even more than he did Apollinaire. Jean, the "faller into step," as one of his friends was cruelly to characterize him, helped him break out of pure hard Cubist discipline, founded on a mental analysis of reality, and get into the visual illusionism of the theater.

A young gypsy-looking southerner, Pierre Reverdy, arrived in Paris in 1910, aged twenty-one. A few months later, at Max Jacob's, he met Juan Gris, and then Picasso, Braque, the sculptor Henri Laurens, André Level, Maurice Raynal, Gargallo, and others. He moved into the Bateau-Lavoir. On March 15, 1917, he brought out the first issue of a magazine, *Nord-Sud,* in which he wrote the first clear, lucid exegesis of the new painting, "On Cubism." It was a sensation. His admiration for Pablo grew as he got to know him better. "Any painter who speaks ill of Picasso is a fake!" he was to say in an exalted moment. The book he did on him in 1924 was a pivotal work.

Diaghilev's ballets till then had been very Russian, largely because of Bakst's flowery, baroque Orientalism in design, and their brilliant colors. But, as one of the first to make French painting known in Russia, Diaghilev was not averse to the Ballets changing. Scandals did not scare him. After all, were they not the vehicle through which the public had come to know modern art? That was why he had commissioned ballets from Stravinsky, Debussy, and Maurice Ravel, who were among the most controversial of the avant-garde composers. In 1912, he had also staged *The Blue God,* a Cocteau–Reynaldo Hahn ballet based on an Indian legend, and he had commissioned the poet to do *David,* which was to be a circus ballet. But, it never materialized.

Changes in Diaghilev's troupe, as a result of a number of dancers leaving, brought to the fore the handsome Leonid Massine, Serge's current flame, whom he wanted to star. For sets and costumes, he had taken on a young Muscovite painter, Larionov, and, hoping to rejuvenate his performances with a scandal like the one created by *The Rite of Spring,* he was negotiating with musicians, artists, and writers who might bring in that new idea. In Diaghilev's eyes, one thing took precedence over all others: to be ahead of the times. *Parade* was the finest opportunity for this.

While Picasso and Satie had known each other for a long time, he and Cocteau now became inseparable, working together as they were virtually daily. Cocteau never stopped lauding the Malagueño's "genius," but he soon realized he was not a compromiser, and that, once his mind was made up, there was no point in arguing. Pablo was quietly modifying *Parade,* to Satie's delight, even though he knew his friend Cocteau would disapprove of his siding with the painter.

"If you only knew how sad I am," he wrote Valentine Grosz on September 14. *"Parade* is being changed for *the better behind Cocteau's back!* Picasso has ideas I like better than our Jean's. What a tragedy! And I am 'for' Picasso! And Cocteau does not know it! What to do? Picasso tells me to go on working from Jean's script, while Picasso works on a script of his own . . . which will be dazzling! Prodigious! I am going crazy and sad! What to do? Knowing Picasso's fine ideas, I am heartbroken to be *forced* to follow good Jean's, which are less good—oh! yes, less good! What to do! What to do!"

The next day, he wrote Cocteau, "Picasso has some strange new ideas for *Parade.* He is wonderful." Jean, who considered the ballet his very own creation, was highly displeased, but he had to go along with Pablo's "wonderful" ideas. The easiest way was to make them his own. And a week later Satie was writing Valentine with relief, "It's all fixed. Cocteau knows all. He and Picasso got together on it. What luck!"

Picasso immediately felt at home in the ballet, about saltimbanques, clowns, dancing girls, and wanted to make a *true* picture of it, without phony sentimentality; Cocteau's "literary" inventions bothered him. *Parade* (literally, "display") is a street scene, such as might be seen anywhere that a carnival or street fair is set up, on the sidewalk level. Acrobats, the little American girl, the Chinese magician in turn all give a taste of their acts while the "managers" carry on their noisy spiels, urging passersby to buy a ticket and come inside.

In his desire to be true to the people, Picasso got the noisy sound effects, which he considered out of place, dropped, as well as the anonymous voice, scheduled to come out of "a loudspeaking hole" and be "a theatrical imitation of the carnival gramophone, a modern version of the antique mask," as Cocteau described it. He also got the poet to reconsider the role of the "managers."

There were three of them, an American, a Parisian, and a sort of Negro mannequin on a yellow horse, hidden behind an amazing concoction of painted and decorated wood and cardboard, intended to dehumanize them. Cocteau called them "human sets . . . Picasso portraits come to life"; and for the painter they were indeed the concrete application of Cubist methods, *tableaux vivants,* living pictures, in the most literal sense.

Pablo's costumes for the Chinese prestidigitator (red, yellow, black, and white, all in hatchings, rays, and spirals), the acrobats out of the Rose Period with blue flames on their tights, and the little American girl in her "sailor suit," were in contrast to the Cubist constructions of the managers. The latter were in equal contrast to the huge popular imagery of the drop curtain. Picasso was supposed to be so insolently aggressive an innovator that Bakst found the curtain, with its naturalism, shockingly "old hat."

In February, before going to Rome to join Diaghilev, Picasso introduced Cocteau to Gertrude Stein, whom he did not know. Picasso did not object to going to Rome and they left on February 17. Nothing seemed more foreign to his tastes and concerns than choreography and ballet companies, nothing less interesting to him than antiquity and museum cities. But, scrupulous to a fault, he wanted to be sure Diaghilev understood and was in agreement with every one of his ideas. Gertrude Stein herself noted, "He was very lively at the prospect of going to Rome."

A mild Roman spring spread its tender rose and mauve over the ruins of palaces and tombs. Cocteau was later to write:

> We did *Parade* in a Roman cellar called Cave Taglioni, where the company rehearsed. We went for moonlight walks with the dancing girls, and visited Naples and Pompeii. We met the lusty Futurists.

But in point of fact he was much more interested in the dancing boys, especially the young Slav god Leonid Massine, and delighted in the daily letters he received from a young St.-Cyr cadet, the poet Jean Le Roy, who wrote him fervent missives. The "lusty Futurists" were very happy to see Picasso again, to show him Rome and tell him all the gossip; Marinetti put himself out for him, dragged him to museum after museum, unable to understand why Pablo yawned at his discourses. Between Futurism and Cubism, there were differences of view that no amount of mutual explanation could overcome, even in the shadow of Raphael or Leonardo. They rather talked about their friend Boccioni, the only Futurist whose talent Picasso had truly admired, killed a few months earlier, and offered their French colleague any help they could give in his new job.

On a photograph of the Sistine Chapel's *Last Judgment,* Pablo's finger followed the contour of a figure. "What a pleasure it is to run a finger along this line! . . . Raphael is the full sky, what serenity in his lines, what domination! Da Vinci did not invent aviation, Raphael did!"

With his agile stroke, Cocteau drew a profile of Pablo with a pipe in his mouth, round eyes under his overhanging lock, and sent it to Apollinaire. In his Via Margutta studio as well as his room at the Hôtel de Russie, Picasso piled up sketches for sets and costumes of *Parade,* weighing his various studies for the drop curtain.

On Easter Sunday, he did a drawing of Cocteau. A strange lead-pencil view of him, in a dressing gown of long vertical and slanted folds, reminiscent of the rhythms of synthetic Cubism and the pasted papers, it is a transitional work between the Cubist drawings and the so-called Ingresque Period, a designation Cocteau disputed for this drawing, "the first in a significant new Picasso manner," as he put it. The hieratic pose, Pisanellian profile, lack of light and shading give a timeless accent to the effigy, drawn, according to Cocteau, "as the bells were coming in."

Picasso also did several drawings of dancing girls and some of his friends, as well as startling caricatures, full of caustic bite, of Diaghilev, Bakst, Massine, and Stravinsky.

> I shall never forget the studio in Rome [wrote Cocteau in his *Rappel à l'ordre*—The Recall to Order]. There was a small crate with a maquette of *Parade,* the tall buildings, the trees, the carnival stand. On a table across from the Villa Médicis, Picasso was painting the Chinese, the "managers," the American girl, the horse that made Mme. de Noailles say it seemed like a tree laughing, and the acrobats that Marcel Proust rightly compared to the Dioscuri.

Picasso drew little of Rome, preferring to concentrate on the people about him. He lived and worked in Cave Taglioni as he might have lived and worked in his Montrouge studio, unaware of his decor, his location, not to mention the colorfulness and grandeur of the Eternal City. He seems to have retained nothing, indeed seen nothing, of Florence, Naples, Pompeii, the churches, palaces, ruins, museums, of Antiquity, the Quattrocento, the Renaissance. But he did take in the hieratic antique goddesses and the sprightly, plump allegories of the baroque ceilings—as would be apparent several years later.

In the heart of the people's Rome—his hotel was on Via del Babuino, between Piazza del Popolo and Piazza di Spagna, not far from his studio—he found the movement and color of a Spanish street. The Italian capital was still a provincial city; its noisy picturesqueness delighted him, with its open-air shows, fetes, markets, terraces of the trattorias at which wandering musicians stopped to play. With his Roman friends and those of the Diaghilev company, Massine, the Swiss conductor Ernest Ansermet, Stravinsky, Bakst, he walked through the streets far into the night. Cocteau, ever sparkling, often irritating, was at home with the corps of dancing men and women, made speeches at the Forum, lectured inside the churches and museums, dissected masterpieces with little short, cutting phrases, and set up a show at the Grand Hotel of Cubist or Futurist works by friends and associates of Diaghilev: Picasso, Balla, Larionov, Gontcharova, Boccioni, Severini, and others.

Stravinsky, telling of the time in Rome with Picasso, for whom he also posed in the studio, says they spent hours on end at the Aquarium. "Both passionately interested in old Neapolitan gouaches, during our frequent walks together we made veritable raids on all the little boutiques and second-hand shops."

Together, the musician and painter also visited St. Peter's and the Sistine Chapel, later enthusiastically telling Ansermet about Michelangelo's frescoes in great detail. Pablo's companion in Florence was Alberto Magnelli, whom he knew from Paris, and who came down to Rome to help prepare *Parade*. The young painter guided him through churches, palaces, the Médicis' burial chapel, San Lorenzo, the primitive paintings, and took him to his own studio to see his latest, resolutely abstract work. Magnelli was deep in his "lyrical explosions."

In April, he scrawled a note to Gertrude Stein: "I work all day long at my sets and constructions of costumes and two paintings I have started and would like to finish before my return. . . .

"I have sixty girl dancers. I get to bed very late. I know all the Roman dances.

"I have done a lot of Pompeiian fantasies, a little on the frisky side, and caricatures of Diaghilev, Bakst, Massine, and the girls. They gave me Chinese presents that came from San Francisco. . . ."

The preparations for the ballet proceeded without a hitch: Ansermet rehearsed the orchestra, while Cocteau and Picasso discussed costumes and stage business with Massine, Diaghilev, and the performers. The curtain (now in the Paris National Museum of Modern Art) was not painted in Rome as has been generally recorded, and the photograph of Picasso squatting among his assistants on the huge composition, as it was being made up, was not taken on Via Margutta. For practical reasons, sets, costumes, and curtain were executed in Paris at a studio in the Buttes-Chaumont district. Picasso insisted on painting it himself—as the program stated—with the help of Diaghilev's three habitual Russian scenic artists, and a French specialist named Socrates. He went and selected the little American girl's costume—the only one he did not design himself—at the Parisian costume house of Williams. All the others were the results of many sketches and studies he made, and when at the last minute Massine added one acrobatic girl dancer so he could do a *pas de deux*, Picasso painted the most graceful kind of azure-blue whorls directly on her leotard.

Everyone noticed the painter's continued attentions to one of the young Russian ballerinas in the troupe, who was very pretty, if not overwhelmingly talented as a dancer. Having fallen in love, he was as usual very outgoing and made no effort to hide his feelings—which shy Olga Khoklova found a bit too demonstrative.

With the troupe scheduled to appear in mid-April in Naples and Florence,

Pablo followed after Olga, then went to Paris at the end of the month to start first full rehearsals of *Parade*. Stravinsky returned to Switzerland, and at the border station of Chiasso, the Italian customs men checking his luggage found Picasso's lead-pencil portrait of him. They asked him what it was.

"That?" the surprised composer replied. "Why, my portrait."

"That's no portrait," said one of the officials. "It's a map."

"That's right, the map of my face, but nothing else!"

But the customs men would not let the mysterious map be taken out of the country. Stravinsky had to go to the Chiasso post office and mail the portrait to Lord Berners, the British ambassador in Rome, who forwarded it by diplomatic pouch to Paris.

The spring of 1917 was a terrible one. The United States had just entered the war, but the offensive on the Chemin des Dames had failed, morale in the front lines was at a low ebb, the first mutinies were beginning to break out in the French army, and back home the "civilians" were also starting to complain: rationing was very strict and pacifist ideas gaining ground. There had been a first revolution in Russia; the Czar had abdicated, and the Petrograd Soviet was clamoring for peace; the soldiers were fraternizing with the Germans all along the Eastern Front.

This was when Diaghilev and Massine presented *Parade*, a ballet in one act by Jean Cocteau, music by Erik Satie, sets and costumes by Pablo Picasso.

IX

"MONSIEUR INGRES"
(1917–1918)

"**B**ACK TO BERLIN! DOPE FIENDS! SLACKERS! FOREIGN FREAKS!" yelled part of the audience. While others shouted back, "Idiots! Scoundrels! Boeotians!" and the Chinese magician calmly took an egg out of his queue, swallowed it, and took it back out of his shoe; he ate fire and made sparks by stamping on the ground. The little American girl made faces and danced a frenzied ragtime step in a deafening cacophony of all kinds of noises. The circus horse (with two dancers under his skin) waddled along and raised a leg. But it was the "managers" that created the worst reaction. People fought in the orchestra, and insulted each other. One dignified gentleman walked out, saying, "If I had known it was this stupid, I would have brought the children!"

Thus, on the night of May 18, 1917, the première of *Parade* at the Châtelet Theatre.

The audience was brilliant. Who was thinking of the war, and the thirty-four thousand killed in Nivelle's mad drive into the Chemin des Dames? This gala evening, with Tout-Paris on hand, was no whit less brilliant than those held in peacetime; only the uniforms of a few men on furlough and the generals in the audience recalled harsh reality. The Châtelet had been sold out two weeks in advance; Cocteau had gotten word to all of his friends and, in order to forestall any criticism, the performance was given for the benefit of the war victims in the East, through a charitable organization chaired by Countess de Chabrillan, one of the great ladies of the aristocracy. Besides, didn't war amputees deserve some entertainment from time to time? Several facing boxes were reserved for them— hostages of the avant-garde, high society, and scandal. Anything could be expected of a trio such as Satie-Cocteau-Picasso; many of those attending brought police whistles, to use in protest if provoked.

The poet was aware of all this, but could see many friends and supporters in the audience; somewhat reassured, he still found it hard to hide his nerves, and scarcely listened to Count Étienne de Beaumont, just back from St. Petersburg with a tale of six thousand people butchered in a few hours by the Bolsheviks.

Picasso seemed calmer, more in control of himself. As for Diaghilev, he was positively in seventh heaven: at the height of the war, to bring together in one audience Cécile Sorel and the widow of Alphonse Daudet, Princesse de Polignac (in nurse's uniform) and Léon-Paul Fargue, Misia Sert and Valentine Grosz, the Philippe Berthelots and the Letelliers—she gorgeous, he the powerful owner of *Le Journal*—the Étienne de Beaumonts and the Chevignés, Leon Bailby and Apollinaire, Maurice Rostand, Paul Morand, and Pierre Reverdy—this was success extraordinary.

In the beginning, everything was fine. It started with the "Marseillaise," after which everyone took his or her seat, to chat and riffle through the program, for which Apollinaire had written the introduction:

> Picasso's Cubist sets and costumes evidence the realism of his art. This realism, or this Cubism, as you will, is what has most deeply agitated the arts during the past ten years.

Cocteau called *Parade* a "realistic" ballet; so Guillaume adapted this to his pet idea of Cubism as the new realism. He went on to say that the "new alliance" among sets, costumes, and choreography, hitherto only more or less well adapted one to another, gave *"Parade* a kind of sur-realism," which might be

> the starting point for a series of manifestations of the New Spirit that will not fail to appeal to the élite, and promises to rearrange our arts and our manners from top to bottom in universal happiness.

But the élite, for the time being, had not yet gone along; it was waiting to see.

Sighs of pleasure greeted the rise of the heavy drapes to reveal Picasso's drop curtain. The huge colored picture was attractive, and the enemies of Cubism forgot their whistles as they took in the fine carnival sights the Spaniard had nostalgically accustomed them to in his Blue and Rose periods. Maybe Cubism *had* just been a bad dream and Frantz Jourdain had been right to call the war its deathblow. Starched shirts, beautiful bare shoulders, epauletted uniforms settled comfortably into their seats.

But not for long. For the music, which had started on a reassuring note as well, quickly changed. Inarticulate noises, wild sounds, a cacophony of dynamos, sirens, trains entering stations, typewriters gone crazy, was now enough to make one cover his ears. Murmuring started. People began to shout, to whistle. Then it calmed a bit, and picked up again.

The appearance of the "managers" was the real signal for tumult. Princess Eugène Murat, her neck swathed in the official colors of the destroyer which she was godmother to, stood up in horror, while Misia Sert, standing in her own loge, clapped her hands off. Massine's fans greeted each of his appearances with applause, answered by the insults of the antagonists. Countess de Chabrillan and Countess de Chevigné looked at each other, trying to determine which attitude to take: to pretend indisposition and make a dignified departure, or stay and see it through so as not to let down the war victims. They were stupefied at seeing the normally perfectly behaved society women hitting one another with fans and bawling each other out like fishwives.

"If not for Apollinaire in uniform, with his skull shaved, the scar on his temple and the bandage around his head, women would have gouged our eyes out with hairpins," as Cocteau was to put it. Diaghilev, who had hoped for a scandal to "launch" *Parade,* had more than his money's worth. The show went ahead as best it could, but ended in utter chaos. Friends and admirers invaded the dancers' dressing rooms and congratulated the authors. Jean could at last breathe easily; Picasso showed no emotion.

With the critics virtually all panning it, Marcel Proust wrote two letters to Cocteau to tell him how much he approved of the ballet, comparing the acrobats to the Dioscuri and calling the horse that "huge swan with the wild gestures." But the true scandal of *Parade* lay in the headline on a newspaper article the next day: "The Three Boches"—meaning Cocteau, Satie, and Picasso! In those patriotic-crazy days, anything hard to understand, violent, tumultuous, incongruous, had to come from the enemy, and the nadir was reached by one Guy Noël, who advised that such "revolutionary arts be reserved for Red Russia, if indeed she will accept them!" It must be noted that, at another charity performance a few weeks before, Diaghilev had raised the Bolshevik red flag during the finale of *The Firebird.*

But true lovers of modern choreography, poetry, music, and painting applauded the happy collaboration of Massine, Cocteau, Satie, and Picasso.

Juan Gris, writing to Maurice Raynal in the trenches, on May 23, said:

> Picasso's set has lots of class and it is simple. *Parade* is not naturalistic, not a fairy tale, has no excessive effects, nor dramatic subject. It's a sort of musical farce in the best of taste and without great artistic pretensions. I even think it is an attempt to do something completely new in the theater. It is a big hit.

Pablo, who stayed away from the Châtelet demonstrations, in the next few days received crank letters accusing him of desertion, treason, provocation, and worse. Montparnasse could only conclude, "He's gone back on Cubism!" A sentence of Bakst's from the program was being widely quoted: "This great painter has found another branch to his art. He is also a decorator."

Picasso's participation in theater had nothing to do with decorating. What most fascinated him in this new experience was the introduction of movement. The "managers," those human Cubist constructions pacing the dramatic development, were of great importance to him; they were quite simply the activating of the paintings he had done between 1910 and 1914. His pictures "burst into life."

Picasso was in love, and as we know he lived each new passion to the hilt. Olga Khoklova, daughter of a Russian colonel, had been born in Niezin (Ukraine) on June 17, 1891. She had had to leave home in order to devote herself to the dance, and her delayed debut with Diaghilev, at twenty-one in 1912, kept her from qualifying for leading roles; she did not really have the makings of a prima ballerina. She was a pretty girl with smooth regular features beneath bandeaued hair; her frank look and a kind of aristocratic restraint appealed to Pablo from their very first meetings. For this son of the bourgeoisie, who in art had come to pass for the prototype of iconoclasm and revolt, could see himself sharing his life only with a girl of his own social milieu.

"Be careful," warned Diaghilev, who had no such problems with his dancing boys. "With Russian girls, you have to marry them."

A few weeks after the *Parade* scandal, the Ballets Russes went to Barcelona for a series of performances, and Pablo naturally tagged along after Olga.

The Barcelona season of the Ballets Russes was to start in June. Pablo stayed at his mother's, but daily was at the Razini Pensión, where the Diaghilev troupe stayed. From one of its windows, perhaps the one in the bedroom of Olga and her roommates, he painted *The Balcony,* a kind of synthesis of the city, with the tall buildings and trees of the promenade, the cranes in the port, the Christopher Columbus monument facing the sea and the extraordinary multicolored sky made up of broad rectangular touches, a daring compromise between Pointillism and Fauvism. In the foreground, the Catalan flag with its broad vertical yellow and red stripes.

Picasso felt he had come home. In addition to seeing old friends again, he was delighted to show them and the town to his new love and the whole ballet troupe. He wanted the dancers to see the truculently lower-class local cabaret life, as real in its way as their theater world was artificial.

The austerity of Cubism was far behind. "Picasso still does good things, when he finds time, between a Russian ballet and a society portrait," Juan Gris wrote to Kahnweiler. Being in the theater had kept Pablo away from many of his Parisian friends. As Max Jacob wrote the couturier-patron Jacques Doucet on January 11, 1917:

> I have not written anything about Picasso. He hates to have things written about him. He hates incomprehension and indiscretion, and I have so much respect and gratitude toward him that I could not do anything that might displease him. Some of his friends have made a living off his name with gossip, stories, and fabrications. . . . Perhaps . . . later on . . . we'll see . . . but much later and, in fact, I rather think never. Our mutual memories are something very sweet, very sacred, and often so sad. . . .
>
> In all frankness, I must say I don't want posterity to remember me as "Picasso's friend," and I fear that a book about him, necessarily more widely accepted than the others, might reduce me to that in the general public's mind.

On June 24, at the Théâtre Renée Maubel in Montmartre, Apollinaire's *Les Mamelles de Tirésias* premiered, and the program, with a cover drawing by Picasso, was in itself a manifesto. The performance was noisy as could be and the press as verbose, if not so bitter, as for *Parade,* about what it called "a Cubist play." The Cubist epigones now did what they had not dared do against Pablo.

Over the signatures of André Lhote, Juan Gris, Lipchitz, Kisling, Severini, Diego Rivera, Hayden, and Metzinger (who, with Gris, had been the likely initiator of it—although it was said Blaise Cendrars might also have a hand in it), they protested to the press "against the unfortunate connection being created between our works and certain literary and theatrical fantasies that it is not for us to judge." *

Letting the Ballets go on to Madrid alone for their engagement, Pablo stayed in Barcelona and worked. Either in the virtually uninhabited old family apartment on Calle de la Merced, or in the studio of another Malagueño painter, Rafael Padilla. He returned to the haunts of his youth with some of the friends of that time, Angel Fernández de Soto, Manuel Pallarés, the Junyer-Vidal brothers, and Reventos. He liked old places and familiar faces, and when any restaurant or brothel they had once gone to closed down he was furious. On the other hand, he could work anywhere, quickly arranging the usual mess around him, by way of protection or refuge.

Pablo just went on switching, as he saw fit, from Cubism to realism, and back. The geometric stylization of the *Woman with a Fan* has as a pendant a series of drawings of women, resting on their elbows, sitting in armchairs, lying down, and heads of girls or women, nimbly and lightly drawn. Olga was often the model, on the balcony of the Razini Pensión, with the view on the Columbus monument, in her bedroom, or in his studio, and they were all done with the same dancing touch, catching the essential with unnerving virtuosity, not unlike that of Matisse.

Woman in an Armchair (in the Barcelona Picasso Museum, where it is titled *Character*) breaks with the graceful display. What he had built, Pablo was now suddenly undoing, or rather composing anew from another viewpoint, more mental than visual; and we have an envelopment of concentric circles strangling or amplifying one another, in blue tones, around a strange human ideogram with features barely indicated. The armchair is recognizable, espousing and directing the orientation of the formal construction that it melts into.

The canvases done in Barcelona, June–November, 1917, mark the appearance of a decorative Cubism which Picasso hagiographers have tried variously to explain away. Actually, it seems quite simply due to his desire neither to disappoint nor to shock Olga. The young ballerina had little artistic culture and knew nothing of the experimental years of Cubism; she had never seen *Les Demoiselles d'Avignon* or perhaps even heard of it, and was totally unaware of the past career of her lover, whom she knew only as the prestigious designer of the Ballets.

New girl, new style: as against the youthful frenzy with which he had disjointed Fernande's face, his lovingly precise likeness of Olga under her mantilla was made to please her mightily with elegantly masterful photographic academicism. The work he now did was intended to prepare her for the disconcerting and challenging world of the Cubists. When she finally got to know Pablo's earlier work, she always hated it, along with that part of his life.

His behavior matched his pictorial modifications. Now he was the dandy, taking out his young fiancée in the familiar haunts of Barcelona. Dark suit, bow

* The protest was not especially aimed at Apollinaire, but mainly at Serge Férat, who had done the sets; his Johnny-come-lately "Cubism," as well as his fortune and social connections, had rubbed the painters the wrong way. Apollinaire defended him in his answer to Gris on June 28, in which he attacked "the bunch of punks who have invaded Cubism," the very ones that, a short time before, he had been glorifying.

tie, white pocket handkerchief, watch chain, straw hat, and cane: Sabartés, looking at a photo of him at this time, was later to exclaim, "Unbelievable, how carefully he dressed!"

The worldwide fame of the Diaghilev Ballets did more to spread Picasso's name than did his paintings; but his return to the city of his debut with the prestige of the troupe lent him extraordinary glamour there. He, who had left for Paris poor and unknown, came back rich and famous, a designer, engaged to a delightful ballerina, under the auspices of an important impresario. Doña Maria felt her confidence in her son had not been misplaced.

Ansermet one evening overheard Pablo, looking at himself in the mirror in dinner jacket about to leave for the theater, mutter: "Monsieur Ingres." He was given a dinner on July 12 by the painters, writers, poets, musicians, and art lovers of Barcelona. There were speeches, and Iturrino, whose paintings had hung with his at Vollard's, proposed the toast. They sang the "Marseillaise" and "Els Segadors," and *La Publicidad* covered it at length in a story headed "Picasso Banquet."

After Spain, the Ballets Russes were to go to South America. Olga resigned and stayed in Barcelona with Picasso. Ansermet said she and he merely showed up at dockside to wave good-bye to the troupe, whom they welcomed on their return, in October. She and Pablo had stayed in Barcelona all summer, and now the Ballets Russes performed again November 5–18. On November 10, a single performance of *Parade* was given, a sensational local event, since it was the only ballet that had Picasso's name attached to it.

It was a total flop. *La Vanguardia* thought that "if it's a joke, it has been carried too far and is in bad taste. We might ask France to extradite the painter, since he is a Spaniard." *El Diluvio,* saying "setting, characters, and music are all Cubist," added, "Imagine! Even the music is measured in cubes!" *La Publicidad* took a whole page to slate it. The effect was one of outrage and consternation: too bad Pablo had been misled by Paris influences to take part in such a hoax! But the article calling for his extradition seemed too much: his friends protested, and *El Poble Catalán,* despite its reservations about the show itself, felt it was "in abominable taste" to express such vehemence against "the greatest painter Spain has had since Goya."

At the *Parade* performance, Pablo's sister Lola and her husband, Dr. Vilato, introduced to him a young friend of theirs, a former student at La Lonja. Twenty years old, he had a good round head, a sparkling eye, and was called Joan Miró. He was very excited at meeting the man all Barcelona considered Spanish painting's most eminent representative in Paris.

"I thought he would ask to see my work," Miró told me, "but he barely spoke. When I told him I had been born right off the Calle des Escudillers Blancs, where he had his studio, he said, yes, it was a good street. . . ."

In 1913, Gargallo had sculpted a very expressive caricatural mask of Pablo, his face wrinkled with a big smile that deepened the features and lighted the eyes with delight beneath the lock of hair across the forehead. With similar ones of Nonell, Reventos, and Gargallo himself, these are in a very modernist setting on the facade of the Bosc Theatre (today a movie house), on Rambla del Prat, symbolizing tragedy, drama, comedy, and farce, the last being Picasso. Showing that he had not been considered especially dour by his fellow Catalans.

On its return, the troupe had gone back to the Razini Pensión, where Olga, for appearances' sake, had stayed; it was just around the corner from Calle de la Merced. A few days after the *Parade* debacle, she and Pablo left for Montrouge, which he found had been flooded in his absence, with several paintings damaged. But, from the moment he took up with Olga, he had known he would be moving. He asked his dealer Paul Rosenberg to take care of it, as Kahnweiler had done before.

Olga was not impressed by the modest house in Montrouge, its sparse furnishing, or the mess in which her lover lived. She was anxious to move to a more "suitable" neighborhood, in keeping with Picasso's reputation. To her a successful artist was a gentleman, and she intended to have a salon, a carriage, and a social life. She agreed to camp out at Montrouge for a short time, only if she could have a maid and other amenities.

Now face to face with Cubism, she found it frightening. Many of the paintings were still rolled up or under seal with the seized Kahnweiler collection, but Picasso was never one to explain, much less try to justify himself or talk about his past. He just carried on with his Barcelonese variations, finished a few works he had started on Rue Schoelcher, did a surprising Pointillist copy of the Le Nains' *Peasants' Meal,* in which the mosaic at times dissolves into abstract spaces, painted several Cubist still lifes with guitar, glass, and fruit dish, as well as some realistic ones, a *Woman Seated, Harlequin, Cakes,* and so on. He also did some amazing "wire" silhouettes of his dogs, chickens, and barnyard rooster.

In a quick sketch done December 9, 1917, Picasso showed himself at the dining table in Montrouge, with his two big dogs beside him. Happy Olga smiles at him across the table, as the maid, behind her, does the serving—a truly reassuring image of bourgeois tranquillity.

For Christmas, Pablo gave his fiancée a charming snow scene of their suburban house akin to the naïve imagery of her native Russia, with stars and snowflakes enlivening the nice synthesis of naturalism and Cubist geometry. A photograph from Spring 1918 that Boris Kochno has shows the elegantly dressed young woman, in a large dress with broad horizontal stripes and a bonnet hat, sitting next to an unkempt Picasso in his usual studio mess. The "slumming" belle is in striking contrast with the artist, and his surroundings, broken-down camp bed, old torn curtains, dirty rags hanging from shelves full of odds and ends, trash bins filled to overflowing.

In April or May, they moved out of Montrouge into the Hôtel Lutétia, at the Sèvres-Babylone intersection of Boulevard Raspail, an enormous hunk of pastry then *the* fashionable first-class hotel of the Left Bank. Apartments being hard to come by in this final year of the war, Pablo here had a large studio with privacy for working, and Olga lodgings for entertaining as befitted their social station. The Montrouge cottage was retained only as a warehouse—and occasional retreat.

The bedroom looked out on the noisy traffic intersection. It was a nondescript neighborhood, but fortunately situated halfway between the painters' haunts of Montparnasse and St.-Germain-des-Prés, the bailiwick of Apollinaire. On January 1, 1918, the poet was taken with serious pulmonary congestion and had to be rushed to the annex of the Val-de-Grâce military hospital, Villa Molière. Disgusted with the Cubists' attitude after the production of his play, he stopped campaigning for any but the best of them: his preface to the Picasso-Matisse exhibition at the Galerie Paul Guillaume was a double paean to the glory of modern painting. The painters of *Les Demoiselles d'Avignon* and *Joie de vivre* were thus conjoined, though they did not fraternize.

From Barcelona, Pablo had sent a small painting of a guitar and a photo of Olga to Gertrude Stein, in the South of France with Alice B. Toklas, nursing wounded Americans. In the accompanying letter, he informed them of his coming marriage. A few months later, back in Paris, Alice decided to use the painting as a tapestry design and asked him how to have it traced. Instead of tracing it, he duplicated the subject on her canvas. Much later, in 1929–1930, Gertrude asked him to trace some other embroidery designs for Alice: he did arabesques on a gray ground circling around some bright-colored spots; these were still to be seen on the backs of two small Louis XV armchairs in her Rue Christine apartment after Gertrude Stein's death.

Pablo was not seeing too many of his old friends, a number of whom, exempted or discharged, preferred the Midi to Paris under the bombings of Big Bertha. The painter's "transformation" (the word used by Ansermet) shocked and disappointed them, and his new life at the Lutétia and in the social whirl with Olga, who abhorred "Bohemianism," set him aside from all but Apollinaire. He too was engaged now and had changed his way of life, but not so drastically as Pablo, for his means were more limited.

After dining out, Pablo often got an urge to go to Montrouge and paint, to the great surprise of Olga, anxious to get home to bed. One night when he had followed the bombing of Paris from his suburban retreat, having no fresh canvas at hand, he grabbed a Modigliani portrait of a young boy and covered it with a still life in full impasto.

Theater and Italy came together in him in an influence akin to the *commedia dell'arte.* Immediately on his return from Barcelona, in Montrouge he drew a *Sitting Pierrot* dressed in a flowing costume and wearing a soft felt hat, which he used for the etching he had promised Max Jacob as illustration for his *Phanérogame* (written in 1905), the story of a man "who flew by flapping his thighs." The *Pierrot* reappeared the next year as a painting (now in the Museum of Modern Art, New York), the traditional comedy character, sad and disillusioned, his mask in his hand, in the purplish glare of the footlights.

But mainly he painted Olga. The most subtly seductive resources of his naturalism expressed her suave beauty with its perfectly expressionless serenity. He made picture after picture of her without ever using them as experimental laboratories for his curiosity and skill, as he had done with Fernande.

On July 12, 1918, at the Russian Orthodox church in Rue Daru, Picasso married Olga Khoklova in a long, complicated ceremony, dripping with gold, incense, and tapers, to the tune of traditional nostalgic chanting. She had specifically requested the religious ceremony in her church; the civil marriage (required by French law) was performed by the mayor of the Sixth Arrondissement, since the bride's legal residence was at the Lutétia, in that district. No one from either family attended; the official witnesses were Jean Cocteau, Guillaume Apollinaire, and Max Jacob.

Two months earlier, on May 2, the painter had stood up as witness, along with Vollard, for the marriage of Apollinaire to a respectable young lady, Jacqueline Kolb, his "adorable redhead." After all their footloose, fancy-free years, both of them were now "settling down," Pablo at thirty-seven, Guillaume at thirty-eight.

When Max Jacob's *Phanérogame* appeared, Pablo was amazed to find himself in it, one of a series of postcards, with "eyes to the heavens," along with Rimbaud, Lamartine, and Rodin. As for poor Max, he fared no better with Olga than he had with Fernande. Associating him with the Bohemian days, she frowned on his presence, accused him of the blackest deeds, and even went so far as to tear up letters of his—especially if they mentioned Mlle. Olivier. Pablo just saw him on the outside.

The newlyweds spent their honeymoon at Mme. Errazuriz' beautiful villa at Biarritz; the donor of the red silk counterpane in Montrouge was now to complete the social transformation of the onetime Bateau-Lavoir tenant. From Switzerland, a concerned and curious Kahnweiler wrote letters inquiring about all the new events in Pablo's life, only to receive greatly delayed and confused replies.

"From 1907 to 1914, there had been teamwork," as Kahnweiler explained it to me. "The absence of Braque left Picasso much disoriented; had Braque been there he probably would have advised him against working for Diaghilev (although he himself also did at a later date). Cocteau was very dangerous, for he saw everything from a society viewpoint. He took advantage of Picasso being alone to grab hold of him. . . ."

"Were you seeing the pictures Picasso did between 1915 and 1918?"

"No, but I heard about them. I saw a few photographs. I was very worried. I could imagine the change that was taking place, for just before the war he had evidenced a desire to return to classicism. It was when he did two *classicist* drawings of a seated man that he said to me, 'That's better than it used to be, isn't it?' But I never thought it would extend to his painting."

"Do you believe Olga influenced this change?"

"Absolutely." But Kahnweiler would not go beyond that.

Biarritz, physically removed from the war, was a fashionable resort. Exiled rulers, Slavic princes, rich Spaniards had strange Byzantine, Renaissance, or baroque palaces there. Before the broad beach, a "Moorish" gambling casino arched its back. In the surrounding piney woods near the lakes, magnificent Basque villas evidenced the survival of local custom despite modern eclecticism; Mme. Errazuriz' Mimoseraie, on the Bayonne road, was among these.

To the great surprise of her friends, this wealthy woman, so exotically beautiful, had insisted on turning her home into a peasant house with whitewashed walls and red stone floors. The long wooden dining-room table was dominated by enormous hams hanging from the ceiling, and the shelves were loaded with victuals alongside typically "back home" kitchen utensils. Meals were served in eighteenth-century silver plate, but the napkins were of coarse cloth. Everything in the house reflected the false modesty that Eugenia felt bespoke her humble origins. Mme. Errazuriz was playing at the peasant girl as Queen Marie-Antoinette had once played at the shepherdess.

In her Biarritz Trianon, portraits of her by Sargent, Helleu, Chartran, and Madrazo hung alongside Cubist pictures by Picasso, and the painter was her "noble savage," while colorless Olga contributed a whiff of the steppes. Yet we must recognize that she early discerned the exceptional personality of the stocky little Malagueño. She annexed him to her existence, sensing his fantastic, paradoxical, contrast-laden character to be not too unlike her own. He too was something of an illusionist, a player, alternately meditative and impulsive, out to provoke, to challenge, to create effects.

This period of his existence has been hushed up by many of his biographers who disapproved of their idol's social compromises. The statue could suffer no chipping. Eugenia Errazuriz is almost never mentioned, although she played a key role in the history of taste. True, it is not thought proper to stress Picasso's avatar of 1917–1918. Decorative Cubism does not have a good name, and what Max Jacob called his friend's "Duchess Epoch" is slipped over.

The coexistence in 1915–1918 of Cubist formulas along with Ingresque classical naturalism, and the arrival at the end of the war of Mannerism, may have led some to believe—and write—that Picasso was a Jack-of-all-manners playing on several keyboards at the same time, a painter unable to choose between a conquering new vocabulary and tradition. It may not be amiss here to quote from what he said in 1923:

> Whenever I had something to say, I have said it in the manner in which I felt it ought to be said. Different motives inevitably require different modes of expression. This does not imply either evolution or progress, but an adaptation of the idea one wants to express and the means to express it.

After the Russian Revolution, the many Russians in Biarritz left; the idyllic atmosphere was beginning to be spoiled, with their abandoned homes requisitioned as rest homes for the amputees and blinded now to be seen everywhere. Pablo was horrified, and turned away, ran home to his hostess's villa, thinking of Boccioni killed, Léger and Braque seriously wounded, Apollinaire with the hole in his head, dragging from hospital to hospital.

On August 16, he wrote Guillaume, sending him a tobacco blossom from Eugenia's garden and saying he was working hard and seeing "lots of fine people." He had decorated one room of the Mimoseraie with rhythmically schematic figures of bathing and dancing girls, enlivened with lines from Apollinaire's *Seasons:*

It was a blessed time we were there at the shore
Going out bright and early hatless bare-toed
And love as it darted like the tongue of a toad
Pierced the hearts of both fools and wise to the core

Love-struck and serene, Pablo was writing thoughtless letters to his friend Apollinaire, detailing the comings and goings of dealers and others of the "élite," while the hard-pressed poet had only three months more to live.

At times free and easy, at others punctilious as a goldsmith's work, Pablo's drawings dwelt on his favored themes: the *Woman in an Armchair* is obviously Olga as seen throughout the many sketches in his pads of alternating still lifes, faces, landscapes, and quick sketches of an almost immaterial Biarritz. Society people were now posing for him, to the delight of his new wife. His portraits of Mme. Paul Rosenberg with her daughter Micheline on her lap, then the girl alone, Mme. Errazuriz, Mme. Patri, the daughter of the Marquis and Marquise de Villaurrutia, Mme. Georges Wildenstein, and others, were flatly naturalistic and plastically quite undistinguished.

But this social round had the excuse of being for the benefit of the wounded, as people were beginning to think of what they would do once the war was over. The wealthy dealers in Biarritz hoped to see a return to classicism. Was Cubism over? The Rosenbergs, with their large stock of Cubist works, demurred. It had to be regenerated, brought up to date—that is, made to conform to order, logic, and clarity.

Pablo, as ever, remained impenetrable. He had just finished a big *Bathers* painting, for which he had done several studies on the beach: a strange composition with very elongated "mannerist" figures that remind one of some of the women he painted around 1901–1903.

Back from a short stay in Brittany, on September 11, Apollinaire answered Pablo, saying how happy he was that his verses had been used in the Biarritz villa decoration (since transferred to an apartment in Marseilles), adding that the poems "I am now doing are closer to your present preoccupations. I am trying to renew the poetic tone, but in a classical rhythm." He, too, had made the turn from youthful challenge to serenity, but he apparently did not understand that with Pablo nothing was ever definitive.

Dada exploded like a bomb in a Zurich café in 1916. Against the horrors of war, the hypocrisy of politics, and the official brainwashing, it was a cry of both revolt and disgust. Had not the best of the younger writers fallen into cheapjack patriotism like the vulgarest academicians? Was not Apollinaire himself playing the national hero, parading his wound?

"I consider that in his person poetry was unable to overcome the ordeal [of war]," wrote Breton, who nevertheless recognized his influence over the youth. Apollinaire had great prestige, and all of the new literature wished to be in his aura. After all, he had been wounded under fire, and decorated.

But Dadaism—which Guillaume did not favor—advocated something more than a tradition renovated through modern classicism. Its superb insolence, eager for anything resolutely "modern," did not flinch from any scandal or aggression in the name of adventure. Young poets were establishing contact with Tristan Tzara and the "historical" Dadaists in Zurich, as Francis Picabia and Marcel Duchamp in New York were bringing the same iconoclastic, nihilist approach to things plastic.

With Man Ray, they were to become leaders of the revolt against traditional art in Greenwich Village. Mere Cubist followers in Paris, across the ocean they seemed symbols of everything defiantly modern and new.

Since Picasso was the symbol of all that in Europe, he suddenly seemed curiously to have lost credence; his "betrayal," going over to the social whirl, was common knowledge in the cafés, where he was often spoken of as "finished." Gris and Max Jacob were not alone in being disappointed in him; Braque felt estranged; yet the Dadaists made no bones of their admiration and respect for him. In *Parade,* they did not see the resignation of a creator but rather the perfect harmony the "newest" of modern painters had managed to work out with their idol, Erik Satie.

Again, Pablo remained untouched by any of these reactions. From his "established" position, he could look condescendingly on the Salon Cubists and their "innovating." For the moment, "society" was adding to his reputation, reassuring Olga, guaranteeing his financial future. His portraits, "cooked up" to flatter their subjects and be photographic likenesses, have only documentary interest. Happy and sure of themselves, the Picassos returned to Paris at the end of September.

> Accepted by public opinion, has Cubism been understood? Has it not rather been adopted as ugly little Chinese dogs recently were, because people were tired of fighting it, and it seemed bizarre, because since *Parade* at the Ballets Russes certain society circles deemed it fashionable, and people did not want to seem to be Boeotians?

The two young authors of these lines, in a manifesto entitled "After Cubism," brought out at the start of November 1918, were the painter Amédée Ozenfant and the architect Charles-Édouard Jeanneret (later better known as Le Corbusier). Having met in May 1917, they had pooled their ideas and ambitions to write this text and to found Purism, so as "to express in one intelligible word the characteristic of the Modern Spirit." If, as they said, "Cubism remained, in spite of everything, a romantically ornamental decorative art," they did not deny its paternity, but went on to seek "the pure element for use in reconstructing organized pictures that seem made by nature itself."

Late on November 9, Ozenfant left his digs on Rue Godot-de-Mauroy to mail some press releases about "After Cubism," and in the evening *Intransigeant* saw the headline, "Death of Guillaume Apollinaire." At the same moment, at the Hôtel Lutétia, Pablo was studying himself attentively in the bathroom mirror, to Olga's surprise. Asked what the matter was, he told her that, as he had been walking along the Rue de Rivoli, a draft had blown a war widow's mourning veil over his face, blinding him for a moment. And he picked up a pencil to make a record of what he had looked like, when the telephone rang. "Apollinaire just died," a voice told. Pablo, livid, put his pencil down. Later, whenever he was asked, "When was the last time you drew your own face?" he would always reply, "The day Apollinaire died."

This terrified look, questioning the mystery, cannot be mistaken. Picasso knew that with the disappearance of Apollinaire not only his youth was ending, but the era of friendships, struggles, angers, Bohemia, and illusion. Henceforth he would be painting for the delight and satisfaction of those he had once defied; there would never again be a chance for a *Demoiselles d'Avignon*—times had changed, and the world with them. The Bateau-Lavoir rebel in his mechanic's overalls and derby hat, waving a revolver, was no longer in order; the young prodigy of the Rose and Blue years was relegated to his sensitive virtuoso's fairy-tale world. Yet he remained forever the demiurge of Cubism. Juan Gris might look down on him, Braque—through his silences—condemn his "transformation," yet, what would they have been without him?

Nothing would be the same anymore. Pablo sent a short note to André Salmon to tell him the news.

The funeral took place on November 13, from the church of St. Thomas Aquinas, with military honors. The next day's papers cited M. and Mme. Pablo Picasso among "those in attendance." On the same day, in a note to Gertrude Stein telling of his friend's death, Pablo informed her that he was moving to the chic 23 Rue La Boétie. He had "arrived."

Despite their social contacts, business relations between Picasso and Léonce Rosenberg were often difficult; and the same would apply to Kahnweiler, when the latter returned to his concern. Pablo always believed his dealers were "taking" him: he had originally broken with Manach because he felt exploited, even though there may have been other, more personal reasons. He also thought he was being used, a reason for his frequent breaks with Gertrude Stein, despite all Leo and she had done for him.

Kahnweiler was always smart enough to let Picasso talk and do as he pleased. The painter knew the dealer was doing what he judged right, in their joint best interests, yet never stopped denigrating, accusing, and abusing him. Kahnweiler understood his way of acting, and each went his way, their relationship never changing, in spite of some stormy sessions.

From 1907 on, there was a kind of tacit agreement between them: they play-acted to each other, saw through each other, and, knowing they were mutually needed, admired and fought with each other like old married couples whose ups and downs go on until death does them part. Picasso died first, and Kahnweiler remained alone with his memories. There was no one to talk back to him.

Léonce Rosenberg was not of the caliber of Kahnweiler, who was perhaps unique in the history of the art business. So Picasso gave him a hard time, and there were many fights, Rosenberg writing him, particularly on December 2, 1918, to clarify his position toward him and other artists that he showed at his Galerie de l'Effort Moderne, or G.E.M. He pointed out to him that he was "with" Picasso and Cubism as far back as 1906, when he bought the first of his paintings from Clovis Sagot, and then bought so many later directly from Picasso. But, he added, "This being said, as a professional I cannot buy any painting however fine at *tomorrow's* price instead of *today's*."

Picasso was not the only one who felt that Rosenberg bought reluctantly and paid a minimum, but, unlike so many of his colleagues who agreed with him but were less well connected, he was able to sell to other dealers or private collectors. They had signed no contract, so Rosenberg had no cause for complaint, and each did as he pleased. As Rosenberg was to put it, "In speaking of relations between artists and dealers, you spoke of class struggle. There is a class struggle between bad workers and bad employers, but for people with a high moral tone, there will never be struggle but always *conciliation*."

Fortunately, picture prices, on the downgrade since the start of the war, were about to go back up, and business would be back to normal. Courageously, Léonce Rosenberg and his brother Paul struggled to impose modern painting—as did some other dealers, Daniel-Henry Kahnweiler far from the least skillful or clever among them.

X

A PAINTER TO
EVERYONE'S TASTE
(1919–1921)

UBISM, REALISM, ROMAN PERIOD, POMPEIAN INSPIRATION, THEATER decoration—wherein lay the real Picasso? As if there were only one that critics, dealers, and collectors might catch in their nets.

"What, after all, is a painter?" he asked. "He's a collector who wants to make a collection by doing the paintings he saw in other collections. That's how it starts, but then it becomes something else."

The war was over. The conscripted artists had returned home, to their studios, though not always to their wives, friends, or dealers. Montmartre had been displaced by Montparnasse, scene of the Roaring Twenties (known in France as *les années folles,* "the mad years"). The prewar generation was home, ready to resume—but after four years of butchery, they wanted calm rather than scandal.

"Escape from Cubism" was the new fashion. Neo-Cubism, "French Cubism" were supposed to take art out of the hands of foreigners, "to serve the spirit, lead to poetry," as André Lhote put it. Remember the xenophobia that greeted *Parade* and *Les Mamelles de Tirésias.* Lhote, that great breaker-down of open doors, was a leader in its "renaissance," with the "cubisters" and hangers-on of earlier days filling the Salon des Indépendants and Salon d'Automne in the 1920–1925 years.

"The Cubist bloc is breaking up," wrote Blaise Cendrars in the first issue of *La Rose rouge* (May 3, 1919), of which he was managing editor. "There is a new beauty." And in the following issue:

> We can already foresee the day when the term "Cubist" will have only a generalized meaning to designate, in the history of the contemporary period, the researches of certain painters from 1907 to 1914. . . .
> Picasso . . . no more searching mind, no fingers or brushes more rapid or subtle. His drive, his skill, his pride, his acrobatics, love, cruelty, elegance, drawing, arabesque, perversity, rarity, occultness, his supersharp taste make him akin to Gilles de Rais . . . above all, the first painter of truth. . . . Like his Harlequins, his painting always wears a mask. . . . Picasso wants no disciples. He knows. He is jealous of the face, the serenity of his painting.

At Vallauris in 1960, pointing to the picture taken of him at one of the Beaumonts' balls, between Mme. Errazuriz and Olga, more triumphantly self-assured than any Spanish torero ever (was it true that he, the bullfight aficionado, had never dared go down into a bullring?), Picasso laughed, his eye atwinkle, "*Comedia* . . ."

Yet now, when none, except the Dadaist iconoclasts who were not yet taken seriously, were trying as he had once done to smash the visual complacency of the "French" Cubists, the comedy, the playacting Picasso was doing suited him. With his fists he had smashed human figures in the *Demoiselles,* with his shoulders jolted the theater and replaced Cocteau's fairly literary and empty conceits with a plastic human reality. And his struggle against conventions, prejudices, against *trompe-l'esprit* (mind-fooling) went on.

Was it all a comedy? Kahnweiler, still in Switzerland, worried over the fact that alone among his painters Picasso had not stuck with him. He understood his being attracted to Léonce Rosenberg's easy money, knowing his fear of recollected poverty. What worried him was the direction he had taken.

On returning to France in February 1920, Kahnweiler, through devoted friends, first tried to get his property back, or at least to avoid its auctioning, for such a sale might knock the bottom out of the Cubist market. Its enemies wished for it; but Léonce Rosenberg thought it would do no such thing. "Infantile . . . consistent with the lack of commercial sense [of this] poor man [who] wound up almost penniless," Kahnweiler years later told Francis Crémieux.

Picasso the man might put on disguises and have fun, but the painting went forward. Olga was one of those who knew and understood her husband the least. She completely missed the creator of Cubism, and his Bohemian Montmartre period so repelled her that she drove away all his old friends. She sowed terror in poor Max Jacob, and was ferociously jealous after the fact of a Fernande that her husband never had anything more to do with. The Braques also were estranged, whereas Olga enjoyed the circle of great Jewish dealers and collectors around the Rosenbergs. When Cocteau introduced the Picassos to Count Étienne de Beaumont, his friend and patron, whose mansion on Rue Masseran was a meeting place for writers, artists, snobs, and society folk, the ex-ballerina felt at last a true Parisienne.

At 23 Rue La Boétie, they occupied two floors, next door to the Paul Rosenberg gallery at No. 21. Their upper floor was Pablo's studio, quickly made as messy as Montrouge and the Bateau-Lavoir, its walls covered with often unframed paintings by Rousseau, Cézanne, Matisse, Juan Gris, Renoir, Braque, and Derain, and his Negro sculptures. In Salmon's description:

> On his floor, you felt free, content. He admitted to it only friends who had been, or deserved to have been, on Rue Ravignan. The carpet was the softest, a carpet of cigarette butts. Servants were forbidden to clean up. Olga herself never went up to Pablo's; he went down to her place.

Which, of course, was the antithesis of his. Perfect order, absolute cleanliness. A setting for an upper-middle-class owner whose slightly raffish taste might account for the acquisition of a few Cubist paintings, sole concession to the profession of the tenant who, in a 1919 drawing, lightly captured the conventional and colorless character of his own dining room: in the center, beneath high windows opening on to an enclosed garden, a large leafed table had a vase of flowers on it. Little other furniture, Olga not yet having had time to fill it: two half-moon cornerpieces, a small table, chair, buffet, and a few familiar objects, a guitar and Negro mask. Later, she would fill her formal dining room with "period" furniture.

She determinedly defended her fief against Pablo and his bad habits. Not always easy to get along with, she was dominating and ambitious, though with no future as a dancer. Her ideal was the "society" parties she gave, at which the Braques, Gris, Max Jacob, André Salmon, or even Gertrude Stein were unlikely to be seen. As for Sabartés, he was away in South America.

As ever a sharp-eyed keen reporter, Pablo drew Olga in high fashion in the Rue La Boétie living room that faced the street, as hostess to Jean Cocteau, Erik Satie, and the young English critic Clive Bell. There is great humor in the precise dry sketch, dated November 21, 1919, catching the forced character of a conventional visit: the three friends sit stiff as mannequins on their chairs around Olga.

Where Kahnweiler never held special shows, Paul Rosenberg loved the gala openings at which Tout-Paris crowded in, to cackle, tear each other apart verbally, and give peremptory opinions of pictures they did not understand. His brother Léonce, whose G.E.M. was on Rue de la Baume, showed recent Picassos from 1919 on, after which Paul had several shows of his work in Paris and then in Rome, London, New York, Chicago, Munich, Zurich, Buenos Aires, Madrid, and so on.

There were two important shows at Wildenstein's (Paris) in 1923 (paintings) and 1928 (drawings). In 1927 the Galerie Alfred Flechtheim in Berlin exhibited drawings, watercolors, and pastels (1902–1927) with an introduction by Jean Cassou. Drawings were also exhibited at the Chicago Arts Club in 1923 and 1928, and paintings in 1930; and drawings and gouaches at the John Becker Gallery, New York, in 1930. Until 1939, all the biggest Picasso shows were to be in the United States; the Rosenbergs, capitalizing on the enormous popularity of painting in the period, opened the international market to him. But from 1923 on, with Kahnweiler back in business, he would start progressively acquiring more and more of the new work, as the Rosenbergs faded into the background after their financial difficulties arising from the 1929 crash.

Paul Rosenberg had never been able to get Pablo to sign a contract with him. All there was was a verbal agreement by which the dealer had to buy so many works per year, in exchange for which he got a "first rejection." What he did not take, or anything earlier that Picasso still had, was free for selling elsewhere. Beyond Kahnweiler, from 1920–1923 on, his main outlets were Paul Guillaume, Jeanne Bucher, and Josse Hessel, then in 1925 Pierre Loeb and André Level, who before managing the Galerie Percier had been the prewar guiding spirit of The Bear Skin. Georges Wildenstein bought many of the paintings, after Picasso painted his wife's portrait in 1918 at Biarritz, but he got rid of them, along with his Matisses, a few years later, because, as he put it, "they gave [him] no pleasure."

Relations between Paul Rosenberg and Picasso were more commercial and social than cordial. Haughty and contemptuous, totally without culture and short on intelligence, Léonce's brother delighted the columnists with the malaprops and non sequiturs he said with the straightest of faces, yet he proved worthwhile as a dealer. He had nowhere near the stature of Kahnweiler, whose intuition and passion for painting and unconditional admiration for Picasso, twice lost, during two wars, and twice found again, were much more important than the famous "business sense" in which the painter so delighted for the freedom it afforded him.

Through the Rosenbergs, Picasso entered the tight world of great dealers, antiquarians, and international experts, and his works went into great American collections and museums. These powerful men, largely Jewish and connected with banking families, formed a caste that controlled most of the international art market; they did much fancy social entertaining, and Olga, to whom painting was almost entirely a matter of social contacts, was very flattered to be part of it. She was amazed that Pablo did not feel the same way.

The exhibitions the two brothers organized had few of the pre-1914 paintings, for the best of those were in foreign collections, such as those of Hermann Rupf or Kramář, or at Gertrude Stein's or in Kahnweiler's sequestered property. The Cubism shown around the world, to the widest audience, was therefore mainly the easiest, most accessible work of 1917–1920, not the austere uncompromising style of the heroic era. The Rosenbergs did not consider that very "commercial," and when the Kahnweiler holdings were sold off in 1921 and 1923, they did not buy a single painting!

Yet Cubism, even watered down and systematized, was still, as it would so long remain, the shocker. It brought protests and mockery. A connoisseur as intelligent as the dealer René Gimpel, although a specialist in ancient art, it is true, was taken aback by what he saw in Léonce Rosenberg's "Cubist lair," as he noted in his *Diary:*

> . . . cubes of canvas, canvas in cubes, cubes of marble, marble in cubes, cubes of incomprehensibility, incomprehensibility in cubes . . .
>
> What was on those canvases? Rubbish made of flat slabs of color, cut up and intertwined . . . (July 15, 1919)

And a few months later, meeting Picasso at the same place, he described him thus:

> The head of the Cubist school is made of blood sausage, ivoried blood sausage. He is under forty, has brown eyes that look like very worn playing chips from a children's game. The tied and untied face of this sausage is cut by six perpendicular lines coming down from the eyes, nostrils, and corners of the mouth.

At Rue La Boétie, Picasso continued painting: all the Cubist/realist variations were not worthy of note, and he did not paint only pictures, but also exercises toward pictures. He would begin a painting, drop it, start another, a third, several at a time, go back to the first, never concerned with "finishing." When he signed and dated them it was just to assert his ownership and keep things straight. Brassaï quotes him in 1943:

> . . . Why do you think I date everything I do? Because it is not sufficient to know an artist's works—it is also necessary to know when he did them, why, how, under what circumstances . . . Some day there will undoubtedly be a science—it may be called the science of man—which will seek to learn more about man in general through the study of the creative man. I often think about such a science, and I want to leave to posterity a documentation that will be as complete as possible. That's why I put a date on eveything I do . . .

Without conscious effort, his reputation had solidified as "master of the modern movement," in the journalistic phrase, "head of the Cubist school." Thanks to the Rosenbergs, an ever broader audience interested in painting, and a new class of well-to-do bourgeoisie trying to "keep up with things," his fame soared, with numerous shows abroad adding to it. However much Cubism dismayed, disgusted, or irritated certain people, it exemplified modern style. The cube was encroaching in architecture, fashions, posters, furniture, decoration, and elsewhere. Yet, *real* Cubism went unrecognized.

Picasso seemed more surprised than anyone else by this, and his surprise, indeed his disarray, took the shape of numerous variations in style from strictest geometricism to naturalism. He was testing himself and also the new circles he moved in, the rich bourgeois, industrialists, bankers, diplomats, dealers, or fancy antiquarians, theater people, dancers, aristocratic patrons, the kind he had never much known before, but who had now discovered him through Diaghilev or the Rosenbergs. He eyed them and himself, and painted them—usually quite conventionally—and Olga and her bourgeois apartment, double symbol of his own social promotion, as if making a trial balance of the sets and actors of his new existence. He was to do the same at Juan-les-Pins and Fontainebleau, where he stayed in 1919–1920, then later in Dinard from 1922 on. In the confused postwar world, with Neo-Cubism carrying (poorly) forward the past, and Dada shaking minds up by calling them to revolt or negation, we can sense that Picasso was concerned about what route to take, but always holding open the possibility of opting for the style best suited at the moment.

The turn he was taking was inevitable. Picasso knew that after the war nothing would be as before; living and painting would no longer be the same. Apollinaire was dead, Max Jacob leaving Paris, Braque, Juan Gris, Léger at a distance, and Kahnweiler was not yet out of his troubles. Pablo was alone, with a new audience and dealers; his reputation had considerably changed, but this did not go to his head. He had no delusions about his "social" life, the people he saw, or perhaps even the paintings he was doing. The body of Picasso's work between 1918 and 1925, in all of the most different styles and manners, is a sort of anthology of his curiosities. As always, he lived in the present, but he was not painting for the present—much less for Count de Beaumont, Jean Cocteau, or the Rosenbergs.

Diaghilev and Massine were looking for the right time to get him to work with them again. Cocteau was disgruntled because Picasso and Satie more often got credit for *Parade* than he, yet he never tarried in his glowing accounts of Pablo. In February 1919 his 1917 *Ode to Picasso* was published in a deluxe edition by François Bernouard, each page bordered in orange-red with the lines of the free verse unevenly distributed within.

Diaghilev had fine recollections of Spain, where society had welcomed him and Alfonso XIII shown himself generous toward the Ballets Russes as few twentieth-century monarchs had toward living art. So he wanted to do something about Spain, naturally with Picasso in mind. In 1916, he had commissioned Manuel de Falla to do the music for a ballet of Alarcón's *Three-Cornered Hat.* When Massine and he in Barcelona first heard the score, they were delighted and promised to make it a ballet for major orchestra—now the more so, since they had discovered a wonderful flamenco dancer, Felix Fernandez.

When they left for London in the summer of 1918, Fernandez went along, and taught the corps de ballet his native dances. But preparations were held up by financial problems and did not really get going until the spring of 1919, when Picasso jumped at their invitation, moving into the Savoy Hotel with Olga and immediately getting to work.

A few weeks before he left for London, the young painter he had met in Barcelona two years before, Joan Miró, came to see him (his first two calls on this first trip to Paris were to the Louvre and to Picasso). Hospitable to him as to all visiting Spaniards, Pablo bought the painting that Miró showed him, a self-portrait.

The Three-Cornered Hat was a ballet on a totally different scale from *Parade:* it had five leads and innumerable supporting roles. The story, laid in southern Spain of the eighteenth century, was full of action, dealing with the endless efforts, through chases, traps, disguises, and somersaults, of a despotic governor trying to carry off a miller's wife. Everything Picasso might have desired: his native province, a love story, and a chance to thumb his nose at authority; yet, to judge by his sketches, he found it very difficult to orchestrate the drop curtain, sets, and costumes. There was not the spontaneous inventive dash of *Parade:* perhaps London's grisaille inspired his fantasy less than the lights of Rome.

Finally, Picasso got the idea of a drop curtain that might act as a sort of second theater: in the arcaded loge of a huge *plaza de toros,* women in mantillas chat with a man in a broad scarlet cape, as a little boy hawks oranges to them; the corrida is ending, the *arrastre* of the dead bull is taking place, and in the background the sun plays on the crowded stands. (This now hangs in New York's Seagram Building.)

His idea was to establish the typically Spanish atmosphere while the orchestra played the overture with its trumpets and drums, its heel clicks and traditional shouts of *Olé!* Then it rose on a set he had long worked at after innumerable gouache and lead-pencil studies. Cecil Beaton, who met him in London, was to describe it as the common denominator of his own Spanish country.

This was no longer Cubism, but schematic expressiveness, with great synthetic power: a pictorial Spain that was ocher, pale rose, and salmon, without picturesqueness or concessions to folklore, of a simplicity calculated to contrast sharply with the baroque curtain fantasy. Diaghilev was enchanted, asking Picasso only to lighten the miller's house a bit, since he felt it was too sad, by adding a vine running up the wall, done on the spot. Most of the set was executed by him personally, though for the curtain he had the help of Vladimir Polunine and his wife, Violet. He signed it: "Picasso Pinxit 1919."

Pablo worked closely on the costumes, keeping all of his studies for them, as he did for most of those for drop curtain and sets. The great ballerina Karsavina, who created the role of the miller's wife, has told how he made one costume right on her after watching her dance for several days in a row: "A supreme masterpiece of pink silk and black lace in the simplest form, a symbol more than an ethnographic reproduction of a national costume."

The Three-Cornered Hat opened at the Alhambra on July 22, 1919. That day, as the set was being put up, Picasso arrived onstage with a stagehand carrying a tray of makeup. One of the dancers, dressed as an *alguazil,* came up to him, greeted him, and waited. The painter selected some makeup and made the dancer up with yellow, blue, and green dots and lines, to look sinister; he did the same with several other supers, and while the principals were made up by professional makeup people, it was with his guidance. He had done several watercolors showing the faces of the protagonists in varied makeups, leaving nothing to chance.

A few months later Paul Rosenberg published a collection of thirty-two stenciled color reproductions of the maquettes of sets and costumes for *Three-Cornered Hat;* each copy of the original edition had a signed Picasso etching in it.

Pablo and Olga stayed in London for three months of social butterflying. The "head of the modern school" was perfectly acceptable to the conservative gentry as Diaghilev's highly inventive decorator. Clive Bell and the economist John Maynard Keynes (later to marry the ballerina Lopokova) shared a charming house in Gordon Square, where they held a party for Picasso and Derain, who had come to London for the ballet *La Boutique fantasque,* for which he had done the sets. They invited mainly writers, artists, and members of London's Bohemia, which Picasso did not much like. On the other hand, Derain was delighted, acting very relaxed and ostentatiously smoking his pipe: he commented sarcastically to Pablo about the latter's having had a new wardrobe made by London's most fashionable tailors. Olga was deeply hurt.

In these three months in London, he accumulated an unbelievable number of studies, drawings, sketches, and filled several pads. The painters who had termed his work with Diaghilev a "betrayal" now wondered whether he had not sensed that getting away from Cubism was a way of breaking not only with a fad, but with the past. That intellectual, austere, uncompromising painting was quite foreign to his present state of mind.

After Cendrars's "The Cubist bloc is breaking up," Cocteau had proclaimed "Down with Harlequin!" (though making an exception for Harlequin costumed

by Picasso): after the death knell, the call to a new order. André Lhote, hardly
suspect of antagonism to Cubism, wrote of Braque's 1919 show at Léonce Rosenberg's: "The atmosphere is morose and heavy as the catacombs. One really feels
something is dying. . . ."

The young painters were now looking for order, and those who did not travel
in the wake of Cubism found Picasso disconcerting, his range bothersome. Bis-
sière, not so young at thirty-four, seemed to speak for them in *L'Esprit nouveau*
when he said they wanted "to replace *analysis* with *synthesis* and thereby return
to *tradition."* André Salmon, once in the van of the vanguard, now also lauded
"order" as in Derain, "the regulator, the most French of artists," a sentiment
echoed by André Lhote in the *Nouvelle Revue française* for January 1920.

A wind of classicism was blowing over French painting, and by great good
fortune Picasso the iconoclast was going the same way. That reassured his current
idolaters, while upsetting those who, through him, had championed the Cubist
revolution. He had gone over to the side of law and order, a highly comforting
fact with Dada rife in the land!

This change in Picasso did not gratify everyone. Returning to France after the
war, Wilhelm Uhde went to one of his shows at Paul Rosenberg's and wrote in
his 1929 book:

> I was looking at a big portrait in what is called the "Ingres style." What did these
> pictures mean? Were they an interlude, a game, fine but not binding, to keep hands
> busy while the soul, weary of the road traversed, was taking a rest? Or was it that in
> a time of hate, when Romance circumspection selfconsciously took a stand against
> nebulous German metaphysics, [Picasso] had felt innumerable people pointing at him
> and accusing him of deep Germanic affinities, connivance with the "enemy"? Was he
> morally isolated in an alien land? Was he trying to find a spot on the specifically
> "French" side? . . .

Picasso's "recall to order" (in Cocteau's term, the title for his 1926 book),
hailed by some, deplored by others, at least had the effect of winning over some
of the academic critics. Seeing the classicism of the former *enfant terrible,* they
concluded that Cubism had been but a necessary prelude to harmonious synthesis. But Maurice Raynal, less ready to change with the wind than André
Salmon, who delighted in this softening of the Establishment, denied any "conversion." He felt Picasso simply revived "the old Spanish custom of marrying
different styles."

And much later André Fermigier was to reinforce Uhde's analysis by calling
this period Picasso's "naturalization file." But the real reasons had already been
given by Blaise Cendrars in his very lucid article in *La Rose rouge* (May 15,
1919):

> Cubism no longer has enough novelty and surprise to act as nourishment for a
> new generation. . . .
> The Cubists are right in the French tradition of cold reason, irreducible stubborn-
> ness, and solemn pomp.

In art, nothing ever starts over, yet Picasso started painting over from the beginning each time he felt the need to. What matter what people said? It was what he did that counted.

He was working on a new ballet, *Pulcinella,* or Punchinello, the burlesque *commedia dell'arte* character with huge hooked nose and humped back, often associated with Harlequin. Massine had gotten the idea when the ballet was in Naples and he saw the delightful satirical zest of the street comedies performed there by a famous Punchinello, Antonio Petito. He invited Petito to dinner with Diaghilev, who, as soon as they got back to Rome, had had old scripts researched, and selected one from 1700, *Four Similar Punchinellos.* Without delay, he told Stravinsky and Picasso about the idea, and they loved it. During one of their walks in Naples they had happened into a small room jammed with people and reeking of garlic, where a farce was being played, starring Punchinello as a swearing, shouting drunk who whispered dirty words to the women as his hands roamed over them. Picasso had been so engrossed by the *commedia dell'arte* that he bought a number of engravings, reproductions of paintings, and postcards on the subject.

Diaghilev wasted no time. He collected all the most typically Neapolitan of Pergolesi's compositions and gave them to Stravinsky, with a request to make a selection and orchestrate it for ballet for Massine. This was in the winter of 1918–1919, but the composer was so busy he did not get to it until later in 1919. In September, Picasso helped his inspiration along by sending him a drawing of Pierrot playing a fiddle as Harlequin accompanied him on the guitar. Only in December, when the Ballets Russes got back to Paris for their annual season, did Diaghilev and Massine, whom Stravinsky had regularly been feeding his score to, fill Pablo in on the scenario for *Pulcinella.*

Full of joyous action and complications, the ballet featured highly characterized "types," right up Picasso's alley. Two girls, their father and their suitors, Pulcinella, the little peasant girl Pimpinella, and her companion Firbo were the protagonists of a plot involving duels, a fake corpse, disguises, chases, and finally a triple wedding. It was real *commedia dell'arte,* a street show, but unlike the two previous ballets it was to give Picasso no end of trouble.

Pablo spent the summer of 1919 with Olga at St.-Raphael on the not-yet-fashionable Riviera. Almost every year, until he finally moved to the South, he tried to go to the shore. The hymn to nature, open air, feminine beauty, now, in Picasso's first Mediterranean cycle, was also a paean to liberty. But how different his seaside nymphs from the ballerinas in their tutus! Lithe and graceful, slim and youthful as are the former, the latter are just as heavy, with huge arms and thighs, inexpressive faces. Their movements too are ridiculous, and Degas, reputedly cruel to his dancers, never went so far as did Pablo in the drawings entitled *Dancers around Olga* or *Three Dancers* (Olga at the left). They were done from photographs at least two or three years old, since Olga had been out of the Diaghilev Ballet since the fall of 1917. In *Group of Dancers* (Olga lying down in foreground), the deliberately stereotyped attitudes make the young women stupid. The stroke, light and fluid, is underlined with hatchmarks and bister-and-blue dotted lines.

Why did he appear to ridicule Diaghilev's ballerinas, whom he so liked and admired, and one of whom he had married? Not at all out of derision, not to lampoon classical dance, it would seem, but because in 1919–1922 reality preoccupied him down to its least detail; he was virtually obsessed with grasping truth. The drawings of ballerinas, like his line portraits—Satie, Berthe Weill, Manuel de Falla, Stravinsky, Olga, in 1919–1920—were simply recorded fact.

Cubism was not dead. Who could demonstrate that better than Picasso? The stark orthodoxy of the prewar period, with its diagrammatic constructions and solid volumes, took on muted harmonies of pastelized colors in decorative cutenesses of a true "period" effect. Did Cubism need air? He opened the window and let Mediterranean clarity pour in.

He was master of the Cubist verb and sole owner as well, a fact he wanted understood. Nothing in common with the others. When the Salon des Indépendants opened on January 28, 1920, the Cubists decided to assert their vitality and show that their art, so recently avant-garde, was now part of history; but Picasso was not among them. Braque was, for the first time since 1908, as were Léger and Juan Gris, appearing alongside Metzinger, Gleizes, André Lhote, Hayden, Villon, Marcoussis, Gondouin, Serge Férat, Herbin, Maria Blanchard, Archipenko, Lipchitz, and Zadkine. A united front of modernity had been formed, with the first revolutionary style of our century at its epicenter.

Having so felicitously done the beautiful nude bathing girls free on the beaches, Pablo at Juan-les-Pins in the summer of 1920 suddenly came up with the trio of monsters harmlessly titled *Three Bathers* (Walter P. Chrysler, Jr., Collection, New York). The extensions and foreshortenings of the jowly cowlike dancers with their outsize joints and wrestlers' muscles, one supine, the other standing with forearms resting on her thigh, watching the third running along the shore, took on a repulsive character. What drove and was to continue to drive Pablo more and more to such distortions? What made him want to replace the playful bathing and idyllic beach time with this triad of horror and nightmare?

Also at Juan-les-Pins he was to do several gouaches and drawings on another familiar theme: rape. A powerfully built centaur, carrying off a naked young woman who is fighting him off, desperately grabbing at his beard and hair. This is Nessus and Deianeira, whose names are often given to one or another of these works in different techniques and styles. Picasso's natural eroticism, his beaming health, his freedom of tone, inspiration, and style have free rein. Terrible Nessus, two-handedly grabbing Deinaeira with his irresistible strength and sensual appetite, is Picasso himself; that is how he acts toward painting, women, life.

Picasso was annexing mythology and history to his own personal theater, introducing into themes a thousand times redone by painters and poets a baroquism of expression and form that combined unbridled gesticulation with the most classical balance, turbulence with measure, eloquence with the madrigal.

Some of the 1919 drawings reflect a strange mannerism, no doubt inspired by the baroque works he had seen in Rome. On several earlier occasions, there had been evidence of his taste for a studied attitude, a decorative excess in expressive distortion, elongation, foreshortening. From the *Woman Ironing* and *Actor,*

1904–1905, to the *Bathers* and *Dancers,* 1918–1919, this mannerism had assumed various aspects; in *Sleeping Peasants,* the couple asleep in almost acrobatic postures reminiscent of baroque ceilings are distorted much as are the dancers. Forearms, thighs, and hips are especially developed, but according to a "colossal" scale that was to give its name to a whole period of his work. This boy and girl, practically rolled into one, spent with love, have just coupled behind the hayrick; the girl's position and dishabille leave no question about that.

In December, the Ballets Russes had a season at the Paris Opéra. On the French first night of *Three-Cornered Hat,* Misia Sert gave a supper for Picasso and de Falla, of which André Salmon wrote:

> Artur Rubinstein embraced Manuel de Falla. Everyone embraced de Falla. Picasso, without whom there would have been no supper, insisted that the hero of the occasion was de Falla. . . .

Then, borrowing Misia's lipstick, he drew a superb laurel wreath on the composer's bald head!

> Picasso was beaming, surrounded by beautiful women dressed in Paris gowns, he himself magnificent in evening dress with a ditchdigger's red scarf as belt; for this other "hour of truth," a fine suit of black light stitched with blood.

From December 1919 to the end of February 1920, when the Ballets Russes left for a season that was to last into April, in Rome, Milan, and Monte Carlo, Picasso, Diaghilev, Stravinsky, and Massine met several times in Paris to prepare *Pulcinella.* The meetings were somewhat stormy, the problems coming mainly, as Stravinsky has told it, from the fact that the final score was not at all what Diaghilev had anticipated, whereas Massine had worked out his choreography to fit not the actual music but what Serge had described to him. There were also quite a few differences of opinion with Picasso.

Picasso had invited Max Jacob to a performance of *The Three-Cornered Hat,* but on his way there, in rented evening dress, the poet, still poverty-stricken, was run over by a carriage. Pablo visited him several times at the hospital, a sacrifice Max Jacob appreciated at its full value. Despite several plaintive statements by the poet, we really do not know what his relations with Picasso were at this time or in the next two decades, yet when Max was dying in the Nazi camp outside Paris in 1944, after so many other appeals had failed, it was to Pablo that he called for help. Too many of their respective biographers have unwarrantedly written so many stupidities about their feelings toward each other that it is best to make no comment. Their story, especially on Max's side, was that of the Poor Man and his Successful Friend—painful, without possible resolution. In March 1921 it became the subject of Louis Aragon's first novel, *Anicet ou le Panorama,* in which both appear pseudonymously.

But when Picasso told Max Jacob, "You are the greatest poet of our time," he brightened his life till its very end.

His relations with Gertrude Stein ended in a quarrel, "they neither of them quite knew about what," says Alice B. Toklas on page 234 of the *Autobiography.*

But there were reasons: Olga; Juan Gris, for Pablo resented Gertrude's intimacy with him and his wife, Josette; probably many more. Now rich and famous, Pablo no longer saw Miss Stein as the patron saint watching over him and his work, which she still wished to be. He denied she had "discovered" him or launched his reputation. She had of course helped him, but had she influenced his work? No. And did she have any rights over him? None.

Pablo was working on *Pulcinella*. He intended to transpose it into a modern period; surprising, in view of his taste for old street shows. He wanted the stage to be a fake theater with forward boxes, as in the pseudobaroque auditoriums of the nineteenth century with their heavily molded and painted ceilings and enormous chandeliers, glittering gold and plush red velvet. The set on the stage was to be an arcaded street centered on a fountain, with a view on the Bay of Naples, Vesuvius in the background. But this construction conformed neither to the actual structure of a theater, since the boxes faced the audience, nor to actual perspective, and to increase the illusion of space the Harlequin coat was twisted.

Picasso was also trying to get into the spirit of Stravinsky adapting Pergolesi: a mixture of artifice and irony based on pastiche. He even thought of dressing the dancers in Empire costumes. But when Diaghilev saw the sketch for the set and the "Offenbach-style" characters, as he put it, with "bewhiskered faces instead of masks," he rejected them out of hand. The painter argued boldly for them, irritating the impresario, who threw the drawings on the floor and trampled them. Then he walked out, slamming the door.

Picasso would never have accepted such treatment from anyone, but Olga's temper had accustomed him to Russian outbursts. Moreover, Diaghilev shortly returned to apologize. The next day, he was all sweetness and charm, and finally convinced Pablo to do it in the *commedia dell'arte* style. Pablo completely redid his set, dropping the fake Italian theater and, with a ludicrous sparseness of means recalling the collage-assemblages of old, dreamed up three schematic screen-houses framing the Bay of Naples and Vesuvius, with a fishing boat in the foreground. The harmony was the same as before, gray, blue of night, and white, with a simple backdrop of gray and black.

Picasso had now gone to the other extreme, stripping the set down almost to banality. The colored visual delight of the costumes, in purest Italian-comedy tradition, overcame the monumental bareness which Diaghilev and Massine disapproved of but had not criticized, lest this time Picasso withdraw for good. Departing from his custom, the latter allowed the Polunines to execute the set without him.

Pulcinella, premiered at the Paris Opéra on May 15, 1920, was a hit. Choreography, set, costumes had all been done in less than three months, but the speed detracted in no way from the overall effect of the production. At the last moment, Picasso got the idea of having a huge white rug in front of the set, for all the action to take place on; it had to be repainted after each performance, so as to remain immaculate. The contrast with the bluish-gray backdrop accentuated the moonlight effect, and the multicolored costumes took on extraordinary plasticity.

When Daniel-Henry Kahnweiler returned to France after the war, in January 1920, the galleries most committed to modern art were La Cible on Rue Bonaparte, Berthe Weill's on Rue Laffitte (and Picasso had just done an amazing "Ingresque" portrait of his pauper-days dealer, a pince-nez covering her steely gaze), Léonce Rosenberg's L'Effort moderne on Rue de la Baume, and his brother Paul's at 21 Rue La Boétie, next door to Picasso. On the same street, at No. 108, Paul Guillaume was starting an amazing career that was to go on in a few years at No. 59; it had solid underpinnings in Negro art, Mme. Guillaume's beauty, Dr. Albert C. Barnes, and Soutine.

La Licorne, run by a dentist-collector and patron, Dr. Girardin, opened its doors in 1921 at 110 Rue La Boétie, while Zborowski, a poor but impassioned Pole, known as a "man of letters," was championing Modigliani and Soutine in his two rooms on Rue Joseph-Bara in Montparnasse. The Frères Bernheim had two places, one at 25 Boulevard de la Madeleine, where they sold academic paintings, and the other at 15 Rue Richepanse, where Félix Fénéon exhibited Neo-Impressionists and Nabis. They had no truck with the Cubists, but the new Neo-Cubist wave found a home at Duret's, Rue Royale, with a February 1921 show of the "purists," Ozenfant and Jeanneret.

Durand-Ruel, like the Hessels, was also unreceptive to Cubism. The former's gallery on Rue Laffitte was the temple of Impressionism, having presented all of its masterpieces, while the latter concentrated mainly on the Nabis, especially Vuillard, whose majestic and cumbersome Egeria was Mme. Josse Hessel. Vollard was still located on Rue Laffitte, but in 1924 was to move to a small private building on Rue Martignac, hard by the church of Ste. Clotilde, while in the same year the Bernheims were to merge their two galleries into one at the corner of Rue du Faubourg-St.-Honoré and Avenue Matignon. Several other galleries were also located in this high-class neighborhood, but their interest in modern painting was restricted to its most reassuring aspects.

Before the war, Kahnweiler and his wife had invited painters and their friends to their home in Auteuil; the Rosenbergs decided to open L'Effort moderne to art and literary meetings on Sunday mornings. Picasso rarely put in an appearance, but Max Jacob swore he would never miss such an event, always good for a big laugh. The Kahnweilers had now found a three-room apartment on Rue de l'Ancienne-Mairie at Boulogne, and resumed their receptions. Juan Gris soon moved nearby, and this brought the old Rue Vignon "stable" plus some young painters out to the outlying peaceful suburb. Sundays at the Kahnweilers' or Grises' meant dancing, music, talk about art, or table turning; Picasso never came to Gris's. "Juan Gris was the only person whom Picasso wished away. The relation between them was just that," wrote Gertrude Stein. The fact was, all other painters bothered Picasso.

Not far from Picasso's, or Paul Rosenberg's, at 29 bis Rue d'Astorg, Kahnweiler opened his new gallery, in the name of his modest partner, André Simon. His old stock was still sequestered and seemed doomed to be sold off. In the new place, he exhibited the prewar names, Braque, Léger, Juan Gris, Manolo, Derain, and Picasso, whose works he started buying again in 1923; he also contracted to represent the sculptor Henri Laurens.

In 1920 André Salmon published his novel, *La Négresse du Sacré-Coeur*, about the Montmartre days of 1907–1910, with Picasso and friends portrayed under various pseudonyms, and a long poem, *Peindre* (To Paint), which had as frontispiece Pablo's portrait of the poet in 1907, though it was dedicated to "André Derain, French painter." Pablo took umbrage, and asked Salmon somewhat bitterly, "Don't you think I'm a French painter?"

Léonce Rosenberg had given the name of his gallery, L'Effort moderne, to a journal and publishing house, and the latter in 1921 published an album about Picasso, restricted to one hundred numbered copies; it had forty-eight illustrations and a text by Maurice Raynal. The reproductions covered work from 1912 to 1919, so that the revolutionary inventor of Cubism was shown giving way to the "classical" painter whose works, thanks to the Rosenbergs, were now in demand by galleries the world over. Raynal in 1921 also wrote the first monograph on Picasso, published in Munich, then in Paris by Crès the following year.

To the general public, Picasso personified the great hoax of modern art; postwar chauvinism helping, he was denounced as an "alien," by such as M. Camille Mauclair, author of *La Farce de l'Art vivant* (The Farce of Living Art), while others attributed his "destructiveness" to "Boche art" or Bolshevism, enemies of "true values," calling his return to "classicism" mere eyewash.

To the younger painters, he no longer seemed avant-garde. They thought there was nothing more to expect from him. Yet some of the critics who had earlier attacked him now held their tongues. Remembering how those who had ridiculed Cézanne or dismissed Gauguin or Seurat turned out to look like fools, they stalled for time. True, Cubism had lost its aggressiveness; it was no longer a scandal or defiance. It was now being called "art to everyone's taste"—a phrase that unleashed a polemical exchange between Maurice Raynal and Roger Allard. If Picasso became a "painter to everyone's taste," the middle-of-the-road critics, who tried to write "to everyone's taste," had to fall in line—and they did.

To show how they felt, the art students of the City of Light drowned Cubism and Futurism in effigy in the Seine.

Cubism finished, dead, buried? Not so fast. If the great magician of the paintbrush had left his experimental laboratory for the social whirl, he sometimes felt an exile in his new surroundings. Was it not in search of his lost identity that he occasionally harked back to Cubism? And was it not also to have a land of his own, that of art, that he turned to Ingres and now toward Greece, the Etruscans, Rome, the baroque, Cézanne, Poussin, Pompeian painting, Michelangelo? . . . "You can't invent something new every day," he liked to say.

The Giantesses of his new phase were idols, as had been the figures inspired by Iberian sculpture and Negro masks; these were the mother goddesses of new-found realism. Jowly women with inexpressive, full faces, heavy limbs, often outsize, great solid breasts, fat hands with sausagelike fingers and wrestlers' ankles, they were sometimes nude and at others dressed in rolling-pleated drapes

*Tristan Tzara, André Breton, Salvador Dali, Max
Ernst, Man Ray, and in the second row, Paul Éluard,
Jean Arp, and two unidentified friends*

(ÉTIENNE HUBERT)

as in classical Greek sculpture. Their pink flesh, with mauve or ocher shadows, their lymphatic serenity often verging on stupidity, were out of antique painting, as on frescoes or vases.

But—might they be "antique" as the *Demoiselles d'Avignon* were "Negro"? That is, the products of a period, a state of mind, an aesthetic and spiritual climate? In 1907–1908, everything was "primitivism," "archaism," "art of Black Africa," and now in 1920–1921, it was "back to the sources," "classicism," "Grecian antiquity." Picasso was to tell Roland Penrose that his penchant for monstrously bloated limbs grew out of a childhood memory: at Málaga, he used to slip under the table in the dining room to gaze with terror as much as curiosity at the huge thighs of one of his aunts peeking out of upraised petticoats. Nor is it irrelevant that at this particular time Olga was pregnant.

Paul, nicknamed Paulo, was born February 4, 1921. This started his father on a new series of Maternities, but the nostalgic grace of the Blue Period now gave way to a plasticism composed of sculptural simplification totally without "sentiment."

Gertrude Stein, struck by the fact that her birthday, February 3, was only one day away from Paulo's, wrote him a "birthday book with a line for each day in the year." Were it not for her being Jewish, she might well have been asked to serve as his godmother.

Perhaps the key to the series of matrons alone or with child, nude or sparsely clad, at a fountain, lying on a beach, or with vase on hip, beyond any reference to antique sculpture, simply lies in an expression of the banality seen in everyday life. These Giantesses were to give body to the idea that Cubism was dead, as Waldemar George was to write ten years later. But, of course, as we know, the "betrayal" went back to 1917. And, actually, if there was such an upheaval in the art world, in 1920, it was due less to Picasso than to Dada. Tristan Tzara had arrived in Paris on January 18.

XI

BETWEEN COCTEAU
AND DADA
(1922–1924)

THAT WINTER MORNING OF 1920 A SMALL, SLIGHTLY STOOPED AND bespectacled young man presented himself at the home of Germaine Everling, the mistress of Francis Picabia. In hesitant French, he explained he was moving in, as the latter had invited him to do several months before when they met in Zurich. This was Tristan Tzara, the inventor of Dada.

The large bourgeois apartment was a mess, since Picabia made a habit of bringing his friends in to talk, eat, drink, and remake the world between naps on the various couches or sofas. Germaine had given birth a few days before, but this in no way deterred the group—Philippe Soupault, Louis Aragon, Paul Éluard, André Breton, and others—who heard of Tzara's arrival and rushed to the Rue Émile-Augier flat to meet the man whom avant-garde circles saw as some kind of subversive messiah. They were disappointed, inevitably: Tzara was ugly, awkward, and unimpressive. Yet he was about to start making things pop.

Without formality, the little Rumanian moved in to Germaine's luxurious living room, and after their first disillusionment Breton and crew were irresistibly charmed by the newcomer. Here was a real leader in the kind of provocations they fancied: Dada was the order of the day.

Picasso's relations with the Dadaists were rather complex: while he painted, they ridiculed painting and belabored masterpieces. Picabia, writing to Tzara in Zurich in March 1918, had said that Pablo was "admired more and more by everyone, and more and more of a success, at what I don't know but those who admire him do." And the founder of Dadaism had tried to use extraneous aural or oral elements in his poems, "to constitute a parallel to Picasso, Matisse, Derain using different *materials* in their pictures."

At this point, the mass press and antagonists of modern art often confused or pretended to confuse Picasso and Picabia because the two painters had somewhat similar names and were both equally famous. Picabia had just changed the title of his magazine from *391* to *Cannibale,* the better to characterize its verbal violence.

In the April and May 1920 issues he sneeringly referred to Picasso working "in his office," and rhetorically asked him, "Picasso, in order to be a Dadaist, don't you think the main thing is not to be a Cubist? . . ."

Pablo let it roll off his back. He knew that the young poets who often came to see him did not consider him an ancestor or a has-been, as some young painters alleged. This, said Aragon, who called on him respectfully, was because "he has a taste for the written word." Picasso drew the frontispiece for his first slim volume of verse, *Feu de joie* (Bonfire).

On December 9, 1920, Picasso attended the wild vernissage of the Picabia show at La Cible. A monster traffic jam was caused by the overflow crowd that included Princess Murat and Breton, Tzara and Léon-Paul Fargue, Drieu la Rochelle and the actress Maud Loty, Aragon and Erik Satie, the Cuban ambassador and Paul Éluard. Cocteau played the drums in an improvised jazz band with Georges Auric and Francis Poulenc alternating at the piano, the poet once more displaying his limitless versatility.

Picabia was the current headline maker; what he had done before with his pictures, he now did through Dadaist aphorisms such as "Cubism is a cathedral of Shit." His onetime gardener Christian Herbler, now a bookseller at St.-Raphael, published a broadside of his own, that said:

> *No more Cubism.* Cubism is nothing but a commercial speculation. Collectors, beware!
> *No more Dadaism.* Dadaism is trying to become a political speculation. Snobs, beware!
> *All that is left is* . . .

And he appended a long list of survivors, including Picasso, Picabia, Cocteau, Aragon, Suzanne and Marcel Duchamp, Auric, Roger Vitrac, Brancusi, Breton, Pierre de Massot, and Stravinsky.

Tzara and friends did not agree with Picabia and his gardener. When the painter thundered that "Cubists trying to keep Cubism alive are like Sarah Bernhardt," * their "transparent newspaper," *Le Coeur à barbe* (The Bearded Heart) replied:

> As long as there are painters like Picasso, Braque, and Gris, sculptors like Lipchitz and Laurens, no one can speak of the death of Cubism without sounding like an idiot.

The Dadaist attacks on Picasso shocked Breton and when, at a Dada soirée, July 6, 1923, Pierre de Massot shouted, "Pablo Picasso, dead on the field of battle," Breton jumped to the stage to defend the absent Spaniard. With a violent slash of his cane he broke de Massot's arm, while Robert Desnos and Benjamin Péret immobilized his victim. It all ended with the cops raiding the place.

"It seems Picasso is with us," Desnos wrote Picabia that night. "He was the only one who said what we expected."

But, back to 1920: it had been a specially fruitful summer. At Juan-les-Pins,

---

* Referring to her frequent and repetitious "farewell performances." (TR. NOTE)

Pablo, with Olga expecting her baby early the next year, continued the series of still lifes begun in Paris in February. He painted giant Bathers and Nudes that combined mannerism and classicism, as well as a few landscapes.

The Mediterranean shore was just as he had dreamt of it during the winter and spring; and now he said, "I don't mean to sound psychic, but it was truly amazing. Everything turned out to be exactly the way I had painted it in Paris. Then I understood that this landscape was really mine."

Superstitious Olga, with her Russian soul, worried lest the Giant Maternities her husband painted be a bad influence over her coming delivery. While he, no less superstitious a Spaniard, saw it just the other way: the women he painted were now hymns to life and joy, soon to be guardians over the baby's cradle.

Where the Maternities of the Blue Period had been thin and painful, those by the expectant father of forty proudly affirmed his virility for all to see. Little Paulo was barely two weeks old when he drew him at his mother's breast, carefully noting the date of February 19, 1921, as he would do with each record of his child's progress. But he went right on with his Maternities, usually in the Giantess mold: when not playing with a child on their laps, these women in antique peplum or robe dreamt in their chairs or read a book, heads resting against the thick sausage fingers of their stranglers' hands.

In May 1921, the whole art world of Paris had only two events to talk about: the sales of the Uhde and Kahnweiler alien properties, to be the real test of modern painting, especially Cubism. The diehards hoped this at last would finish off the movement the war had not been able to kill.

Max Jacob, meanwhile, was reading with sadness, "I have come to look at you, life of our suffering, dear Poor One, with the delightful thought of that mutual past, from which I alone have been able to escape. . . ."

Why did Aragon, such a nice young man, send him a copy of his novel, *Anicet ou le Panorama,* just published, that tells the story of two men: Bleu, who was to become a famous painter, while poet Jean Chipre was to remain poor and unknown? Several years after the poverty they shared in youth, they meet again. Bleu says cruel things that only Picasso might have uttered, and Chipre is as resigned as Max himself. But his memories, even if sad, brighten his life; his mistake was to elaborate on them aloud to Aragon. *Anicet* is a baroque, disconcerting, and yet fascinating book; its author's defense is that the keys could be apparent only to those in the know.

Picasso-Bleu, fulfilled as man and artist, famous and rich, now has the one joy he still had not known: fatherhood. Max Jacob-Jean Chipre goes into exile, a penitent resigned to the daily mortification of poverty. And life follows fiction: Max had decided to forsake Paris for the little village of St.-Benoît, "near a Romanesque basilica sprouted in a wheatfield on the Loire."

Pablo and Max had a last meeting in November 1921. While the painter was cordial, it was clear this kind of reunion was distasteful to him. Max was disappointed at not having been asked to be Paulo's godfather, since Picasso had been his at his baptism; he tried to be affable, and talked volubly to cover his embarrassment, trying to clear the air with jokes. But as soon as Pablo left he broke into tears. A little later he told Kisling that that day something broke in him: "To me, Picasso was deader than Apollinaire." "A very little while after this," says Alice B. Toklas,

we were somewhere at some picture gallery and Picasso came up and put his hand on Gertrude Stein's shoulder and said, oh hell, let's be friends. Sure, said Gertrude Stein and they embraced. When can I come to see you, said Picasso, let's see, said Gertrude Stein, I am afraid we are busy but come to dinner the end of the week. Nonsense, said Picasso, we are coming to dinner to-morrow, and they came.

The dinner was no happier than his meeting with Max, and his relations with Gertrude Stein did not improve; for a number of years, they would see each other only occasionally, Pablo continuing to bad-mouth Gertrude, as he did everyone else. Those who had known him when he was poor and unknown got the worst of it, as if he resented their having seen his plight and helped him. Kahnweiler alone was spared, and yet, even he . . .

The Uhde sale took place May 30. A short time before, L'Effort moderne had, very knowledgeably, done a big group show of works by the creators of Cubism, their disciples and followers. In the Uhde lot, there were thirteen Picassos, seventeen Braques, five Dufys, Metzingers, Juan Grises, Herbins, Marie Laurencins, Légers, and Douanier Rousseaus. To the general amazement, Léonce Rosenberg had accepted appointment as one of the experts at the sale. This "inelegance" (or was it "conflict of interest"?) shocked many, and some who went to the Hôtel Drouot for the auction were just lying in wait for the dealer. When he came in, Braque jumped on him, swung him around, and gave him a number of kicks in the behind. Ozenfant tried to intervene.

"You're defending the bastard!" Braque yelled at Ozenfant, and turned on the painter, landing a haymaker in his midriff and knocking him into the arms of André Level. He apologized the next day, and that was the end of it. But Léonce Rosenberg decided he had better take boxing lessons.

The Uhde sale brought in 247,000 francs against an anticipated 90,000. Cubism triumphed. And the Kahnweiler liquidators decided to split their sale into several events, each one offering just enough paintings to saturate the market. As expected, this progressively diminished the interest, and each lot brought less than the previous one, when they were held June 1 and November 17–18, 1921, July 3–4, 1922, and May 7–8, 1923.

"No market in the world could have withstood such an avalanche," Mr. Kahnweiler was to say. There were 132 Picassos, 118 Braques, 56 Grises, 43 Légers, or in all more than eight hundred paintings, apart from drawings, watercolors, prints, and miscellany. Several American collectors bought things, especially the works of Juan Gris, but the big French collectors and dealers, the Rosenbergs in the lead, passed. Nor was the French government interested; the museum directors did not even attend!

Alphonse Kann and André Lefèvre took advantage of it and strengthened their collections. Raoul La Roche and the Belgian René Gaffé bought worthwhile works, the banker La Roche being represented at the sale by young Jeanneret (Le

Corbusier). Through friends, Kahnweiler bought back some of his own possessions that he most prized, the French buyers of record being largely such young writers and artists as Breton, Éluard, Tzara, Michel Leiris, Armand Salacrou, and the architect André Lurçat.

It was in 1921–1923 that two of the greatest European Picasso collections came into being, Hermann Lange's at Krefeld, Germany, and Dr. G. F. Reber's at Lugano, Switzerland.

The Uhde and Kahnweiler sales were great publicity for Cubism and helped spread the market for contemporary painting. They showed it had appeal the world over. Despite the press and so many hostile critics and dealers, Cubism was not only alive, but valuable! The four Kahnweiler auctions brought a total of 647,800 francs, against an anticipation of only half that amount. With the proceeds of the Uhde sale added, the total is nearly 900,000 francs, no laughing matter. Cubism, so often written off as dead, was in the best of health. (In 1967, the value of the Kahnweiler sales was expertly estimated at between nine and eleven billion old francs, or some $20,000,000.)

Diaghilev had been planning a Spanish ballet entitled *Cuadro flamenco* and asked Juan Gris to do the sets and costumes. Very ill, the painter hesitated a long time, but then in April 1921 finally agreed to go to Monte Carlo for Diaghilev. On April 25, he wrote Kahnweiler the plan had been dropped: "I don't know just what happened." What happened was that Picasso had made it known that Gris was too sick to do the job in the time allotted, and stepped in and took over. To make his point, he immediately sent some sketches along to Diaghilev, who had to give in.

To make up for it to Gris, who still did not know the truth, he asked him to stay on and do portraits of his lead dancers, Maria d'Albaïcin, a Spanish gypsy, and Slavinsky, as well as the painter Larionov. When Gris did find out what Picasso had done, he left Monte Carlo for his home at Bandol: he never expressed any anger or reproach to his fearsome compatriot, but his letters to Kahnweiler suggest how this depressed him.

Diaghilev could not stand up to Picasso: violent, quick to anger, and despotic as he was, he took anything from the Spaniard. The latter did not know the scenario of the ballet, but that mattered little, for the Andalusian dances and songs Diaghilev, his secretary Boris Kochno, and Stravinsky had selected while in Sevilla were familiar to him.

For the set, Picasso simply used the one Diaghilev had turned down for *Pulcinella*—which accounted for his ready-made sketches. And this time he actually created the interior of the red, gold, and black rococo theater, with people in the forward boxes, previously rejected. The curtain no longer rose on a scene of the port of Naples, but a standing-room area with flowered panels. Even if such a theater existed in Spain, it hardly fitted the folk ballet Diaghilev was doing, colorful, sparkling, and full of southern comfort. The costumes were the traditional ones of Andalusian dancers, singers, and musicians, with Picasso adding colors and details of his own.

On April 1, in Paris, Pablo had done an exact, very Ingresque portrait of Leon Bakst, but shortly thereafter turned to a much lighter, more supple, airier stroke, barely touching the paper, to capture the very feminine grace of Diaghilev's charming new secretary and later librettist, Boris Kochno; two men, two styles.

The first performance of *Cuadro flamenco,* at the Gaîté-Lyrique in Paris, May 22, 1921, met with a lukewarm reception, as did its opening in London a few days later. Really not much more than a recital of native dances and songs, it was to be the last Diaghilev production Picasso worked on. It was dropped at the end of the season, and the director found nothing new that Picasso wanted to do. Pablo missed Massine, who had left Diaghilev in January 1921, and he never liked taking big chances.

Picasso took a villa at Fontainebleau to spend the summer with his wife and child. Everybody had started going to the Riviera, and he wanted privacy. Olga had a hard time after her delivery, but Paulo was a bouncing baby, as the many portraits Pablo did of him show. He had no intention of making a spectacle of him to society—and even less to his lady friends.

The little 1830 house and garden had been rather haphazardly selected through an agency; in the Picasso drawings of it, it is very much of the Louis-Philippe period, like a set for a Labiche comedy. On one, Olga is playing the piano in the parlor; on others she has Paulo in her arms or on her lap: happy family scenes of a quiet summer in the country.

Picasso worked industriously: landscapes, Bathers, portraits, Giantesses, classical figures, still lifes came one on top of the other. But the quiet country home was where he did one capital work, long elaborated as the *Demoiselles* had been, through numerous preparatory studies; *Three Women at the Spring* was the first synthesis of his antique-ish compositions (the second to be 1923's *The Pipes of Pan*), and all through the early states we can follow the development of his thinking, his experimental groupings of figures and relationships with the background, all the problems of space and color. Contrary to what some have written, this was nothing new with Picasso—it only seems so because this time they dealt with a "classical" composition.

But what prodigious activity! His life is in these painting, drawings, portraits; social life takes much less of his time, and Olga seems weary, detached, and, despite having a nurse for him, very busy with her baby. Braque, Derain, Léger, Vlaminck were now also "made" painters, Paul Rosenberg's business was thriving, and Kahnweiler's was about to start doing so again.

There are more and more Picasso shows and collectors. Prices are rising; Rosenberg puts 80,000–100,000-franc price tags on recent works. René Gimpel, in 1930, would pay 110,000 francs for a 1903 gouache, *The Blind Man* (Fogg Art Museum, Harvard University), and note in his *Diary* that Georges Bernheim had asked 200,000 francs for a Picasso of the Blue Period.

Picasso spent the summer of 1922 at Dinard with Olga and Paulo: different climate, light, setting; delicate, lifelike portraits of his son, Breton landscapes, and seascapes. The happy family life accounted for many mother-and-child paintings; some Cubist still lifes piled up their strict geometricism enriched with bright colors, underlined by vertical or horizontal streaks that suggested the cut and crosscut of engraving. His women were losing some of their matronly heaviness, their inexpressive faces, awkward gestures, becoming more graceful and flexible, suggesting a change in Picasso's canon of femininity.

At the end of September, Olga was taken suddenly ill and needed an operation; Pablo rushed her to Paris by car, she was operated on, and recovered rapidly. Paulo and the nurse had stayed in Dinard; he went to fetch them and his accumulated works.

Jean Cocteau's *Le Secret professionnel* had just been published, with a portrait of the author by Picasso, still his "good-luck charm," as Sabartés says Cocteau called him. He hoped one day to repeat their *Parade* collaboration, perhaps with his new adaptation of Sophocles' *Antigone*.

Charles Dullin, the actor Pablo had met years before at the Lapin Agile, was doing the play at the Montmartre Théâtre de l'Atelier, which he now managed. The première was to be December 20, 1922, set by Picasso, music by Arthur Honegger, costumes by Gabrielle Chanel, then at her height. Two days before the opening, Pablo had still not brought in his set design. Begged by Cocteau, nagged by Dullin, he remained serenely calm, while the rehearsals took place with no idea of what the stage would look like. Finally, he came in and produced a crumpled piece of paper, saying to a bemused Dullin, "Very well. Here's your set." Which it was. Wrote Cocteau:

> Crumpled canvas the color of blueing made the stage into a cavern, with openings on either side; in the center, high up, a hole behind which the chorus declaimed, through a megaphone. Around this hole, I had hung the masks of boys, women, and old men painted by Picasso or executed [by me] from his models. Beneath the masks hung a white panel . . .*

When the canvas was hung, Picasso took a stick of sanguine and rubbed it against the panel, which, because of the texture of the wood, turned into marble; and then in ink, he created three Doric columns.

> The existence of these columns was so sudden, so surprising that we burst into applause.
> As we left the theatre, I asked Picasso if he had calculated their approach, if he had closed in on them, or if he, too, had been surprised by them. He answered that he had been surprised, but that you always calculate unconsciously, that the Doric column results, like the hexameter, from an operation of the senses, and that perhaps he had just invented such a column in the same way the Greeks had discovered it.†

André Breton disapproved of Pablo's work with Cocteau, since he was trying to interest him in his Revolutionary Salon. For him to prefer, as Breton wrote Picabia, to decorate the flighty "frivolous prince's" *Antigone,* seemed most

---

* Jean Cocteau, *Le Rappel à l'ordre,* translated by Richard Howard in *Professional Secrets,* edited by Robert Phelps. New York: Farrar, Straus & Giroux, 1970, p. 84.
† *Ibid.,* p. 85.

distasteful. And he and his friends turned out at the theater to demonstrate, but Picasso put a firm stop to that idea.*

In 1923, according to Gertrude Stein, he seemed as happy and fertile as in his Rose Period, and everything was rosy. On March 22, Satie wrote Count and Countess de Beaumont: "I spoke to [the Picassos] about the *Divertissement.* They are willing to participate . . ." This turned out to be the ballet *Mercure,* a few months later, with all the invention, fantasy, and originality of *Parade*—Picasso with Massine, but without Diaghilev. Or Cocteau.

When summer came, Picasso took a villa at Cap d'Antibes, to which he invited his mother. Doña María, who had never been to France, had not seen him in several months nor ever met her two-year-old grandson. Pablo had remained in close contact with his family, and visited them several times with Olga, who liked Barcelona because it reminded her of their early love.

Pablo did a portrait of Doña María: she was Spain, with its grave and noble face, its melancholy beauty, and the slightly sad look that seemed to anticipate her country's tragic fate. Gertrude Stein, who met her here, found that "Picasso looks extraordinarily like her." The two women, without a common language, extolled Pablo to each other hour after hour as they watched little Paulo make sand pies on the beach.

Almost half a century later, Jacques Baron, who had been one of the young Surrealist poets, in his *L'An I du Surréalisme* (Surrealism, Year One), 1969, recalled visiting Rue La Boétie:

> The living room, or dining room, was entirely taken up by a child's toy electric train. "It's a wonderful train," Picasso said. "I'll show it to you later." The studio was one fairly light room of the apartment that could just as well have belonged to a house painter.
>
> . . . All was chaos: completed and uncompleted canvases of all dimensions, many with their faces to the wall, ragged chairs and armchairs, brushes, tubes of color, paint pots of course, but their closeness or distance was strange, newspapers and magazines strewn about, wire and all kinds of metal pieces, from old tincans to corrugated sheet iron.
>
> At the time, Picasso was being very mild, which worried Aragon and Breton. He painted ladies with children on their laps. The ladies were fatter than nature, but the children were normal. . . . I remember one small oil, in work, on the easel. As if a nostalgic recall of Cubism: a packet of tobacco, pipe, and bottle made of great sticks of color dotted with periods and commas . . . On the wall, the famous bull's head made of a bicycle seat and handlebar. The materials came out of life's use, human débris, people's discarded objects from which the artist made new things.
>
> [Back in the living—or dining—room] Picasso, kneeling on the rug, was happy as a child and as a king to make the little locomotive and cars go forward, back, and stop.

And the painter referred to Ingres's picture in which the Spanish ambassador

---

* Although often lumped with the Surrealists by some literary historians, Cocteau (after a very brief first association with them) had virtually nothing more to do with that group. They used him as one of their regular targets. Indeed, it was Éluard who in 1930 created a public scandal at the dress rehearsal of Cocteau's *La Voix humaine* at the Comédie-Française, with a catcall referring to his homosexuality. (TR. NOTE)

Picasso and his son Paulo, 1923
(Collection of Sir Roland Penrose)

*Picasso, his mother Doña María, and his wife Olga at
Antibes, 1923 (Collection of Sir Roland Penrose)*

comes in while Henri IV, on all fours, is giving his children a ride on his back.

"I'll paint one like that," he said. "President Poincaré (or Deschanel) playing with a ten-year-old boy on his shoulders and the Spanish ambassador, Quinones de León, coming in unexpectedly. Maybe that's what we have to paint today, huh?"

Count Étienne de Beaumont had set up and commissioned a ballet season held in May–June 1924, at the Théâtre de la Cigale, in Place Blanche, using the title of Apollinaire's onetime magazine, *Les Soirées de Paris* (Parisian Evenings). Diaghilev did not like the idea of such emulation, but magnanimously allowed his troupe to participate and enthusiastically applauded the "Suite of Plastic Poses in Three Parts" called *Mercure.* With score by Erik Satie, choreography by Massine, and drop curtain, sets, and costumes by Picasso, it opened on June 18, 1924.

Composer, choreographer, and painter all had one idea: to repeat the *Parade* scandal in reverse, the shock coming not from the audience, but from the show itself, devoid of any "subject" or story, deliberately banal, chaotic and disjointed in character, to aggressive music and amazing inventions by Picasso, who once again made tangible his extraordinary gifts as director, theatrical creator, and painter. Even more than with *Parade,* in which he was making a debut and was in constant conflict with Cocteau, this show was all his. While painting the stage curtain and sets, as the dancers rehearsed, he did a very Ingresque lead-pencil portrait of Beaumont, having done his wife three years earlier.

Growing out of numerous preparatory sketches, the *Mercure* curtain was very simple; the sinuous line describing the silhouettes of Pierrot and Harlequin against a set of geometrical flat surfaces was as gracefully light as a flight of birds. The hiatus between these arabesques and the colored shapes, accentuating the movement of the figures, was an old Picasso idea that Léger and Dufy had borrowed. He had tried it out in a sketch for a setting for Gounod's *Philemon and Baucis,* but Diaghilev had so disliked it that he had preferred to cancel the ballet.

The whole show was based on this disassociation between arabesque and color, for which the curtain prepared the not-very-receptive audience. The dancers' outlines stood out against wire elements affixed to flats that invisible stagehands moved around during the various tableaux, giving their movements a syncopated character in harmony with Satie's score. The set seemed to be moving more than the actors.

The public did not understand any part of Picasso's original gags or the humor of the show that turned mythology into a wild series of farcical tableaux fit for an art students' ball. Satie's music was no less witty than Massine's unbridled choreography. As usual the drop curtain had nothing to do with the show itself. Pablo thought this one of the dynamic elements of the conception, but the Paris élite jeered at it. On opening night, Cyril Beaumont, considered the oracle of the dance, called *Mercure* an "unbelievably stupid, vulgar and insipid" ballet, whereas in fact Pablo, Satie, and Massine displayed in it as much imagination and verve as they had in *Parade.*

Marie Laurencin said she just didn't get it, didn't know why Picasso "changed solids into wires. . . . He takes himself too seriously because he's Spanish." But Apollinaire's onetime inamorata saw the ballet under bad conditions: she had been having horrible toothaches for several weeks.

The Surrealists demonstrated noisily. They accused Picasso of working "for international aristocracy"! It was true that Count de Beaumont had had printed on the program that the ballets were "for the benefit of the Fund for Assistance to War Widows and Committee to Help Russian Refugees." And he had even asked President Millerand and his wife to act as sponsors, as well as Premier and Mme. Poincaré, Marshal Foch, and other VIPs, highnesses, society fashionables, and ambassadors.

Picasso was outraged by the Surrealists' attack, and Breton promptly repudiated it; he sent *Paris-Journal* a "Homage to Picasso," which all the Surrealists signed, even those who had demonstrated. Auric and Poulenc also signed, in addition to Aragon, Breton, Max Ernst, Benjamin Péret, Desnos, Soupault, Vitrac, Joseph Delteil, and the rest.

It said that, "following so many meaningless occurrences in the domain of art and thought," they wished to express their "profound and total admiration for Picasso, who, disdaining all consecrations, never ceased creating modern malaise and giving it its highest expression." After lauding *Mercure,* they added that the painter, "unlike those surrounding him [these words in boldface type] appears today as the eternal personification of youth, and the incontestable master of the situation."

Two days after the opening, on June 20, 1924, Diaghilev at the Théâtre des Champs-Élysées premiered a "danced operetta" by Cocteau and Darius Milhaud, with sets by Henri Laurens, and costumes by Chanel, *Le Train bleu.* The drop curtain was by Picasso, who had simply allowed one of his 1922 distempers, *Two Women Running on the Beach,* to be enlarged for it. It had been executed by a specialist, the Russian émigré Prince Chervachidze, but Pablo insisted on signing it personally and inscribing it to Diaghilev, who was so moved by this that he thenceforth used it as curtain for all his ballets.

The neo-Cubist cycle of still lifes begun at Dinard was going right ahead, and he also did a lot of drawings, many of which, women's figures especially, were nothing but the imprint of a brush dipped in paint. The delicate, bright, and saucy nymphettes were replacing the mother goddesses: the portly robust matrons of bovine look departed his harem and were replaced by Venuses, to whom young Paulo played Cupid. Pablo painted each phase of the boy's growth.

He also returned to his Harlequins, the most famous of which are the one the Spanish painter Salvado posed for in the costume Cocteau had worn when he came to see Pablo in 1916, now at the Paris Museum of Modern Art; the one at the Kunstmuseum Basel, in Switzerland, which came from the Staechlin Collection; and the one called *Seated Harlequin,* in the Niarchos Collection.

He also dressed Paulo as Harlequin in a pretty costume of yellow and blue lozenges, a lush ruche about the neck, and seated him on the corner of a Louis-Philippe armchair; he disguised him as a torero with a background of suggested

"Seated Harlequin" 1923 *(Musée national d'Art moderne—Paris)*

(GIRAUDON)

arcades of an arena, for he was also turning his attention back to bullfights. Several of the 1921 drawings foreshadowed this; those of 1923 mainly show the bull goring a horse, and sometimes the torero is the victim of their brutal encounter. The dead-horse theme periodically recurred in Picasso's work.

Now Paul as a Pierrot: the Harlequin had been sad and looked bothered, while his white-suited and -collared mate, jauntily wearing his pointed hat, fists on hips and one hand holding his mask, had the cocky air, combining pride with challenge, of Pablo in the bare-waisted photograph taken in the Rue Schoelcher studio in 1913.

He spared Paulo the awful Cubist disjointing that his later children were to suffer; Olga probably would not have stood for it. The little boy's portraits have a freshness, purity, and grace that express not only childhood innocence, as did the *Child with Pigeon* of 1901, but also a father's tenderness toward his son and the serenity of a happy household. This peace covered all of the work of this period, symbolized by *The Lovers* of the Chester Dale Collection, *Village Dance*, *The Sigh* (a resting dancer so titled by Cocteau), *The Pipes of Pan*, the Harlequins, saltimbanques, and numerous portraits of Paulo and Olga. Yet, the faces never smile.

Cocteau was preparing a book about Picasso. Their friendly relations had somewhat cooled; the Surrealists, periodically praising the painter, were firing their hottest shots at the poet. He, in the last years, had devoted himself entirely to the life and work of a strange boy named Raymond Radiguet, who not only deceived him with women, but spent nights in whorehouses. When Radiguet died, Cocteau almost went mad with grief.

He had long wanted to do such a book, but learned to his chagrin that there was no point in asking Pablo about himself. In the summer of 1923, having wired to ask him his birth date, he got a telegraphed reply: "What's yours?" That being the case, he would have to go it alone.

The *Train bleu* enterprise got Jean back to work, though he still grieved for Radiguet. One day, coming to see Pablo at Rue La Boétie, he noticed that the elevator had a trademark in it, "Ascenseur Heurtebise." He heard a voice say, "My name is on that plaque," and thereafter Radiguet became "Ange Heurtebise" (Angel Wuthercut) to him. But the incident brought him closer to Picasso, who, like many of his friends, felt the vision he had had came from his opium smoking, and advised him to take a cure.

In his long poem *Plain-Chant*, one of his most beautiful, he devoted several highly laudatory stanzas to Picasso and now read them to him: Picasso would have enjoyed them more had the author not interspersed them with direct questions to him about his life, his work, and his ideas about art, only to bandy the answers about. "The trouble with Cocteau," Pablo said, "is that you have to watch out what you say in front of him"—and he never forgave him for writing that when they visited other painters' studios in Montparnasse, the artists would turn their canvases to the wall, lest Picasso use them as ideas for his own.

The Pipes of Pan (which he kept for his own), after the *Three Women at the Spring,* is the second great synthetic work of his "antique" period. André Fer-

*"Three Women at the Spring" 1921 (summer)
(Collection, The Museum of Modern Art, New York.
Gift of Mr. and Mrs. Allan D. Emil)*

migier calls it a "Poussin done from nature," a "Cézanne of the best vein"—but how can we not see it also as a further proof of Picasso's disconcerting diversity? Apart from his own early predilections, many masters' works, from Perugino to Poussin, from Corot to Cézanne, have kinship with this Arcadian pair. They are two young men with rough-jointed peasants' bodies, strangely "wooden" limbs, one standing, the other sitting beside him, playing his rustic musical instrument; behind them, there are cubic elements, steps, and flats, that enclose the sea. No idealization, but powerfully balanced classicism, as Picasso with simple means revives the pastorale and gives it a sort of country nobility embodying both strength and melancholy.

> No attitude, no gesture but is a plastic result of the means employed. No head, body, or hand but are by their shape and positioning a uniquely useful element in the expression of the whole, no meaning beyond the plastic constitution of the picture,

wrote Pierre Reverdy in his *Picasso* (1924), which appeared the same year as Cocteau's. "Picasso is imitating Corots and Romanizing them," wrote Max Jacob to Michel Leiris. In fact, Picasso was bidding adieu to antique humanism.

Amazing as it may seem, none of his newspapering friends ever thought of interviewing him: not Apollinaire in the Cubist days, or Salmon, Roger Allard, or Maurice Raynal. The first to do so, in 1923, was a Spaniard, Marius de Zayas, who had done a lengthy piece on his compatriot in New York when his first American show was held ten years earlier. The interview, done in Spanish and approved by Pablo, was translated into English and published in *The Arts* (New York), May 1923, as "Picasso Speaks."

It contains some very significant and revealing passages about the artist's behavior and his ideas:

> I can hardly understand the importance given to the word *research* in connection with modern painting. In my opinion to search means nothing in painting. To find, is the thing. . . . The one who finds something, no matter what it might be, even if his intention were not to search for it, at least arouses our curiosity, if not our admiration. . . .
>
> The spirit of research has poisoned those who have not fully understood all the positive and conclusive elements in modern art and has made them attempt to paint the invisible and, therefore, the unpaintable.
>
> They speak of naturalism in opposition to modern painting. I would like to know if anyone has ever seen a natural work of art. Nature and art, being two different things, cannot be the same thing. Through art we express our conception of what nature is not. . . .
>
> Cubism is no different from any other school of painting. The same principles and the same elements are common to all. The fact that for a long time cubism has not been understood and that even today there are people who cannot see anything in it, means nothing. I do not read English, an English book is a blank book to me. This does not mean that the English language does not exist, and why should I blame anybody but myself if I cannot understand what I know nothing about?
>
> I also often hear the word evolution. Repeatedly I am asked to explain how my painting evolved. To me there is no past or future in art. If a work of art cannot live

always in the present it must not be considered at all. The art of the Greeks, of the Egyptians, of the great painters who lived in other times, is not an art of the past; perhaps it is more alive today than it ever was. Art does not evolve by itself, the ideas of people change and with them their mode of expression. When I hear people speak of the evolution of an artist, it seems to me that they are considering him standing between two mirrors that face each other and reproduce his image an infinite number of times, and that they contemplate the successive images of one mirror as his past, and the images of the other mirror as his future, while his real image is taken as his present. They do not consider that they are all the same images in different planes. . . .

Arts of transition do not exist. . . . Many think that cubism is an art of transition, an experiment which is to bring ulterior results. Those who think that way have not understood it. Cubism is not either a seed or a foetus, but an art dealing primarily with forms, and when a form is realized it is there to live its own life. . . . If cubism is an art of transition I am sure that the only thing that will come out of it is another form of cubism. . . .

Cubism has kept itself within the limits and limitations of painting, never pretending to go beyond it. Drawing, design and color are understood and practiced in cubism in the same spirit and manner that they are understood and practiced in all other schools. Our subjects might be different, as we have introduced into painting objects and forms that were formerly ignored. We have kept our eyes open to our surroundings . . .

In the postwar, not yet "roaring," years, when Montparnasse was just beginning to dance to jazz and be the rendezvous of the piebald artists of the world, riotousness, aggression, violence stood for Dada, which Picasso was of course not at outs with, but alongside which he seemed a quite bourgeois painter. For Apollinaire, he heralded a synthetic renewal that would include painting, poetry, and music in the revived "great tradition." Breton had long shared this Apollinairian view, but Dada had opened his eyes to what novelty really was: the adventure of the imagination rejecting established rules and conventions, undertaking spontaneous creation of untried means of expression.

The world had changed and art had changed in content, meaning, and end. In 1919, the German architect Walther Gropius had founded Das Staatliche Bauhaus Weimar—commonly called the Bauhaus, or Construction Building—which had a curriculum based on the search for functionalism not only in architecture, but in everyday things, graphic arts, advertising, theater, life-style, and so on. It was a revolution, or perhaps better a renovation, of considerable magnitude, which France, to its loss, would ignore because of its being "Boche." Yet it might have spared the French the ridiculous ornamental rhetoric of the 1925 period, with its sorry Exposition des Arts Décoratifs (whence present-day Art Déco), that summing-up of all the mistakes, clumsiness, and ignorance of French "creators." "Not having found a style, the period retreated into decorativeness, and reveled in it," as Jean Cassou would write.

Before the war, in studios or galleries, Picasso had sometimes come across a long skinny young man whose blade-sharp face was lighted by two bright and rather mocking eyes; both nonchalant and attentive, he was a painter of unoriginal Cézannish canvases that did not make much impression. A brother to Jacques

Villon and the sculptor Raymond Duchamp-Villon, Marcel Duchamp had kept the original family name.

Beginning in 1910–1911, he changed his manner, mixing Cubist decomposition with Futurist dynamism in his works, and trying to convey movement through the juxtaposition of simultaneous or successive states, only to end up abandoning painting. At the New York Armory Show of 1913, his *Nude Descending a Staircase* had been the epoch-making scandal, but the very next year his "ready-mades" established him as an "anti-artist." These everyday objects, designated works of art by his whim alone, challenged the easel painting and damned what he considered turpentine intoxication. At the same time, he was making a strange construction founded on simple calculations and unusual objects, *The Large Glass.* This antipicture, or rather "non-picture," was, like *Les Demoiselles d'Avignon,* to remain unfinished; by 1923, Duchamp had given up all "artistic" activity.

Matisse, Derain, Bonnard, Braque, Dufy had entered upon their own classicism: a kind of happy medium, a balance of sorts, a certain clarity giving their works more appeal than innovation. These creators from the heroic ages of living art were now operating their painting business like executives. French painting was in hibernation. The postwar period was a siding, the Surrealist scandals alone acting as salutary and exciting diversions, while public and conservative critics alike saw in them only the jokes of the impotent, the provocations of cranks or vagaries of madmen.

Through the magic of a poet, André Breton, Surrealism would restore their inventive power and their influence to the two great prewar Cubists, Braque and Picasso. Fernand Léger alone did not do as his friends, no "vacation from painting" for him in the Twenties; his sets for the Darius Milhaud-Blaise Cendrars *Creation of the World* led him into fundamental reconsideration of his development: he understood that the new world of technics would need its own new art, and that the painter could no longer just be a manufacturer of more or less delightful varicolored rectangles, but had to be an actor in, perhaps even prime mover, portrayer of, that world.

So, while Braque, Matisse, and Picasso remained studio or laboratory artists, he went into the street to find "the state of organized intensity," the shock signals of vitality, energy, modernity. His pictures were not to be landscapes, or still lifes, or figures, but surfaces. Realism? Just a matter "of lines, masses, colors," said Léger. In order to concentrate on canvas as much power as possible, with the simplest means, linear contours, pure flat colors, no storytelling, isolating the object outside its context, "I took the object, blew up the table that Braque and Picasso had kept. I put that object in the air, without perspective, without support."

At one of the Kahnweiler auctions, where several of his things were on display, Léonce Rosenberg whispered to a friend, "One can't say it, but Léger is the greatest."

To Picasso, the present was within himself; to Léger, around him. Dazzled by the machine age, he was also an indefatigable walker, prowler through great cities. Cendrars said of him, "We really tangled with modern life. Together, we plowed into it." But they did not get far. After the *Ballet mécanique,* which Léger filmed without a scenario in 1924, he said: "A spot magnified a hundred-fold forces upon us a new realism that must be the starting-point of a modern development of plasticism." But easel painting is not film; it is a fixed image of no great proportions, enlargement of which runs into the frame, quantity expelling quality. Léger expected people to take to this art and understand it, see their lives in it, but they did not; that was the tragedy of his life and work.

Picasso, friendly with him since 1910, never classed him among the "historical" Cubists. Kahnweiler's friendship for Léger, and his interest in his painting, were always arguable to Pablo, but Léger was no Juan Gris, and Picasso never dared take him on. "There's nothing beyond the first glance," he would tell Kahnweiler. "Léger always says painting is like a glass of rough red wine, but there's more to it. It takes blood."

Several times, in the 1922–1925 period, Breton tried to bring the two together, unsuccessfully. Léger kept away from Pablo, having heard the disagreeable things he said about his work. It did not matter that Kahnweiler told him he acted that way toward all artists; Léger, frank, generous, and uncalculating, was adamant. When Nadia Léger kept after her husband to get together with Picasso in the Fifties at Vallauris, all that ensued was one brief encounter, never repeated.

Now, the "crazy years" were at hand. It would be Cocteau, Montparnasse, Coco Chanel, Art Déco, Charleston, cocktails, and the mixed-up politics of the Third Republic—with Surrealism in counterpoint. The "in" place then was Le Boeuf sur le toit ("The Bull on the Roof"—named for a Cocteau ballet), where all the celebrities of the day, from every walk of life, rubbed elbows in an unbelievable tohubohu. And there, in the midst of all the noise, a young man, Maurice Sachs, reported hearing "the hate-filled, rancorous voice of Picasso, followed by his hail-fellow-well-met face, his friendly laugh that could turn evil, and give way to his short witty quip, cutting as the lash of a whip."

XII

"BEAUTY
WILL BE
CONVULSIVE . . ."
(1924–1930)

HY DID ANDRÉ BRETON MAKE PICASSO ONE OF THE "PATRON saints" of Surrealism?

"My favorite painters are Ingres and Derain and I greatly appreciate the art of Chirico," he had written to Tzara in January 1919, also naming Braque and Juan Gris, but not Picasso.

A friend of Apollinaire's, whose weaknesses and limitations he knew, as early as 1916 Breton had written a poem to Derain. All his contacts with artists were to reveal, beyond his love of discovery and surprise, of mystery mixed with the unexpected, a tolerance in sharp contrast to his intransigence in matters literary. For all that Picasso refused to go along with the idea of a Revolutionary Salon in 1922–1923, Breton had not given up hope.

In the beginning, Surrealism had brought no new elements into painting. A traditionalistic revolutionary, Breton saw creation primarily as an adventure of the mind. In an earlier generation, Hippolyte Taine had written:

> The image, like the sensation it duplicates, is of an hallucinatory nature. And the hallucination, a seeming monstrosity, is the very texture of our mental life.

The relationships between our mental movements and the metamorphoses they bring about open new paths to man in the field of the irrational and unconscious, which seem stimulating to pursue and picture. Beyond pure visual sensation there appears a new investigatory possibility: the hallucinatory sensation. Did not abstract painting question the existence of the outside world? This abstract art seemed to justify Breton's theories. Yet Kandinsky had many times asserted it was not a product of instinct, whereas Breton's concern was for the "automatic image" to be called forth by "automatic thought." This, he said, would free the "savage eye" just as it freed man's deeper, unconscious mind, from the constraints of logic. It opened the gates of mystery.

Never did anyone wish more intensely than Breton to enter and explore the recesses of the being: revealing "inner man" and giving his instinctive drives the same creative dimensions as his thought-out manifestations, Surrealism was to push passionately toward an extraordinary evidentiation of what had never been seen, never even been conceived. Each artist recognized by Breton would be expected to adapt his nature to this quest, to capture in the image a clairvoyance as intense as that of the poets' words. "The imitation of visionary faculties" found in trance or ecstasy, the unbridled condition of half-sleep, providing automatic writing, might equally lead to pictorial creation.

As Breton was to write in his *Le Surréalisme et la Peinture* (Surrealism and Painting) (1928):

> It is not possible for me to consider a picture as anything other than a window about which my first concern is to know what *it opens upon*, in other words if, from where I am, "there is a good view." I like nothing better than what extends before me as *far as the eye can see.*

This conception was not far from Picasso's own.

Breton had only slight interest in the later forms of modernity; Futurist dynamism, Picabia's machinism, Duchamp's ready-mades sinned by being beyond his control. He was never able to win back the two New York Dadaists, Picabia and Duchamp. And his book would ignore the Futurists and Dada; yet the painter to whom he never ceased referring was the one who most resisted capture.

Picasso's neo-classicism and his work with Diaghilev had disappointed Breton, but in the way the painter conceived the sets of *Mercure* he discovered inventions that got to him through their poetic, playful content, a new sense of "wonderment." Picasso's "unusual predestination" seemed so obvious to the poet that he never tolerated anyone expressing the slightest reservation about it—at least until he joined the Communist Party in 1944.

"If Surrealism is to adopt a moral line, it has only to do what Picasso did and will continue to do," he wrote—only to drop the word "moral" when the book was reissued in New York in 1945: Pablo had just joined the Party.

Which Picasso did he mean? The Cubist, the neo-realist, the lover of primitive art, the illusionist of *Parade?* His extolling of the Cubism of the 1910s may be surprising, but Breton was to get around that by calling Picasso a Surrealist of Cubism, and more specifically lauding

> the great gray or tan structurings of 1912 the most perfect type of which, no doubt, is *The Man with the Clarinet* of such fabulous elegance . . . the tangible proof of what we continue to affirm, namely that the mind obstinately speaks to us of a *future continent* and that each of us is always able to accompany an ever-more beautiful *Alice in[to] Wonderland.*
>
>   . . . Picasso, creator of tragic toys for adults, has made man greater and, in sometimes appearing to exasperate it, put an end to his childish agitation.

Yet Breton's feelings for Picasso were not without misgivings. He tried to

"Woman in Chemise in an Armchair" Paris, autumn 1913 (Collection of Mrs. Ingeborg Pudelko—Florence)

(GIRAUDON)

reassure himself, by trying to get his young disciples to agree that "To us, of course, what matters today is Cubism. Essentially Picasso and Braque." They were aghast at such "conformism": after all, weren't Picasso and Braque last year's moderns—indeed, prewar vintage?

Breton's warm endorsement of Cubism, even if sometimes with reservations, was due to the fact that a Cubist picture did not look like anything ever seen before. It was based on what Apollinaire had lauded: surprise. But he felt Picasso and Braque were different from all the other Cubists, and he was not so sure about Braque, with his *papiers collés*. "In a year or two perhaps we may not be able to speak his name," he defensively speculated in 1928.

The Surrealists especially liked Picasso's 1913 *Woman in Chemise in an Armchair*, a prefiguration of their own "wonderment," which Éluard would write about most lyrically. Many Surrealist exhibits were to feature it.

Breton was really too "serious" a man for Dada: he feared audacity and resented rowdyism. Besides, he needed solid foundations for his Surrealism, and Picasso was the only great prewar creator who remained sufficiently controversial while having wide enough acceptance.

So, the first Surrealist exhibition, at the Galerie Pierre in November 1925, ignored Duchamp and Picabia, whom he had not been able to take into camp, whereas Picasso appeared alongside Klee, Masson, Arp, Miró, Man Ray, and Pierre Roy. However, knowing how Pablo felt about such things, Breton got the paintings from friends.

Pablo was quite content with the flattering attitude of Breton (whom he often ran into in the summer of 1923 at Cap d'Antibes) and the Surrealists, and was grateful that so many of them had bought up his works in the Kahnweiler auctions (those were the ones that found their way to the Pierre exhibition). Their agitation reminded him of the "scandals" of Cubism in his earlier days, and he was now seeing poets as he had fifteen years before.

At the beginning of March 1925 he left with wife and son for Monte Carlo, where he saw Diaghilev and the ballet troupe. As usual, he did many graceful drawings of the performers. Back in Paris, probably in May, he returned to a large composition he had begun before he left, a capital work called *Dance* that was to remain in his studio until January 1965, when it was acquired by the Tate Gallery through the good offices of Roland Penrose. A celebration, but also a parody, of the choreographic shows to which for several years he had devoted himself, this painting, as important in his work and life as *Les Demoiselles d'Avignon*, was reproduced along with it in No. 4 of *La Révolution surréaliste* (July 1925).

The handsome young gods and nymphs whose idylls Pablo had followed with his pen now changed into strange disjointed puppets with attitudes not unlike those of the whores in the Carrer d'Avinyo. Picasso had just begun *Dance* when he heard of the death of one of his dearest old-time friends, Ramón Pichot; that event was immediately reflected in the work in progress, and the ritual of the dance became a kind of strange funeral ceremony. The silhouette of the dead man stands out, moveless and somber, on the right, holding the hand of the

"Dance" *Monte-Carlo, Paris, spring 1925*
(Tate Gallery, London)

(GIRAUDON)

bacchante on the left, who is agitated by a kind of frenetic delirium, like the professional keeners at Catalan village funerals. The middle dancer balances the scene by her cruciformity.

Dance spelled the end of his neo-classical period and for a long time of his theatrical contributions. At the same time, he was renewing his autobiographical painting, his personal diary; henceforth, his affective life, pains, joys, loves, revolts would again express themselves directly, as they once had, in his work. Almost as if the anarchic, iconoclastic forces of Surrealism had impelled him, forsaking the logic and harmony of preceding periods, to go back to his own interrupted revolt, his own iconoclasm. That was Surrealism's main effect on Picasso. He was never to recognize this, at least openly, or admit the key place of Surrealism in his work. We may even wonder whether Breton himself always understood that Surrealism/Picasso rapport.

Breton (as he was to write) believed Picasso "joined" the Surrealists in 1926, adding, in 1961:

> Picasso turned toward Surrealism on his own, and did what he could to meet it halfway. As evidenced by part of his 1923–1924 output, many of the works between 1928 and 1930, the metal constructions of 1933, the semi-automatic poems of 1935, right up to *Desire Caught by the Tail* in 1943.

In 1955, when Kahnweiler showed Picasso the proof of the catalog of the retrospective to be held at the Paris Museum of Decorative Arts, Pablo asked only one alteration, concerning that very Surrealist influence. He denied any such influence on three works, where it was suggested: *Dance, Guitar* (assemblage of scraps, 1926), and *Woman Seated in an Armchair* (1933). On the other hand, he owned up to it in the Minotaur drawings of 1933.

As Kahnweiler pointed out, his work always had a coherence not found in the Surrealists'. They, of course, carried subjectivism to the extreme: the point was less to communicate than affirm their hostility to the outside world, and subject it to their will. Was not a creative work, as Breton put it, "the product of an excretory faculty"? It was part of life; there was no break between the real and the imagined, for the artist's role was to add to the real what his imagination suggested, apart from reality, yet born of it. Whence the most eminent and dangerous of creative ambitions: the man was not only *in* his work, he *was* the work.

Picasso had been back from Monte Carlo for two months when he was shown that *Révolution surréaliste* for July 15 with his *Dance* and *Demoiselles d'Avignon* (the latter erroneously dated 1908). His past was catching up with him: these young Surrealists, whom he found "interesting," worshiped great men and masterpieces. Olga, who had never seen the *Demoiselles* before, was appalled by her husband's youthful aberration that Breton had convinced him to dig out and mount. For a collector, and an important one, wanted to see it: M. Jacques Doucet.

Doucet was both ridiculous and appealing. The famous couturier, with no culture whatsoever, was in some ways reminiscent of Vollard, who, equally uneducated, like him had tremendous flair. On the other hand, unlike the dealer,

Doucet was handsome, and his amours were a great part of his life. After the loss of his beloved in 1912, he sold his fine eighteenth-century collection, moved from Rue de la Ville-l'Évêque to Avenue du Bois (later Avenue Foch) and in his new mansion set to collecting modern art. His avant-garde acquisitions in a few years were as fine as his earlier collection, although opinion was now divided as to whether he was a madman or an opportunist. In part, this new art interest was meant to attract the pretty young things he could invite to "come up and see" his Ruhlmann furniture, Legrain or Rose Adler bindings, or Douanier Rousseau's *Snake Charmer*.

He took to the Surrealists, made friends with them, subsidized their books and magazines, and employed Breton as an art scout, to write him letters, as detailed as possible, about works he advised him to buy. If he liked the description, he took the trouble to go and see them.

That was how he happened to deign to come to Rue La Boétie with Breton to look at the *Demoiselles*.

When, after eyeing the studio somewhat as Louis XIV must have done LeBrun's, he asked an intimidated Pablo to name his price, and Picasso muttered an astonishing twenty-five thousand francs, he accepted without batting an eyelash, promising "Two thousand francs per month, starting next month, until the whole amount is paid." *

Picasso was speechless, but Breton soon realized the price had been too low, and he advised his friends, such as Derain, whom Doucet visited the very next day, to double their asking figures. Breton was responsible for Doucet's getting not only the Rousseau and the Picasso, but a Seurat sketch for *The Circus*, Chirico's *Disquieting Muses*, Duchamp's *Glider* . . . and *Rotary Demisphere*, important works by Picabia and Miró, and a second Picasso, *Woman with Sherbet*.

The Surrealists' doings interested Pablo much more than their paintings. The aggressive demonstrations, their rude attacks, their calls to revolution "first and always," their pamphlets and slaps delighted him. How timid he and the Cubists had been in their day! The Bateau-Lavoir had been pretty tame by comparison. He played host to the Surrealists, as to visiting Spaniards, in his studio on Rue La Boétie, but neither group was invited into Olga's flat.

From 1923 to 1926, Pablo made several visits to his family in Barcelona, in 1926 probably going by way of Céret to see Manolo, who, after lean years, was beginning to be successful. On one of his Barcelona trips, at Dalmau's, Pablo was struck by the paintings of a young man, Salvador Dali, especially one called *Girl's Back*. He mentioned the name to Paul Rosenberg, who wrote Dali asking for photographs, but never even received an answer.

What *Dance* conveyed was the anxiety, the instability, the uncertainty troubling Picasso. There is an element of panic in it. Like the *Demoiselles*, it is made up of two discordant parts: both hymn to life and funeral cortège, this farewell to

---

* The painting was first to be publicly shown in New York at Jacques Seligmann & Co. in 1937, returning on loan to Paris in 1960 and again in 1967. It was acquired by the Museum of Modern Art, New York, through the Lillie P. Bliss Bequest, 1939. (The original sale to Doucet amounted to $1775, paid at the rate of $142 per month.)

a whole period of his existence gave the painter a chance to cast up a sort of trial balance. From the *Demoiselles* to the still lifes on a stool before a window, all of Cubism was summed up here.

Dance has been said to evidence some psychic ailment. The painter was exhausted, constantly nagged by Olga, who was getting more and more difficult. The little ballerina had now become a violent, tyrannical woman, hating everyone, accusing her husband of unfaithfulness, Kahnweiler of shortchanging them, seeing enemies everywhere. There were more and more frequent painful family scenes; sometimes he actually thought she was losing her mind, which affected his own moods. He became subject to deep depressions and terrible rages, haunted by fearsome ideas, as reflected in some of the 1925–1926 drawings, grimacing female faces with threatening teeth, mad eyes, ravaged features. But then serenity returned, and the sharp broken line gave way to enveloping arabesques, curved rhythms rolling about the faces.

Pablo was to be even more surprising with his *Guitar* (now in the Paris National Museum of Modern Art). Aragon wrote, in *La Peinture au défi* (1930), a preface to a Galerie Goëmans exhibit in March, which did not include the *Guitar:*

> . . . Picasso did a very serious thing. He took a dirty shirt and attached it to a canvas with needle and thread. And since everything he does turns to guitars, it became a guitar. He made a collage with nails sticking out. . . . I heard him complain then that all the people who came to see him and saw him make use of old bits of tulle or cardboard, strings or corrugated iron, and rags picked out of a garbage pail, thought they were doing him a favor by bringing swatches of magnificent fabrics *so he could make pictures of them.* He didn't want those; he wanted the real trash of human life, something poor, dirty, scorned.

This was literary phraseology. Picasso did not at all feel that he was desacralizing painting by using trash, nor did he think he was appealing to a broader public by using everyday materials. What he was doing merely showed his curiosity, his liking for diverse objects, which we know he had always piled up in his studio. The older, dirtier, more broken, dusty, useless, the more he appreciated them. It was while taking a bath that on the floor he had noticed the sacking he made into the *Guitar*—and with his ever-present sense of defiance he said he intended to set razor blades around the edges so anyone who picked it up would cut his fingers!

These were the "crazy years," the Roaring Twenties, when Montparnasse was such a "moveable feast" that "established" artists fled the tourists, pseudo-artists, and affluent paper-rich bourgeois from the world over. It was no longer the semi-country area he had lived in with Éva. There were nightclubs all over, the most famous of them Le Jockey, that opened in the fall of 1923. There were so many foreigners that a painter named Guy Arnoux, with a studio on Rue Huyghens, a block or so behind the Café du Dôme, put a sign on his door, reading "French Consulate."

Night life was the style of the moment, but Braque, Matisse, Derain, Gris,

Picasso were not among those often seen with the loud-singing, fast-living models and others who had become queens of the night. The all-night orgies terrified poor Max Jacob, who, on returning to his monk's cell near the Benedictine monastery, chalked on its wall, "Never go to Montparnasse." Which did not keep him from returning to its pederastic pleasures.*

In January 1926, a twenty-seven-year-old Greek named Christian Zervos started a magazine called *Cahiers d'Art;* he met Picasso at the same time and his whole life changed as a result. No one, save Sabartés (but his case was exceptional, since Pablo's success was compensation for his own failure), would so venerate the painter or show him so much abnegation. Yet, unlike other admirers, Zervos always maintained his lucidity.

Zervos had come to France before World War I, studied in Marseilles, then Paris, and taken a doctorate with a thesis on the philosophy of Plotinus. He had also been secretary to Anatole France. After working for a publisher named Morance on a small collection of monographs of contemporary artists, he launched his magazine with the publisher's help, subtitling it, "A Monthly of Artistic Events." Despite this modest description, it became the tribune of modern art, especially of Picasso.

Unfortunately, there is a small paying audience for such journals, and *Cahiers d'Art* survived, literally, only by accident. Seriously injured when run over by an automobile, Zervos collected enough in damages to allow him to keep it afloat for a period. It mixed articles on Braque, Léger, Laurens, Matisse, Chagall, African art, the "idols" of the Cyclades, and the *nuraghi* of Sardinia, with an abundance of documentation on Picasso, always in first place. The wide range was not its least attraction.

In 1934, he was to publish a book on Greek art that scandalized traditional historians and archaeologists because he concentrated mainly on fourth-century sculpture, until then held to be "archaic" and thus negligible. The attacks by academics were so violent that the book became a best seller and he made money on it. This he put into *Cahiers d'Art,* which, since 1929, was also the name of a gallery in the Rue du Dragon run by a delightful young lady named Yvonne Marion, who became Mme. Zervos. After World War II, mainly, he followed his Greek book with many others on art subjects both classical and contemporary, as well as publishing works by Breton, Georges Hugnet, and Paul Éluard, to whom he was especially close.

But the great work of his life has remained the complete catalog of Picasso's works he brought out from 1932 on, the twenty-third volume (paintings and drawings, 1962–1963) being completed when he died on September 12, 1970, eight months after the death of his wife. This gigantic enterprise had a difficult start: Zervos, believing everyone was as interested in Picasso as he, had made much too great a pressrun, most of which had to be junked, and in order to carry on he had to sell his collection of Cubist paintings as well as his apartment near the Porte d'Auteuil, something that Pablo learned only many years later.

_____

* As a few years later he was to tell the translator, he was hard put to find priests to confess to, for he could not return a second week to the same father to tell of the same sin. (TR. NOTE)

But that was how he succeeded in bringing out, volume after volume, that "compleat Picasso," which was to be supplemented only by several catalogs of youthful works when these later came to light. Beyond the *catalogue raisonné,* he also devoted several books and special issues of *Cahiers d'Art* to Picasso exclusively.

To the latter, this gigantic work seemed perfectly natural; he was overjoyed every time Zervos and his collaborators showed him photographs of recently discovered or never-before-photographed old works, examined them carefully, commented on them, and so on, but never once asked Zervos whether all of this represented any financial strain. He did, however, make him gifts of several big paintings—but, unlike what happened with virtually all his other associates, he never once made a portrait of Zervos.

He almost did one of Yvonne. It was at the Rue des Grands-Augustins. Pablo had prepared his color crayons when she arrived; unfortunately she had mentioned the plan to a painter named Fernandez who, meaning no harm, came along to watch. Picasso put the crayons down and never returned to doing the portrait; all he did draw was Yvonne Zervos' hands.

"When André Masson calls one of his sculptures *Metamorphosis,*" Kahnweiler said, "it is because it shows a human being undergoing a metamorphosis into an animal, vegetable, or mineral. But there is nothing like that in Picasso, you can believe me. In the emblem he invented to represent 'naked woman,' the components are all there but merely rearranged otherwise than they would be in an actual woman's body."

The *Seated Woman* in the James Thrall Soby Collection at the New York Museum of Modern Art, the *Still Life* stripped down to abstraction (Juan-les-Pins, 1925) (in the Vicomte de Noailles Collection), the *Painter and His Model* which he kept as his own, and many other works of 1925–1926 bear out Kahnweiler's words. His imagination was at its height in the ferociousness of disjointing; as he dismembered the woman there appeared at times a desperate reaching for serenity, if not tenderness. One is surprised to discover on a sketch-pad sheet of Summer 1925 a phallic symbol along with two breasts with nipples in erection and a belly button. It is reminiscent of some fabled animal seen in an erotic nightmare, or the obscene semiotics found in obscure corners of cathedrals or the paintings of Hieronymus Bosch. In 1925–1930, Picasso was nearing his fifties, his domestic life was on the wane, and his sexual gluttony was becoming obsessive. He who had never lacked for women now doubtless worried that age would reduce his amorous capabilities and physical performance. After all, was not the entire universe he had built based on desire?

Picasso was nowhere in the Exposition of Decorative Arts of 1925, but Cubism was everywhere—or rather its ridiculously commercialized caricature. "People tell me, 'You're the one responsible for it,'" he commented acidly. "And the worst part is, they think they're flattering me. Just imagine Michelangelo having dinner with friends who say, 'We just ordered a fine Renaissance buffet with your Moses on it!'"

The great innovating movements of the postwar period, the ones that really upset given ideas—De Stijl, Russian Constructivism, the Bauhaus, abstract art—were absent from the Exposition. As was Le Corbusier. He was there only in the display he had himself taken for *L'Esprit nouveau,* the magazine he and Ozenfant published. The painting combined the conservatism of the official Salon, as reproduced in the colorplates of *L'Illustration,* and the safe kind of modernism practiced by Segonzac, Derain, or Favory.

The pioneers would do their work elsewhere, elsewhere build the world of tomorrow. For France, 1925–1930 were wasted years, those of aborted promises. Beginning with Art Déco, she rejected the present and lost her place as art leader for the future.

What the Bauhaus set out to do was ignored or ridiculed. What was to be learned from the Boches? Yet that was a key part of the future: the work of art was no longer an easel piece, a decorative panel, an isolated object, but one of the components of modern life, city planning, architecture, furnishing, environment, theater, movies, and so on. It was bringing into being a special dimension of artistic creation that Léger had grasped (but not followed up on) in filming the *Ballet mécanique,* and which Picasso missed. Except for his theater work, he was never to go beyond picture and decoration in their traditional meanings.

It would seem that Picasso was a victim of the artistic apathy in immediately postwar France, as well as his distrust of others and the hostility mass audiences showed him. Unafraid to violate millennial rules of painting, like most great revolutionaries he respected tradition and order, and saw himself more as liberator than disrupter. A prisoner of the "imaginary museum" inside which he was the eternal iconoclast, Picasso, in reality a nineteenth-century painter, was the last of the great masters of the past. Living alongside the inventors of the present, he passed them by: Kandinsky, Duchamp, Malevitch, Schwitters, Mondrian, the first great masters of the future.

From the sets and costumes for Diaghilev to the *Dove of Peace,* from *Guernica* for the Spanish Pavilion at the 1937 Exposition to the *Icarus* mural in the Paris UNESCO headquarters, by way of the Picasso Museum in Barcelona, he never turned down anything, none of the numerous requests to illustrate books, or the even more numerous shows and retrospectives around the globe.

"No one in the official world wants to hear of Picasso," wrote René Gimpel in his *Diary of an Art Dealer.* When Jacques Doucet died in 1929, no one considered whether his *Demoiselles d'Avignon* should be retained for the French national museums; it was eventually acquired by the Museum of Modern Art and no one contested its going to New York. This was the time when the head of the French public collections, after his losing fight against the acquisition of a Toulouse-Lautrec, had exclaimed, "A fine Louvre you're making for us!"

The first time a Picasso was officially acquired by France was in 1950! Until World War II, one painting of his was in the Musée du Jeu de Paume (devoted to foreign schools of art), the portrait of Gustave Coquiot. Pablo himself had made a gift of the 1901 painting to the State in 1935.

After the postwar lull, he was the only prewar painter who could be held up

*"The Milliner's Workshop" Paris 1926 (Musée
national d'Art moderne—Paris)*

(GIRAUDON)

against the Surrealists, the only one whose power of renewing himself and inventing remained intact despite success, fortune, and bourgeoisification. He was to tell André Masson, as the latter told me, that the dream and fantasy content of Surrealism never appealed to him. Were there to be dream painters, as there were painters of horses or flowers? he asked. And when Masson cited Max Ernst, he replied that he thought his collages were ridiculous. "Imagine," Picasso guffawed, "a dove coming out of a stationmaster's arse!"

The 1925 *Studio* is a still life that mixes realism and geometricism; the theater influence is appreciable and there are antique plaster fragments reminiscent of the previous period; the whole thing bristles with both baroque and static shapes. The 1926 *Painter and Model* on the other hand appears like a skein of inextricably intermingled arabesques against a background of big separated flat surfaces.

While celebrating creative activity in *The Studio* and *Painter and Model,* just as his own family life was falling apart and a new love was entering—and complicating—his existence, he was also inventing the image of a couple with much solider and more durable union, though symbolic of a peaceful conflict, a clash. The relations between painter and model are based not on sex but on the eye, which, progressively, is to become the sex surrogate. Not that Picasso was impotent or abashed: indeed, he remained the triumphant male whose attentions many women coveted; but two organs were none too many for one with his overflowing vitality—what with time growing short.

An anecdote told him by Léger delighted him. A new model had come to him, a young girl who, once stripped, turned out to be brimming with touching gracefulness, a picture of unblemished freshness and purity. "Well? What did you do?" Picasso asked. "What would you expect?" Léger replied. "I raped her."

Like any good Mediterranean, Pablo hated turning fifty. The approach of that fateful date upset and depressed him. So, beginning in 1925–1927, after a rather long period of calm and sometimes of soft torpidity, he now embarked on an era of anguish, distress, and fear. And at the same time he started his period of metamorphoses. Reinvention would henceforth be the motive force of his aesthetics and ethics, but now based on cruelty, violence, ugliness.

Look at the Women, the Bathers, sometimes called only Figures, that dot the years 1926–1930, cropping up in the summers spent at Cannes in 1927 or Dinard in 1928–1929. These Picasso *jamais-vus,* terrifying and grotesque as they are, are also unbelievably daring. In that woozy period that was discovering nothing, inventing little, and being satisfied with the banal and vulgar, he set up his monsters as so many challenges dotting the joyful beaches of the privileged of the world. The summer of 1927 meant endless sheets of paper with bathers whose deformations underlined the obsessions of those troubled years. What remained of their real anatomy was cut up and distorted in the light of a double constant concern: phallus or clitoris, sometimes both. The clear sculptural intent was to become more concrete with the years.

That same summer at Cannes he drew a series of projects for monuments, which, he said, might be set up along the Croisette. They were assemblages of

"Figures at the Seaside" January 12, 1931 *(private collection)*
(GIRAUDON)

powerfully molded shapes, all in sharp juttings, with atrophied limbs or slinky sex organs, pierced with holes. He continued these drawings at Dinard the next summer, introducing variants that made the monuments even more fantastic; he conceived extraordinary scaffoldings topped by large bubbles with holes and complicated by all sorts of tentacles, ambulacra, or fins, all to convey as much mystery as possible.

These inventions, resumed in Paris in the fall in the form of small sculptures, then wire constructions, exude a tragic atmosphere; they stand before empty horizons suggesting Tanguy—the Tanguy of marine horizons with scattered bones—and Chirico. They were published as "Picasso Projects for a Monument," in *Cahiers d'Art* in 1929, and they could not fail to appeal to Breton and the Surrealists. The Cannes and Dinard monsters are uncomfortably akin to those Max Ernst and André Masson were painting and drawing at the same time, or Arp's reliefs. But Pablo was actually closest to Miró.

The young man, on his first visit to Paris in 1919, had come to pay obeisance to Picasso. Later trips had acquainted him with the Dadaists and Surrealists, and then he settled on Rue Blomet, where his compatriot the sculptor Gargallo had lent him his studio. He made friends with Reverdy, Max Jacob, and his neighbor André Masson.

At Miró's first Parisian show, at the Galerie de la Licorne, in April–May 1921, Picasso had encouraged the blushing beginner. From then on, he was never to lose sight of the strange world of the young painter whose boundless imagination had forsaken the baroque naturalism of his early days in favor of a ballet of little brightly colored figures—men, insects, imps—suspended in midair like puppets. The Surrealists took to his dreamlike microcosm, so fantastic, gay, attractive, and bizarre; they turned his Galerie Pierre exhibit of June 1925 into a demonstration of their friendship. Picasso came again, and in November in the first Surrealist Exposition at the same gallery their works were side by side in the group show.

Picasso's eye was quick to assimilate what it could from the young Catalan's paintings. The round-eyed ectoplasms on deserted beaches, with aggressive phalluses, almond- or bean-shaped heads flying in space, surrounded by lighthearted arabesques like so many Ariadne's threads in that weightless universe, the vibrions and larvae of Pablo's 1926–1928 painting come directly out of Joan Miró's magic shop, but in the transfer they have lost their fantasy, turned sad and ambiguous. "It can be held that Miró had a largely determining influence on Picasso," Breton has said. Naturally, he was never to admit this debt and would rain derision on his friend, while always demonstrating indefeasible friendship toward him. One day, looking at a Miró in a Cannes gallery, he was to say, "For an awfully long time now he's been running after the moon dressed as a little boy." But was that really adverse criticism?

Juan Gris, who had been ill for a long time, was now reaching his end, and had to be rushed from Puget-Théniers to Boulogne in January 1927. Picasso had never let up in his animosity toward him. He once angrily asked Gertrude Stein at a Gris show at the Galerie Simon why she stood up for his work, when "you know you don't like it." She merely turned her back and walked away.

Gris died on May 11. Picasso and Olga were among the first to come to pay their respects, Pablo overwhelmed, for every Spaniard who died was like a piece of himself that was gone. He said, "I had painted a big black picture. I did not know what it meant, but when I saw Gris on his deathbed, there was my picture."

But, as Alice B. Toklas described it:

> . . . Picasso came to the house and spent all day there. . . . Gertrude Stein said to him bitterly, you have no right to mourn, and he said, you have no right to say that to me. You never realized his meaning because you did not have it, she said angrily. You know very well I did, he replied.

On May 13, Gris was buried at the Boulogne cemetery, with his son, Kahn-weiler, Lipchitz, Maurice Raynal, and Picasso as pallbearers. Now, in Cubist painting, and at the Simon Gallery, there was only one Spaniard.

While much of the popular press was unreceptive to modern art, L'Intran-sigeant, the leading Paris evening newspaper, took a great interest in it, often to the surprise or indignation of its readers. The editor-in-chief, Fernand Divoire, was an interesting man who had given carte blanche for a column each Monday by "Les Deux Aveugles" (The Two Blind Men). Under that byline, they ran articles on and interviews with Chagall, Le Corbusier, Léger, Rouault, Van Dongen, Matisse, Picasso—in a word, the very people whose work was dis-missed or disdained by most of their readers, who really thought the authors were blind. They were in fact Maurice Raynal and a young Greek called É. Tériade (real name: Efstratios Efeftheriades), who had come to France in the middle of the war, at eighteen, to study law, but had very quickly taken up with painters and poets. In 1926, he had joined Cahiers d'Art, recently launched by his countryman Zervos, who put him in charge of the modern-art department, allow-ing him thereby to meet the great artists he would later work with for his mag-nificent art books, notably Picasso.

Pablo was not one of those who came off best: he hated interviews and would write nothing on art himself. Nevertheless, in November 1928, he did let Tériade come to visit his studio and showed him some curious wire constructions with little heads on top, saying, "This is kind of the way I would like to do the monument to Apollinaire." Then he showed him his sketchbooks, especially the ones from Cannes 1927 with the monuments projected for the Croisette, that Tériade compared to "sculptures of stone bone remains."

"See," said Pablo before one of them. "It is generally taken for a seated woman. It's a leg of lamb, a potato, a fork, and a pickle!"

They looked at paintings. Pablo told how a garageman at Juan-les-Pins had asked him to pay for the damage he did by painting on his walls. When told that Picasso got paid for such works in Paris, he exclaimed, "Go on! You're not going to tell me that Parisians are such fools as that!" He also talked painting, and was quoted at great length in the newspaper (November 26):

> "When you stick colors alongside one another and trace lines in the air that don't

correspond to anything, at best that's decoration. In this period [pointing to a 1910 picture, 'from the Kahnweiler auction period'], we were passionately concerned with being exact. We painted only from a vision of reality that, through hard work, we tried to analyze plastically.

"What an effort every picture was at that time!

"I always stuck with that search for exactness in my own researches. There is not a painting or drawing of mine that does not exactly reproduce a vision of the world. I would like some day to exhibit my synthetic-form designs alongside those of the same things I did classically. You would see my concern for exactness. You would even see that the former are the more exact.

"I have a horror of all that abstract painting! Abstraction is such a mistake, such a gratuitous idea."

Four years later, the experience was to be repeated, and Tériade quoted him in *L'Intransigeant* (June 15, 1932):

"After all, nothing depends on anything but oneself. The thousand-rayed sun you have in the belly. The rest is nothing. That is all that makes Matisse Matisse. Just that he has a sun in his belly.

"Pictures are always made the way princes make their babies with shepherdesses. You never do a portrait of the Parthenon, or paint a Louis XV armchair. Pictures are made from a shack in the Midi, a packet of tobacco, or an old chair.

"The whole interest of art is in the start. Once started, it's already over.

"Somebody asked me how I was going to arrange my show, and I said, 'Badly.' Because whether a show, or a picture, is well or badly 'arranged,' is all the same. What counts is the spirit of continuity of ideas. And if that spirit is there all the rest takes care of itself.

"Nothing can be done without solitude. I have created a solitude for myself that no one knows about. It is very difficult to be alone today, because we have watches. Did you ever see a saint with a watch? I've looked all over without finding one, even among the patron saints of watchmakers."

At Dinard, during the summer of 1928, Picasso did a lot of little brightly colored pictures featuring a microcosm of ideograms in varicolored striped bathing suits, at all sorts of pastimes on the seashore, such as playing with a ball. By plastic means alone, without any recourse to imitation, he reconstructed the free joyful midsummer beach atmosphere, the heat of the sun, transparent sky, and heaviness of the perfectly blue motionless sea. He usually did one, or two, of them a day, all carefully dated. But on August 12 and 13 he interrupted this playful series with two women's masks of greatest purity, inspired by Hellenistic Greece, but more directly by the face of his new consort. Thus from time to time, the vertigo died down and stabilized; it was the time of metamorphoses. He was reinventing anatomy. The remodeling of man, completed by 1927–1928, was accompanied by a return to movement. These scenes are dynamic, with bright happy colors full of precise expressiveness in their daring. The figures, made of small multicolored pinheaded sticks, the spots, dots, stripes dance extraordinary, joyfully chaotic ballets. The Dionysiac vertigo of *Dance* is present in this frenzied world of little beings dressed in the striped bathing suits already fashionable at the time of Douanier Rousseau; but trouble is brewing behind the euphoric display, and the picturelets of Dinard, like the grimacing masks and monsters, are so many landmarks on the road to *Guernica*.

Picasso had shocked, upset, scandalized—now he frightened.

Naturally, Breton and the Surrealists were enthusiastic! Picasso alone, of those who preceded the war, signified to them: with authority, without compromise, while Braque, Matisse, Derain, even Léger were now in the semiretirement of glory.

Sex stimulation was the basic motive force of his lyrical flights; desire, with him, was violence, dismemberment, tumult, indignation, excess. No sentimentality: the Dinard women are not seductive; their vulvas, underlined with obsessive precision, are hardly attractive. But they are there, their reason for being and their emblem; to Picasso the very sign of life.

Torturing the shapes of women was an old habit of his, but even when pitilessly disjointing their anatomy, he had always respected their essentially human appearance, even kept a bit of their seductiveness. But now he put such hate into killing or ridiculing the vestiges of an already seriously shaken femininity that we must suspect other motives than purely plastic ones. A sentence in the *Diaries of Anaïs Nin* of May 1945 may give a key to Pablo's behavior with women: Alice Paalen, the wife of the Surrealist painter Wolfgang Paalen, who was Picasso's mistress, is quoted as saying that one of his joys was to deny women their climaxes. As Éluard wrote in transcribing a graphological analysis of him in 1942: "Loves intensely and kills the thing he loves."

Picasso was inventing an ante-human humanity, one with primitive man, wild beasts, now terrifyingly reintroducing the Giantesses. When asked why these visions of horror, he quietly answered, "To rid me of things that people can't see."

Sometimes humor crept in, and ugliness gave way to caricature. Striking colors with very "modish" refinements dressed up the pneumatic curves of the *Bather Playing Ball*, chasing the ball in her mauve swimsuit with yellow triangles. Her elephantinely graceful attitude, simultaneously painful and comical, is accentuated by the spongy bulbs of her body, her head like a rabbit's snout, round eye and upstanding ear, and the touching landscape about her, the beach cabanas, the verdant cliff with the flagstaff, and the tricolor waving against the blue-gray sky.

The strange thing about this repertory of monsters is that they never quite completely make a break with reality, and Picasso provides them with all his color resources. So that, once the deformations, disarticulations, and disjointing are accepted, one can only admire the variety of the fantastic iconography with the frequently recurring positions. For instance, the woman with head thrown back and mouth open, later to reappear in *Guernica:* Sexual surrender? Sacrifice? Perhaps both.

Salvador Dali, whose early works Picasso had seen in Barcelona a few years before, came to Paris, with his aunt and sister, in the spring of 1929, and wanted to see only three things: Versailles, the Musée Grévin waxworks, and Picasso. The Spanish Cubist Manuel Angelo Ortiz took him to Rue La Boétie and, as

Dali tells it, he and his "fellow Catalan" immediately sensed that each had met his equal.* Picasso's version, if any, has never been told.

After 1933, Ambroise Vollard, with whom Pablo was now on the best of terms, had set up in a private townhouse at 28 Rue de Martignac (Seventh Arrondisement). It was not what was called an "artistic" neighborhood; there were no dealers there, no artists' studios, but Vollard considered the location, within earshot of government ministries, embassies, and the aristocratic Faubourg-St.-Germain, a great step up in the world.

After buying the fifteen etchings of Picasso's *Saltimbanques* in 1913 (they were done in 1905–1906), he shied away from Cubism and until 1923 bought only five more plates, although in 1927 he did take fifteen more, of "classical" type, of which twelve, along with the line-and-dot combinations of 1926, were used in 1931 in *The Unknown Masterpiece.* Pablo then did thirty etchings for Ovid's *Metamorphoses,* to be followed by a number of other books: *Lysistrata* (New York), Éluard's *La Barre d'appui* (The Handrail), Buffon's *Natural History* (delayed until 1942), and *Afat,* seventy-six sonnets by Iliazd, all illustrated with etchings.

An unexpected theme now appeared in Picasso's work: the Crucifixion. In his youth, and even more recently, he had used the figure of the Christ crucified, but he had never gone into the totality of the Calvary episode.

Born Catholic, and one of his uncles being a canon, he had been baptized and (although he was married in his wife's Russian Orthodox church, which his mother took as an affront) his son was given Catholic christening and took first communion in 1933. Yet, Pablo saw one religion as being as good as another and the lack of any, no problem. Which did not mean he was without metaphysical concerns; Fenosa told me Picasso was "obsessed by God," the contrary of what most of his friends said, but he added quickly: "God, to him, meaning what accounted for Creation, what made man." And his faithful friend of half a century added, "He always talked about God."

He would tell Françoise Gilot, "There may be something to all that stuff about churches," as he dragged her into the one at Antibes, to make her "swear here that you'll love me forever." He had a deep feeling that some fatality outside of humans directed and led us. To accept one's destiny, to believe in that fatality, and thus to identify with it. Which might well be called God.

The studies Pablo made in preparation for the small 1930 oil called *La Mise en croix* show that his preoccupations of the Dinard days had not abated. Some of the figures, such as Mary Magdalen, are deformed and convulsed by a sort of rage; several 1929 notebooks are filled with them. He was haunted by similar doubts as he approached the subject of Christ. Perhaps as an exorcism. Who knows? "Who knows" was always a key phrase in his deportment.

From time to time, he would visit Max Jacob in his retreat at St.-Benoît-sur-Loire. These visits always upset the poet, for Pablo would bring along a beautiful woman, and the recluse felt he was being shown off as some kind of freak.

* Cf. *The Unspeakable Confessions of Salvador Dali,* as told to André Parinaud, translated by Harold J. Salemson (New York: William Morrow & Company, 1976), pp. 74–75.

Picasso's Hispano-Suiza was a local sensation when the "Paris people" got out of it, and Pablo's generous help, slipped to him unobtrusively before he left, only made Max feel worse.

One day, coming out of the basilica, Max pointed to its Romanesque sculptures and told a friend, "See, that's what Picasso wanted to do."

Pablo had been struck by a reproduction of the *Isenheim Altarpiece* by Grünewald in the Colmar museum, and in 1932 made several drawings inspired by these convulsions and nightmares of the Middle Ages. To him, the Crucifixion was not a pious image. As he told Brassaï:

> I love that painting, and I tried to interpret it. But as soon as I began to draw, it became something else entirely.

The death of Jesus, too, is "something else entirely." Narrow minds may see these drawings as blasphemous—but it is Spanish blasphemy that is in his work, with all its violence and roughness, its smell of blood and taste of death. Picasso reached the paroxysm of a delirium both sacred and sacrilegious, probably the acme of paradox—or of cynicism—but especially, in the painting dated February 7, 1930, the most overwhelming expression of his bowing to fate.

Picasso continued to inspire sarcasm and anger. All the official bastions of anti-modernism, seeing red in what they called the poisoned miasmas of Bolshevism, aimed at him as the horrid symbol of that invasion. And he met hate as he had glory, with indifference and detachment.

Camille Mauclair, the onetime Symbolist poet and artistic progressivist, author of books on Fragonard, Greuze, Rodin, and Albert Besnard, was now the mouthpiece for the attack on "false living art," and the right-wing papers parroted his pamphleteering, replete with obsessive anti-Bolshevism and visceral anti-Semitism. His fulminations against the "foreigners" found a good reception in the Royalist *Action française.* And in his blind hatred he lumped the "amazing nonentity" Matisse, Derain, Vlaminck, and Dufy's "corkscrews," in with Lhote, Léger, Van Dongen, Chagall, Chirico, Soutine, and Kisling—but his most violent diatribes were reserved for Picasso. His unforgettable "M. Picasso is famous for having invented the picture without up side or down" was applauded in *Le Figaro* and *L'Ami du Peuple* just as similar bilge was carried in the Hearst papers in the United States.

It is no laughing matter, for Mauclair actually was voicing what many felt, and what good students at the Beaux-Arts were being taught daily: Picasso was a hoax, his fake reputation, artificially built up by international Jewry, would not last; and the "modern" art dealers were impostors or crooks (mostly Jews, anyway).

A well-to-do young Swiss named Albert Skira, urged for some time by his mother to settle down and do something lucrative instead of running around, opted for publishing.

What would he publish? she asked. A book illustrated by Picasso, was his undaunted reply. And off to Paris, where he did succeed in seeing the painter at Rue La Boétie.

When Pablo asked him what book he wanted him to illustrate, the answer was, "A book about Napoleon." Picasso said he was not interested, and laughed it off.

But, the story goes, the mother came to Paris, interceded with Picasso, and nagged him until he changed his mind. Picasso finally agreed that someday he would do it, if the young man came up with the right book. From Pierre Matisse, the painter's son, Skira got the idea of doing Ovid's *Metamorphoses*. Neither he nor Picasso had ever read it, but it sounded like a very good idea.

Albert Skira got hold of a copy, and gave it to Picasso, who riffled through it. A few phrases and stories caught his eye. Amazingly, he agreed, and did the engravings: in this hard period of monumental rigor with stable austere structures, when Pablo was producing mainly monsters, the *Metamorphoses* brought forth again the antique light and joyful vein.

Deliriously happy, Skira joined forces with Tériade, who left Zervos' *Cahiers d'Art* to work with him, but he was terrified that Picasso's mind might turn to other things, and he might fail to complete the plates for the book. So he set up offices in a neighboring house on Rue La Boétie, the better to keep an eye on him.

"Each time I finished one of the copper plates," Pablo said, "instead of going to the phone, I took my bugle and went to the window, to blow Ta-ta-ti, ta-ta-ti, ti-ta-tati-ta-ta—and, presto! There was Skira!"

The illustrations for the *Metamorphoses* were printed at Louis Fort's: the dancing arabesque, grazing the contours of nude and free beautiful bodies, followed the whims of the painter's inventiveness. The limber rhythms bespoke an irresistible joy in living; here more than anywhere else there was justification for the famous phrase attributed to him, though Picasso may never actually have stated it in just those words: "I do not seek; I find."

This return to antiquity was a brief détente in the corpus of his work. Even in brutal or bloody scenes—Cephalus inadvertently killing his wife Procris, Meleager slaying the boar of Calydon, Perseus and Phineus struggling against Andromeda, and so on—he avoided excess, stressing sweetness, serenity, and elegance; his touch was incomparably seductive, with power such that, if he described the scene, he also brought into being light and space.

Then suddenly, his sexual obsession came again to the fore; the classical plates that he went on with after the *Metamorphoses,* at Vollard's urging, were suddenly marked by nightmares and violence. *Man Disrobing a Woman* and *Rape* translate the exasperation of a male harassed by desire; the line was jerky, nervous, the bodies became angular. What episodes of his private life were being expressed in these plates? For he was still continuing to write his private diary.

XIII

MINOTAUR AND
SLEEPING BEAUTY
(1931–1932)

PICASSO HAD TURNED FIFTY, AND DID NOT LIKE IT. HE IRRITABLY brushed aside the telegrams and birthday cards that piled up. The summer had been spent at Juan-les-Pins with Olga and Paulo, who was now all that kept him and his wife together. In one of fate's ironies, it was his very classical portrait of Olga, done at Montrouge in 1917 during their honeymoon, that had won him the Carnegie Prize, the previous year, the highest international award in the plastic arts.

However, he refused to go to Pittsburgh to accept it. He hated long voyages, and America did not especially appeal to him. Besides, he was not too happy over the work selected; the creator of Cubism being crowned for a "sensible" portrait, even a sentimental one, a perfect likeness—was that not a very backhanded compliment? He preferred to look the other way.

In order to be able to work quietly outside Paris, and have green spaces at his disposal, he had bought the Château de Boisgeloup, near Gisors in the *département* of Eure. It was very imposing, but what he mainly wanted it for was the outbuildings, for he planned going back to sculpture.

In Barcelona, his mother had worrisome problems. Doña María Ruiz had sold some four hundred of his youthful drawings to one Miguel Calvet for the negligible sum of fifteen hundred pesetas. The buyer had quickly turned them over to the Galerie Zak in Paris for 175,000 francs. Several had already been sold, but Pablo, who was furious, had filed suit against Calvet for swindling the old lady. He personally appeared at several dealers', accompanied by plainclothesmen, to try to repossess his drawings. In several of the places, he met with stern rebuffs, and one of the dealers even pointed out that he was scarcely showing proper gratitude to a profession so largely responsible for his fortune and fame. Picasso left without replying.

He immediately informed his mother and sister that no one had any right to dispose of youthful works of his that they might have. The suit against Calvet

*Portrait of Olga Picasso in an armchair   Montrouge
1917, artist's collection*

(GIRAUDON)

was tried three years later, in 1934; though he won, he was never able to get the drawings back.

The "Vollard Suite" is the high point of Picasso's graphics between the two world wars. The famous dealer had ordered a hundred engravings that he did between 1930 and 1936, printed by Roger Lacourière. Pablo liked to visit the engraver's picturesque workshop, at the foot of the Sacré-Coeur, an occasion for a walk through the neighborhood, alone or with a friend (in later years Sabartés, when he came to work for him).

Sometimes he took beautiful fur-clad ladies through these old and deteriorating streets. They might not enjoy this dip into the poverty of his past, but how could they resist the Ogre? This became a test for his consorts, both the "official" ones we know of, and others. Their reactions played no small part in how long their liaisons lasted and how intense they became.

This "Vollard Suite," at first glance, is disconcerting. It had twenty-seven plates on unrelated subjects done in 1930–1936, plus seventy-three grouped by theme: *The Rape* (five engravings, April–November, 1933), *The Sculptor's Studio* (forty-six plates, forty engraved March 20–May 5, 1933, six in January and March 1934), *Rembrandt* (four plates, July 27–31, 1934), *The Minotaur* and *The Blind Minotaur* (fifteen plates, May 17–June 18 and September 22– October 22, 1933), and three portraits of Ambroise Vollard.

For all the differences in theme and style and the fact that the plates were engraved in periods stretching over six years, the "Vollard Suite" has unquestionable unity. (It was printed in an edition of three copies on parchment signed by author and publisher, two hundred and fifty on Montval paper with the Vollard watermark, and fifty with the Montgolfier Paperworks watermark. The dealer having died in 1939, a large part of the edition that remained unsold was acquired during World War II by Georges Petit. Since 1950, the first of the series, signed by Picasso, have been commercially available.)

In the studio, the bearded sculptor works at top speed, his female companion alongside him; Picasso had returned to sculpture shortly before this and quite naturally these engravings were inspired by his work of the time. Like those of *The Painter and His Model,* they are less a personal diary than a sort of accompaniment or obbligato to his behavior, his work, what he is and is doing.

The sculptures the artist is working on are not always those of the model; while at times, nude and embraced, in tender abandon they look at a small bust or head on the workstand, more often his work in progress is a young horseman, a bacchanale with bull, or even a "Surrealist sculpture." He looks at the work; she looks at him. As Picasso joked, "She is saying, 'I never looked like that.' "

Thus the problem of creation is posed. Pablo at times had referred to it, in conversation, with a few brief, paradoxical, or sphinxlike sentences, expressing himself in witticisms or semi-admissions. In the engravings what he reveals are not only his concerns with figuration, but also with reality in general, man's relation to nature, and to woman, not so different one from the other. In one 1933 plate, the bearded sculptor crowned with ivy lies nude alongside the equally nude model whom he thoughtlessly caresses as he studies his work, representing two young horses in loving struggle. The symbolism is evident.

The tortured face of the man, the creator, contrasts with the serene or untroubled one of the woman, the creature (when she is not asleep). They look at the work but never at each other, as if the problem of communicability, of communion, went not from one to the other of them, but through the creation. Their bodies are often tenderly intertwined, and since they are nude we are given to believe their intimacy is total, though their thoughts are elsewhere; the alternation in the studio of realistic and abstract works informs us on the meaning and content of their concerns. This was the first time that Pablo was revealing the give-and-take between actual and invented form, which had obsessed him since his early days. For he, who, as he said, could "draw like Raphael" or Ingres and always asserted his devotion to realism, also knew that creation could only be invention and that, in Baudelaire's words, "anything that is not distorted is insignificant."

Were the truth of art and the truth of nature reconcilable?

In a 1927 engraving entitled *The Painter with His Model Knitting,* the artist, on his canvas, has transformed the model's skein into a purely abstract calligraphic maze. However, it can be assumed that in this case the model was not inspiring, since she is a scarcely appetizing old woman; so Picasso turned from the subject to the object.

Several of the Vollard plates deal with Rembrandt. "Just think, I made a portrait of Rembrandt!" Picasso said to Kahnweiler, who had come to see him. "It was another case of bad varnish. I had an accident with a plate and said to myself, 'It's spoiled. I'll do any old thing on it.' I began scribbling, and out came Rembrandt . . . ."

Kahnweiler noted this conversation in his diary on the date of February 6, 1934. "I started to like it, so I went on," Picasso continued. "I even did another one later with his turban, furs, and elephant's eye. . . . I'm going on with that plate to try to get blacks like his; you don't get that at one sitting." The four Rembrandt plates of the "Vollard Suite" were done between July 27 and July 31, 1934.

"Picasso's *Minotaur,* carousing, loving, and fighting, is Picasso himself. He is laying himself totally bare, in what he hopes is complete communion," Kahnweiler said.

The Man-with-the-head-of-a-bull, synthesizing antiquity and Spain, had hectored him for a long time. In 1913, Apollinaire spoke of "Picasso's hybrid beasts that have the conscience of Egyptian demigods." After the war, the Minotaur appears in a collage done January 1, 1927, later made into a tapestry, and in a later painting. He suddenly surged into the etchings of Spring 1933. First he took part, muzzle erect, in an orgy in the sculptor's studio, wallowing with the beautiful naked women. He also appeared as the cover of the first issue of Skira's magazine, *Minotaure,* and on four plates inside in which, scepterlike, he brandished his symbol of virility, the double-edged phallic dagger.

But the monster in the "Vollard Suite" does not long enjoy the pleasures that his ingenuous bestial nature have led him to. Wounded, he falls to the arena floor, his suffering wild and inhuman, yet moving and tender. Having tried to be part of man's life, he was betrayed, and now, a blind, pitiful monster, he is guided about by a little girl holding a dove or a nosegay. In the starry night, he raises his huge head with the dead eyes, beating the air with his great arms, a stick in one hand, as the passersby ignore him. This admirable velvety-black aquatint ends the story of the Minotaur.

While he was working at these engravings and returning to sculpture at Bois-geloup, important shake-ups were taking place in his country: Catalonia had proclaimed an independent republic on April 14, 1933. Like almost all Catalan intellectuals, Picasso was on the side of democracy, though Kahnweiler was to describe him as, until the Civil War, "unbelievably apolitical." Once, asked about his politics, he had said, "I am a royalist. Spain has a king, so that makes me a royalist."

Ilya Ehrenburg told how enthusiastically he had welcomed the Russian Revolution: an anarchist sympathizer like most of his youthful congeners, he had demonstrated in the streets against repression and colonialism. The Ferrer affair upset him deeply, but he never really became *engagé*. When he lived in Montmartre, he was afraid he might be deported if suspected of anarchist sympathies. And his brush with the law, over the stolen statues from the Louvre, left him a haunting bad taste.

The Surrealists had tried to involve him in their own political demonstrations, especially protesting the Moroccan war in 1926, in which they took a position close to that of the Communists, but he held off. That same year, Éluard, Aragon, Breton, and Péret had joined the Party, but in 1930 the Surrealist group, disagreeing with the resolutions of the International Congress of Revolutionary Writers held at Kharkov, broke with Aragon and Sadoul, who had attended it. The publication of Aragon's poem "Red Front" in the French edition of Moscow's *Literature of the World Revolution* caused the magazine to be banned from France, and on January 16, 1932, the poet was indicted for incitement of the military to disobedience and incitement to murder. Picasso signed the protest against this, one of the rare things he ever signed before World War II, along with Le Corbusier, Braque, Matisse, Léger, Bertolt Brecht, Thomas Mann, Federico García Lorca, and even Jacques Benoist-Méchin, who less than a decade later was to be a Vichy government minister and notorious pro-German. Aragon never forgot that friendly gesture of Pablo's.

Boisgeloup was now his domain, his refuge for quiet work, far from family arguments and invasions by fans, dealers, reporters, or friends. He did several very realistic landscapes showing the imposing structure of his seventeenth-century castle, the village, and the church with its great shade trees. Apart from an elegant but dilapidated Gothic chapel, Boisgeloup had huge stables and barns that he turned into sculpture studios. But the many large rooms of the main house remained quite empty, except for some pictures, usually his own, hung on their walls.

On the top floor, he fitted out rooms for himself, Olga, servants, and eventual guests, but his wife rarely visited there, finding it horribly depressing. He, on the other hand, was delighted with it, not only because he could work in peace, but even more because when he went out of the château he could leave his painting or sculpture at the point it had reached, knowing that no one would bother it by tidying up. This and his sumptuous Hispano-Suiza with its white-gloved chauffeur were constant reminders of his rise in the world. Yet he would never have dreamt of showing off by building a private townhouse such as Braque had, or driving Bugattis at eighty miles an hour as Derain or Vlaminck did. Or taking long trips to Tahiti, like Matisse.

To Boisgeloup, Pablo moved the press on which Louis Fort printed the plates of *The Sculptor's Studio* and others, notably the Rembrandts. For long periods, Picasso drove out there each day and left only at night. His friend Julio Gonzalez helped him with the sculpture, and sometimes they stayed on for several days, Julio's manual dexterity serving Pablo's inventiveness. And he felt better, "as happy as in 1908," he told Gonzalez. 1908: that is, *Les Demoiselles d'Avignon,* the Bateau-Lavoir, Fernande, poverty, friendship.

Kahnweiler was the one who suggested working with Gonzalez: Pablo wanted to do a monument to Apollinaire, in iron, which his compatriot had been working with so masterfully for several years. He called on him at his studio in Rue de Médéah (Fourteenth Arrondissement), and easily convinced him, for Gonzalez was in straitened circumstances. In an article Gonzalez wrote about him in *Cahiers d'Art,* 1936, he called him a "man of form," adding that in his earliest Cubist paintings

> he presented form not as a silhouette nor as a projection of the object, but by bringing to the fore planes, syntheses, and by the cube, as a "construction."
> . . . I often observed that there was no form that left him indifferent. He looks at everything, on any pretext, for all forms represent something to him, and he sees everything with a sculptor's eyes. . . .

Had Pablo himself not said that if his Cubist paintings were cut up, one would get sculptures?

Shortly after Apollinaire died, Serge Férat had started a committee to put up a monument to the poet. An auction had been held at the Hôtel Drouot, with manuscripts, paintings, sculptures, and other types of objects sold to raise the funds for it. Unfortunately, they were insufficient. Picasso, who had agreed to do the monument, made some maquettes, but some members of the committee objected. According to Paul Léautaud, editorial secretary of the stodgy *Mercure de France,* its director, Alfred Vallette, and his wife, Rachilde, asked whether some of those involved were not "too bizarre . . . 'furriners,' Cubists, Bolshevists, Dadaists, and assorted other 'Boches'?" *

Perhaps no one had bothered to inform Pablo that Apollinaire's widow, Jac-

---

* This may be taken with a grain of salt, since Léautaud, despite his friendly association with Fernande Olivier (he wrote the preface to her book on Picasso), became a notorious anti-Semite and xenophobe. (TR. NOTE)

queline, and Férat intended this monument to adorn the poet's grave in the Père-Lachaise cemetery. Originally buried in the military section, his body had been moved to a private plot bought by his widow. Pablo, always terrified of death, quit working on it when he heard this. Without advising those concerned. And time went by. Every year on November 9, he attended the observance of the anniversary at Apollinaire's tomb, and the monument was discussed, but nothing happened. Finally, with Jacqueline's agreement, Férat himself designed the head-piece erected there.

Some years later, Picasso revived the idea, thinking the City of Paris would give him a spot on a square near where Apollinaire had lived. But he had mis-judged the retrogressiveness of Parisian councilmen, to say nothing of some of Guillaume's friends. The Apollinaire monument, in maquette form, remained at Boisgeloup, as he and Gonzalez had left it. In 1972 Pablo authorized the Museum of Modern Art of New York, with his cooperation, to realize the monu-ment as he had originally conceived it, and that is where it now stands.

For a long time, Pablo had not felt so relaxed as here; his domestic scene at Rue La Boétie had been hell. Argument followed battle, and Pablo himself told how on one occasion he had dragged Olga over the floor by her hair. He no longer attended her social affairs, or wore the nice respectable clothes she had insisted on: he buried them in a trunk, where they may still be to this day. Years later, he explained the failure of their marriage with "She expected too much of me."

The Boisgeloup stable studios had become junk heaps; the wildest found ob-jects were there, with bolts, pots and pans, car fenders or twisted hoods every-where, springs underfoot, wires treacherously projecting. From this debris, held together with plaster and wood, came constructions of extraordinary freedom of form and invention, such as the *Woman with Raised Arms* (1932), *Head of a Warrior* (1933), *Woman with Leaves,* and those amazing little articulated dolls made of bits of wood and fabric, cheek by jowl with no less singular totems out of some forgotten ritual.

His inventiveness knew no bounds: with a penknife he carved out of bits of wood wiry characters with little chiseled heads and long-stretched limbs that later, like the metal-junk constructions, would be cast in bronze. Here we again have the primitive man, the wizard who could turn the humblest material into an idol and sacralize it; in the same way, in 1932–1933, he imagined huge plaster heads with prominent noses and eyes, some of them over two meters high! Several of these powerful and observant heads appear in *The Sculptor's Studio,* as objects of the contemplation of questionings of artist and model, at times presiding over their sexual congress.

At Boisgeloup, Picasso had few guests. In winter, he worked till nightfall in the large unelectrified studios; in summer, friends such as the Kahnweilers or Leirises—the young ethnologist and sometime Surrealist Michel Leiris had mar-ried Kahnweiler's sister-in-law—the Raynals, Braques, Gonzalezes, Zervoses or-ganized picnics on the terrace. Paulo played with the dogs, while Olga sulked;

she had noted, among the heads her husband had modeled, one of a woman that intrigued her, because it did not seem invented.

Picasso enjoyed this relaxation; until they left for Paris, he chatted with his friends in the shade of the great trees or in his studio before new works. Yet, one could feel his nervousness, his concern; more and more, he was moving away from Olga's hold and the social demands she had so long made of him.

One day when Roland Penrose was at Boisgeloup, Picasso showed him one of the Heads he had recently done and told him how he had been working on a wire construction that came to life only when his oil lamp threw its shadow on the wall, making a woman's profile. "I went on, added plaster, and gave it form," Penrose quotes him as saying: it looked strangely like the one that intrigued Olga.

"When you work, you don't know what is going to come out of it," he said. "It is not indecision, the fact is it changes while you are at work"—a turn of mind that a number of young artists accepted as gospel. And again, "At the start of each work, there is someone working with me. Toward the end, I feel I have worked on it all alone."

The extremely modest, almost self-effacing Gonzalez put it this way:

> As I see it, the mysterious side, the nervous center, so to speak, of Picasso's work are in his sculpture. It is the sculpture that has made people talk so much about his work, and earned him so much fame.

To this "someone working with" him, Picasso owed an elegance of volumes and decorative lyricism to which he added his own barbaric roughness, his daring choice of materials and shaping of forms, which, with him, even when moderate in size, always appear monumental. His sculpture flows from his primitivism, animated, sublimated by an almost magical conception of the power of things, whether some piece of junk, or everyday objects adapted or as is, integrated into his constructions.

On Boulevard Haussmann, in front of the Galeries Lafayette department store, on January 8, 1927, he had noticed a pretty blond girl, aburst with health; and looked at her, and looked at her. She was seventeen, with luminously blue-gray eyes that struck him. He followed her, accosted her, spoke, and she listened. "Miss, you have an interesting face. I would like to do your portrait. I am Picasso." Famous as the name was, it meant nothing to her, since she had not been concerned with painting. Nor had she thought much of love. "I was a bit of a ninny," she says today. But he persisted. "We will do great things together," he said, when she met him two days later at the appointed place in the St.-Lazare subway station. He told her he was married, but she did not care; she thought the whole thing amusing, and the man very nice. It reminded her that, a few years before, her mother had loved a painter; the coincidence made it all easier, brought closer the foreigner with the strange accent who was twice her age, yet seemed especially attractive. Especially because of the red-and-black tie he wore, which she has kept.

Her name was Marie-Thérèse Walter; she lived outside Paris, at Maisons-Alfort, with her mother, and was sweet and "a good girl."

Everything worked out as Pablo wanted it to. She let herself be carried away, aware though she may have been of the complications and troubles that might result. For the moment, there was happiness . . . and, reliving that period today, that happiness remains her most precious possession, even as she says, with a pale little smile, "I always cried with Pablo Picasso." For he was "wonderfully terrible."

He was literally crazy for her youth, her wholesomeness, her unquestioning surrender. His new conquest had a beautifully firm figure and the transparent blond flesh he had fantasized in his youth, seeing Pre-Raphaelite paintings. She was as nonchalantly sensual as Fernande, happy as Éva, startled and attentive as Olga was when first he met her. She had the disconcerting naturalness of women who take life as it comes, not thinking of what lies ahead.

Picasso had decided to get divorced. Marie-Thérèse discouraged him, since they were happy as they were. Olga, still not knowing, but suspecting something, was wild with rage when her husband suggested a separation. In order not to prejudice his case, he was as noiseless as an Indian about his new love. Unable to do without her, he asked her to come secretly to Dinard to be near him, while he spent the next two summers there with Olga and Paulo; and in 1930 she was to follow him to Juan-les-Pins, where, as in Brittany, she was put up a stone's throw from the Picassos' apartment.

Except for 1936, when they were to spend nearly two months in greatest mystery in a villa at Juan-les-Pins with their daughter, Maya, Pablo, on the pretext of the divorce proceedings that kept dragging out, never actually "lived with" Marie-Thérèse. After she moved into Vollard's house at Tremblay-sur-Mauldre, and to Boulevard Henri-IV in Paris, he stayed with her from Friday evenings to Monday mornings, and later, when Maya was in school, the Thursday afternoons she had off, and demanded that Marie-Thérèse write him every day. He himself sent her letters or delirious love notes, often illustrated with sketches, bouquets of flowers, with "I love only you," "I love you a bit more every instant," and "Beautiful love of my life, Marie-Thérèse of my heart." And this went on during his affair with Dora Maar, then with Françoise Gilot, he delighting in being Ogre and Sultan at the same time, relishing the ambiguous situation, the occasional stormy confrontations between the women filling him with sadistic satisfaction.

Marie-Thérèse adored Picasso, and still does, living on with her candid and forgiving naturalness in the memory of the being she feels was diabolical, which he was to her as to the others. Yet she tempers her after-the-fact imprecations with understanding references to the "poor dear." Almost a half-century after they first met, she is still bedazzled; she is still the same girl full of dynamism and laughter ("Pablo Picasso did not like for me to laugh," she says. "He was always saying, 'Be serious.'"), to whom he was neither famous painter nor married man, but just her complicated happiness.

In his loves as in his painting, Pablo expressed both his destructive aggressiveness and his love of life, a life without respites, in which he enjoyed moments of calm and happiness only if violence, cruelty, and despair lent them their indispensable counterpoints. Marie-Thérèse endured much from him, as would Dora Maar, Françoise Gilot, and some others less well identified. All three, however different in nature, got the same shock treatment. One was saved by her freshness of soul, another by prompt retaliation; but the third, Dora, would bear the scars of it throughout her life.

With Jacqueline Roque it was to be something entirely different. Picasso, when he met her, was past seventy, in the toils of the ultimate demands of sex. In eroticism, the best and worst of it, his tragic instinct and love of challenge, his cruelty and violence, bitter, wild, and desperate, would find a way to exalt and satisfy the amazing lust for life that was in him. Which, if we can believe the drawings and engravings of the "Jacqueline years," the companion of his last active manifestations amply stimulated.

Of Picasso's five "official" wives, beginning with the first legal one, none was to be as discreet as Marie-Thérèse Walter, nor any benefit less from his fame; she was to cause him the least grief and return in tenderness all the humiliations, wrenches, and suffering he imposed on her. She was probably the one to whom he was most deeply and lastingly attached—in his fashion, most often surprising or revolting.

Their affair long remained secret. Many of his friends were unaware of her, and of Maya. Kahnweiler assured me he never suspected her existence till after World War II; this was necessary so as not to jeopardize Pablo's divorce, and he enjoyed the secretiveness. He had his young mistress come and live right near him on Rue La Boétie, for the proximity of the Galerie Simon on Rue d'Astorg gave him excellent pretexts to go over that way. There was little chance Olga would criticize him for it, as she had always said he did not keep a close enough eye on his dealer.

This new love was a veritable fountain of youth for him. He was joyous again, playful, and the affair, which in the eyes of the law ranked as contributing to the delinquency of a minor, since she was no more than seventeen, titillated him with its equivocal and clandestine character. He made many portraits of Marie-Thérèse, cagily hiding her initials in them, and invited her out to Boisgeloup. Other times, on her bicycle, she would be waiting for him on the Gisors road, in the evening, on his way back to Paris. With her, he was back to his old Bohemian ways and sloppy clothes: their meetings were in suburban bars or discreet hotels of the environs of Paris. She even got him to go boating on the Marne—which might well have amazed his friends, had they seen him . . .

To the Ogre, she was dream, and comfort. As they did not cohabit, she represented escape; but once his break with Olga was final, and Marie-Thérèse became no longer a desire to go after, but a reality possessed, things changed. What had been fancy free now was habit, and, as Françoise was to write, "Marie-Thérèse replaced Olga as the one to escape from . . ." This was when Dora Maar came into his life.

The paintings inspired by Marie-Thérèse at the beginning of their affair were made of full enveloping curves, healthily, harmoniously voluptuous. The monsters had been exorcised. Picasso was visibly delighting in the spell of his charming regular-featured model, her waving hair, firm globular breasts, belly and thighs rounding into hairy plumpness. The pleasures of bed benefited him and his work.

Her presence at Boisgeloup was concretized in many Heads, often of considerable size, one of them with an aggressively phallic nose and vulva-shaped mouth that revive sexual obsessions which had seemed extinguished. The equivalence or permutation of faces and genitals was nothing new with Picasso. Behind the quiet dreams of Marie-Thérèse, new demons lay aborning . . . He would say:

> To displace. To put eyes between the legs, or sex organs on the face. To contradict. To show one eye full face and one in profile. Nature does many things the way I do, but she hides them! My painting is a series of non-sequiturs. . . . *

Gertrude Stein was writing her memoirs. While Picasso was buying Boisgeloup, she had bought a charming country house in the Ain Department, at Bilignin, which, despite the distance, replaced Rue de Fleurus. That was where she started her book, in the guise of the Autobiography of her friend Alice Toklas. On one trip to Paris, she asked Pablo to listen to a few pages of it about him; Olga came along. Miss Stein, sitting beneath her 1906 portrait, began reading: their first meeting, the posing sessions at the Bateau-Lavoir, friends of those days, and so on. When she mentioned the name of Fernande Olivier, Olga, who had been fidgeting on her chair, turned livid with anger and walked out. Picasso stayed put, and asked her to go on.

"You ought to go after her, and call her back," Miss Stein said. "All of this was so long ago." Grudgingly, he went looking for her, but Olga was gone. For months thereafter, she refused to see Gertrude, saying she had affronted her wifely honor. What could Pablo do but go to Marie-Thérèse and tell her his troubles? For almost twenty years, she admirably filled her triple role of lover, confidante, and sister of charity, so that one day her pitiless but bewitching torturer was to write her, "You were the best of all wives"—and undoubtedly mean it.

Olga was long obsessed by the imminent appearance of a book of memoirs Fernande had written about her affair with Picasso. Three chapters had run in Le Mercure de France, titled "Recollections of the Picasso Milieu." The publishing house of Stock accepted the manuscript, but then dropped it, probably under pressure from Picasso, nagged into it by Olga. Other publishers also rejected it, until finally in October 1933 Stock did bring it out somewhat abridged, with a preface by Paul Léautaud—perhaps because Pablo had raised their hackles by offering them money to keep it off the market.

Olga carried on wildly with Pablo over it, but hardly with justification, for Fernande was very discreet in what she said of her life with Picasso, if not necessarily true to fact. She had had only eleven francs to her name, she wrote, when she left Picasso, and now, twenty years later, was not much better off. After trying various trades, including reciting poems at the Lapin Agile, she was

---

* Coq-à-l'âne: "cock-and-bull stories"; or literally, "cock-to-ass." (TR. NOTE)

now living by her wits, her ripening charms still attracting much flattering masculine attention.

The master's fame kept growing, with exhibitions around the globe, his name variously meaning scandal, revolt, or hoax, and the prices of his works going up accordingly. Fourteen of his works were shown in the New York Museum of Modern Art "Painting in Paris" show, January 19–February 16, 1930. Nine were in another exhibition there May 17–September 27, 1931, and that same year, he had three others shows in New York galleries, as well as exhibits in London, Cambridge (Massachusetts), Chicago, Hanover, Munich, and Paul Rosenberg's in Paris. Notices were mixed, with the mass public generally against his "distortions," and when his "classical" works were shown they were greeted with comments of "See, he *does* know how to draw" or "That proves he's pulling our legs."

One day at the Salon d'Automne he stopped suddenly before a painting and said to a friend, "That must be by a Spaniard." It turned out to be Peinado, recently arrived from his native Ronda and on view for the first time in a Parisian Salon; Pablo asked that he come to see him and made him a member of his intimate circle.

The master was vastly amused to hear that at Madrid's San Fernando Academy, which he had attended thirty years earlier, teachers carefully avoided mentioning his name. Shortly before, through the painter Pruna, he had met a twenty-five-year-old sculptor named Apel-les Fenosa, the son of a small Barcelona tinsmith. His strange first name had been given him by his parents as a tribute to a Catalan poet friend of theirs, quite well-known at the time of his birth; he had one sibling named Palmyra, after the Greek city, and another Oscar, after Oscar Wilde. Fenosa remembers how cordially Picasso welcomed him, and the paintings he showed him and Pruna, the largest being that of three women marvelously traced in white on black, and how enthusiastically they reacted to them.

"Picasso was so happy to see us like his works," he says, "that he suddenly went into two or three pirouettes of joy!" And a few minutes later, half seriously, half joking (how could one tell with him?), he confided to them: "I had said to myself: 'If they don't like this, I don't know what I'll do anymore!' "

Pruna insisted Fenosa show the master his own work, so he closeted himself in his little room on Rue Oberkampf for a month, but was able to come up with only four small pieces to show timorously to Picasso.

"He put them on top of the radiator and crouched down in front of them," Fenosa relates. "He looked at them without a word for half an hour. I was terrified . . . Finally, he asked, 'Have you shown them to Level?' "

André Level, onetime organizer of The Bear Skin, now owned the Galerie Percier, Rue La Boétie, and of course Fenosa had shown them to no one. Picasso said he would, then added, "You need money more than compliments. Come back tomorrow. They'll be sold." And indeed they were: Level had bought them, and Pablo gave Fenosa the money. "Since then, he never dropped me," Fenosa adds.

Picasso's devotion to the young Catalan seems strange, particularly since the latter was no innovator but a portrayer of rhythmic, measured, mainly female human forms. He did more for him than for any of the many others he encouraged. For years, until Fenosa had it made in his own right, he supported him financially and morally. Fenosa lived by and off him, and yet he remained faithful to his own poetic charm, his decorative arabesques with their smooth plantlike rollings, and was influenced neither by Picasso nor by any of those around him. Instead of submissiveness or blind admiration, Fenosa repaid the generous Picasso with very deep gratitude and an equal amount of respect.

Pablo bought, or disposed of, many of his friend's works; when he died, he left 120 of them. He used every kind of ruse to help him without appearing too obvious.

Once, when they were at the Café Flore together, Fenosa recalls, Pablo said, "Got anything to do today? Come with me to Robiquet's." This was the name of his bronze caster in suburban Malakoff. Pablo shook various hands at the workshop, chatted, then sat down at a worktable with a ball of wax, which he then shoved over to Fenosa, saying, "Here, while I'm working, keep busy."

Pablo went out, and Fenosa almost mechanically shaped the wax into a statuette. When Picasso returned, he exclaimed, "Bravo! I'll buy that!"

"He realized," says the sculptor, "that I was really down on my uppers, and used that trick to give me some money. He had no business at all at Robiquet's that day."

Picasso's generosity and encouragement toward Fenosa are in sharp contrast to the scorn or cruelty he showed some other artists. What was Fenosa to him? Did he have a soft spot for him as a person? For his work? Even Fenosa cannot answer that. Picasso counseled him, "Make a sculpture a day, and make them cheap. The only real friends you will have are the ones who make money off you."

And Cocteau told him, "When Picasso gives you money, he is giving you his heart." A heart that, by some rare phenomenon, Apel-les Fenosa was given in its entirety.

The great Picasso retrospective at the Georges Petit Gallery on Rue de Sèze, in June 1932, was an event. It was the first complete showing of his corpus of work in Paris. Another, just as significant, was also taking place at the Kunsthaus in Zurich.

The selection of the Georges Petit, not very receptive to modern painting but specialized in established masters, the solemn character of the opening and its high-society guest list, the sumptuousness of the heavy gilt frames used to show the pictures to best advantage against the royal purple of the walls, all bore the mark of the Rosenbergs and Paris's high-luxury trade. Instead of the usual critics, prestigious dealers, the Bernheim brothers and Étienne Bignou had been asked to do the preface of the catalog. They called the show "as complete as possible . . . desired by the international élite, . . ." featuring a "central personality of the School of Paris."

Picasso, who always liked for his exhibitions to have a museumlike character, was delighted; he himself selected the paintings and saw to their arrangement. Several of his friends disapproved of the theatrical nature of the setting that was in such contrast to the provocative nature of most of the work. It was, to say the least, surprising to see Cubist constructions, Giantesses, and Picasso's disjointed and distorted figures in a setting more suited to society portraits or official Salon genre painting. Some, such as Raynal and Salmon, bemoaned the fact that Pablo was being increasingly dictated to by his dealers, that he did nothing without their approval, and worried over their reactions.

Indeed, he often answered, "What will Rosenberg think?" when called upon for something—but it was also often a handy way to dodge an issue. For he was as reluctant as ever to make decisions or let his choices be known. Sole master of his own creations, in private life he needed approval, acquiescence in what he did. This also allowed him to avoid a share of the blame for any failure.

The vernissage of the Petit Gallery was a Parisian social success, but the critics were less than overwhelmed. Georges Charensol was one of the few to see it as "the most important aesthetic event of these past thirty years." Only Zervos, whose *Cahiers d'Art* was, after all, Pablo's own fief, shared that view.

Germain Bazin, a young Louvre curator who with his colleague René Huyghe ran a magazine, *L'Amour de l'Art,* very much devoted to "respect of classical values," wrote:

> Picasso has drawn up his balance sheet. . . . Picasso belongs to the past. . . . His downfall is one of the most upsetting problems of our era.

And Jacques Guenne said in *L'Art vivant:*

> Like a *couturier* twice a year Picasso trots out the collection of his mind. In cosmopolitan Paris, he has played the role that Boucher held in the days of La Pompadour. . . . Picasso is but a delightful barbarian. He is descended from M. Ingres in the way railroad cars are descended from the Acropolis.

Yet the painter's prestige, his ascendency, impressed Guenne, who, though not blinded by it, did recognize

> . . . the mystical action he exerts upon all of us. . . . He is the artist who has best avoided compromising himself while making believe that he was forever taking sides. The Institute would not dare condemn him, and the Surrealists claim him as one of their own. He has created a sort of artistic Esperanto that each can interpret according to his own conscience and tastes. And a religion too. It is the unselfconsciousness with which he displays decadence that gives him his strange nobility.

Another critic, Pierre Courthion, averred:

> Against the walls of the rooms I saw something quite other than a reassuring spectacle. I had before me—drawings, colors, matter, and rhythms—a world torn, dominated by the Nietzschean idea of I know not what final order dredged up out of disorder itself.

The Zurich exhibition was no better received than the one in Paris, and it was the occasion for Jung to pontificate that Picasso's painting in his eyes amounted to the expression of a classic case of schizophrenia!

Jacques-Émile Blanche's society paintbrush was all softness, but this friend of Marcel Proust's had a pen that could be sharp. Writing about the retrospective (after inspecting the 236 paintings, watercolors, and drawings, covering thirty years of work), he said:

> Perhaps he too quickly demanded that we accept him without reservation. . . . Picasso no longer surprises, any more than the music of Stravinsky, his brother-in-arms at the vanguard of the shock troops. Too committed to be able to turn back, they are forced always to keep going ahead.
>
> The cruelty, the quasi-mechanical processes, the sexual obsession that some detect in Picasso's slightest sketches, the outstanding traits of his art, correspond to the needs of the present spirit and express it.

On entering the gallery, he had bumped into the painter himself, putting the finishing touches to the hanging; Pablo turned to him and, somewhat mischievously, asked him how he liked it. "Wait," Blanche replied. "I'm overwhelmed." And Picasso amiably became his guide, showing him the *Nude in Black Armchair,* dragging him from one canvas to another, toward Cubism, then away in the direction of a fine Ingresque nude.

A woman's torso from which, Blanche noted, pure white had been banished, made them stop: Picasso said he had wanted to create "the most luminous white," and the surprised visitor countered that the white was made up of blues and roses. Then, prudently, he stopped. He was, after all, already exhausted . . . He collapsed on an inviting bench and peered down the length of the great hall, where only the heavy gilt frames kept him from seeing every detail of what he called those "heroized easel paintings." And he came to realize:

> There are so many kinds that anything one might say that would be right for one of these pictures would be wrong for another. . . . Each manner, each stage of the Picassian journey requires the critic to change his position.

Still, in an attempt at impartiality, despite the knocking-about he had felt from style to style, he concluded:

> Recapitulating my feelings, it would seem that the latest avatars of the Protean creator of Rue La Boétie give the key to the enigma. Taste, taste, always taste, manual dexterity, Paganini-like virtuosity, the caprice of a craftsman who, from a bit of string, and some brass, concocts a piquant and poetic ingenious object. . . . He can do anything, he knows everything, succeeds at all he undertakes. . . . Child prodigy he was; prodigy he is in maturity; and prodigy of old age to come, I have no doubt. . . .
>
> But let him see what happened to Stravinsky, let him reflect on the awful consequences risked by those who put all their stock in novelty.

This long quotation fairly well sums up what most of the press and public were saying, as sampled in the earlier citations. The man was a demoniacal magician; his latest trick was the most fascinating, but the next might be even more so. No painter had ever so varied his styles. There was not one Picasso, but ten, twenty, always different, unpredictably changing, and in this he was the opposite of a Cézanne, whose work, the rigorous expression of his thought, followed that logical, reasonable course to fruition.

Picasso was not proposing any new art, but a succession of vocabularies, ranging from the classical to the most unheard-of. He was perpetually juggling "possibles." "Painting is stronger than I," he noted in a notebook. "It forces me to do what it wishes." And then, in 1966, he completed his thought: "I don't say everything, but I paint everything."

From 1932 to 1936, his picture production slacked off; in 1935, at the worst of his domestic wrangles, he even stopped painting completely for several months. But he was never inactive; now he was doing engravings and sculpting at Boisgeloup.

His affair with Marie-Thérèse did not interfere with his making a trip to Barcelona in the summer of 1933 with Olga, Paulo, and the dog. They arrived from Cannes on August 18, Picasso himself driving the Hispano-Suiza, as the chauffeur, Marcel Boudin, had been sent back to Paris. To befit their social position, the Picassos had rooms at the Ritz, and on August 22, after the family reunion, went off to Sitges, from where he returned delighted.

Only his mother, in Barcelona, sensed something was wrong. She, of course, had never liked the "foreigner," and in 1917 had done her best to discourage the marriage. Newspapermen, rushing to interview him at the Ritz, had no success; they had to content themselves with articles entitled "Picasso Won't Talk" and descriptions of his warm welcome at the hotel to friends of bygone days, Manolo, the Soto brothers, the Junyer-Vidals, Pallarés, Jacinto Reventos, Juan Vidal-Ventosa . . .

He took his young son to see the enormous pseudo-Renaissance palaces at Montjuich, and museums, the Romanesque murals he had once so admired in mountain churches, now moved to the Museum of Catalan Art to avoid their deteriorating. They also visited the Pueblo, with its typical bits of Old Spain left over from the 1929 International Exposition. His sister Lola's sons Fin and Xavier Vilato went along with Pablo and Paulo, and delighted in their uncle's recollections of his youth and childhood.

In October 1932, the government of the Generality of Catalonia had acquired from the city's most famous collector, Luis Plandiura, a large part of his holdings for the Barcelona Museum of Modern Art. It included a score of key Picasso works, mainly from his youth, which Plandiura had bought directly from him (they were friends and appear together in a photograph taken at the Galerías Layetanas in 1917). Among them were the portrait of Lola, *The Divan* and *Woman with a Shawl* (1899), *Lovers in the Street, Woman Before the Mirror,* and *La Diseuse* (1900), *Cancan Dancer, End of the Number, Streetwalker with Hand on Her Shoulder* and *La Nana* (The Dwarf Dancer) (1901), the portrait of Sebastián Junyer (1902), *Woman with Lock of Hair* and *Mother and Child with Scarf* (1903), the portrait of Mme. Canals (1904), and others. This superb lot, along with the *Harlequin* that he donated to the Museum in 1919, was to constitute the first step toward the "Picasso Museum" that no one at the time might have dared dream of.

In the summer of 1934, he again took his wife and son to Barcelona, and for a long roundabout trip through Spain.

XIV

"THE WORST TIME
OF MY LIFE . . ."
(1933–1937)

On a wooden plank, he had thumbtacked a section of crushed and pleated paste-board similar to those he often used for his sculptures. On top of this he placed one of his engravings, representing the monster, and then grouped around it some lengths of ribbon, bits of silver paper lace, and also some rather faded artificial flowers, which he confided to me had come from an outmoded and discarded hat of Olga's.

THUS BRASSAÏ, PICASSO'S OFFICIAL PHOTOGRAPHER AT THE TIME, TELLS in his book (*Conversations with Picasso*) how they concocted the cover for the first issue of *Minotaure,* published by Skira and Tériade, which appeared on May 25, 1933.

Pablo at the time was engraving the plates of the *Minotaur,* several of which show the fantastic inspiration of Surrealism. His big show at the Galerie Petit had had so many pictures close to that spirit that several critics called it one of the major events of Surrealism. The robots and monsters of the Dinard period, the terrifying *Naked Woman in Armchair* (1927–1929), *Woman Bather* (1930), the series of bones and metamorphoses reminiscent of the creations of Miró and Tanguy, were of course, quite as much as his wire sculptures and junk-objects, influenced by Surrealism. Picasso denied it, but we know how much his denials meant. As for Breton, such associations between Picasso and his movement delighted him quite as much as Pablo's arm's-length attitude, for he felt such behavior to be more naturally Surrealist than any forthright affirmation. In effect, Picasso really "joined" Surrealism by the game he played toward it.

Breton's esteem remained as great as ever; he appreciated the fact that Picasso had selected the Minotaur as one of the major themes of his graphics, for the Surrealists had taken as their own the ancient myth in which they recognized some of their most cherished ideas. The monster, revolting against the gods, broke the limits of being, defied established laws, and was the very symbol of the Greek word *hubris,* which they interpreted to mean "in revolt against authority." The Minotaur seemed to them the embodiment of an unconscious force struggling against Theseus, the man of reason who, finally, by getting hold of Ariadne, would be able to get through the labyrinth and kill the beast.

Picasso's monster was quite something else. Having always loved animals and lived among them, Pablo could not make one a villain. His Minotaur, god and beast, had the natures of both, revealing sometimes one, sometimes the other. He was closer to the bull in the bullring, powered by dark eruptive forces, than the Greek myth; brutal and cruel, yet if one of the beautiful nude girls he lusted after succeeded in taming him, he could be charmingly seductive. Defeated, he became pitiful, which was how Pablo portrayed the Blind Minotaur, led by a small girl with a dove; his terrible blindness when, head raised, he swung his arms so wildly, made him even more terrifying in his heavy hesitant gait. This bestial Oedipus is one of Picasso's most upsetting creatures. Yet his Minotaur and the Surrealists' were one and the same.

In succeeding issues of the magazine, Derain, Dali, Magritte, Matisse, Miró, and others, like Theseus of yore, were called on to do battle with the monster on its already famous cover. There were eleven issues until May 1939, the first being almost entirely devoted to Picasso, whose "extra-pictorial production" Breton had presented under the title, "Picasso in His Element."

In his own poetically incantatory tone, he detailed the sculpture of the master of Boisgeloup, and it is one of the poet's finest pieces about his unconstant and paradoxical friend, illustrated with Brassaï photos of Pablo's latest statues and views of the Boisgeloup and Rue La Boétie studios.

This was the first time Picasso had ever given a photographer access to the places he worked in; he had taken a liking to Brassaï and invited him to the circus at their first meeting. Tériade had hired the young Hungarian picturizer of Paris night life and unusual sights to photograph the sculptures for publication in book form, and Olga asked him to photograph young Paulo. He made several shots of the father, looking enigmatic under his rebellious lock of hair, with his dark "down under" look, posing in front of Douanier Rousseau's *Yadwigha* that he had bought so long ago from old Père Sagot. Brassaï noted that it was the concavity of his eyelids that gave him that hallucinated look; Pablo had a way of opening his eyes so wide that they seemed to become abnormally big and threatening.

That first issue also contained the drawings Picasso had been led to by the *Crucifixion* of the *Isenheim Altarpiece.*

Under Picasso's sign, Surrealism, like the tamed and "redeemed" Minotaur, finally made the difficult turn and "came back into art," while he was going around in circles. Having completed *Minotaur* and *Minotauromachy,* he revived their most dramatic themes at Boisgeloup in the summer of 1934, in several pictures full of violence and blood portraying the fighting bull and bullring confrontations. In the fall, total switch: he painted girls or women reading or writing, eyes down toward their tables, or, perhaps wearied of such intellectual pursuits, heads dropping and falling asleep. No great creative exaltation in these paintings; they seemed to reflect a certain weariness of his own.

Picasso's painting mirrored the epoch, alternately indifferent and fevered, in which, while in Germany and Italy fascism took on threatening proportions, the democracies sank into apathy or displayed beatific optimism. In Spain, the factions were tearing each other apart, riots following riots; churches burned, convents were looted, anarchists struck. France was suffering deep crises, scandals that made the "good people" sick. A spirit of surrender or bitterness was creeping into the literature of Céline, Mauriac, Malraux, Montherlant, Bernanos, forerunners of Sartre's *Nausea*. And the same in art: but now there was more and more talk of "sensible values," "vital forces"—manhandled and debased humanity had to be resurrected, humanism restored to the saddle . . .

Picasso naturally was called one of the "destroyers," as the conservative *L'Amour de l'Art* continued to carry on the "good" fight, and René Huyghe did not blanch to write: "Picasso has lived in the ecstasy of the self-repeating miracle, and in golden reliquaries displayed for our fervor the bitten nails of his talent." Huyghe, brilliant museum clerk, highly cultured and brightly intelligent, was the very type of young bourgeois who saw a whole world crumbling but refused to accept change. "After the Picasso shipwreck, how many fine pieces of wreckage will make us regret the captain's consciencelessness?" he wrote, while Germain Bazin, in the history of contemporary art that Huyghe edited, opined:

> Picasso's case throws a profound light on the essential ill of a period; his diabolical soul seems to suffer from the lack of the divine of which the twentieth century consummated the ruin. . . . He plays at being smarter than God, his pride driving him to ape the Creator. . . . His work is heroic in that it is the supreme witness of man struggling against matter. No wonder, then, that a period made him its champion, its troubadour, its hero . . . it found in him the most critical manifestation of what it was suffering from. . . .

During the winter of 1934–1935, Christian Zervos went to Boisgeloup several times and had long conversations about art with Picasso. Before publishing them in *Cahiers d'Art,* he submitted his notes to the master, but Pablo declined to read them. Here are some of the comments:

> The main thing, in these days of moral poverty, is to create enthusiasm. How many people have read Homer? Yet, everyone talks about him. That created the Homeric superstition. A superstition in a sense creates precious excitement. Enthusiasm is what we need most, both we and the young.
> A picture lives only through the one who looks at it.
> I would like for no one ever to be able to see how my picture was made. What does it matter? What I want is only for an emotion to be imparted by my pictures.
> One works with few colors. What makes them seem numerous is that each was put in its right place.
> There is no abstract art; everything is figurative.
> The painter paints through an urgent need to discharge his feelings and his visions.
> Everybody wants to understand painting. Why don't they try to understand the singing of birds?
> I don't know why everybody is concerned with art, trying to call it to account. Museums are so many lies. Most people in art are impostors. . . .

To the pictures already in museums, we added all of our own stupidities, our mistakes, the defects of our spirits. We made poor ridiculous things of them.

What we need is total dictatorship—a dictatorship of painters—the dictatorship of a painter to suppress all those who deceived us, the cheaters, the objects of deceit, the habits. . . . But good sense will always get the upper hand. We ought to rebel against *it*. . . .

If Picasso was in a quandary in this winter of 1934–1935, there was an additional reason: Marie-Thérèse was unexpectedly pregnant. Always one to share joys and sorrows with a friend, in this he was alone. Marie-Thérèse was merely an innocent bystander, if one may make so bold.

Maître Henri-Robert, one of France's leading barristers, was handling his divorce, but since Olga and Pablo had been married under community-property rules, if they parted everything they owned had to be appraised and split between them. This proved too complicated, so the proceedings were dropped. Olga and Paulo moved out to the Hôtel California, in the Rue de Berri, practically around the corner from the studio, and Marie-Thérèse, expecting in the fall, stayed at her mother's in suburban Maisons-Alfort.

This was when Pablo bethought himself of Jaime Sabartés, his close friend in youth, probably the only one who might share his problem and help him with it. A faithful admirer of Pablo's, serving him might help Sabartés forget his own failure. His bad eyesight had made it impossible for him to persevere as a sculptor, and his poetry, journalism, and other writings did not give him the satisfaction he could get by allying his personality to Picasso's triumphant one.

Sabartés had been a reporter in Venezuela and Uruguay, a correspondent for leading European papers, and he had married and had a son. He had painted and done pyrogravure in New York, and written two books on South American politics and mores, yet he had never lost his awareness of Pablo's blazing success. Now he received a real SOS, dated July 13, 1935: "I'm alone at home. You can imagine what has happened and what still is ahead of me . . ." Picasso wanted him to move in with him and share his life, take care of practical problems concerning the divorce for him, and handle his business affairs, dealers, the press, collectors, and so on.

On October 5, at the Belvedere Clinic in Boulogne, Marie-Thérèse gave birth to María de la Concepción, it being her idea to name the child after his little sister who had died at age four in La Coruña. She was to be known to the family as Conchita, until she herself diminutized her name into Maïa (Maya). Pablo and one of Marie-Thérèse's sisters went to the city hall and registered the birth, "father unknown"; a few years later, when she was baptized, Picasso, never one to be bothered by contradictions, stood up as her godfather!

The happy event brought only a brief lull in the lovers' troubled life. Pablo, delighted to have a daughter, helped Marie-Thérèse change and wash diapers, entertained the child who looked so much like him, and observed her at length sleeping in her cradle. The mother, now aware that Pablo would never get a divorce, spent her nights crying.

Indeed, Pablo, convinced that his life's work could not be appraised and split up, postponed the divorce indefinitely—permanently. For all their flare-ups, he was to see Olga often, get daily nagging letters from her, and, like a good Spaniard, go on honoring her as his legitimate wife, respecting her as the mother of his son.

Sabartés agreed to come as soon as practical. After stopping off in Barcelona, he arrived in Paris on November 12, 1935. Picasso was at the railroad station waiting for him, wearing an old raincoat, his cap down over his eyes. Their life at Rue La Boétie was quickly organized: they had a lot to talk about after twenty-odd years. Pablo, still never ready to go to sleep, would drag the conversation on into the night . . . even after they retired, still wandering about, hoping that maybe his friend might still be awake . . .

Picasso now was writing. Having stopped painting, and needing an outlet, he turned to the pen. "They tell me you are writing," his mother wrote him. "I think you could do anything. If some day I am told you are saying Mass, I'll believe that, too." Gertrude Stein's reaction was different. She did not fancy him as a rival in literature. Their relations, always subject to ups and downs, had been particularly strained recently; she was close to thinking that he was writing only to annoy her. On reading his first attempts, she told Salvador Dali that she could not abide painters' lack of poetic sense—and he promptly carried the word back to Pablo.

As she related it in *Everybody's Autobiography,* they met at a Braque show at Paul Rosenberg's and, after admitting she had said that to Dali:

. . . You see I said continuing to Pablo you can't stand looking at Jean Cocteau's drawings, it does something to you, they are more offensive than drawings that are just bad drawings now that's the way it is with your poetry it is more offensive than just bad poetry . . . you never read a book in your life that was not written by a friend and then not then and you never had any feelings about any words, words annoy you more than they do anything else so how can you write . . . well he said getting truculent, you yourself always said I was an extraordinary person . . . ah I said catching him by the lapels of his coat and shaking him, you are extraordinary within your limits but your limits are extraordinarily there . . . it is all right you are doing this to get rid of everything that has been too much for you all right all right go on doing it but don't go on trying to make me tell you it is poetry . . . well he said supposing I do know it, what will I do, what will you do said I and I kissed him, you will go on until you are more cheerful or less dismal and then you will, yes he said, and then you will paint a very beautiful picture and then more of them, and I kissed him again, yes said he.

Pablo went on writing. He would later write his play, *Desire Caught by the Tail,* during the icy winter of 1941 under German occupation, when morally and physically he was unable to paint. And other literary texts would grow out of similar personal problems. On the other hand, he would often use not words but drawings, to "correspond" with his children after his break with Françoise Gilot.

He had often pondered the worth or expediency of a creator substituting one medium for another. Writing, to him, was as much a visual exercise as painting; his words, his sentences were so many graphic images and, using varicolored crayons or inks, he played with their colors as he did in a picture. So his written pages, in his own words, looked like "a parrot's feathers."

He wrote in Spanish, almost without punctuation, but using longer or shorter dashes to separate thoughts. He once told Braque, at lunch in his studio, that "punctuation is a G-string covering the shameful parts of literature." Then he dropped even the dashes—and capitalization.

He consulted Sabartés: "What do you think of my writing without separating the words?" And immediately went to it, all in capital letters, running together the whole text of one of his many portraits of Sabartés. Zervos a few months later published it as illustration of a back cover of *Cahiers d'Art*.

This was a bad time, in which he lost his temper over the slightest irritation, taking his anger out on Sabartés, who gradually became used to his role as whipping boy. What had been Olga's apartment now became an annex to the studio, encumbered with the same mess of junk of all kinds. In the mirror above the mantel, between glass and frame, all sorts of notes and cards were slipped in, as Sabartés said, like "so many little flags." A bronze sculpture in the room seemed to him like a Christmas tree, with all the ornaments Pablo had hung over it: champagne corks, pompoms, wire, a little doll, a plume, a puppet's dunce cap, and obsolete bank notes—each a reminder of some event, date, place. "It was a sort of tangible notebook," Sabartés wrote.

Gradually, Pablo began to go back up to the studio again, but still did not work. He turned his pictures this way and that, looked at them, spent hours day-dreaming, and talked to Sabartés.

On December 12, 1935, about 11:00 A.M., he was sitting in the dining room while Jaime was setting the table in the kitchen. Pablo had fired all the help, keeping only a cleaning woman, and now they ate all their meals in there. Suddenly, the door swung open, the dog Elft ran in followed by her master waving a piece of paper: "Look, here's a portrait of you!" Pablo said.

Sabartés was surprised by the lack of punctuation, so they left the reading till after their lunch, since the writer himself was the only one who could give the proper cadence and rests. He read aloud to him, in Spanish:

> Live coal of friendship
> clock which always gives the hour
> joyfully waving banner
> stirred by the breath of a kiss on the hand
> caress from the wings of the heart
> which flies from the topmost height
> of the tree of the fruit-laden bower
> when the gaze turns its velvet toward the window . . .*

—the most beautiful declaration of friendship Pablo ever made. Sabartés, over-whelmed, was unable to speak, his nearsighted eyes overflowing with tears. The

* Translated by Angel Flores in: Sabartés, *Picasso, An Intimate Portrait*.

thirty years of maltreatment by his boss that were to follow were paid for here and now, in advance.

His cogitations had led Pablo to decide he ought to write pictures and paint poems. Breton made no mistake, when he prefaced his friend's poems in *Cahiers d'Art,* "This poetry cannot fail to be plastic to the same degree that this painting is poetic." The mix of tactile image, visual image, and aural image gives Pablo's poems amazing intensity.

In *Cahiers d'Art* Breton published several of the poems, translated into French by him, with his preface and a laudatory text by Sabartés: the torrents of colorful images concretized into cascades of tumbling, rolling words, truly automatic surges, delighted the Surrealists and won Pablo the friendship of one of his most inspired supporters, the later mentor of his political commitment, Paul Éluard.

As during the previous interregnum, after Éva and before Olga, Eugenia Errazuriz was on the scene again. Pablo was wearying of Marie-Thérèse; he felt she did not care about his problems or help him solve them. But had he not always kept her apart from them? Eugenia, on the other hand, was privy to them all, and although their intimacy may not have exceeded the privilege of sharing his meals in the kitchen, she lightened his burdens and prepared him for coming emotional involvements. Sabartés, who did not like any woman who got close to his friend, helped keep her at a distance, but she reappeared from time to time.

On an entirely different level was Marie Cuttoli, whom he had met in 1934. The wife of a senator from Algeria who was an important politico of the Third Republic, she had discovered native North African handicraft at Constantine and Sétif, and around 1920 set up an embroidery workshop in her home, employing young local girls. She tried to simplify the work they did, and commissioned Lurçat, then a young painter in his thirties with a passionate interest in tapestry, to do a very sober design of yellow and green spots on a wide white ground. This contrasted so with the overembroidered work of the times that Mme. Cuttoli's rugs were a sensation at the 1925 Exposition of Decorative Arts, the ambassador of Japan being her first buyer, and Jacques Doucet her second.

With Lurçat as adviser, she set out to revive the flagging old tapestry industry and opened a gallery on Rue Vignon, where Kahnweiler once had been. She approached the painters whose works she owned, to make tapestries from their oils: Braque, Léger, Miró, and Picasso. After she got to know Picasso better, Mme. Cuttoli was to collect a number of his works, the nucleus of her fine array of contemporary art.

For the moment, Picasso was reluctant, but she was persistent, and had very persuasive charm. He finally agreed to have the *Farm Woman* of 1932 transferred to wool, followed by *Two Women,* a superb 1934 collage. But this led nowhere, nor was there any real sense in copying paintings and showing the tapestries under glass as if they were paintings themselves. Lurçat and Miró were the only ones to do original cartoons for her before Marie Cuttoli, sensing her mistake, abandoned imitations. The two copies of Picassos remain as documents, milestones toward the rebirth of painters' tapestry, which Lurçat a few years later was to initiate.

In 1936, Picasso's *Minotaur Running* was woven at the Gobelins factory, and toward the same end he did a huge collage entitled *Women at Their Toilet,* one of his finest works of 1937–1938, but it was never woven. The project was resumed in 1970.

Still at loose ends, Pablo did a "word portrait" of Eugenia for her birthday, and saw a good deal of Braque and his wife, now friendly again, as well as Zette and Michel Leiris, Kahnweiler's sister-in-law and her husband, who kept an eye on the painter for him. "But no one else," Sabartés insists. At times, Pablo read them his poems, in French or Spanish.

Apart from these close friends, he occasionally saw Breton, Tzara, who in Spring 1935 prefaced a show of Pablo's 1912–1914 *papiers collés* at the Galerie Pierre, Benjamin Péret, Éluard, the Zervoses, and a few Spaniards, including the sculptors Joan Rebull and Fenosa. Ambroise Vollard was sometimes there when the poems were read, but they promptly put him to sleep. Vollard's insipid company drove Picasso crazy, but it was hard to avoid him, since Pablo regularly worked for him.

In Spain, a group known as A.D.L.A.N. (*Amigos de los Artes Nuevas*— Friends of the New Arts) wanted to hold a series of shows of his work. Nothing of his had been seen in his native land for a long time, except for one show at the Pinoteca Gallery in Barcelona, in October 1932, shared with Ramón Casas. Their first exhibition, to take place in the capital of Catalonia in February 1936, required extensive preparation. The Spaniards virtually took over the studio to get things ready, so he went to Boisgeloup, where—in his own very peccable French—he wrote a preface for it, published in *Cahiers d'Art.*

When Sabartés pointed out to him that it was full of mistakes, he answered, "So what?" Did he want him to remove everything that was personal to him, just to conform to some grammatical rules? He was echoing what Braque also believed: "In painting, too, the rules come later."

There was quite a crowd at the opening of the Picasso show at the Sala Esteva in the heart of Barcelona, on February 18, 1936. It was his first comprehensive show in his native land, finally allowing his countrymen to see his recent work. Sabartés, Gonzalez, Miró, and Dali came down from Paris, but not Pablo. In the evening, Radio-Barcelona featured Luis Fernandez, Gonzalez, Miró, and Sabartés, talking about their friend, and Salvador Dali called the work shown "a crack express train arriving in Barcelona forty years late." Then Doña María came on and, in a voice choked with emotion, talked about her son.

The show's organizers (headed by the architect José-Luis Sert) had deliberately stressed the creative periods of his work, omitting the Blue and Rose, already known in Barcelona. But the opening was marked by two unusual aspects: it was held at 10:00 P.M., with admission charged.

Students and intellectuals were exuberantly enthusiastic. Not so, press or public: unfamiliar with modern art or Picasso's development, they were less than lukewarm, even shocked. Nor was Éluard's lecture, delivered on February 17, made to enlighten them: very poetical, it was over the heads of the uninitiated. Here too, students and intellectuals alone were receptive.

La Publicidad published Picasso's portrait of Éluard done January 8, with the inaccurate legend, "A Week-Old Drawing by Picasso," over a text by J. V. Foix. Other papers were either silent or hostile. The regular art critic of *Mirador,* "The Weekly of the Élite," let his editor, Justo Cabot, speak in his place: under the headline, "Picasso Poorly Served," he expressed widespread reactions. People thought a poor selection had been made, its "ugliness" not representative of the painter's great talent, and even in *La Publicidad* one M. A. Cassnyes deplored the fact that he had not carried his experiments to their logical conclusions!

Pablo's poems, read over Radio-Barcelona by Ramón Gómez de la Serna, convinced many listeners that their famous compatriot perpetrated hoaxes in mixed media. But in Madrid, where the show was next presented, the critic Guillermo de Torre prefaced the catalog with a vibrant text, and the enthusiastic and fervent young poets Rafael Alberti, José Bergamín, and Federico García Lorca celebrated "the toreador of painting."

The Barcelona opening had coincided with the Popular Front's victory in the February 18 elections, and a kind of Spanish Spring was blooming in the working people's joy: the painter and democracy were entwined in the same fervent chant. "Picasso the Marxist!" was what the students had shouted at the Éluard lecture the day before the voting, and that hardly reassured the "élite."

After months of silence and reclusiveness, Picasso started going out again. With Sabartés and the dog Elft, he could be seen at the Deux-Magots, the Flore, or Brasserie Lipp, and of course more and more people now came to see him. Dealers, reporters, collectors, admirers—especially of the female gender—photographers, and seekers after favors of all sorts showed up, to be sorted out by Sabartés and admitted or sent away, according to the master's moods.

But Picasso, now the subject of all kinds of rumors, on March 25, left for the Riviera, not yet sure where he would stay. He would send his address to Sabartés, who was to write him in the name of Pablo Ruiz. Then Marie-Thérèse and little Maya came down to join him, for he still thought someday there might be a divorce without splitting up the paintings. In order not to prejudice his case, he swore Jaime to absolute secrecy; he alone was to know where they were: Villa Ste.-Geneviève, Avenue du Dr.-Hochet, Juan-les-Pins.

But he could not forget his worries. Sabartés was concerned by the many letters —usually one a day—he sent, something very unusual for him. It seemed to mean his friend was exercised, unstable. On May 14, a wire announced his return to Paris. Not a word about Marie-Thérèse, and only short replies to Sabartés' queries about his work of the past six weeks. But his trunk was crammed with paintings and drawings.

When he opened it, a few months later, Jaime would be speechless with surprise and admiration. In less than fifty days, Picasso had covered the entire gamut of a confounding diversity of sentiments, feelings, and impulses. His imagination had not ceased being stimulated, in no less amazing a variety of styles and techniques. Most of these works would remain unknown until Pablo had David Douglas Duncan photograph them in 1956, but we still do not know all of the paintings and drawings he did during that time.

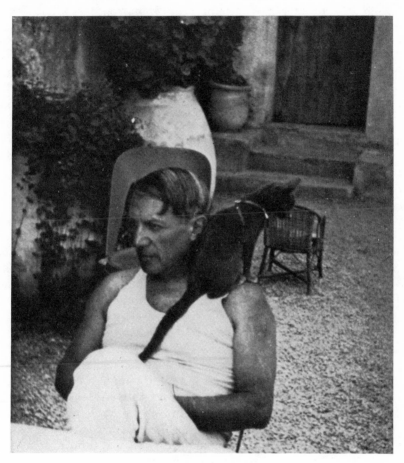

Picasso at Mougins, in 1936
(Collection of Sir Roland Penrose)

Never, in all of his "intimate diaries" of painting, had he so laid himself bare. Perhaps that is why he kept these works hidden so long, why some are still in the vaults he had stored them in—in order of size.

They start, at the beginning of April, with some amazing crescent-shaped profiles of Marie-Thérèse, in multiple variations. On April 5, a drawing: the Minotaur moving a load of the most heterogeneous things on a handcart, including a disemboweled mare, with head dragging on the ground. The next day, he turned it into a painting: the load on the cart is intriguing, looking like a matador's banderillas. "Not at all!" Picasso exclaimed. "That's a framed painting that the Minotaur doesn't want to leave behind. And the mare is not disemboweled; she has just foaled! See the little head and little red legs? That's the foal!"

On April 7, he turned to the family theme that he was to come back to several times during the month, sometimes including the Minotaur. Was there something personal in the bearded man looking at the baby in the cradle or its mother's arms? He is holding the mask of a horned god, while she is crowned with flowers, as Marie-Thérèse is in several portraits. This sad reminder of the new family that dare not speak its name is not without sexual obsessions. On April 16, he covers several sheets of paper, some of them sketches for paintings, with phallic variants.

Then, another theme: woman at her dressing table. Painted April 9 the first time, with drawings and paintings the following days, including erotic allusions in an oil of April 11. On April 13, two portraits of Marie-Thérèse, one bursting with colors, fragmented like a church window, the other a simple ideogram with curved rhythms, an even more simplified one on April 15. Beyond his beloved, he is seeing not only the intimate being, but the essence, the original core.

April 15, a still life: vase of flowers, pitcher of wine, fruit, bread. From one family to the next, everyday necessities remain the same. The woman may go by, the love change, but life goes on. These domestic subjects grow more complex: the father hugging the child passionately to him. A woman walking forward on the beach as the prone Minotaur eyes her curiously; she walks in solemnity, strangely clad, and seemingly reciting. In between, more portraits of Marie-Thérèse, each in its own style, different from the last, and its special technique, her attitudes and facial expressions seeming to follow a curious dramatic progression. On April 25, she is downcast, overwhelmed, weeping with face in hands. To reappear on April 26, triumphantly striped in bright colors, a hat on her head and a smile on her lips. Mona Lisa restored in a moment of happiness . . .

Then everything suddenly collapses. What tragedy inspired the scene painted in blue-gray on blue, April 29? Two nude women, confusingly intermingled, embracing, one holding the other, as if dead, at the seaside. Is this a lifesaving incident? A death scene? On May 4, a drawing elaborates: the two women are holding up a third, nude and swooning, their anatomies stressed with implacable precision in the most intimate detail . . .

Before one painting of a dark woman seated on the floor of a windowless bedroom, seeing herself crowned with flowers in a dark mirror, he was to say thoughtfully, much later: "This was the worst time of my life."

That painting was done April 30. May 2, same theme, while the day before he had painted two totally reinvented heads. But the woman, engrossed in detecting her face in the opaque mirror, does not see the monstrous striped creature that has just come into the room. May 8 and 9, the Minotaur is thrown to the ground in a bullfight. On May 10, a horse is trampling him, while a pure-faced woman watches the scene unfeelingly. On May 15, Picasso is back in Paris.

Let us not try to explicate this "worst time" of his life, or interpret its drawings and paintings. The only dominant fact is the constant presence of Marie-Thérèse's face, which in so many more-or-less reinvented versions he kept for his own, hidden so long. Hers seems to him the most harmonious, the most *logical* face and figure he ever painted; she is also the embodiment of uncomplicated sensuality, plain happiness, unbeset by problems. With her, he can forget his worries.

Judging from the pictures, among all his women, Marie-Thérèse was the one he most seems to have enjoyed making love to.

As soon as he was back, he went to work on the drawings promised to Vollard, "no one knows since when," for Buffon's *Natural History*. Almost every day he and Sabartés went to Lacourière's, where the drawings, as soon as finished, were engraved in aquatint. He watched every step of the operation, asking questions, suggesting alterations, gracefully accepting the decisions of the technicians whose skill he appreciated. The studies of animals, so dear to him, took Pablo's mind off his problems; thanks to his prodigious visual memory, he did them all without models. With these drawings, his feet were back on solid ground.

He also went back to his walks in Montmartre, gravitating to the Bateau-Lavoir, as if irresistibly attracted, sometimes dropping in on present tenants, more often cutting up old touches with Frédé at the Lapin Agile: the old man had only two more years to live, until July 1938.

Paul Éluard, with whom Pablo had become very close, celebrated May 15, 1936, Picasso's return, as the day he again saw "him I don't forget, him I won't ever forget." They had known each other a long time, but circumstances had kept them apart. A wonderful poet whose open sensitivity was a far cry from Breton's puritanism. Éluard like Pablo had lost a Russian wife—Gala, who had left him for Dali. After the shock of war, and a brief Dada period, he had made a seven-month voyage around the world in 1924, joining the Surrealists on his return, and the Communist Party in 1926. In 1929, on a Parisian sidewalk, he had met a penniless girl, ready to sell her body rather than starve and sleep in the streets. She was an Alsatian called Nush (real name: Maria Benz), whom Éluard fell madly in love with. She had been a hypnotist's stooge in a circus and Éluard was to say that for several weeks she refused to sleep with him, out of shame at not being a virgin.

Now everything changed: the poet was mad for her irregular-featured face topped by tousled hair, her delicate shape quite different from Gala's robust beauty. Nush, so much more knowledgeable, was readily amenable to the equivocal sex arrangements he fancied. She was to be always faithful to him as he remained ever faithful to love.

Picasso, aroused by the total congress of body and soul between Nush and

Picasso and Paul Éluard

(CARTIER-BRESSON—MAGNUM)

Éluard, since he had to hide his own feelings for Marie-Thérèse, threw himself desperately into one-night stands in an attempt to appease his Ogre's appetites. Later, at Éluard's suggestion, Pablo's relations with the couple, and perhaps other couples as well, would be different—and much more complicated. For now, Éluard, with his limitless admiration for Picasso, was all sweetness; his soft voice, slow and precious gestures, all the somewhat feminine aspects of the poet's makeup, intrigued and moved Pablo, his very antithesis. He was grateful to him for having trumpeted his fame in Spain.

Paul spoke in the same velvety warm tones of love, painting, Communism, Surrealism, brotherhood, and like Pablo he wanted to use language to break the prisonlike chains of reality and invent a human, exclusively human, that is, fraternal, world. To Pablo, he would say, "You hold flame in your hands and paint like a fire," comparing him to Prometheus, while Pablo in turn was to say that his friend's poetry spoke the "language of fire."

Pablo promised to illustrate Paul's book of poems, *La Barre d'appui* (The Handrail). One day at Lacourière's, watching the plates being pulled for *L'Histoire naturelle,* he took a copperplate, divided it into four equal parts, and in each quarter engraved a composition in a different style: Nush's portrait, a bird-bodied young woman before a very detailed seascape made of cursive signs looking like Arabic writing, a portrait of Marie-Thérèse asleep and crowned with flowers, and finally in the last his own handprint. Before the plate was cut in four to have the pictures printed separately, thirteen copies of the composite plate were pulled.

Many of his old friends were now to be found in the cafés of St.-Germain-des-Prés or Montparnasse. Entire evenings spent talking in the noisy, smoky atmosphere were a delight to him after the months of solitude and retreat; they let him forget himself. To Sabartés, with his weak eyes, they were torture, which Pablo may well have been aware of. But Sabartés never dared leave him and go home. This "café period" took Pablo back to his Bohemian days. His son, Paulo, now fifteen, would come along, unable to comprehend how his father could know so many people. Picasso never ordered anything but a split of Évian mineral water—which he often did not even consume—and around midnight, when the gang broke up, Sabartés going home to wash his tired eyes, the indefatigable Pablo would take Elft for a walk to the Gare St.-Lazare, to watch the night trains pulling out.

One day in January 1936, at a nearby table in the Deux-Magots, he noticed a girl whose calm, serious beauty struck him. With black hair and large dark eyes, she was much in demand, but her distant air put off most of her would-be suitors. Born of a Croatian architect father and a French mother, and raised in Argentina, she was back in France, where she had been introduced to the Surrealists by Georges Bataille. A painter and photographer, Dora Markovitch, known as Dora Maar, naturally spoke Spanish, and the first time Pablo said something to her she answered in his own tongue.

Éluard got them together. Dora Maar, who was no child, obviously knew just what Pablo was after; when she welcomed the Ogre's attentions, it was with eyes wide open. One day, as he sat next to her in the café, she took off her black gloves embroidered with little pink flowers, and while he spoke played mumblety-peg with a sharp little penknife on the table between her fingers. Sometimes she missed, and a drop of blood formed on her hand. Fascinated, Pablo asked her to give him her gloves, which he later kept in a showcase at his studio on the Rue des Grands-Augustins, among his souvenirs.

He asked her to come and take photographs at Rue La Boétie and Boisgeloup. Then he resorted to one of his tried-and-true tactics, going away with the current mistress while putting off till his return the conquest of the new one. When Marie-Thérèse went to Juan-les-Pins to join him, she did not even know Dora existed, and vice versa. But several paintings he did down there show more or less directly that, despite the importance given to Marie-Thérèse, Picasso now had divided feelings.

On his return to Paris, Pablo renewed contact with the beautiful photographer, whose entry into his existence was to make a complicated situation even more complex. Between the legitimate wife, being divorced, and the official mistress, who had borne him a daughter he adored, Dora slipped in, as through a narrow chink. With her robust body in full bloom, her madonnalike face without a smile, and her slow, noble, calculated gestures, she had an impulsive nature, given to sudden rages, thoughtless violence, and she would be the only woman known to be able to stand up to our Malagueño, look him in the fiery eye, and oppose his devastating tantrums with Baudelairian furies of her own that exacerbated her lover's lusting senses. But such a hypersensitive regimen could not be undergone for long; in the end, Picasso would win: Dora would break.

It was June 3. The summer nights were fine and warm, and they went from café to café, all terraces crowded. Pablo, wild for Dora, wanted to leave with her and the Éluards for the South, but he went right on seeing Marie-Thérèse regularly, giving her no inkling of his feelings.

On the evening of July 18, word came that trouble had broken out in Spain, then more precise news of a military rebellion begun in Spanish Morocco and threatening the régime. The very next day, many of the Spaniards living in Paris were knocking at Picasso's door, some determined Republicans, others favoring the army and order. He who had never given politics much thought did not hesitate: he spontaneously took sides with the defenders of democracy, that is, liberty. No hesitancy this time; he knew where he stood. And he was not alone; millions stood beside him.

Franco, who headed the rebellion, was well known. Fat and big-bellied, he was no leader, but a corridor tactician, especially dangerous because he cloaked himself in mystery. Could one forget how he had smashed the revolt of the Asturian miners?

The Republic under attack had to marshal its forces, and with this in view President Manuel Azaña named Picasso director of the Prado Museum. Did he or anyone think Pablo would come to Madrid to take the job? Not really; it was a symbolic appointment. It could not help but impress the democracies waiting to see which way the wind would blow in Spain, and they were quick to see how important art was to the legal régime, since it put its treasures in the keeping of the most famous of contemporary Spanish painters.

Pablo was overwhelmed: the Prado was one of the world's great museums. It was there that he had first been taken by his father to see the works of his country's great masters, which later he would make student copies of. Director of the Prado was for him, who scorned honors—but never turned them down— a title that hit him where he lived. But how could he fill the position? How preserve the museum's masterpieces from war? For he never for a minute thought of going to the spot.

In France, as in Spain just a month before, the Popular Front won the elections in March 1936. In the euphoria of victory, the Léon Blum régime decided to make July 14 a great working people's celebration. Among other attractions, a huge and boring theatrical pageant by Romain Rolland, written in 1901 and celebrating the fall of the Bastille, was to be put on at the Alhambra Theatre, with stage music written by Jacques Ibert, Georges Auric, Honegger, Darius Milhaud, and others.

Two young intellectuals, Jean Cassou, a great admirer of modern art and artists, a poet and essayist working in the offices of Minister of National Education Jean Zay, and Léon Moussinac, journalist and film, theater, and art critic, suggested Picasso to do the drop curtain for Rolland's *14 Juillet*. He accepted but, since time was short, offered a recent gouache, dated May 28, 1936, of a human eagle holding in its arms a dead Minotaur dressed in Harlequin's garb. Somewhat to the rear, a bearded man, draped in a horse's hide, carried on his shoulders a triumphant youth crowned with flowers, the whole scene taking place on a deserted shore with a half-collapsed building of several stories in the right background. The low-key harmony was of subtly matched blue-gray, rose-gray, and earth tones. The execution of the curtain was entrusted to Pablo's friend Luis Fernandez.

Spain was at war. The Moors, shamelessly emblazoned with the Sacred Heart, were ravaging the country, to the words of the Archbishop of Toledo, "The love of the God of our fathers has armed half of Spain!" In that cause, the people of Spain were to be sacrificed to the holy alliance of the powerful, the rich, the Church, and the military. At dawn, August 19, Federico García Lorca was executed by a firing squad.

Spain was at war, Spaniards were dying, and the director of the Prado was blissfully tucked away with Dora Maar on the Riviera. Bowing before the inevitable, she had given in to the Ogre. But since she lived at home, and had not informed her parents, she had to "go to visit a friend at St.-Tropez" so as to rejoin her lover. Driven down early in August by Marcel in the Hispano-Suiza, he had taken rooms at the Hôtel-Restaurant Vaste Horizon at Mougins, a small village above Cannes. This time, "I am not incognito; you can give my address to anyone," he wrote Sabartés.

The Éluards, the Zervoses, the Paul Rosenbergs, Man Ray, René Char all visited him there, to swim at Golfe-Juan or drive through the upcountry. Paul and Nush Éluard were his closest companions for the summer, and since Paul in love

Picasso with his friends at Mougins: Valentine Penrose, Lee Miller, Dora Maar, a friend, Éluard, and Lise Deharme (Collection of Sir Roland Penrose)

could truly possess only what he shared, and love what he offered another, he gently eased Nush into Pablo's arms. This was not the first time she had complied with her husband's sexual vagaries, to the great indignation of Breton, whose morals did not countenance such conduct. Nush was very nice about it, and loved Éluard the better.

It was quite simple: the poet was replacing the traditional conception of exclusive love in marriage with love for and by others. His gift to Picasso of the woman he so passionately loved could only sublimate their friendship, for there was nothing underhanded or calculated in Éluard's behavior. But when Dora Maar got to Mougins, things normalized. Although Pablo was not one to be satisfied with a friend's offering, he liked Nush immensely, and until the end she was to remain present in his life and work, and he was to write several poems about her.

He was painting little, strolling about, chatting, drawing from time to time, and following the news from Spain in the papers, with more curiosity than involvement. One day, he and Dora and the Éluards went to Vallauris, where ceramics had been made since Roman days. Pablo watched the workers turning the clay and then baking the pieces, at one of the potteries, and inquired about details, fascinated by this art that was new to him. Back at Mougins, Éluard incorporated an allusion to this in the poem, "À Pablo Picasso," that he was writing.

A minor accident in a car driven by an Englishman taking Picasso back from Cannes interrupted the calm of the vacation. He was more shaken up than hurt, but he took a fortnight to get over it. Around September 20, Marcel drove him back to Paris. His visits to Marie-Thérèse were resumed, while the Dora affair went on.

Madrid was being threatened by Franco, and the government rent by factionalism; but still wanting to preserve the Prado masterpieces, it sent them by truck to Valencia for transshipment to Geneva. The Franco planes were to hit the museum several times.

José Bergamín came to Paris to tell Picasso how the move to Valencia had gone, and he exclaimed, "So, I am the director of an empty museum!" When the poet mentioned having unrolled a canvas to discover it was Velázquez' *Las Meninas,* Picasso was deeply moved: "How I would have liked to see that!"

Dora, now a fixture in Pablo's life, first appears in his paintings in the fall of 1936. Like Marie-Thérèse, she was not actually cohabiting with him, but returned at night to her parents' on Rue de Savoie. She was not subjected to the usual visit to the Bateau-Lavoir or the confrontation with his past work, which she was already familiar with, but she had to put up unquestioningly with his visits to Marie-Thérèse and, on his return, his dithyrambic paternal ecstasies over Maya. As well as long scornful diatribes on sterile women—in dubious taste.

A few weeks earlier, Picasso had moved Marie-Thérèse and their daughter into a house of Vollard's at Le Tremblay-sur-Mauldre, some fifteen kilometers from Versailles. Though it was empty and required complete furnishing, this was a convenient way to get her at a distance so as not to interfere with his relations

Dora Maar at her studio at the Rue de Savoie
(BRASSAÏ)

with Dora Maar. Yet he still visited her several times a week and, as in Olga's day, spent each weekend with her, drawing children's pictures for Maya. He also did drawings for Marie-Thérèse's mother, who sometimes stayed there, usually cutout and colored masks. His notebooks were full of sketches of this "happy family."

Vollard had intended the house for Rouault, but the latter had no use for it. Pablo, on the other hand, fancied it, and in the winter of 1936–1937 he was to do a series of still lifes there.

On September 11, he drew a charming pen-and-ink portrait of Dora, "by heart," as he noted next to the signature and date. On November 24, in an oil, she was represented with the hieratic and somewhat distant air that had first struck him at the Café Flore. There were more portraits of her, her features distorted for greater dramatization: he tamed her thus by enclosing her in the endless traps of his contradictory styles. But now he needed a larger studio, for he had been commissioned by the Spanish Republic to do a great mural for its pavilion at the Paris International Exposition of Arts and Techniques, to be held in May.

Dora heard of an immense studio available not far from her parents', at 7 Rue des Grands-Augustins. It was atop an old seventeenth-century house that, before the French Revolution, according to legend, had been part of the Savoie-Carignan mansion, the one in which Balzac had situated the action of his *Unknown Masterpiece.* As if fate had intended this for him, Pablo did not hesitate a moment, and rented what was now known to neighbors as the "Barrault attic," because the young actor had occupied it for a few months.

News from Spain was worse than ever. The Loyalists were retreating everywhere, as Franco, supported by German and Italian units, gained the upper hand. Atrocities proliferated; each city taken by the so-called defenders of Christian civilization suffered executions and looting. The foreign legionnaires were especially adept at this, as they showed at Badajoz. In the west, La Coruña was invested, and to the southeast the attack on the coast around Málaga was getting under way.

On February 8, Málaga fell, and Arthur Koestler, who witnessed the weeks of battle there, was to recount the event to Picasso, telling how over a hundred thousand refugees fleeing the city were strafed and shelled by Italian planes and ships. The squadron commanded by André Malraux fought one of its last engagements over Málaga.

In February and March, Pablo spent several days at a time at Le Tremblay. On February 12, he painted *La Baignade* (The Bathing Party) there, reconstructing the mechanistic anatomies of the Dinard period, although with rounder volumes; aggressively phallic forms, limbs like pincers playing with a little boat while on the horizon, above the sea, a face appears—huge head with tiny eyes, mouth, and nose—a disquieting watcher.

At Rue La Boétie, Dora had succeeded in getting rid of Sabartés. Picasso tried to hold out, but in vain. In mid-January his old friend packed his bags and left the apartment they had shared for fifteen months. He moved to an apartment on

Rue Jean-Dolent (Fourteenth Arrondissement, and his *amie* moved in with him. But he continued to handle Picasso's business affairs. The morning he moved out, Pablo got up and left early, which he never did. "We said good-bye as if I were to be there when he returned," Sabartés noted; and added, "When I came back, I would have to ring and, like a beggar, wait for a crumb of friendship."

Courage was something Picasso did not display, any more than any kind of sensitivity; Sabartés' departure hurt him, but he never said so. Except perhaps in his writing or painting . . .

The later deportation of his friend Desnos by the Gestapo, or the death of Nush, were to "upset" Pablo less than purely banal little domestic events that affected him directly, for all his deep feelings about them. He once made a scene over Brassaï's using "his" thumbtacks.

The Barrault attic was no ordinary place; it was not reached by the fine wrought-iron stairway of the house, but by a dark threatening spiral staircase. On the way one came to a sign identifying the offices of the owners, *L'Association des Huissiers de la Seine* (The Society of Process Servers of the Seine Département), and since Pablo felt this might disconcert his visitors, he pinned a sheet of paper on his own door, reading, *"C'est ici"* ("This is the place").

The door led directly into a room he had immediately converted to his usual junk shop, and the next room was equally encumbered, paintings and sculptures everywhere, a Matisse leaning against a Modigliani on the floor. An inside stairway led up to the studio proper, another huge room as crowded as those below. Here Picasso worked and saw his friends, as earlier Barrault had lived there and held rehearsals of the Groupe Octobre to which he belonged, putting the whole company up when the work lasted too late.

From the studio, one could see a row of small rooms, apparently more orderly than the others, indeed somewhat "decorated." Pablo lived and ate there, and slept in a bed covered with an expensive fur throw, which several ladies have described. He even had a bathroom installed.

The amazing part was that there was another door opening on still another staircase, no less hidden and threatening than the first, reserved for close friends. This theatrical arrangement, also customary for secret assignations, delighted him, and he played on it like a virtuoso. In one little room of this Feydeau-Kafka farce-nightmare, he set up the handpress he had bought from the engraver Louis Fort: it was his "engraving workshop." That superb press, its arms equipped with rubber handles molded by hundreds of inky hands, was to go with him through many avatars.

Warmly wrapped up in winter, for it was hard to heat the huge studio, and in a sailor's striped jersey and shorts in summer, he entertained those Sabartés had let through to see him. Marie-Thérèse might come in one door, Dora the other, and never meet—even if Bluebeard did occasionally make a mistake on purpose. His paintings too had double accommodations, double entry.

Gradually, the portraits of Marie-Thérèse of the early months of 1937 underwent distortions that were less and less flattering; her curves began to get flabby, her face aged and wrinkled with unbecoming teeth. On the other hand, in a drawing dated March 1937 and entitled *Dora Maar Asleep,* the new inamorata appeared in all her glory; she had even taken from her predecessor what seemed to have been her own characteristic, and one of her most delicious attractions, her sleep.

XV

GUERNICA
(1937–1938)

GUERNICA, SUNDAY, APRIL 26, 1937: THE LITTLE TOWN OF SEVEN thousand inhabitants was symbolic, for it was under its famous oak that Spanish sovereigns, or their representatives, swore to respect Basque rights. This was market day, and the main square and surrounding streets were especially busy. At 4:30 P.M., bells rang out the air-raid alarm; there had been several before in the region, but Guernica had not been touched. The front was less than twenty miles away, but there was no target of military importance in the town.

At 4:40, a first wave of Heinkel 111s came in, strafing and bombing, followed at twenty-minute intervals by waves of Junker 52s, dropping incendiaries. Screaming with terror, people fled the burning town, but the planes followed them into the fields, mowing them down. Until 7:45, Franco's German air force kept after Guernica, leveling its center, killing 1,654, wounding 889.

The entire free world was revolted by this Nazi exploit. Picasso, as man and Spaniard, doubly felt the horror of it. This was the shock that reawakened his long-dormant political conscience. A Royalist when Spain had a king, as he once told Kahnweiler, he turned Republican the more easily because the new régime had not stinted its favors to him. What Éluard had told him of the welcome extended by intellectuals and students in Barcelona had deeply moved him— especially that shout of "Picasso! Freedom!" that the poet said he had so often heard.

The "detached" artist Pablo had been, the aesthetic narcissist, turned into a "committed" painter, the first and most vehement, most passionate in Spain since Goya, whose blazing genius he was carrying forward a century and a half later. Pablo, attached to his country by every fiber of his being, had never, as has been said, "lost" it. Spain always fed his art, picaresque, darkling Spain, festive, deathly Spain, with its songs, its walls, its moans of love or bloodshed.

That was where he was from—and nowhere else. Whatever the distance between them, he always remained abreast of the doings of his kith and kin. And in that closed, restricted world, war had broken out: everything that was the Spain

"Guernica" *(1937, May — early June). On extended*
loan to The Museum of Modern Art, New York, from
the estate of the artist

of his heart was shaken up and smashed. When the Spanish Republic asked him to paint a great composition for its display at the May 1937 International Exposition, it had implicitly hoped the work would speak for its cause. Writing in *Cahiers d'Art,* for March of that year, José Bergamín had clearly instructed the painter:

> Our current war of independence will give Picasso, as the earlier one had given Goya, conscious fulfillment for his pictorial, poetic, and creative genius . . .

His Spain expected from him a manifesto painting, a cry of revolt, a song of glory, a call to arms.

And he was not to fail it. *Dream and Lie of Franco,* in January, in among the serene portraits of Marie-Thérèse, was a word-and-picture indictment that fulfilled Bergamín's hope: Goya's outcry had found its echo.

Franco, at the behest of the Republic, in 1934 had brutally smashed the revolt of the Asturian miners, killing almost a thousand civilians, thirty thousand going to jail throughout the country, while neither Picasso nor anyone else protested. Now, with the help of his Nazis and Blackshirts, he was instituting in the peninsula a régime of terror which if victorious would exterminate all those who had expected the Republic to bring social justice, brotherhood, and freedom. Every day Pablo's countrymen, his family and friends, were dying, while others were imprisoned and tortured. The blood the Francoists shed was his own; his studio was now a rendezvous for Spaniards in mourning, seeking advice, or in need of financial help that he never refused. Those who were enlisting with the Loyalists, he bade Godspeed, and gave them letters of recommendation. From Spain came requests that he urge the Léon Blum régime in France to come to the assistance of its sister republic, and he served on committees, signed petitions. In vain. France and England watched the death throes of Republican Spain without lifting a finger.

Franco was the summation of all the nightmares that had haunted Spain: darkness and death. He was the hideous heir to the Inquisitors, the torturing Conquistadors of America, the obscurantists, fanatics, the sick and crazy crowned heads, all those who denied life, the enemies of happiness and freedom who, over the centuries, dotted the tragic destiny of Black Spain, living at the edge of Europe with its autos-da-fé and Black Masses. Witchcraft had long infested it, and Franco now picked up where those tools of Satan left off, in the repulsive, obscene, and grotesque picture of him that Pablo drew. He was a hairy monster with threatening fangs, soft flesh, wearing the *requete* cap as he faced the Spanish people, embodied in a fuming bull.

The pamphlet is made up of two sheets, the first with nine engravings, the second five, measuring 9 x 14 cm. per panel (12⅜ x 16⅞₆ in. per sheet). They were done on January 8 and 9, 1937, and printed immediately. A second state, with aquatint added, was pulled on May 15, and a third on June 7.

Picasso often heard from his mother, who described the ravaged churches and convents, the raped nuns, strangled priests; generally the Anarchists were the culprits. The situation in the Catalan capital was very confused, as the factions tore at one another. May saw bloody riots, followed by strikes. Communists and

Anarchists were not reluctant to shoot at each other; the ceaseless dissension, with the ensuing political complications, was a hindrance to the war effort. Not all of the Ruiz Blasco family was on the Republican side.

Pablo agreed completely with Bergamín and his Spanish friends: the great work commissioned from him had to constitute a statement of position, but spring went by without his having determined what shape it would take. All those in authority in Spain had not acquiesced in the selection of Picasso, fearing that his work might seem hermetic to the crowds expected at the Exposition, but he was supported by José-Luis Sert, the architect of the Spanish Pavilion, who had organized his recent shows in Spain; the poet Juan Larrea, who headed the Madrid government's propaganda office in Paris; and the young intellectuals and artists who were faithful to the Republic.

The first reports of the bombing of Guernica were printed in Paris and London the next day; the correspondents of several newspapers had witnessed the savagery of the wanton destruction, and, however much the Francoists tried to blame "Basque incendiaries" for it, these lies fooled no one—not even such right-wing papers as the *Écho de Paris,* which had taken up a collection to present a sword of honor to Colonel Moscardo, defender of the Alcazar in Toledo.

The crime of Guernica was a front-page story in all papers published in free countries, to virtually total condemnation, Franco propaganda notwithstanding.*
Ce soir for May 1 published pictures of the burning city, and many Spaniards came to Pablo's studio with the paper, cursing or weeping. That very day, he began the first studies for the great painting, which the event had triggered. He did not know exactly how it would come out, but he now had within him the exaltation and rage which, added to his own human suffering, were to be the yeast of the work aborning.

José-Luis Sert was the first to see these rapidly done sketches on blue paper, born in rage on May 1: confrontations of shapes some of which are aggressively sexual, men and beasts disemboweled and screaming, first draft of the mortally wounded horse that was to occupy the center of the final composition. The same day, a drawing in very pure line gives us an idea of the symbolic themes Picasso wanted to bring together: the majestically serene bull, the screaming disemboweled horse, mouth wide open, a tiny winged steed emerging from its wound, the

---

* The Francoists, and the French right-wing press, tried then and since to minimize the crime of Guernica. Two journalists, Bernardo Gil Mugarza and Vincente Talon (*España en llamas,* Madrid, 1968), with thirty years' delay, went through the official records of the town, to discover that less than two hundred people were killed on April 26. Official records are notoriously untrustworthy in wartime, and with time and hostile municipal authorities at work, they would be infinitely less meaningful. The evening of the bombing, many foreign war correspondents of all persuasions visited the ruins and attested to the number of dead; twenty-seven Basque priests, nine of whom had been eyewitnesses, confirmed their reports. There are still many people in Guernica who saw it happen. But, in addition, there is the testimony of the German fliers to whom that day's raid was merely one sortie among others, notably the fighter-pilot Adolf Galland (*The First and the Last,* London, 1955) and Marshal Goering, who confessed that for the Luftwaffe Guernica had been a proving ground (Juan-Antonio Ansaldo, *Mémoires d'un monarchiste espagnol* [Memoirs of a Spanish Monarchist], Monaco, 1953). No one on either side ever claimed that the city constituted a military objective.

woman, a sort of fighting Minerva, lying dead beneath the horse. Above, the bust of a woman peering from a window and lighting the scene with a lamp.

On May 2, Picasso drew and painted separately a cameo of the horse's rearing, screaming head with open mouth and outsize teeth. The battle was joined between painter and tragedy: studies followed one another in a sort of frenzy, Pablo being visibly possessed by the subject. He was expressing not only his revolt but also his pity, as in the admirable figure of a woman drawn on May 8. She is dragging on the ground, head back, shrieking her pain as she wildly hugs her bloody dead child. Looking at the drawings placed against the canvas, he was to say, "I wish they would crawl right up into the picture, like cockroaches."

Dora Maar photographed each study, each step of the work which was forever to embody the crime of Guernica in its title.

Picasso's coming out for the Republicans was quickly known; he became the standard-bearer of the Spanish people's resistance to Fascism. The Catalan students had been right to couple Picasso and Freedom.

In May–June 1937, the North American Committee to Aid Spanish Democracy and the Medical Bureau to Aid Spanish Democracy sponsored a show of Spanish war posters in New York. Picasso gave a statement to a young critic, Elizabeth McCausland, printed in *The Springfield Republican,* July 18, 1937, in which he said that, contrary to what Franco propaganda asserted, the embattled Spanish people took great care of their artistic treasures. He was giving the lie to right-wing propaganda.

> Everyone is acquainted with the barbarous bombardment of the Prado Museum by rebel airplanes, and everyone also knows how the militiamen succeeded in saving the art treasures at the risk of their lives. . . . On the one hand, the rebels throw incendiary bombs on museums. On the other, the people place in security the objectives of these bombs, the works of art. In Salamanca, Milan Astray cries out, "Death to intelligence." In Granada, García Lorca is assassinated. . . .

The Prado masterpieces were saved, just as Picasso, symbolizing the Republic's devotion to spiritual and artistic values, was curator of the museum. The Spanish people were fighting not only for their own freedom, but for what Spain with its prestigious heritage represented in the world. Spanish people and Spanish art were inextricably one and the same.

He made clear to one and all that

> The Spanish struggle is the fight of reaction against the people, against freedom. . . . In the panel on which I am working which I shall call *Guernica,* and in all of my recent works of art, I clearly express my abhorrence of the military caste which has sunk Spain in an ocean of pain and death. . . .

The first idea for the composition, drawn in pencil on paper, was done on May 9. Further studies underlined the importance to him of the screaming horse and the woman carrying the dead child. On May 10, he drew a head of a bull-man, impressive in its calm, symbolizing as in *Dream and Lie* Spain courageously, confidently facing Fascist aggression. There was a striking contrast between this head, with its unconquerable pride, and the images of terror and panic of the woman and horse. On May 11, the final composition was set on the canvas stretched from one wall to the other of the Rue des Grands-Augustins studio. Unfortunately, though huge, the studio was not high enough, and the 11-feet-6-inches-by-25-feet-8-inches canvas had to be slanted slightly, to allow him to complete the upper portions from a ladder, using long brushes.

During its execution, the composition was to undergo several modifications of detail, but the overall picture remained virtually unchanged. Dora Maar's photographs follow those modifications: the seven successive shots, between May 11 and early June, also illustrate the painter's behavior and mental processes. He began with that "vague idea" he had once told Kahnweiler was the way to start.

In the first studies, under the impact of shock, he let himself go to automatism, but the carefully dated drawings, going right on to completion of the painting (and, for some of the themes, even beyond), through their violence, power of suggestion, and breaks in style, reflect his deepest psychic reactions. Picasso's entire nervous system was shaken up without his yet having any idea where these eruptions of his inner self would lead him. He was allowing free association until the disparate elements of his wrath might coalesce into a synthesis. The event itself was being reinforced by its overtones; he was not avoiding the massacre, but when he got around to the canvas, eleven days after the first studies, Picasso had already established a certain distance between the shock of the event that triggered the work and his minutely established inventory of all the sufferings and horrors of war.

André Breton was to write of it, "The question no longer is, as once it was, to know whether the picture *holds up,* say, in a wheatfield, but indeed whether it holds up against every day's newspaper, open or folded, which is a jungle." *Guernica* is black and white, as were the pictures Picasso had seen in the papers, where the headlines, telling of the crime, were shocks of black ink on white paper. For many years, the TV images that brought the day's events into even the humblest abodes were also to be black and white. As Jean-Louis Ferrier said, *Guernica* "is the first painting of the mass-media era. Practically the only one to date."

Intensely and violently modern in its direct visualization of the event, the work leaps across time to join hands with the medieval apocalypses, which in the manuscripts painted by the Spanish monk Beatus de Liebana also expressed the great fears of the people. Its triangular composition recalls the pediments of Greek temples or Roman tympana. Beginning with improvisation, Picasso had achieved synthesis: the outcry turned witness—to the crimes of both the Fascists and those who, out of cowardice, left them unpunished.

He has never deigned to explain any of its innumerable symbols. So the evocative power of *Guernica* remains without any clarifying overlay: it affects the viewer's sensibilities directly without any intervening screen. The title itself refers to the original shock, not to the content of the painting in which, despite the realistic character of the scene and the many spoken allusions, nothing *precisely* represents the massacre of April 26, 1937. While Picasso carefully signed and dated each preliminary study, he never signed or dated *Guernica*. This "true allegory," as Courbet might have termed it, not only transcends the event, it also exorcises time. Every war, every crime committed by the "military caste," from Lidice to Sakhiet, from Oradour to My Lai, is anticipated and condemned in *Guernica*—for such great works are both the announcement and the recall of what we have not known, have not seen or personally experienced. Picasso's witness aims not to express the *reality* of war, but its *truth*. Now and forever.

Guernica reawakened him to "sentiment." Beyond the cerebral cogitations of Cubism, he was going back to the most painful works of the Blue Period. He who could be cruel and cynical with friends, pitiless with his women, was touched to the quick when Mankind was concerned. To him the tragedy of his country involved the fate of Everyman. Indifferent to World War I, largely unconcerned by the proclamation of the Spanish Republic, having heretofore painted only what touched his own life, his personal feelings, he was now won over to a cause. Never having hidden his indifference, he would not hide his commitment either; once *engagé,* he would be so body and soul, totally honest in his passions. "Picasso," said Claude Roy, "wears his heart on his canvas."

Against his usual custom, he allowed many friends and visitors into the studio while doing *Guernica:* the work seeming to him a message and manifesto intended for the widest possible audience, he felt it natural that it should come to life before everyone's eyes—he even (unheard of!) asked for advice. Amid his sketches all over the floor, Picasso, in shirt sleeves and brush in hand, commented on the work for the friends who were with him; José-Luis Sert, Juan Larrea, José Bergamín, Jean Cassou, André Malraux, Maurice Raynal, Zervos, Paul and Nush Éluard. The poet was one of those who had gotten Pablo committed; the two men saw a great deal of each other, and it is certain that many of the *Guernica* symbols, difficult for us to make out, originated with Éluard, daily present at the work, who was to write an admirable poem on "the victory of Guernica," and later the commentary for Alain Resnais's film.

Among the visiting journalists, occasional young, pretty women might be asked to stay on with the painter. Dora Maar closed her eyes to the ravenous appetites of the Ogre, who still went on seeing Marie-Thérèse regularly. Both of them appear in *Guernica.*

He often pointed out some change to a visitor in the studio. He had contemplated using color at one time, and tried pasting in bits of paper: striped or flowered paper for the dresses of the weeping, shrieking women, one for a while even having a tea napkin as a scarf. But the idea bothered him. One day he cut a teardrop out of red paper and tried it on various eyes, finally putting it on the bull's. But then he took it off: the red splash weakened the impressive inwardness of the monochrome. Jokingly, he told José Bergamín it would remain the "furtive tear."

One may wonder whether Marie-Thérèse Walter was aware of Dora's presence in Pablo's life, for even when he was in Paris, he went right on sending her torrid notes full of pledges of eternal love along with bouquets and sketches. Each note, from the very start, had been preceded by a monogram linking her initials, *MTW*, with *P* for him, and then *C* for Conchita, after the birth of their daughter. This continued despite time and new loves.

She regularly wrote him, since he insisted he could not live without her letters. When she came to Rue des Grands-Augustins, he showed the devil's own ingenuity in keeping her from meeting Dora. Marie-Thérèse was too wide-eyed in love to see through him. As for Dora, though she was aware of her rival, he had assured her that there had long since ceased to be anything between them—which did not keep him from occasionally reading her some of Marie-Thérèse's letters, even as he would later to Françoise Gilot.

One day while he was painting it, he announced to Marie-Thésèse: "*Guernica* is yours." She believed him; but did not know where she could put it. He often made this kind of promise, no sooner said than forgotten, somewhat the way an actor says his lines without meaning them. With enough expression, they "get across." With Picasso, there was a touch of sadism in this: to deceive, humiliate, disappoint, all added up to the same thing—to destroy. Nor were his women the only victims of these cruel hoaxes, intentional or not. When Maya was twenty, her father told her to go to Cartier's and pick out whatever she wanted; she did, but her father never sent the money along, and she had to do without the jewel.

The last mission of André Malraux's squadron in Spain had been the protection and rescue of refugees from Málaga in January 1937. He visited Pablo in Paris a few weeks later, and came again several times while *Guernica* was in the works: they spoke of Goya, the battles Malraux had been in, and death. In the course of his work, Picasso had carefully studied the *Tres de Mayo,* the double lighting of which fascinated him: moonlight on the village and the hillock before which the men condemned to the firing squad scream with rage and fear, and the lantern placed behind the riflemen. The latter lights only the one man standing in the foreground, arms raised, face expressing revolt, trousers and shirt immaculate—as if crucified.

Picasso continuously mentioned Goya to Bergamín, Alberti, Éluard. He knew his work better than that of any other artist. He told a painter friend, "The funny part is, when Goya came to Paris he did not go to see Delacroix, but Horace Vernet!" While Vernet was indeed his Parisian guide, it is likely the son of the onetime ambassador Fernand Guillemardet, whose portrait Goya had done in 1798, took him to see the painter of the *Massacre at Chios*. Although Pablo also voiced his surprise over this to Malraux, the latter never checked it out.

When Malraux told Picasso he thought he had made good use of his subject in *Guernica,* for all his lack of concern with subject, Pablo answered that he believed in themes rather than subjects, and then only if they were symbolically expressed. And what did he mean by theme? The symbols themselves. In *Guernica:* war, death, Fascism, country, mother love, and just plain love—since he included Marie-Thérèse the sweet and Dora the weeper.

Was the bull symbolic of evil (Fascism), or of the Spanish people? We might opt for the latter, but Picasso told Jerome Seckler of *New Masses* (March 13, 1945), "the bull is not Fascism, but it is brutality and darkness"—which is no great help.

Juan Larrea saw the disemboweled horse as a symbol of Spain, while Picasso said it was the people. Yet, as the passive victim of bullfights, it might well symbolize sacrifice and anonymous death, unnoticed and disregarded. However, in *Dream and Lie,* it was Franco who was identified with the horse, while Pablo seemed to be expressing empathy with the Minotaur. Had he not several times identified with that animal himself?

All this ambiguity explains much of the disappointment of some Spanish Republican authorities when they first saw *Guernica.* Now so familiar as to appear classical, at the time it was not quite what they expected. But what did they expect?

Juan Larrea says they considered *Guernica* antisocial, ridiculous, and unsuited to the proletariat's wholesome mentality. They even thought of dropping it from their pavilion, but felt that would be offensive to Picasso. When it was shown in New York in 1939, *Art Digest* headed its report: "*Guernica* misses the masses, but wins the art critics." But after the war Clement Greenberg could still write that the immense painting is like a pediment with a battle scene that has been run over by a poorly functioning steamroller.

On the other hand, Ilya Ehrenburg, *Pravda*'s Spanish correspondent, on his way home stopped at the Exposition to see his friend Picasso's painting, and wondered, as he was to recall:

> How had he captured the secret of the future? . . . The Spanish War was an old-style war; doubtless the Luftwaffe looked on it as grand maneuvers, but the Guernica raid was a small operation, like the test of a pen before you start writing . . . Picasso's canvas has all the horrors of the future, raising to infinity the atomic cataclysm, the world reduced to rubble, the triumph of hatred, despair, the absurd, nothingness.

Where the Spanish officials complained of *Guernica*'s not being realistic enough, Ehrenburg countered, "Reality demands to be treated from higher up, not as a mere episode, but viewed from the very heart of the tragedy."

Guernica has the same kind of dislocation, the same tragic disorder as Picasso had put into the Crucifixions he derived a few years before from Grünewald's masterpiece. For it is indeed another crucifixion, that of a whole people sacrificed as Christ Himself had been. Yet it was in the name of this God of Love that Franco's soldiers, with the Church's blessing, were putting Spain to the sword! Making *Guernica* one of the most powerful works of sacred art.

During the course of his work, Picasso was visited by the great English sculptor Henry Moore and Roland Penrose. As they were deep in a discussion of the old problem of reality expressed in the fiction of painting, Pablo suddenly disappeared and came back with a long streamer of toilet paper, which he stuck to the hand of the fleeing woman on the right: she suddenly looked like someone caught in the act of defecating, and taking to her heels without realizing how ridiculous she looked. "There," he told them. "No question now about the most common and primitive effect of fear."

Most spectators' reactions at the Exposition were colored by their own political allegiances in the war. But some Catholic intellectuals, such as François Mauriac, Georges Bernanos, Jacques Maritain, and some priests and religious, though not of the Left by any means, could not stomach the coalition of Fascist leaders, Moorish mercenaries, and high churchmen: they came out on the Republican side. Pablo's commitment was not so ideological as theirs: he was personally affected by the crime of Guernica.

Christian Zervos devoted a whole issue of *Cahiers d'Art* to *Guernica*, presenting Dora Maar's series of progressive photographs and a selection of Picasso's studies. Naturally, it was all a tribute to the painter, with articles by Jean Cassou, Georges Duthuit, Pierre Mabille, Michel Leiris, Bergamín, Zervos, and Éluard's eloquent poem, "The Victory of Guernica," as a pendant to his friend's paintings.

At the same time, a great restrospective show of the main artists and movements of our century was being held at the Petit Palais under the title of "Masters of Independent Art." While it brought together many of those artists whom the French government had systematically ignored (Picasso, Braque, Juan Gris, Léger, Picabia, Villon), it put its main stress on modernist realism, so-called human values (Segonzac, Waroquier, Maurice Denis, Derain, Maillol, Despiau, Vuillard, and others), and the organizers exerted all their hypocritical faculties to try to show the "humanistic" side of Fauvism and Cubism, rather than their revolutionary character. Thus, Lhote, Marie Blanchard, and La Fresnaye were given very extensive representation.

Thirty-two works, including two sculptures, gave an objective overview of Picasso, though he was far from the most favored of those shown. He had a room of his own, but it was off to one side, where the President of France, at the official opening, was not taken: Cubists, Surrealists, and abstractionists were not to be allowed to offend the presidential eyes! This ostracism brought forth some protests. At the instigation of the Zervoses and a few other interested parties a countershow was organized on the ground floor of the Museum of the Jeu de Paume, called "Origins and Development of Independent Art," to do justice to the modern movements. Hastily put together, on a virtually nonexistent budget, it was no more effective than the one at the Petit Palais—and it was criticized for including too many foreigners, such as Picasso!

Yet, looking at *Guernica* at the Spanish Pavilion, a woman was heard to say, "I don't understand what it means, but it does something to me—as if I were being hacked to pieces!"

With *Guernica* completed, Picasso returned to one of the themes that had most concerned him during its execution: the weeping woman. His numerous tragic studies (based on Dora Maar), drawn or painted, with their twisted or shrieking mouths, and their double eyes streaming tears, are overwhelming in power and intensity. As Marie-Thérèse had been the woman of his return to calm and serenity, Dora became his vision of tragedy. Her whole unstable character suited her perfectly to the combination of the grotesque and the desperate that appeared beginning with the various heads of Weeping Women in early June. Screaming or crying, heads thrown back or biting on their kerchiefs, these women scarcely look human; their eyes are out of their heads, tears large as peas streak their cheeks, and their mouths are distorted into horrible grimaces.

Their affair was dizziness at danger's edge; they loved and destroyed each other to the utmost. A sensitive, impulsive, intelligent artist, she drew deep sensual pleasure from embodying tragedy in the work of the century's greatest painter. She took a somewhat morbid delight in being the victim of the double Picassian-Spanish trauma. He, having remained profoundly attached to Marie-Thérèse, periodically returned to the regeneration, the recreation of her love, resulting in serene, sweet, brilliantly colored works. The conjunction of his meeting Dora and the outbreak of war in Spain changed all that: "She Who Sleeps" was relegated to the privileged domain of memory, as "She Who Weeps" became the obsessive reminder of the painful, tearful present. Dora represented *what happened to* Picasso, *what happened to* Spain—for which, he would never forgive her.

Leaving *Guernica* to the preplexed critics and public, he took Dora, and a new Afghan hound he had just bought, Kazbek, to the Hôtel Vaste Horizon at Mougins, where the year before he had been with the Éluards. In Spain, with the fall of Bilbao, things went from bad to worse, and Pablo painted Mougins houses in raw, almost childish colors, flowers, skies yellow as Van Gogh's sunflowers, and Dora's face.

But he was anything but serene; his only light moments were when he described the Italian Blackshirts as "seeing the enemy with their behinds." In Madrid, on July 3, an International Writers' Congress, organized by Ehrenburg and two other Soviet writers, Fadeyev and Alexis Tolstoi, brought together Ernest Hemingway (writing *The Fifth Column*), Malraux, Bergamín, Rafael Alberti, Tristan Tzara, Antonio Machado, and other prominent intellectuals of many countries. It had been suggested that Picasso be invited, but it was too obvious that he would decline. The Loyalists were grateful for the money he sent, and the help he gave their friends in France, his statements and paintings; asking more would be too much.

In June 1937, the French government, amazingly, had bought a *Still Life with Pitcher* by Picasso, at a public auction, for 56,500 francs. But in November the Artistic Council of National Museums had rejected it, by 12 votes to 5. Was this another official slap at the creator of Cubism? Not exactly, for he himself had felt the painting to be less than his best, and asked that it not be shown in the Jeu de Paume, to which it was supposed to go. His suggestion that they "buy a different one" was taken as a sign of greed, rather than a desire for quality; no other was bought, and that was the end of that.

To make things worse, he and Sabartés were now on the outs. After moving out, Sabartés was deeply hurt, and, when he answered a summons to testify in the Picasso divorce case, Pablo turned against him completely. Sabartés countered by spreading all kinds of nasty rumors, which were naturally repeated to Pablo, who closed the matter with one of his sharpest barbs. "What did Sabartés ever do in life?" he asked. Then, after a pregnant pause: "He has me, that's all . . ."

The year before at Mougins he had lived in a small, almost bare room; now he took a huge one with a balcony, and turned it into a studio—that is, a hopeless mess no one was to disturb. He worked all day, swam, had Marcel drive him to Nice or Monte Carlo, and spent time in the countryside with Dora and their friends. A favorite evening pastime was crusing the streets of old Nice, whose sordidness reminded him of Barcelona's *barrio chino.*

Mornings were often spent at the beach, sun and sea bathing with Dora, and watching pretty bathers dash by, as he lightly undressed them with his pencil. A beautiful American photographer, Lee Miller, who had been Man Ray's student and friend, and Roland Penrose, whom she was later to marry, shared these innocent pastimes, far from the warring world. Dora took pictures of Pablo stripped, sun worshiping, a bull's skull in one hand, a stick in the other, with eyes closed, like the Minotaur. Lee, an expert lenswoman, immortalized the lovers side by side, their torsos above the water, powerfully carved male and female figureheads, he nervous, she full-chested, like sea-gods looking us and the future in the eye, Picasso unshakably confident, Dora smiling stereotypically with a somewhat troubled look. The Picasso family album and life-style documentation was growing apace.

When Éluard one morning asked what he had been doing, he replied, "Portraits." During this summer, he painted mainly faces, from memory, although the models were nearby. Tragic or serene, generally distorted and tortured, they were a gamut of variations of expression, in which as usual he mixed invention and daring, emotion and calm; they were Éluard, Nush, Lee, and especially Dora. And once again they began to combine full face and profile. This method, applying to people the descriptive technique that analytical Cubism had used only on things, gave Dora's face, and especially her eyes, increased intensity.

The violent, angular *Woman with Cat,* with its sharply contrasting colors, is a double challenge: the grotesque appearance of the woman in her outlandish hat and clothes and the repulsive character of what she is doing and laughing uproariously about; for she is breast-feeding a kitten on her lap. Picasso claimed to have seen this happen. Dated August 30, 1937, it was painted at Mougins.

In mid-September, he decided to go back to Paris. The Éluards had gone, and there were few people about. Accompanied by Marcel, who had somewhat replaced the absent Sabartés as confidant and aide in his often complicated situations with women, he made trips to Antibes, Nice, Menton. Some days he asked to be let off at certain places, to be picked up later at designated locations, after what he said were long walks. But, years later, Marcel still wondered what those long walks were all about.

Except for the commissioned *Guernica,* and the *Dream and Lie of Franco* graphics, Pablo had not painted a single canvas about the war, the daily bombings of civilians, the hundreds of people summarily shot, the Fascist repression in the occupied cities. Though he would not admit it, he worried about reprisals against his mother and family if Barcelona fell. He had asked Doña María several times to move to Paris, but she refused to flee.

In Mougins, Dora had found two delightful Spanish girls, whom she hired as Pablo's Paris chambermaid and cook, since the Rue La Boétie apartment had been badly neglected after he fired the help. He was delighted, the more so since the elder sister, Inéz, was truly beautiful. (She was to play an increasingly important role in his life, serving as a model. After marrying Gustave Sassier, a young Parisian "refugee" in the South in 1940, she would display great tact in handling the Dora–Françoise Gilot transition. Each year at her birthday, around Christmas, Pablo gave her a new portrait he did of her.) Back at Rue des Grands-Augustins, he returned to work. He had left Paris exhausted by *Guernica;* the stay in Mougins had relaxed him, but now he was about to get into the swim again.

When Kahnweiler came to see him, he showed him through the studio and the rather run-down apartment, which needed lots of work, saying, "It's just like Rue Ravignan." For he tried to hold on to his young days, his beginnings, ever haunted by the impoverished Bohemia which he constantly recalled, to the varying distaste of his successive women, who resented their obligatory pilgrimages to the Bateau-Lavoir. He still had the creaky, shaky easel on which he had painted *Les Demoiselles d'Avignon* (today in one of the studios at Notre-Dame-de-Vie in Mougins).

In October, he took a trip to Switzerland, never clearly explained, but probably connected with his now having a Geneva bank account. Bernhard Geiser, later to catalog his engravings, suggested that he visit Paul Klee in Bern, an idea that delighted Pablo. He had never met the painter, who was one of his admirers and had hoped to meet both him and Braque on his first trip to Paris in 1912, but had been too shy to call on them. He had later been impressed by the great Picasso retrospective show at the Zurich Kunsthaus in 1932.

Since 1933, Klee and his wife had lived in a small Bern apartment, of which the biggest room was his studio, a grand piano virtually filling the dining room. His fame had come late, and he knew he was already incurably ill.

Pablo was deeply moved; they shook hands warmly, but found little to say, despite all they had in common, having both carried imagination—Klee the invisible, Picasso the visible—to its heights, and both seeing art as a way of knowledge, a revelation of world and self.

"He was magnificent, very dignified, and worthy of respect for his attitude as well as his work," Pablo was to say. He looked at length through Klee's folders of drawings, while the latter, somewhat taken aback by his guest's silence, held aloof. All his life he had been afraid that the influence of Picasso might intrude on his own inspiration, and felt some mistrust of the robust man, vitality oozing from him as he looked at each drawing as if to make its secrets his own. How different from Braque, who, a short time earlier, had also been there! With Picasso, for all their empathy, rapport did not set up. To clear the air, Mme. Klee sat down to play some Bach on the piano.

The two men embraced when they separated, but without a word to bind them in friendship or admiration. Pablo told Geiser, after the visit, that Klee's workroom looked more like a laboratory than a studio. A few years later, asked by the Swiss publisher François Lachenal about his impression of Klee, Pablo answered, "Pascal-Napoleon." Meaning that he combined spirituality and strength of will, passionate asceticism and intense energy.

This trip must have taken place between the tender oil-and-pastel portrait of

"Weeping Woman"   Paris, October 1937 (Collection of Sir Roland Penrose)

(GIRAUDON)

Dora he did on October 1 and the poignant *Weeping Woman* dated October 26. The latter work was the tragic finale of the series begun while he was doing *Guernica*. The face, beneath a ridiculous hat, is distorted by corners viciously bent in, their points causing tears to flow down the cheeks like long deep wounds. The haggard eyes, ringed by enormous lashes, under arched eyebrows, seem to leap from their sockets. Yellow, green, purple, or blue, the ill-assorted pieces of the mask of pain crash into one another in a strident mosaic. To hush her sobs or moans, the toothless mouth is tearing at the handkerchief the woman is holding; and down the nape of her neck is Dora's silky wavy hair, which she, and Breton's wife, Jacqueline, had been first, among the Surrealist "bluestockings," to wear streaming down to their shoulders.

For this despairing Gorgon was Dora, too. In several of his pictures, she wears that little beanie of a hat, then in style, but rarely had such violence nightmared her face. Nor was Pablo to subject any of his other mates to so cruel a savaging, and one may wonder what this represented, as of October 1937, in the stormy development of the sorry Pablo-Dora affair. The vivid colors, unsuited to the suffering face, remain disconcerting, as do the details that toss in an unexpected comic relief: the red hat with its bluebell, the budlike ear, the huge-fingered hand.

In December, Tériade brought out *Verve,* a new art magazine that was a doubtful venture in such troubled times. American-financed at the start, by a publisher who wanted to boast of "the most beautiful art magazine in the world," Tériade struggled to get full control, which he finally did, thanks in the beginning to his secretary and sole assistant, Angèle Lamotte, and after her untimely death, to her sister, Marguerite Lang.

It truly was "the most beautiful art magazine in the world," and it brought together the greatest artists, writers, art historians, and poets. Picasso was duly represented, but since Zervos devoted entire issues of *Cahiers d'Art* to him, Tériade justly felt he ought not to compete in that area. Moreover, he felt closer to Matisse, Braque, Maillol, or Bonnard, that is to say, the kind of purely Latin hedonist classicism represented in literature by Paul Valéry and André Gide. Picasso bothered him, as also did Paul Claudel, whom he considered fascinating and admirable, but excessive. Tériade was attracted both to the avant-garde, which to him had meant mainly the Surrealism of *Minotaure* (and there were no Surrealists in *Verve*), and humanism. He wanted to combine past and present, certainty and experiment, and often pulled off that difficult undertaking.

The contents of the twenty-five issues of *Verve* from 1937 to 1960 include such diverse names as Georges Bataille, Bonnard, Braque, Chagall, Roger Caillois, Claudel, Derain, Giacometti, Matisse, Masson, Malraux, Hemingway, Henri Laurens, Maillol, Valéry, Henri Michaux, Picasso, Miró, Rouault, André Suarès, and Sartre. Only after World War II did Tériade devote any special issues to Picasso: Summer 1948 (Nos. 19–20), Winter 1951 (25–26), Fall 1954 (29–30), for each of which Pablo did the covers.

On December 19, 1937, *The New York Times* published Picasso's appeal to the American Artists' Congress taking place in New York, in which he recalled the measures the Spanish government had taken to protect its artistic treasures in "this cruel and unjust war." While the Rebels bombed museums, the Loyalists risked their lives to safeguard artistic masterpieces, so he urged:

> It is my wish at this time to remind you that I have always believed, and still believe, that artists who live and work with spiritual values cannot and should not remain indifferent to a conflict in which the highest values of humanity and civilization are at stake.

On New Year's Eve, December 31, while others were celebrating, he painted the first of the three fable-pictures in which he turned from denouncing the horrors of war to moralizing. In a very soft-harmonied green-gray and blue painting, the Minotaur, shot with an arrow, is dying on a sandy beach, as three Muses, sailing by, see him and stop to look at him.

January 1: two of the Muses are gone. The third is still helping him. Coming toward the Minotaur, who painfully raises up, she holds out a drink and a mirror to him.

January 2: the Muse is sinking into the water, only her face with closed eyes still visible, as the seated Minotaur watches. How long will he have to wait, alone, for this compassionate one to return, or will she ever?

The seascape was the one seen from the heights of Mougins, and Pablo kept these three paintings for his own.

Suddenly, his model changed. On his return from the Riviera, he had resumed his frequent calls on Marie-Thérèse. Maya was now a delightful two-and-a-half-year-old, whom his lively paternal passion turned into a great many portraits, both fine, elegant pencil drawings and violently distorted paintings. The ones done at the beginning of 1938, despite the disjointing of the face seen both full and in profile and the lack of gracefulness he imparts to the childish body, are delightfully tender and, what is more, admirable likenesses.

Paulo had been born in a period of relatively relaxed production, and Olga would not have tolerated her husband subjecting his son's face to the customary anatomical tortures. Maya, on the other hand, had appeared during a tragic period in which Picasso was becoming more and more conscious of the parallel between the fate of his work and that of the world. Whether playing with a boat, a hobbyhorse, or a doll, like any little girl her age, her face reflects traces of the tragedy she is unaware of; there is worry in her eyes and the way she convulsively clutches her toys to her, so that we sense that, despite her innocence, she too is the image of a world in trouble and man torn asunder.

The four portraits of Maya of January 1938 were undoubtedly done at Le Tremblay-sur-Mauldre. Still lifes of dizzying dynamism followed in March. Their whirling, convulsed forms suggest that the painting had gotten away from the painter. They alternated with bright loud roosters. And more variations on Dora's face, now more serene. But not for long. For Pablo, lacking any respect whatever for her beauty, gives her Kazbek's pointed snout. Then, more poetically, she becomes a horned bird! Again, not very elegant.

The battle for Teruel had taken place; after some false hopes entertained by

"Portrait de Maïa" (*María de la Concepción*) *Paris*
January 16, 1938, artist's collection

(GIRAUDON)

Pablo, it had finally fallen to Franco, now free to attack Aragón and Catalonia. On March 11, Hitler took over Austria with the Anschluss. Still, the democracies stood by. On March 16, Franco's planes hit Barcelona: seventeen raids, leaving thirteen hundred dead, two thousand wounded. The newspapers announced that every neighborhood of the city had been hit, and Picasso, like his Spanish friends come to Rue des Grands-Augustins, was wondering whether his mother and family had survived.

Despite Dora Maar's continued association with many of the Surrealists, and his own, since he preferred poets to painters (only two of the latter, Beaudin and Masson, really being close friends of his between the two world wars), Pablo did not take part in the International Surrealist Exhibition, organized by Éluard and Duchamp at the Galerie des Beaux-Arts in January 1938.*

This famous gallery belonged to Georges Wildenstein, whose wife's portrait Pablo had done twenty years before at Biarritz. In the interim, "Monsieur Georges," who was related to the Rothschilds, had bought several Picassos, as he had Matisses, Derains, Légers, and others, and later sold them, saying they "did not please" him. But the very classical portrait of his wife had a place of honor in his New York home.

One afternoon in April 1938, Sabartés bumped smack into Pablo, walking his dog, at St.-Germain-des-Prés. They had not seen each other for months, but the meeting was so sudden that all old spats were forgotten, and they fell into each other's arms, embracing Spanish-style. Pablo introduced Kazbek, who had taken the place of Elft, now retired to Boisgeloup, and gruffly, to mask his embarrassment, said, "Don't you ever get down this way? Come on along. I'll show you my new studio in Rue des Grands-Augustins."

Sabartés said he was busy, and he would come another time. They met several more times, but Jaime still stayed away from the studio, anxious to avoid Dora. Pablo chuckled at the idea of her surprise and fury, but Jaime stalled for time.

At the end of June, he got a note from Pablo in colored crayons, that he said looked like a little flag. Each sentence was in a different color, red, yellow, green, orange, blue, and so on. "Friend Sabartés," it said, "you promised to come. I know you don't like to meet people; if you want, we could meet secretly whenever you say. Come of a morning to Rue La Boétie. Write me here. Your Picasso."

And he added that Paco Durio, that old friend of theirs, wanted to see him, and was coming *to his studio* the next Tuesday, July 5, around four o'clock. This time Sabartés had no excuse: he understood that Pablo was still living at Rue La Boétie and Dora at her parents', on Rue de Savoie. Rue des Grands-Augustins was the workshop, the place to meet friends.

It had been a splendid spring. On June 25, Paris was as warm as midsummer. On a rose ground mottled with flowers, Pablo painted Dora in a new hat, a straw sunbonnet, and a lace blouse, and there were more portraits, no less brilliant, the following weeks. When people grew ecstatic over her boldly elegant attire, he joked, "If she had actually gone out in that blouse, they'd have locked her up for the summer."

* Cf. *The Unspeakable Confessions of Salvador Dali*, pp. 189–193. (TR. NOTE)

Early in July, following that perky series of sunbonnet pictures, he and Dora were off to Mougins again with the Éluards. He did several portraits of Nush, Dora, whom he had not exactly been kind to in recent months, and Inéz, the beautiful young chambermaid they had brought back to the village where her family lived.

XVI

ONE MORE
MOMENT
OF HAPPINESS
(1938–1939)

T WAS A SWELTERING SUMMER, THE WEATHER IN KEEPING WITH THE storm-laden international situation. The Spanish Republic had nothing left but Catalonia, Madrid, and some southeastern provinces, and its territory was split in two. The Fascist specter cast its aura of blood and death across the peninsula.

One of Picasso's oldest friends, André Salmon, correspondent for *Le Petit Parisien* in the Franco zone, vaunted the deeds of the new Crusaders; Pablo long refused to speak to him, and only in his last years did he again shake hands with that weeping, repentant poet.

France had its traditional summer-vacation euphoria: Hitler had 1,300,000 men under arms and was announcing his intention to annex the Sudetenland, to mild democratic protests. In Mougins, as Picasso put it, the vacationers were all sucking lollipops: he painted men and women with all-day suckers or ice-cream cones, their gluttony as hateful as if they were tearing prey to bits. Their nostrils are unusually distended, eyes wide, enormous tongues emerging from the toothless mouths, their thick fingers like fangs or palm leaves. His anger and fear also brought back the overstuffed monsters of *Dream and Lie of Franco,* and others out of *Guernica,* which, in this summer of 1938, was on display in Scandinavia.

Pablo went to Nice, where Matisse had recently moved. The friendly enemy of the heroic years was now a sort of pope of hedonistic realism. Yesterday's revolutionary was enjoying his success; a whole section of French painting derived from him and acknowledged its debt, but the glorious septuagenarian now synthesized the art of living and the joy of painting. Where each step in Picasso's work was a new start, usually without follow-up, in Matisse it was a deeply thought-out affirmation, carried to its extreme within a harmonious whole. The former Fauve still believed what he had said half a century before: "Composition is the art of decoratively arranging the various elements the painter can use for the expression of his feelings." He symbolized reasonableness, clarity, and taste.

Against Pablo's *trompe-l'esprit* painting, against his violences, obsessions, and cruelties, Matisse was doing *rassure-l'oeil:* the turmoil of the times was not to be found in his work, nor was he *engagé*. Nothing in his pictures but reassuring human emotions.

Matisse was not expressing himself; he was communicating. While all about him felt that war was impending, he painted nonchalant young women, windows open on the Mediterranean, happy landscapes, opened flowers, sprightly still lifes. He had just moved into a fine light apartment in the onetime Hôtel Régina on the heights of Cimiez, above Nice. Picasso visited him there, caustic but respectful, his eye darker and more penetrating than ever.

Matisse, his physical opposite, received him among exotic plants and birds. Order and clarity reigned in his rooms, through which furtively passed the beautiful Russian girl said to be his favorite model and mistress. Picasso quickly took it all in, as Matisse watched, not without concern, as if he might upset or change it all. Or even pilfer it.

Our ex-Cubist would often ask, "What is Matisse up to?" But he did not show the same interest or curiosity about Braque. When, on meeting the latter, he said, "We have to have dinner together one of these days," his old pal knew how little it meant. They did see each other now and again, usually at Henri Laurens', the latter having been bypassed by glory and finding the going hard. Marcelle Braque liked Picasso, and tried to encourage their meeting: the sculptor's wife, Marthe Laurens, was a wonderful cook, whose meals made them forget their differences, the disagreeable gossip, and life's hardships.

What Picasso and Matisse had accomplished followed parallel developments, differing in methods, content, and goal. Pablo liked the idea that this painter of women and happiness had remained so "French," and that he was able to give color so much expression so brilliantly. He owned several of his *very fine paintings, some bought from Rosenberg, and others exchanged with Matisse. The latter gazed upon his several Picassos without comment, whereas our Malagueño muttered acid barbs about his.

Pablo went to see him two or three times, saying the last time, "We have to do this often; I enjoy it." "From then on," commented Matisse, "I never saw him again."

The only thing they had in common was their dealer, Paul Rosenberg. After one of his Picasso shows, Rosenberg showed the press clippings to Matisse, who remarked bitterly, "They don't insult me the way they insult him. They let me off easy. Naturally, next to Picasso, I still seem like a young girl."

Things were worsening, and war seemed imminent. *Guernica* was scheduled to be shown in London under the auspices of a committee of writers and artists for the Spanish Republic. Roland Penrose, who was in charge, cabled Pablo to ask what he ought to do in the circumstances, and Picasso replied full speed ahead. Was *Guernica* not the very outcry against war and its horrors? It opened

on schedule at the New Burlington Galleries, flanked by seventy-seven preparatory drawings and paintings. Herbert Read, in the *London Bulletin,* hailed the
"monument to disillusion, to despair, to destruction":

> It is not sufficient to compare the Picasso of this painting with the Goya of the
> *Desastres.* Goya, too, was a great artist, and a great humanist; but his reactions were
> individualistic—his instruments irony, satire, ridicule. Picasso is more universal, his
> symbols are banal, like the symbols of Homer, Dante, Cervantes. For it is only when
> the widest commonplace is infused with the intensest passion that a great work of art,
> transcending all schools and categories, is born; and being born, lives immortally.

The Munich conference averted the war threat, but the democracies had shed
their honor by allowing Hitler a free hand. In Spain, with the Ebro still ablaze,
the government decided to dismiss the International Brigades, which held a last
parade in Barcelona on November 15, cheered by the people who strewed their
path with flowers—flowers on the corpse of Spain.

Shortly before Munich, literally terrified by the threat of war, Pablo had had
Marcel drive him to Le Tremblay-sur-Mauldre, where Marie-Thérèse lived with
Maya. He was convinced that the first blow of the war would be the bombing
of Paris and that it was safer in the country. He painted and drew there, returning to his studio only after the crisis passed.

After the successful show at the New Burlington Galleries, at the request of
the Labour Party leader Clement Attlee *Guernica* and its preparatory studies were
shown at the Whitechapel Gallery, in the workers' district, so that the masses
might get to know Picasso's work and form their own opinion about it; after that,
Leeds, Liverpool, and finally New York, where *Guernica* was hung in the Museum of Modern Art along with *Les Demoiselles d'Avignon* in the greatest Picasso retrospective ever. In that same year of 1939, there were other Picasso
shows in six private New York galleries, in London, Chicago, Los Angeles, San
Francisco, and at Paul Rosenberg's in Paris.

When Pablo got together with Sabartés again, he asked him to come back, to
help him by typing up his writings—more a pretext than a real reason, but Pablo
always was devious where deeper sentiment was involved. He stalled about actually letting him get to work. The main thing was to have him back, almost as if
they were living together again, although Sabartés did not move in to Rue La
Boétie, but arrived usually around noon. They talked endlessly, Pablo showed
him his paintings, read him his poems; they wandered about Paris or drove out
to Le Tremblay, where Picasso kept many of his paintings and sculptures. In the
evening, Marcel would drive Sabartés to Versailles, where he caught a train to
Paris.

Around this time, Picasso bought up all the early works of Fenosa that were
on show at the Percier Gallery, so that his friend might receive his share of the
sale. It is notable that Pablo really only encouraged and helped artists who were
not very original—not Miró or Antoni Clavé in their youths, but Peinado, Fenosa,
Manolo, those whose work was least in a category with his own. He often lauded
mediocre artists, posing for pictures with them, and stating how delighted he was

that Oscar Dominguez or his nephew Vilato was "painting Picassos." He never aimed his barbs at such as these—only at Braque, Matisse, Bonnard . . .

In the gift that his heirs, following his instructions, turned over to the French museums after his death, there were only "masters," old or modern, but few works by young artists. Youth never interested Pablo much—and the feeling was mutual.

As soon as he returned to Paris at the start of October, Brassaï began the picture essay on Picasso, his work, his habits, friends, and studios, for *Life* magazine. Dora Maar was furious at not having been commissioned to do it, but actually she had recently been doing more painting than photography.

Picasso, with Sabartés and his varied but numerous retinue, often ate at Brasserie Lipp with other friends, then going across Boulevard St.-Germain to the Flore, where he was greeted by such habitués as the Prévert brothers, Aragon, the Éluards, the Groupe Octobre actors, Jean-Paul Sartre, then teaching at the Lycée Pasteur in Neuilly, Simone de Beauvoir, Dr. Jacques Lacan, and André Masson. He generously signed autographs on exhibition catalogs, or photographs, even sometimes adding a sketch, if he liked the person asking. He might say a few words to some bashful girls, give encouragement to a Beaux-Arts student, saying, "I studied at the Fine Arts School myself." Or joke with Sabartés about some youthful recollection. He told Éluard, "I've done so many portraits of Nush, and the only good one is the one I did without the model. By heart." On November 16, in the Rue des Grands-Augustins studio, he gave a watercolor of his left hand to Peinado, inscribing it to him.

Brassaï did not snap him only in cafés or restaurants, at St.-Germain-des-Prés with Kazbek or friends, but also in his studio; yet Pablo would not let him shoot while he was actually working. He had set up Louis Fort's press in an unheated room after bringing it from Boisgeloup, and the lack of heat was an excuse for going to Lacourière's back in his beloved Montmartre.

His works still were a journal of his life: having visited the Zervoses at Vézelay in October, he drew a *Naked Farm Woman Lying Down,* on which he based the painting, *Reclining Nude,* that Zervos interpreted as a transposition of their village: "The two feet are the roads, the left leading to Clamecy, the right to Avallon. The belly is Place de la Foire, where the town begins. The arms are the two roads leading to the basilica, and the head the church itself."

Shortly after this, Picasso had an attack of sciatica that kept him in bed; he had to drop the still lifes he was doing. The weather was terribly cold, and many friends came to see him, each with another cure for his condition. Sabartés spent his days at his bedside, and Pablo told him he was so grateful that when he was well he would paint him between a naked woman and a very skinny dog.

With the approach of Christmas, old memories came back to mind; in his bed, surrounded by his flood of mail and all kinds of newspapers, Pablo remembered his father, and worried over his mother, now past eighty, from whom he had not heard in some time. The papers said there were more than a million refugees in Barcelona. Food was in short supply, and Franco tried to demoralize the defenders by dropping loaves of bread from the air. Pablo was completely upset by events at home—the more so since some of his countrymen spread rumors that he had not done all he could for Spain, or even that he was trying to cozy up to the Fascists. And now Barcelona was under fire and Franco's principal objective.

In bed and in pain, he could not keep his mind quiet. One morning, when Sabartés arrived, he found the bed covered with drawings. When he voiced his surprise, Pablo told him that he drew to forget his pain, while waiting for breakfast, and then kept on drawing till the breakfast was cold. As for the pain, "it never leaves," adding with a mischievous smile, "not like you."

Dora Maar spent most of her evenings with him, but their rendezvous were hardly romantic. "She comes to sit up with a sick friend," Pablo said.

Sabartés, making conversation, asked him how he knew a picture was finished. He replied:

"Have you ever seen a finished picture? A picture or anything else? Woe unto you the day it is said that you are finished! To finish a work? To finish a picture? What nonsense! To finish it means to be through with it, to kill it, to rid it of its soul, to give it the final blow: the most unfortunate one for the painter as well as for the picture."

One time, Sabartés said he'd like to see himself as a sixteenth-century nobleman with a plumed hat to hide his bald head. "I'll do it," Pablo said, and a few days later showed him triumphantly a sheet of paper on which, on Christmas day, he had drawn him with a ruff around the neck and a plumed toque atop his head; the paper was so bad that, in trying to darken the blacks, he had torn it. The next day, complete transformation, and there he was as a monk in his habit, but drawn so lightly that the line barely showed on the paper. "Welcome, Brother Sabartés," was how he greeted him. But then, that same December 26, he did several more portraits of him, including a second one as a nobleman, but with his baldness intact.

While he was ill, Pablo did one of his tenderest portraits of his daughter, *First Snow.*

An electrical treatment finally cured Pablo's pain, and he was able to get up. His first concern was to go back to Montmartre and start working at Lacourière's, at times spending each day there. He wanted to publish as a volume a collection of his recent graphics, drawings, and poems, pictures and words being just complementary forms of expression to him.

Vollard was enthusiastic about the idea and they had many long talks about it, but Pablo as usual delayed a final decision: he would say there was plenty of time, the main thing was getting the work done. He often would drop one idea to pursue another: for a while, he turned away from engraving and was interested only in monotypes. And no point in trying to woo him away, or he would drop everything. Nor would he follow any organized work habits or hours, doing his engraving anywhere, anytime, and wondering why the workers were not always available to pull prints at any hour of day or night. Lacourière would stay on with Picasso as late as he wished, but the men left at six o'clock, much to Pablo's dissatisfaction.

Sabartés told me how, one day when Picasso was doing an engraving on the corner of a table with the sun shining in his eyes, he cleared the table to give him more room. Pablo immediately abandoned the plate he was working on.

The war was at Barcelona's gates; its fall was anticipated any day. Refugees flooded toward the French border, while the Rebel troops closed in from south and west. On January 26, Barcelona was taken, as Madrid and Valencia would be in March.

A few days before Barcelona fell, his mother, Doña María, died—along with Spain. And a past that Pablo would never see again. Franco had stolen his country —let him keep its ruins and ghosts, the three hundred thousand dead soldiers, the four hundred thousand dead civilians, the hundred thousand shot at the orders of the generals, the bishops, landowners, bankers, country squires, and dukes, who had come down from the Velázquez and Goya paintings to plunge into the sewers of Fascism. The painful voices of Federico García Lorca, shot by the Falangists, and Antonio Machado, dead at Collioure after dragging himself, dying, across the frontier with his old invalid mother, had been stilled with Spain itself. With the fall of Barcelona, the victors repealed Catalan autonomy and forbade the use of the language. On March 15, Hitler was entering Prague and making Czechoslovakia part of the Greater Thousand-Year Reich.

Picasso now decided to move to Rue des Grands-Augustins, the work ordered by Dora having been completed, including central heating. He would live in the two floors connected by the spiral staircase. However, this did not mean he settled down. Everything remained in total disorder, and the engraving studio was virtually never used. His paintings and those of his collection were scattered all about; the place was always full of Spanish refugees—and, however much the bother, he never turned one away. Sometimes, he had to take refuge himself at Rue La Boétie or Le Tremblay, and let Sabartés handle the hapless mob.

The collection of poems and graphics had fallen through, as he had disagreed with Vollard on how to handle it, but other books were being planned. The engravings intended for that first collection have remained unused, and when Bernhard Geiser, editing the catalog of his graphics, asked to see them and photograph them, Pablo did not know where they were—somewhere in his massive disorganized files.

During several stays at Le Tremblay that winter he painted cut-up, disjointed women, shrieking or weeping, terrified, sometimes convulsed, and among them now some diabolical creatures, such as the cat cruelly devouring a bird in several of these oils. "That subject obsessed me. I don't know why," he was to confess.

But we know why: that awful, menacing, hallucinating animal was a harbinger of misfortunes yet to come: it was to reappear in his work in October 1962, at the time of the Cuban missile crisis.

Though deeply affected by his mother's death, he did not reflect it in his work. He corresponded frequently with Lola, but only on personal matters. Everyone

was well, and his many youthful works were safe, as was his voluminous correspondence with his mother (none of which he ever allowed to be published).

On July 21, Vollard's chauffeur-driven car had an accident; the dealer, dozing
as usual on the back seat, hit his head against a small Maillol statue behind him,
fracturing his skull; he died that night in a Versailles hospital. Pablo left for Paris
forthwith, and since Vollard's chauffeur, like his own, was named Marcel, he told
Sabartés he would never ride in an automobile again—a pledge immediately forgotten. The days before the funeral he spent at Rue La Boétie, dining at Lipp's
and going for the evening to the Flore or Dôme—staying till they closed.

On his return home from the Vollard interment, July 28, there was a wire
inviting him to a bullfight the following Sunday at St.-Raphael; he delightedly
asked Jaime to go south with him. Antibes was very quiet, what with the dearth
of tourists as war clouds threatened; Marcel had driven Sabartés and Pablo down.
It was Sabartés' first contact with the Riviera, and he loved the light, the sun,
the beauty of the scenery. Dora did not even object strenuously to his reappear-
ance. She never went with them on their long drives to Nice, Cannes, Monte
Carlo, or Juan-les-Pins.

Picasso had bought a huge canvas in Nice and set it up in the main room of
Man Ray's apartment, used as his studio. He did not yet know what he would
do on it, but for the time being it hid the atrocious wallpaper on several of the
walls. He intended to do a number of paintings on the canvas and then cut it up.
And so to work.

Sarbartés would call for him at day's end, as usual, trying to come as late as
possible so as not to disturb Pablo in his work. But he was dispirited: his mother's
death, the Franco victory, the refugees and what the French government was
shamefully doing in interning them, were so many reasons for worry and depression. Yet he painted furiously, "so as not to throw myself out the window,"
as he told Sabartés.

Dora was not much consolation to him at this time, their feeling for each
other having turned quite superficial and even their physical relationship strained.
Her difficult makeup irritated him and, while he still appreciated her intelligence
and culture, her beauty had palled, as Marie-Thérèse's never had. Dora Maar was
indeed the scapegoat of his own emotional trials.

One evening, he and Dora were walking in the port at Antibes, as the fishermen prepared their boats for a night's work. They were hanging acetylene lamps
which shone above the water, attracting the fish they then harpooned. On the
quay, girls were cycling by, and on the way home Dora had bought ice cream,
which they ate as they watched the dark night with the moon shining on the
old city and its towers. The lights of the boats twinkled across the waters.

As soon as he got home, he set to painting the scene. *Night Fishing at Antibes*
(Museum of Modern Art, New York, from Mrs. Simon Guggenheim Fund) is
a "painting from life," directly recorded, with the fishermen, the port, the boats,
the girls with bicycles, one of them being Dora eating her ice-cream cone, the
moon shining above, all there. This extraordinary synthesis of several different
simultaneous visual shocks with diverse lightings—moon, stars, boats' lanterns—

"Night Fishing at Antibes" (1939, August) Collection, The Museum of Modern Art, New York. Mrs. Simon Guggenheim Fund

in phosphorescent yellows, blues, greens, and purples, also superimposes several different feelings, the serenity of the night, indifference of the summer-clad girls, and cruelty of the fishermen, harpooning their catch with tridents. The whole thing merges together, into a sort of semipoetic, semidramatic epic, the visionary character of which, as ever in Picasso, has a foundation in fact.

He might well have explored this hallucinatory expressionism further, had not the Nazi-Soviet Non-Aggression Pact come like a bolt from the blue on August 23. War now seemed inevitable, and the question, Should one return to Paris? That evening, cafés in Antibes were empty, trucks rumbled by, taking troops to strategic points, and people stayed glued to their radios.

On August 25, Pablo suddenly decided to leave, going by train with Dora and Sabartés, while Marcel came up by car, with the rolled-up canvases, luggage, jerricans of gasoline, and all the food the vehicle would hold.

Friends flocked to Rue La Boétie the minute they heard he was back, so he fled to Le Tremblay, empty because Marie-Thérèse and Maya were on vacation at Royan. He was terribly worried: What to do if war came? What would become of his paintings, most of them scattered around the world in different shows? At Rue des Grands-Augustins, he wanted to make order of the works at hand and pack up things he wanted to keep, but did not know where to start. So he paced back and forth, chain-smoking, as Dora did likewise, quite unruffled.

The morning of August 29, he decided to get out of Paris, several high-placed officials whom he had seen the day before having assured him war was imminent. Thinking of Spain, he was mainly fearful of bombing raids. His feverish impatience reminded Sabartés of what he must have been like as a child, watching the clock to get out of school and home to his paintbrushes and one of the old man's pigeons.

Marcel drove them away toward midnight on September 1, Picasso, Dora, Sarbartés with his lady friend Mercedes, and Kazbek. The driver was to return later for the luggage. They headed for Royan, simply because Pablo had lived through World War I, and everyone of his generation thought first of retreating toward the Atlantic coast. Also, Marie-Thérèse and Maya were there.

It was dawn when the Hispano pulled in to Saintes. They had breakfast at a café and went on toward Royan. Suddenly, there was the sunny, silvery ocean in a comforting landscape that gave Picasso the feeling of security the sea had always afforded him.

XVII

"THE GATES
WERE
BEING GUARDED . . ."
(1939–1943)

BEFORE BEING ALMOST TOTALLY DESTROYED IN 1944, ROYAN WAS AN outdated little city, mixing all kinds of styles and periods, that struck Pablo as a stage setting without actors. Now it had room for many refugees, as the owners of so many of its summer villas were gone. He and Dora moved into the Hôtel du Tigre, at the corner of Boulevard Georges-Clemenceau and Boulevard Albert-Premier. Marie-Thérèse and Maya were living in a villa, called Gerbier de Joncs, where he visited them as often as possible, telling Dora he had rented a studio there—Marie-Thérèse still not even knowing of Dora's existence, while the latter had no idea she and her daughter were in Royan. Sabartés knew all about it, but said nothing, fearfully expecting the worst.

Refugees arriving after August 25 were not issued permits to stay, since the town had been designated a frontier area, so Pablo, with Sabartés and Marcel, drove back to Paris to get the required papers—immediately issued him by his friend, the future prefect and ambassador André-Louis Dubois, at that time assistant head of the national police. When things got really tough, that old anarchist Picasso always found some magistrate or policeman to protect him. Once, it had been prosecutor Granié; now the second in command of the *Sûreté* during the occupation, in person or through intermediaries, would act as his guardian angel. In two days, they were back in Royan.

September 1, Hitler invaded Poland, and France and England were at war with Germany.

The first drawings Picasso did in his new improvised studio were of requisitioned horses he had seen on the road back from Paris, or out his window, headed for slaughter. Always an animal lover, this upset him: he was sure the horses understood what was happening to them, as in bullfights they were sacrificed to the violence and cruelty of men.

The setup was makeshift, but as long as he had colors, brushes, ink, and crayons, he could get by; surroundings meant little to him. He found a small easel in the Royan auction house, and bought it, even though Sabartés told him it would not do. It delighted him and, while in fact he would never put it to use, that was enough. He would just as soon paint with his canvas set up on a chair, regardless of the inconvenience. And the trees blocking his light made no difference to him. His palette was the seat of a chair.

When the sun went down, the room got dark; this was Sabartés' cue to go up after his friend. The day was ended. They would take a walk through the town with its now almost-doubled population and sit on a bench on Quai du Bac before going to the Café le Régent to hear "the communiqué." News went from bad to worse: Poland caved in in a few weeks, and men were digging trenches along the beaches, which led Sabartés to ask him whether he thought they were to be used as bomb shelters.

"Only you could think of such a thing," Pablo sneered. "No, my friend, no! . . . You don't understand. These are excavations to see if they can find trenches—and that's all. You'll see. As soon as they find one they'll take it to the museum and if there is no museum, they'll build one on purpose."

As the days dragged on, and Sabartés complained of boredom, Pablo told him, "Write—any old thing—just for your own amusement, if need be. You'll see how it'll cheer you up." And Sabartés began his *Picasso. Portraits et Souvenirs,* which was to appear in 1946, a living chronicle of the painter's doings as seen in veriest detail by his closest friend, whose uncompromising admiration readily accommodated deliberate omissions and otherwise doctoring the truth to suit its author's taste.

On October 18, 1939, Pablo painted a *Woman in an Armchair,* ample and tortured, twisted every which way as if her flesh were an inflated goldbeater's skin, with arms bent around her head in a position then dear to him. The *Still Life with Sheep* that he had done on October 6 was brutally realistic, and in a pad full of drawings done between September 30 and October 19, there are a number of sketches of sheep's skulls, some with threatening teeth, even some detailed studies of the jaw, "outside part" and "inside part," as he noted in the margin.

This same pad also had a whole series of drawings of crossed, circled lines, drawn with extreme lightness of touch, in which he appears to be reverting to the geometrical constructions of 1930–1935. Then, with the mental and manual agility so characteristic of him, he goes on to fantastic inventions, characters with reinvented faces, done with a cruelty sometimes reminiscent of what he had done to his Dinard victims. After that, this destructive frenzy gives way to the grotesque: huge horn-noses, wide double sets of eyes, swollen puffed bodies. The erotic aspect also comes in clearly through the phallic concern.

Unable to stay in one place, Pablo left with Sabartés for Paris at dawn on October 12, Marcel driving. They stayed until October 26, with side trips to

Boisgeloup and Le Tremblay to inspect his sculptures and paintings in those places. There were letters from American friends telling him of the success of the Museum of Modern Art restrospective in New York, along with clippings; the catalog was a sumptuous volume of over two hundred pages, with 214 illustrations.*

Sabartés' fears were soon justified: one day Marie-Thérèse saw Pablo get out of a car with Jaime and a young brunette she did not know. He came over to her and kissed her, much to Dora's surprise. The next day, Marie-Thérèse wanted to know who the woman was, and he evasively mumbled, "Some Spanish refugee . . ."

But both women quickly found out the truth and from then on were engaged in a secret war, while Pablo alternated from one home and one mistress to the other, with his usual disconcerting nonchalance, his diabolical love of the ambiguous, ever associated in its growing refinements with his destructive instinct, the obverse of his sexual urge. Which also had to be shared.

Now his court was set up again, and he was happy. He was living with Dora and seeing Marie-Thérèse and Maya daily. He had his customary walks with Sabartés, and at the Régent, instead of Lipp or Flore, the split of Évian water tasted the same as at St.-Germain-des-Prés. He went back to Paris twice again, December 5–21, then February 5–29, 1940; and one final time, from mid-March to May 10.

Alone among his Parisian friends, Jacqueline Breton was at Royan, with her daughter Aube; she chose to stay here because her husband was in the medics at Poitiers. She was very friendly with Dora, but Pablo insisted on introducing her to Marie-Thérèse, since Maya and Aube were about the same age. The two girls quickly became playmates. Dora was furious and for some days refused to talk to Jacqueline, the matter not being helped any by the fact that Jacqueline looked so much like Marie-Thérèse as to be often mistaken for her.

This was the time of the "phony war," and Picasso worked as if unconcerned by events, either within his own circle, where Marie-Thérèse and Dora were at loggerheads, or in the world. As in 1914, he was left alone again now, but in an exile of which we cannot tell whether he enjoyed or resented it, for the pads reflect no specific reaction.

He began another on January 10, 1940, with a series of drawings freely inspired by Delacroix's *Women of Algiers,* which he would interpret in his own way some years later. Then, back to the invented, re-created female anatomy, the hands behind the head spreading harmonious enveloping curves or crisscrossed geometric rhythms across the pages, with heads, breasts, and pubises clearly outlined as precious reference points.

Well-fleshed or schematic, these nudes were his daily preoccupation, until, in March or April, they gave way to very linear studies of the matador's horse, then women on a high chair. Their breasts are sometimes outside their blouses, and their heads rest on their hands, in the way he several times had shown Dora.

He took this pad to Paris with him in March, and finished it May 26, a few

* Alfred H. Barr, Jr., *Picasso: Forty Years of His Art.* New York: Museum of Modern Art, 1939.

days after the final German offensive, with the head of a woman and the skull of a sheep.

In January, he had rented the fourth floor of a villa, Les Voiliers, facing the sea on Boulevard Thiers. The owner, Mlle. Andrée Rolland, had been reluctant to consider the little man with the foreign accent the rental agent was sending over, what with the war and all, but her prospective tenant said, "I understand you paint. Then perhaps you've heard of me," and wrote out his signature on a piece of paper. "I was overwhelmed," she wrote in her book about him, *Picasso et Royan* (1967).

The well-lighted rooms were sparsely furnished and he piled in all sorts of other pieces, bought at auction or in secondhand shops, that he generally put to unexpected uses. But he did not start working there for several weeks, as Marie-Thérèse's had better heating. Meantime, Dora painted in their hotel room.

From his window at Les Voiliers, he could see all the gingerbread Belle Époque architecture, and said to Sabartés, "Wouldn't this be great for someone who thought he was a painter?" And on their walks, they solemnly discussed "art," "culture," "beauty," "genius," and "originality," leading Pablo to assertions such as "Primitive sculpture has never been surpassed. Have you noticed the precision of the lines engraved in the caverns? . . . Assyrian bas-reliefs still keep a similar purity of expression."

"Why?" Sarbartés wondered.

". . . man ceased to be simple," Pablo explained. "He wanted to see farther and so he lost the faculty of understanding that which he had within reach of his vision. When one reflects, one pauses . . ."

Picasso, who, according to Mlle. Rolland, "was conscious of his value and his superiority," sometimes stopped by to visit his landlady, who lived with her mother one floor below, twitting the spinster for her abhorrence of bullfights and her dog Médor's snarling encounters with Kazbek. But no one but Sabartés and Kazbek ever went up to Pablo's apartment.

Royan was small, and Marie-Thérèse and Dora could not always avoid each other. Sabartés did his best to keep them apart, but his having no use for either of them and his *amie* having taken up with Marie-Thérèse only complicated matters. He long remembered the Royanese period with shivers.

One day Maya's mother, passing by Les Voiliers, saw the door ajar and went in. Mlle. Rolland heard her and came out to find her staring at a palette placed on a piece of furniture in the vestibule. To Marie-Thérèse's questions, she honestly replied that she did not know whose it was, nor had she seen anyone go up. A few minutes after Marie-Thérèse left, Dora came by and picked up the palette that she had simply left there while running some errands. But she never went to the fourth floor.

On January 21, in wash and India ink, Pablo did an unprecedentedly violent bullfight scene; the contrasts between lights and darks are heightened by variations in techniques and styles that reinforce the dramatic intensity of the whole, which, like so many other works of this period, derives from *Guernica*. The subject is one of his most frequent ones: the bull charging the armed picador,

328 /   "THE GATES WERE BEING GUARDED . . ."

but here the animal is majestically superb and once again the horse is to be the victim of the confrontation.

One pad was hardly enough to hold his drawings done January 20–30, over eighty in number. They are variations on the seated woman, dressed or nude, with or without her arms behind her head, then nude and squatting, followed by studies of heads and hands. From a light line he goes on to little confetti or vermicelli touches that impart vibrations to the form.

On March 4, he began a new pad with a wonderful, extremely voluptuous drawing of a nude woman, next to which he wrote a text beginning:

> mouth edged with fishhooks wolf trap mauve rose orange extended hand from a field of oats pinning the edge of the cloth stitched with screams of slaughtered sirens expiring
> cornucopia fingernails tearing the skin of clouds wiping off furniture beneath the plough of the slice of buttered bread . . .

Growing progressively accustomed to Les Voiliers and the new space and light, on March 6 he painted one of the key works of this period, *Woman Dressing Her Hair* (Collection of Mrs. Bertram Smith, promised to Museum of Modern Art, New York), a monstrously enormous female with a repulsive body, as were those of the bathers and seaside women before the war. Her parts seem to be made of lathed wood, and she has a giantess's thighs and feet the plant of which is painted with disconcerting realism. Nevertheless, this woman sitting in a cell in which she can scarcely move, assumes the languid airs of Matisse's odalisques, of which she is a caricature; she is stretching, and behind her terrifying head with its clashing eyes, its mouth twisted off to the left and drooling with pleasure, her tentacular arms meet in her hair. Her nose is non-existent, a mere bone slicing the face in two; one breast grows out of an armpit, the other on a shoulder; and—on one side only—her ribs make circumflexed striations, while the soft blue flesh of her buttocks oozes over a kind of violet-and-black seat.

Was Picasso crying out here in anger? He told Sabartés, in their wide-ranging talks:

> "Beauty is something strange, don't you find? To me it is a word without sense . . . Do you know exactly where its opposite is to be found? If someone were to show me that there exists a positive ugliness, that would be something else . . .
> "The Renaissance invented the size of noses. Since then reality has gone to the devil. Look how influential words can be: when I say *realidad* (reality) I think of *realeza* (royalty). One must recognize frankly that since the Middle Ages there has not been a single *real* (real, regal, or royal) figure which could pass the test. Who could paint a king today just as he is? . . ."
> "[Genius?] It is personality with a penny's worth of talent. Error which, by accident, rises above the commonplace.
> ". . . In the museums, for example, there are only pictures that have failed . . . Those which today we consider 'masterpieces' are those which departed most from the rules laid down by the masters of the period. The best works are those which show most clearly the 'stigma' of the artist who painted them."

The pad started on March 4 is full of nudes. At times, these drawings of unlimited fantasy have a few handwritten notes, mainly concerning colors, that show he intended to make a painting of the subject, or change some earlier work in terms of these new specifications. For relaxation, he, so unreceptive to the "charms of nature," would often lean out his window and draw the sailboats tossing on the water.

One day, during the boredom of the "phony war" period, he extolled to Sabartés the work of a sign painter:

". . . The painter contributed all that was his; the time, the place and state of mind do the rest, as in this case. But I am interested only in the painter's work because, thanks to it, I can see him and I am certain that the poor devil put all his five senses into producing it. . . . Thus when we [Picasso and his Cubist friends] used to make our constructions, we produced 'pure truth,' without pretensions, without tricks, without malice. What we did then had never been done before: we did it disinterestedly, and if it is worth anything it is because we did it without expecting to profit from it. . . . We put enthusiasm into the work, and this alone, even if that were all that were in it, would be enough . . . We departed so far from the modes of expression then known and appreciated that we felt safe from any suspicion of mercenary aims."

In the middle of March, he and Dora went to Paris, to take care of various business, notably his alien status, find out whether the unusually cold winter had done any damage at Rues La Boétie and des Grands-Augustins, and see a few friends. He also had to consult his lawyer about that interminable divorce matter. But now, what did it matter?

He wrote Sabartés that he was working, painting, and being bored, and wanted to be back in Royan, and the notes he sent Marie-Thérèse overflowed with tenderness. Paris, with its sandbagged monuments, blue lights, whispered rumors about an impending end to the war, Hitler's "sickness," the coming revolution in Germany, and so on, depressed him. The papers gave out silly stories about the army's rocklike morale, General Gamelin's conviction of victory, army entertainments, and the slow wasting away of Germany's ill-equipped and ill-fed soldiers! And on April 3, he wrote Sabartés that he had painted three still lifes with fishes, scales, a crab, and eels, that made him miss the marketplace in Royan.

And so, as so often when he was trying to recapture an image, or colors, or odors, he turned to paint: on March 19 he did *The Soles,* and the following days *Sea Spider* and *Sea Eels.*

A showing of his watercolors and gouaches was to take place at the M.A.I. Gallery, which Yvonne Zervos ran, to open on April 19, and he wrote notes on the invitations to various friends.

In the habitual St.-Germain-des-Prés cafés, he found those friends who had not been called up and the foreigners, Georges Hugnet, Man Ray, the Zervoses, Brassaï. Éluard, Breton, and Aragon stopped off when on furlough; Éluard was planning his *Les Fleurs d'Obéissance* (Flowers of Obedience), which was to have Picasso drawings, and he was making arrangements for it. Since December

1939, Hugnet and Zervos had been publishing a magazine called *L'Usage de la parole* (The Use of Words), and for their April issue—the last, as it turned out—Pablo did some drawings to illustrate Pierre Reverdy poems.

In April, he painted four Women's Busts, dated April 10, 11, 14, and 21, and drew the *Bird-Minotaur* (Dora as the Minotaur—for once showing some affection for her). On May 5, a wonderful drawing, *Nymph and Satyr,* which, along with *Squatting Man and Nude Woman,* recaptured the delicate "antique" inspiration of Ovid's *Metamorphoses.*

On May 10, at 5:30 A.M., the Nazis swept into and through Belgium, Holland, and Luxembourg, and the war was on for real. By May 13, they were heading for Paris; the panic began, and on the evening of May 16, Pablo and Dora returned to Royan, now filling with new waves of refugees, including the painter Mané Katz, whom he had known in Montparnasse, and the American architect Paul Nelson, both of whom were planning to sail from Bordeaux to America. And Pablo locked himself up in Les Voiliers, avoiding the overcrowded public places, and the likelihood of meeting people he did not care to see.

On June 3, he started a new pad, doing broad-stroked drawings of the café he could see from his window above the port, to become a painting two months later, and superb, royal portraits of Kazbek. Royan was occupied on June 23, with the air high command moving in to the Hôtel de Paris, right next to Les Voiliers. Two days later, the day of the armistice, he did a pencil portrait of Maya, wonderfully capturing the innocent gracefulness of the child, which drove out his recent monsters and his worries. He dwelt on her hair bow, her big light eyes, delicate features, her apron with its funny illustrations, and showed her asleep, sucking her thumb.

One day an officer stopped to ask the breed of his dog, and Pablo mumbled his reply, but now, afraid he might be stopped again—or worse, asked to visit with them in case they recognized him—he felt he had to get away. The more so since, the day the Germans came in to Royan, he had made a blistering reply to a lady, a friend of Mlle. Rolland's, who had expressed her enthusiasm at the success of the Nazis and Franco. But the roads were so crowded travel was impossible: he was forced to stay, and be near the hated enemy.

> "This is a race apart" [he told Sabartés one day as a regiment paraded by]. "They think they are very wise, and perhaps they are. They have made progress—and so, what? . . . Anyhow, one thing is certain and that is that we paint better. Fundamentally, if you notice carefully, they are very stupid. . . . So many troops, so many machines, so much power, so much noise to get here! We arrive more quietly. . . . Why can't they do what we did? They probably even think they've conquered Paris! But we, without moving from here, took Berlin a long time ago and I believe they will not be able to dislodge us."

Pablo had no use for Pétain, who had been French ambassador to Franco, and he would never join Vichy any more than he would de Gaulle.

He continued drawing, to fight off depression and boredom. Robot heads, with metal ponytails behind by way of hair, and threatening, screaming jaws, once more revived the mechanical monsters of the Thirties. But on June 17, the day Pétain announced that "fighting must stop," his pencil turned tender again to draw another profile of Maya, pure as an Ingres.

What drove him to violence, what to sweetness? What kind of feelings moved him, and what was happening to his inner self? The tragic events which, like so many others, he was witnessing, may well have motivated his plastic externalization, but they were not reflected in it. As in *Guernica,* he had recourse to metaphor, more what he remembered than what he saw. What he was offering for consideration was not evidence but rather collateral material.

A brush drawing of July 11 seems exactly to project his recollections: it shows a man throwing himself with extraordinary violence upon the body of a nude woman beneath him, legs spread, arms raised, head back, to choke her, or rape her. The painter's brutal instincts, exacerbated by events, must have gone through several steps, represented by the Heads he had drawn during the preceding weeks, before crystallizing in this wild death scene.

On the morning of August 15, a sentry in front of the Hôtel du Golf, where the *Kommandantur* was located, was shot down; and the same evening someone, probably shooting at the Hôtel de Paris next door, fired into the apartment beneath Picasso's. The German reaction was furious, but quieted down somewhat when the French police convinced them that when the shot was fired a German fighter plane was doing aerobatics over the beach. Picasso said, "It was fired downward, and from very near by." So the staff at the Hôtel de Paris decided to forget about it.

But these incidents brought to the attention of the authorities that Picasso was an alien, and he decided to go back to Paris as soon as possible, as he advised Marie-Thérèse, who stayed behind, and Dora, who was coming along. Sabartés, of course, was part of the baggage.

That day he left Royan with Sabartés and Kazbek, Marcel at the wheel of the Hispano, loaded down with rolls of drawings, paintings, and bric-a-brac, Dora following by train. Shortly afterward, Marie-Thérèse called on Mlle. Rolland and asked whether Pablo had paid his rent, asking to be informed if he should forget. Mlle. Rolland commented, "She was trying to be of service, but also wanted it known how intimate her relationship remained with her daughter's father."

Why did Picasso return to Paris, when friends urged him to go to the United States, where he enjoyed a great reputation, or to Mexico? He could have stayed there safely till the end of the war. But no one who knew him could expect him to do this, first because he liked his old haunts, his restaurants, cafés, studios, and friends, and secondly because he could not bear to be parted from his paintings.

Whatever may have been said about his lack of civic consciousness, deciding to stay in Paris under German occupation represented a kind of courage. He had never made any secret of his feelings about Hitler's ally Franco, and *Guernica* had denounced the criminality of Nazi fliers to the entire world. As a painter, his works were among those confiscated in Germany as "degenerate art" and sold at Lucerne in June 1939, but his worldwide reputation spared him the humiliations inflicted on other "decadent" artists.

In Paris, in an attempt to reconcile some of the intelligentsia, the Germans would tempt Pablo several times with offers of extra food and fuel. Despite the terrible cold in his huge studio on Rue des Grands-Augustins, he turned away one such offer from the German embassy, relayed by the writer Ernst Jünger, serving as an officer in Paris, with "A Spaniard is never cold."

The French defeat and German occupation were no harder on him than on most Frenchmen. But he was a foreigner, who owed nothing to France, where for almost forty years he had been made to feel an outlaw of art, subjected to sarcasm, wrath, and insult. There was no link between him and the French people, who saw nothing in his painting to attract or exalt them—but, of course, that was just as true for Matisse, Léger, or Braque. Pablo simply was more outrageous and, being foreign, suspect, yet they all enjoyed total freedom to create, more out of indifference than through respect or admiration. Under German occupation, Pablo got the same favored treatment. The attacks on him came not from the occupants but from certain French "collaborators" or artists who on several occasions violently attacked him and brought pressure on dealers not to exhibit his Cubist or expressionist works, termed "Bolshevik" by the paladins of the New Europe.

When the Germans decreed the banning of all works that did not accord with their own aesthetics, he did not react; nor did anyone else. There were indeed some who saw this ban as a salutary measure which would restore wholesomeness to French art, hitherto polluted by "foreigners." Pablo's concern always was only to have as much peace as possible, to be able to paint without hindrance. He did let some Germans visit him, mainly artists who were on duty in Paris, and allowed them to take his photograph, as he later would the Americans. Or would have Russians or Chinese.

In the fall of 1940, the Germans decided to inventory all bank vaults. Picasso was summoned to the one in which he had two rooms, on Boulevard Haussmann, so the authorities could inspect his collection of Cézannes, Matisses, Renoirs, Douanier Rousseaus, and others. The dealer Pierre Colle, who went with him, told Jean Cassou that the Germans were amazed by what to them were nothing but daubings. They looked them over, asking, "What's this?" or "What does this mean?" as much in amazement as anger. Picasso, livid, kept still; Colle mumbled totally incomprehensible answers to them.

All of this upset him, but Pablo finally got back to work and resumed old habits, although the curfew made him turn in earlier than he had been used to. He stayed at Rue La Boétie at first, but then decided to stay at Rue des Grands-Augustins, because he got home so much more quickly when the Lipp or Flore had to close. At a secondhand shop he had found a huge coal stove that had been the very devil to get up to his studio, but he unfortunately never got fuel enough to keep it going properly. This cast-iron delight of his, which he compared to a Negro sculpture, was an almost unused witness to those difficult years.

He worried about his friends, some of whom were back in Paris and others gone, or about to go, to America. Apart from the group of Spaniards centered on him, he saw few artists and rarely went out. He did not need "entertainment." His relations with Dora had normalized, but Pablo did not hide his growing need for some variety. Yet, she was the principal model of the Women in an Armchair he was to paint over a period of months, as well as many other works. Olga was at a hotel with Paulo; Marie-Thérèse was still in Royan with Maya; and the Rosenbergs were in the United States. Kahnweiler, who had left Paris on June 12, 1940, was living with his wife and one of his sisters-in-law in a small house called Le-Repaire-l'Abbaye, near St.-Léonard-de-Noblat, about twenty miles east of Limoges, where most of his paintings had been sent. Boisgeloup, so long unoccupied, now housed Germans, but it was French soldiers who, during the "phony war," had thrown Picasso's sculptures out of the windows, or shot holes in them!

A number of Picassos had been in the great Jewish collections the Germans had seized, notably those of Paul Rosenberg and Alphonse Kann; they were less appreciated than the Fragonards, Bouchers, Renoirs, or Degases, most of which Marshal Goering appropriated for himself. The works of Picasso, Braque, Dufy, Matisse, Dali, Soutine, and other "wild Expressionists" were relegated to the rearmost, and least accessible, room of the Jeu de Paume Museum, which served as a sort of refuge for so-called degenerate art. Paul Rosenberg's finest Picassos were there, mainly dating from the "classical" period of the Twenties. Later, they were to be traded among various German, Dutch, Swiss, or French dealers having older or Impressionist works more acceptable to the masters of the Third Reich. Pablo may have taken advantage of this trafficking to buy back some of his old paintings, through intermediaries.

Sometime in 1942, his alien registration card lapsed and, not wanting to go through the Spanish embassy, Pablo got in touch with André-Louis Dubois, who, although relieved of his *Sûreté* job by Vichy, still had strong connections with the police. He saw a good deal of Pablo, and now sent him a high official of the force (since become well-known as a writer), who handled the matter expeditiously and quietly, as he would do also for Éluard and other intellectuals the Germans had reason to distrust. Pablo remained his grateful friend afterward.

Dubois was also able, through his good relations with Señor de Lequerica, the Spanish ambassador to Vichy, to spare Pablo and the small group of fellow Spaniards under his wing the harassment the Germans might otherwise have visited on them because of their virulent anti-Francoism. No mention was made of *Dream and Lie of Franco* or *Guernica,* and that constituted one aspect of Pablo's "resistance": fame and friendship kept him out of temptation as well as danger.

A constant guest at the German embassy, where the "Francophile" ambassador, Otto Abetz, was doing his best to enroll the Parisian intelligentsia, Maurice de Vlaminck was one of those who fell for ambiguous political and aesthetic promises made him. He thought—quite inopportunely—that here was a good chance to get even with that old rival Picasso, whom he had long detested. And

on June 6, 1942, in *Comoedia,* he published an article so extreme, and so unusual, that the editors not only stated that it represented only his own personal
views, but also that they would "out of impartiality" run the opinions of another
painter, André Lhote, on the problems Vlaminck raised, particularly "the case
of Picasso." True, Vlaminck had not beat around the bush:

> Pablo Picasso is guilty of having dragged French painting into the most fatal dead
> end, into undescribable confusion. From 1900 to 1930, he led it to negativism, im-
> potence, death. For alone with himself Picasso is impotence incarnate . . . He bor-
> rows from masters of the past, and even contemporaries, the soul of creation which
> he has never had . . .
> Without hesitation, one can put a name on each of his reminiscences. It is obvious
> who is behind each of his many and disparate "manners." . . . The only thing
> Picasso can't do is a Picasso that's really a Picasso!

Going on in the same vein, Vlaminck not only confirmed the occupying power's
hatred of "degenerate" art and pointed the finger at Picasso, but also attacked
the critics who showed him "infinite tolerance" or "limitless admiration," to
say nothing of the public, "stupefied, mystified, and misled by such hot air."
And Vlaminck, knowing Pablo could not reply, and his friends and defenders
were away or silenced, went on:

> For several generations of artists Picasso choked off the "spirit of creation," faith,
> sincerity in work and life. For, if it is agreed that a work of art need not prove any-
> thing "socially," certainly it has to be human, to teach a lesson.

André Lhote's reply, printed the following week, was extremely dignified:

> One would have to be truly naïve to believe that an article, even one written by an
> artist, could change anything in the development of painting . . . One would have
> to be a fool to think that "youth" pays any attention to the invective that artists, fol-
> lowing a regrettable tradition, indulge in flinging at each other over their easels, or
> that it waits for the coarsest insult or the nastiest barb, to make up its mind . . .

He concluded his piece with praise of Cubism—which in his own way he
had been practicing for some thirty years—by saying that he was "empowered
to state that Cubism will be mainly whatever it pleases French artists to make
of it."
Yet a survey of many artists by Gaston Diehl in the same publication the
following December showed how many young people were less attracted to that
movement than to the manner of a Bonnard. As for the elders—Vlaminck included—they were remarkably restrained; not one mentioned the name of Picasso,
who, as Diehl pointed out, "is one of the rare ones who willingly go to and
carefully observe the exhibitions by younger artists." The writer had not felt
impelled to include Pablo in his survey, knowing that he never responded to
interviews anyway, but he was the instigator of a protest by younger artists
against Vlaminck's views, that was also printed in *Comoedia*—and Pablo appreciated it.

The 1942 tracts fell flat, to the regrets of many who saw Picasso as a supporter of Bolshevism, an enemy of "collaboration" and the New Europe, and publicly called for an end to the "Gaullist" meetings taking place in his studio, as they claimed. Through Picasso, they were aiming at an entire purge of art, just as Hitler had freed German art of "Jewish poison."

Picasso was not in a mood to paint; like a caged lion, chain-smoking, walking by himself or with Kazbek, at best meeting a few friends in little bistros unlikely to welcome any Germans. He stopped going to any of the galleries he had previously followed rather regularly. Most of the dealers he knew were Jews, and some had been supplanted in their own galleries by chiselers better avoided, for they were often mere stalking horses for the Germans and their French "collaborators."

It had been a rude winter. Back from Royan, Marie-Thérèse needed an apartment for herself and Maya, for the Germans had taken over Vollard's house at Le Tremblay. There were vacancies, and she found one very close to the Rue des Grands-Augustins studio: she could practically peer in and see what went on there. But she was also offered one on Boulevard Henri-IV, and Picasso immediately urged her to take that: she understood, and bowed to his request once more. He would still spend weekends with her, and expect her daily letters.

He was seeing Olga again, but on days when he visited her he was· in a terrible mood, despite his delight in seeing Paulo, the official reason for the renewed contacts. Thursdays and Sundays belonged to Marie-Thérèse, since Maya was home from school those days. Pablo had asked the Spanish sculptor Rebull, whom he met through Fenosa, to do a bust of Maya, and since they regularly met at Marie-Thérèse's, they became close friends.

As soon as he got back from Royan, Pablo had begun to write: he had notebooks filled with jottings that he read to friends from time to time. Painting and writing periods alternated or mingled, according to his moods. On Tuesday, January 14, 1941, during a deadly icy evening, after a day of hard work, he opened a school notebook and began writing the bits of ideas that came to him, without logical continuity. On the first page, he did a drawing of himself at his table, glasses on his forehead and pen in hand, in a bird's-eye view. It was a kind of frontispiece for the body of the text, of which he still had no idea; the sentences just came, without order or grammar, for he played with words as he had done with paper, wire, junk, or anything else he decided to turn his hand to. He was familiar with the Surrealists' method of automatic writing, having used it in poems and drawings, and almost unconsciously now the sentences that he laid out word by word turned into a grotesque and tragic farce that he titled *Desire Caught by the Tail.**

His absurd humor owed much to Lautréamont and Raymond Roussel, whom he had probably never read but had heard much about in the old days from Apollinaire. On the other hand, he was very well acquainted with Alfred Jarry's work, and owned some of his manuscripts. *Desire* also reflected the atmosphere

* Translated by Bernard Frechtman, as *Desire, A Play* (New York: Philosophical Library, 1948).

of the occupation, and its characters, Tart, Skinny Anguish, Fat Anguish, Two Bow-Wows, Onion, and Big Foot, were obsessed by three things: hunger, cold, and sex. Those were the themes of the plot in which the free-flowing words unfurled torrents of wildly funny, poetic, or dramatic images. With his visual sense, Picasso displayed as much daring and dash here as in the collages, which his writing technique resembled; but there are few allusions to painting, except for one about the *Demoiselles d'Avignon,* which, says Big Foot, "already have thirty-three long years of their annuities."

Sabartés says that the lampoon was "written purely as a pastime," and it is nothing like Picasso's conversational tone. Indeed, he never spoke in flowing images but in brief phrases marked by pithy formulations that suddenly shed light on his thought and work. His conversation was incisive, biting, his barbs not intended to shock or amuse, but to convey a kernel of truth. Picasso, like Degas, was not one for witticisms or *bons mots;* when he expressed an opinion on the work of a friend, without indulgence, he was never witty or funny, but went directly to a trait of character or behavior, delineating an attitude. Passing judgment.

Little by little, Dora Maar's face was reappearing, in many drawings done in the winter of 1940–1941, then in 1941 when the arrests of resisters and the executions tragically accelerated. Suave, haughty Dora followed Dora in cubes or as a bird, among these realistic or geometrical anatomical variants, and then in May he did a portrait of Nush Éluard.

The poet and his wife stayed in Paris until the end of 1942, while he published *La Dernière Nuit* (The Last Night) and *Poésie et vérité 1942* (Poetry and Truth 1942), in which his famous poem, "Liberty," appeared for the first time. Before going underground, he rejoined the Communist Party, which he had left a few years before. They saw Pablo daily, either at the Grands-Augustins studio, where friends often forgathered now in addition to the habitual Saturdays, or in the cafés and restaurants of St.-Germain-des-Prés, where one might find the Aragons, René Char when he was in Paris, Youki and Robert Desnos, Jacques Prévert, Georges Hugnet, Raymond Queneau, Dominguez and the usual Spaniards (Fenosa, Rebull, and so on), Michel and Zette Leiris with word of Kahnweiler, Jean-Paul Sartre with Simone de Beauvoir, and others.

Picasso was obsessed with woman, monstrous, grotesque, cross-eyed, or trumpet-nosed, sometimes in Dora's old flowered hat, but always drawn or painted to fit his mood, and from time to time, since indeed she was very pretty, having her pure profile, deep wide eyes, and thin mouth that rarely laughed. The most repulsive of the female heads were violently impastoed, their texture thick and labored, its application in small sticks hammering away at the features.

Although having had trouble getting back to work, Pablo now did not let up; true, during the three years of German occupation he spent in Paris, he hardly ventured beyond the small closed world of his studio and the nearby cafés and restaurants. He showed his face nowhere, accepted no invitation, and ignored suggestions to exhibit. He had nothing but sarcasm for some of his friends who endorsed the "European" cause, like the ever visible Jean Cocteau, who took up the torch for Arno Breker, Hitler's official sculptor, whose huge athletes tailored to the Nazi ideal of manhood had all the attributes to appeal to him. Jean was a major attraction at Breker's show in May 1942.

This unfortunate display, plus his "Salute to Breker," published on the front page of *Comoedia* for May 23, 1942, were widely held against Cocteau; many of his friends cut him dead. Pablo and he had been on the outs for years, for Picasso had said unusually unkind things about him, and Jean let him know how hurt he had been. Rumor had it that at the intermission of a play at which the Picassos ran into Cocteau's mother, Olga apologized profusely, much to her husband's mortification.

In 1943 (when it had become apparent that Germany would lose the war), Cocteau was to change his attitude. Ever adept at turnabouts, he did one of his most dazzling: he renewed contact with Pablo and, at Liberation a year later, they were as close as ever they had been.

Picasso produced so much, with such diversity, during this wartime, that it is hard to detect periods or styles; the different series overlap, themes intertwine as the tireless inventive mind runs its course. Within the succession of women's heads or seated women with or without hats, appears a series of line drawings on the death of a horse during a bullfight, and several nudes.

On August 19 and 30, he did two wonderful portraits of Nush Éluard, bosom bare, in a subdued scale of grays, ochers, and greens. The more moving of the two, with its eyes lowered, a slight smile on the childish lips in the triangular face, and its tiny breasts, clearly expresses her fragile charm; she is surrounded by a soft light caressing her person, not flesh-, but shroud-colored. Pablo gave it to Éluard as a present, and it had a place of honor among the paintings, photographs, and objects that lined his apartment in Rue de la Chapelle; today it is in Paris' National Museum of Modern Art.

But the monsters kept appearing. Then Cubism made an unexpected comeback in some new and very geometrical women in armchairs. Beginning in Fall 1941, he started a series of two nude women, in a bedroom, one lying down, the other seated or standing before her. Anatomies, poses, and decors might change, but the guiding idea remained the same, and would still dominate a few months later in *L'Aubade* (done on May 4, 1942), now in the Paris Museum of Modern Art.

Turning the bathroom into the sculpture studio, since it was the only heatable room in the huge apartment, he spent long hours there and in it in 1943 created the famous *Bull's Head,* made of a bicycle seat and handlebar. As Brassaï reported him saying:

> Guess how I made that head of a bull. One day, in a rubbish heap, I found an old bicycle seat, lying beside a rusted handlebar . . . and my mind instantly linked them together. The idea for this *Tête de taureau* came to me before I had even realized it. I just soldered them together. The thing that's marvelous about bronze is that it can give the most diverse objects such unity that sometimes it's difficult to identify the elements that make up the whole. But that's also a danger: if you no longer see

"L'Aubade (Nude with a Musician)" Paris, May 4, 1942 (Musée national d'Art moderne—Paris)

(GIRAUDON)

anything but the head of a bull, and not the bicycle seat and handlebar that formed it, the sculpture would lose its interest.

A big head of Dora Maar, the one which, cast in bronze, was to be the Apollinaire monument in Square St.-Germain-des-Prés, stood on one stand in the studio, next to a wary limber 1941 *Cat,* and other pieces. The 1943 *Skull* or *Flayed Head* is among his most overwhelming sculptural works; half-rough, half-polished, the surface of the face is plowed by gaping excavations in place of nose, eyes, and mouth. An amazing dramatic intensity issues from the fleshless, yet bruised, lumpy face, akin to stones rolled and shaped by stream or sea.

He did not like the pictures of the recent sculptures, most of which were stored at Boisgeloup. He said they "looked better in plaster" and that he had had them cast only because Sabartés insisted that no other way could they be preserved. In order not to arouse German curiosity, they had been taken to and from the foundry one by one, by friends, in private cars or on the Métro.

One day he showed Brassaï a high-fashion mannequin from the turn of the century that had been headless and armless, until he added a left arm from Easter Island that Pierre Loeb had given him and a right arm and head he fashioned himself.

A few months later, he was to paint the food-laden buffet at the Catalan's, the restaurant of those dark years. In one of the last things he wrote before his arrest by the Germans (resulting in his death), Robert Desnos quoted Picasso in *Contrée* (Paris, 1944):

> I had been lunching for months at the Catalan's, and all those months I looked at his buffet, thinking nothing except, "It's a buffet." One day, I decided to make a picture of it. I did. And the next day, when I got there, the buffet was gone, its place empty. I must unwittingly have appropriated it by painting it.

January 19, 1942, portrait of Dora Maar; April 4, one of Inéz, the chambermaid-housekeeper who, since marrying Gustave Sassier, was living in a small apartment in Picasso's building, so that, though living separately, they were always available, and Pablo could hold long Spanish conversations with the young woman, show her his work, and ask her advice, which on occasion he followed. The portrait of beautiful Inéz he inscribed to her newborn son, Juan, his godchild.

Now a new motif appears, out of the still lifes: the head of an animal cut off and placed on a table. In January, he had done a gouache version of *L'Aubade:* a nude woman lying on a divan, as near her another woman lifts a curtain that reveals her charms to view. There is a frame at her feet.

Julio Gonzalez, who had long been sick, died; and on March 27, 1942, a pale winter sun shone on the cortège leaving his little house at Arcueil. Picasso, one of his oldest friends, took part in the funeral with Fenosa and Fernandez; the funeral service at the humble parish church upset him, he told them. To him, the death of Gonzalez was part of the tragedy of Spain, the war, the occupation, the disappearance of so many others.

Gonzalez' work had not fulfilled his early promise. His collaboration with Picasso had in the end profited only that great devourer of people and forms.

A few days later, he said of Gonzalez to Fenosa, "I'm the one who killed him." In tribute, he painted a series of seven pictures portraying, against great green or purplish geometric flats, a striking dramatic bull's skull. Fernandez says that the background was suggested to Picasso by the play of light through stained-glass windows during the funeral service. To Pablo, the seven were the "Death of Gonzalez."

Contorted so that she may be seen in all of her profiles at the same time, the nude woman of *L'Aubade,* in the definitive version dated May 4, 1942, was stretched on a divan with a striped cover, while her companion, all points, triangles, and folded paper birds with striations or solid coloring, played a mandolin sitting on a chair beside her. The simultaneous aspects of the ocher-colored nude are translated into linear planes or sharp-crested facets. The nocturnal harmony, highlighted with bright colors, is strictly rigorous in its hues.

This composition illustrates one of Pablo's concerns as concretized over several years in so many drawings and gouaches: the double nude. In August 1941, he had several times done a naked woman lying on a bed, her friend sitting alongside her and watching her sleep, a theme he now went back to, transforming the line study into a thicket of pencil strokes reminiscent of some of Giacometti's "smothered" drawings.

The girl friend watching over the nude woman suddenly undresses in the gouache of January 2, 1942, and draws the curtain back to reveal her friend's anatomy. But four months later she was dressed again, had lost all femininity, and was playing a mandolin. Later, the two women friends would return in various forms and styles, from classicism to geometricism, no longer just looking at each other, but doing their hair, or talking. Sometimes a man replaces one of the women; or else, the women are taking a child through its first steps, and then back home are washing their feet. They go through these ablutions without the slightest gracefulness, bothered by an anatomy that makes things no easier. In *Reclining Nude and Woman Washing Her Feet* (Art Museum, Worcester, Massachusetts), the subject is reduced to the barest essentials: squared-off wooden mannequins transform the Baudelairian theme of women lovers into a confrontation of barbaric totems in a bedroom lighted by a storm lantern on the floor.

On July 16 and 19, the painter started the long series of drawings and washes, to be resumed in later periods, that deal with *Man with the Sheep,* the big two-meter-high statue that, after over a hundred preparatory studies, he would do in a single day in February 1943. The month of August was spent in thick-textured still lifes, energetic but austere, with flowers, fruit, and then some heads. And the pigeon reappeared.

Linked to his earliest childhood memories of the Málaga square where they flew around the great plane trees outside his windows, and his first drawings under the direction of Don José, who painted them so often and suggested them as models to his son, pigeons had been present throughout his life. The drawing of November 5, 1942, was a prelude to a whole series done during that autumn, realistic as well as geometric pigeons, on chairs, and elsewhere, eventually leading to *The Dove of Peace.*

The October 9 portrait of Dora Maar is one of the most moving he ever did of this consort whom he so often mistreated. His hardness and cruelty toward her appeared not only in the tortures he inflicted on her reproduced body or the aggressively monstrous character he often gave her face; in every way, he was a heartless inquisitor to her. Knowing her to be extremely nervous, subject to wild manic-depressive extremes, he nevertheless continually drove her to distraction.

Dora, it can be said, took everything at his hands. Royan, where Marie-Thérèse attracted all eyes as everyone fawned over Maya before her proud daddy, had been hell to Dora. To have to endure pity for being neglected, double-crossed, while he was living with her and not the other woman, had been intolerable. Scenes ensued; slapped with full force by the Ogre, Dora would lie unconscious on the ground, while he shouted insults at her. Several times, her violent nervous fits gave him a fright—quickly forgotten.

Some feminine faces, conscientiously drawn, allow us to suppose that in 1942–1943 he paid some attention to certain pretty young women: these he did not torture or distort; his famous realism celebrated their beauty. But, while he often treated Dora without any consideration, he could also be charming, full of unexpected thoughtfulness and kindness. Often, of a morning, he would phone to invite her to lunch; since running afoul of other ladies at his studio, she no longer dropped in there, but met Pablo in the street, and they then went off to a restaurant to join their friends. Mysteriously, whenever Pablo was talking on the phone to Dora, Kazbek evidenced delight, running to the door and asking to have it opened. No matter what strange names Pablo used for her, or what outlandish things he said, Kazbek could always recognize that it was she; yet when Picasso took or made other calls, Kazbek ignored them.

In the portrait of October 9, 1942, Dora is wearing a green- and red-striped dress, with white collar, that sets off her bust; she looks both troubled and resigned. Her face is like a mask, with a strange fixed stare in the eye; the open-nostriled nose and small, delicate, unsmiling mouth, which identify her on even the most monstrous "portraits," are precisely drawn. Dora, distant, as if in some other world, seems more a vision than herself; she seems to be enclosed in the cell in which for some years Pablo had been placing his models, and this time he carried his cruelty to the point of painting bars in the background, with a jar of water and a hunk of bread. What a symbol it was of the life she was leading, having changed so now that her friends no longer recognized her: once smiling, lively, full of fun and humor despite her reserved nature, she was now sad and fearful.

While she was posing at Rue des Grands-Augustins, her mother became seriously ill, so the trouble in her eyes was understandable. Once again, fate was on Pablo's side, giving him a break from the portrait, for the time it took for Dora's mother to die. When he started in again, he removed the prison bars and bread and water, and perhaps intensified the suffering on her face. At any rate, he skirted the tragedy, but did not enter it; Dora's features remain serenely suffering, her dress perky, the emotive power of the specter-figure concentrated inside it. Dora had learned to keep quiet, not to verbalize her feelings; she was allowed to cry out, chew on her handkerchief, or weep only in her lover's pictures.

In 1945, he was to tell André Malraux:

Dora, for me, was always a weeping woman. Always. . . .
. . . And it's important, because women are suffering machines. . . . When I paint a woman in an armchair, the armchair implies old age or death, right? So, too bad for her. Or else the armchair is there to protect her. . . . Like Negro sculpture. Innocent painting exists. The Impressionists—in any case, the Promeneurs—are an example of innocent painting. But not the Spaniards. Not Van Gogh. Not me. . . .

He had so masterfully contrived it that Dora and Marie-Thérèse had never bumped into each other at Rue des Grands-Augustins. Sometimes of a Sunday, when he was at Boulevard Henri-IV, Dora would phone him there. When Marie-Thérèse asked him who had called, he would answer, "The Argentine embassy."

Having no choice in the matter, the two women tolerated each other's existence; each had her appointed days, hours, weekends, or trips. It was not a fair split, since Dora, now the official mistress, got the lion's share, being generally accepted as his mate. She lived near him, might bump into him in the neighborhood, or be summoned at a moment's notice, but Marie-Thérèse had a trump card: Maya.

When Dora selected a dress at her regular couturier's, Pablo ordered a duplicate sent to Marie-Thérèse. One day, the deliveryman made a mistake, and brought Marie-Thérèse the one intended for Dora. Marie-Thérèse, convinced that Pablo had had it done on purpose, phoned him, only to be told by Inéz that he was not in; so she hotfooted it to Dora's, where she was most unwelcome. Meanwhile, from the next room, Pablo listened to their whole catty/bitchy exchange. That afternoon, Marie-Thérèse was at the studio.

"You've been promising to marry me for so long," she told him, "it's about time you got divorced."

After the morning's incident, Pablo had been expecting anything but that, and countered, "At my age, you know, it would be a little ridiculous, and besides there's a war on, which complicates matters a good deal."

This was the tenor of the conversation, when Dora in turn arrived unexpectedly, and flew off the handle at the presence of Marie-Thérèse.

"Look, Picasso," she thundered, "you're in love with *me,* and you know it."

Whereupon Pablo tenderly put his arm around the neck of Maya's mother, and said, "Dora Maar, you know very well that the only woman I love is Marie-Thérèse Walter. Here she is, and that's that."

Dora could not believe her ears. Marie-Thérèse, equally taken aback, melted with tenderness. And Pablo went right on talking. So Marie-Thérèse, in her newfound self-assurance, turned to Dora and ordered her to leave. The latter refused. Picasso reveled in the drama he saw developing, as the two women faced off against each other. Marie-Thérèse repeated her order to get out; Dora demurred again. So Marie-Thérèse grabbed her by the shoulders, and Dora slapped her.

She got a louder slap in return and was pushed out the door, without Pablo reacting at all.

Once Dora was gone, he simply said to Marie-Thérèse, "You know how much I love you."

And, as she sadly recalled the incident, "Then he gave me my five kilos of coal and I went home. That's all."

Thanks to well-placed connections, Pablo had been getting a super-ration of coal, but since he always burned the whole ton right away, the studio was generally freezing. As long as there still was coal on hand, Marie-Thérèse would come daily to collect five kilograms of it that she carried herself on the subway. When he was in a good mood, he would open the wardrobe and show her the gold ingots piled up in it, and at least as many big bars of good yellow soap that she had stocked up on before the war. And say to her, "You see that gold. If anything happens to me, take it, it's yours."

"I'd rather have the soap back right now," she would answer, being reduced to the same abominable ersatz as everyone else. But he would close the wardrobe, on both gold and soap.

After that Dora–Marie-Thérèse showdown, things went back to being just the way they were. Had Picasso been aware of what he was doing? At any rate, he had hurt the one least able to take it.

"Picasso's palette is in mourning," Maurice Raynal had said. Gray, mauve, black, and dark brown were now dominant, without shimmer or brilliance; the paintings of Spring 1943 are bathed in a sort of twilight pall. The only agreeable note: the first steps of a child, Inéz', whose progress Pablo followed wondrously. But the drawings and canvases on the early life of the round-faced baby are not tender; Pablo referred to little Juan as "Churchill," and turned him into a kind of toad with outsize hands and feet, and two disparate wide eyes in a round face. The young woman awkwardly helping him put one foot before the other came off no better.

Events inspired Pablo to do several still lifes, some reflecting the sorry deprivations of the dark years, empty cooking pots, percolators for the ersatz known as "national coffee," plates and glasses watched over by a candlestick as if at a wake. The others show how the hungry went about trying to improve their fare, as in the *Tomato Plant* that Picasso noted on a windowsill, or *Fruit Dish with Cherries,* suggesting a rare treat. The buffet and serving table of Le Catalan belong to this series of "slices of life."

"I did not paint the war because I'm not the kind of painter who goes looking for subjects, like a photographer. But there is no doubt the war is present in the painting I did then. Perhaps later some historian may show how my work changed under the influence of the war. I don't know how."

Pablo was the one who discovered the restaurant later known as Le Catalan, hard by his Grands-Augustins studio; it catered largely to bricklayers and construction workers for whom the owner, Arnau, outdid himself in culinary exploits. As a Catalan he could do no less than his utmost in appreciation of his

Andalusian neighbor's assiduous patronage, and the latter introduced several of his friends, among them Georges Hugnet, the poet, who henceforth held Friday evening get-togethers there with friends and acquaintances collected at the various St.-Germain-des-Prés bistros. In that way, the nameless little restaurant, which after the war was to become a rendezvous of Tout-Paris, now welcomed Picasso's entourage, everyone from Éluard to Reverdy, "Baron" Mollet to Desnos, Prévert to the actress Lise Deharme. Even Jean Cocteau appeared there, with Jean Marais, begging acceptance again after his ridiculous fawning on Arno Breker. Éluard refused to shake his hand, but Picasso, amused by him and more tolerant, let him sit down. He had Cocteau where he wanted him.

It was at Le Catalan's, or "chez le Catalan," as Picasso had baptized the place, that Léon-Paul Fargue, lunching with him and Hugnet on April 28, 1943, suffered the stroke that was to leave him paralyzed. There was singing and even plotting, as well as eating there, and one day food inspectors arrived while Pablo was treating his friends to steak on one of the week's three meatless days: both he and the owner were heavily fined, and the restaurant was closed for a month.

One Sunday morning in January 1943, Pablo made an unusual visit to Dora Maar's on Rue de Savoie, to bring her a copy of Buffon's Histoire naturelle, which had been started some years before by Vollard and finished by the publisher Fabiani. The latter, notwithstanding the war, had succeeded in beautifully completing the superb work, with its thirty-one aquatints, the first of which had been pulled five years earlier.

Pablo sat down before a table at Dora's, looked around at his mistress's paintings hung on the walls, as well as the imaginary animals he had drawn on the walls themselves, using as starting points any spots she had made while painting. On the open book before him, he began incredibly quickly to draw heads of antique heroes and all sorts of familiar animals. Wherever there was a blank page, he filled it completely with a drawing, a face usually half-realistic, half-invented. On the frontispiece, he did Dora as a bird and signed the facing page with a Catalan pun: Per Dora Maar tan rebufon (For Dora Maar, so supercharming), bufon, the Catalan for charming, being close enough to Buffon to make it funny. Then, here and there, he added a skull surrounded by skeletons and snakes, screaming heads, and a scrawny bird expiring. These illustrations that he superimposed on the Natural History were in turn to be published in 1957 as 40 dessins de Picasso en marge de Buffon (Forty Picasso Drawings Alongside Buffon).

Parisian electricity was rationed in January 1943, thirty Métro stations were closed, an exhibition called "Lotteries of Yesterday and Today" opened at the Orangerie, the street in the Sixteenth Arrondissement named for Heinrich Heine was renamed for Johann-Sebastian Bach, there was a big do at the Palais de Chaillot to celebrate the tenth anniversary of the Third Reich. But no one talked about what had happened to the Nazi armies at Stalingrad.

On February 8, five students, accused of having launched an anti-German demonstration at the Lycée Buffon, were shot by a firing squad.

Paris was laid open to the Gestapo and their "collabos." Jews and Communists, "terrorists" or those so-called, were hunted down, arrested, tortured, deported. French Fascists paraded on the Champs-Élysées and proclaimed their faith in German victory and the New Europe. The daily execution of Resistance people could be heard each dawn, as Paul Éluard wrote:

> What do you expect the gates were being guarded
> What do you expect we had been locked in
> What do you expect the street had been closed
> What do you expect the city had been conquered
> What do you expect it was dying of hunger

Who was it that first spread the rumor Picasso was Jewish, or half-Jewish? Fortunately, because he was Spanish, although notoriously anti-Franco, the Gestapo had not bothered him. If not Jewish, he had certainly been the friend of many Jews, which was no less reprehensible: Kahnweiler, the Rosenbergs, Gertrude Stein, Max Jacob. When someone asked him in confidence whether he actually had Jewish blood in his veins, he replied, "No, but I wish I did."

One morning at Passy, André-Louis Dubois got a phone call from Dora. To her "They're at Picasso's," he replied, "I'll be right over." His friends had not worried for nothing; the attacks and betrayals had hit home. At Rue des Grands-Augustins, Dubois found two men in green raincoats who demanded his identification papers. Satisfied, they let him by, and left. As he quoted what Pablo told him, "They insulted me, called me a degenerate, a Communist, a Jew. They kicked at the paintings. And then they said, 'We'll be back.' That's all." *

Arno Breker is supposed to have said, "Picasso will not be touched." He later denied it, and indeed minimized, if not completely denied, any close friendship with the painter, or doing him any favors. A thorough investigation of contemporary witnesses, German as well as French, seems to indicate that Hitler's official sculptor intervened with the Gestapo only once, on behalf of Maillol's mistress-model who, arrested for being Jewish, was released.

One day, Brassaï brought Henri Michaux, who wanted to meet him, to Picasso's; Pablo showed them a series of recent pen-and-ink and wash drawings, covering all sorts of subjects out of his inexhaustible imagination: heads and busts of women, pigeons, chairs, what have you. They seemed animated by some amazing secret life, an inner flame that burned or ate away at them. As he was taking them out, Brassaï asked Picasso whether his ideas came to him fortuitously, or whether they were planned.

> I don't know [he quotes him]. Ideas are just simple points of departure. It's rare for me to be able to pinpoint them, just as they came to my mind. As soon as I set to work, others seem to flow from the pen. To know what you want to draw, you have to begin drawing it. If it turns out to be a man, I draw a man—if it's a woman, I draw a woman. There's an old Spanish proverb: "If it has a beard, it's a man; if it doesn't have a beard, it's a woman." Or, in another version: "If it has a beard, it's Saint Joseph; if it doesn't have a beard, it's the Virgin Mary." Wonderful proverb,

* A.-L. Dubois, *Sous le signe de l'amitié* (In the Name of Friendship), Paris, 1972.

isn't it? When I have a blank sheet of paper in front of me, it runs through my head all the time. Despite any will I may have in the matter, what I express interests me more than my ideas. . . .

Every time I draw a man, it's my father I'm thinking of, involuntarily. For me a man is Don José, and will be all my life . . . every man I draw I see more or less with his features. . . .

Matisse makes a drawing, then he makes a copy of it. He recopies it five times, ten times, always clarifying the line. He's convinced that the last, the most stripped down, is the best, the purest, the definitive one; and in fact, most of the time, it was the first. In drawing, nothing is better than the first attempt.

The war did not interfere with the many Picasso shows in the Americas: Chicago, 1940 ("Picasso: Forty Years of his Art" at the Art Institute) and 1941 (Katherine Kuh Gallery); New York, 1941 (Bignou Gallery and Museum of Modern Art), 1942 and 1943 (Paul Rosenberg Gallery), 1943 (Pierre Matisse Gallery); *Guernica* at Columbus, Ohio, 1941, and at the Fogg Museum of Art, Harvard University, 1941–1942, the latter also showing Picasso with Frank Lloyd Wright and Maillol in 1943; Phillips Memorial Gallery, Washington, 1944, as well as the Sociedad de Arte Moderno, Mexico City, and elsewhere. The Mexican show had prefaces by José Moreno Villa, Augustín Lazo, Carlos Merida, and José Renau. And two traveling exhibits of Picassos toured American university campuses in 1941–1942 and 1942–1943.

The year 1940 saw the simultaneous publication in Paris and New York of Jean Cassou's *Picasso*. In 1941, *Personal Revolution and Picasso* by Louis Danz, dealing with *Guernica* and his reactions to the Spanish War, appeared in New York; in 1942, *Picasso sin tiempe* by Juan Marinello in Havana, *Picasso, el artiste y la obra de nuestro tiempo* in Buenos Aires; in 1943, *Cinquanta disegni di Pablo Picasso* (Fifty Drawings) at Novara, *Picasso, scultore* by Enrico Prampolini in Rome, and Robert Desnos' *Picasso: Seize peintures 1939–1943* (Sixteen Paintings), in Paris.

Through the Leirises Pablo heard regularly from Kahnweiler, but, out of caution, they did not write each other, for the dealer, both a Jew and a protector of "degenerate" artists and their works, was a prime Gestapo target. His place of refuge was in the heart of the area where the Germans and their French Fascist allies were fighting it out with the *maquis* of the Limousin. Despite several alarms, Kahnweiler was never in real trouble, but in February 1942, Leiris, tipped off by friends, told him he would do better to change his retreat. Anonymous letters to the Gestapo had stated that a Jew was hiding firearms at Le-Repaire-l'Abbaye.

There were several searches, without result. The frustrated Nazis looted the house, carrying off jewels—but overlooking the paintings. The true identity of Henri-Georges Kersaint (Kahnweiler's alias) was not discovered. But he decided it was prudent to move; he and his wife settled with friends of the Leirises at the hamlet of Lagupie, between Marmande and La Réole, about fifty miles southeast of Bordeaux. They had several narrow escapes when the Germans surrounded the town and burned houses they alleged had "terrorists" in them. But for all that, Kahnweiler was able to work in relative tranquillity, and here he wrote the book on Juan Gris published in 1946, as well as several essays.

In Paris, Louise Leiris (known to her intimates as Zette) had succeeded in buying her brother-in-law's gallery, which had been condemned as Jewish property, after Kahnweiler's partner Simon, also Jewish, took refuge in Brittany. There were complications, for someone wrote to the Bureau of Sequestered Jewish Property stating that, since Mme. Leiris was Kahnweiler's sister-in-law, this could be only a dummy purchase; but she was able to prove she had worked with and for her brother-in-law since 1920 and it was therefore quite natural for her to want to acquire ownership. In fact it was not a dummy sale, as the duly notarized deed attested. The Germans acquiesced, and she became owner of the Rue d'Astorg gallery, which remains in her name.

The Leirises saw Picasso almost daily, in part because Kahnweiler was afraid he might fall for the lures of one of the new, inexperienced but daring, dealers who, having taken over sequestered Jewish galleries, were riding high, getting the Germans the paintings and art objects they wanted. One of them had in fact gotten to Pablo, who in a thoughtless moment agreed to a deal with him, and actually sold him several paintings or drawings. The dismayed Leirises immediately bought a large number of their friend's works so that lack of funds might not tempt him to become a regular "supplier" of their dangerous rival.

Several Germans, collectors or just art lovers, came to see Picasso at Rue des Grands-Augustins. One day, on the stairs, Éluard came face to face with an officer of the Kommandantur, and thought Pablo had been picked up. He, however, was amused at his friend's concern over him. "Sometimes Boches came to see me, claiming they wanted to admire my pictures. I gave them postcard reproductions of *Guernica,* saying, 'Take it. It's a souvenir!' " he told Simone Téry in an interview that appeared in *Les Lettres françaises* for March 24, 1945, headed "Picasso Is Not An Officer in the French Army."

Dora Maar tells of Pablo visiting her one day when she was painting a still life that included an alarm clock. "I'll show you how to do the clock," he said, and drew an exactly realistic version of it: body, hands, legs, and alarm bell. Then another, with certain distortions, the face now ovoid, hands crossing, and then a third and several more in which, progressively, the clock turned into some totally imaginary fantastic thing. Finally Picasso opened the clock, and its inner works became an amazing dancing girl: the alarm clock was still there, but it had given birth to creation. This was not a new procedure with him; he had always liked opening boxes to see what was in them. That was how he was to show *The Catalan's Buffet.*

Georges Hugnet very frequently joined Pablo for meals at the Catalan's, Gafner's, or other neighborhood restaurants. The encroaching little man, a charming poet once close to the Dadaists and Surrealists, who had broken with most of them, had written some revealing texts about his painter friends, and owned a large number of their works, a remarkable collection from Cubism through Surrealism.

"What a period this is!" he said to me between drinks of red wine around

1960. "Painters don't give anything away anymore." For they had spoiled him.

Picasso liked the company of this amusing and thoughtful young fan, who had dubbed him the "inventor of fire." With Éluard, Desnos, and Reverdy when he was in Paris, he was part of the court of poets in whom Pablo found much friendlier resonances than in professional critics. At times René Char put in an appearance at the Catalan's or Rue des Grands-Augustins, but as an officer in the Resistance he had to stay out of Paris, too risky at the end of 1943.

If amused by Hugnet, Picasso was also very generous to him, and did wood-cuts in 1942 for his *Non Vouloir* (The Non-Will) and 1943 for his *Le Chèvrefeuille* (Honeysuckle), which, in addition to six woodcuts, had twenty-five special pulls of them in three colors, plus an etching.

Suddenly, in July 1943, there appear pen-and-ink drawings of the tip of the Île de la Cité, Square du Vert-Galant dominated by the statue of Henri IV at the foot of the Pont-Neuf. Had he turned landscape artist? In the following months, he did several other drawings and paintings of this spot, then some equally "classical" Parisian scapes: Notre Dame, the Seine and its bridges, and so on, of which he told Malraux in 1945:

> "I did not do many landscapes in my life; these came about on their own. There was a lot of talk in those days, 1943–1944, about the possible destruction of Paris. I often walked along the Seine with Kazbek, especially between the Pont-Neuf and the Pont Saint-Michel, a spot I know well. One day, all those things came together in me almost unwittingly and I did a synthesis of them."

None of these landscapes was done on the spot.

He drew a very great deal, having always at hand or in a pocket different-shaped pads that he covered with sketches, filling them at an incredible rate. All styles, techniques, subjects sprang pell-mell from his ever-alert inspiration. A number of the pads are clearly erotic; the older he became, the more Picasso was haunted by desire, women's genitals obsessing him, and beyond the tradi-tional coital positions he drew the most unlikely amorobatics that could be in-dulged in only by figures whose anatomy permitted. There was no pornography in these drawings, for Picassian eroticism is openly enjoyable, neither unwhole-some nor turgid; sex, love, and the use one put them to were perfectly natural to him. At least for now.

At sixty, he was as lustful as at twenty, and women flocked to him without his even trying. He availed himself of all he wanted, however he wanted; ex-periments repeated with varying partners were merely "verifications" of a virility that was to remain so long triumphant, which he was always ready to expatiate about in euphoric detail to friends, notwithstanding the fact that he might have with him some earlier beneficiary of his attentions. After Dora Maar's first at-tempt at suicide, he did become more discreet in his demonstrativeness, and less open in public recountings.

When a woman bored him, he turned absolutely odious toward her; if she became distant, he was furious; if she reproached him, he would beat her. In good Spanish manner, to him woman was a slave; he was concerned only with his own feelings, desires, needs, amazed that they might also be hers; woe to her if she showed any personality of her own. He was sure that once repudiated his mate could not survive him; that had happened to Fernande—who had left him of her own accord—and Olga, who now dragged their memories of the Ogre with them like a ball and chain. Marie-Thérèse placidly accepted a back seat and resignation, while Dora was still holding out. But not for long.

Jacques Prévert was a frequent visitor. With his lugubrious eye, his flaccid jowls pulling down his lips, the ever-present cigarette butt dangling from them, his exhausted look accentuated by his hesitant step, he was strangely both funny and sardonic. When he talked—which was sparingly—he seemed to be making a superhuman effort. Sometimes, at Pablo's request, when friends were there, he would recite one of his poems, in a catastrophic, jerky, but poignant way: his funniest performance was reading aloud from René Benjamin's brown-nosing book to the glory of Marshal Pétain, *Le Grand Homme seul* (Great Man Alone). Sidesplitting.

On one such day, July 3, 1943, Pablo had just finished an especially difficult painting, an inside view of the studio with, in the foreground, the unused radiator and a pipe going up, as the window opens on to the tiered rooftops of Paris and the sky. Prévert said to Brassaï:

> "Look at that. Any other painter would have omitted the radiator, thinking it was ugly, vulgar, 'unesthetic.' He would have stressed the 'picturesque quality' of the old walls and roofs, but it's precisely that radiator that dominates this canvas. Picasso wants to tell the truth, before anything else. Look, he's even painted that old rag hanging on the wall."

That was the terrible lucidity of a painter who knew the price and weight of things. And he went right on producing, painting, drawing. Periodically in the many works the same pigeons, women's heads, women seated, landscapes of the Vert-Galant, sheep's skull, rooster, and death's-head came back. Then other heads with flopped-over noses, as in the 1906–1907 faces, and Maya, women in hats, still lifes with coffeepot, candlestick, mirror, skull, new "vanities" of a time of mourning.

Nursing women, women helping their children walk, washing their own feet, wearing complicated flowered hats such as were then fashionable, and women lying nude on a couch, plus the *Woman in a Rocking Chair* (August 9, 1943), make up a terrifying catalog of anatomical aberrations, distortions and deformations that are brutally, icily cruel.

Sometimes the woman did have a woman's face, but only the more pitilessly to be judged, to be more *readable*. Over all, the female figures of these war years express Picasso's apparent departure from general male feelings toward a woman, desire, pleasure, passion, to be replaced by those that painting alone dictates. For Pablo, from this time on, was progressively enclosing himself more and more within his painting, living through and with it; while keeping columnists, gossipmongers, and torchbearers—ever more numerous, more sycophantic— athrob with his public life, his joining the Communist Party, attending peace congresses, his new loves, bullfights, family bathing at Golfe-Juan, and all the rest, he was getting deeper into the skin of his last great avatar: that of the providential man, the man of destiny.

From August 1944, in the very first days of France's liberation from the German grip, basing himself on Poussin, the most rigorous and logical of all the classics, he invented a second classicism: autobiographical classicism. His vital functions, pulsations, respirations now were paintings; he would never again let up, taking only the shortest respites, when traveling, or obliging his Communist friends by speaking here or there. His final thirty years were to be a dizzying, breakneck race toward creation. That alone. And totally that.

The last line of the book his friend Hélène Parmelin wrote in 1959, *Picasso sur la place,** quoted him, "You live a poet's life, and I live a convict's." The years 1941–1944 were the prelude to that penal servitude. Heaven be blessed, in order to lighten his labors, the sixty-two-year-old Ogre was about to have in his bed an appealing creature, intelligent and uninhibited, thirty-nine years his junior; while waiting for her to say yes, he went ahead with pen-and-ink and wash sketches for his *Man with the Sheep.*

* *Picasso Plain*, translated by Humphrey Hare (New York: St. Martin's Press, and London: Secker & Warburg, 1963).

XVIII

"LIFE
WITH FRANÇOISE"
(1943–1946)

IN MAY 1943, ALAIN CUNY, THE ACTOR, WAS HAVING DINNER WITH TWO girls at the Catalan's. At a nearby table, Picasso was talking to Dora Maar, Marie-Laure de Noailles, and some man. He noticed the two young girls and tried to attract their attention by talking loud. As he knew Cuny, he finally went over to their table, carrying a bowl of cherries, and offered them some.

When, at his request, Cuny introduced the girls and they told him they were painters, Don Pablo burst out laughing. "That's the funniest thing I've heard all day," he exclaimed. "Girls who look like that can't be painters!" They protested that at the very moment they were having a joint exhibition in a gallery on Rue Boissy-d'Anglas, and Pablo invited them to visit his studio.

And that is how Françoise Gilot, who was to be his mate for ten years and bear him two children, met Picasso. Or that, at least is how she tells it in *Life with Picasso,* her book written with Carlton Lake. Others say she had known him for some time before through a painter whose *amie* she was.

The day after the meeting at the Catalan's, Françoise and her friend Geneviève, visiting from Montpellier, climbed the spiral staircase to the Grands-Augustins studio. Mistrustful Sabartés opened the door and asked whether they had an appointment; unimpressed when they said yes, for every pretty girl claimed to have an appointment, he made them wait, while he went to inquire.

He never could tell; Pablo made all kinds of dates, and kept very few of them. If they were to be at the studio, like as not, he would duck out just before the appointed time, leaving Sabartés to make up an excuse. And sometimes reappear before Jaime had got rid of the visitor, then putting on an act and blaming Sabartés for having forgotten to remind him or misinformed him. He even pulled this kind of act on Julian Huxley when the latter was Secretary General of UNESCO.

But he was in to Françoise and Geneviève. Before he came out, they looked the studio over, slightly surprised by its disorder and especially by the pile of junk filling a whole corner. On the walls were a Vuillard, one or two Douanier Rousseaus, a Modigliani, and Matisse's well-known still life of the bowl of oranges on a rose tablecloth with blue background. "Oh, what a beautiful Matisse!" Françoise exclaimed. To which, Sabartés, who had come back, replied, "Here, there is only Picasso."

In a few moments, Sabartés led the two girls up the inner staircase. Pablo, in a striped sailor's jersey and ill-fitted pair of old pants, was with several friends. He greeted the girls most demonstratively, then took them back down to the studio from which they had just come, to show them around in detail. In the engraving studio (the bathroom), he gave them a short course in technique, but, despite their hopes, showed them none of the paintings standing facing the wall. Only when they were ready to leave did he take them back into the room where the paintings were and turn two or three around for them, one of a cock crowing lustily, and another, as Françoise wrote, "of the same period, but very severe, all in black and white."

As they were leaving, he smilingly asked them to come again. "But if you do come, don't come like pilgrims going to Mecca. Come because you like me . . ."

A few days later, at the gallery where she and Geneviève had their show, Françoise was told that Picasso had been there that morning, looked silently at the pictures, and then left. They were surprised and upset, for it probably meant he did not think much of them. This was important to Françoise, who wanted to see him again.

So, one morning about a week later, she dragged Geneviève to Rue des Grands-Augustins again, and Sabartés this time was so amazed to see them bring a pot of cineraria that he let them in directly. "Nobody brings flowers to an old gent," Picasso laughed, but then noticing that Françoise's dress matched the petals, he added, "You think of everything . . ."

This time, he showed them much of his work, and the most recent: stark, somber still lifes, versions of *The Catalan's Buffet,* nudes, Vert-Galant landscapes, children taking their first steps, then other, more richly colored still lifes with legs of lamb, skinned rabbits, sausages, and so on, all the things that wartime Parisians were being deprived of. And finally, the tortured, disjointed, tragic portraits of Dora Maar.

"I saw your exhibition," he told Françoise. "You're very gifted for drawing. I think you should keep on working—hard—every day. I'll be curious to see how your work develops. I hope you'll show me other things from time to time."

Françoise returned to Rue des Grands-Augustins, alone, several times. The Ogre, as could be expected, was delighted with such assiduity, and appreciated her youth and beauty. She indeed was doing everything to win that appreciation. One day, when she came in dripping with rain, he even dried her hair for her. As she commented in her book, "Of course, Picasso didn't have a situation like that handed to him every time." But there would be others. To Sabartés, Françoise was another one with "hot pants," and he detested her, as he did all of Picasso's women—but as usual said nothing.

Under Françoise's pen, their courtship comes out all sugar and honey; the attentions she attributes to Picasso are not typical of him, for he treated women rather cavalierly. But she attracted and intrigued him, so he inquired about her: twenty-two, from a very good bourgeois family in Neuilly, she frequented painters and was the mistress of one of them, whose angular, tense canvases were causing a good deal of comment. When Pablo asked Sabartés to check on that, he ducked the assignment by claiming he could not because of his weak eyes!

Pablo was furious with him, for he was beginning to have doubts about Françoise's professed modesty, innocence, and distaste for people. As luck would have it, Brassaï had met her two or three years before, at the studio of a fellow Hungarian, the painter Endre Rozsda; she had been friendly and invited him to dinner at her parents'. Her industrialist father did not approve of her dropping out of the university to paint. Brassaï delighted Pablo with his account of the verve with which she defended herself against her father, her passionate opinions on art. "She has been dying to show you her pictures for a long time," he said.

Dozens of girls and women weekly came to show their pictures to the master, some briefly, others at greater length—when given a tour of the apartment, and the studio upstairs. One day, when Picasso was called away for a moment, one of them quickly shed her clothes and slipped between the sheets. He sent Sabartés to get rid of her.

Françoise's visits became more frequent, as the two of them studied each other, weighed the situation. Was the time ripe for an affair? Pablo showed her his "museum," first step in the ritual initiation. She tells how, pointing to a wooden foot on one of the shelves, he said, "That's Old Kingdom. There's all of Egypt in that foot. With a fragment like that, I don't need the rest of the statue." Then the Ogre "very gently" pushed her to one side of the case where there were several pebbles with female profiles cut in them, as well as a bull's head and a faun. "I did those with this," he said, taking out of his pocket a single-bladed jackknife, with the Opinel trademark on the blade (Françoise recalled even that minor detail!).

When she asked about another object, he identified it as a fine-tooth comb, and said he might give it to her but, after running his fingers through her hair, he told her, of course, she would not need it. But the studio visit seemed to pall. Perhaps he was wearying of the girl who, when he made a tentative pass at her, did not shy away, but calmly replied (as her best defense, she claims), "I'm at your disposition." That, indeed, was forcing him to assume the role of an *ordinary* seducer and resort to conventional, therefore humiliating, moves toward the young thing he so desired and wanted to force into submission. "How do you expect me to seduce anyone under conditions like that?" he demanded. "If you're not going to resist—well, then it's out of the question. I'll have to think it over."

He thought it over, and decided he had to go along. On later visits, there were all the mechanical moves: once he tried to maneuver her to bed; she dodged. Another time he brought up the Marquis de Sade in order to shock her; she expatiated back on Restif de la Bretonne and Choderlos de Laclos. Still another morning, he lured her up under the eaves to see the view and, coming up behind her, took her breasts in his hands. She did not react. As a last resort, he pointed to an "enormous phallus, about seven feet long, with baroque subsidiary decoration" that some workman had whitewashed onto a wall across the way, and asked her what she thought it was. "It didn't seem to me to be at all figurative, I told him," she writes. When she later turned and faced him, "He was slightly flushed, and he looked pleased."

She left on vacation to visit her friend Geneviève near Montpellier, and says she did not return to Picasso's till November. He apparently did not write her, but did not feel he needed to, for the outcome was now ordained. When, finally, he got her into the bedroom, and began undressing her, he was to make a painter's point. "I want to see if your body corresponds to the mental image I have of it." Unfortunately, he felt obliged to add, after seeing her nude, "You know, it's incredible the degree to which I had prefigured your form."

On August 9, a friend came to tell him of the death of Chaim Soutine. Rushed to a Paris hospital from Champigny-sur-Veude, in Touraine, where he had taken refuge with his consort, Marie-Berthe Aurenche, Soutine had died of an operation for a stomach ulcer of long standing. He was being buried in the Montparnasse Cemetery. Pablo had never been very close to the enigmatic, distant Russian, whose tortured, earthquake-wracked paintings expressed his hallucinations and obsessions so overpoweringly; but now, with Cocteau, he walked in the meager cortège and, for all that he was repelled by death and funerals, stayed for the interment, among the group of people he did not know, so many of whom were trying to hide the yellow star they were forced to wear.

Summer vacations were things of the past. Was that why, in order to feel closer to nature, trees, water, and sky, Pablo was drawing and painting his Vert-Galant and Seine landscapes, with their calm delight in living? Françoise, in the South, was still only an intangible future conquest, a very charming and titillating idea. Dora was at hand, haughtier than ever, no longer worried about his lapses with feminine callers. Friends came and went, as they could, those from the Resistance when they did not feel endangered, the others when they did not think they would disturb him. The Catalan's was the place to meet, "Picasso's dining room."

Thursdays he visited Maya and her mother on Boulevard Henri-IV, so Sabartés made no appointments for that day. He also regularly saw Olga, whose almost daily letters brimmed with lamentations and diatribes. There was also much in them about André-Louis Dubois, who kindly and diplomatically acted as go-between for the separated couple.

Paul and Nush Éluard were there infrequently, for he was deep in the Resistance and had to be very careful. As head of the National Writers' Committee for the northern zone, Éluard at the beginning of 1943 had met in Paris, in an apartment on Boulevard Morland, with Aragon, Elsa Triolet, and Georges Sadoul, representing the committee for the southern zone, to unify the two movements. He had helped Jean Lescure edit the volume entitled *L'Honneur des Poètes* (The Honor of Poets), which Les Éditions de Minuit brought out clandestinely, and under the pseudonym of Maurice Hervent contributed two poems to it, *"Chant*

Nazi" (Nazi Song) and "Courage." From November 1943 to February 1944, he and Nush would be forced to hide at the Psychiatric Hospital of St.-Alban, in the Lozère, shielded by his friend Dr. Bonafé. But Éluard had already begun the slow, patient job of getting Pablo to join the Communist Party. What a triumph that would be, under the noses of the German occupants!

Zervos, whose Rue du Bac apartment had been requisitioned by the Germans, was also in hiding; yet he succeeded in seeing Picasso, and hoped to bring out the drawings Pablo had recently done on some magnificent Japan paper he had discovered by chance and bought for its weight in gold: Pablo had them in a cordovan leather binder, with impressive nailheads and ironwork. Georges Hugnet came by assiduously, along with Brassaï, the photographer and memorialist of those dark years of which he has given us the most valuable account, and also the Leirises, "Baron" Mollet, Prévert, André Beaudin and Suzanne Roger, Valentine Hugo,* Raymond Queneau, Camus, Sartre and Simone de Beauvoir.

Since their reconciliation, Cocteau was present from time to time, but he was afraid of bumping into "Gaullists" who might attack him for complaisance to the occupant. He claimed that in exchange he had gotten the German authorities to exempt film workers from being conscripted for labor. To try to erase it all, he was deep in legend and myth, writing *Renaud and Armide, The Eternal Return* for Jean Marais, and *The Eagle Has Two Heads.*

One day Cocteau, who was no favorite of the collaborationist press despite his "Salute to Breker," was attacked on the Champs-Élysées for not having saluted the flag of the Legion of French Volunteers (anti-Communist fighters in Wehrmacht uniforms) going by. He was beaten and came home with bruises all over his face, but lucky not to have been searched, for in his pockets were leaflets from Éluard's committee. The "frivolous prince" now qualified as a "resister."

Pablo was frequently seeing his son, Paulo, a big, unflappable redhead, more Russian than Spanish, unimpressed with the old man's fame. Married and a father himself, he was looking for a trade he had not yet found, but did not seem worried about it. Saturdays, Picasso's "at home" day, the studio filled up with all kinds of people, who seemed to know one another but nevertheless worried Sabartés, ever afraid there might be a Gestapo agent among them.

On October 21, 1943, Jean Paulhan wrote to André Suarès, ". . . while the latest Picassos are disappointing, Braque and Rouault were never so great." The Picasso oeuvre in the occupation years was so diverse that this seems a very hasty judgment, but the very variety of it was an embarrassment. One would have to become accustomed to it, for this was the way Picasso was going: his works, deliberately, almost consciously, were invaded, dominated by the genius of Evil, another aspect to him of Old Age, Decay, Death. The youth and beauty of Françoise and the birth of their two children would exorcise them for a period, but they would reappear when that interval was over.

The female figures painted during the occupation are remarkable not only because of their horrifying character, but also by the fact that almost all of them

---

* This is the Valentine Grosz of the Diaghilev *Parade* period, since then married to Jean Hugo. (TR. NOTE).

"The Man with the Sheep" (bronze) Paris 1944

are enclosed in rooms, some of them prison cells. Pablo was suffering from not being free to move about, feeling more or less spied upon, shadowed, despite his reputation and high connections, at the mercy of an arrest, an assault. He went out little, leaving the St.-Germain-des-Prés area only when he went to Marie-Thérèse's; the curfew and night patrols haunted him.

Éluard, who was soon to leave Paris in order to evade arrest, was present when he turned to a work that he did in a single day, by way of contrast and relief: the *Man with a Sheep*. Pablo had asked a Spanish friend to get him some modeling clay, and as soon as he had it he set to work. He who never got up before morning's end was at his workbench by 7:00 A.M., and was not to stop till nightfall. As he kept "building up" the figure, he had to reinforce the armature, which was too light to hold the mass of clay. The statue threatened to tip over and had to be supported with loops, the animal bound with wire, which helpers did while Pablo went on with his work, giving full value to the bust of the man, his simultaneously robust and nervous stature, his masculine assurance. The sheep, seeming to try to break away from its bearer, bleating, strains its neck. As in Picasso's magnificent preliminary studies.

December saw a proliferation of cutout and scratched papers. Françoise was back. Wasn't she beautiful, wasn't she nice? he asked Brassaï. Her long, pure-featured face framed with brown hair began to appear in the drawings of that icy winter. His fingers freezing, Pablo could scarcely work, and friends who came in found him wrapped in a mackinaw with a cap down over his eyes. At noon, as usual, he would phone Dora Maar to meet him at the Catalan's; afternoons, more and more often, there was Françoise at the studio, bringing her most recent work to show the master.

On February 22, 1944, Robert Desnos was arrested by the Gestapo. A few weeks before, Pablo had finished the etchings for his *Contrée*. First held at Fresnes, Desnos was transferred to the Royallieu Camp at Compiègne, then deported to Germany, where he was to die in a hospital of typhus, shortly after being liberated.

Just at this time, after six months of "walking all around each other," Françoise became Picasso's mistress; as she put it, "It was a cold gray February day, but my recollection of it is filled with midsummer sunlight."

Max Jacob, too, had been arrested. The only Jew at the monastery of St.-Benoît-sur-Loire, he had worn his yellow star with Christian humility, avoiding neither the sarcastic smiles nor the hateful glares of those about him. For years, he had been writing Pablo long letters that went unanswered, but he talked about him to all his visitors, infrequent though they were now because of the occupation. It was always "Dear Pablo" or "Pablo, my darling," even though poor Max never failed to add, "He did me so much harm." On January 25, 1943, he wrote to Marcel Béalu, "What explains my forty-one-year friendship with Picasso is that we made a pact: Whatever anyone tells you about me won't count, and vice versa."

When his safety was seriously threatened, his friends the Salmons urged him to leave St.-Benoît and move in with them in Paris. He thanked them, but

specified that if he had to hide somewhere someday it would be at Picasso's, "as is only natural." But he never got to do it. On February 28, six days after Desnos, he was arrested and taken to the camp for Jews at Drancy. He immediately wrote Cocteau, who got in touch with Salmon, Henri Sauguet, Sacha Guitry, Pierre Colle, and Pablo, who dropped Max a brief note.

Cocteau tried to reach Otto Abetz, writing two manifestoes that were filed with the German embassy. Pierre Colle begged Pablo to intervene there, but Picasso answered, "We don't have to do anything. Max is an elf; he can fly out of there without us." But he could not: on March 5, Max Jacob died of pneumonia at Drancy.

Michel and Zette Leiris, who lived around the corner on Quai des Grands-Augustins, decided to hold a reading of the play Pablo had written three years earlier. Camus was selected to "stage" *Desire Caught by the Tail*, that is, he would describe the nonexistent sets, announce the acts, and introduce the antagonists, a cast such as no theater in the world could have dreamt of:

Tart	ZANIE AUBIER (ACTRESS ZANIE CAMPAN)
The Cousin	SIMONE DE BEAUVOIR
Skinny Anguish	DORA MAAR
Fat Anguish	GERMAINE HUGNET
The Two Bow-wows	LOUISE LEIRIS
Big Foot	MICHEL LEIRIS
Round End	JEAN-PAUL SARTRE
Onion	RAYMOND QUENEAU
Silence	JACQUES-LAURENT BOST
The Curtains	PUBLISHER JEAN AUBIER

There were several rehearsals, before a delighted Picasso.

The allusions to current privations, especially the food shortages, were even more cruel in the spring of 1944 than three years before. Phrases such as "I'm taking some more sturgeon. The pungent flavor of these dishes keeps my depraved taste for spicy and indigestible foods in a state of high suspense" or "Your buttocks are a dish of baked beans, and your arms a sharkfin soup" were symptomatic of the period's concerns.

Big Foot, in the middle of writing poems, stops and says, "When you come to think of it, there's nothing like a good mutton stew." And Tart describes herself:

I've got six hundred quarts of milk in my sow tits. Ham. Salami. Blood sausage. Tripe. And my hair covered with chipolatas. I've got mauve gums, sugar in my urine, and my gouty hands full of the white of eggs. Bony cavities. . . . lips twisted with honey and marshmallows. Decently dressed, clean, I wear with elegance the ridiculous clothes that are given to me. I'm a mother and a perfect whore and I can dance the rhumba.

The "performance" was held at the Leirises' on March 19, 1944. The "actors" were perfectly up in their parts, and although in street clothes they succeeded, with the help of Camus's commentaries, in creating the situations and costumes

At Picasso's after a private showing of "Desire Caught by the Tail" June 16, 1944 From left to right: Dr. Jacques Lacan, Cécile Éluard, Pierre Reverdy, Louise Leiris, Zanie de Campan, Picasso, Valentine Hugo, Simone de Beauvoir. Seated on the floor: Jean-Paul Sartre, Albert Camus, Michel Leiris, the publisher Jean Aubier, and Kazbek, the dog
(BRASSAÏ)

the playwright intended. Indeed, it would have been difficult to follow to the letter such stage directions as ". . . covered with soapsuds, they jump out of the bathtub . . . dressed like everybody else of that period . . . Tart comes out alone, completely naked but with stockings on." In the last-named part, Zanie Campan was especially remarkable; but then, she was the only professional actress in the lot.

Pablo enjoyed his triumph. After the show, he took them all home to his studio, including the audience, among whom were the Braques, Reverdy, Valentine Hugo, Jacques Lacan, Paul Éluard's daughter Cécile, Brassaï, and Sabartés. All were treated to a show of Pablo's latest works and given a Brassaï photo as a souvenir, and an enthusiastic Picasso even went so far as to take out of his treasure chest a yellowing manuscript, Alfred Jarry's *Ubu cocu* (Ubu Cockold), which he displayed as a tribute to the one who had inspired his play. (Among other things in that treasure chest, Brassaï was to report, was the manuscript of Apollinaire's *Bestiary,* illustrated with all sorts of animals done by Picasso.)

Dora Maar now noticed an unknown face in Pablo's drawings. This was an unmistakable sign; Olga had been similarly informed of a new entry into the Ogre's life. With his usual slyness, he let those drawings lie about. He never kept from anyone, least of all from the fading favorite, the identity of a new love, his male vanity being impervious to the despair or anger of others.

He was supervising Françoise's artistic growth:

> Sometimes he would have me do things for composition [she wrote]. He would give me a piece of blue paper—perhaps a cigarette wrapper—and a match, tear off a bit of cardboard and say, "Make me a composition with those. Organize them for me into this," and he would draw a form on a piece of paper to indicate the size and shape. "Do whatever you want, but make a composition out of it that stands on its own feet."

Another time he told her:

> You must always work not just at the limit, but always a little short of your possibilities. If you can handle three elements, use only two. If you can handle ten, forget five of them. That way you compose with greater care, greater mastery, and give the feeling of having some strength in reserve.*

Touching, these art lessons while Europe went up in flames: two pigeons tenderly in love despite the bombs, one slightly shopworn but cooing convincingly to his love-struck little dove. In the Grands-Augustins aviary, friends did not quite know what to make of it: the Leirises held off, pending Kahnweiler's reaction to this resurgence of youth in Pablo. Sabartés, as usual, fumed, doing his best to get rid of Françoise, whom he hated.

Paul Léautaud, the magazine editor and writer who had done the preface to Fernande Olivier's book (and been largely responsible for her writing it), cared

---

* Translated directly from the French version; the English on p. 58 of *Life with Picasso* is somewhat freer and, it seems to us, less in tone with the original. (TR. NOTE)

little or nothing for Picasso's painting, but met him each year at the annual commemoration of the death of Apollinaire. In a strange way, the reactionary libertarian admired Pablo's disregard for conventions and his unfettered individualism, and perhaps misread his views. In his very detailed diary, Léautaud tells of meeting Picasso on Rue Jacob, April 7, 1944, and how Pablo crossed the street to talk to him:

> He had let his hair grow, down to his collar. The hair was completely white. But not at all on an old man's face. Seen from the rear, he must look old. Strange idea. I had never noticed how small he was. His charming face was full of mockery. We found we agreed on one point, which I expressed to him: the first three years of the war, I had not been particularly concerned about it . . . But that now it was no longer the same, I was involved, upset, worried, almost disquieted . . . "Isn't that so?" Picasso replied. "I feel exactly the way you do."

After the Normandy landing in June, the Allies were marching on Paris, and the Germans, following a few weeks' resistance, were in retreat. Pablo was frightened; recent raids on the La Chapelle district and the Gare du Nord had caused serious damage at Lacourière's and marred one of his paintings, *Still Life with Japanese Lantern.* He was once again contemplating leaving Paris, storing his works in a safe place, but in this apocalypse, there was no safe place. So, he took refuge in work. And in love.

Perhaps trying to retain something of the ever-more-threatened city, he did several more characteristic Parisian landscapes (again Pont-Neuf, Vert-Galant, Notre-Dame, and Île de la Cité), now gray and blue, silent and serene beneath a starry sky, as are the candlestick, vase, and pitcher he was painting on Chardin's and Cézanne's simple wooden table. In their company, he was awaiting the end of the nightmare.

If one did not know the events of July–August 1944, no trace of them would be found in our Malagueño's work; however, he did do a new painting of the vigorous tomato plant he had already done several months before. Perhaps it was symbolic: though captive, the plant had blossomed, its green fruit now a brilliant red—the color of blood, also of celebration.

His studio was a beehive of comings and goings, and in the dramatic events of the day he did not even notice the disappearance of Dora Maar. Like everyone else, he was waiting, nerves on edge. The closer the Allies got, the greater the fears: What if the Gestapo came after him and he went the way of Desnos and Max? The "collaborators" were well aware of his friendship with the "resisters," and last-minute reprisals were a constant possibility.

The first street fighting gave no reassurance; he left the studio, to hide out at Marie-Thérèse's, there to await the liberation of Paris. There were violent skirmishes in the Boulevard Henri-IV neighborhood, and to take his mind off them he drew Maya's face and heads of women. Then, suddenly, on August 24, just as the first barricades were being thrown up and everywhere in the city thousands of men and women turning street fighters were getting ready to rise, he painted a watercolor after Poussin's *Triumph of Pan* which is also filled with revolt, anger, and joy, a bacchanale of drunken bodies, men and beasts intermingled, a sort of fantastic paean of glory to life triumphant.

As Paris was gaining its freedom, August 24–29, Picasso returned to that theme, with its brilliant colors flying, its irresistible strength buoying it up: this frenzied page was saying what his painting of tomorrow would be. An era of his life was finishing with the end of the occupation, the return of freedom. An era in art, too. Pablo was sixty-three.

When the danger was over, he returned to Rue des Grands-Augustins. Was he aware of the welcome the first American GIs to reach Paris had in store for him, along with his friends of the Resistance? Come to maturity before World War I, born eight years after the death of Manet at the height of Impressionism, old enough to have known Van Gogh and Seurat or studied with Gauguin and Cézanne, here was a painter who symbolized all that his adopted country was regaining in its euphoria and hope; he was "liberated" art.

Hemingway was fully aware, on August 25, 1944, that Pablo Picasso was the providential man for the art of the future. Coming into Paris with the American army, he rushed to Rue des Grands-Augustins, only to find its famous tenant away at Marie-Thérèse's. What gift could he give Picasso that was less banal than a carton of cigarettes or a case of Spam? In a flash of inspiration, Papa Hemingway left a case of hand grenades with the building's concierge, to be given to the great exploder of modern painting.

Éluard, clandestinely back in Paris for some time, now could smilingly reappear with Nush at Pablo's studio, where he greeted them effusively. Éluard brought a whole raft of Resistance intellectuals with him, for this was the time to finalize winning over Picasso, which he had worked at during the occupation. The studio was constantly full of enthusiastic GIs and respectful Free French soldiers; the Catalan's was coining money; one day a uniformed young lady appeared, especially welcome: Lee Miller Penrose, war correspondent for *Vogue*.

Also among the visitors was the war photographer Robert Capa, who shot Pablo among his recent works, with the *Man with the Sheep* and plaster casts of several other sculptures, but Capa seemed to delight in avoiding his model's more "scandalous" own works, preferring those in his collection, by Renoir, Degas, Modigliani, Rousseau, and Matisse.

There were group tours of Picasso's studios as there were of the Eiffel Tower, Versailles, or the Louvre. Sabartés was ideal for the role of grumbling Cerberus, keeping out the gate-crashers. Inéz, and sometimes even Françoise, helped the hostesses of these tours and the charming interpreters who were supposed to comment on the master's works and translate the GIs' endless questions to him, such as:

"Mr. Picasso, how did you get to seeing women with three eyes and two noses?"

Mr. Picasso's reply was a hearty laugh.

"Mr. Picasso, how come you sometimes paint horrible people, and at other times very fine portraits—what do you call 'em, classics?"

"Well," he told them, "it's like when you make an experiment in chemistry. I work on some subjects as if I were in a laboratory. Sometimes the experiment works; and I go on to another, so as not to repeat myself. I always try to discover new things."

To help them understand, he told a story: two young people, a French lad and a Spanish girl, were in love with each other, and very happy, although neither one understood the other's language. One day, the Spanish girl decided to learn French, and the whole mystery of their love was destroyed. The gaping GIs nodded: they had "understood Mr. Picasso's" painting; now came the picture-taking and autograph-signing sessions. After they left, Pablo would discover they had left him cakes of soap, cartons of cigarettes, chewing gum, the luxuries of the day.

Of course, Cocteau was soon on the scene again, now with Jean Marais in the uniform of the French Second Armored Division. The poet was concerned: Would he have his successes as before, appeal to the youth, and be able to come up with more and more novelties? He wondered whether he would be "purged." But, then, Picasso was no "purer" than he: he had had German soldiers visiting his studio, sold canvases to dealers who worked hand in glove with Nazis, known Arno Breker, associated with Ernst Jünger; after all, like the vast majority of Frenchmen, he had put up with the Germans, and held still so as not to be bothered and go on working.

Éluard, never friendly to Cocteau, put a stop to this speculation with one sentence: "He was one of the rare painters who behaved properly, and is still doing so." As later he was to write Penrose: "Picasso paints more and more like God, or like the Devil." Could one do anything against either of *them?*

In the Communist *Les Lettres françaises,* Louis Parrot commented at this time:

> If there is one man whose fondest memories have been revived by recent events, it is certainly the painter Pablo Picasso who recaptured in the Parisian insurrection all the heroic popular images of old Spain . . . At Place de l'Hôtel-de-Ville one of the first tanks to pull up had a name whitewashed on it: *Guernica.* The officer who alighted was Spanish . . .

This excited tone was typical of the times and not restricted to France: the first news of liberated France sent home by the correspondents of *Time* (September 11, 1944) reported that Picasso was "almost white-haired . . . had a new bathroom, a six-months-old baby" and had steadfastly "refused to sell to Germans officially." Since, to Americans, Picasso was identified mainly with *Guernica* and the resistance to Franco Fascism, such news was welcome and moving (the baby came from the overwrought imagination of someone misinterpreting the pictures of Inéz' son).

And just as he was being venerated in America as the living symbol of modern art—while the greatest creators of the present, such as Malevitch, Mondrian,

Duchamp, or Kandinsky, were virtually ignored—he was for very similar reasons being lauded to the skies by the intelligentsia of the French Resistance, largely Communist in politics, whose leading thinkers were Aragon, Éluard, Parrot, Vercors, Jean Marcenac, and the like. Such ambiguities did not bother him: they were the public counterpart of the ones he privately promoted among Dora Maar, Marie-Thérèse Walter, and Françoise Gilot.

Indeed, he enjoyed being one of the few Resistance heroes known by name. He did a drawing for page one of the album the poets and painters of the Resistance got up in tribute to General de Gaulle, and was not taken aback to be the second most popular public monument in Paris for the GIs after the Eiffel Tower. But on one of the photos from that euphoric 1944 autumn, with drawn features and white hair down to his collar, as Léautaud had noted, his watch chain, and his tanned, wrinkled hand on the breast of one of the Women he had sculpted at Boisgeloup, he looks more survivor of the past than harbinger of the future, his eye more serene than incendiary.

His way back into reality was to give in to Éluard's urgings and join the Communist Party. Éluard had been aided by unforeseen circumstances. During the occupation, he had asked Michel Leiris to give asylum to Laurent Casanova, one of the underground Communist chieftains, who had escaped from Germany, where he and his wife, Danielle, had been deported, and was being actively sought by the Gestapo. Leiris, not uncourageously, agreed. Only a few of his friends were told who was staying with him, among them Picasso, who was deeply impressed by the quiet strength and intelligence of the man; his persuasive talk put the finishing touches to the groundwork laid by Éluard. The latter and Aragon, once Liberation came, found the rest easy; the only thing was to sign, seal, and deliver him—before the return of Kahnweiler, who did not want to see Picasso make such a political commitment.

Other friends tried to dissuade him, too, getting around Sabartés, who merely shrugged his shoulders as a gesture of powerlessness. Pablo's Establishment protector, André-Louis Dubois, who tried to talk him out of it, quotes him in his book:

"These are hard times. Serious events are ahead. We haven't finished with the Nazis. They've given us the syph. A lot of people caught it, without even realizing it. And we'll see it soon enough. And what about the poor, all the poor? Are we going to leave them to them to batten on? Well, they're not going to put up with just anyone and just anything. They'll defend themselves, there'll be strikes, troubles, and during that time you want me to stay up on my balcony, watching the show? No, that can't be. I'll be down in the street with them."

He told Françoise, "I came into the Party as one goes to the fountain," and when the Spanish painter Pedro Flores asked him what he had gotten out of joining what was known as "the Party of those shot at sunrise," he answered: "I found my youth again."

Everything was ready. During the last days of September, Éluard, meeting

Penrose at Pablo's, whispered in the Englishman's ear: "I have great news for you: in a week it will be announced publicly that Picasso has joined the Communist Party."

The "big news" made page one of *L'Humanité* on October 5. Two days later, the Salon d'Automne opened, with a vibrant tribute to the greatest of living artists, the symbol of "liberated art."

Seventy-four paintings, most of them done under the occupation, and five sculptures bore testimony, at the Musée d'Art Moderne, to Picasso's protean genius. For four years, the public had been out of touch with him, many having even forgotten what his insolent painting was like. Now here were *L'Aubade, Woman with Artichoke, First Steps, Chair with Gladioli, Woman with a Bouquet, Still Life with Bull's Head, Little Girl with Doll, Butterfly Hunter, Skull and Pitcher, Woman Washing Her Feet, Man with Sucker,* and so on; and among the sculptures the *Bull's Head* made with a bicycle handlebar and seat, *The Cock, The Cat,* and several Women's Heads from Boisgeloup days.

Never, in a long time, people felt, had an artist gone so far in assaulting vision. Nor ever had an artist so violently mixed political commitment, pictorial creation, and current events. But there was something else: Picasso's painting, held by the Nazis to be "degenerate" art, not only identified with newfound freedom but came out as an indictment and a conquest in the service of the Communist Party. And this at the very moment when the Party was using all of its power to get the country purged.

Conservative bourgeoisie, deeply attached to its intellectual as well as visual comfort, had never accepted Picasso, that symbol of the scandals and challenge of "modern" art. That bourgeoisie, having largely gone over to the Vichy régime and passively put up with the occupation because it guaranteed "law and order," could not help reacting violently to what it saw as a provocation, the more intolerable because the painter had so spectacularly joined the Communist Party. There were violent demonstrations at the Salon d'Automne.

A horrified André Lhote wrote in *Les Lettres françaises:*

> Some brainless young people looking like Doriot-Fascists, who had had better things to do than join the Resistance, and some gentlemen of advancing years and overly pious minds, ran through the Picasso Room yelling, "Money back!" and "Take 'em down!" And indeed they did take down some of the paintings, which they would have trampled had the artists who were there not snatched them from their hands.

And the "Resistance" press, mainly Communist, let loose against the demonstrators, perhaps a bit too hastily dubbed "Fascists." The National Writers' Committee protested in a declaration signed by Aragon, Éluard, Mauriac, Paul Valéry, Jean-Paul Sartre, Georges Duhamel, and others, not all Communists by any means. They did not hesitate to pronounce the demonstrations, which grouped various elements of the traditional Right with students from the Beaux-Arts, as "acts of the enemy."

The enemy, as it happened, was youth, and not "the gentlemen of advancing years and overly pious minds," and Picasso, who understood this perfectly well, was very upset by it. He was also furious that the Party had not protected him better. He was never to get over that "liberated" Salon d'Automne.

A few months later, Jean Lurçat, Rémy, and Jean Agamemnon, all distinguished Resistance heroes, denounced these Salon demonstrators and certain "noisy student gangs" in the Latin Quarter, saying that "Picasso was a significant, and, what is more, active, Resister"—a somewhat unexpected tribute. They added, "It is more convenient to massacre a watercolor than to freeze one's feet in the marshes at the front."

Other young painters and students, among them Françoise Gilot, vied with one another for the honor of standing guard before the Salon d'Automne Picassos to protect them. But that did not keep a gang of Beaux-Arts students from returning on a Sunday afternoon and taking some of the pictures down again.

In the course of his existence, Picasso had often been insulted by backward bourgeois, attacked from the benches of the Chamber of Deputies or City Council, accused of the worst misdeeds and smothered in slander; but that young people, future artists, should try to take down and cut up his paintings upset him terribly. Of course, they were the products and victims of their academic teaching, and their "professors" at the Beaux-Arts did all they could to pass Pablo off as an unworthy dauber, guilty, according to the right-wing press, of having degraded French art (an opinion even Matisse once echoed). But still, the attitude of these woefully misled young people remained incomprehensible to him. On the other hand, he accepted as inevitable that as a result of his joining the Party some American collectors forsook him and his prices took a dip on the American market.

So, at the behest of Kahnweiler, now back in Paris and not at all happy about the unfortunate consequences Pablo's "commitment" might have for him, Picasso decided to explain himself to his American friends. An interview with Pol Gaillard was published in *New Masses*, October 24, and more fully in *L'Humanité*, October 29–30, as follows:

WHY I JOINED THE COMMUNIST PARTY

Joining the Communist Party is the logical conclusion of my whole life, my whole work. For, I am proud to state, I have never considered painting as an art of simple entertainment, or escape; I wanted, through line and color, since those were my weapons, to go deeper into the knowledge of the world and men, so that that knowledge might free each of us increasingly every day; I was trying in my way to say what I considered truest, most correct, best, which naturally would be the most beautiful, as all great artists well know. . . .

I went to the Communist Party without the least hesitation, for after all I had always been with it . . . and if I had not yet officially joined it was out of "innocence" in a way, because I thought that my work, the giving of my heart were enough, but it was already my Party. . . . I have always been an exile, now I no longer am; until the day when Spain can welcome me back, the French Communist Party opened its arms to me, and I have found in it those that I most value, the greatest scientists, the greatest poets, all those beautiful faces of Parisian insurgents that I saw during the August days; I am once more among my brothers.

Some felt that if he had made this gesture when his fellow Spaniards were fighting for their freedom, or when the Germans were occupying France, it might have carried more weight, however courageous and generous it was now— but it was not considered proper to utter such remarks. No one knew that all he had done was watch the Battle for Paris from behind a screen at Marie-Thérèse's. And Parrot wrote, again in *Les Lettres françaises*:

> A few days ago, this man that Jean Cassou in his book on the painter of *Guernica* characterized as an artist "hungry for solitude," decided to join more closely in the life of other men. . . . His art will doubtless gain in depth at the contact of a reality in which he will find, if that were necessary for him, inexhaustible subjects of inspiration.

Picasso did not need the *parti des fusillés* to give him inspiration, and this kind of plaudit seemed rather farcical to him; yet he very conscientiously played the part of a militant member, which befitted this "public" period of his existence. He was no longer hungry for solitude, as Cassou had once written, but now for dialogue with his fellows. That was his way of being in the swim—now that his painting no longer was.

The post-Liberation period brought Pablo more intimate joys than the group visits of Americans or renewing ties with old friends: this was the period of the nymphets.

His taste for adolescent girls remains one of the secrets of his private life, to be respected at least to the extent that he never publicly took credit for his plucking of such green fruit. This was not restricted to just this period, but in the tumult and disorder of that fall and winter, it was more pronounced than usual. These nymphets escaped Sabartés' notice as they ducked in to the Grands-Augustins studio, and Françoise never caught them. Anyway, who could be suspicious of such ecstatic schoolgirls, rebelling young bourgeoises or Party vestals, with their ponytails and high-set breasts, looking for autographs or asking him to sign mysterious petitions? Not all, it is true, came with dalliance in mind—but who could resist the Ogre's appetite?

One of them called on him as president of the National Student Front of Lycée Fénelon, and editor of its paper, *La Voix de Fénelon*. Very young and very blond, she later depicted herself as "a silly little thing," but her way of telling it rather showed her to be ingenuously calculating. Taking the bait, Pablo made her more than a one-afternoon stand, like so many others, and accepted her as a friend, confidante, and collaborator—if we are to believe her lyrical account, for she became a poetess. He did do a number of drawings of her, some of which leave no doubt as to their extreme intimacy.

Other adolescent girls danced their mating dances around the Ogre at the same period. He used Rue La Boétie to let these springtime loves revive his autumnal ardors. To make himself younger, Pablo had his long white hair cut, which gave him more than ever the copper appearance of an old Etruscan.

One of the nymphets much later told me this tale: Pablo did her portrait in the soft jumble of bedclothes where she lay nude and fulfilled, and made her a present of it. But what could she do with it? She could neither take it to her parents' apartment nor give it back. She wanted to keep it, for it was both a fine drawing and cherished souvenir, and valuable to boot. So she hid it. Time went by. Our nymphet flowered into womanhood, was married, and divorced, and decided to sell the portrait. It was appraised at a very high price, but unfortunately did not have his signature. Through a friend, she sent it to Picasso to be signed—only to have him state, to her amazement and fury, that it was a fake, and that he would not sign it. This was how so often his amours ended—in some evil action.

Picasso was still a magnet for Spaniards. Fenosa, the master's discreet and furtive shadow, Manuel Angeles Ortiz, Hernando Vines, Pedro Flores, Dominguez, Peinado, Borés, all were frequently about, as well as Joan Rebull, who made a specialty of bringing new faces such as Grau Sala, Clavé, or Creixams. And there was Pablo's nephew Xavier Vilato, a painter in his own right but unfortunately too familiar with his uncle's work. All these Spaniards, and especially the Catalans, were always welcome, much to the displeasure of Sabartés, who tried more and more to make Pablo his exclusive property. But while Jaime mumbled that the master was not home, all the boss had to hear was a Spanish accent, and he came flying. In a way, Picasso and his "secretary" were an "act": each one played true to form, and only the most uninitiated could be fooled.

Antoni Clavé was an exception among the recent group: a pure-blooded Catalan, he had got his start in Barcelona doing decoration and posters, fought on the Aragón front in the Civil War and, in January 1939, fled across the French border with the sad remnants of the Republican army. Interned by the French, he was freed a short time later, and lived by his wits in Perpignan and later Paris, where he illustrated some books and tried to do some lithography. In 1942, Pedro Flores and Grau Sala had introduced him to Picasso, and he came back several times, but only on D-Day, June 6, 1944, did they have their first real get-together. For three hours, Picasso showed the thirty-one-year-old painter all his recent paintings, drawings, and sculptures, revealing his total genius to the young man who had always admired and respected him at a distance. Grau Sala and Rebull were there, too, entranced, and when it was over, Picasso shook Clavé's hand, saying, "Let me see your work. It's so long since I've seen any of it . . ."

Picasso had never seen the younger man's work and this went straight to Clavé's heart. A few months later, when he had a show at the Galerie Henry Joly, and Pablo attended, their friendship was sealed for good. When he had achieved fame, and was one of Picasso's cronies, he still never dared show him the paintings Don Pablo had once guilefully said he had not seen in so long. Even on Picasso's eighty-fifth birthday, when a newspaper in Nice asked Clavé to illustrate its front page, in tribute, he refused, feeling unworthy. "In his presence," he said, "I was never able even to sharpen a pencil." Picasso recognized this respect and fervor and repaid it with friendship to the end of his days.

In the fall of 1944, Albert Skira, who had spent the whole of the occupation in Geneva, brought out a new monthly in newspaper form, *Labyrinthe,* whose twenty-three issues were to see the most prestigious names appear in defense of living art. The revelations of the postwar period rubbed elbows in it with the heroic pioneers of *Minotaure*. The first issue paid tribute to Picasso, printing the lecture Éluard had given in Barcelona in 1936, illustrated with reproductions, a picture of Pablo in his Boulevard de Clichy studio in 1901, and a manuscript poem by Éluard, dedicated to him, "L'Oreille du taureau" (The Bull's Ear).

Pfc. Jerome Seckler, a GI who was also an amateur painter, was among the first Americans to visit Picasso. An ardent admirer, he was especially anxious to "explain" the master's work to his army buddies. He found symbolism everywhere, with a consistency that irritated but also amused Pablo. The latter showed him great patience and forbearance—not always his predominant traits.

Seckler's account is not to be shrugged off. His reactions reflect the attitude of certain young Americans, and he reports on the painter's behavior at a time when, in place of the customary intimates, events filled his studio with a mixed bag of foreigners to whom he was a myth. The myth in the flesh listened courteously, perhaps even with some curiosity, to these strange new men who were doing to him just what he had done to man: dissecting him, taking him apart.

Seckler first interviewed him on November 18, 1944, then again on the next January 6, when Picasso okayed the notes he had made at their first meeting. His article, published in *New Masses* of March 13, 1945 (slightly abridged; the full typescript of the original is now in the library of the Museum of Modern Art, New York), conveys an informal colloquy, with Pablo at pains to try to define the painterly truth about himself.

To Seckler, the *Butterfly Hunter* (1938) seemed "a self-portrait—the sailor's suit, the net, the red butterfly showing Picasso as a person seeking a solution to the problems of his times . . ." The butterfly being red appeared to have political significance and "the sailor's garb" to indicate "an active participation in this effort." Pablo countered that he had not used red for political significance, and "If it has any, it was in my subconscious!"

Pointing to *L'Aubade* (or *Nude with a Musician*), Seckler found it obscure, and asked Picasso why he painted "in such a way that your expression is so difficult for people to understand."

"You're a painter," Picasso explained, "and you understand it's quite impossible to explain why you did this or that. I express myself through painting and I can't explain through words."

Again, "Now is the time in this period of change and revolution to use a revolutionary manner of painting and not to paint like before . . . the proof that my paintings are revolutionary is how the students rise up against me. They would strip me naked and lynch me. '*Picasso à poil! Picasso au poteau!*' "

As Alfred H. Barr, Jr., sums it up in his *Picasso: Fifty Years of His Art:*

Throughout these interviews Picasso held his ground against Seckler's persistent effort to get him to admit that his paintings carried conscious political implications. Picasso admitted the possibility of unconscious symbolism and the interest and value of some symbolic interpretation by others: "embroidery on the subject—it's stimulating." But he refused to consider the idea of changing his style or subject matter to meet any possible social or political obligations. In the end, however, he agreed that there was a connection between art and politics.

The editor of *New Masses* reported that Seckler's interview "created more discussion and controversy than any other article we have ever published." Rockwell Kent, in a sense Pablo's American counterpart (the best-known "committed" U.S. artist), attacked Picasso in the left-wing magazine on April 3, ridiculing the *Still Life with a Bull's Head*. He said of the candlestick that "my little granddaughter of six could do as well." And as a realistic artist he found the palette and book "stupid," while saying the bull "doesn't look the least bit like a bull" (a very debatable opinion, at best).

As in France, Pablo was getting caught in the middle of the controversy on whether class-conscious, socially significant art had to be immediately intelligible to the masses. The "silent majority" (as it was later to be known), hating modern art of all kinds, of course felt that his new avatar as a Communist just proved what they had always thought: he was an irresponsible hoaxster. But even among his political sympathizers and comrades in the United States, many decried his adherence to what had been called a decade earlier "the cult of unintelligibility" (shown by the "Letters to the Editors" columns of subsequent issues of *New Masses*).

There was a rumor in the United States that General de Gaulle had gotten the French government to commission front-line work from Picasso and several other artists, including Daragnès and Fautrier. This was incorrect; Pablo was never a "military artist."

Gertrude Stein and Alice B. Toklas had come back to Paris, the former more than ever an overfed Roman Senator, the latter a bony Wicked Witch. They had spent most of the occupation at their home in Bilignin, and later at Culoz, treated with kid gloves by Vichy and especially Marshal Pétain, because their good friend Bernard Faÿ, French translator of *The Autobiography of Alice B. Toklas,* was administrator of the Bibliothèque Nationale under the Pétainist régime. Gertrude had been worried about her collection of art at Rue de Fleurus, which both the Nazis and the French, Jewish Property Custodians had their eyes on. Pablo got to Faÿ for her, and the latter persuaded Count von Metternich, the Nazi "protector" of works of art in occupied territories, to put Miss Stein's apartment and studio under official seal, thus keeping her treasures intact. Come the Liberation, she had no trouble making out that she had "resisted," and while Faÿ went to prison as he deserved, she was idolized by the GIs as she had been by their fathers of the Lost Generation.

She was invited to give talks to soldiers, and her solid good sense and examples of courage went over big. Once her assignment was completed, she went back to Paris, where she and Alice took it on themselves to get Bernard Faÿ out of prison, and in order to protect his property, which seemed about to be requisitioned, if not looted, they moved into his estate at Luceau, in the Maine.

When she returned, Gertrude left Rue de Fleurus, moving to Rue Christine, where she was Picasso's neighbor, and he saw her and her collection again. They went back to their prewar game of needling each other, she bitter and disillusioned but always violently lucid, he perfidious and cruel, never missing the chance to remind her she had never really discovered anyone, not even him. "When there was Matisse and Picasso to discover, things were simple, weren't they? But then you went on to Gris—which was down a notch. After that, your 'discoveries' didn't amount to much . . ."

She bit her lips and did not reply. She was wearied of trying to stand up to him and, like most Americans and almost all his old friends, could not accept his having become a Communist. She thought it stupid and unsuitable, while Alice detested Françoise. Soon the GIs who toured from one of the two historic monuments to the other were the only remaining link between Gertrude and her one-time "little Napoleon."

One day, as she and Alice were shopping in a neighborhood grocery, a group of soldiers yelled to her, "Miss Stein, Mr. Picasso is looking for you." Going out, she saw Pablo waiting for her, delighted, in the middle of the street, and he insisted on going with her on all the rest of her errands. In each shop, as the people recognized him, long a neighborhood fixture, the butcher, the baker, and the greengrocer doubled her permissible ration, as Pablo whispered, "See what fame is, Gertrude?" To which she replied, leaving him speechless for once: "The main thing, Picasso, is that we're both defending mankind."

On March 24, 1945, readers of *Les Lettres françaises* thrilled to these words, written, the paper said, in Picasso's own hand on two pages of a pad, for Simone Téry, who had interviewed him:

> What do you think an artist is? An imbecile who has only eyes if he is a painter, ears if he is a musician, or a lyre at every level of his heart if he is a poet? . . . Quite the contrary, he is at the same time a political being, constantly alive to the heart-rending, exciting, or happy events of the world, wholly creating himself in their image. How would it be possible not to be interested in other people, and in the name of what ivory-tower nonchalance could one remain detached from a life they bring you so copiously? No, painting is not made for the decoration of apartments, it is a weapon to be used offensively and defensively against the enemy.

It was titled "Picasso Is Not an Officer in the French Army," in rebuttal to that earlier rumor, and constituted a real offensive against the "enjoyment" painting of Matisse or Bonnard. But who was the "enemy" he meant? What crusade could this wild individualist be the head of? Nothing in his painting seemed a "weapon." Or was he just taking precautionary measures against eventual Party pressures on his mind and the themes of his work?

His relations with the Party remained good until the matter of the Stalin portrait in 1953. The Party had the good sense to parade him as a star without ever making artistic demands on him. Even at the time of "socialist realism," the

Central Committee left him pretty much to his own devices, not always to the satisfaction of the "mass base," to soothe whose perplexed feelings they put forward the calendar art of Fougeron, Boris Taslitzky, Amblard, and the like. Picasso never hid his low opinion of them.

Some Party stalwarts would later find it hard to reconcile the double acceptance of that kind of painting while glorifying a Picasso whose work was not only just the opposite, but incomprehensible to boot—and relegated to obscurity in Russian museums, where the magnificent Picassos of the Shchukine and Morosov collections were shunted aside as "Western bourgeois decadence." But it was still only 1946.

When Laurent Casanova, whom Picasso had met at the Leirises' during the war and who was now the Communist Minister of Veterans Affairs, in opening the "Art and Resistance" exhibit in February at the Paris Museum of Modern Art, glorified "the great artists who had found in the heroic action of our brothers the elements of a new modern art," he turned to Picasso. The painter was exhibiting *The Charnel House,* which he had not long since completed, and a tribute *To the Spanish Republicans Who Died for France.*

Pablo was paying his dues. For several years, he would with most laudable conscientiousness carry out his duties as a card-carrying Party star. He who detested reporters and interviews answered the weirdest questions about his "commitment," and despite his distaste for travel went to Peace Congresses at the Paris Stade Buffalo, Wroclaw, Warsaw, beneath his well-known pigeon, now *The Dove of Peace.* A crowd-phobiac, he appeared at mass meetings and even read addresses, was active in the France-Spain Committee, which sometimes met in his studio, and the Spanish Aid Committee, signing appeals, donating works to be sold for many causes, on occasion bidding them in himself—or having it done for him by Kahnweiler—if the auction had not brought a high enough price, then donating the cost to the cause.

Moreover, he did get something in return. First of all, the popular fame that had so long escaped him and which Léger, who was also a Party member, was never to know, even though his art was so much closer to the people than Pablo's. When Pablo gave the Communist Municipality of Vallauris his *Man with the Sheep,* there was a big unveiling celebration, and chairman Laurent Casanova intoned, "Salute to Picasso, our brother in arms!" to the sculptor's delight. He got the same delight the following month (November 1950), when at Warsaw he was awarded the Peace Prize along with the Turkish poet Nazim Hikmet, Paul Robeson, and Pablo Neruda, who stated, "The Picasso Dove is flying over the world . . . No criminal birdcatcher will henceforth be able to impede its flight!"

Much has been written about Picasso's relations with the Party, yet they were simple enough. He was happy to have a family, but he also felt free to speak ill of the hateful family that bored him. If the family paid him back in kind, he got furious or unhappy. There was a certain amount of disingenuousness about it all.

When Georges Tabaraud, editor of the *Patriote* of Nice, called on him while he was doing the portrait of Joliot-Curie for a Congress of the Peace Movement, Pablo asked, "Was he right to devote so much of the last years of his life to action for peace? Would it not have been better, for the Party, if he had remained the foremost of the great physicists?" And himself answered:

> Physicist or painter, we are all workers, all knifegrinders. The worker sharpens the blade; I sharpen my pictures. I do not paint for the people. If I did, it would mean I was on the outside. But I am on the inside. And being on the inside is not just any old thing. One does what he thinks best. That's what counts.

And another time, he told Tabaraud, "Even if they didn't want me, I'd still hang on to the Party."

One day in the winter of 1944–1945, while the Battle of the Bulge seemed to be going most badly, Picasso was having dinner with Cocteau, who asked him: "If the Germans were to come back, what would you say to them now that you've joined the Communist Party?" Pablo thought a few seconds, then smiled mischievously, and said, "Why, Jean, I'd say, 'Can't you tell that was just a joke?' " And he gave a great shove to some imaginary listener.

Françoise Gilot, now part of his life, had not yet given in to his urging to move in to Rue des Grands-Augustins. She acquitted herself honorably of several tests, the visit to Gertrude Stein under the inquisitorial eye of Alice B. Toklas, then the pilgrimage to the Bateau-Lavoir. He told her what all the places in Montmartre reminded him of, and even took her to see Germaine Pichot, his old friend Ramón's widow, now living in penniless old age; he left her some money, and told Françoise she had once been one of the most beautiful women in Montmartre—a kind of roundabout warning.

Dora Maar tried to fend Françoise off, but unsuccessfully. Her reign, which had been tottering, was now at an end. The newcomer was no Marie-Thérèse who had willingly agreed to share, mainly because her principal concern was Maya. She and Dora were now both has-beens, and if Françoise was not antagonistic to them, it was probably because she realized that there was a difference between sharing Pablo's bed and reigning on the throne.

The Ogre had turned headstrong, haughty Dora into a submissive slave, a shadow of her former self. She stayed and painted at her Rue de Savoie apartment, ready to jump when he phoned to say to come to lunch or dinner at the Catalan's. All he had to say was "Come." This became as natural to her as the *ménage à trois* had become to Marie-Thérèse. But she was childless—and Pablo never let her forget it.

Françoise felt sorry for Dora, but also afraid of her nervous fits that ended in scenes. One night a police patrol had even found Dora wandering along the Seine: she told them she was looking for the little dog Picasso had given her, that had been stolen. After her mother died, Dora started having attacks of mysticism, reproaching Pablo for his sins, and he finally had to ask Dr. Lacan to look after her.

Françoise made the mistake of going to an exhibit Dora had at the Jeanne Bucher Gallery in Montparnasse in April 1945, and almost sent Dora into one of her depressions; but the upshot was that Picasso, misunderstanding the circumstances, became peeved at Françoise, and avoided her for several weeks, while she in vain waited for him to phone and make up.

Dora took advantage of this to get back into his good graces: on June 15 she was with him at the Théâtre Sarah-Bernhardt, where the Roland Petit Ballets presented the Henri Sauguet–Boris Kochno *Les Forains* and Prévert's *Rendezvous,* with sets by Brassaï. Picasso had agreed to do the drop curtain, but had not been able to find time for it, so he let Kochno select one of the still lifes that fitted in with the character of the ballets, to be enlarged for it. Kochno took a small canvas dated November 18, 1943: a candlestick with a lighted candle next to a carnival mask, on a summarily suggested table. Its big black outlines and smoky black, blue, mauve, and beige harmony enlarged felicitously.

Since the Romain Rolland *14 Juillet* in 1936, Pablo had not done any more theatrical work. The only thing he had done was to tattoo a broomstick pyrographically with circles and spirals to be Jean Marais's scepter in *Andromaque* at the Théâtre Édouard-VII in May 1944. But now he was taking an interest in the Roland Petit Ballets, as he had not since the days of Diaghilev—and Olga. He was much concerned about how Brassaï's highly evocative pictures of Paris nightlife had been adapted into the *Rendezvous* setting. So he agreed to do a cover for the ballet program, to be printed, according to his instructions, from two plates, the Muse's face filling the whole page with her hair as an arabesque frame, and the text in between.

When not with Dora or Françoise, visiting Marie-Thérèse or Olga, seeing friends, dealers, sycophants, GIs, Spaniards, or Communists, Picasso was working. He sold his canvases to Kahnweiler and to Louis Carré, whose gallery in Avenue de Messine was now one of the leading ones in Paris. The two dealers were often at the studio but, thanks to Sabartés' savoir-faire, they never bumped into each other. Pablo also had to handle a new generation of American dealers, for whom he was not abstract enough—but who bought anyway, by the carload.

He still had his table at the Catalan's, but there was now a new owner, a Frenchman named Maurice Desailly, whose portrait Pablo did, as he had done his predecessor's, and it was on the wall where Arnau's had been. Desailly added another shop across the street, and officially named it Le Catalan, after which fashion took over, and Picasso was to stop coming, except occasionally when he knew for sure that only his friends would be there.

For the nonce, he frequented the place, having as his guests Camus, Reverdy when he was in Paris, Gertrude and Alice if he was on speaking terms with them, André Beaudin and Suzanne Roger, and the Leirises. Others who patronized the place were Cocteau, with his charming new secretary Paul Morihien and their entourage of aesthetic lads, Jean Genêt and a few other ex-cons, Sartre and Simone de Beauvoir, Elsa and Louis Aragon. Jean Paulhan, editor of the *Nouvelle Revue française,* sometimes turned up, but as he was close to Braque, Pablo was suspicious of him.

Paulhan had taken an early fancy to Braque and dared, unpardonably in Pablo's eyes, to put him and Rouault on the same level as Picasso. When his *Braque le*

Patron (Braque the Master) came out in 1946, Pablo fumed—more because of the unfortunate title than because of the contents (for he never read it). As for Paulhan's demonstration of what Cubism was, Pablo found it the more stupid since he himself did not admit that Cubism existed. Nor did Braque; but the "intellectuals" always found words where in fact there was only painting. As Malraux did, for example . . .

Malraux and Paulhan, a few years before, had shared an admiration for Fautrier; now it was Dubuffet in his forties who was Paulhan's new young hope. To Pablo he was a pale imitation of Permeke and Gustave de Smet. "Just Belgian painting!" he called it to André Lhote, who reported it to an amazed and irritated Paulhan. From then on, when Dubuffet was mentioned, Pablo would reply, "Never heard of him!"

Nothing irritated Pablo more than to see the Catalan's invaded by the new flock of bothersome, chattering *précieuses* named Louise de Vilmorin, Marie-Louise Bousquet, or Denise Bourdet, dragging behind them their retinues of snobs, dressmakers, writers, Resistance veterans, and fashionable homosexuals. One evening, to insure Picasso's privacy, Desailly closed his door to outsiders, and the painter was able quietly to have dinner with a colonel just back from Germany, who in his pathos-laden voice described the apocalyptic ruins, the starving population, the pillaging and rapes by the Russians. Pablo listened avidly, of course: it was Col. André Malraux.

He had appeared at Rue des Grands-Augustins, thin of face and somber of eye, and Picasso had been taken aback by the uniform of the "Alsace-Lorraine" brigade, the black beret he had worn since the days of the Spanish war, the insignia, boots, and wide belt ("but no medals," as Pablo noted). Almost thirty years later, Malraux in his own synthetic way would recount that afternoon of May 1945, as he did in his "reportage" on his visit to General de Gaulle on December 11, 1969, mixing his own words with those of his interlocutor, so that one can no longer distinguish when he or the other is talking. On this day, Malraux was still only a famous novelist and an "adventurer" distinguished for his daring in Spain, the Resistance, and the final battles of World War II. The painter had just recently joined the Communist Party, whose bitter enemy Malraux was to become. But the latter had not yet had his supreme revelation: he was not to meet de Gaulle until August 1945.

Malraux did not write his account of their meeting until some months after Picasso died. During Pablo's lifetime, he hardly mentioned it, generally making reference to him only in connection with other art forms or artists he was more interested in. Picasso's Communist allegiance he was bitter about, albeit jestingly. The Malraux account, published in the spring of 1974, was of course not meant to justify his shortcomings or his mishandling of Picasso in the ten years he had served de Gaulle as Minister for Cultural Affairs. The State does not have to explain, much less exonerate itself: it *is* The State. Since he no longer represented it, what Malraux had done or not done during his ministry was now history, above and beyond individuals. As a writer, in his statement, he was making up again, not with Picasso-the-man "who did not like de Gaulle," but with the painter he had admired, and whose political and emotional commitment, at the time of the Spanish war, he had shared.

With Picasso gone, Malraux was free to go on about the "Saturn of Metamorphosis," whom he had avoided for so many years—for, between 1945–1950 and 1958, they met very few times, and beginning in 1959, when Malraux entered the Cabinet, no more at all.

That visit in May 1945 was enough for the writer, as in the case of de Gaulle, to do a "reportage" in which he quotes his interviewee not in the simple, direct sentences he used, as everyone knows, but in a kind of visionary rhetoric and majestic tone quite out of keeping. We hear not the true voice of Picasso, but the one Malraux superimposes on him; his narrative is meant less to show the motivations or reactions of the painter than to allow for the writer's verbal inflation as he gives his own ideas on art in general and Picasso's art in particular. Our Malagueño never with Malraux, or anyone else, indulged in the kind of socio- or symbolico-aesthetic digressions in which each speaker in turn acts as spark plug while the other soars over the summits, in the manner of December 11, 1969, at La Boisserie.

When Malraux writes, "It had been in the Grands-Augustins studio that we first spoke of the Museum Without Walls," we know right away who is talking. We are given fair warning: the conversation is to take place on the highest of levels, not that of individuals but of civilizations and Art, not of people but of their statues and gods, not of life, painting, or creation, but of Fate. Which is, in a word, to say that it will be Malraux's rhetoric handling both questions and answers, while Picasso is shunted aside. Through the writer's voice and tone, we hear neither the painter nor the man: just the Myth.

Malraux reports that Picasso had cut off his forelock, but that this did not change the expression of his face, nor "the same out-of-this-world eyes in the surprised-Pierrot face." Then he looks at the Parisian landscapes his host had painted toward the end of the occupation.

> . . . "Do they surprise you?" he asked. "It's true, I'm not a landscape painter. These particular landscapes came to me just like that. I spent a lot of time walking the quays during the Occupation. With Kazbek . . ."

In his own book, Brassaï also tells the story of the Malraux visit, at which he was present: he dates it May 11, 1945. The things Picasso said about the landscapes come out about the same in Brassaï as in Malraux, but the latter gives them his personal dimension. Malraux does not mention the presence of Brassaï or Nush Éluard, whom Pablo introduced to him. How important are mere mortals when such deities meet each other?

Brassaï on the landscapes: "[Malraux] is especially impressed by their colorings: symphonies of tone in grays and beige, ranging from deep to cool, with skies of gray-mauve-blue . . ."

Malraux on the same: "The palette, different from what I had known before, surprised me. His *Vert-Galant* with its trapezoid treetrunks and sea-urchinlike greenery, captured in flight the banks of the Seine between its knives . . . Almost happy, these pointed landscapes. Not to be trusted."

In showing him *The Sweethearts, The Blue Hat,* and several other recent works, Picasso "smiled, ironical and concerned," saying, "What do they mean?" A springboard for the writer, who records:

"You know better than I," I said. "They mean what nothing else could mean. In one chorus, they all shout it."

I added, not without a slightly bitter admiration: "They also mean, 'Written on prison walls,' " and finally that, over a period of so many years, these intractable works had created a world of painting that had never before existed: obviously very different from the architectural Cézannian world of Cubism.

To which, according to Malraux, Picasso replied:

"Cézanne's Louvre must not have been much different from mine. What is different is precisely what is not in the Louvre.

". . . In our heads we have a museum that is not the Louvre, sure. That is like it. That is not like it. But watch out: only in our heads. Intellectuals are not bothered by that. On the contrary. Painters *are* bothered by it. The idea of a picture . . ."

"In this case, a recollection or reproduction . . ." [Malraux interrupts].

". . . is not a picture" [concludes Picasso].

Malraux pointed out the true meaning of the Imaginary Museum, the "necessarily mental location" of the works that govern any creator of forms: "We do not inhabit it; it inhabits us."

When Picasso says of the little pebbles he had sculpted into statues, "I did these with a little knife," Malraux comments, "Ageless sculpture."

As day began to wane (at Colombey, on December 11, 1969, at about the same hour, it would be snow falling), the tone turned to a sort of poetical, prophetic incantation, a reverie on Art, the Imaginary Museum, styles, resemblance, Rembrandt, Goya ("'What would he have thought of *Guernica?*' Picasso wondered. 'I think he would have been rather satisfied. I live with him more than with Stalin.' "). This Picasso-Malraux dialogue is the monologue of one character with concordant voices: the man of destiny.

When Picasso had a meal in a restaurant, with friends, or other guests, he would draw on the paper tablecloth. Or else cut a piece out of it, fold it, and then tear it, turning the torn or juxtaposed papers into fabulous creatures. One day, in front of Éluard, he turned three pieces of paper through skillful arrangement into a sort of wide-eyed monster, with limbs spread; the poet reached for it, but Pablo blew on the unconnected bits of paper and they flew away. Before his friend's discomfited look, he burst out laughingly, "That's one you can't catch, Paul!"

Picasso would also draw on the paper cloth with a wine-soaked finger or a fountain pen, going from one spot to another, making designs that he heightened with mustard, coffee, or gravy. "See, I can get yellow, brown, or black like that," he said. And soon, before his friends' amazed eyes, a whole part of the table became the field for a fantastic creation; some tore them off to put in their pockets—another Picasso for their collections! He liked the idea, or took umbrage, depending on his moods.

Cocteau would enviously admire the way, with virtuosity equal to his imagination, he could invent ever-new forms. He was fascinated. Max-Pol Fouchet relates how during one lunch at the Catalan's Pablo thus drew a chick and an owl in one unbroken line without ever taking his finger off the table. The others present were no less impressed than Cocteau, who, livid with jealousy, suddenly said, "Let me duplicate it." He inspected Pablo's work, the chick and the owl, and turning his head away, on another corner of the paper cloth did exactly the same drawing with his pen, also in one unbroken line. Fouchet saw this as "a symbol of both Picasso's genius and Jean Cocteau's skill, his special knack," as Pablo had the last word, "Sure, but I did it first!"

In contrast to his previous major love affairs, the arrival of Françoise Gilot in his life had not, at least for the moment, filled his work with joy and happiness. The Winter 1944–1945 canvases are dramatic as can be. While during the entire German occupation he had felt and expressed the tragic circumstances only through the screen of allusion or metaphor, now that France was rid of the Nazis, he became aware of the war, but, as with *Guernica,* he recorded the event by indirection.

The Charnel House (Museum of Modern Art, New York) is not the war, but its consequence or effect; the bodies piled up in an unbelievable chaos of mixed-up members, battered or crushed heads, arms frozen in a final gesture of supplication or tearing away, are not necessarily those of fighters; there are women, children, old people—for the ongoing war had as many innocent civilian victims as combat casualties.

But, when one looks closer, the room where these victims lie is a kitchen with open door, while floating in the air, simply drawn in charcoal, is the Cézanne or Chardin table with pitcher and bread. Painted in black, gray, and blue, with large blanks and marginal parts done in line, to form dancing arabesques that suggest curls of smoke, *The Charnel House* is without the monumental sweep or power of conviction, without the overtones of *Guernica.* It does not have the horror that Picasso had so often portrayed on his faces; it is at peace. The massacre is over, in its aftermath all is ash- and sky-colored, in the haggard light arising from this awful pile. One arm is up, one hand outstretched, open, toward the table and bread. Everything is going to begin again, hope, liberty, life . . .

The Charnel House is contemporaneous with another series of still lifes with pitcher, candlestick, skull, enamel cookpot, and so on, all especially dramatic, and several views of Notre-Dame done between February 27, 1945, and the end of April. The latter are cut into sharply outlined triangles, so that, as Antonina Vallentin put it, "the landscape seems to be seen through a network of steel beams."

The Charnel House allayed the fears of those who thought his joining the Party would change his style and approach. To think so was not to know him well. His decision remained outside his work; it committed the man (or did it?), but not the painter. Picasso's was not a Communist vocation, just an avocation.

And the Communists were unhappy. Shown at "Art and Resistance," *The Charnel House* did not satisfy those who expected a historical painting, an "event," as the Spanish Republican leaders of 1937 had hoped for in *Guernica*. They found it disconcerting, hard to grasp, and incomplete. *To the Spanish Republicans Who Died for France* was equally disappointing, and despite the dutiful praise in the Communist press, there was widespread bitterness. Some spoke of "hoax" and "booby trap." "It doesn't look right," said one panjandrum about the tribute to the Spaniards; echoes of this and his friends' reactions to both works shocked and hurt Picasso; but his troubles on that score were far from over.

On May 23, he did three realistic "likenesses" of the Party head, Maurice Thorez.

Dora's health was more and more precarious, and Pablo asked Françoise to avoid her so as not to upset her, yet insisted that she move in with him, which Françoise was reluctant to do. So he took Dora and left for Cap-d'Antibes, to stay with the Cuttolis. Peeved, Françoise went to Brittany, but she had hardly gotten there when she had a letter from Pablo, "Please come at once. I'm terribly bored." He had rented a room for her at his friend the engraver Louis Fort's at Golfe-Juan, but Françoise said no. Only that November did she realize it was "almost a physical impossibility to go on breathing outside his presence." She returned to his studio at Rue des Grands-Augustins on her birthday, she says, November 26— and the Ogre thought he now had his young prize where he wanted her.

Since coming back to Paris, Picasso had resumed lithography in the Mourlot brothers' shop on Rue de Chabrol, near the Gare de l'Est. There were three Mourlots, Fernand being the manager, head and soul of the great caravanserai from another era which had once housed the Bataille printshop, famous, apart from its purely commercial work, for doing all the theatrical posters ranging from Polin's music-hall singing turn to Sarah Bernhardt's *Phèdre* as seen by Mucha. Their father, himself a lithographer, had bought it in June 1914, and when he died seven years later left it to the three sons, the eldest, Georges, being mainly the businessman, while Maurice left to become a painter, and Fernand ran the craft side of the shop. He found that "by far the most agreeable," and was to be responsible for the greatest artists of the time coming there to work on their color lithography, which he guided to international renown.

It was Braque who one day mentioned Fernand Mourlot to Pablo; the latter, ever intrigued by new processes, jumped at the chance. He had done a little lithography before the war and wanted to get back to it. Sabartés got in touch with Mourlot, who came to Rue des Grands-Augustins one morning. Picasso listened attentively to the master lithographer's technical explanations, and told him, "I'll be there the day after tomorrow."

The date was November 2, 1945: he stayed for four months, coming in each morning at eight-thirty or nine, which was unusual, as he preferred not getting up before noon. The first day, he brought some paper collages he had prepared the day before, and took his place near a press with Mourlot and the best old worker on his staff, M. Tutin, who had been specially selected for the Picasso assignment. Pablo made his drawing on the lithographic stone, Tutin pulled a first proof, and the artist said, "I like that." Then, lighting a cigarette, he asked Mourlot to show him around the shop.

After inspecting everything, talking to everyone, he chose a corner he would work in. The workers at first expected to see him for a week, two at the most. But every day the shop was open, he was there. Marcel drove him up, he walked about the neighborhood a bit, and then checked in.

His day started with a round of hellos, then to his corner, where he was joined by Tutin, and Jean Célestin, who was assigned to work with him. Unfortunately, Tutin detested Picasso's art; it nauseated him; and Pablo as a result naturally was spurred only to do wilder and wilder things on the stone. Tutin would kick, say it was not feasible, and then go ahead anyway: usually, the result was remarkable.

As Fernand Mourlot put it, "Picasso looked, listened, and then did exactly the opposite of what had been shown him—and it worked." That was always his way; his lithographic method was contrary not only to the customs but also the rules of that craft. But Pablo got around difficulties with ease because he started from the principle that a creator might do anything, since everything that existed was his to use. And besides, he had unheard-of passion for his work. Even today, craftsmen such as Célestin or Henri Deschamp—Tutin being retired—remain amazed by what they saw of Picasso's prodigious activity and his skill.

He refused to cover his mouth so as not to spray saliva on the stone: "Saliva makes blanks," he said, and one day when a little line he had made around a head cracked, the technicians repaired it. When he came back, he spotted it immediately, saying he had not done that, and they proudly replied, "No, we fixed it up." "Well," he said, "you're not supposed to fix it up." "And he was right," Mourlot commented. "Everything counts. It makes no difference, and it makes all the difference in the world."

Pablo's first lithograph was the collage done the day before, a woman's head, followed on the same day (November 2, 1945) by three others in varying techniques, then more women's heads, and boys' heads, and some still lifes and bull-fight scenes. Between November 2 and December 30, he was to do sixty-three lithos, including all their states, not counting the illustration of Pierre Reverdy's *Chant des Morts* (Hymn for the Dead). The major part, however, was the women's faces, inspired by Françoise when, at the end of November, she finally came back to him. The first color attempts were dated December 15 (*Still Life with Three Apples*), and resumed again in January and February 1946.

There were other themes, too: as usual, the two nude women friends, one sitting and one lying down, in varying styles and techniques, birds in flight, bull-fights, and finally the bull that became the subject of a famous "series."

"One day he started on that bull," Jean Célestin recalls. "A wonderful, very plump bull. I thought that was it. Not at all. Second state. Third. Still plump. And then more. But the bull was changing. He was fading away. Losing weight." Or, as Henri Deschamp told it to Hélène Parmelin: "Picasso removed more than he added. He was cutting up his bull at the same time. Making cuts in him. And each time we would pull a proof. He could see how perplexed we were. So he would joke about it. And go on working. Yet another bull, with less and less to him. He'd say, 'Look, Henri. This is what the butcher ought to have. Then the housewife could say, "I want this bit, or that one." ' In the end, the head was like an ant's."

With the eleventh state (the final one), on January 17, 1946, all that was left of the bull was an ideogram. Jean Célestin, who watched that "plump" bull reach this state over a period of a month and a half, still remembers it with awe: "I could not help thinking: he's ending where he ought to have started. I did not understand . . . But what Picasso wanted was that very bull, and in order to get to that bull of his own, he had to go through all those other bulls as others saw them. The last bull truly was Picasso's bull."

All the time that he was working at Mourlot's he asked Sabartés and his close friends not to say where he was. This "disappearance" upset many other friends, who thought he was hiding out with some girl; not least the Communists, who were always worried about his possibly getting away from them. But, naturally, the truth got out fairly quickly, so he forbade anyone coming to see him there— except Éluard, and then Aragon, which reassured the Party.

On February 14, he did a black-and-white *Seashells and Birds.* The twenti-eth and twenty-first, he drew a *Composition with Skull* and made experiments in lithographic processes with wash, crayon, and scraping knife. A *Bird,* as ele-mentary as it is expressive, concluded these four months of work. He would return to Rue de Chabrol only on June 14, to start a new series—celebrating Françoise.

Reverdy's *Le Chant des Morts,* published by Tériade, had been begun at the start of 1945. Picasso had at first done a few drawings in the margins of the manuscript, but then he wanted to see his own hand alongside the poet's, as graphic counterpart and competition to his friend, while adding to the depth of meaning of the poems. Reverdy wrote out a fair copy, and Pablo went to the very heart of Reverdy's spontaneous inspiration. The two creative hands were con-fronted and conjoined in a free give-and-take which, in the words of the Greek poet Odysseus Élytis in *Verve,* attained on Picasso's part "the mysterious gravity of a ritual act that seemed imposed on him by some unknown religion."

In November 1945, Pablo made his first tests on stone, washes printed in red, black-and-red lithographs, washes on paper, all but one immediately erased. The first blood-red arabesques for *Chant des Morts* were put on the stone in January and February 1946; the next year, he did some more plates, at home, on zinc; then in the winter of 1947–1948 on zinc plates that Mourlot brought him to Vallauris, where by then he was living. He worked on a large terrace at Georges and Suzanne Ramié's, with no one to disturb him, or in inclement weather inside one of their shops. He was dissatisfied with certain prints, and new lithographs had to be made so that the illustration of this great long poem, made up of 125 lithographs, including two for the cover, was not finished until March 1948.

When the edition was all printed, Pablo asked a bemused Tériade to scrap it and start over, since he envisioned it now differently! But the publisher—with some little trouble—talked him out of that. It was exhibited in December 1948 at the Louis Carré Gallery, the only book Picasso did for his friend Tériade.

During the war, several exhibits of his work had taken place in America, although not in Europe, especially not in France, where the Germans controlled all artistic events. At their insistence, a 1901 Picasso, *At the Races,* full of turn-of-the-century Impressionism, had been withdrawn from the show the very day that an exhibit called "Parisian Scenes and Figures" was opened at the Charpentier Gallery in 1943.

The first Parisian show of his recent work was held at the Louis Carré Gallery in June 1945, the catalog including poems by Éluard and critical pieces by Fagus (his 1901 article), Apollinaire, Zervos, Aragon, Cocteau, and Jean Cassou. Also some quotations from Picasso statements. The Resistance-born press was in seventh heaven.

Not so in London, where Picasso and Matisse were jointly exhibited at the Victoria and Albert Museum. There were rather lively controveries, for apparently British art critics and public had not understood much of the achievements of modern painting. But at least their reactions could be appreciated for their frankness, whereas in France everyone had to fawn. No criticism of Picasso's genius, however mild, might be voiced in those days.

That first Louis Carré show proved the continuity of Picasso's art during the war years, how his style had developed and grown along its lines of constancy. The next one, in June 1946 at the same gallery, went the other way, showing that the painter, with his ever-renewing inventiveness, performed in every technique, every genre, every medium. The provocative and protean character of his work had, it seemed, been forgotten—so there was surprise, and in some cases disapproval. Wrote Jacques Lassaigne:

> Far from signifying a development, each of the exhibited works seems like a denial, as well as an opening on to still uncertain possibilities . . . They do, after all, represent that kind of pan-availability that does basically remain the Picasso temperament.

What of Dora and Françoise? The former was finished, and Pablo had found a way to ship her out. On a picture shown him by a friend, he had noticed a house built on the ramparts of a village in Provence, Ménerbes, and decided to buy it. It was not expensive, and the painter topped off his handy cash with one of his recent still lifes. Then, having gotten-title to it, he made a gift of the house to Dora Maar—keeping a set of keys for himself.

With Françoise, things were just beginning, but in Pablo's life nothing was ever simple. She was quickly initiated to all of his tricks and traps. When he insisted she come to the Flore, she knew he thought Dora would be there, and that an awful scene would ensue. As he brought forward his new conquest, he had a way of saying to the discarded mistress, "You remember Françoise, don't you?" that might call forth any kind of explosion.

Picasso in love, at sixty-plus, was no more retiring about his triumph than he had been at twenty-five, when every man's eyes undressed Fernande as he escorted her into the Lapin Agile. But Françoise was anything but a sexpot: in her jumper, pleated skirt, and low-heeled shoes, she fully warranted Dora's sneering reference to her as a "schoolgirl." Pablo, doing more and more portraits of her, using her as model for all of his nude or dressed figures of the period, on May 5, 1946, turned her into a "Flower-Woman."

Originally, this *Femme-fleur,* as Françoise tells it, "was sitting on a long, curved African tabouret shaped something like a conch shell," rather realistically painted. But he decided, "No, it's just not your style. A realistic portrait wouldn't represent you at all . . . You're not at all the passive type. I only see you standing." And he started to simplify, lengthening the body, rounding the face. Let her take it from there:

> He painted a sheet of paper sky-blue and began to cut out oval shapes corresponding in varying degrees to the concept of my head: first, two that were perfectly round, then three or four more based on his idea of doing it in width. When he had finished cutting them out, he drew in, on each of them, little signs for the eyes, nose, and mouth. Then he pinned them onto the canvas, one after another, moving each one a little to the left or right, up or down, as it suited him. None seemed really appropriate until he reached the last one. Having tried all the others in various spots, he knew where he wanted it, and when he applied it to the canvas, stood aside and said, "Now it's your portrait." He marked the contour lightly in charcoal, took off the paper, then painted in, slowly and carefully, exactly what was drawn on the paper.

Thus the birth of *The Flower-Woman* (Françoise Gilot Salk Collection).

She is a long thin stem, like a metallic sculpture at the top of which is a round face like a ceramic plate, with large light eyes, and all around hair held in by good-sized opened petals. The young woman's round breasts are the fruits of the wonderful plant that also has two arms, or two branches in phallic form, a somewhat discreet but utterly Picassian allusion to the pleasures Pablo found with his model, and it is all painted in pastel tones to reflect the tender character of the picture, which Picasso was to say he would "reproduce infinitely."

In April, he spent a few days with her at Golfe-Juan, at M. Fort's, where Françoise was resting up from a recent fall. Marcel drove them on a visit to Matisse, and Pablo tried to convince her he could not go on without her. A few months before, he had a firm grasp on her, but she had escaped again. Did any other woman ever act that way toward him? Was this kid going to stand up to him very long, when so many other beautiful women were swirling about him, offering themselves both forcefully and shamelessly? He was furious with her, even threatening to throw her into the Seine!

Since each had now proved how attached he or she was to the other, and what a gift they had for melodramatics, the time had come to settle matters. Françoise told him she was ready to write her mother and grandmother that she was leaving them, to live on her own. Actually, Pablo dictated the letter, and posted it himself.

A few weeks later, mid-July, when he told her they would be spending the summer in the Midi, she thought he would say at Cannes or St.-Tropez. But he left her speechless by announcing that they would be going first "to Ménerbes, to Dora Maar's house."

XIX

OH,
THE GREAT DAYS!
(1946–1948)

O N THE BEACH AT GOLFE-JUAN, PICASSO, LYING HALF-NAKED WITH Françoise, watched the beautiful young women with their lithe bodies pass back and forth at the water's edge, diving in, running about with equally bronzed young lads, or playing ball. Or else lying sunbathing, dreamy and languid.

Fine summer. Great days . . . Pablo's love was at the stage of happy beatitude. His new conquest was young, endowed with somewhat animal beauty, not radiant but in full bloom. Françoise, though not without grace, was not given to impulsive displays of affection, and love did not sweep her off her feet. She did not appear sensual, or rather did not call forth sensuality, but rather seemed to restrain it, perhaps fully aware that she had other attractions.

The stay at Ménerbes had seemed endless to her. Why had Pablo insisted on taking her to this pretty Provençal village with its huddled, sun-baked houses perched on a shiplike rock? "I'm the one who gave that house to Dora Maar. There's no reason why I shouldn't use it," he had said. She could only bow to his wish. And the days there went by in dull succession; Pablo seemed to be putting her to a test, for up to now he had almost exclusively seen her with friends in Paris—never in *tête-à-tête*.

She watched her stocky, alert, devoted sexagenarian, possessive like all Spaniards, proud of the beauty he could show off, as of her charms that he displayed in the many nudes he did of her. So sure of himself, of his fate, of his love! He was overwhelming in his confidence, a mere corollary of fate in his eyes. Wildly egotistical, cynical, cruel, a real torturer of others, especially those closest to him, taking sadistic pleasure in bragging to the current woman about her predecessor's accomplishments.

In their long walks at Ménerbes, telling Françoise about Dora, reading her Marie-Thérèse's daily letters, ecstatic over Maya's development, and never hesitant to reread several times the most intimate passages, reveling in their lyricism,

"Somehow I don't see you writing me a letter like that," he would taunt her. "It's because you don't love me enough. That woman *really* loves me. . . . You're too immature to understand things like that. . . . You're still just a girl."

What was his game? Françoise wondered as she bit her lip and held her tongue. Dora's house, Marie-Thérèse's letters, Picasso's comments were all a bit much for a honeymoon, especially under the eagle eye of Marcel, who although blasé was wondering how this one would turn out. Behind Pablo's back, she decided to hitchhike to Marseilles, where she had friends who would stake her to a ticket to North Africa. But of course the car that picked her up on the road was Picasso's, an ironic Marcel at the wheel. To her amazement, the lord and master reasoned rather than remonstrated with her, painted her a beautiful word picture of their future, and concluded, "What you need is a child."

Bastille Day was a big event down there; Pablo delighted in the local torchlight tattoo. "I never saw him more excited than he was as he watched those rugged blacksmith types, most of them stripped to the waist, blowing his beloved bugle and waving their torches," Françoise wrote. The next day he did a large gouache of the parade.

Marie Cuttoli put in a well-timed appearance that took their minds off their troubles—which had not really upset Pablo. Since he could not imagine any woman being anywhere but in seventh heaven by the very fact of his presence, and everything he did or said seemed wonderful to him, he wrote Françoise's behavior down to her youth and improper rearing. She needed training, he was to tell Marcel. And he would train her—after which, she would fly the coop.

Mme. Cuttoli invited Picasso and his *amie* to visit her at Cap-d'Antibes, to the relief of Françoise, finally shed of Ménerbes. By the same occasion, they would be able to see M. Fort in his little house at Golfe-Juan, and be at the seashore, which they both enjoyed. As he did the feminine company there. So, he rented the two upper floors of Fort's house, Marcel went back to Ménerbes for the luggage, and a new Mediterranean cycle began for Picasso.

Pablo bathed, dreamt, and drew in the sun. August was glorious and the beach was not crowded; some days, Françoise and he had it to themselves. Mythological inspiration had quite naturally returned with verve and grace; his fingers were now fashioning leaping fauns, nymphs, centaurs, some at the seaside, some fighting with arrows. *Fauns and Women, Fights of Fauns and Centaurs, The Wounded Centaur, Dance on the Beach, Busts of Centaurs* were, among others, some of the titles of the clean-lined, admirably free drawings that he did. Sometimes he enhanced them with large flat applications of color, as if the sun were pouring its brilliance on to the joyful and/or (not really) cruel scenes. No doubt about it, this was happiness.

The photographer Michel Sima was staying at Dor de la Souchère's and suggested that his friend the curator get hold of Picasso and ask him for something for the museum. The professor was reluctant, but Sima dragged him down to the sunning couple on the beach. They chatted a while, and then, as Dor de la Souchère humorously tells it, Sima "popped the question."

"Oh, sure, I'll find some drawing for you," Pablo agreed. And they went on to other subjects, like paintings and commissions. "Strange," Pablo commented, "I'm cut out to work on large surfaces and no one ever commissions me to." *

Dor de la Souchère rose to the occasion, suggesting the huge surfaces in his museum, and they headed directly up there. The rooms one flight up were virtually bare. Pablo said nothing. He was bare-chested, in shorts, with Françoise, Dor de la Souchère, and Sima around him. The light played on the immaculately white walls, rose brick floors, and ceiling beams. A bee flew in and buzzed about. Through the windows, the old city could be seen, with its narrow streets and tiled roofs, as well as the port, the bay, and, in the distance, mountains. Typical cries in the local dialect could at times be heard. Could Picasso fail to be reminded of his youthful studios in Barcelona, similarly located?

Later, he was to tell Dor de la Souchère, "If you had said to me, Let's make a museum, I wouldn't have come. But you just said: Here's a studio. You had no idea what might be done with it. That's why it worked, because you didn't try to imitate a museum."

In this studio, Pablo was to work "like a madman," to quote Dor de la Souchère, for five months, August–December 1946. He set himself up on the third floor, where he made arrangements to be able to paint during night hours; he and Sima went and got huge pots of boat paint, coarse brushes, and ordered three-meter-long sheets of asbestos cement. He was ready . . .

How could Picasso not have been singing? It was summer, the war was over, a new love was at his side. He was back on the Mediterranean, where for over thirty years, with his successive conquests, he had lived so many of the happiest months of his existence, in the fullness of passion shared. What he was creating in the solitude of the old museum to which Dor de la Souchère had given him the keys, and where he spent the best parts of both his days and his nights, was a huge lyric poem in bright allegro, a hymn to life filled with fantasy and humor. Around the *Joy of Living,* more nymphs, fauns, other creatures danced other rounds in simple lines, spare masses, calm and soft colors, without excessive brilliance, recreating the themes of his neoclassical period, now reevaluated in a new dimension.

During this time at Antibes he also took to doing knife carvings on pebbles and flotsam gathered on the beach. Previously, at Ménerbes, on a walk with Françoise, he had come upon a piece of bone and picked it up, saying to her, "That's Adam's rib. I'm going to draw an Eve on there for you," and on it he had sculpted a little squatting woman, horns on her head and a face as round as her breasts. At Antibes, he brought owls, fauns' or bulls' heads, mythological characters out of the sea-washed and rounded stones he collected.

"Now, of course, they should be cast back into the sea," he was later to tell Brassaï. "Think how astonished people would be, finding pebbles marked with symbols like these . . . What riddles they would pose for archaeologists!"

Paulhan's book, *Braque le Patron,* made Pablo see red. For several days he could not get over it. And not a soul was defending him! For years, the editor had been hacking away, imperceptibly but precisely, in conversations and articles, at Picasso's preeminence in Cubism. Each time, of course, Pablo was informed, being shown an article, or a letter (one from Paulhan to Marcel Jouhandeau, for example) somehow turning up. Pablo, of course, would respond with disparagements of poor Braque, who was in no way responsible for this Paulhan campaign.

Thus, he snidely told Paulhan's friend Maurice Toesca one day, "Braque is just a female Picasso!" and opined to Malraux that "What Braque is doing now is no longer anything like what I do. For him, the battle is over . . ." His former fellow-traveler of the heroic years took all this philosophically. He knew Pablo too well to be concerned. As with Matisse, Picasso's mockery or sarcasm was a cover for the admiration—and envy—he felt for what each of them had that was their own, beyond his grasp.

The Communists had gotten some upsetting reports about the mythological flights of "Comrade Picasso," which seemed to them not to conform to the Party line. He made short shrift of that, saying, "At Antibes I did what I could, and I did it with pleasure, because for once I knew I was working for the people."

Françoise in her book recalled a tiny seafood shop owned by a woman who "was so wide and her café so narrow there was hardly room enough inside for her, so she stood outside trying to drum up trade." There being no more crowd so late in the season, she would dip into her stock of sea urchins every so often, to the delight of Pablo, who did four pictures of *Woman Eating Sea Urchins*. He also did a *Sea-Urchin Eater* and used this shellfish in numerous still lifes. From January 1947 on, the sea urchin was to meet with his owls, face to face in several of the pictures.

The great amount of work Picasso turned out between August and December of 1946 let him move somewhat away from his Parisian circle. His friends and the Party understood he was honeymooning. Éluard was the one assigned to keep an eye on him, but their close friendship made his company a pleasure. Not so for Françoise, who resented Éluard's holding her responsible for Dora Maar's mental illness; and Nush, she thought, was intriguing against her. Pablo thought only of enjoying Françoise and his painting.

The war period had seen the disappearance of some of the great contemporaries, Klee in 1940, Delaunay in 1941, Mondrian and Kandinsky in 1944. Matisse was now a virtual invalid. Bonnard, crushed by the death of his wife, was also to go, in January 1947.

Abstraction, not so long ago ignored or held to be a hoax, was now riding high, in the first waves of what was to be a tidal sweep. In the minuscule Galerie l'Esquisse, on Quai des Orfèvres, the young were discovering Kandinsky, who had had but one show in Paris during his lifetime, in 1929, totally unnoticed. As for Picasso at the Salon d'Automne, a few Beaux-Arts students, aided and abetted by extreme right-wing elements, threatened to sack the gallery, mumbling, beneath their ostentatiously patriotic accouterments, "The Germans would never have put up with this." Which was true. Nor would they have allowed the large Galerie Drouin, on Place Vendôme, to give the first major Parisian exhibition of abstract painting, or in March 1946 the first comprehensive Kandinsky retrospective.

But the popular press was all Picasso. His show at the Louis Carré Gallery was almost unanimously hailed—with only a few speculating on who would be next. Some saw as his successor André Marchand, making Pablo see red again—not entirely for artistic reasons. The young critics were now discovering (or perhaps, better, rediscovering) Calder's mobiles, introduced by the top current writer, the Father of Existentialism, Jean-Paul Sartre. Those who favored realism put forward the name of Gruber, whose *misérabilisme*, though somewhat literary in nature, answered some demands of the day. The only painter whose personality and works, both equally "scandalous," were reminiscent of the Picasso of the early days was Dubuffet. His show, wildly titled "Mirobolus, Macadam et Cie, Hautes Pâtes," at the Galerie Drouin, came just before Picasso's at the Louis Carré.

The great New York Museum of Modern Art Picasso retrospective, doubtless the most complete and finest ever put together, was held in 1946. Its organizer, Alfred H. Barr, Jr., did a catalog-album, *Picasso, Fifty Years of His Art*, a veritable compendium of his life and work. The book had immense influence not only in the United States but throughout the world, and remains to this day the model for such huge collections that attempt to encompass the whole of an oeuvre, its motivations and content.

In 1945, Ramón Gómez de la Serna, in Madrid, had published his *Completa y verídica historia de Picasso y el cubismo*, while Ceferino Palencia had also done an important study published in Mexico City. Sergio Solmi's *Disegni di Picasso* appeared in Milan along with Emilio Zanzi's *Redenzione di Picasso*. But the most original work of the period was by the Catalan critic Alexander Cirici Pellicer, *Picasso antes de Picasso* (Picasso Before Picasso).

In 1946, there were *Picasso, The Recent Years*, by Harriet and Sidney Janis, and *Picasso and the Ballet*, by William S. Lieberman, both published in New York; Christian Zervos' *Picasso*, Milan; and, at last, in Paris Jaime Sabartés' *Picasso: Portraits et Souvenirs* (published in New York as *Picasso: An Intimate Portrait*, translated by Angel Flores, Prentice-Hall, 1948), which mixes some excellent pages about the youth and beginnings with the most regrettable, and often ridiculous, of inventions. There are many mistakes, often deliberate, as well as omissions and confusions; his "rearranged" Picasso is far from the truth, which never seems to have been Jaime's principal preoccupation. His role—at times with Pablo's connivance—was to flesh out the Picasso myth, and take care of old grudges.

Henceforth, indeed, the "true" Picasso was to prove more and more elusive. Now came the day of the praisers, heralding that of the hagiographers, and it would be a long time before anyone dared touch the statue; those who did usually did so out of so blatant an anti-Communism as to make them meaningless. Time alone would bring percipient analyses of the man and his work. Interest in him and it would wane—and when rekindled in 1958–1960 would not always be of the best kind.

As usual paying little attention to what might be written about him, Picasso did, however, at times talk to some writers, usually replacing some true circumstance with a made-up story he felt to be more in character: his own statements about himself are in a sense the least trustworthy. But he did give an interview to a critic for the leftish *Arts de France* (No. 6, 1946) which, if not novel, bore out some of his past views:

> I am not in search of anything; I only try to put as much humanity as possible into my pictures. Too bad if that offends a few idolaters of the conventional human image . . . What, after all, is a face? Its photograph? Its makeup? Or the face as some painter portrayed it? What is before, inside, or behind it? How about the rest? Doesn't each of us see it in his own way? . . . I never painted anything but what I saw and felt . . .
>
> . . . Everything in painting is just a sign. So, what counts is what is signified, not how it is done. Yet there is a big difference between the sign and the word. The word "chair" doesn't mean anything. But a painted "chair" is already a sign. Its interpretation can go on infinitely . . .
>
> See these drawings? They are not the way they are because I was trying to stylize them. But what was superficial disappeared of its own accord. I was not doing anything "on purpose . . ." Of course, the only key to that sort of thing is poetry . . . If lines and shapes rhyme and come to life, it is in the way a poem does . . .

Since he never allowed notes to be taken during the interviews he gave, the words put in his mouth are a poor reflection of his thought—more often expressing the interviewer's opinion of him. The one formal plan, toward 1960, to have Dora Vallier transcribe his views came to naught, because he would not tolerate her making on-the-spot notes.

Picasso and Françoise returned to Paris in October 1946; before leaving for the Midi, from June 14 to July 13, he had done a series of portraits of his *amie* at Mourlot's. With oval face, almond-shaped eyes, well-formed mouth, heavy hair and long neck, she looked somewhat distant, indifferent, not to say stupid. She was, of course, intelligent. But, for Pablo, what matter? He made no secret of his passion for her, and on June 15 he had done, complete with paper cutouts, a *Françoise as the Sun* denoting the light that shone from her. To make his meaning more explicit, he completed this solar lithograph with a series of drawings showing two turtledoves mounting each other . . .

Back in Paris, he was again among friends but, except for the usual Spaniards, there were few painters among them. The young were notably absent. He might have their respect, but he belonged to another world, and his love for realism was irrelevant to their growing abstractionism. He had told his *Arts de France* interviewer:

> There is youth and youth . . . Youth has no age . . . Some of today's youth seem older than painters who died several centuries ago . . .

These obvious commonplaces were merely intended to create a gulf between them and him, as when he stated several times, "There is no such thing as abstract art." What indeed did the young have in common with this old man, keeping people abreast of the constancy of his sexual urges, his sympathy for the masses, and his insolent love of life? When Nicolas de Staël was looking for answers to the inner torments that turned his pictures into pathetic conflicts of forms, he went not to him but to Braque, whom he called "the greatest of living painters in the world." Nor did lyrical Wols and Mathieu, geometrical Dewasne, or baroque Atlan, the great hopes of the avant-garde in 1946–1947. We can only be amazed that such gentlemen as Claude Roger-Marx and André Warnod in *Le Figaro* lamented "the disastrous influence of Picasso and Matisse on the young." They were talking about the wrong generation.

Pablo was delightedly informing his friends that Françoise was pregnant, expecting this blessed event to afford him new ardors and new joys, as well as new paintings. She was less delighted.

Pablo had recently started changing: he had lost the long hair that came down to his shoulders; his drawn face was firmer, his hollow cheeks rounder, his gaze somewhat less intense. He seemed now more assured, weightier; in the photo taken at Toulouse in the winter of 1946, which he inscribed to Sabartés, who was on it with him, Picasso is indeed "Don Pablo" in his warm mackinaw, muffler, and beret. He looks the solid Spanish landowner, the *campesino* whose brow would wrinkle and eye cloud up at the thought of an unsatisfactory harvest.

There were not too many paintings in 1946–1947. True, the large panels at Antibes had taken up much of his time. Local reaction to them was far from entirely favorable, and when the château, finally refurbished, was opened to the public, there were to be protests and even attempts at vandalism which, unlike the Salon misdemeanors of 1944, could not reasonably be written off as the doing of French Fascists, Royalists, or collaborators.

It was now time to familiarize Françoise with the several vaults he had at the Banque Nationale pour le Commerce et l'Industrie (BNCI). When the guard there smiled broadly, and Pablo asked him what the joke was, Françoise relates that the man answered:

> "You're lucky. Most of the customers I've seen here in my time come in year after year with the same woman, always looking a little older. Every time you come in, you have a different woman and each one is younger than the last."

Next she was treated to a visit to Boisgeloup, empty for years now but still filled with most of Pablo's large statues. Paulo went with them. A few months later, in 1948, Picasso let the sculptor Adam move in there; he had also lent this artist a studio he had rented near his Rue des Grands-Augustins home to use for storing paintings.

Gertrude Stein had been taken seriously ill at Bernard Faÿ's at Le Luceau and rushed to the American Hospital at Neuilly, where she died July 27, 1946. Picasso heard of it while down south. He dropped a note to the grieving Alice B., but he was principally concerned with Gertrude's magnificent collection that contained so many of his own precious works. Miss Toklas, as legatee, kept it intact in large part until her own death in 1966, following which, in 1967/1968, the principal ones were bought by a syndicate made up of Friends and Trustees of the Museum of Modern Art, New York. Picasso never again saw its thirty-nine works of his most conquering periods.

Early on November 28, a phone call to Rue des Grands-Augustins informed him that "Little Nush died." Pablo broke down. Dora, who had also heard, arrived shortly thereafter, sobbing. Sabartés discreetly dismissed an American reporter who had a date to see Picasso. More grieving friends came in. Nush Éluard had collapsed on the street while doing errands, and her husband, in Switzerland, had been advised by wire. But since the telegram read "Madame Éluard," he had thought it referred to his mother.

Paul Éluard was so distraught, his friends feared he would lose his mind. Pablo and Dora went to the little apartment in Rue de la Chapelle where Nush lay, her husband shaking her gently as if to wake her. Nush had once been in a circus act with a hypnotist who put her to sleep and then placed huge stones on her chest and hammered them to bits without her feeling it. Now Éluard was convinced she was in such a cataleptic state and would soon come out of it.

When friends finally got him out to dinner in a restaurant, he was still sure the doctor had made a mistake in signing the death certificate, and he even convinced Picasso that when they got back to the apartment, there would be Nush alive.

The spring output was not too significant, everything being in abeyance until May 15, 1947, when Françoise had a son, Claude.

In January, there had been owls, as well as Inéz and her child, in several of the lithographs done at Mourlot's. They had alternated with mythological scenes such as *Fauns and Female Centaur, Centaurs Playing, Centaur and Bacchante with Faun,* and the women's heads, pigeons, and still lifes that were the subjects of a few paintings between February and April. His lithographic activity was most varied until the summer when, at Vallauris, Pablo did several zinc plates. A funereal ideogram of April 20, *The Black Bull,* had a massive body attached to a tiny head with pointed horns. The two nude women, one seated, the other lying asleep, on May 11, became the subject of a gray-and-black composition of sober beauty that was printed in fifty copies.

Picasso had been struck in a book by a reproduction of the Lucas Cranach *David and Bathsheba* from the Kaiser Friedrich Museum in Berlin. He used it as the basis of one of the re-creations he would be so fond of in the years ahead. He deeply appreciated this German painter, whose *Venus Bitten by Wasps* was in the fine collection of his friends Charles and Marie-Laure de Noailles.

David and Bathsheba appealed to him in its mixture of eroticism and ceremony, which he tried to capture in the series of lithographs begun on March 30, 1947, continued exactly a year to the day later in 1948, and then March 6 and April 12 and 17, 1949, covering more than two years.

This interpretation of *David and Bathsheba,* for Picasso, was the start of an indulgence in exuberant excessive costume, baroque fashions, later to lead him to the knights in wildly complicated armor and their heavily caparisoned steeds. He had always had a soft spot for disguises, liked to dress up in them, and did not blench at parody, however grotesque. He loved to have others join in the masquerade, and the strange hat on one of Bathsheba's ladies-in-waiting probably reminded him of the ones he used to put on Dora Maar. Besides, the theatrical character of the event as Cranach had presented it, transported to a framework and costumes of his own day, also appealed to Pablo; he gave the scene a "decorative" character that was accentuated by the arrangement of lines and excessiveness of dress, especially the delightfully outlandish hats with their plumes merging into the greenery.

It often happened that he came back, after quite lengthy periods, to one or another picture or print, and when he did he would carefully note the dates of execution on their backs. He had unquestionably forgotten his March 30, 1947, lithograph of *Bathsheba*, in its five states, when he came across the zinc a year later at Mourlot's. In its final state, the zinc had been worked on with a scraper, and he continued in that technique, skillfully arranging whites and blacks. Another year later, on March 6, 1949, he made few alterations, but when he brought back to Mourlot on April 12 the zinc that he had taken home with him, the whole spirit of the composition was changed.

Scraping tired him out, so he preferred erasing the blacks with gasoline, leaving the graven line, and he started from that drawing to complete the scene with wash and scraper.

In November 1948, he asked for the sixth state, dating back to March 30, to be transferred to the stone. He set the latter up on the big stove in his studio and left it there for several weeks. As Fernand Mourlot worried about what had become of it, Picasso told him he did not dare touch it: "It scares me." Which did not keep him from going back at it with a scraper again, arranging and rearranging the orchestration of blacks and whites, playing like a virtuoso on the tight network of arabesques, enthralled by the archaic spirit of the composition.

He left *David and Bathsheba* when he went south in June; prints had been pulled from the stone, but it was put aside in case he should want to come back to it, which he planned one day to do. He never did, however, and this state of May 9, 1949, remained final.

Picasso was delighted and proud to become a father at sixty-six. His son looked very much like him and was to look even more so as the years went by: same dark eye, square face, and smooth complexion. He was solid and well built. Come summer, they were all off to Golfe-Juan, Pablo stopping for a bit in Avignon, but then rejoining his "family," which now included not only Françoise and Claude, but also Maya, whom Marie-Thérèse more and more often "lent" to her father, and Paulo with his young wife and their children.

Olga, powerless but not inactive, stood by as all this was going on, writing virtually daily letters to the man who still by law was her spouse, mixing her Franco-Russian jargon with bits of bad Spanish to go into diatribes, reproaches, accusations, affection, regrets, and advice. Pablo was furious at these often overlong letters, yet read them all to the end; he punctuated his reading with Catalan insults and no less forceful comments. He blustered that they were making him sick, but each time Inéz brought in a letter from "Madame Olga," he rushed to tear it open; that was part of the game, as a few years before had been his weekly visits to his abandoned wife.

All of his wives and women, Sabartés, Paulo and family, and a few of the traditional Spanish parasites lived off him, to say nothing of his staff. He complained of this constantly, not hiding what he called his miserliness, and accused everyone, Kahnweiler foremost, of taking advantage of him; he took all of his fury out on poor Sabartés, who each night went home to his mate in their little apartment in the Fifteenth Arrondissement; she never set foot in the studio. But Jaime was not unhappy: he was living in the shadow of the greatest painter of the century, who kept repeating he could not live without him. Even with his temper, Picasso would be fine for Jaime to get along with, were it not for his women—Picasso's, of course.

Sabartés always hated the ones who shared Pablo's existence, whatever their position, whether the "recognized" ones or the one-night passersby, the latter being less repugnant to him, because of their very impermanence. He would gladly have found a new woman for Pablo each day, if he could be sure she would not return. Like the valets in farces, he had a special penchant for mystery and secrecy (the result, he said, of the fact that during the war any visitor unknown to him had seemed surely to belong to the Gestapo, or after Liberation to British Intelligence or the U.S. secret services). One day when Brassaï came in, Françoise relates that she asked him, "Ah, you've come to photograph all the sculptures?" only to have Sabartés reprimand her, "It's nobody's business how long he's here or what he's doing." When she replied that she had known Brassaï longer than she had Picasso, Sabartés snapped, "Then see him outside and ask him."

Jaime's antagonism toward Françoise did not end with the birth of Claude—quite the contrary, for the baby was frightened by Sabartés' thick glasses and howled whenever he came near. Inéz equally resented Mlle. Gilot, for as soon as Picasso had his own son, his interest in hers diminished. And she often showed her jealousy.

For some time, he had been besieged by an important American dealer, Samuel Kootz, whom Pablo used mainly as a threat to Kahnweiler, to raise the latter's prices. But Kahnweiler would not be moved; he detested Kootz, who in New York was pushing abstract art, so alien to him. Kootz had arrived at Pablo's, self-confident and voluble, waving the just-published book by Harriet and Sidney Janis, demanding to know whether the pictures reproduced in it still belonged to Picasso and what he wanted for them.

This delighted Pablo, who immediately sensed he might make good use of the enthusiastic millionaire with his cigars thick as chair rungs and his briefcase stuffed wth dollars. It would let him play hard to get not only with Kahnweiler but also with Louis Carré, Paul Rosenberg, whose business was not so good, and others (Léonce Rosenberg was to die shortly, on July 31, 1947, in a Neuilly clinic).

Kootz had no Picassos, but his gallery, opened in 1945 at the corner of Madison Avenue and 57th Street in New York, a leading avant-garde showcase, displayed the works of such American artists as Gottlieb, Glarner, Motherwell, Baziotes, and Browne. Since buyers were not rushing for these works yet, Gottlieb had suggested to Kootz that he go to Europe and get some Picassos to head his line-up and give stature to the gallery. That was how on a morning in December 1946 he had arrived at the home of Brassaï, whom he knew, got him out of bed, and virtually forced him to take him to Picasso's, to the dismay of Sabartés, who saw the whole operation as lèse majesté.

Kootz did not know what dealing with Picasso meant; he soon saw that his cigars and bankroll were cutting no ice, and that another approach would be needed. Picasso played for time by leafing leisurely through the Janis book, commenting at length, criticizing the quality of the reproductions, and leaving his visitor on tenterhooks. Kootz could hardly stand it, and kept vaunting the virtues of his gallery and his painters, while Sabartés somewhat scornfully translated. Finally, he came to the point: What was for sale? Sabartés turned a few pictures around, Kootz enthusiastically asked their prices, and, when told, immediately answered "Sold," each time. To which Picasso retorted, "Come back in June, and we'll see."

Now Pablo had someone to outbid Kahnweiler, Rosenberg, and Carré, especially Kahnweiler, who, he felt, was taking more interest in others, such as Léger, just back from America, whom Picasso detested. But his dealer was not one to be pushed around; he refused to raise his prices for the paintings, agreeing only to bring out and sell fifty-copy editions of the Mourlot lithographs. When Sam Kootz returned, Picasso sold him nine paintings, at top prices, and Kahnweiler was beside himself. The American came back to Rue des Grands-Augustins several times, each time carrying off some prizes, and in the summer of 1947 even visited him with Mrs. Kootz at Golfe-Juan. This time Picasso refused to accept payment for several paintings at the agreed-upon prices, took Sabartés to task for the deal, and finally turned on Kootz, accusing him publicly of "gypping" him.

Still, he did not break with Kootz, and continued to sell him paintings, so numerous, in fact, that Kahnweiler began to be worried, raised his prices, and in exchange was given a virtual exclusive on all the paintings, under conditions he has never been willing to reveal. Pablo went right on playing them one against the other, more for the intrigue of it than for the profit: his finest work, except during the actual years of the two world wars, always went to Kahnweiler. As Françoise related it in her book:

> . . . from time to time he would say, "I'd like Kootz to have that painting." When Kootz came to call, Pablo would tell him to go to Kahnweiler and pick up the painting he had earmarked for him. . . .
> One year he had Kootz ship him . . . a white Oldsmobile convertible, in exchange for a painting. That way he was able to tell Kahnweiler, "Oh, I gave him a picture because he sent me an automobile."

In Golfe-Juan, Picasso, Françoise, and little Claude with nursemaid were leading a peaceful life in M. Fort's house. Our young-old father-husband was reminded of the days when he had vacationed there with Olga and Paulo. Each year, at the end of July, nearby Vallauris feted its potteries, flowers, and perfumes. In 1946, at this fete, Pablo had met Georges and Suzanne Ramié, owners of the Madoura factory, who were fighting hard to revive the local ceramic art. He had spoken with them at length, and liked them, and they had timidly invited him to visit their workshop. Ever intrigued by new artistic techniques, he had gone there, asked all kinds of questions, tried his hand at the craft: it was July 26, 1946, a date they would never forget, when at Mme. Ramié's suggestion Picasso picked up two balls of clay and fashioned two bulls and a faun. They were baked a few days later, and he was asked to come and see, but never did. The Ramiés thought it had just been a lark for him.

For several years, he had been friendly with Jean Cassou, who had published several works about him. A very active Resistance member, Cassou had been named by the Algiers Committee to be Commissioner for the Republic in the Toulouse region. On the night of August 19–20, 1944, his car had been attacked by a German patrol and, under an assumed name, Cassou had been taken, at the point of death, to a hospital. It was months before he recovered, and by then the reestablished French government named him Curator of the Museum of Modern Art, to start virtually from scratch.

Cassou set to the herculean task of filling the museum's collection, which, because of lack of interest of previous Fine Arts bureaucrats, was almost without any living art. He turned to those artists he knew, first of all Picasso. The museum occupied the buildings between Avenue du Président-Wilson and Quai de Tokyo, built for the 1937 Exposition. It was to take over from the Luxembourg Museum, which, pell-mell, housed only "official" art. The French national collections owned only one Picasso, the 1901 portrait of Gustave Coquiot, and other contemporary masters were not much better represented. Moreover, the Picasso was kept at the Jeu de Paume, with the "foreign schools."

"I won't sell you anything," Picasso told Cassou. "But I'll give you something." And he made a date for him to come back. When he did, the amazed Cassou was confronted with a gift of twelve pictures. Aragon, who was along, was no less stunned. Before the two men's speechlessness, Picasso asked, "What's the matter? Are there too many?"

It was Aragon who gave its title to *L'Aubade,** the famous 1942 painting in a geometrical style of majestic simplicity, showing a woman playing a mandolin to another lying on a divan. Among the others included were *The Milliner's Workshop* (1925), *The Muse* (1935), *Still Life with Oranges* (1936), a *Woman's Portrait* (1938), *Rocking Chair* and *Still Life with Cherries* (both 1943), *Woman in Blue* (1944), *Enamel Cooking Pot* (1945), and a *Figure,* neither dated nor signed. Two years before, Paul Rosenberg had given the museum a *Still Life with Antique Head* of 1925.

Following this Picasso donation, Éluard, in memory of his wife, gave Cassou the wonderful portrait of Nush of August 19, 1941.

This spectacular and impressive acquisition did not move the government to go after any additional Picassos. The French museum administration merely bought a 1914 gouache-and-pasted-paper, *The Glass,* in 1950; its Commission of Artistic Recovery the same year added an unsigned *Woman's Head* (1924); and

* Literally, "Morning Music" or "Morning Love Song," known in English as *Nude with a Musician.* (TR. NOTE)

in 1952 the collector Raoul La Roche donated two Picasso still lifes, of 1914 and 1924. The administration did, however, buy one piece of ceramic, *Vase with Dancers,* bearing the artist's fingerprint, on June 24, 1950.

After the paintings had been hung at the museum, Pablo accepted Cassou's invitation to inspect their presentation, which he approved; he even repaired one canvas that had been accidentally streaked. That was the sum total of his relations with the Musée d'Art moderne. A few years later, Cassou asked him to help on a project dear to his heart, an exhibition of his sculptures, but it never materialized.

Apart from the Musée Grimaldi at Antibes, the Musée d'Art moderne in Paris was the only one in France with any overview of Picasso's work. He was well over sixty, his reputation for years had been great throughout the world, yet French officials were still leery of him. There was reluctance in high places when the city of Antibes decided, with a little prompting from him, to name the museum after him. They were afraid that thus honoring a living artist might create a dangerous precedent!

The whole of the Picasso oeuvre owned by the Musée national d'Art moderne (some eighty items at the artist's death in 1973) was significant, but in no way comparable to those of the great, well-endowed American museums which own some of his major works. Not only did France not bid on any of them; it did not even try to stop them from leaving the country.

Following his 1947 gift to Cassou, Picasso's relations with French officialdom did not change, except, perhaps, as a result of several unfortunate incidents, to get worse. At his death, he willed nothing to the national museums, although his heirs, Jacqueline and Paulo, gave the government thirty-seven paintings from his collection and eleven monotypes by Degas, some of these paintings becoming the subject of much dispute.

In the summer of 1947, abstract painting caught on in Paris, and the abstract/objective argument split dealers, critics, and artists, while Picasso, uninterested and unconcerned, bathed with his family at Golfe-Juan.

Why not go over to the Ramiés' and see what had become of those pottery experiments from last year? A half-hour later, Suzanne Ramié was amazed to see Pablo and Françoise get out of their car in front of the factory. She and her husband had seen them a little earlier sunbathing on the beach, said hello, and mentioned those pieces that had been sitting there for months. His curiosity had flared. Why not drop back to Madoura one of these days? Well, he had work to do at the Antibes château. He'd see if he could find time . . .

When he did come, he had with him dozens of sketches done during the winter for more ceramics. Not only had he not forgotten, he was ready to go on with the work. "If you'll give me a workman to help out with the technical side, I'll come back and work seriously," he told them.

Yet, he wanted to complete what he had started at Antibes. Dor de la Souchère was not showing the public the panels he had already painted and was planning to complete, because the building was in such disrepair, and he had no money to restore the rooms. The curator talked to the mayor, M. Pugnière, who could see the importance of this job, and they went to Paris together to see the Historical Monuments administration. Dor de la Souchère was amazed that the magic words, "Picasso is working at my place," were met with indifference. Only after months of stalling, and all kinds of paper work, did the French Building Department make available fifty million francs (then $100,000) with strings attached.

Senator Cuttoli and his wife, who had important government contacts, did what they could to help La Souchère, and told Picasso that the government would feel better disposed if he were to make a gift of his paintings to the Antibes Museum. Françoise tells how Cuttoli suggested this during a luncheon at Golfe-Juan, and the painter flew into a rage. Had he not even been told that things would go better if he got naturalized? The national museums were displeased because he had done his work in a small municipal museum, apparently unworthy of interest. Why not extend his future generosity to the National Museum of Modern Art, which was of a different caliber than the half-ruined Château of Antibes that no one ever went to? The man in charge of all the national museums, Georges Salles, was an old friend, and would be able to "reroute" the works Picasso had done at Antibes to Paris—but the artist absolutely refused to hear of this.

That luncheon at Golfe-Juan had been very hectic. As Mme. Cuttoli recounted it, "Pablo had misunderstood my husband. He never suggested that he forsake his Spanish nationality. That would have been insulting. But when Picasso is angry, there is nothing for it, and that day he was especially wild. My husband didn't know what to say, and was most bothered. Since Picasso refused to make any outright donation, my husband finally found a formula: he suggested he legally entrust them to the State, which left him ownership while the government kept and protected them. They could not be moved without agreement of both parties. This Picasso accepted."

Georges Salles also agreed, and Picasso, under Marie Cuttoli's urging, "entrusted" a number of paintings and drawings to the Grimaldi, while she in turn made it a gift of several works she owned, notably the famous *Two Women* tapestry that had been made in her own workshop in the old days. Later, Picasso was to add to these some more drawings and ceramics, and would often come to visit "his" rooms and Dor de la Souchère, usually with friends.

On June 19, 1948, Pablo wrote Marie-Thérèse Walter, "I learn to paint all day long. I even think I've made some progress. I'm making painted sculptures."

Few painters have been interested in ceramics for, with few exceptions, they have seen it only as an ancillary endeavor. To Picasso, who for the past months had been painting little and seemed somewhat weary of pictures, it was a revelation; that was why he had worked so hard the winter before. Now he needed a stimulant, particularly a craftsmanlike stimulant; there were times when the workman came to the surface in him. He delved into all aspects of the technics of ceramics, but, not content to mold simple shapes, he handled the clay so innovatively that the workers were at a loss, and he had to "bend" the material himself, remembering pottery that he had seen in his youth at Málaga. Intensely visual, he dredged up all sorts of things he had seen, what he knew of old Mediterranean traditions, from Crete, Mycenae, and ancient Greece, even Persia and the Orient. His artistic vocabulary borrowed from all of them, to form one style: his own.

His hands could accomplish wonders. Of course, he had worked in clay before, and sculpture had no secrets for the wizard, as he fashioned vases of bacchantes with arms for handles, she-fauns who were bottles or pitchers. On the bulge of a jar or in the curve of a cup a nude bather appeared, a faun danced, a centaur reared . . . Nothing could resist his eye and hand; in a trice, he became the main attraction and soul of the pottery, all the workers working with and through him. Immersed in the piece he was doing, he would comment as the latest ones came out of the kiln, "See, we oughn't to have done that . . . This is better . . . Look. See, this is how it ought to be done . . ."

"It was terrific," one old worker said. "He made us want to 'hump it,' and believe me, we hadn't been shirking!"

The main turner, M. Lagar, sounded like the workers at Mourlot's or Lacourière's, with a Provençal accent added. "One day," he says, "I was turning a piece over a meter high when Picasso came into the shop. 'Oh, what's that you've made me?' he asked. 'What a beautiful shape!' He came closer and with four thumb strokes turned it into a woman, a beautiful brilliant nude, then asked for some clay turds and made her two arms. It was finished . . ."

He had rediscovered the secrets of this great folk art, its simplicity and directness, but unfortunately before long would abandon his early creative verve with its spontaneity, fantasy, and whimsical humor for a more sophisticated manner, which little by little, because of the quantity of production and the repetitive procedures, would tend toward systematization. Some days he did twenty or twenty-five different pieces, and the Ramiés, basking in his glory and the attendant prosperity, echoed all others in praising his work to the skies.

In one year, October 1947–October 1948, working at the Ramiés' each afternoon, he turned out almost two thousand pieces; 150 of them were exhibited in November 1948 at the Maison de la Pensée française in Paris. This was an event: under the wing of the Party, his idolaters flocked enthusiastically to it, while he and Françoise merely dropped by the day before the opening to approve the layout.

A photo by the UNESCO photographer Chamude, through one of the glass cases at the Maison de la Pensée française, shows Picasso in dark beret and cape looking at some of the works. The attentive old gentleman seems both sharp and distant, like those who see beyond things; he no longer is called upon to create an oeuvre, that is, to give answers, but, being one of those privileged ones whom humanity expects always to upset or overawe them, to assume a destiny. Because life gives them orders; and the opposite of life—its destination as well—is death.

Léon Moussinac set the tone for the celebration of Picasso, seeing in the ceramics

. . . the harbinger of the social role the artist will play in tomorrow's society . . . Clay and fire, in Picasso's hands, become for us the living representation of matter and mind, their struggle and their victory . . . (*Les Lettres françaises,* December 2, 1948)

Jean Bouret, in *Les Arts* (November 26), had been more temperate:

Picasso's experiment moves us . . . mainly because he felt the need to go back to sources, to make contact with the manual side of this art [ceramics], to manufacture it. One would think he had needed a new strength which the earth alone could give him. . . .

Picasso, as usual, remained unmoved by the approbation, particularly passionate among women writers. His work at Vallauris, like the Antibes panels, was only one phase of his activity; he was wallowing in the themes and myths of the Mediterranean, enjoying a pantheistic Arcadian sensuality. His Party comrades were allowed, at a distance, to watch him on the beach through constant coverage in *L'Humanité,* and know that each day he went to work at the Madoura factory —even in the heat of August!

A worker among workers, he was quick to stand a round of drinks for the ceramic and pottery workers who, like their predecessors at Mourlot's, felt that because of "Monsieur Picasso" they were first in the world. Which did not keep him from answering, when a newswoman asked him whether he had learned much from the potters, "What could they teach me, since they know nothing?"

Pablo's infrequent visits to Paris during the first ceramic period of 1947–1948 were largely spent at Mourlot's, Lacourière's, Kahnweiler's, or with friends. In Vallauris, in order to be closer to the workshop, he had taken a little house at the top of the village, La Galloise, resembling a railroad-crossing guard's shack. There he was finishing his illustrations for the Reverdy and Góngora poems, being vsited by Miró, and going to see Matisse at Vence. Tériade sometimes came over from St.-Jean-Cap-Ferrat, or Pablo went to see him, meeting Braque or Reverdy there. Once or twice a month, Fernand Mourlot would come down from Paris with zinc plates, and take back the ones Picasso had cut since his last visit; that was how *Le Chant des Morts* was completed.

The work at Madoura had appreciably reduced Picasso's painting output, but engraving still delighted him. Besides the Góngora etchings, in 1947 he did six plates for Iliazd's *Escrito,* and after finishing the Reverdy in 1949 made thirty-eight burins for *Carmen,* and in 1950 thirty-two etchings for Aimé Césaire's *Corps perdu.* In 1952, there were ten etchings for Adrian de Monluc's *La Maigre,* in 1953 six burins for Maurice Toesca's *Six Contes fantastiques,* in 1955 six celluloid cuts for Tristan Tzara's *Haute Flamme,* in 1956 thirty-three drypoints and burins for *Chevaux de minuit* by Roch Grey, and three drypoints and three lithographs for Max Jacob's *Chronique des Temps héroïques.* In 1950, he had done nine lithographic plates for the publisher Pierre Bordas, to illustrate Tzara's *De mémoire d'homme.*

After the lithographic surge of 1945–1946, etching was a different exercise for Pablo—if not a new technique, at least one renovated by the work he had done at Mourlot's and his recently acquired new experience with lines, rhythms, and light contrasts. Engraving allowed for more complex, deeper "cooking up" than did lithography; it could also be the testing place or continuation of painting, and sometimes its further deepening—a black-and-white transposition of what he had accomplished in color. It was rigor, ascesis, direct dialogue between oneself and the plastic phenomenon.

From 1949 to 1953, he did many, many etchings and drypoints for writer and publisher friends: René Char, Claude Roy, Tristan Tzara, Sabartés, Éluard, Pablo Neruda, André Villers, Hélène Parmelin, Reverdy, Cassou, Aragon, Jean Cocteau, P.-A. Benoît, and others. His 1952 lithographs were mainly those of *The Unclasped Hands* that he did for the poster of the Second World Peace Congress at Vienna in December (dissatisfied with them, he finally selected instead an etching of *Dove Flying*) and a couple of Doves.

When Pablo was in Paris in November, Mourlot asked him to do a portrait of Balzac for a deluxe edition of *Père Goriot* that André Sauret was planning. Mourlot had come to see him at 7 Rue Gay-Lussac, an apartment he had bought in Françoise's name and, just in case, had brought along what was needed for the work. The next morning, Pablo phoned him: during the night he had made eight lithographic drawings, in ink on transfer paper, numbered I through VIII, as well as three large compositions, all variations on Balzac's superbly expressive face, which came through in a surprising "likeness," for all of Picasso's graphic exploits.

A few days later he was back in Vallauris for a short stay, doing three portraits of Paloma, Françoise's second child, born to them three years before. From Balzac to the little girl playing with her doll, the experimental gamut was the same, and Pablo's inventive spirit, ever based in reality, remained equally lively. As Éluard wrote:

> All of Picasso's models look like their portraits. His drawing restores things to their truth, for out of an infinitely variable appearance, made up of myriad flashes, he distills one constant, eternalizes the sum of the images, totalizes his experiences.

The Communists were delighted that Picasso, far from locking himself in an ivory tower as he used to, mixed with the masses, and behaved in a way they could approve of. Éluard came often to Vallauris. After the awful shock of Nush's brutal death, he kept pursuing her memory in the places where they had been happy together. Picasso was not one to calm or discourage this obsession, but he did not hide the fact that Paul often got on his nerves with it—the more so, he said, since Éluard was secretly getting his jollies with a young couple.

He was the Party's "eye" on Pablo, as the Leirises had been Kahnweiler's. The Communists, deep in an active antiwar campaign, properly felt that the painter of *Guernica* ought to be part of it: the "dirty war" that had begun in Indochina in December 1946 was again the object of their propaganda. Pablo, urged by Éluard and his old friend Ilya Ehrenburg, agreed to attend the Congress of Intellectuals for Peace, at Wroclaw, Poland, in August 1948.

Since he hated travel so, and had scarcely been out of France, it was a meaning-

Picasso and Françoise Gilot at La Galloise
(DOISNEAU RAPHO)

ful gesture, whatever motivations or meanings may be imputed to it. For he was leaving Vallauris in midsummer, in the middle of his work. Nor was he asked merely to be an extra: he was to be a star at the Congress and make a public speech.

On August 22, Picasso left Golfe-Juan in his car, driven by Marcel, stayed three days in Paris, and then, with his chauffeur, flew to Poland, accompanied by Éluard and Vercors. The day before he left, August 24, Jules Moch, Socialist Minister of the Interior, presented "Monsieur Pablo Ruiz Picasso" the alien-category Silver Medal of French Gratitude "for signal services rendered to France."

He stayed in Poland about a fortnight, during which Éluard never let him out of his sight. The first four days were spent at the Congress at Wroclaw, then three in Warsaw, two in Cracow, and the last six again in Warsaw for official receptions and ceremonies. The press enthusiastically greeted the arrival of Picasso with Éluard and Vercors, as well as Irène Joliot-Curie, Fernand Léger, Pierre Daix, and Maurice Bedel. Writers, artists, poets, professors, and intellectuals of every category and all countries outdid one another in their tributes to "the greatest of living painters," "the workers' friend," "our brother Pablo Picasso," as Maurice Thorez called him.

Ehrenburg, who had gone to the airport to greet his friend "Chort," the devil, as he called him, took him in charge, acted as his guide through Warsaw, slowly recovering from its wartime ruins, and with Vercors, Éluard, Pierre Daix, and a few others, went with him to Cracow, where the Czartoryski Museum, closed since the start of World War II, was reopened in his honor. They admired Leonardo's *Lady in Ermine,* and when Vercors started to expatiate in front of Rembrandt's *Landscape with the Good Samaritan,* Pablo interrupted with "Cut it out. Against talent, none of that stands up . . ." They also visited the Wawell Castle and the concentration camps at Auschwitz and Birkenau.

Picasso met many artists, mainly architects. The painters, who mostly practiced "socialist realism," were rather reticent toward him, considering him a "bourgeois artist" and filthy capitalist: either his painting repelled them or they held it to be unintelligible to the masses. As for the ones in the avant-garde movements, they felt about him as did the young French artists: he was a has-been who did not interest them, good only as window dressing.

The Soviets, in spite of Ehrenburg, were also visibly leery of him. The novelist Fadeyev, speaking for their delegation, told him that frankly he could not make out some of his works.

"Why do you choose such inaccessible forms?" he asked.

"Tell me, Comrade Fadeyev," said Picasso, "were you taught to read in school?"

"Of course," said the nonplussed writer.

"How?" asked Picasso.

"Well, B-A, BA . . ."

"B-A, BA, the same way I was taught! But did anyone teach you to understand painting?"

Fadeyev laughed at the joke, and agreed he had been stupid—but that was the last Picasso heard from him.

Through earphones, Picasso devotedly followed the Congress sessions, and seemed to be enjoying it, until he jumped at hearing Fadeyev call Sartre a "typewriting hyena." He tore his earphones off, while the French delegation became livid with rage. Some wanted to leave and go back to Paris, but it was finally smoothed over, and Pablo made his speech in defense of Pablo Neruda, imprisoned in Chile. On September 2, in Warsaw, the President of Poland gave him the commander's cross with star of the Order of Polish Renascence, "for his eminent contribution to the work of international cultural cooperation and his efforts in the field of Franco-Polish friendship."

Before leaving, Pablo bought embroidered sheepskin coats for Françoise and Claude; he painted his son wearing his on October 23. One evening at Warsaw's Hotel Bristol, where they were staying, Ehrenburg posed for Picasso, who drew his pencil portrait so fast that the Russian was amazed. "I've known you for forty years," Pablo laughingly reminded him. While there, he also did a portrait of a pretty young Spanish woman, Mercedes Arcas.

He had promised Françoise that he would write often; he did not, but each day sent her a telegram ending "BONS BAISERS." This being a working-class kind of salutation that neither Pablo nor Éluard would have used, it meant that he had asked the chauffeur Marcel to handle this daily chore. "When he returned," she says, "I was in a black mood."

While he was performing for the Party at Wroclaw, the French press of the same stripe was carrying on a violent campaign against abstract art, which some intellectuals claimed had "sold out to the Americans"! They were all for "socialist realism," first known as "new realism," which was represented by very mediocre artists. The "bourgeois" papers, and the traditionalist, nonabstract galleries, looking for a non-Communist young artist to hold up against the Party's hacks, hit upon Bernard Buffet, a starving young painter who worked in a monochrome misérabilisme that was not without character. He was awarded the Critics' Prize for 1948.

There were other names being mentioned, although not yet well known, as those of the men of talent in the small avant-garde circles and galleries: Mathieu, Bryen, Hartung, Wols, Schneider, Soulages, Poliakoff, Atlan . . . Were they the masters of tomorrow? Not one of them considered himself akin to Picasso, who one day was to be heard to say, "Balthus is the most important of the French painters."

His Little Hubert and Thérèse Blanchard along with two Mirós were the three works by living painters in the lot Picasso's heirs gave to the Louvre.

XX

WAR
AND PEACE
(1949–1953)

"**P**ICASSO IS DINING AT PICASSO'S" SAID A HUGE SIGN HANGING from the mantel of La Galloise, the ordinary, and only relatively well appointed, house he had selected at Vallauris. The place was alive with friends come for the housewarming.

He had moved here, not only to be closer to the Madoura factory, but also to get away from Olga, who had followed him to Golfe-Juan, where, making friends with Mme. Fort, the wife of Pablo's engraver-landlord, she did her best to importune Françoise. She accosted her on the street, shouted curses at her, and created such public scandals that Picasso asked his friend Senator Cuttoli to have a word with the police about Olga. Marie Cuttoli thought he even considered having her locked up . . .

The police kept her quieted down, until the day when she engaged in a hair-pulling contest with Françoise on the Golfe-Juan beach. Picasso was used to "his" women fighting over him, but never before had there been such a spectacle of it—especially with one forty years older than the other.

Françoise, beside herself, was not helped any by Pablo's wry amusement at the whole affair. Paulo was also living in Golfe-Juan, uninclined, after his failed marriage, to earn a living; his father had to keep him employed. He was to become the chauffeur after Marcel was fired for using one of Picasso's cars for a family outing, smashing it against a tree. Besides the Kootz Olds, there was a Chrysler, a present from an American friend. And had it not been for Olga's machinations, Pablo might have been quite serene, surrounded by his *cuadrilla* of Françoise and Claude, Paulo and Marcel. There was soon to be a second baby, Paloma, born April 19, 1949, and a new member of the group, a boxer dog named Yan.

Claude was now his favorite model, as Maya and Paulo had been in their day, and as for them he made toys, wood or cardboard dolls that he daubed with paint, or broke up cardboard boxes to make funny figures. There are numerous portraits of the boy, many of them with his mother.

Woman against Starry Background (February–March 1949) shows a pregnant Françoise seated in the armchair that earlier had held Olga, Dora, and several others. Hieratic, vaguely distant, with her fine well-fed infanta's face, she good-naturedly let Pablo be as cruel to her artistically as he wished.

We see her posed before an admirable night view dotted with stars, her features bathed in light, wide-open uneven and slightly terrified eyes, as Dora's used to be when the Ogre stared at her, small round mouth, all admirably "caught" by Pablo's brush . . . But suddenly he dropped this canvas to start another: on the same day, he portrayed her face in a tragic greenish phosphorescence, head all surrounded by a network of red wires barbed with excrescences. Here a brown spot, there an ocher streak, knotted forms, chaotic masses—all of which may have masked some drama in his life.

There was violence, a sort of iconoclastic determination, such as Pablo had not demonstrated for a long time, in these pictures of Françoise that seemed to bring back a whole past of nightmare and obsessions. Perhaps the domestic difficulties—painfully recounted by her in *Life with Picasso*—were at the basis of these furies. Was Pablo taking revenge on his young mistress's face for the inevitable quarrels that the ambiguity of their relationship and the difference in their ages more and more often triggered? Two lithographs of March 8 aggressively dissect her features into grotesque trunklike masks; they are titled simply *Composed Face*.

The Communists were preparing a World Peace Congress to be held in Paris at the Salle Pleyel in April 1949, and for several months he was constantly attended by the Party intellectuals. Apart from Éluard and Aragon, Jean Laffitte, Jean Marcenac, Jean Kanapa, Léon Moussinac, and others were always at his side, and Pablo, who hated or avoided almost everyone, found their devotion very touching. After all, the younger artists and critics paid little attention to him except for his shows, and he appeared most often in the gossip columns.

Bonnard, who had just died in 1947, Villon, Matisse, Braque, Léger, Rouault, even Derain despite the problems he had had after his conduct under the occupation, were the masters the young respected and often even admired. None of the gossipmongers would dream of trying to interview Braque turning somersaults on the beach, Matisse feeling up Lydia, or Derain in Montparnasse coming out of his girl friend's place, a young girl friend who had just presented him with a child, at about the same age as Pablo! But the latter was always out front, to be seen, heard, ogled, photographed. It was no surprise that Hélène Parmelin, whose unquestioning admiration for him is beyond cavil, titled her book of anecdotes and impressions of him *Picasso sur la place* (Picasso on the Square) (in the English-language edition: *Picasso Plain*).

He had not much use for Aragon, whom he found precious, especially since the latter never stopped raving about Matisse, Matisse's colors, Matisse's light, Matisse's sense of taste and order so wondrously classical and French—everything that made our Malagueño envious of his old rival. To Aragon's displeasure, he

Dove of Peace lithograph   Paris January 9, 1949

constantly reminded him what a shy young fellow he had been when he came up the Rue La Boétie elevator to beg a frontispiece for his first "slim volume" of verse.

Pablo had even less use for Aragon's wife, Elsa Triolet, because her Russian accent was so much like Olga's, and he set her down, not unreasonably, among the bluestockings. The Aragons at times brought the top Communist leaders—Maurice Thorez, Jacques Duclos, or Laurent Casanova—to see him. Picasso was both irritated and flattered, but he knew so well how many people, beginning in the first instance with Kahnweiler, would be furious at his seeing them and being photographed with them, that he greeted these visitors with delight.

In Spring 1949, Aragon came to him at Rue des Grands-Augustins to select a drawing for the poster for the World Congress of Partisans of Peace, Paris, April 20–23. Pablo opened his folders to him. Riffling through, Aragon noticed a lithograph done at Mourlot's in January—January 9 to be exact. It was a pigeon huddled upon itself, its feathers silky lustrous, white on black ground, with a small tuft of feathers behind the head. The tones of the lithograph were very delicate, a result Pablo had achieved by mixing lithographic ink with wash.

Aragon took one look at the pigeon: pigeon to dove, dove to peace, was but one more step. And thus was born the Dove of Peace, henceforth destined to circle the world. It was almost noon; Aragon rushed to the printer's with the print. A few hours later, *The Dove of Peace* was coming off the presses.

"Poor guy!" mused Picasso, over Aragon's delight. "He doesn't know the first thing about pigeons! The sweetness of the dove, some laugh! There are no crueler animals. I've had doves here that pecked to death a little hen-pigeon they didn't like. They pecked her eyes out! They tore her to bits—horribly! Some symbol for the peace movement!"

Nevertheless, when he saw the proofs of the poster, he said, OK for the *Dove of Peace*. To his great delight, his Party comrades would bring that lithograph to a worldwide audience. Who else could have done it? Who else was that interested in him? It was the Party that had come to his support, helped him contend with his fame, brought him forth on platforms before the people, among intellectuals and artists of the world, let him speak out for an imprisoned poet—and poets had always been his life's companions.

In July 1950, for the Second World Peace Congress, to be held in London, he did a *Dove in Flight,* of which he executed several versions the same day before deciding on the last, more vigorous than its three predecessors through his using the stick of lithographic ink without wetting it.

He drew more doves in October 1952 for the Third Congress, to be held in Vienna in December. He had first planned a poster called *Clasped Hands,* a circle of hands and arms forming a chain around the dove in flight, but he did not like that, and instead did a superb "exploded" Dove against a rainbow background. To his amazement, the heads of the peace movement turned it down as unintelligible. People, they said, would not understand the dove cut up in various pieces flying through space, and it would be misinterpreted! (" 'They' say people will think the dove is atomized!" he grumbled, hurt and offended.)

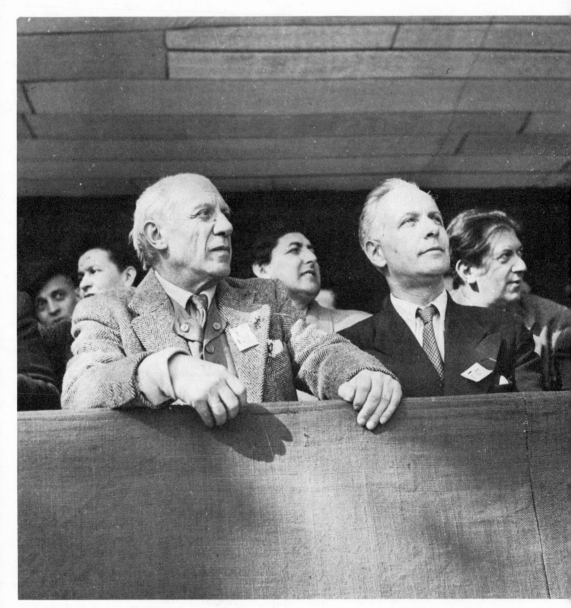

Picasso and Aragon at the World Congress of Partisans of Peace, May 1949

(ROGER-VIOLLET)

But the Picasso Dove became known and familiar to everyone, even those opposed to the "Red peace," those who felt Picasso was just another Communist hoax, and thought the two main eyewashes of our time deserved each other.

But Communist euphoria before his *Dove of Peace* was almost delirious; Pablo Neruda, freed from prison, proclaimed, "Picasso's Dove is flying around the world, and none can stop it in its flight . . ."

Georges Salles, knowing that several members of the Council of Museums disliked Picasso's painting, had the canvases Pablo gave to the Musée d'Art moderne transported to the Louvre, not only so they might see them, but also because the artist had asked to see his works alongside some of the Louvre masterpieces before the latter were rehung, now that they were back from their wartime hideaways.

Pablo got there with Françoise at 11:00 A.M., an unusually early hour for him. Salles tells of taking him to where his paintings were and how the guards then carried them down to the various halls. "Put them near some Zurbaráns," said Picasso, in a voice trembling with emotion. Several were set up near *St. Bonaventure on His Bier,* one of the Spanish golden-century works that meant most to Don Pablo. Nearby were the Velázquezes, the Murillos, the Goyas. He looked them all over, silently, while those present tried to divine the reaction in his intensely impressive eyes. Finally, in a quiet, as if pacified, voice, he said, "See, they're the same thing." And repeated, "The very same thing."

He also had them set up near various Delacroixes and Courbets, but when asked whether he wanted to try the Italian schools, he thought a few moments, and then said all he would have liked was to see a Cubist painting alongside an Uccello—but they had no Cubist work at hand, so he concluded, "That's enough for today."

He and Françoise walked back to Rue des Grands-Augustins along the Seine, Pablo not uttering a word. There were friends at the studio and, after a bit, as if coming out of a dream, he related the trip to the Louvre and the experiment he had tried: what struck him most was seeing his pictures near the Zurbaráns, and the fact that the great Spanish masters' works did not eclipse his own. After all, he said, they were all one family.

Meanwhile, as Antonina Vallentin points out, *The Dove of Peace* was becoming more popular than Millet's *Angelus,* more ubiquitous than the traditional Post Office calendar. The clearest, most appealing work by the most incomprehensible of painters, the least likely to reach the people, was now conquering the world—not only from museum to museum, and exhibition to exhibition, but on factory and workshop walls, in the humblest of dwellings, students' rooms, workers' centers . . .

But the peace symbol was not appreciated by official America. And some of the Party scribes did their best to harp on the "poisoned arrows" that the State Department might try to shoot it down with. Much of it just verbiage—but it upset Kahnweiler, who was afraid of Picasso's losing American collectors and museums. For all that the Dove became the symbol of the American peace movement, however, the Philadelphia Academy of Fine Arts gave the lithograph its

Pennell Memorial Medal when it was exhibited in New York at the Buchholz Gallery in the fall of 1949.

On August 6, 1950, on the main square of Vallauris, the little town where Picasso lived and worked, which he was to make famous, his *Man with the Sheep* was unveiled. For several months, the bronze had waited in the abandoned chapel of an old priory built by the monks of Lérins. Now, beneath the plane trees in front of the church, the crowds gathered in sunshine and dust: young and old, girls in bright dresses, potters, tourists; the Party represented by Laurent Casanova, reading a manifesto-speech that stated the CP stand on art; the municipality headed by the mayor, M. Derigon; Picasso in rumpled trousers and white shirt with sleeves rolled up; Françoise, wearing a flowered shirtmaker; Éluard; Tristan Tzara; the young local poet André Verdet, reciting a poem. Up on a balcony, behind the statue, above a banner reading "To Picasso, Grateful Vallauris," Jean Cocteau with his friend Mme. Weisweiler, the screenwriters Pierre Bost and Jean Aurenche, and others; and in the evening under Japanese lanterns there would be dancing around the *Man with the Sheep.*

"You know," Picasso was to tell Verdet a few months later, "my *Man with the Sheep* looked much better in that old chapel . . . It had a tone to it, it took off . . . Here, on the square, it's diminished. Don't you agree? Besides, the pedestal isn't right for it, it's too big. The statue disappears up into the trees. Funny—the *Man with the Sheep* doesn't breathe as well in the greenery as it did back between the old chapel walls . . . There, it came from way off . . ." And then he added, laughingly, "You know, one night I felt like getting up secretly and going down there and painting the *Man with the Sheep.*"

Verdet, who, after writing poetry, was to become a painter and sculptor, was a kind of symbol of friendship and poetry for Pablo in old Vallauris. They had met in St.-Paul-de-Vence, when Pablo, sitting on the terrace of the Café de la Place, with Jacques Prévert, noticed that one of the boules players he was watching had a concentration-camp number tattooed on his forearm. Prévert, who knew him, introduced them, and Pablo and Verdet became close friends, sharing many interests, pretty vacationers and local belles not the least among them. Verdet wrote some beautiful poems about the painter, as well as fervent analytical studies and tributes. Pablo did not forget him when Verdet, still suffering the aftereffects of his deportation, had to go to the mountains at Le Sappey, above Grenoble, for a rest cure in 1953.

One morning, he relates, the hotelkeeper woke him to say, "Monsieur Verdet, there are two young ladies downstairs to see you." He was expecting no one, and it was April Fool's Day; he thought it was a joke and went back to sleep. The innkeeper called again, and Verdet finally got up and went downstairs, to find what he calls "two superb panthers, two American girl students, one a brunette, the other blond, who said to me, 'Monsieur Picasso sent us. He said you were bored up here in the mountains, and we were to entertain you. And to make sure we'd do as he said, he kept our passports . . .'"

The two young ladies really did "entertain" Verdet for four whole days, throwing their hearts and souls into it, and then went back to Paris, where Picasso returned their passports, since they had completed their mission. While there, they also "entertained" the old faun; his drawings of them, to quote Verdet, revealed that he too had become privy to the most delectable details of their anatomies.

Cocteau at Vallauris for the *Man with the Sheep* do was openly playing footsie with the Communist Party, but since he had performed many another political somersault in his day, no one was too impressed by it. His honeymoon with Picasso, resumed at the end of the occupation, was at its height; he sang the praises of the painter everywhere, but of course could not avoid some regrettable witticisms. Now making his home at Mme. Weisweiler's sumptuous estate, Cocteau, on coming to see Pablo at La Galloise, waxed ironical about the "ostentatious simplicity" of Picasso's place. "One has to be able to afford luxury, in order to be able to scorn it," Pablo shot back.

In 1949, Kahnweiler's book on Picasso's sculptures came out, illustrated with Brassaï's remarkable photographs. There had been a number of other recent books or studies on the various aspects of his oeuvre, by Christian Zervos, Walter Erben (at Heidelberg), Juan Larrea (New York, on *Guernica,* with work photos by Dora Maar), Sabartés and Éluard (on the Antibes Museum paintings, with Michel Sima photographs), Bernhard Geiser (on the lithographs, New York), Georges and Suzanne Ramié (on ceramics, Geneva), Tristan Tzara, Jacques Lassaigne, Giuseppe Marchiori (Venice), Jean Bouret (drawings), Juan Antonia Nuno Gay (Barcelona), Gerhard Walter (Stuttgart), Blanche-Juan Taurines-Mery (on influences on Picasso), André Verdet (on the *Man with the Sheep*), and Maurice Gieure, among others.

Two issues of Tériade's magazine *Verve* were devoted to him, the first in 1948 reproducing the Antibes works along with Picasso's statements to Tériade originally printed in *L'Intransigeant* on June 15, 1932, and the second, in 1951, entitled "Picasso at Vallauris," carrying paintings done from 1949 to 1952, landscapes of the town, portraits of Claude and Paloma, Françoise, and the like.

Fernand Mourlot's *Picasso lithographe,* with a preface by Sabartés, carried the lithographs done between 1919 and 1949 in their various states.

Just before the opening of the Paris Peace Congress, Françoise gave birth to her little girl, on April 19, 1949, and Pablo decided she should be called Paloma, the Dove. So, once again, his life, his work, his political activity had a common denominator. The baby looked very much like her radiant father. "Still making babies at my age, ridiculous!" he exclaimed. But the increasingly numerous family squabbles, the frequent blowups were now forgotten; for a time, the many ladies flocking to the vigorous almost-septuagenarian were shunted away. A blond poetess, who the minute he closed his eyes forever was to detail publicly the ecstasies she had shared with him, although those around him remember seeing little of her (which can only be to the lovers' credit), now temporarily kept at a distance. Picasso was all wrapped up in his family life.

The violence of the February–March canvases now abated or dissipated; the

Just as he improvised sculptures, Picasso makes himself a pair of hands out of local rolls aptly known as "picassos"

(DOISNEAU RAPHO)

two *Composed Figures* of March 8 contrast with most of the lithographic production of the period, marked by the tumultuous *Great Bullfights* with their
stormy blacks.

However, the whole world did not join in the respect and veneration that
Picasso's most enthusiastic admirers felt he deserved. The English remained aloof
to him, and on April 28, 1949, at the annual banquet of the Royal Academy, the
outgoing president, Sir Alfred Munnings, after lambasting Matisse, took off
after the aesthetic fakers of the so-called Paris school, and told, over the airwaves,
an anecdote about how he and Winston Churchill had agreed that, were they to
meet Pablo Picasso on the street, they would straightaway kick him in the rear!

The result was a scandal: disliking, even criticizing Picasso was permissible,
but not with such totally un-British want of finesse. Several artists and intellectuals sent him and Matisse an expression of their sympathy and support, the
signatures including those of Raymond Mortimer and Cyril Connelly, Graham
Sutherland, Henry Moore (whom Sir Alfred had also slated in his speech),
Douglas Cooper, Philip Hendy of the Tate and John Rothenstein of the National
Gallery, and editor-critic John Lehmann.

Shortly before this, by way of Kahnweiler, Picasso had received a cable signed
by the Museum of Modern Art curator of painting and sculpture James Johnson
Sweeney, Stuart Davis, and Jacques Lipchitz, prompted by some U.S. congressmen
alleging that modern art was all a Communist plot. It read:

SERIOUS WAVE OF ANIMOSITY TOWARDS FREE EXPRESSION PAINTING SCULPTURE
MOUNTING IN AMERICAN PRESS AND MUSEUMS STOP GRAVE RENEWED PRESSURE
FAVORING MEDIOCRE AND UTILITARIAN STOP ARTISTS WRITERS REAFFIRMING RIGHTS
HOLD MEETING MUSEUM MODERN ART MAY FIFTH STOP YOUR SUPPORT WOULD
MEAN MUCH TO ISSUE COULD YOU CABLE STATEMENT EMPHASIZING NECESSITY FOR
TOLERATION OF INNOVATION IN ART TO SWEENEY 1775 BROADWAY

Despite the prepaid-reply coupon, he tore it up, commenting to Françoise in part,
"Art *is* something subversive . . . Once art becomes official and open to everyone, then it becomes the new academicism . . . Only the Russians are naive
enough to think that an artist can fit into society . . . Rimbaud or Apollinaire
in Russia are unthinkable. That's why Mayakovsky committed suicide . . ." He
regretted that his American friends had wasted their money.

When André Verdet visited Matisse, the latter told him, "Picasso's sincerity
is total, even when he's just having fun. He alone can allow himself anything.
He can put down anything, for he is always within the laws."

Pablo purred with delight when this was repeated to him. But Matisse could
be cutting, too; although warmly praising Picasso to André Masson, he added,
"He has no palette." And when Masson related the exchange to a Provençal
newspaperman interviewing him, that was the only sentence he picked up.

Nothing could have hurt Pablo more, and Françoise told Masson he had spent
a sleepless night over it. Seeing Pablo at the Deux-Magots a few weeks later,
Masson went toward him, only to have Picasso turn his back on him. When
Masson suggested to Kahnweiler that he would write Picasso and put the phrase

back in context—which was highly flattering to him—so as to clear himself, the dealer assured him it was no use, Picasso never changed his mind.

They had been friends for thirty years. Picasso had called Masson his "legitimate son," but they were never to see each other again.

Several portraits of Françoise attest to the "knotted" graphism, punctuated with intersections and knots, also found in two February 1948 canvases called *La Cuisine*. Their starting point is the kitchen at Rue des Grands-Augustins, where Pablo and his family ate almost all their meals. Within the astounding network of straight and curved lines, unfolding and intertwining like a maze seen from above, infrequent realistic reminders struggle with the ideogram-birds, all equally caught in the trap of rhythms. This is one of Pablo's most curious works; all illusion of perspective has been dropped, the lines never meet or cross, the linear play has something fascinating about it, and we realize the extent to which, while being accused of having forsaken inventiveness, he was concerned with graphic and spatial problems.

One might be reminded of his illustrations for the Balzac story or Reverdy's poem, but here we have new paths he is marking out, not recalls, and these two canvases are extremely important in his development. As he told Brassaï:

> An artist should observe nature but never confuse it with painting. It is only translatable into painting by signs. But such signs are not invented. To arrive at the sign, you have to concentrate hard on the resemblance. To me, surreality is nothing, and has never been anything but this profound resemblance, something deeper than the forms and the colors in which objects present themselves.

Beyond this, he instructed Françoise:

> If one occupies oneself with what is full: that is, the object as positive form, the space around it is reduced to almost nothing. If one occupies oneself primarily with the space that surrounds the object, the object is reduced to almost nothing. What interests us most—what is outside or what is inside a form?

In June 1949, he returned to Vallauris, but before leaving, at Mourlot's, from April 6 to May 29, he did a whole succession of lithographs, accompanied by poems, the text in all capitals, and the numerous illustrations at times opposite and at others not. They were assembled by fours, not necessarily chronologically.

The compositions include owls, eagles, fauns' heads, still lifes, women, mythological episodes and landscapes, profiles of youths, baroque bouquets, nudes, bullfights, children's faces (probably Claude's), realistic themes, wild inventions with re-created anatomies in which full-blown arborescences mix with organic crisscrossings—fantastic delights, tender naturalism, knotted graphism and beautifully deep-black tachism, the touch now serene, now quirky, lithe arabesque contrasting with tight hatchings, every jerk of his hand translating the impulses of his senses—a prodigious repertory of infinite variations! He employed everything at hand—ink, pen, wash, lithographic pencil, gouache on transfer paper. If our civilization were to disappear and one day this album of fourteen untitled plates were found, who could ever imagine it was done by one man in fifty-three days?

At La Galloise, he did nothing to avoid confrontations between Marie-Thérèse and Françoise, which he enjoyed, although the women did not. He was indulging in more and more escapades, going off to Nice, Cannes, St.-Tropez, even to Paris for a few unexplained days. The ladies involved are known: some of them have told their stories, some Riviera hotelkeepers spilled the beans, but none was less discreet than Pablo himself. Very often he signed his own name and that of his current companion in the establishments' guest books. Éluard at times arranged matters, with unknown women, or women friends, continuing the somewhat ambiguous role he had begun at the time of Nush and continued ever since.

In Vallauris, Picasso worked at several studios: at the Ramiés workshop for pottery, and on Chemin du Fournas in an L-shaped onetime perfume factory he rented in 1949. He split the building in two, one side for painting, the other for sculpture, over twelve meters (nearly forty feet) long, with adjoining rooms holding wooden shelves for his ceramics. In front was the so-called donkey plot, named for the two donkeys Pablo had bought to eat up the obstructive weeds: in so doing, they so well fertilized the plot that it grew over with daisies and wild mint, giving the place an unexpected floral touch.

Naturally, the whole studio was immediately turned into his usual junk shop, its disorder covered with spider webs so thick they seemed like fishnets, in contrast to the monklike simplicity of La Galloise, which had only the barest of furnishings, an occasional plate or lithograph of his on the white walls.

The painting studio was also huge, the table in its center, according to André Verdet, looking as if it had "been squared by Van Gogh," with all his painting and engraving equipment plus assorted other tools, pots, vials, cans on it. A huge potbellied stove here, while another stood in the sculpture studio, that old-iron repository with ten, twenty, thirty, fifty, or more examples of every kind of oddment, spare part, or discarded metal—as well as bits and pieces of ceramics, tin cans, bicycle chains, handlebars, pram wheels, pulleys, and you name it. To say nothing of endless nails and barbed wires on which ladies caught their skirts or snagged their stockings. When he wanted an excuse, Picasso would claim that in one of those cans he had stashed away a little key, which he had never been able to find again.

He usually got there late in the morning, alone or with friends, walked around the sutdio, picking up one thing or another, twisting, turning it in his hands, taking another, talking, gossiping, while his fingers began to make an assemblage. Sitting down, he would push ahead with his work, saying, "You go on. I'll catch up with you." And the friends would leave one by one.

Alone, he would work; if he had company, he would stop it, and go down to the beach to join Françoise and the children. In the afternoon, he returned or went to the Ramiés'. At the Fournas studio, from 1948 on, he did several of his large sculptures, an *Animal Head,* a *Centaur,* several *Female Forms,* made of assembled discards as are *The Glass,* the extraordinary *Pregnant Woman, Woman with Baby Carriage,* and the famous *She-Goat.*

Starting in Summer 1949, he turned more toward painting than ceramics, getting his main inspiration from his children, Claude and Paloma, as well as

"She-Goat"   bronze, Vallauris 1950

their mother, who appears in so many portraits. There was also a long hiatus in the lithography, but when Mourlot came down in April 1950 to ask him for a cover for Volume II of the four-volume *Picasso lithographe,* he said, "Wait, I'll do it for you tomorrow." As Mourlot tells it:

> The next day, he closed himself up in the studio. I was a little surprised, for he had neither grease pencil nor brush. He found a solution: he put a little water into the lithographic ink tray and with his finger dissolved the hardened ink, to do an amazingly faithful portrait of Claude and Paloma . . .

That was the afternoon of April 16, 1950. Mourlot reminded him that for months now Tristan Tzara had been waiting for illustrations for his poem *De mémoire d'homme* (Within Living Memory); whereupon, using the same system, Picasso traced the nine lithographs of fanciful flowers, butterflies, dragonflies, and toads that were so impatiently needed by the publisher, Mourlot's son-in-law, Pierre Bordas.

The year 1950 saw Picasso paint two of his capital canvases: *Portrait of a Painter, after El Greco,* in February, and *Young Ladies along the Seine, after Courbet.*

The El Greco was in the provincial museum at Sevilla, and Pablo had never seen it, but had a reproduction of it. What interested him about it was not only to transpose the volumes and rearrange them, starting from total destruction of the picture's coherence, but, as he put it, "to render the lunar light" typical of the great Toledan.

He succeeded admirably in this. The restructuring of the canvas is a prodigious feat of baroque inventiveness, as well as a tour de force of psychological and plastic intelligence, for the essence of the original has been retained. For external resemblance, as he had done several other times Picasso substituted internal resemblance, so perfectly captured in the Cubist portraits of Uhde, Kahnweiler, and Vollard. Of course, here the process was different, the model being not a human but a picture; as it were, he put a tracing over El Greco's painter and applied his own touch to it, thereby freeing the essence, the spiritual content of the work. His line dives down inside the picture and wrenches its secrets from it.

This "nocturnal" work constituted Picasso's return to Spain.

For the *Young Ladies along the Seine,* he just chanced on a reproduction. Pablo admired Courbet for having defied the traditions of academicism by daring to show figures in uninhibited attitudes and contemporary clothing, out in the open. His canvas was a statement, and Pablo's would be, too, but from another angle. He kept everything of Courbet's, down to the tiniest detail, but used it all in an entirely different system of signs that closeted reality and transformed it for a new dialogue emanating from another image.

He underlined the feeling of serenity, the relaxation under the shade trees along the water, but the sensuality of the original, the "cool flesh" aspect of Courbet, disappeared. Pablo wanted to express not an episode of life, but all those moments of rest, calm, happiness he had known and now tied together in a bunch of baroque forms with colors truly Oriental in their sumptuousness. What

"Young Ladies along the Seine, after Courbet" 1950
(Kunstmuseum—Basel)

(GIRAUDON)

he was portraying was not anecdote, but the *totality*. And as with the El Greco portrait—which he said was done a few weeks before these *Young Ladies* or *Demoiselles*—he was concerned more with essence than appearance.

In the 1948–1950 period, painters were engaged in a fruitless struggle: socialist realism *versus* abstract art, with Communist writers preaching the former —comprehensible, moral, uplifting, and politically "committed." The result, unfortunately, was crushing mediocrity, praised as being preferable to the abstract work of those who had "sold out" to the Americans.

Picasso, a Communist and proud of it, was not comprehensible, and the masses who saw him on platforms alongside Thorez, Duclos, Casanova, or Aragon did not understand his work. He wanted no part of socialist realism, and no one dared ask him to. Besides, if anyone had been "bought" by the Americans, it was he, whose paintings brought top dollar from museums, collectors, and dealers, while the abstractionists, at least in France, rated no great prices—not, certainly, before 1953–1954.

On June 25, 1950, North Korea crossed the 38th Parallel and occupied Seoul; two days later, President Truman sent troops to support the South Koreans, and the Communists immediately started a campaign against "American aggression."

Picasso had not been much moved by events after the Spanish War, which had affected him directly. The 1940 rout, the exodus from Paris and German occupation, the tortures and murders by the Gestapo, the *maquis* Resistance and Liberation had touched him only to the extent that they interfered with his work, upset his habits, threatened his security. Like the vast majority of Frenchmen, he knew little of what was actually going on. Troubled by the arrest and sad fate of some of his friends, such as Robert Desnos or Max Jacob, he had also been overwhelmed by the revelation of the truth about the Nazi concentration camps, the gas chambers, those visions of hell and apocalypse. He avidly queried the deportees who returned, but when one of them told him of their sufferings, he retorted with a reminder of what the Spanish refugees went through when they crossed the Catalan border with the Franco troops at their heels, to end in the horror of French internment camps. All of that was what he had tried to put into *The Charnel House*.

The French war in Indochina, that "dirty war" his Communist comrades were denouncing, was far away, and he had little understanding of politics. He gave to various causes, when asked, grudgingly, vowing each time was the last, but still giving, money or pictures. However irritated at being pestered, he would rush to meet a deadline with a front-page drawing for *L'Humanité*'s Christmas issue, or for the Nice *Patriote* on the anniversary of the Spanish Republic or the October Revolution, do posters, draw propaganda portraits of Party heroes or victims of Fascism, from Joliot-Curie to Henri Martin, from the Rosenbergs to Beloyannis and Grimau. Cursing those who brought them, he signed petitions and other Party-sponsored statements; but always only at the last moment, to have the pleasure of hearing Aragon or Auguste Lecoeur beg him by phone to hurry up and do it.

But no one ever asked him his opinion of socialist realism, even though he was both painter and Communist. He could not understand why, and when he asked the Communist leaders, he got evasive answers. He told Hélène Parmelin, "In painting, it seems to me I might be able to say things to quite a few people. But no one asks me to. Why?" Then, resigned, sighed, "Well, the only thing that counts is to save the revolution!"

He was, in fact, no less indifferent to Korea than to Indochina, having only the vaguest notion of its geography or what might be motivating the Americans to intervene. On January 15, 1951, while doing a series of edifying scenes of family life, mainly Françoise, the children, and the Vallauris landscape bursting with colors, he started a canvas he was later to call *Massacre in Korea* (and which he kept for his own).

Were the Communists responsible for his doing this big work, which was to condemn the war and further their anti-American propaganda? Not directly; but indirectly, for sure. Roland Penrose writes that

> His communist friends had grown to expect a gesture from him condemning this new outbreak of violence, and it was hoped that he would paint a picture which could be used to blame the Western powers as aggressors.

But the canvas remained untitled for months, as noted by Kahnweiler when he visited Vallauris in March 1951. It was named *Massacre in Korea* only just before being exhibited in the Salon de Mai of that year, although Penrose says it was titled before being done, and Claude Roy, who was seeing a lot of Picasso at the time, says that in September 1950 he was working on something called *Korea.*

"Overwhelming with human pity," was how Kahnweiler described it, but the Communists did not much care for it and, after it was spread across the full breadth of page one of *Les Lettres françaises,* their position was to mention it as little as possible. The comrades were of one mind: Why could he not follow the Party line like everyone else? Why still paint unintelligibly, hermetically, and, what is more, repulsively? How could they accept both Fougeron's *In the Country of Mines* and this *Massacre in Korea?*

It fell to Jean Marcenac to set it all straight in *Les Lettres françaises,* under the innocuous title of "The Lesson of Picasso and the May Salon." Calling the picture "modest" and characterizing it as "a sketch," he wondered "whether this Picasso is worth more than another or less. What is certain is that, of all his works, with the influence they have on painting, few are so important"—which clarified and explained nothing. No one wanted to "stick his neck out." The irreconcilable socialist realism and Picasso had both to be made acceptable—which required a wilier dialectic than Marcenac was able to muster.

The very next week, in the same *Lettres* (May 24), Marcenac was at ease and relaxed as he covered *Les Constructeurs* in "Fernand Léger and the Workers of Beauty." This was not very clever—nor could anything have offended Picasso more. When he heard that Lecoeur, secretary of the Central Committee, had asked that Party publications mention *Massacre in Korea* as infrequently as possible, he decided on a showdown. But he got no satisfaction.

This was the same Lecoeur who a few months before had called for maximum publicity about the Fougeron exhibit, "In the Country of the Mines," a lamentable paean of glory to socialist realism, which had so appealed to the Party intelligentsia. Fougeron had been invited to the northern mining region by the miners' union, headed by Lecoeur, and had turned his "on-the-spot" sketches into reportage-like scenes of mining life. However good the intention, the result was flat and appalling.

The Party, which had financed the exhibition at Bernheim-Jeune Galleries, went all out in promoting it, André Stil, in *Les Lettres françaises,* demanding that his critics show as much care as Fougeron himself and "not lightly judge an effort that commands respect, for which the painter outdid himself." Since all of this could only rub Picasso the wrong way, it was decided that on February 5, a few days after the Fougeron show closed, they would hold a "Tribute to Picasso, Winner of the Grand International Peace Prize," also honoring the late novelist Jean-Richard Bloch and filmmaker Louis Daquin, equally prizewinners. Frédéric Joliot-Curie chaired the meeting; Yves Farge and Vercors spoke; and Fernand Léger read an address to Picasso, lauding *Guernica* and the Dove. But this was not the end of the matter.

No event was depicted in *Massacre in Korea,* the disconcerting work that had started the May Salon controversy. It might have been any place, any time, in any era. The robots commanded by a sort of medieval knight armed from head to toe, firing point-blank at naked men and women while terrified children ran away, were straight out of the cuirassed warriors Picasso had drawn in January 1950, and done in lithographs in February–May. If one wants to place the *Massacre* in the history of art, Goya's *Third of May* and Manet's *Execution of Maximilian* offer a sort of lineage.

Massacre in Korea is not Spain, nor does it reflect the "Picasso furioso" of the old days. This faraway war with its destruction and death did not directly involve him. Was that not why he made the gunners anonymous, the scene timeless? And the victims naked, with nothing to indicate their nationality or origin? They were all women, all men, pressed together, lined up, resigned, terrified; even the landscape is geographically characterless. As in *Guernica,* there is a monochrome harmony, light steel-gray with slight yellow and green scumbles. Like the *Demoiselles d'Avignon,* Picasso held *Massacre in Korea* to be unfinished.

A few months later, in Vallauris, Picasso set it up out of doors, and contemplated it, to try to see why the Communists had boycotted it. "Even if nobody liked it, it was really something, wasn't it?" he pondered. He might not be following "the line," but did a painter, especially one named Picasso, have "a line"? Yet there was no one to explain to him why it was attacked, much less what he, Pablo Picasso, represented to the Party.

He had thought his joining would release him from his creative loneliness, and it had given him broad currency, but his comrades viewed him mainly as a star. Paradoxically, as a Communist, the Communists made him feel even lonelier: they venerated the man but ignored, or pretended to ignore, the work when it did not conform to Party aesthetics, and inside the Soviet Union he fared no better. He suffered when Communists failed to appreciate his work, to analyze it and explain it to the Party members; even Éluard did not dare try, while Aragon mixed hollow dithyrambs with the most elemental kind of exegesis. A glance at the back issues of *Les Lettres françaises* shows how the champions of "committed" art misunderstood what Pablo wanted, never dreaming it was the same thing they strove for: all they could give him was courteous applause, banality, or silence.

He took it out on socialist realism: he slated the apologists of Fougeron and the like, whose articles he read in the *Lettres* and other Party organs, and ridiculed Soviet painting, with its historically uplifting paintings by people who considered him "decadent." Georges Tabaraud, who can be suspect of ill-feeling neither toward Picasso nor toward contemporary Soviet art, tells us that when he painted *War* and *Peace* Pablo was contemplating a reproduction of a painting by that most *pompier* of official Soviet painters, the famous Gerassimov.

When Kahnweiler was at Vallauris, Picasso had shown him his recent ceramics and the winterscapes of the little town, dark and hard, with their ochers, browns, and pale greens, the chimneys of the potters' kilns crowned with gray plumes. The warriors and knights surprised the dealer, who saw their kinship not only to the still-untitled great canvas, but also to the comic strip of *Ivanhoe* in *L'Humanité*.

Kahnweiler watched him do a lithograph of a knight in armor and a page that he described as "very Pinturicchio-ish." This was on the evening of March 12, between 5:00 and 8:00 P.M. "Well, the little page again!" Kahnweiler commented.

"Yes," Pablo replied, "I wanted to do him even better. Besides, why does one work? For that. In order to do something better; look [outlining the page for Kahnweiler with his finger], I wanted to show he was walking. Run your eye up the left leg and then down the right; you'll see he's walking."

As Kahnweiler further noted in his diary, Françoise pointed out that the shield was not historically accurate. Pablo insisted it was, adding that the knight's skinny neck was not possible in reality, but "no one would notice it." Françoise said he had no documented knowledge of knights' attire, yet the details were breathtakingly precise: his visual memory was as fantastic as ever. After years, he could still visualize the slightest detail, and when he did the Buffon plates at Lacourière's, he had no animals before him for models, yet everything is perfectly exact. Beaudin, who saw him do one, after all these years has never gotten over it.

Pablo and Kahnweiler would cut up old touches, going back half a century, evenings after dinner. While they both claimed to feel they had not changed since their youth, Kahnweiler noted that Pablo talked as one afraid of growing old.

But the next day, back in the studio, he showed the dealer his latest paintings, portraits of Françoise and their two children, views of Vallauris with what he called the smoke of the kilns like big black goldbeater's skins, the admirable *Night Landscape* with its sweet serenity, the *Young Ladies along the Seine, after Courbet.*

"A picture that tells a story really isn't so bad," Pablo commented. Then they

Picasso in his studio at Vallauris, "Landscape in the Midi" on the floor before him, and "Night Landscape" behind him. 1951

talked of this and that, of Communism, and he said, "I'm a Communist so there will be less misery in the world."

The fact was, Picasso was enthroned in his own myth. In an October 1950 preface to a show at the Maeght Gallery, Michel Ragon, a twenty-six-year-old champion of abstractionism, wrote:

> Picasso, the idolized star, attracts as many tourists to Antibes as the Eiffel Tower in 1900 did yahoos come to Paris. But where is his influence? . . . The young are dropping away from this "bothersome genius." . . .
>
> The artist today is building a new world. Picasso will soon be considered by the new generation as Delacroix was by the young Impressionists of 1865. He is no doubt the last great realistic painter. It will be necessary to unteach Picasso to the public. . . .

Going on to compare Picasso to the man who invented the garbage pail and, in France, left his name to it, the rude young whippersnapper came back to the assault in March–April 1951, in a magazine called *Contemporains* (Contemporaries), tearing down the "Man-with-the-Sheep-between-His-Teeth," for obvious shock effect. He also satirized the many preparatory sketches for the Dove of Peace and, treating it like any other commercial poster, wondered whether we would now have to see exhibits of "art" of every successful advertising campaign. He concluded:

> I can perfectly well conceive what Picasso may have been to Apollinaire's generation, but what the devil! Apollinaire today would be old enough to be my grandfather! Why don't we follow his example and turn our attention to our contemporaries?

In a way he was right: showing *all* Picasso, without regard to what was finished work and what just drafts, could only do him a disservice. It was not *all* good. He had become the symbol of modern art to the general public who hated it— hated it the more for being so indiscriminately tossed at them. Pablo, so concerned about what the Communists thought of him, could not care less what gallerygoers thought—in sharp contrast to the conscientiousness of a Matisse, Bonnard, or Braque. He would never (as Rouault did) burn his unfinished works to keep them off the market. Legend and enthusiasm were enough for him.

Yet, before any show of his work, he often asked to see the layout, decided where pictures ought to go, spent hours on the phone to Kahnweiler or his staff, or the organizers. When it was hung, he demanded photographs of what it looked like, and all the press clippings—which mostly he did not read.

But the star of the Fifties, with his worldwide reputation, was no luckier than the obscure artist of 1908. Or maybe the public simply is not lucky. For in this century it has had no luck with Matisse, Mondrian, Kandinsky, or Duchamp, or with Brancusi, Laurens, or Le Corbusier. Their glories are all based on a series of misunderstandings.

But, let us get back to Vallauris. Pablo had long planned to build a Temple of Peace near Céret, and when he stayed in French Catalonia on several occasions in 1953–1954, his friends tried to bring it to fruition. It was to be on the peak of Fontfrede, superbly overlooking both Spain and France. But in the meantime he also planned to "do something" in the abandoned chapel of the priory of Vallauris, where his *Man with the Sheep* had stood before being installed on the square.

"They asked me to decorate the place," he told André Verdet. "I've given a little thought to what I'd paint. On one side *War,* on the other *Peace,* but the walls will have to be fixed, they're very damp, and then I can get to work."

"That's battle painting," Verdet replied.

Pablo clouded up, then retorted violently, "Cézanne's apples are battle painting, too! Every picture, every rhythm, ever color is a battle. A battle against oneself, against painting. Don't you do battle poetry?"

On March 31, 1952, the Greek Communist Beloyannis was shot by a firing squad in Athens. The Party had carried on a fierce campaign to try to stop this crime. Picasso, in Paris, had joined in the protests, unfortunately unavailing. When he read the news dispatches of the hero's last moments, he told Claude Roy, "It's like a Goya picture. Horrible . . ." They decided they would write a statement of protest that their friends could also sign. They took a sheet of paper, and Roy began to write, but Picasso got up, went down to his studio, and came back shortly with this:

> The glow of the oil lanterns lighting up the night in Madrid on the May evening the noble faces of the people shot by the rapacious foreigner in Goya's picture have the same grain of horror sown in handfuls of projectors on the bared chest of Greece by governments sweating fear and hatred. An immense white dove sprinkles the wrath of her mourning over the earth.

That, too, was out of Goya.

Picasso also told Roy of wanting to decorate the Vallauris chapel, and in April he began the preparatory drawings. The municipality had agreed to make the necessary repairs, and he knew he would have full freedom of action.

It had not been so in the case of the country canon who, canvassing artists to decorate his church at Plateau d'Assy, had come to him after having already enrolled Braque, Léger, Lurçat, Chagall, Matisse, Rouault, Bonnard, and others. Pablo, being in one of his better days, showed him a big drawing of a woman with a disjointed, tortured face, a figure of terror and death, calmly telling him it was "The Holy Virgin."

The canon was completely taken aback. After his first dismay, he dared ask timidly whether the master might not have something a little more "classical," a little less aggressive. Even an old work, no matter—obviously having in mind the Blue or Rose Period, which at least would create no problems nor antagonize his ecclesiastical superiors or visitors. Picasso held his tongue. Arms crossed, eye dark, he stared at the canon looking at the lacerated, tormented woman's face, and finally averred, "Rivers never flow back upstream . . ."

Here at Vallauris he did not plan to go backward either, but rather to forge ahead. He never repeated himself, never reprised an old theme in order to turn it into a pastiche in light of later developments. Now, as always, he would be able to say, "Look at me changing . . ."

One day, André Verdet wrote at the time, he had been to visit Picasso, and, walking in the donkey yard, Pablo in shorts, bare-chested, tanned as a king of Thebes, told him:

> "Nature is full of wonders. One has to know how to want, to know, to seek, to see, to find . . . Do you want to see the temple at Angkor? Look . . ."
>
> His hand lifted a thick tuft of long grass. That tuft revealed other plants with intricate leaves and coniferous pods in myriad layers that suddenly brought to mind the admirable image of a Cambodian temple. Beyond belief. It was all there, bigger than life, the architecture, the masses, the decorations, the symbols.
>
> "Yes, one just has to *see*," Picasso said, "to see and be faithful to everything about us, attentive as if putting a watch together; invention starts from there . . ."

But what he needed now was communication, participation. He wanted to show the Communists—and others—that he could tell a story and that, unlike the abstractionists, whose pictures to him were mere decoration, he could be a *modern* storyteller, as in their own time Titian, Tintoretto, Rubens, or Delacroix had been. Men talking to other men in direct and true vocabulary.

On April 28, 1952, Picasso started a first sketch pad of studies for *War* and *Peace;* he finished it on May 1, with fifty-eight drawings done in India ink and pencil. A second pad was filled May 5–11, and then a schoolboy's notebook, originally intended for Claude's scribblings, filled with 175 pencil sketches done between July 19 and September 14. As he told Claude Roy:

> "I had filled entire pads with sketches, details, but I did not have a single overall sketch. I started with *War*. What I experienced at first was the loose jerky career of one of those provincial hearses, impoverished and squeaky, that you see going through the streets of little cities. I began at the right, and all the rest built up around that image. . . .
>
> "For months, for years, like everyone else I had been obsessed by the threat of war, filled with anxiety and hatred. *Massacre in Korea* had been a first result of that. That picture threw people, and did not appeal. But I myself have begun to see it for what it is, and I know why it met with surprise: I had not done *Guernica* over again— which was what people were expecting. Here I have not repeated *Guernica* either, nor *The Charnel House,* nor the *Massacre* . . ."

Since the two panels were to follow the vaulting of the cradle-shaped sides of the chapel, the sun at the top of *Peace* would not be at the top of the picture, he added, but over the heads of spectators:

> "It's not very light in that chapel, and I would almost wish they did not light it, so that visitors would carry candles in their hands, walking along the walls as if in prehistoric grottoes, discovering the figures, while the light danced on what I had painted, a little candle's light."

Picasso worked for months in the Fournas studio, seeing no one, always carrying the key with him; only when he had reached full awareness of his subject and its details did he begin to execute the job panel by panel.

War is cruel, and especially stupid, combining horror and foolishness, which is why he portrayed it as a hearse, a grotesque image of the double tragedy of war and death, so intimately connected; the horses pulling the carriage trample books symbolic of civilization and culture, while in the background there is a hideous cortège of killers silhouetted against the gray-and-black night. But on the left, at the edge of a wheatfield, rises the warrior, image of justice, whose scales he is carrying, and of peace, whose dove adorns his shield.

With this announcement of peace, mankind is seized with delirious joy. Women dance contortedly, as if moved by some frenetic agitation, as children play, one of them leading the capering Pegasus of *Parade* dragging a plow, displaying virile attributes, symbols of fertility. On the right, a happy family in a flowered garden is enjoying the return of happiness, one woman preparing the meal, another nursing her infant, the man writing. At the extreme left, an adolescent is playing a pipe, as did the fauns of the Antibes *Joie de vivre*. They are all naked as the day the earth was born, and the sun shines with all its most brilliant rays. As he told Claude Roy, showing him the endless preparatory studies for the chapel:

> "When I was working on this series of drawings, I would look back over my sketchpads every day, wondering, 'What am I still going to teach myself that I didn't know before?' And when it was no longer I talking, but the drawings I had done, when they had gotten away from me and were defying me, then I knew I'd reached my goal. . . .
>
> "If peace wins in the world, the war I've painted will be a thing of the past . . . The only blood that flows will be before a fine drawing, a beautiful picture. People will get too close to it, and when they scratch it a drop of blood will form, showing that the work is truly alive."

This physical existence of the work of art was something Pablo often talked about. One day he had said, "Real pictures, if you put a mirror before them, will cloud it, with living breath, because they do breathe."

During the work, he was so excited with how it was going, and the physical exertion in moving the heavy ladders about from one panel to another, that he pointed out to a visitor that "no house painter could cover such a surface in so short a time." The visitor, Geneva professor Jean Leymarie, also tells of Picasso riffling through a special issue of *Le Point* devoted to him, with contributions by Maurice Raynal, Kahnweiler, Tristan Tzara, Édouard Pignon, Roy, Pierre Reverdy, and amusing photographs by Doisneau. Picasso was especially moved by the Reverdy prose, telling of the poet's early friendship with "this athlete of very surprising stature," who "from the first day was subject to every kind of attack, every insult, the worst calumnies." Ending, despite sober reservations, by lauding the "image, destined for glory throughout all time of this man who at his highest moment was the marked man, the tree to be felled—and yet was able to remain standing—my dear friend."

Vallauris: The Temple of Peace, seen in totality, 1952
(FAILLET-ZIOLO)

Like Leymarie, who, a few days later, on Pablo's birthday, October 25, was to read this text to his students, Picasso was overcome by it. He had often resented Reverdy's preferring Braque to him, nor did he understand the poet's slow progression toward Catholicism, his retreat to Solesmes at the abbey where he attended Mass every morning and even vespers. Yet Reverdy had said to a friend who termed Cubism too intellectual, "No, Picasso was never an intellectual; he is an eye!" And, "They say he throws an egg against a canvas and signs it Picasso. He is right: he's the only one who can afford to do this, because he cannot help doing it with genius."

Hard as Picasso may have been for so sensitive a man as Reverdy to have an unclouded friendship with, yet, as Kahnweiler has related, "Only when Reverdy talked about Picasso did he use the term 'genius.'" He had always been sorry not to have been a painter, sculptor, or ceramicist. One day in 1948 he decided to inscribe some of his poems on clay tablets and fire them at the Ramiés' in Vallauris. These ceramics were shown at the Madoura Gallery in Cannes, and Picasso took many of his friends to see them; he owned several, and hoped to see them published; one of them compared him to a wild seed that made deserts to sprout.

In 1949, the Paris Musée d'Art moderne was planning a big Matisse exhibition. The day before the vernissage, Picasso, being in town, phoned Jean Cassou to ask whether he could come in and see it, then and there. Cassou agreed and a quarter of an hour later Pablo arrived, to be greeted by Pierre Matisse and his father's secretary, Lydia Delectorskaya, as well as the curator. As they were entering the first hall, Picasso stopped, his dark eye roaming over the recent pictures hanging there, and said simply, "That's good. I was a little afraid . . . Because he's getting old, isn't he?"

The others just looked at each other. As the Spaniard went slowly from one painting to the next, he repeated, "That's good." But anyone knowing the Picasso touch would know that he had not come to the show just to put his own stamp of approval on it.

There was some small talk at the end of the visit, and as he was saying good-bye to the painter's son and secretary, Pablo suddenly asked the latter, "What is Matisse working on now?"

"He's working on a chapel," she replied.

Picasso, who was well aware of that fact, drove home his barb: "Oh, so he accepted a commission! Whoring, eh?"

Cassou cut the embarrassment short by taking Picasso into his office. Once there, our Malagueño told him, "What I said wasn't very nice. But, just the same, doing a chapel! . . ."

Pablo was never able to admit that Matisse might have conceived and executed the Chapel of the Rosary at Vence as a friendly gesture to the Dominican sisters. Especially since the painter had written the Bishop of Nice on June 25, 1951, the day it was consecrated, that he considered this sanctuary his masterpiece.

Picasso was all out in his criticisms of Matisse, and Aragon went right along, so that when the poet visited Matisse the latter had to remind him to act

with a bit more decorum. Yet, in all fairness, it must be reported that when Matisse first mentioned the project he told a friend, "I'm going to do a chapel. And I know one person that's going to upset."

Could Pablo have been unaware that as early as 1908 Matisse made reference to "the so-to-speak religious feeling I have about life"? He too had gone in for Christian art in the series based on the Grünewald *Altarpiece,* and painted or drawn several Crucifixions. In 1954, when his friend Henri Laurens died, he even contemplated sculpting a large Christ for his tombstone in Montparnasse Cemetery, though this never came to fruition.

By an amazing coincidence, when Matisse began to draw the stations of the cross for his chapel, at Vence, he too took careful note of the masterpiece at Colmar. What Picasso was unable to admit was that his old rival had done that chapel with the sole resource of light; this he could not have done, and that made him furious. Matisse alone among their contemporaries could have done this: and in the chapel at Vence there is nothing, or almost nothing—very pure, schematic lines simply suggest the stations of the cross, the Holy Virgin, St. Dominic, with some yellow and blue staining the windows; and the changing light is what creates the effects desired. At the Vallauris Temple of Peace, on the other hand, lines, colors, contrasts all come from the traditional painter's bag.

Picasso could not forgive Matisse his own inability to take over the latter's sensitive and so felicitously expressive vocabulary. He got even with witticisms, barbs that in fact were only a reflection of disappointed love. Matisse understood, and did not hold it against his rival, for their geniuses, indispensable one to the other, thrived on this love/hate relationship. They were to fight, to tear at each other, until that very last visit the Ogre of Vallauris made to his dying friend, when not a word was spoken, but he bent over and kissed his hand.

The person who told me the story sobbed as he did.

Picasso had visited Matisse's chapel while he was doing it, and he wanted to see it again after his death. He went in, in silence, accompanied by a few friends. Behind a counter, an old nun was selling postcards and souvenir booklets. Someone recognized him, and whispered, "That's Picasso." The nun, hearing this, looked up and asked if it were really so.

She walked over and looked at him. He was obviously moved. "I'm so happy to see you here, Monsieur Picasso," she said, "because Monsieur Matisse often talked about you. One day he pointed to the paintings and said to me, 'I don't really know what they're worth, but there's only one person who's entitled to criticize me, and that's Picasso.' "

Thus, the two master painters of the twentieth century, Matisse and Picasso, one to the other.

At La Galloise, between pictures and loves, both tumultuous and changing, Pablo, some ten years after *Desire Caught by the Tail,* wrote a second play, *The Four Little Girls.* It was the period of his quarrels with Françoise and his problems with the Party, with Claude and Paloma to take his mind off his public and private troubles; as against the winter of 1953–1954, when Françoise was to take the children and leave him, now he was expressing himself in writing.

He was playing with words, puns, associations, images, with his usual drive and somewhat more lyrically than in *Desire.* Many of his verbal inventions may have had their origins in the conversations between Claude and little Paloma, playing near their father or posing for him.

The 1950–1951 Picasso sculptures, *Pregnant Woman, Woman with Baby Carriage, She-Goat, Owl, Little Girl Skipping Rope, Goat Skull and Bottle,* like his paintings, were all connected with his private life. The first two are Françoise; the she-goat really existed and even was the occasion of a quarrel between Pablo and her because it was actually a billy goat, and Françoise had to give it to some gypsies because of its stench. The owl hooted at night and had long since become one of Pablo's familiars. As for the little girl skipping rope, they saw her every day as they went to Rue du Fournas.

They were made of the pieces of junk piled up in the studio, among which Pablo selected, playing with the scraps as if medically examining them, until suddenly they came alive under his touch, becoming head, belly, arms, hand, child, animal . . . Claude Roy tells of taking a walk with young Claude, who stopped to pull a hunk of metal out of a garbage pail, saying, "Papa might be able to make use of this."

The *She-Goat* is a symbol of fertility.

Fertility, fecundity, transmission of life, maternity—all themes that since youth preoccupied Picasso and were the subjects of countless watercolors, drawings, engravings, paintings. Like one of the victims of *Massacre in Korea, Baboon with Young* has a belly big with imminent childbirth.

The goat's head returns in *Goat Skull and Bottle,* made from pieces of corrugated cardboard that Picasso put to use by taking advantage of their every irregularity and tear; the eyes are the heads of two large bolts, and the horns bicycle handlebars. The bottle alongside serves as a candlestick. In the manner of primitive artists for whom the visible and invisible had equal value, the radiation of the candle's flame is represented by long needles. The same title, *Goat Skull and Bottle,* was used for still lifes of the same period in steel gray with subtle variations enclosed in a network of "broken" rhythms; the overall effect is that of a broken mirror.

Paul Éluard died on November 18, 1952. Less than a year and a half before, Pablo and Françoise had been his witnesses at his marriage in the St.-Tropez city hall to Odette, known as Dominique, Lemor, whom he had met while on a trip to Mexico.* He had been ill for several years and finally died of angina. Picasso, in Paris, went to the funeral, held under Party auspices, sitting in the front row of the stand put up before the entrance to Père-Lachaise for speechmaking. It was very cold, and he was dressed in a huge overcoat, a muffler up around his ears, and being squeezed between Dominique Éluard and Elsa Aragon, he kept warm enough. Aragon, Cocteau, Claude Roy, Fernand Léger, and the Party leaders surrounded the poet's wife and daughter.

The quarrels with Françoise were becoming more and more frequent, as were

* Françoise Gilot, on page 299 of her book (in English), says, however: "I think Pablo and I were with Paul Éluard the day he first saw Dominique . . ." (TR. NOTE)

his absences. She was not about to let herself be made a fool of by an old man hungering for fresh meat. Nor he to give up his sacrosanct freedom. The children were the only things that still kept them together: he adored them, played with them for hours on end, and endlessly painted and drew them.

But life at Vallauris was like a circus, with everyone getting into the Picasso act: friends dropped in unexpectedly, bringing others, whom often he did not even know—to say nothing of dealers, collectors, newspapermen, tourists, would-be photographers, autograph seekers, all wanting to see the strange animal. If in the mood, he was hospitable, entertaining them or taking them all out to dinner. And from time to time he threw his arms around a friend of a score of years' standing, Jean Cocteau, Prévert, Marcel Duhamel, or Kahnweiler, whom Marcel had picked up at the Nice airport. Or it might be Aragon with Elsa, or Charlie Chaplin.

But, when not so inclined, he refused to see anyone, working all night long at the Fournas studios. He had invited Édouard Pignon, a painter friend from before the war, and his wife, Hélène Parmelin, to come and live "a painter's life" in all simplicity near him. The young woman, a talented novelist, turned chronicler of all the master's actions, and recorder of his *mots*. Until the end they were to be his closest associates. Pignon wrote:

> I will always remember, a few days after we got there, his coming into the studio he had put at my disposal. I heard his voice coming out of the depths of the corridor, "May one look in?" He came out of the shadow of the house and his gaze fell on the large charcoals and watercolors of my *Dead Worker,* pinned to the studio wall. His dark eye seemed to bore into them like a gimlet, searching. I suddenly felt shy as an adolescent . . .

From time to time, Picasso would take out his recent paintings, and set them up in the grass outside the studio walls. The way he had in the old days with Braque at Sorgues, and spend hours talking.

The sun caressed the geometrical faces and the broad flat stretches of brilliant color in the portraits of Claude and Paloma, the views of Vallauris, still lifes, the extraordinary *Moonlight at Vallauris* that looks like a pyrotechnical display of trees, swirling stars, and sky.

In a lecture given in London about Picasso, to mark his seventieth birthday, Éluard had described this painting on October 11, 1951, as follows:

> He copies the night as he might copy an apple, from memory, at night, in his garden at Vallauris, a quite ordinary garden on a slope. . . . I know in advance that these Vallauris nights will have nothing of the easy graces of Provence, but I am certain that after having seen them I should never again be able to experience a night in Provence without feeling it as it exists in his pictures. Picasso's drawing reestablishes things in their own truth, for out of an infinitely variable appearance, out of billions of snapshots, he distills a constant, eternalizes the sum of the images, totalizes his experiences.

Picasso did two portraits of Hélène Parmelin (*Mme. H.P.*). On one she is stooping, as if coiled in on herself, with a triangular face and an ambiguous smile, framed by an ample mass of blond hair, long cascading spaghetti whose supple arabesques contrast with the angular, "broken" character of the body, outlined with stresses suggesting stained-glass technique. On the other, conversely, she is all curves and roundness, with waves of straw-colored hair, sumptuous breasts and the buttocks of the Callipygian Venus. She preferred to keep the former.

The portraits were placed out on the grass, and Mme. H. P. looked at herself, while Picasso and Pignon off to the side argued animatedly. As she describes it:

> . . . Each in turn got up from the grass where they were continually sitting or lying down, to go up and shake their fingers right over a bit of the canvas, in the way painters do (the finger a millimeter off the surface) that so upsets guards in museums.
>
> . . .
>
> Picasso looks at the canvas and tells me he rendered me just as I am. But that was not what he should have done at all. And next time he'll do me as I am.
> Listening to him, seeing him, knowing how he is at work, painting appears as the instrument of a dazzling way of knowing, and magnificently impossible. Each finished canvas opens up a horizon more difficult than that of the day before.
> That is what gives his journeyman work so severe a feeling, sometimes also so tragic. Nothing is ever easy for the painter to whom everything is easy . . .

Picasso was doing the large *Woman with Baby Carriage* sculpture, inspired by Françoise pushing Paloma's carriage, when the Braques arrived. It was a real carriage with the child and woman made of assembled junk, a cast-iron chimneypiece, cake molds, cheese grater, corrugated-iron pipe, and a gas-heater ring. The woman looked like a barbaric idol of hieratic deportment, with a tiny little schematic-featured head on top of a long neck.

The Braques had been driven down from Paris by Claude Laurens, the sculptor's son, and had made a detour through Sorgues to revisit the little town where, in 1912, with Pablo and Éva, they had spent such a happy, fruitful vacation, the year collages were invented. Picasso was delighted to see "little Claude," to whom, on his sixth birthday in 1915, he had given a coloring set. "No day has ever gone by without my thinking of Braque," he told him. And they cut up old touches, until Cocteau arrived, ending the friendly reunion with his usual high jinks.

All the 1950–1951 sculptures are not assemblages: for example, the Owls, the Women's Heads, and the Doves. The *Pregnant Woman* is his monument to fecundity, naked, with taut muscles, small high head, arms hanging at the sides, proudly displaying her smooth swollen belly and round breasts. This woman had previously been one of the group shot in the *Massacre in Korea,* and he long kept a meter-high casting of her on his studio worktable.

Among friends, he was always happy, having fun. He had always liked to put on disguises, and they would bring him costumes or hats from everywhere, picturesque or wild, that he wore and sometimes reproduced in pictures. He also liked to dress up his women and children, making masks for them, as well as for his surprised visitors. Hélène Parmelin tells how once when she was in bed with a sore throat at Vallauris, in came Picasso, Pignon, and Paulo dressed as Spanish *penitentes* and exaggeratedly aping the *De profundis* of a holy procession. At the beach, Picasso would cut up, dance, and have Claude and Paloma splitting with laughter as he dragged them into the water.

Once when Aragon came to the studio with Elsa, winded from climbing the steep street, and the local Party bigwigs, Pablo rushed him over to the *Baboon with Young,* saying, "Get a look at your ancestor!"

A Parisian antiquarian was there one day, when Picasso suddenly asked, "Are you tattooed?" The painter was bare-chested, as usual, in a pair of shorts, which he topped in the evening, "to go out," with a striped sailor's shirt. When his visitor said he was not, Picasso said, "Then take off your jacket and shirt! I'm going to tattoo you."

This was the beginning of a whole tatooing period—done actually in gouache —when every time a friend came by Pablo covered his chest, back, face, and legs with various signs and figures, fauns, cupids, nymphs, or demons. Starting at the chest or umbilicus, he would trace hilarious, if erasable, faces. Making him the inventor or forerunner of "body art."

Kahnweiler and the Leirises often came to Vallauris. For all that Kahnweiler was a friend of so many years, he remained *the* dealer to Pablo, and as such their relationship, though cordial, was very complex. The painter still insisted he was being "gypped" by him, fooled and betrayed, but the dealer had Picasso down pat, and paid no heed to such talk. He was used to it . . .

The fact was, they were "gypping" each other, both conscious of playing the game, old and solid as their friendship, of each foiling his adversary's traps— which were set knowing full well they would be foiled. This two-character play was their best mutual creation. As different from one another as could be, in all respects, what they held against each other was just what made them re-ciprocally indispensable. The antagonisms between Picasso and Kahnweiler were their strength, the cement of their understanding, and if we are to believe the amusing anecdotes Françoise Gilot tells of how Pablo "rehearsed" with her how he was going to get the better of his dealer the next day, he toyed with her just as he did with Kahnweiler. But the latter was not taken in, while she was.

In Spring 1952, Kahnweiler held a show of Françoise's paintings in his Rue d'Astorg gallery. Pablo came by the day before the vernissage, to check how everything was hung; Louise Leiris had asked a few friends in and a great time was had by all.

This was bullfight time; Pablo and his tribe never missed one. During the season, he was fanatical about it: every Sunday, they trekked to Nîmes, Arles, Aix, Fréjus, where a huge, teeming, varicolored crowd cheered the master as well as the corrida. He would arrive like a prince, driven by Paulo, smiling happily, his sombrero on his ear, surrounded by his court, saluted by the car horns, calls, shouts, whistles, applause, and sometimes even a brass band. For weeks they talked of nothing but the bullfights at Vallauris, Picasso saying that he was too busy and would not be able to go. Until Saturday morning, when he exploded with "You're not going to keep me from going to the bullfights, you know!"

And Paulo, who knew the routine, already had a batch of tickets. The Old Man, as he called him, would rage at "having to drag friends along," then go out and invite the first familiar faces he saw, and a parade of cars took off from Vallauris on Saturday night or Sunday morning.

In each of the cities there was a group of friends who faithfully forgathered at Picasso's corrida. Françoise, carsick as an aftermath of Paloma's birth, would be pale as a corpse but Pablo, radiant, ignored that, embraced the new arrivals and clapped them on the back Spanish-style, shook hands, greeting with equal euphoria aficionados and rubbernecks, to say nothing of the carloads of Parisians who came down for the bigger occasions.

As soon as Pablo got into town, he had to go to the toril and see what the bulls looked like, then to the hotel where the toreros were staying, to see them. One of the most serious moments was the discussion with the breeder about the characteristics of each entry—followed by a group luncheon.

In Nîmes there was a traditional huge paella for the Picasso party, given by André Castel, big boss of the local corridas. Present would be John Richardson and Douglas Cooper, who, at his Castille château not far away, had a superb Cubist collection; the Leirises, Georges Bataille, Jean Cocteau flanked by Édouard Dermit and Mme. Weisweiler, André-Louis Dubois and his guests, Coco Chanel and Serge Lifar, the Vilatos, Pignons, Ramiés, and more. Also a delegation of Spaniards from Barcelona.

On one Sunday that Picasso was never to forget, Oscar Dominguez and Marie-Laure de Noailles spent the whole bullfight gorging themselves right behind him, while he furiously tried to concentrate on the corrida as was his wont. That day, it became too much for him, and he finally turned away from the arena toward the shameless gluttons. Françoise was on the point of throwing up over the fumes from their garlic sausage, while Prévert kept calling them "fucking idiots" between his post-paellian belches. Pablo, his eye more somber than ever, unleashed a blistering series of Spanish insults at Dominguez—and the latter grabbed the sandwiches, the sausages, the bottles of beer, and everything else, and flung it all into the arena. For a moment, everything stopped. But the painter was a Spaniard—and a friend of Picasso's. The whole stadium burst into thunderous applause, and the bullfight went on.

Pablo himself had to admit it had been a *beau geste.*

Knowing that Françoise could not stand the sight of blood, he would often advise her against coming. Since she knew what that meant, she would acquiesce. Later, in Jacqueline Roque, he was to find a subtler companion, who smiled graciously as he covered her shoulders with the cape of honor that had just been presented to him. While he yelled, exclaimed, protested, jumped up, banged his fists against the railing or his knees, she would quietly put her hand on his arm. When he calmed down, she could read the expressions of distress, anger, admiration, or glee on his face.

In the evening, it was back to Vallauris, after a generally grandiose dinner well washed down with wine in a restaurant previously selected by Paulo, who acted as organizer for the paternal feastings. When the corrida was at Nîmes, the evening would be spent at the Château de Castille, where Douglas Cooper, the generous host, brought together everybody who was anybody in Paris, London, or the Riviera to join with the master.

Kahnweiler regularly showed Picasso's recent works, each vernissage being an event, first at Rue d'Astorg, then later in Rue de Monceau in the new Louise Leiris Gallery, opened in 1957, which Pablo never saw. Almost every year, in January, Kahnweiler, Louise Leiris, and the gallery manager Maurice Jardot, himself a remarkable connoisseur of the painter's works, presented Picasso's own selection of his new productions. He had a complete set of photographs of the Rue de Monceau gallery and at each show he was sent full photographic coverage of the ensemble as well as each panel, with the canvases displayed where he had himself planned.

Tokyo in 1951 had a showing of the 1937–1950 pictures, with 1905–1951 etchings and lithographs exhibited at Basel, Essen, Friburg-in-Brisgau, Hamburg, Munich, Nuremberg, and Stuttgart. The Palazzo Reale in Milan in 1953 offered visitors a simultaneous viewing never to be duplicated, of *Guernica, Massacre in Korea, War* and *Peace,* among two hundred paintings, thirty-four illustrated books, and several hundred drawings, engravings, ceramics, and sculptures. "Picasso has bemused Italy," wrote Claude Roy in review, "outdrawing Rita Hayworth in *Gilda.*"

That same year at the National Gallery of Modern Art in Rome, the President of Italy officially opened the show (something the President of France was not to deign to do until 1971—for Picasso's ninetieth birthday).

Also in 1953, the Stedelijk Museum of Amsterdam exhibited lithographs, watercolors, and bronzes. In 1954, Picasso's graphics were presented at the Liège Museum in Belgium by Tristan Tzara, and the Kunsthaus in Zurich by Bernhard Geiser and R. Wehrli. In Paris, the Berggruen Gallery show, with introduction by Kahnweiler, had the 1903–1907 drawings, and the Maison de la Pensée française again had an Aragon preface for its "Picasso: Two Periods, 1900–1914 and 1950–1954." The São Paulo Museum of Modern Art also had an impressive show of the recent paintings in 1954.

Notwithstanding market fluctuations, the prices of his canvases had steadily increased since that amazing bid of 11,500 francs in 1914 for *The Acrobats* at the *Peau de l'Ours* sale. The alien-property sales of the Kahnweiler and Uhde works had in no way impeded the rise, since in 1925 a still life sold for 11,200 francs had constituted a record for a painting of medium size at the time. In October 1927, the heights were attained with the *Harlequin Family,* a 1906 gouache, going for 52,100 francs.

"Kahnweiler, I have good news for you," Pablo quipped to his dealer. "I've raised your rates!"

In 1930, for the account of the Toledo, Ohio, Museum, René Gimpel paid 110,000 francs for the Blue Period gouache, *The Blind Man.* Works from that and the Rose Period were the most sought-after, with Fauns and Harlequins outranking the Cubist canvases, symptomatic of world taste in the time between the two world wars.

In 1937, a *Still Life with Blue Pitcher* went at auction for 56,500 francs, and the following year a Blue Period *Maternity,* a pencil drawing with watercolor, brought 6,500 francs.

During World War II, prices still rose: 1943, 60,000 francs for a *Seated Woman;* 1945, 160,000 for a *Beach Scene;* 340,000 in 1946 for a still life. Drawings and watercolors were following the same upward curve: 37,000 francs in 1947 for a Blue Period drawing of *Head of a Woman* and 140,000 for a sanguine *Maternity.*

Starting in 1949, the Cubist paintings, now regarded as "classics," started to fetch high prices, but when the youthful works were sold it was their rarity that shot the figures up. Thus, in 1950, an 1897 *Pyrenees, Spanish Side* brought 225,000 francs, and a 1907 portrait of Max Jacob 535,000. About the same amount was paid in December 1952 for a 1940 *Portrait of a Woman,* on paper remounted on canvas.

At the Girardin auction in December 1953, *At the Beach* went for 2,350,000 francs, and a portrait dated 1942 in pastel and wash for 190,000.

The exhibition at the Milan Palazzo Reale was a triumph, and for the one in Rome, Jean Cocteau, who happened to be there, was asked to pay a tribute to his friend Picasso:

> Excuse me for speaking to you standing up and off the cuff [he said, with deep emotion], but I consider it indecent to sit down at a table to talk about a man who lives standing up, and is very rarely to be found sitting still . . .*

Pablo naturally went to neither Milan nor Rome, having other things on his mind; he was more and more involved with his blond poetess, who went everywhere with him and was only too happy to inform all and sundry about how intimate she was with the master. But she was not his only problem; life with Françoise was slowly coming unstuck.

Worst of all were the threats of requisition that hung over his apartment in Rue La Boétie, where he had not lived since the war, but which was full of furniture, pictures, everything that he had accumulated for years and which no one was permitted to touch. He even forbade anyone to use the apartment, although that would probably have obviated the threat of seizure. As long as his friend André-Louis Dubois was Prefect of Police, nothing happened, but things were not the same under his successor, who was both violently anti-Communist and woefully uninterested in modern art. He alleged that the apartment was no longer occupied, since Picasso was merely a tenant, and the painter, moreover, had two other residences, at Rue des Grands-Augustins and Vallauris, to say nothing of Boisgeloup, which he had given to his son.

To top it all off, Marcel, who often used the Oldsmobile for personal ends, had smashed it against a tree outside Paris. As the boss's confidant and accomplice in his amorous adventures, Marcel thought the part he played with such tact

---

* Tape-recorded, this improvisation was later printed by Cocteau as an afterpiece in his *La Corrida du premier mai* (1957). It is one of the most sensitive and truest pieces among all that the poet wrote about his friend Pablo.

made him immune to any reprisals—but the ladies, each for her own reasons, demanded his dismissal. Picasso hesitated, but then, to Marcel's amazement, fired him. He bought a Hotchkiss and let Paulo become his regular chauffeur, the son also rebuilding the old Hispano-Suiza, seating eight or nine, which the Old Man now used to take the gang to the bullfights.

Despite all the strings he pulled, Pablo had to move out of Rue La Boétie, a TV producer taking over the apartment. Sabartés was in charge of the moving, which took several days. The furniture was put in storage, along with pictures and sundry objects piled into seventy huge crates. A certain number of paintings, some precious objects, and various souvenirs were moved to Rue des Grands-Augustins, but for want of space there Pablo had to have some of them moved into the two apartments he had bought for Françoise, on the fourth and fifth floors at 9 Rue Gay-Lussac, just off the Luxembourg. She lived in the lower, while Inéz with her husband and son occupied the upper.

Picasso had stayed there several times with Françoise and the children, although he did not like the place. He did little work there, almost daily going to Rue des Grands-Augustins or to Mourlot's, Lacourière's, or elsewhere. During one of these winter stays, he caught cold and developed a pulmonary congestion. Claude and Paloma took sick too, and Picasso was out of circulation for several weeks. Once back on his feet, he returned to lithographs and to drawing.

Yet, for all his glory and adulation, Picasso felt lonely, at ease only with such old friends as Kahnweiler, Sabartés, Pignon, or Michel Leiris; and even among the Party people he was uncomfortable. He preferred the younger ones, for the elder treated him "like a pope and an idiot," and changed the subject whenever he tried to discuss the Party's ideas on art.

When Pierre Daix, the journalist, returned from deportation to Germany after the war, and was secretary to the Party chieftain Charles Tillon, Éluard had introduced him to Picasso. Now, Pablo would question him about the Party's attitude toward him, toward youth, the international situation, socialist realism, and so on. He had been deeply hurt by Party reactions to *Massacre in Korea,* and in these discussions with the Party-liner Daix, Picasso the man showed himself as he truly was: concerned, scrupulous, anxious for the truth, seeking confidence and human warmth. His tribe of courtiers, necessary as they were to him, weighed on him; great stars can rarely do without supporting players when age catches up with them. Françoise, forty years his junior, had added no one of her generation to their group, and at Vallauris as in Paris they were always surrounded by the same interchangeable group of courtiers.

In the paintings he was doing, of the children and Françoise, there were broken lines, sheared-off volumes, something both violent and sharp, as if Picasso were venting a grudge against form for, no doubt unconsciously, being the vehicle of his rancor, his angers, his defeats . . . This woman he had desired, and then possessed, no longer looked at him; in the pictures, she turned her head from him, and her profile lost its purity, its serenity . . . she didn't even look at his children anymore. She had gone away, was now part of a world that was not Picasso's world, and he could never forgive that.

Yet, whose fault was it? He had been so demanding, so excessive, trying to enslave her, while at the same time playing fast and loose. When sick, he required her to take the same treatment he took—so that, by the time he got well, she had to take to her bed. She lost weight ("You were a Venus when I met you," he nagged. "Now you're a Christ—and a Romanesque Christ, at that, with all the ribs sticking out"), and he lost interest. Some of the hangers-on, sensing the end was near, carefully cooled toward her so as to take his side—but he, of course, had no intention of breaking things off; he never did: he just set up something new alongside.

Likewise in art. Abstraction had triumphed, most of the younger people had adopted it, but this was in no way reflected in Picasso's painting or conduct. Is that surprising, after all? Should a seventy-year-old painter bend to the fad of the day? Of course not. Braque, always so discreet and respectful of the work of others, had quipped to him, "Abstract painting is just society painting. But its prices are concrete!" Pablo went him one better, with an equally ridiculous comment to Pignon: "Just imagine an abstract hunter. What could an abstract hunter do? Certainly not kill anything!"

Joke though he might, abstraction was on his mind. Had he not been abstract long before the others? In the hermetic period of Cubism. By now abstraction was an anachronism, out of date, but that did not keep him from talking constantly about it—usually in a pretty silly way—somewhat the way his enemies talked about him.

But now he had only one dominant obsession in everything he said: his sex apparatus and how to make the most of it, thereby to live, even to survive. He no longer desired Françoise, and found in others delights she no longer furnished, so she ought to be smart enough to understand and let him do as he pleased. Making love and painting, to him, were one and the same, the same expenditure of energy, the same virile joy. Sex and painting in his eyes spelled action.

On March 8, 1953, he did an important canvas, *Woman with Dog against Blue Background,* part of a cycle of paintings and drawings in which violence vies with cruelty. This is a far cry from the Flower-Woman, the fine pure portraits of Françoise; perhaps under the influence of one of his inamoratas—one of whom played an important part in 1950–1953—he had a revelation of the change that had occurred in his *amie,* not only physically (after the birth of Paloma), but also mentally. He, of course, never changed, just remained the pitiless domestic tyrant, the sultan with childish whims, the nabob with his servile followers, the Ogre of outsize appetites, since he was the center of the world, The Painter, Modern Art, Picasso.

The woman in the picture had violently grabbed the dog by the paws (it was his boxer, Yan), pinned it down, and sported a victorious smile on her face topped by her coil of hair—Françoise's chignon. The furious boxer bared his teeth in rage, fought back, but she was too strong.

On March 5, 1953, Stalin died, and Aragon phoned Picasso to get a front-page portrait of him for *Les Lettres françaises.* Published March 12, it created an awful scandal. Letters flooded in from Party members, saying the painter had made a sort of Asiatic playboy out of Stalin, and on March 18, after a protest from the Soviet embassy, the Party Central Committee, on motion by Auguste Lecoeur, "categorically disapproved" the portrait.

This scandal had hardly broken when the press invested La Galloise: American reporters were the most numerous and most sanguine. Would Picasso remain a Communist after such a disavowal? His local comrades wondered how he could have been disciplined without even a hearing. Pablo himself shut the door on the press with his statement, "This is a matter between the Party and me."

Françoise was away in Paris during all of this.

Pablo felt the Party rebuff keenly, and it was not the first time. Remember *Massacre in Korea,* the "exploded" Dove, and the Fougeron affair: the Party's adoption of that painter had been hardest to take; Pablo was still upset by it. Now, talking to Pierre Daix, who was to run afoul of Party discipline twenty years later with his *What I Know about Solzhenitsyn,* Pablo said, "I brought my bouquet of flowers to the funeral. They didn't like it. That happens, but usually people don't catch hell for bringing flowers that others don't like." And he went on:

> At first I was going to do Stalin naked, like a kind of hero. But if I had done him nude, I'd have had to put in his cock. They would have bawled me out for giving him a big cock, and said, "You did the same thing with Franco!"
>
> My Stalin was young, that's all. Wasn't that how he had looked? Of course. But now that's not the one they want—they want him old, and white-haired . . .

Suppose Pablo had given him a laurel wreath? They would not have put up with that, either, and yet, he told Daix, "You'll see, when they need a portrait for dictionaries, they'll use mine."

A warm letter from Maurice Thorez smoothed things over a bit—and the affair ended with the quite pitiful "self-criticism" that Aragon published in the *Lettres* for April 9.

On her return from Paris, Françoise took him violently to task, to his amazement telling him the portrait was a terrible mistake and he was in the wrong. He could hardly believe his ears: for the first time, she was taking sides against him. When his associates pointed this out to her, she blew up, saying no one cared about her or her painting, that Pablo was a has-been, and the painters of her generation were doing the painting of the future. They were what the Party needed. She had joined the "Worker-Painters" group that Franz Masereel had founded in Nice, and was taking part in a few weeks in its first offering at the St.-Denis Museum.

Never before had Françoise talked that way about the Party and the workers. Why the reversal? Was she not equally entitled to be supported by the Party and exhibit under its aegis? Could the brilliant young Communist essayist, a friend and eulogizer of Pablo's, with whom she was so often seen, have been responsible for these new attitudes of hers?

Back in Paris, Pierre Daix told the Aragons about Françoise's violent reaction, and to his surprise they defended her. "She found a good pretext for breaking up with him," the novelist said. "It will be for political reasons . . ."

As for Picasso, he refused to have anything more to do with them, and was not to see Aragon again until 1971, after Elsa had died.

There was something amiss now between the painter and his Party. He could not understand the Khrushchev purges, or what "de-Stalinization" meant. When he asked for explanations, he got evasive answers that shocked and upset him. As he said, "When I ask Thorez, 'What's going to happen now?' I always feel he's going to answer me, 'Take your pail and go play in the yard.' "

The last was no joke, but a true expression of his frustration. He was anxious to question Hélène Parmelin when she returned after five weeks in the Soviet Union at the XXth Congress, the "de-Stalinization" one, and came to see him at La Californie, where by then he was living with Jacqueline in Cannes. She was ready to tell him "all about it," but that was a hard thing to do with him, because he always asked questions that went beyond that "all." So, like a good Party member, she preferred not to relate what her explanations had been, or his questions, his irritation, his rancor or confusion.

Picasso at the time was painting Paloma playing, still lifes, Vallauris land-scapes, heads of women, in short what was before his eyes—a somewhat deadly period, in which one feels he was painting just to keep painting, as a person eats only to keep alive, out of organic habit and need.

One day in January he amazed the workers at Mourlot's, on whom he dropped in as he did whenever he was in Paris: in a corner of their shop, he looked over the zinc plates about to be scrapped, and was taken with one of them, a halftone screen that had been used to print the poster for the exhibition of nineteenth-century painting from Lyons held at the Orangerie in November 1948. It was the portrait of an Italian woman painted by Victor Orsel.

Delighted with it, he took it home and brought it back the next day, "Picas-sized": the woman had not been greatly changed, though some of her features were stressed with a black outline, but all around her were strange characters, fauns making all kinds of faces and playing all kinds of flutes to try to tempt this serene young person in native costume, while a nude woman, arms crossed, on the sidelines, watched bemused.

At Vallauris, he had gradually gotten away from ceramics. In 1951 and 1952, he did only a few pieces: a plate with a fish against a colored background, a profile of a goat, a vase with goats, a still life with spoon on a flat plate on December 22, 1952, a dish with a very schematized face on it and inscribed "Vallauris," on March 10, 1953, a bullfight on a round plate March 11, then nothing more until September.

Picasso had not forgotten the invitation from Jacques de Lazerme, son of the Catalan poet Carlos de Lazerme, to come and visit him and his wife in Perpignan. He arrived there on August 12, 1953, with Maya, and they put him up in a beautiful pale pink suite in their mansion, which they had originally shared with Jacques's late poet-father. But Pablo first took off to a bullfight at Collioure, then popped back to Paris, and returned on September 5, with not only Maya, but also Paulo, Xavier Vilato, and a whole retinue, completely taking aback the Lazermes, unused to King Picasso's ragtag court. The pretext for this second visit, this invasion, was a bullfight in Perpignan. The next day he was joined by Totote and Rosita Manolo and other friends.

The Communists in Céret took this occasion to organize a reception in honor of the painter, who delightedly came there with the Pignons and Paulo. After speeches and toasts in white wine, the master was asked for a drawing, and on a large sheet of drawing paper he did a pen-and-ink drawing of a dance beneath the dove: *The Sardana of Peace.*

A few days later he returned to Vallauris, where, during a violent argument, Françoise informed him she was leaving him. He would not believe it, because this was not his way. What would she do without him? What would become of her? Can a woman desert the father of her children? Especially when Picasso had "given" Claude and Paloma to Françoise to make a woman of her.

When she said she was taking them along, he did not understand. Ogre, nabob, tyrant—he was speechless. For the first time in his life, a woman stood up to him, worse, thwarted him in the love he bore his children. And upset all his ideas about women, love, relationships, life; ideas as old as ancient Iberia and its conventions and prejudices that made his mate into a man's slave, his object, and nothing more.

To him, a woman who was not a mother was incomplete; he had been pitiless, though faithful to his own logic, in the way he had thrown up to Dora Maar that she had no children. Olga was the Mother Supreme, since he had married her, and Paulo superior to Maya and Françoise's offspring, because he was "legitimate." Pablo alone could undo that hierarchy as he alone could undo the ties he himself had made. No one else. Especially not the woman who for the past few months had been slipping away from him, no longer even inquired where he had been when he stayed away for days on end, made him no scenes over it, nor questioned the female faces in his drawings and pictures which, ostensibly, were those of her rivals. When he called her "a monster of indifference," he was being supremely offensive, for no one had the right to be indifferent to Picasso.

He may or may not have known what people were saying: that she was having an affair with the young writer who, nonetheless, was often to put his pen in the service of the master and his glory. That she was seen a lot at the beach with a young Greek student . . . Was he forgetting that he was over seventy? He was suffering like the blinded Minotaur, and moaning his complaints to Sabartés, Kahnweiler, the Leirises, Dominique Éluard, the Ramiés . . . to test their reaction, sneering, "You know, Françoise is leaving me!" But the words that seemed banal were like so many daggers to him—for if she left, the children went, too.

War and *Peace,* symbols of this period of his life, were still in the Fournas studio where he had done them. When Luciano Emmer came to shoot his film about him, titled *War and Peace,* Picasso painted directly on the arch of the Vallauris chapel a figure of war and a huge dove, murals which remained even after the panels were put up. Why did it take six years for the two big compositions finally to be installed, and unveiled, and the Temple of Peace opened to the public? The reactions of visitors, when the Vallauris paintings were shown, had disappointed him: the "committed" painter was much less popular, and what the Communists had to say, after the Stalin portrait business, did not help matters any. The dream of unity and brotherhood he wanted to express through *War* and *Peace* foundered on incomprehension and ambiguity. War was never going to be a thing of the past.

There was also the fact that the municipality of Vallauris was Communist, while the French government was anti-Communist. When the paintings were affixed permanently, Pablo could not make up his mind to do the composition for the rear, between the two panels. In a fit of pique, he forbade anyone to enter the chapel and even had a dark veil hung before the entranceway!

In October 1953, the Lazermes, in Paris, saw him several times. Pablo was more than hospitable to them at Rue des Grands-Augustins, insisting that his Perpignan hostess accept as a gift a Cézanne and a Juan Gris! Naturally, she refused.

He was alone, and did not want to go back to La Galloise, which belonged to Françoise. Yet he did go back there in November, embittered, sad.

And old.

On November 28, he did several drawings of a young woman undressing before a painter who has eyes only for his work . . . Then he stopped for several days, until December 14, when he went back to a drawing begun on November 27: a model seated, nude, and before her a hairy painter. Once that was done, he could not stop: between then and February 3, 1954, he was to do 180 drawings on the theme of The Painter and His Model. They are the sad song of an old man, feeling the loss of his youth, of love, of beauty. A sarcastic intimate diary, pitiful and tragic—the Picasso heart laid bare.

XXI

JACQUELINE,
THE GENIUS-GUARDING
SPHINX
(1954–1955)

"MATISSE IS DEAD."

That news, telephoned on the morning of November 3, 1954, awakened many old memories in Picasso. After Françoise left, and before the new love took shape, during the period that Michel Leiris called his "season in hell," he had gone to the Régina several times to visit his old friendly enemy in the light-filled room, brimming with exotic plants and doves, brilliantly enlumined by the fireworks of his recent paper cutouts.

Derain had died, too. Hit by a car on the road near his home at Chambourcy, he had been taken to the hospital at St.-Germain-en-Laye and closed his eyes without getting to see the young woman he loved so deeply, who had presented him with a child a short time before. Pablo had been very close to him, in the earliest days, during the Diaghilev Ballet period. Time had since gone by without their friendly relationship reviving. During the war, Derain had opted for "collaboration," and made his unfortunate trip to Weimar. Pablo after that had refused to shake hands with him, and they never saw each other again.

Maurice Raynal was gone, too, a friend of over half a century, a clearheaded, nonflattering critic. And Henri Laurens.

"Matisse is dead; he left me his odalisque," Picasso said, and this would soon prove more than a joke. In the following year, Matisse's presence was apparent in the amazing series of *Women of Algiers,* after Delacroix, the studio scenes, the portraits of Jacqueline in Turkish costume or Arlésienne dress. With Matisse gone, there was now available a whole inheritance of light and colors, brilliant tones with jarring constrasts of yellows, reds, greens, and blues, suns and gardens, beautiful languorous nudes, Edens of blossoming flowers, cooing doves in

*"Joy of Living"   Antibes 1946 (Musée Picasso,
Château Grimaldi—Antibes)*

(GIRAUDON)

broad bright interiors . . . Picasso made haste to claim it. His Mediterranean had been peopled by monsters and schematic, hybrid, poorly articulated creatures, like those of the capering *Joy of Living* in the Antibes Museum; now they were to be more human, the women under Pablo's brush assuming graceful undulations, joyful, clicking ornaments.

No one stood in his way any longer; Picasso had a free hand. His dialogue with the world became a monologue with himself. The basic impulse of the *Women of Algiers,* the *Rape of the Sabine Women,* by way of *Las Meninas* and the *Déjeuner sur l'herbe,* was as Matissian as could be—it was woman, too desirable, too multiple, too physical as well, whose simultaneous celebration and destruction he sought, knowing, as Matisse before him did, that she was beyond his reach.

Picasso also took over the exoticism and, beyond his ingenuous dream, the Orient which the painter of odalisques had made his own: an Orient of imagery but also of hothouses, those interior scenes that Pablo would enjoy proliferating as soon as he moved into La Californie, an added Oriental element in his repertory with its baroque Byzantine Art Nouveau and its tropical garden. Through decorative or constructive sumptuousness of color Pablo broadened the Matissian spell, but he was unable to avoid the dangers of mannerism; only the Spanish resurgence, during the short Vauvenargues period, was occasionally to ward it off.

With Françoise gone, Picasso at loose ends did not long remain womanless. The cycle of drawings begun November 28, 1953, and completed February 3, 1954, reflected his loneliness and spiritual discomfort, but no physical deprivation. He led a feverish sex life; that "immense masquerade," which, according to Leiris, was "part English Christmas pantomime, part *Commedia dell'arte,* and part *danse macabre,*" was also a retesting of his manly potency.

Abandoned by Françoise, he knew he had been deceived, and that was only justice, for he had never hidden his own infidelities—but he would not admit that justice. As proof, his huge output of drawings and washes, up to twenty in one day, displayed actors, clowns, acrobats, monkeys, naked women, through all of whom he was telling his story, weeping, laughing, satirizing himself, but also making confession.

Painfully. Yet insolently too. For he was struggling. The time might be nearing when he would have to give up loving, enjoying sex, women, climax, give up living. One is reminded of Baudelaire "through the darkness of night" looking "back into the deepest years," of Goya in his dramatic series of *Caprichos,* expressing his own passion through satire, politics, and suffering, making use of certain themes that Picasso was to reprise.

He continued to be haunted by the idea of his "visual diary." Now, in addition to artist and model, there was the corollary: creative impotence. These two, actually identical, themes provided the sad or comical incidents of the romance of which, whatever its aspect, he was the hero. Yet, he portrayed himself only as victim though still able to accuse and jeer. The Painter and His Model are old age and loneliness facing youth, beauty, love, as well as the creator facing the creature who but for his ability to give form to the formless would be nothing. She is as dependent on him as a work of art on its author. There is a whole cruel nostalgic ballet of these old men and young girls, the former myopic, kinky, obese, lustful, the latter teasing, sensuous, reticent, mocking, evasive, the better to exhaust the panting suitor, holding his big belly in both hands, or surprised that Cupid should come to her wearing an enormous mask, yet accepting with delighted protest the onslaughts of these Amors in ever uglier masks . . .

Before his easel, the bearded painter, collapsed in an armchair, overwhelmed by his incapacitating impotence, watches the gorgeous naked girl, who, with finger to lips, orders him to keep quiet. Another, ugly enough to scare you, hairy and wearing glasses that practically touch the canvas, pays no attention to the three sumptuous nudes apparently posing in vain. A third is painting a magnificent creature whose arms behind the back of her neck brace her chest to bring out the firm rounded breasts, while a worried colleague seems to be contemplating the work of art being created, out of the frame . . .

The critique of creativeness which leads Picasso to replace the attractive model by meaningless scribbles, and the painter by a clown or a monkey, is a hymn to woman. Can there be a purer beauty, a more splendid image of youth than the one whose blooming suave outline is limned on Christmas Day, 1953? The unfinished body, with its Hellenic-profiled head, its ponytail hair, has two lightly sketched breasts—and the rest is just space, the infinite flesh of the whiteness of paper, whiter than a milk spot.

When the painter disguises himself as a clown, it is the better to make fun of what he is trying to do—or he may be a monkey, quietly painting while that same beautiful naked model eyes him with amusement. His eye sees only the pointed breast darted toward him and his mouth that has the same breast shape.

Then back come old man and clown. Where the Barbary ape had stupidly offered his lips and short little arms to the flourishing beauty two heads taller than he, the old man accepts his decrepitude less comfortably. He gets older and older, hairier and hairier, potbellied, broken-down. He nearsightedly presses his goateed snout toward the displeased beauty sitting on the stool; he sniffs at the proffered flesh which another bearded oldster is gazing at without amenity.

How can one decipher all the thoughts, the recollections that went through Picasso's brain and hand while he was doing this pathetic carnival? Just what is taking place in the studio between painter, clown, ape, and model? What is the meaning of the scene of the hefty wrestler lifting up a Rubensesque nude, in front of some clowns and another nude woman, doubtless his other partner? On the porcelain-tiled terrace with its Matissian palm trees, what are these gestures of the nude odalisques near a hookah, one looking comical, the other as pure of profile as a Grecian vase? In a virtually identical scene, the woman has on a grotesque old-man's mask while he is wearing her attractive young one, as a monkey in the background, outraged, turns his head away.

This game of masks in the presence of the monkey has an important place in Picasso's drawings. Do the old man and the pretty young nude exchange masks because they can't trade ages and powers? What is mere amusement for her is bitter derision to him. Where the game gets complicated is when Harlequin, taking off his huge bearded oldster's mask, shows the amazed woman and monkey his real face—that of a young leading man made up as for a Japanese No play.

A deformed dwarf wears a mask resembling the naked girl's face; she replies, kneeling to reach his level, with the mask of a handsome virile man.

An old man, sitting tailor-fashion, potbelly abulge, smiles salaciously at the naked girl seated opposite him. This color-crayon drawing is dated January 27, 1954. Had wisdom become the finale of the art of love? All innocence and purity, the adolescent girl is a figure of exquisite grace.

From full-flowering beauty to nymphet, the whole gamut of femininity beneath his fingers dances a ballet of seduction. Of all seductions. Those that need a mask, and those that don't. The complicated and furtive ones, the subtle and the familiar, the sensual and the carefree. Infinite variations in which the figures turn the dramatist of *Guernica* and *The Charnel House* into a bitter sybilline moralist to whom each image is a fable. Woman needs to be loved in order to exist, as the model needs to be painted, but it is man, the creator, who brings life to them, and whether young or old, handsome or deformed, or making use of a clown or monkey, caricatures of himself, he is the irreplaceable demiurge, and woman must submit to his desires. Those of his appetites as of his impotence, of his sex as well as his gaze. For that alone counts, since man by wearing a mask can disguise himself at will.

Toward the end of the set, Picasso, thanks to color crayons, was able to give a light-fingered polychrome to the limpid dancing arabesque. The nervous, jerky, scratchy line, the spot, the runnings, the wash and gradations gave way to an Ingresque linear precision harking back to the "wire" drawing of the 1920s. The last drawing, February 3, 1954, shows the nude model with a mask of classical beauty seated before the bearded painter with his tousled head, looking at his painting—not a portrait of the pretty girl but a mocking image of himself. Is not art, as he had once told Sabartés, the child of sadness and pain? And of lies.

Through this November 1953–February 1954 cycle, Picasso was approaching the drama of creation. It has absolutely extraordinary tension and power of concentration and analysis, qualities that were to remain present in all of his drawings and engravings until the very end.

Michel Leiris wrote about this series:

> Never had more artistic genius been put to work to make fun of art, and never had it been so peremptorily demonstrated that, in the final analysis, nothing had been changed of the essential, held in check by physical decline, prior to the evil of absolute separation—for the one who can do whatever he wishes with his brain and his ten fingers.*

Pablo had broken off his "diary" for a few hours to celebrate New Year's Eve, December 31, 1953, at a restaurant in Vallauris with the Lazermes, the Pierre Brunes, Totote and Rosita Manolo, and a few other friends he had invited.

---

* In "Picasso et la comédie humaine ou les avatars de Gros Pied" (Picasso and the Human Comedy, or the Avatars of Big Foot), the introduction to *Verve*, No. 28–30, special issue reproducing the 180 drawings done November 28, 1953–February 3, 1954.

The "season in hell" had in no way dimmed the ardors of the faun: his appetite had for some time been fixed on a pretty young brunette with regular though somewhat sharp features, an aquiline nose, and almond-shaped eyes. There was something hieratical and mysterious about her that awakened his concupiscence, and he saw a great deal of her, since she was the hostess of the Madoura pottery.

Jacqueline Roque, divorced from an overseas bureaucrat, lived with her four-year-old daughter, Catherine, in a villa at Le Suquet. She was free to come and go, and was more often at the beach than at the Ramiés', which was where Pablo went to see her between liaisons. She, in turn, called on him at La Galloise when Françoise was away.

He greatly missed the children, whom Françoise had taken with her to Paris. She agreed that he might see them whenever he wished, but they were so young and his life was such that this was not easy to arrange. He did several canvases based on Claude and Paloma, as well as some drawings: the little boy and his sister drawing, a familiar image of the old happy days, following the series completed in February, as yet another homage to creation. Here, no more bitterness, anger, revolt, but paternal affection expressed with remarkable economy of means.

Two canvases done in the waning days of 1953 show a very schematic man, silhouetted in black, going into a bedroom at La Galloise: back to the sun, he is going toward a bed on which a naked woman is sleeping in an exposed pose. Here was Picasso trying to forget his loneliness, his sadness, and his hunger: in ever renewed sex bouts with beautiful new partners. A toy belonging to the children has been left behind on a shelf, a homely reminder of the broken home. The *Nude in the Studio* (December 30) is a woman lying in the limber pose of Matisse's odalisques, in which he has superimposed the truly Picassian monochrome structuring of broken rhythms and acute angles over the colorful decorative themes (rugs, fabrics, curtains) that had been so dear to the master of Cimiez.

One day on the street in Vallauris, Picasso met a girl with a lithe slim body and a ponytail, referred to as "the English girl," because on the Riviera any slim blond girl had to be English, and besides, her escort, Toby Jellinek, was an Englishman. Twenty and French, born at Boulogne-sur-Seine, she had met Toby at the Summerhill school; her name was Sylvette David.

"What a delicate doe," was Pablo's reaction. The ladies of his court panicked, but this was no affair: he just wanted Sylvette to pose for him. Overwhelmed and delighted, she agreed—prudently bringing Toby along.

Pablo was moved by the long-necked sylph in the black slipover that revealed her tiny bosom, wide flowing skirt, and ballet pumps. An islet of purity and candor in the feminine archipelago, a good pretext for a series of eighteen portraits in which, as against the way he had once experimented with Marie-Thérèse, Dora Maar, or Françoise, he sought no metaphor, or any intermediaries between the model and him. The dialogue went directly from the painter's eye to his hand, from the model to her image never dissociated from reality, even when decomposed according to Cubist principles, with some of the characteristic Picassian procedures: double imaging and interpenetration of the features full-face and in profile, in stylization verging on schematization.

He appears literally to have been fascinated by Sylvette's grace, to the point of not daring to touch her. After the previous winter's "season in hell," she was a sort of messenger of youth, beauty, happiness, but the old man sensed all the dangers of seduction, of "prettiness," and therefore in some of the Sylvette portraits he did not hesitate simply to obliterate her face with one vertical sweep.

In the series of pictures he painted of her, along with the many drawings, he experimented with every medium. Sylvette went through various stages of the Picassian vocabulary: doubled up, reconstructed, outlandishly elongated or, on the contrary, squashed down, cut up into rectangles or segments. But whatever he does to her, she never loses her powers—or, rather, Picasso, under her spell, lets her keep them, perhaps in an effort to exorcise the monsters still abroad and threatening. Even faceless, she looks out at the future.

All the portraits of Sylvette are done in a camaïeu monochrome of silvery-soft blue-gray.

On June 3, 1954, he painted a new female figure, but this was no longer Sylvette, the blue and blond passerby of a springtime, but a strong woman with a hard face of sharp lines and masses, atop a long rectangular neck. Her compact body is all in acute angles, her hands clasped around her knees. Behind her, the space is cut up into broad geometrical planes. There is frank harmony in the grisaille of head and hair, with its peremptory plastic authority in contrast to the blues, reds, yellows, and dark browns of the overall picture.

The monumental aspect of this portrait is striking; it is his first of Jacqueline Roque. Picasso had made her into a Sphinx.

The Vallauris bullfight that year was to be a special success. Early in July, with Paulo, he went to visit the Lazermes at Perpignan to invite them to this celebration, which he was to preside over after a triumphal tour through the little pottery town, standing in an open car with Penrose, Cocteau, Prévert, André Verdet, and all his customary jesters, waving to the delighted populace. Pablo and his friend Pierre Beaudouin, the tapestry expert and producer, both had half their heads shaved, and the barbers working for the Spaniard Arias, who had the exclusive concession of haircutting and shaving the master, were as usual dressed as matadors—for the high point of the festivity was to be the bullfight with "trophy presented by the great painter Picasso": a piece of Madoura ceramics. The corrida might be substandard, but Pablo was having a better time than he had in ages.

Beside him in the stands were Françoise and the children, an unsmiling, hard-faced Françoise—as well as Jacqueline Roque, who smiled agreeably every time Pablo expressed his amusement at the matadors' clowning. There was also Paule de Lazerme, laughing or smiling as befitted each occasion, wearing a solid gold necklace with a bull's head, which Pablo had designed and had made as a gift to her.

When Douglas Cooper saw it, he offered to buy it from her—but, of course, she would not sell it.

Then the master left for Perpignan with Maya, for a nice quiet summer at the Lazermes'—until Jacqueline arrived unexpectedly. Picasso refused to let her stay with him at the Lazermes', and sent her to a hotel.

He was painting. At night, he and friends would go to dinner at René Pous's Hostellerie des Templiers at Collioure, watch the sardana being danced in the square; and it was as if he was back in Céret. He even considered moving here from Vallauris, took two rooms to work in at the Villa Miranda, a Templiers annex, and went swimming on the beach with his children. He told Jacques de Lazerme he would like to buy "a big house like yours," and selected the imposing château of St. Elmo up above Collioure in all its repulsive splendor—but it belonged to the departmental government and was not for sale.

Firmin Bauby had set up a small art center at Perpignan, the San Vicens Pottery, which Pablo, accompanied by Jacqueline, found greatly to his liking. He decided to start a ceramics project to decorate the Temple of Peace planned for Fontfrede Peak, above Céret, facing Spain. He had visited the mountain in the summer of 1953; a monument to bullfighters was to be put up there at the time, but he had convinced his friends that a Temple of Peace would be more appropriate . . . yet it was eventually erected not here but at Vallauris.

The inhabitants of the latter place had not taken to the idea of his moving away. The Pignons, the Leirises, with the Ramiés, tried to enlist Jacqueline in their cause, sensing her coming election to the master's favor.

On the other hand, at the Lazermes' in Perpignan, René Pous's at Collioure, or Firmin Bauby's at San Vicens, Pablo, surrounded by ladies-in-waiting and gentlemen at his beck and call, played alternately the role of Ogre, Sultan, or Nabob. If new persons struck his fancy, he added them to his retinue: when three pretty girls asked him for his autograph at San Vicens, he told them, "Go have your hair done; dress your prettiest, and come to dinner at a friend's." That evening, the amazed damsels were among his guests at the Hostellerie des Templiers —among fifteen, twenty, or more, for en route he had recruited a group of tourists and even some of the locals, whom he invited in Catalan.

A radiant King Picasso signed the Golden Book, made little potato figures that he colored with the ladies' rouge and lipstick and articulated with matchsticks, and even went into the kitchen to lend a hand. Local artists came to pay tribute to him, flashbulbs crackled, the fiesta was on. A guitar was heard and a voice singing a *copla,* and later the sardana was danced in the square beneath the starry sky.

On August 15–16, he chaired the Collioure festivities as he had those at Vallauris a few weeks before. But none of this kept him from painting or drawing, at the Miranda, or at his Perpignan hosts', where he drew Paule de Lazerme several times in Catalan costume, as well as doing portraits of Totote and Rosita Manolo. But after the wild days, he cried for some peace: "Turn the phone off and close your door, Jacques," he requested. "Act as my screen."

The Vallauris clan redoubled their efforts and in the summer of 1954 the Lazerme home was the field on which his future was decided. The hosts, abetted by Firmin Bauby, did their best to convince him to stay, emphasizing the many plans he had for San Vicens, when he finished his work at Vallauris. During one such session he cut his name and the date, August 20, 1954, into an aloe leaf in the garden.

Jacqueline had moved out of the hotel and into the Lazermes', where Françoise was also staying with Claude and Paloma. One night, the house was shaken with a terrible scene between a furious Picasso and Jacqueline; the next day, she quietly boarded the train, out of Perpignan. At lunch, to some fifteen rather subdued guests in the great dining hall, he expressed delight at her departure.

The phone rang. Jacqueline, calling from Béziers: he refused to speak to her. A few minutes later she was calling again, this time threatening suicide. Finally, at his host's insistence, he stepped into Lazerme's study and took the call. "Let her suit herself," he said when he came back. "I think I made her understand. I'm through with her." To all those present, Jacqueline Roque seemed eliminated.

Two days later she returned: "He said suit yourself. So here I am back." She stayed; he acquiesced, first furious, then resigned, finally flattered, at the presence of the shrewd, intelligent woman who insinuated rather than imposed herself, called him her god in public, kissed his hands, and equally charmed his hosts with her manner, tact, and indomitable will. Not for nothing did Totote Manolo call Jacqueline "the first woman to lead Picasso around by the nose."

Three months earlier the Maison de la Pensée française had unveiled one of the largest and most meaningful of Picasso shows, covering two of his key periods: 1900–1914 and 1950–1954. The works from the earlier period were from the Serge Shchukine Collection (which the Soviets, after taking power, had split between the Moscow and Leningrad museums) and the Gertrude Stein Collection, kept up by Alice B. Toklas. This was the ideal face-off between the Picassos of yesterday and today.

The pre-1914 assemblage had first-rank works, such as the 1903 *Celestina*, *Harlequin and His Mate*, *Old Jew*, *Little Girl Acrobat on a Balloon* from the 1905 Saltimbanque period, *Little Girl with Basket of Flowers*, the first Picasso Stein had bought in 1905, the two famous 1909 Cubist landscapes, *The Reservoir* and *Houses on the Hill*, a study for the *Nude with Drapery*, the *Farm Woman* painted in 1908 at La-Rue-des-Bois, the famous 1914 collage *Student with Pipe*, the no-less-famous Cubist portrait of Vollard, and so on.

"Picasso is harder to talk about than anyone else," wrote Aragon in the preface to the show. "Whatever one states, he immediately denies . . ." The exhibit demonstrated this to a T.

A few days after it opened, Shchukine's daughter, Irène Keller-Shchoukine, who had never protested before, took out an injunction against the show, and laid claim to her father's collection, nationalized thirty-seven years before. After a hearing behind closed doors, her petition was denied, but the show was closed and the ex-Shchukine pieces taken down, a precautionary measure to insure their safe return demanded by the Soviet embassy. Pablo sent several replacements, so the Maison de la Pensée could reopen.

Yet, despite his comrades' insistence, he was never to express himself about this case, which he said did not concern him, except to aver that "Mme. Keller-

Shchoukine's claim does not seem warranted." He had not even taken the trouble to come to see those old works of his: they too were of no concern. The fate of paintings is independent of that of the painter. "People don't understand what they have when they own one of my canvases," he told a friend. "Each one is a vial of my blood. That's what they're made of."

Yet the show was the occasion of many commentaries, the unforgiving old critics once again regretting his abandonment of his early realism for his "monstrous" and "inhuman" art. Claude Roger-Marx, in the *Revue de Paris,* September 1954, wrote:

> The war without truce that has been going on within him since his early years, the scorn he always felt for others and for himself, the mistrust he always had for his own facility, all drive him to eschew the wholesome, the normal. . . . His work methods inevitably lead to destruction, his metamorphoses are the opposite of natural metamorphoses: the butterfly turns back into a larva, the frog into a tadpole, man into fetus . . . Wherever Picasso is, breakage occurs . . .

Jacqueline was now a part of his private life, having tactfully moved into it after Perpignan, soon making herself indispensable, irreplaceable. Yet, not all his friends welcomed her; though she was intelligent, they felt her to be devious, and her passionate devotion to Picasso often seemed out of place. Aware of this, she held her peace, as she gradually built up her own entourage, tiny but active, parallel to his. Soon there was a Jacqueline atmosphere, Jacqueline decisions and decrees that enclosed Pablo in a network of solicitude and tenderness, to become in time a solid protective wall isolating him from the world, from his oldest friends, and even, except for Paulo, from his children.

Thus, under Jacqueline, the genius-guarding Sphinx, without let or hindrance his work would go on to the last day, his full pack of wizardry, seduction, and insolence in which she was to remain the last beloved face.

His portraits of his new helpmeet, done as soon as they returned to Paris, were a sort of revenge his male vanity took for Françoise's departure. This sovereign woman with her straightforward look, intelligent, sensitive, sure of herself and her power, replaced the fragile, faithless, detached female. The new reign was to be one of fervor and respect. Pablo, in his pictures, showed her a reverence he had never displayed to any of his previous women except Olga: no excessive distortion, no torturing cruelty, but a calm and, in the early 1954 canvases, loving realism. No one could ever doubt his love for her.

She was not known to many in the fall of 1954. The few visitors to the Grands-Augustins studio saw only portraits of Mme. Z. The one dated June 3, sent to the Maison de la Pensée française show, was simply titled *Portrait of a Young Woman.* Aragon gave it double-edged praise, saying, "I can hardly say who is stronger, artist or model. I would put my money on that young woman." He was not mistaken.

The Communists invited Picasso to the book sale of the National Writers' Committee, which they had taken over. It was a long time since he had taken part in a public demonstration of the sort, and he was gratified to see the admiration and curiosity the crowds exhibited toward him. Several times, it took force to restrain assaults on the stand at which he was autographing works about himself; according to his mood or the individual involved, he on occasion added a bit of drawing. The Communists, who had feared some backlash from "the masses" after the Stalin portrait, were reassured; but the Writers' Sale attracted more students and society women than workers.

Guests became more frequent at Rue des Grands-Augustins. His long stays at Vallauris, the break with Françoise, and events of the past summer had kept him away from his many Parisian friends; now they came up his spiral staircase every Saturday, his traditional "at home" day—all the old mixture of yore, and already Jacqueline, discreetly in the shadows, was beginning to sort them out.

It was back now to the Catalan's, the Flore, and Lipp, and to visit Kahnweiler and Mourlot. There was a tour up to Montmartre to Lacourière's, and the visit to the Bateau-Lavoir, to relive those old memories once again. They went to several galleries, to the Museum of Modern Art to check on how the 1946 gift had been hung and say hello to Jean Cassou. They bumped into an ecstatic lady who reported having been at the Writers' Sale, which, she said, was "like believers flocking to a miracle."

"If it had been," Pablo replied, "I wouldn't have gotten a blister from signing autographs."

As when each of his friends disappeared, Matisse's death sent him into a period of silence. When the painter's daughter, Marguerite Duthuit, phoned to tell him about it, to her great chagrin he would not speak to her, though he had a wonderful portrait Matisse had done of her in 1908. But, silence or no, he suffered cruelly from the void left by this loss. For Matisse had been more than a companion, he had been the brotherly rival of his entire life, the only one he put on a level with himself, who had his own wonderful secret world of forms, figures, and colors.

Picasso had some admirable canvases by the master of Cimiez, some of which he had swapped for years before, others that he had bought. At Vauvenargues, several hung in his dining room; at the Grands-Augustins, then at La Californie and at Mougins, the superb *Still Life with Oranges* had a place of honor on an easel in his studio. "The finest picture I know of," Picasso called it. Each year, on New Year's Day, Matisse sent him a crate of oranges, which he laid out before the picture, and no one was to touch. "Matisse's oranges," he would say with awe.

On his visits to him at Vence, and later at the Régina, he had admired a mahogany medal cabinet his friend had had made for storing his drawings. After his death, Matisse's children gave it to Picasso, who was deeply touched by the gesture: to friends, he often compared the clean-cut, straight, perfectly crafted and balanced cabinet to Matisse himself, also, as Pablo said, "made of precious wood."

The death of Maurice Raynal also affected him greatly, though there again he did not let it show. The critic had just finished a new work about him, and the day Picasso heard of his death he told another friend that each day he made a habit of silently ticking off the names of all his best friends, and he felt guilty, because that day he had left out Maurice's.

"But that doesn't mean you killed him," said his friend.

"Oh, to be forgotten is worse than to be dead," he replied.

With the death of Henri Laurens, May 5, 1954, a whole segment of his youth crumbled: they had been introduced to each other by Braque in 1915 at Léonce Rosenberg's, and Pablo had always esteemed the sculptor's great conscientiousness, his impoverished but dignified life, his refusal to compromise or take shortcuts. Picasso had always done whatever he could to help Laurens out. It was he who got Diaghilev in 1924 to commission Laurens to do the set for the Cocteau–Darius Milhaud operetta, *Le Train bleu*, about Riviera beach life. Laurens accepted, but only with the greatest misgivings: he had never been on a Riviera beach.

Busy at other things, Picasso never did get around to doing the Christ he had planned for his friend's grave in the Montparnasse Cemetery. When the sculptor's son decided to make a public gift of his father's works, he came to Picasso for advice. Tériade had been urging him to give them to St.-Jean-Cap-Ferrat, where he owned a magnificent estate which Laurens had several times visited. But Pablo said, "No, it has to be in Paris."

Technical problems intervened, and the Laurens gift was not unveiled until June 1973 at the Museum of Modern Art, with Picasso already two months dead.

On December 13, 1954, he started a series of canvases on the theme of Delacroix's *Women of Algiers,* a painting that had obsessed him for years, but which he did not bother to go back to study at the Louvre, where he had seen it years before.

Those carefree belles in their heavy harem atmosphere, with their languorous, supple, solid bodies, full bosoms, gazes peeking out through thick brows, were so many Jacquelines, like her discreetly sensual and pacifying, fleshly and delectable despite an evident and probably professional passivity. For two months, he fought with the Delacroix, decomposing it, recomposing it, analyzing it, arguing with it and making up. He moved the figures around, one especially fascinating him, the one at the right with the hookah, who looked so strikingly like Jacqueline. He transformed the Oriental serenity into a wild outburst of rhythms, volumes, cones, and cubes. In place of Delacroix's veiled eroticism, he portrayed overpowering sensuality: a good sign, the old man was not getting out of the saddle, and wanted the world to know how much enjoyment Jacqueline afforded him. *The Women of Algiers* are a public announcement of shared pleasures of the flesh.

But what detours he had to go through to get there!

The series of fifteen canvases done December 13–February 14 went through every one of the stages of Picasso's amazing inventiveness and prodigious appetite for forms. The black servant appeared and disappeared, the supine woman changed, nude and as if knocked over on her girl friend's lap, laid open, swoon-

Portrait of Jacqueline with crossed hands June 3,
1954, artist's collection

ing, obsessively looking as though she came from Ingres's *Bain turc,* only to be disjointed into these smooth round rhythms as she spread her sex open . . . In this female couple, Pablo was carrying forward his variations on the waking woman seated beside her reclining sleeping companion, begun several years before.

The rearrangements went on: the grisaille of several versions contrasts with the glowing colorfulness of others, the outlines of bodies are heavy and gross in some cases, light and dancing elsewhere. Geometrical constructs give way to full volumes, only to return again, after a brief Matisse passage (in the January 25, 1955, version), as broken rhythms. These successive variations are not different states of the same picture, but facets of a theme in which Picasso was mixing his old-time "manners" and his new conquests in a kind of inventory—a "pilgrimage," Antonina Vallentin calls it—going through his oeuvre, checking at each point on his own powers and his connections with Delacroix, as he had done for Courbet, Cranach, Poussin, or El Greco, before getting to Velázquez and Manet. He was establishing a kind of dialogue, an exchange with them that had nothing to do with plagiarism, pastiche, or pastime. A few years later, Baj and Lichtenstein would do the same with Picasso.

He put an end to the conversation—or confrontation—on February 14, 1955, with a composition neither more nor less definitive than the earlier ones, but which seems a sort of compromise between realism and Cubism, between sumptuous decorativeness of color and strict decomposition of light. The dissymmetry between the woman with the hookah seated majestically on the left, in her glitteringly colored costume and her nude breasts, treated with a freely transposed naturalism, and the right-hand side of the picture with the geometrically shaped juxtaposition of the sleeping and waking women, is reminiscent of *Les Demoiselles d'Avignon.* The color scale is that of Matisse, as is the spirit, bespeaking his calm, luxury, and *volupté;* what is left from Delacroix, apart from the point of departure, is only the deepening penetration of space with a structural complexity new to Picasso.

A few months later, Kahnweiler phoned to tell him an American had bought the fifteen *Women of Algiers:* they had been exhibited in Paris at the retrospective show held at the Museum of Decorative Arts, then at Hamburg, Munich, and Cologne. Picasso at the time was at La Californie in Cannes, and was much amused at the idea: "That whole harem at one American's!" he exclaimed. "That's too many women for one man!" He was not wrong: the buyer soon sold the lot, today separated among several collections and museums.

Thanks to the master of Romanticism, Pablo regained his creative drive. And thanks to Jacqueline, whose portraits continued to proliferate: the ones done in November 1955 in "Turkish costume" (a red bolero with bright embroidery given to Picasso by a Japanese lady) flow from both Matissian Orientalism and *The Women of Algiers.*

When Roland Penrose remarked on the lack of a connecting thread through the series of pictures, Pablo said, "Let others find one, if they wish." Then he took out a recent aquatint: a group of several figures, some of them grotesque old characters, others younger, watching an artist working at his easel, and said:

> Tell me what this means to you, and what that naked old man with his back to us is doing there. Everyone who has seen it has made up a story for him, but I don't know what's going on, I never do. If I did, it would be all over for me.

In recent years he had engraved many etchings and drypoints for writer and publisher friends, René Char, Claude Roy, Éluard, Pablo Neruda, the young publisher P.-A. Benoît of Alès (Gard) who created precious bibliophile works with very meager means, Cocteau, Reverdy, Jean Cassou, Aragon, and others. Several of the 1954 lithographs are related to the themes of the "season in hell": *Three Women and Bullfighter, Two Models, Pose in Clothes, The Painter and His Model,* and so on. In January 1955, while doing the *Women of Algiers* series, he did two lithographs on blackened stones also suggested by the Delacroix painting.

Nineteen fifty-five was a year of great Picasso exhibits: Munich, Haus der Kunst, "Picasso 1900–1955"; London, Marlborough Gallery, drawings and bronzes; Paris, Museum of Decorative Arts, 150 canvases, from the 1899 *Self-Portrait* in watercolor and charcoal to *The Women of Algiers;* the Bibliothèque Nationale, showing his graphics oeuvre.

The show at the Arts décoratifs was his first official restrospective in Paris. Even though not held in a state museum, it was held under sponsorship of the Ministry of National Education, which designated Maurice Jardot, the manager of the Louise Leiris Gallery, to organize it. He was wise, or prudent, enough to warn visitors (122,000 against 850,000 only eleven years later):

> It is not impossible that the art of Picasso, like that of Rimbaud, may remain unassimilable for a long time, that it may be essentially unsuited to become the conformism of any period or society whatsoever. For it is a refractory, rebellious art, outside the law (that is how noble it is!), an art which daily demonstrates its wonderful vocation of freedom. . . .

The selection of the works revealed a wish to stress the expressionist side of Picasso's oeuvre; the painter of pathetic deformations, the insolent aggressor against beauty was put forward, yet the series of *The Women of Algiers,* if it did not convert the enemies of the Minotaur, proved that beyond his "ferocity," as one critic worded it, he was an unequaled orchestrator of forms gifted with plastic inventiveness well served by a brilliant freedom of line.

There were also several books about Picasso in 1955, by Wilhelm Boeck and Sabartés, Frank Elgar and Robert Maillard, Vercors on the works in the Leningrad and Moscow museums, Bernhard Geiser on the graphics, and this would go on in the years to come. Only the Soviet Union failed to publish anything about him.

No artist boasts so vast a bibliography, mainly laudatory. And Christian Zervos was carrying forward his methodical catalog of the oeuvre, periodically supplemented. In 1966, Georges Boudaille and Pierre Daix published in Neuchâtel a *catalogue raisonné* of the 1900–1906 period, to be followed by a second volume on the Cubist period, 1907–1914.

And who was Mme. Z? Everyone wondered about the enigmatic portrait shown at the Arts décoratifs, and when the model's identity was revealed to the public (Pablo's friends knew, of course, who she was), columnists had a field day. Fortunately, gossip scrambles the facts, not always best to tell, and in the end we were to know little about Jacqueline Roque, who was terrified of "keyhole peeking" and succeeded in keeping her privacy. So everyone was amazed when one day she said to some visitors at La Californie, who were gazing at her wonderingly, "Don't you know me? I'm the latest Egeria!"

A rare manifestation of her sense of humor.

Olga had died at Cannes on February 11, 1955, and was buried in the Protestant cemetery, attended by Paulo and a few friends. Shortly before, she had done a touching thing: she had sent Jean Cocteau a photograph taken in Rome in 1917, with the poet and painter on either side of the radiant young woman she then was. On the back, she wrote, "Rome—Minerva" (the hotel they had been at). And Cocteau added, "Picture taken in Rome during preparations for *Parade* in 1916 [he was a year off]. Olga Picasso sent it to me this morning."

Wearied of Paris, the constant flow of visitors to the studio, the persistence of reporters, the naggings of favor seekers, Pablo took Jacqueline back to the Riviera, where they stayed at a hotel in Cannes. Dor de la Souchère visited him there and invited him to the Antibes Museum, which he had rearranged around the *Joy of Living* panels. But Picasso demurred. "That great adventure," as he called it, was over—part of a period of his life that had ended, ended infinitely sadly.

Today M. de la Souchère, living alone in the vaulted rooms on the ground floor of the Château Grimaldi since the death of his wife, speaks with melancholy of Pablo's visit. Changing his mind a few years later, he came with Jacqueline and some friends, to see the Museum. Both painter and curator were deeply moved by the many memories locked away there. La Souchère whispered into Pablo's ear, "This is Françoise's cemetery." And the painter replied, "Yes. And you're its best keeper."

The wound he had felt when she left him closed only slowly. But when, in collaboration with the American journalist Carlton Lake, she wrote the book in which, without great discretion, she told of her *Life with Picasso,* that put an end to whatever he may still have felt about the mother of his children. To a Spanish friend, who mentioned the book, he said, "She's a woman I knew a long time ago." The tone suffered no reply; it was both harsh and distant.

Olga's death, after years of illness, put an end to a whole part of his existence; he secretly carried within himself all of his past, for despite his tyrannical character, his cruelties and egotism, he lived intensely through his memories. That is why he remained so deeply attached to his youthful companions, such as Sabartés or Pallarés, why he said, whatever house he might live in, there was always a spare room for Braque.

The past was also Kahnweiler, Totote Manolo, Ilya Ehrenburg, Josette Gris. And even old André Salmon, whom he had refused to see after the Spanish war, in which as a war correspondent he had glorified Franco. Visiting the Pignons at

Sanary, where Salmon lived, he had asked that he be brought over. They met again in tears that Salmon wiped away only as they toasted their lifelong friendship in endless glasses of rosé wine.

"Picasso is a sentimentalist," Sabartés said to me, "while Braque wasn't." And that was true: Don Pablo might hide his heart, yet it always throbbed; if he sometimes seemed without one, it was not toward friends, admirers, or the needy, but only toward his women. He has been dubbed a "monster," and some say that toward the end of his life he was especially odious to his children—except for the one "legitimate" Paulo—and grandchildren. Others have held Jacqueline responsible. But all this ignores the fact that, Picasso being Picasso, his logic was not the same as other people's. Many of his reactions, incomprehensible or repulsive, were based on fear—fear of others and of his own complexities of character.

Pledges of love were common currency to him. Marie-Thérèse Walter got them repeatedly over almost twenty years, yet he never ceased humiliating and deceiving her; he mocked Dora for being sterile, and shamed Françoise with the birth of Paloma having weakened her health and—*Picasso dixit*—ruined her looks. He turned away at Matisse's death; when Paulo left his wife, he allowed his grandchildren to be unprovided for; and when the Spanish Republicans in exile had Jean Cassou ask him to accept the Order of Liberation, he did not even reply.

Fear of giving himself, of laying himself open. Fear of seeming weak. Fear of acting human, when his inhumanity was what protected him . . . Fear of being laid bare going hand in hand with his fear of pain. He literally panicked at the idea of being sick, losing his faculties, being held to inactivity or immobilized by an accident. The serious surgery Matisse underwent after months of being at death's door, Dufy's crippling arthritis that he went to Boston to have treated, Derain's sad end, the senility of some others whose works were now nothing more than scribbles—all haunted him. What a contrast between the aggressiveness of his work and the worries of the artist, to say nothing of the rather conventional private life he led, love affairs apart! Stormy petrel that he was, he was all for marriage, quiet home life, children, the fervent attention of friends. He was a stick-in-the-mud, self-centered, parsimonious, cautious, in a word, "bourgeois," and totally without adventurousness—except in his pictures.

The studied tranquillity of his existence, which he was able to establish so early, is surprising. How different from the dramatic destinies of a Rembrandt, Van Gogh, or even Cézanne, despairing of ever achieving "realization" and knowing no surcease in the quest for it. Compared to them, or to Delacroix, Courbet, Manet, Braque, or even Matisse, Pablo seems a shy creator, circumspect, able to ward off all contingencies by a great prudence of position (especially evident when he became a Communist) and many helpful protections in high places. If his tranquillity as a painter was threatened, he panicked; the unexpected was always catastrophic, as was anything that "disturbed" him. During the occupation, he was constantly terrified; and finally called on his friend Dubois to see that he was not bothered. That he should have been glorified as a

Resistance member was not the least of the post-Liberation paradoxes. Nor his ironic delight in being acclaimed for it.

His extraordinary creative power never underwent any stoppage, and the overabundance of his daily output, the kind of torrential flow that constitutes his oeuvre, especially in the final period, so obviously disconcerted the critics that they opted for not trying to judge it. Except in terms of its vitality, virtuosity, diversity, and multiplicity.

Pablo wanted to return to the shores of the Mediterranean, and Jacqueline and he selected a large 1880 baroque-style villa, a pretentious but roomy layer cake with gingerbready wrought-iron balconies and "turn of the century" ornamentation that enchanted him. La Californie, as it was called, had belonged to a famous champagne grower, and was located in a wealthy residential neighborhood above Cannes. The rooms were large with broad bay windows facing a very fine garden. Pigeons came to rest on the balconies, and the calm would have been complete were it not that on summer nights the wind wafted over bits of conversation from the *"Son et lumière"* shows put on at the Isles of Lérins. Picasso was intrigued by them and always said he'd go and take a look one day; he never got around to it.

At Vallauris, La Galloise and the Fournas studio had been practically wide open; La Californie had a fence around it and watchmen whose job was to say no one was home, according to Hélène Parmelin. Those who got by were often told inside that the master was resting, working, or out—only to have him dash out on hearing a friendly voice and shout welcome!

Picasso quickly turned La Californie into the same kind of wild maze as his earlier studios; necessary furnishings—beds, tables, chairs, wardrobes, and bureaus—were reduced to the barest minimum. Of course, no "decorating," but the traditional Picasso bivouac, the successive loams of his long existence piled up without chronological order, especially poetical in this setting with its harsh light and stubborn aromas of mimosa and eucalyptus.

In the garden, Picasso was to set up several of his bronzes, *She-Goat, Man with the Sheep, Pregnant Woman,* women's heads and busts from the Boisgeloup days, *Baboon with Young,* and others. There were more indoors, sometimes brought out on the porch to be photographed with the boxer Yan or the goat Esmeralda—a real goat that was kept in the hallway of the second floor—and later Lump, the Dachshund given him by Douglas Duncan, and the Dalmatian Perro. In the entranceway, the 1944 bronze *Cat* calmly eyed this domestic menagerie. In what had been the main living room, now Pablo's studio (though the whole house, actually, was his studio), a bust of Dora Maar presided over tall cages of cooing doves.

Claude and Paloma were to come several times for long stays at La Californie. Pablo played with them, dressed them up, dressed himself up, painted them in several pictures, watched them draw, or ecstatically listened to their chatter. One of the nicest parts of the day for the children was when their father awoke at 11:00 A.M. Paloma recalls how he would have her climb up on the bed and "steal" his extremely frugal breakfast (a bowl of coffee or hot milk and a bit of bread). After which, they all headed for the beach, and he had a high time with the two of them as well as Jacqueline's daughter, Cathy—who called him Pablito—and her little friends, and on occasion Juan, Inéz' son, who had been invited for his vacation. Paulo and Maya, now respectively thirty-four and twenty-six, also came to Cannes, the former usually at month's end.

Meals were simple, light dishes with little to drink. When Jacqueline and Pablo were alone, lunch and dinner were quick affairs. He ate very little, drank water or very light wine, but he liked to treat his friends royally and honor his guests. His favorite indulgence was chocolate ice cream; and on noteworthy occasions he would take over the cooking himself, making some specialty from his native land.

La Californie was to be the last act of the Picassian show, the finale of the big parade before retirement to Mougins. The circus was giving its last performances, the court living its final hours of glory, as Versailles had done before the fall of royalty. Titles, favors, and privileges still were in full force. Fawners, favor seekers, parasites, hagiographers, and jesters knew they were being watched, judged, weighed, and sorted out by the genius-guarding Sphinx and her favorites. Who among them would avoid being purged in the last great-age cutoff?

Work and fun went on without clashing. The noisy hot Sunday bullfights, from Nîmes to Fréjus, with the best toreros of the day in the arena, and the sublime Luis-Miguel Dominguín, whose visits to La Californie with his beautiful movie-star wife, Lucia Bosè, were always deeply enjoyed. The birthday parties each October 25, and the potters' festivals at Vallauris. Gary Cooper, arriving with his wife, his daughter, and his mother-in-law, and bringing Pablo a wonderful cowboy Stetson and a six-shooter. Kahnweiler and the Leirises visiting to see the latest works of the master and of Xavier Vilato, who respectfully submitted his to his uncle, and Totote and Rosita Manolo, Douglas Cooper working on a book, Sabartés, who regularly sent down the canvases, drawings, engravings, collages, mock-ups, and other items Picasso called for, shipped in crates from the Rue des Grands-Augustins studio.

Jacques Prévert visiting, and Pablo on September 26, 1956, doing a huge caricature portrait of him, his eye heavy with world-weariness, his eternal cigarette butt stuck to his lip; and twenty-five more such portraits on the following days.

Jean Cocteau, light of foot and voluble, whom Pablo adored cutting off in midsentence, to see him turn pale, his long diaphanous hands in suspense along with his words. The Belgian Academy had elected him to the seat that had been held by Colette; he had been made an honorary citizen of Milly, gone to Rome to open an exhibition of his works, and become a member of the prestigious Académie française, where in his acceptance speech he had lauded "the magnificent loving insults a Spaniard has aimed at the human face." His plays were being revived almost everywhere; he had been awarded an honorary doctorate by Oxford and was about to decorate the fishermen's chapel in the port of Villefranche, about which Pablo twitted him with bitter sarcasm.

Cocteau was offended, but said nothing. "The great disturber of traffic," as he called Picasso, was his oxygen. "Like Penelope, he has a mysterious gift of being able to knot the thread without ever coming to the end; he has faery hands, what else can I tell you!" said the poet, by now unable to speak two sentences without referring to the painter, as he kept writing him, phoning him, spurring him on, a regular gadfly to the great man, whom he both irritated and amused. One day he brought around an ambassador's wife, who unlimbered the silliest of comments before Picasso's pictures. "Are you angry at me?" Cocteau asked next day on the phone.

"Not at all. But she's spoiled my pictures for a month," Pablo replied.

Vladimir Pozner came to see him, too, to get the drawing Pablo had promised for the poster for Joris Ivens' film, *Song of the Rivers,* which Pozner had written. The theme was to be hands of workers of all colors, which gave Picasso an idea: "I've always wanted to do hands," he was saying, "lots of hands. We might make four. How many races are there? Four? People always forget Red Indians, but I always include them. We could have four hands, or else one hand with four colors . . ."

As he spoke, he did five successive drawings, with colored crayons and Pozner's fountain pen, showing four hands laid out like the open petals of a flower. "Will it be clear that these are hands?" Pablo asked.

Then several more drawings of hands and flowers, flower-hands, and hand-flowers. In all colors. He had done the first one about ten-thirty, Pozner said, and by noon there were fourteen of them, "the hands becoming prettier and prettier, and the flowers, too. The colors symbolizing the races had disappeared, and now they were green and red and yellow and blue." Picasso said:

> Now, I could spend my whole life drawing hands and flowers. That's the way it always is. If you kept writing on a sheet of paper, it would be entirely black. The same goes for painters. If you go through to the end—the real end—you'll be facing a blank sheet. If Chaplin went all the way with his films, there'd be film with nothing on it . . .
>
> . . . You work, and there's an art lover behind you, who decrees, this one is good, this one is bad, this one is finished. A kind of guardian angel who keeps you from going on. When you work yourself, you never know whether it's bad or good . . .
>
> Only the young folks graduating from schools and academies know what's good and what's bad. They always know, in relation to something. It's "good" if the likeness is good, if you can recognize the model . . .

By 3:40 P.M., Picasso, who had been at work over five hours, finished the twenty-first, and last, drawing, the one about which, as Pozner wrote, "Picasso's guardian angel had said: enough." He signed and dated it, September 20, 1955.

When Pozner thanked him, Pablo kissed him on both cheeks, saying, "What for? I only did what you asked me to." *

Thus, Picasso daily drawing or painting—for himself, for a friend, for Kahnweiler, for the Party, in order to live . . .

And for Jacqueline, the ever discreet and attentive Jacqueline, holding a grow-

* Vladimir Pozner, "Picasso comme il travaille" (Picasso While He Works), in *La Nouvelle Critique,* No. 130, November 1961.

ing place in Pablo's life and activity. She was there when he worked, when he saw visitors, with his friends, his children, those who wanted favors, those who were under obligation, the dealers. First in the background, then more and more in evidence, finally indispensable. What has not been said and will not be said about her?

It was rare for Picasso to go to meet anyone at a railroad station: he had done it long ago for Sabartés when the latter first joined him in Paris, and then thirty years later when Jaime came back to work for him. On November 10, 1955, he was meeting Sabartés again, at the Cannes station. Jaime was not alone, but brought Juan Vidal Ventosa, one of their youthful days' companions whom he had not seen in over twenty years, and who passionately embraced Picasso. Two young Barcelona picture dealers, Miguel and Juan Gaspar, and the latter's wife, Elvira, were also along: it had been Sabartés' idea to bring the Gaspars, whose gallery on Calle Consejo de Ciento, in the center of the Catalonian capital, was one of the most important in Spain.

Pablo was happy and moved to see Ventosa again; a year older than his host, he was well dressed and distinguished, and did not look his age. At La Californie, or at Vallauris at the Ramiés', Pablo danced attendance on him. Clavé had come down from Paris, too, and now they were all talking about the city where they were young together, about the happy years and those of civil war and oppression.

There had not been a Picasso exhibition in Barcelona since the one that opened on Christmas Eve, 1948, at the Galerías Layetanas, with sixteen 1901–1904 canvases and twenty-six 1946–1947 lithographs. The Gaspars were determined to exhibit their countryman's work on a regular basis, and with Don Pablo that kind of thing went fast: the first Sala Gaspar Picasso show, October 6–19, 1956, was a considerable success.

The second, bringing together several characteristic examples of the painter's varied activities (paintings, engravings, sculptures, and ceramics), opened a year later. After that, each year the Gaspars showed recent Picasso works that he selected for them. This renewed his links with the city, and in 1957 he made a gift to Barcelona of sixteen ceramic pieces that were held in its Museum of Decorative Arts, pending transfer to the Picasso Museum.

His 1959 absence from the potters' festival was to make tongues wag, and it similarly did when he failed to attend the oft-postponed opening of the Temple of Peace on September 19. He had in fact left Vallauris, and local consternation ran high, for, as the local paper naïvely wrote, "Picasso is for this town the equivalent of an advertising and publicity budget such as few of the biggest cities could afford!" There was talk of Jacqueline making scenes of jealousy because he was away too often, and a provincial magazine even reported they had split up. But his friends and entourage insisted there was nothing to that rumor.

His ceramics output had greatly slowed down; nothing between the rounded cupels he had done on January 30, 1954, and the one called *Bullfight Scene*, November 21. Another series of these dishes at the end of March 1955, some plaques or plates with dancers, bathers, or young pipers. Finally, on the little porcelain wall plaques, Jacqueline's face appeared . . .

Large earthenware vases in white faience with funny heads, wall plaques with beach scenes, round plates with wild or threatening fauns snickering on them, and all sorts of other amusing faces: *Woman's Face in Shape of a Clock, Face with Grille, Face with Leaves, Sleeper, Clock with Tongue,* and fishes, fauns on horseback, a geometrical *Jacqueline at the Easel,* and baroque centaurs, tormented faces, square faces, and a *Geometrical Face with Lines.* Irony, invention, perky polychrome, Picasso was enjoying himself and entertaining us; then suddenly, starting in Summer 1956, no more work at the Ramiés—not again until three years later, June 11, 1959.

On that day, in a few hours, he did four large platters with scenes of bull-fighting in black, white, and red ocher, and a face, done in the same harmony.

XXII

THERE IS
NO
PICASSO MYSTERY . . .
(1955–1957)

"**S**PEED! . . . ACTION!" ANY NUMBER OF TIMES EACH DAY WOULD start the cast doing a take at Nice's Studios de la Victorine, a take to be almost endlessly repeated over and over again.

"OK . . . Cut!" put a halt to it.

But on this summer's day of 1955 the words were addressed to no ordinary star, no seasoned actor: on the set, there was only a little man with a stocky naked upper body, tanned, sweating, and drawing to order on a huge screen of white paper. Henri-Georges Clouzot was shooting *Le Mystère Picasso.*

The famous director should never have attempted this film. Not that he lacked the necessary talent, good will, or surely admiration for his subject—but by stressing the virtuoso side of Pablo he was revealing the painter's secrets while travestying them, turning them into legerdemain or gestural acrobatics. In trying to describe Picasso's creative process—a virtual impossibility—Clouzot showed only the surface and reinforced the feeling of facility of execution which so many of his adversaries have derided. The camera in a few minutes could not give a true account of Picasso's amazing creative activity; it could show only a few glimpses of it, a few steps. Picasso laid bare by Clouzot is no longer an inventor, but just an actor, worse, an illusionist demonstrating his most successful tricks; the doubts, hesitations, scruples, doublings back, empty spaces—all those things that are the drama of creation—just do not come through. The painter is too sure of himself for an audience that is much less sure he is not having them on. When he stops in his work, saying, "Well, I'll leave it like that," he has to be taken at his word. For he is the sole judge of himself. But by what right does Clouzot have him say, "I don't worry about the public"? The whole film is fraught with such inconsistencies, such mistakes.

Le Mystère Picasso is the revenge of Clouzot, painter *manqué,* on Don Pablo, genius.

As a filmmaker, Clouzot had long wanted to portray Picasso, and the latter had been agreeable, but he wondered whether the camera could not be something more than a recording instrument as it watched him at his work and set down the successive phases. Dora Maar, in her still photographs, had shown the step-by-step development of *Guernica;* the movie camera with its more fascinating power might be able to restore movement, actually take the place of the painter's eye and hand. In a word, what Picasso hoped was that Clouzot might reveal the path followed by one or several of his works, simultaneously or successively; in trying to cover too much, the director played him false. That falseness is evident in the fact that, when the movie was finished, Picasso went on working on *Beach at La Garoupe,* which he had painted on camera.

This was not the first film devoted to him. Alain Resnais had intelligently explored *Guernica*—albeit in a questionable manner, turning the huge painting into an exercise of his own cinema style. Luciano Emmer, more respectful and more didactic, had attempted to re-place each of the master's periods in its historic context. The Belgian art critic Paul Haesaerts had been less ambitious: his *Visite à Picasso,* the first movie to show the painter at work, had the virtues and shortcomings of a home movie. Georges Sadoul wrote that it "hardly went beyond anecdotal, familiar reportage." Perhaps because Haesaerts was not a professional filmwright.

This was not true of Clouzot: he was to make use of Picasso with full technical power, as well as a remarkable sense of mass appeal.

After not having seen each other for fifteen years or so, Picasso and Clouzot in the summer of 1952 had met at Nîmes in Dominguín's hotel room while the bullfighter prepared for a corrida. As they were leaving, Clouzot whispered something to Pablo, who replied, "A fine idea. Let's talk about it again. I'd like to do something with you someday."

Three years later, living at St.-Paul-de-Vence, Clouzot went to visit Pablo, and they discussed their project several times: Pablo was interested, but not quite ready.

One morning he phoned the director to say he had just received some bottles of a new kind of ink from the United States, and had immediately done a brush profile of a goat with it. Holding it up to the light, he had seen that the drawing came out as well on the back as on the front of the paper. Clouzot, delighted, came over that afternoon. "Can't we start, then?" he asked.

This new process would allow the camera freely to show the back face of the drawing while the artist worked at it in front; in a way, it was the perfecting of the technique Haesaerts had essayed in having Pablo paint on large glass plates with white paint, so that in the transparency one saw both the artist at work and the work he was doing.

Like Picasso, Clouzot was enthusiastic over this new possibility, and immediately visualized his film, the painter absorbed in the act of creating. There were a number of preparatory sessions at La Californie, with Picasso, Clouzot, the latter's crew, and of course his cameraman Claude Renoir, grandson of the painter ("Every time I hear someone call Renoir, it does something to me!" Pablo said). It was early summer, an especially torrid one, and everything was finally ready. The score had been commissioned from Georges Auric, hardly the ideal composer for a film on Picasso, and what he eventually did was rather characterless. "Representational music for a film that was not," as Claude Mauriac was to appraise it.

Pablo never wanted to stop when the director called "Cut!" and as long as there was a short end left in the camera he went on drawing: a fish with a belly-ful of flowers, a chicken with spreading plumage, or fauns and nymphs having their sport on top of each other, along with a goat, on a huge vertical panel that would be the backdrop of the film. He was bare-chested, in shorts, and bright-eyed.

Clouzot was overwhelmed: never had he thought that the seventy-four-year-old painter might have such stamina. Picasso would stand hours on end before the white sheet, painting or drawing in the suffocating heat, solid of footing, never stopping the work in hand except to turn to another. He rested only when breaks in the shooting schedule allowed.

A bouquet appeared on the canvas. Then two feet. A corolla became an eye. A cock, a fish followed one another. Or the fish turned cock, flying away to make room for an owl.

Jacques Ripouroux, the camera operator, moved in closer. Maya handed her father his brushes, while Clouzot kept watching and puffing on his pipe. The heat was becoming unbearable. After a "Cut!" Clouzot asked Pablo how he felt about it. "Fine, but it's still too external," Picasso replied. "We have to take more chances. What if we do fall on our faces? Let's go the limit." Or, another time, he urged him to try to catch "the truth at the bottom of the well."

André Verdet was making notes for a diary of the filmmaking, which he was to publish as *Picasso à son image* (Picasso in His Own Image). Prévert, visiting the set, said, "This film could go on for hours. After a few minutes, any notion of time disappears."

One day Picasso told Clouzot he was going to "do La Garoupe," one of the Cap-d'Antibes beaches where he sometimes went swimming. To Picasso, to "do La Garoupe" was to sing a hymn to life, to the joys of summer, the beauty of present-day water nymphs, sun, vacation, happiness. An old man's tribute to free and carefree youth, as well as his chosen habitat, the Mediterranean coast.

"We have to show all the pictures that there may be behind one picture," he told Clouzot. And for this closing sequence Clouzot decided to use Cinemascope.

Picasso began by structuring his canvas with a solid geometrical construct, a framework whose points of support were the horizon; to the right a circle with a character in it, to the left the roof of a house. Now the camera was alongside him and this of course interfered, forcing him to stop work frequently for changes of setups, or to let the colors dry; the work rhythm could not follow his normal tempo.

Unable to remain idle during the breaks when he had to leave *La Garoupe* alone, Picasso was doing drawings on large sheets of paper set up on easels off camera. So his mind remained alert and his hand active, while lightings were arranged, angles selected, camera reloaded, and the canvas fanned to get it to dry more quickly.

The director called "Action!" and Pablo was back at "the beach." His physical endurance amazed everyone: when working, he had never known what it was to be tired. The structure of the picture grew, the figures appeared, the beach became active, peopled. The umbrellas dotted the sand. A café awning, in the foreground, framed the work.

A water-skier traced a wake on the ocean's surface.

A girl in bathing suit, and her male companion, leaned against the awning support. Swimmers' heads appeared above the water, one of them disproportionate.

The bathing beauties became larger, ampler. One woman, a round-headed black silhouette against this extravaganza of varied colors, was sitting at the extreme right. To the left, the house whose roof he had first drawn in became a charming cottage surrounded by trees, then disappeared.

"Cut!" He stepped back, looked it over. Through for the day.

Every day, to quote him, he "changed everything." The camera recorded these changes for the spectator to see. The geometry of the beginning softened up, the canvas lightened, simplified. The two bathers turned into imposing blue-and-white geometrical constructs cut out of paper and pasted over the earlier ones.

A large sheet of paper, also pasted over the right side of the canvas, allowed for structural alterations without destroying the previous state. A second water-skier flew through it over very schematic swimmers.

Around the two bathers, the picture continued changing. Colors, style, disposition of the figures altered incessantly. The harmony was white, azure, and night-blue, with a fragment of red-and-yellow from the café awning at the upper right. "Picasso made me understand that white was the color of darkness," as Clouzot put it.

The bathers were not all that solid, and were replaced by a mythological nude couple, bacchanalian dancers painted on another sheet of paper to be pasted on to the canvas.

Behind them, a large violet rectangular screen suddenly popped up.

Then it disappeared. Black took over all of the canvas, completely transforming it about the dancers: the characters stood out as light silhouettes against the ink-blackness of the night.

Picasso tore off the sheet that hid the right-hand part; the character seated at the far end reappeared. Also the bathers. But he had to rebalance the composition: the scale of the characters was changed. The harmony was now blue, azure, gray-blue, with broad splotches of red and yellow for the awning, sand, an umbrella, the bikini-clad swimmer's halter. At this point, it had reached its extreme of solar intensity.

Picasso contemplated it a long time. Then suddenly he dipped a heavy brush in turpentine and erased almost the whole thing. Turning to an appalled Clouzot, he said, "It's bad . . . Very bad. I'm not satisfied. But that way people will see it's not so easy." And then, "I'll start in again."

He began again, further simplifying the composition, schematizing the figures, the ensemble now suppler and more concentrated; all the elements of the earlier versions having been reevaluated according to new criteria.

Stepping back, he put down his brushes, sat down, and announced, "This time, it's finished. But I'm going to do another *Garoupe.*"

"Roll'em . . . Action!" On a large white canvas of the same format as the earlier one, he immediately replaced the linear framework of the original composition by huge geometrical flat spaces of blue, yellow, red, orange, and purple, representing the principal structural zones in which the figures were to be placed, the two bacchantes in the middle, the large seated woman at the right. And so, starting from abstract elements, he "built" reality, step by step.

The elements themselves gradually became "natural," sea, sky, beach, sun-soaked tents. The bathers, reduced to their essentials, took shape inside and outside the colored planes. Picasso worked very fast; he picked up the canvas where he had left it in the first version, but by starting from its internal schema he deliberately omitted the whole narrative side, the holiday accouterment, the sentimentality. What emerged under his brush, now peremptory and self-assured, where the earlier composition had presented such problems, was a synthesized, flowering La Garoupe beach, without cuteness or curlicues. The creator's spontaneity had regained its lively freshness.

In this second version of *Beach at La Garoupe*, painted in fourteen hours, Picasso employed the emblematic vocabulary of *Les Demoiselles d'Avignon*, *Dance*, and *Guernica*. It was now two o'clock in the morning, and a storm had broken out after the torrid day, turning into a steady fine tepid downpour. Backing out of the camera frame, Picasso lit a cigarette, and those present could see by the flame of the lighter that his face looked haggard.

Suddenly he was faint. "Catch me, I'm going to fall," he said. The terrific effort he had put on before the cameras brought on a siege of hypertension that would require extended rest. Yet, he would come back to the film studios to trace his signature on a big white canvas, for the fade-out.

For weeks, he was not allowed to leave La Californie, rising late, taking long siestas, seeing no one, doing no work. He kept abreast of all the papers, even a weekly which, by dint of untruths, errors, and approximations, classified his works, under the heading "Picasso and Women," according to his successive muses—not excluding Sylvette David! "Mail call" was what he was most interested in, devouring the correspondence, as well as the periodicals, that came in. The first letter, almost every day, was from Sabartés, whether in Paris, Barcelona, or elsewhere. The others, postmarked everywhere, went from hailing "the world's greatest painter" to denouncing "the demon" or the "murderer of painting."

Some also criticized his becoming a Communist, at times in violent terms. And there were questionnaires from newspapermen—mainly Americans—requests for photographs, autographs, money, subsidies, donations to causes, and authentication of some painting or drawing (generally from a photograph). "I have a wonderful memory. I remember every one of my works," he boasted, but that was not always true. In one letter, a furniture manufacturer offered to "redo" his whole house in "ultra-modern," gratis, just for the publicity value.

The huge villa had become the latest Picassian storehouse: the mess from the Rues La Boétie and des Grands-Augustins, on top of the Fournas bric-a-brac, had been multiplied by ten—since there were that many larger rooms available! Paintings on easels or on the floor, sculptures everywhere, ceramics, baskets, wrappings, and what have you, fighting for space on the nondescript pieces of furniture. African masks hung alongside bullfight posters and Douanier Rousseaus. A whole family of Bathers, looking like funny semaphor towers, stood about, made of wooden crating, canvas stretchers, legs of couches, doors, broom handles, junk.

There were painted or drawn portraits of Jacqueline like beacon lights in various parts of the "junk shop," the head of Dora Maar that was to become the Apollinaire monument, a 1906 *Nude* with hands clasped behind her head, another Jacqueline, a bull's head, more Jacquelines.

Picasso's consort was not in very robust health. She tended to be ailing, which worried and exasperated him. He never could abide sick women, but her indispositions were often foretold by tense, feverish portraits.

As Pablo was to say to John Richardson, he then painted healthy pictures of her when she was sick—he never understood why he was always ahead of the fact.

In the fall of 1955 and early winter he started several more Jacqueline portraits, and then proceeded to "inventory" his home in a series of Studios, of La Californie Interiors, begun on October 23 and lasting intermittently until June 1956.

Picasso had taken this opulent leisure-class residence with its magnificent tropical garden, neighboring medieval, Byzantine, or Art Nouveau palaces (sometimes a combination of all three styles), and huge reception halls, and turned it into a campsite for millionaire gypsies—and this double atmosphere was what he restored to his fluidly painted pictures, done with delicate "juices" in which the white of the canvas often remained bare. They are wonderfully free. True interior landscapes.

There are numerous Matissian reminders in these Studios, as, despite consciousness of structure, the ornamental tendency wins out and Pablo gives full value to the exotic climate of La Californie and true character to each object. The Orientalizing style of the interiors, in the beginning at least, was in harmony with Picasso's hedonism of those months of relaxation. A "Mozarabic chapel," Antonina Vallentin said of one of them, and Pablo agreed there was something of that there, the whole curving arabesque style confirming it.

These Studios, sometimes including Jacqueline, became progressively less sunny, giving way to black, ocher, and white, as the winter's disorder was replaced by a tragic void. John Richardson says it was raining that April of 1956 and Pablo was morose over not being able to go to the bullfights. The main living room of La Californie looked like the monastery of Yuste, where Charles V spent his declining years, having it draped in black for his eventual funeral. "A friend of my father's, a painter, used to say, 'When you don't see anything, you use black,'" Picasso said, echoing Titian's "He who does not know how to use black will never be a painter."

When that series of Studios was over, La Californie had truly become Picasso's.

Three years later, Charles Feld, director of the Éditions du Cercle d'Art (which has published the finest books of Picasso reproductions), brought out a facsimile of the pad on which the painter worked November 1, 1955–January 14, 1956, with an introduction by Georges Boudaille. The vast majority of the brush or crayon drawings in it are of the Studios; day by day, we can follow the preparation, the graphic commentary, of the canvases done during the same period. Portraits of Jacqueline alternate with interior scenes: in the "Turkish costume" seen in several canvases, she runs the gamut from realism to distortion with the resigned acceptance of a victim ever in thrall to the painless tortures of her inquisitor.

Dark and cluttered at first, the studio airs out and loses some of its mess, assuming the gay colors of a Matisse palette, and the eye is regaled by a pyrotechnical display of yellow, blue, red, and green crayons, flanked—in the chance arrangement of a daily pad—by two pen-and-inks after the portraits of Catherine of Mecklenburg by Cranach and Charles of Morette by Holbein. One more portrait closes the pad, done in pen-and-ink to simulate etching, Rembrandt's *Man with the Golden Helmet.* What Picasso mainly tried was to render the light-and-shadow effects by using only clustered or intersecting hatchmarks.

Always curious about all techniques, Picasso got interested in that of a Norwegian sculptor, Carl Nesjar, and invited him to come to La Californie and show him his sandblasted concrete work. Perfected in Oslo by the architect Erling Viksjö and the engineer Sverre Jystad, it had been used for buildings in their country. When he had learned about it, Pablo gave Nesjar carte blanche to cast his subjects, merely asking for the right to give advance approval to each work selected. The first entrusted to him were three drawings which Nesjar produced for the new Oslo Government Building that Viksjö had put up, and then he did a three-meter-high "proof-sculpture" from a Picasso maquette at Gon, a village near the port of Larvik, Norway.

There were several more monumental statues: for the Colegio de los Arquitectos in Barcelona (1960–1961); at Kristinehamm (Sweden), where in 1965 on the shores of Lake Vänern an immense wide-eyed *Cutout Figure,* five meters high, was put up atop a circular pillar; the *Déjeuners sur l'herbe,* of huge cutout figures known as "folded sculptures," more than three meters high, now in the Moderna Museet in Stockholm; the *Profiles* at the South Lycée in Marseilles; and a large engraved wall at Douglas Cooper's Château de Castille.

But the most striking of all was put up in 1962 at the estate of Kahnweiler, Le Prieuré at St.-Hilaire, near Étampes: *The Angel,* done from a Picasso cardboard maquette. It was so named by Nesjar and his friend the architect Johannessen because the figure, over five meters high, with its broad arms spread out like wings, stands near the ruins of a Romanesque chapel it appears to have under its protection.

One winter day of 1955, in Paris, Patrick O'Higgins, secretary to "Madame" Helena Rubinstein, the famous cosmetics magnate (and art collector) was amazed to see scattered about her room "the most extraordinary assortment of embroidered evening dresses, elaborate opera cloaks, Spanish shawls"—the more unseemly in that she had just lost her husband, Prince Gourielli.*

Marie Cuttoli, it turned out, had finally arranged for Picasso to do a portrait of La Rubinstein—in exchange for the latter's promise to rent the first vacant apartment in a building she owned on Quai de Béthune to another celebrated Cuttoli friend, no less than Georges Pompidou, future President of France—and Pablo wanted to paint her in "something really ex-tra-va-gant!"

Once on the Riviera, Madame wondered why they did not hear from Picasso, whom she referred to as "the devil." And O'Higgins explained that each time he phoned a different voice (obviously Pablo's own in various disguises) answered, "Monsieur is asleep" or "swimming" or "at the bullfight" or even "gone to Paris."

Ready to take the bullfight aficionado by the horns, she went to La Californie, appropriately outfitted: "Under an opera cloak quilted in shades of orange and lemon with calla lilies and sprigs of mimosa, Madame wore a medieval tunic of acid green velvet."

The gardener who answered their ring, after mumbling "No one's at home," took one "horrified look" at Madame and ran to alert Jacqueline.

"They fell into each other's arms," O'Higgins writes, and Jacqueline led them "into a huge room cluttered with canvases, rocking chairs, and enough flotsam to furnish a thrift shop."

Pablo was all warmth and affection for Madame, introducing her to his other guests, who, in addition to Paloma and Kahnweiler, included "a tall, lanky man who not only looked like Gary Cooper but who was Gary Cooper" and his wife and daughter.

After some banter, Pablo gave her an appointment for a sitting at six o'clock the next evening, "the light, then, is just right. Besides I never work until six." And the next three evenings, she was there at that hour, and Picasso did sketches —taking what he called "police notes"—that she imprudently voiced the hope would "make a nice portrait."

"Who says I'll paint a portrait?" he shot back. Later, after commenting on her (and his own) big ears, which he said meant they would "both live forever, like elephants," Picasso informed her the portrait might turn out to be "a posthumous work . . . Either you die first or I do . . . Either I paint it or I don't . . ."

Barred from the room while the work was going on, O'Higgins was entertained and shown about the premises by Jacqueline. He was amazed at the

* This episode is based on the chapter titled "Picasso's a Devil!" in *Madame,* by Patrick O'Higgins (New York: Viking Press, 1971).

ubiquitous movie magazines in which, she said, Pablo "likes to study photographs of his heroes . . . then they are real to him because he seldom goes to the cinema."

He also noted that Jacqueline always referred to Picasso personally as "Pablo" or "Don Pablo," reserving "Picasso" as the designation for the artist or for his works.

Thus, in "Don Pablo's Treasure House," she showed him art by Cézanne, Renoir, Degas, Douanier Rousseau, and then "Picasso's own," and casually informed him he would never do the portrait of Madame, explaining:

"He's just sketching her as a reference for a series of lithographs. He likes to use real people and Madame, Madame Rubinstein is . . . larger than life."

Jacqueline volunteered to him that Pablo was "the most considerate, sensitive, elegant person I've ever known and—besides being a genius—he's the only lover I've ever really wanted"—this, despite the fifty years of difference in their ages.

With Anglo-Irish practicality, O'Higgins asked her, "Has he provided for you? . . . If he died . . . then, what happens to you?"

"Who cares?" came the typical Frenchwoman's reply.

Helena Rubinstein died in 1966, seven years before Picasso. Officially, she was aged ninety-four, though some claimed she was five years older than that. He never painted her portrait.

There was now a new character in the Picasso circus, a Neapolitan tailor named Michele Sapone, doing business in Nice since 1948. Pablo admired a gaudy coat he had made for André Verdet, and after he called on him at La Californie he became known as "Picasso's tailor."

Shrewd and crafty, he quickly realized that, for all his wild attire, Picasso dressed very carefully: even when putting on some costume, it was not hand-me-down. As early as his Barcelona period, Pablo had had unusual and strangely matched outfits made for him by Soler, whose family, it will be recalled, he painted several times.

Once Sapone became attached to Picasso, he remained part of his entourage until the very end: for him, he went back to his native Italy to get special fabrics, or to the Yugoslav or Greek mountaineers who made handwoven woolen materials soaked and pressed till they were thick and hard as felt. And he discovered all kinds of corduroys, a special favorite of Pablo's.

At each visit, Sapone carried off a lithograph or drawing, sometimes several. He had made a habit of coming to his customers with a book of swatches under one arm and an autograph album or Golden Book under the other. What they drew or inscribed in the latter was like money in the bank, for their names included Magnelli, Clavé, Giacometti, Prévert, Cocteau, Hartung, Pignon, Villon, Arp, Borsi, César, and the like. Only Dubuffet had refused to see him, answering his phone solicitation with "Picasso? Never heard of him!" In Chagall's case, it was the artist's wife who turned him away.

Sapone never measured his customers, and the suits did not always fit, but "Picasso's tailor" could not be concerned with such minor details, any more than

Picasso was. He was delighted with the tailor's originality and imagination and his wardrobe grew, not only for daily wear, but also for disguises. When Sapone brought a magnificent bridal gown back from Italy for Jacqueline, Pablo tried it on first . . .

Daily, without appointment, Sapone would drop in at Picasso's, bringing a bolt of cloth, or an overcoat or suit, and leaving with some art work. "You work for me, and I work for you," Picasso told him; their "collaboration" left the little Neapolitan tailor with a collection of Picassos even more numerous than Picasso's Sapones. Of all those works that went through his nimble hands, the tailor kept a hundred or so, he says, to say nothing of the inscribed books and albums. They constituted his daughters' dowries, the price of an art gallery in Nice, and a nice nest egg for the future. (Sapone, art dealer, might have made some of his customers laugh—but it came to pass, though in another avatar. His daughter Patricia married her first cousin, so the art dealer is the tailor's nephew and son-in-law . . .)

Spring (March 20, 1956) brought a rare freshness of color to the celebration of rebirth. It was the year of Pablo's seventy-fifth birthday, celebrated all around the globe. But Kahnweiler, who had hoped to mark the occasion by opening the new Galerie Louise Leiris at 47 Rue de Monceau, had to postpone his plan, for the overview Pablo planned for it was not ready. The show took place the following year—marking the fiftieth anniversary of his opening on Rue Vignon—and presented a kind of compendium of living at La Californie: studios, portraits of Jacqueline, children, and gardens.

Woman in a Rocking Chair (March 25) was obviously Jacqueline, decomposed into discrete volumes, like a broken-up jigsaw puzzle, like God in a Romanesque mandorla, and majestically centered in the rhythmic scroll of the rocker.

When he was finished with the Studios, Pablo turned to the entomology of his garden, doing dragonflies, grasshoppers, crickets, gnats, butterflies, with great precision on sketch pads or detached sheets—but he still retained humor enough to draw a bull climbing up a plant stem toward the shining sun.

One afternoon Prévert and his wife arrived at La Californie—no great event since they lived at Antibes and often dropped in on the Picassos—but that was the day Pablo "discovered" the poet whom he had known for over thirty years, and drew the first of his twenty-six portraits of him to be done in twenty-one days. On February 7, 1957, he was to do eleven washes of bullfights in a single day, and on July 5, when the water joustings took place as usual at St.-Tropez, he did eight India-ink drawings of them during the one day. On May 20, 1958, he was to do thirteen studies of leaves, flowers, and plants. July 19, the famous pianist Artur Rubinstein, his friend since the Ballets Russes days, came to see him, and Pablo, starting a fresh pad, did twenty-one portraits of him in a few hours. The last was just a few crayon scribbles with two little circles, but at the bottom of it, he wrote, "Very good likeness portrait of Artur Rubinstein."

Much has been written about this virtuosity of Pablo's, and his adversaries made the most of it. Yet, it is in itself less amazing than the fact that he was always ready to show these quick jobs to anyone, rather than keeping them to himself. He not only dated them, but successively numbered the ones he did on the same day, showing that he felt time to be an important factor.

A young photographer from Arles, Lucien Clergue, had been introduced to Picasso by Cocteau and become a frequent visitor at La Californie. He was the first to suggest a show of the master's recent works in his native town. To make him happy, Pablo agreed to see the curator of its Reattu Museum, colossal, truculent Jean-Maurice Roquette, who immediately appealed to him because of his Southern enthusiasm, his unmistakable accent, and his naturalness. They agreed on Picasso's lending thirty-eight drawings, mostly unexhibited before, to be added to the loans of several local collectors. The show was held in the summer of 1957, to considerable acclaim. But it did nothing to improve Pablo's relations with "official circles." The bureaucrats of art who once considered him a worthless dauber now ignored him on the pretext that he was a Communist!

> Napoleon was born at Ajaccio, August 15, 1769.
> Picasso was born at Málaga, October 25, 1881.
> Constant, the valet of the former, told stories about the Emperor's cold chickens and white trousers. I used to shine the shoes of the latter, when there was polish to be had, around 1900, without thinking that my shoebrush was making me part of History. He has changed the shape of houses, clothes, the theatre, posters, and store-windows, sculpture and pictures . . .

Thus, Max Jacob in his "Chronique des temps héroïques" (Chronicle of the Heroic Days), written in 1936 and published in October 1956, while Pablo's seventy-fifth birthday was being celebrated. That extract opened the tribute to him in *Les Lettres françaises,* which also included a poem by Pablo Neruda and some recollections by Aragon.

On his birthday, Picasso went to the Madoura pottery with Jacqueline and Jean Cocteau, and all the potters assembled to celebrate with him: he cut the seventy-pound cake on which he had blown out the seventy-five candles with three breaths. Then his fellow workers made him a present of a copper potter's wheel, he thanked them, and Georges Ramié made a little speech. After which, the master went home to resume his interrupted labors.

At the behest of Ilya Ehrenburg, the Soviets had decided to observe Picasso's seventy-fifth birthday, and the writer went to Cannes to work on it. The Moscow Museum of Modern Art was to show a selection of a hundred-odd of the master's canvases, judiciously, but skillfully chosen. Picasso, officially invited to come to the USSR, declined, sending a message of thanks to the organizers.

This first Picasso exhibit in the USSR is never mentioned by his biographers, even those who are Communists. It is not listed among his foreign shows, and when, on this birthday, also the opening day of the exhibit, *Les Lettres françaises* published Ehrenburg's preface to the show, it did not so identify it.

Only from the writer himself do we know of the impressive success of the exhibition. The officials who had him organize it also let him open it, as president of the Association of Friends of French Culture. Ehrenburg was deeply moved as he formally cut the red ribbon across the doorway, but he had no sooner done so than the excited crowd started storming in. "Try to calm them," the distraught director of the museum asked him. "They'll trample one another!"

"Comrades," Ehrenburg announced over the public-address system, "you've waited twenty-five years for this exhibition. You can wait twenty-five minutes longer!"

Moscow crowds are well disciplined; order was restored in a hurry, and three thousand people saw the exhibit that first day. There were just as many each day, and more on Sundays, for the three weeks that the show ran.

Picasso's "distortions" offended the youth; in a way the Soviets were reacting as the good bourgeoisie of 1874 had to the first Impressionist pictures, but they were confused because of their respect for Picasso the man, the Communist painter, the "comrade of genius." Could a good Party member really paint that way? And if one did so paint, could he be a good Communist, since Communism rejected such art?

As in Paris, the Moscow "masses" did not understand.

A few days before the unveiling, on October 13, *Izvestia* published a piece by an eminent member of the Soviet Academy of Fine Arts, Solokovskalo, violently protesting against those who defended Western art, or like the critic Kamensky criticized the Association of Artists of Revolutionary Russia. Had the latter indeed not had the effrontery to say that its members' works were "dull, soulless, close to photographic naturalism"? The Picasso show could only revive such old antagonisms, the ever-growing attendance merely increasing the concern of the socialist-realist painters. Molotov himself wrote an article to ask them not to depart from this Party line.

There was to be no further Picasso show in the USSR for ten years, until his eighty-fifth birthday in 1966.

De-Stalinization was on the way, and a certain amount of liberalism was creeping into world Communism. Many, though not all, Communists were reconsidering their values; in Hungary and Poland there were considerable upheavals in the summer of 1956, resulting in gradual relaxation of discipline for the Poles but one of the greatest tragedies of Hungarian history.

With the brutal Soviet crushing of the Hungarian uprising in November, many intellectuals and artists were nonplussed. Picasso, under a barrage of messages asking him to "denounce Budapest," felt objective information was wanting and at a loss as to what attitude to take. Once again, his Party leaders left him on his own, but this time they were as much at sea as he. His friends were terribly upset: many publicly tore up their Party cards. On November 22, *Le Monde* published a letter to the Central Committee of the Party, signed by ten Party members, intellectuals or artists: Picasso, George Besson, Marcel Cornu, Francis Jourdain, Dr. Harel, Pignon and Hélène Parmelin, Paul Tillard, Prof. Henri Wallon, and Prof. René Lazzo. Recent events, they said,

confronted Communists with burning questions of conscience that neither the Central Committee nor *L'Humanité* had helped them to solve . . . interpretations of the events in Poland and Hungary exacerbated a dismay of which the consequences had been rapidly felt . . . requiring the calling of a special convention to discuss, realistically and honestly, the innumerable problems facing Communists today.

Publication of the letter, attributed to a "leak," made quite a stir, and the Central Committee, fearing more than anything a public resignation by Picasso, did its best to minimize it. Thorez and Roger Garaudy denounced the position taken by "certain intellectuals who have lost sight of the class struggle." *L'Humanité* stated that "those who signed . . . may have a different opinion. They may even cling to it in spite of the facts, but they have no right to impose their viewpoint on the Party through illicit means." The Central Committee's evasive answers did nothing to help the situation. Pablo was contacted by several discreet emissaries, as well as getting letters from Thorez and Casanova, but there was never any danger of his resigning.

A few weeks later, Georges Tabaraud, editor of the Nice *Patriote,* and Moscow's local "eye" on Picasso, was at lunch at La Californie with Yves Montand and Simone Signoret. The stars were among the Communists who had come out against Soviet intervention in Hungary, and Montand was very vocal in reaffirming his condemnation of it. Tabaraud defended it, and the argument waxed hot and heavy (as photos made by David Douglas Duncan show). Picasso took in every word, watching each of them carefully in turn, noting reactions and gestures, but never saying a word himself.

The house was in total silence. The master was at work. The pigeons were cooing on the balcony of the studio in which he was setting himself up against Velázquez, redoing *Las Meninas.* From time to time, Lump, the Dachshund Duncan had given him, barked briefly; the third-floor studio was off limits to him because he had several times tried to do in the pigeons who went freely in and out of their coop, protected by a metal grille, but easy of access. Jacqueline was resting, the she-goat was munching grass in the yard, a pair of Bengalees were in their cage on the mantel of the main living room near cut-up pieces of sheet iron, masks, or children's toys. Yan, the boxer, was stretched out on the tile floor. It was a hot, heavy summer.

When Picasso was working, friends who phoned to let him know they were coming over were asked to call back later, but exceptions were sometimes made for Kahnweiler, the Leirises or Pignons, Penrose, David Douglas Duncan, and Sabartés, more a Spanish Mr. Pickwick than ever (which was how Pablo was to draw him for the title page of his book, *Les Ménines et la vie* *), and of course Sapone, who never phoned ahead of time.

Roland Penrose, on page 371 of *Picasso: His Life and Work,* quotes the artist (indirectly) on the work:

> Velasquez can be seen in the picture, whereas in reality he must be standing outside it, he is shown turning his back on the Infanta who at first glance we would expect to be his model. He faces a large canvas on which he seems to be at work but it has its back to us and we have no idea what he is painting. The only solution is that he

* Jaime Sabartés, *Les Ménines et la vie* (*Las Meninas* and Life), Paris, 1958.

is painting the king and queen, who are only to be seen by their reflection in the mirror at the far end of the room. This implies incidentally that if we can see them in the mirror they are not looking at Velasquez, but at us. Velasquez therefore is not painting las Meninas. The girls have gathered round him not to pose but to see his picture of the king and queen with us standing beside them.

What attracted Pablo especially was that *Las Meninas* was a trick picture: the complex relationships between the different parts of the composition, the watcher and the watched, and those looking at all of them, implied a new relationship between the reality of the work and that of the outside world. Don Pablo entered into it as Velázquez had into the closed, tight abode of the King of Spain, where nothing was as it was elsewhere, because it was Spain, the King's, and Velázquez.

From then on, his face was drawn and gloomy, as it was whenever he was undertaking a struggle. No more visitors, no noise in the house; anything unexpected, however minor, loomed as a catastrophe. Jacqueline, recuperating from an operation, found it hard to put up with this atmosphere, even tenser as a result of a pain in the leg that Pablo suffered from most of the summer. Fortunately, there were the unscheduled arrivals of Duncan, coming back from all over the world, loaded with caviar, smoked salmon, or whiskey. At each visit he would snap hundreds of pictures, and then be off again.

Fortunately, too, there were bullfights . . . But, between bullfights and *Las Meninas,* it was, as reported by Hélène Parmelin, a nightmare:

> What an appalling business! he would say. One always thinks that to do a painting is just to paint. . . . And yet it's worse than death in the ring; it is death in the ring. . . .
>
> *Las Meninas* were furies which dogged us along the roads to the corridas; to the huge luncheon-tables in Nîmes; to the *paellas* on the Camargue; and to Marseilles where, by dint of searching, we found the only place where one could eat real *langoustes pourries,* served by the ladies who owned the restaurant. . . .

He began *Las Meninas* on August 17, 1957, with a huge canvas measuring 1 meter 94 by 2 meters 40 (77 inches by 95 inches, approximately) that constituted taking possession of the Velázquez. All its elements are there in a monochrome steel gray-blue atmosphere that disjoints and rebuilds the room flooded with light. The painter, on the left, has become a sort of hairy bewhiskered totem, and in the background is the silhouette of the courtier going out the open door; at the extreme right, front, a sort of ectoplasm in arabesque—and the dog Lump. The essentials of the Prado painting are there, only the plastic relationships being modified by the format, width in Picasso replacing what was height in Velázquez. Whence the flattening of the bare spaces of the ceiling, and the change in scale of the painter, a kind of monument to painting filling the whole left side of the canvas.

He did nineteen successive studies of the Infanta, before considering the ensemble again and taking up its separate details. Having thus gone round the job, he was ready to get into it and inventory it. He began with the serving-

*Bullfight at Vallauris: Picasso with Jacqueline Roque,
Paloma, and Claude, and behind him, Jacques Prévert.
1958*

(DORKA)

women, then went on to the little jester at the right in the Velázquez, kicking the wolf-dog quietly seated before the dwarf-woman. His attitude, the position of his hands and leg, suggested to Pablo that he might be playing an invisible piano, so he showed him at a keyboard lighted by two candles, dressed in a strange red gown. His head is a large white spot without the slightest feature on it, prolonged by an equally long white plait down the back. As Penrose quotes him (page 374):

"I saw the little boy with a piano," he said to me. "The piano came into my head and I had to put it somewhere. For me he was hanged so I made him hang. Such images come to me and I put them in. They are part of the reality of the subject. The surrealists in that way were right. Reality is more than the thing itself. I look always for its super-reality. Reality lies in how you see things. A green parrot," he continued, "is also a green salad *and* a green parrot. He who makes it only a parrot diminishes its reality. A painter who copies a tree blinds himself to the real tree. I see things otherwise. A palm tree can become a horse. Don Quixote can come into *Las Meninas.*"

The Infanta reappeared on December 30. Alone. With infinite grace, in a green-gray harmony highlighted with rose spots, she makes a closing curtsy to the long series of *Meninas* and the year that is ending.

Pablo deftly intermingled the "painted" and "drawn" parts, the latter strangely childlike. The "sacrilegious" plan of demythologizing the masterpieces, sometimes thrown up to him, is not apparent at all. He is no more savaging Velázquez than he had Delacroix, or would Manet or David. It takes a singular lack of comprehension to see his analytical enterprises as "latent Dadaism"—if Dadaism equals negation.

What mainly interested him in masterpieces was taking them apart ("Opening the watch and spreading the works on the table," as Jean Cau put it), to see what made them tick. Once inside, he isolated each part, so as to reassemble the whole according to what he had perceived. Analysis and synthesis thus went hand in hand, and Velázquez' *Meninas,* multiplied by forty-four new interpretations, became a huge fascinating set of mirrors around a little girl in too heavy a dress, with hesitant gestures and an irregular-featured face with two little round eyes that we may suppose look enviously at the window in which Picasso's pigeons stand for what she will never know: freedom.

One day, Jacqueline phoned the Pignons at Sanary to ask whether they were coming to the bullfight at Cannes the following Sunday, October 6. There were no corridas at this season—but Jacqueline went on, "I mean the only one, the special one, ours . . ."

Thinking they had understood, they drove to La Californie the next Sunday, arriving about the same time as the Leirises and, as she puts it, "We all had our minds on *Las Meninas* as we talked of this and that, everyone, including Picasso, knowing full well that this and that were *Las Meninas* . . ."

Diabolically, he confided, "This is where I ought to bring out *Las Meninas,* if I were going to bring them out."

But he didn't. It was getting dark. They all went inside, still chattering about this and that. They had some supper, but without appetite. They were all tired and all wondering whether he was finally going to show them the damned *Meninas,* which by now they all cordially detested.

Finally, at midnight, the Picassos, as well as the Leirises and Pignons, the latter falling off their feet, went to their rooms. Pablo came into the Pignons' and told Hélène that Jacqueline wanted to kiss her good night. When Hélène came back a half-hour later, her husband and Pablo were lying on the twin beds, and Picasso was saying, "Well, I'll show them to you tomorrow. I guess it's too late tonight . . ."

Knowing Picasso well, Pignon replied, "Not too late for me, at any rate. Let's go . . ."

"OK," Pablo answered, "let's go. But it's cold up there, so put something on. I'd thought it was too late, but if you want to . . ."

Up they went—without Hélène, dying to see the paintings, but not included in the invitation. She went back to join Jacqueline.

Two A.M. Three. The two painters upstairs were talking; the easel could be heard being moved about. Finally, they came back down. Hélène, exhausted, her mind whirling with her own imaginings of what *Las Meninas* might be, no longer had the strength to ask her husband about them . . . But then he started to tell her on his own, and he described them in a sort of Picassian nightmare that kept them awake most of the balance of the night.

In the morning, Pignon started describing them to the Leirises. And again to Hélène. And as the day went by, Pablo diabolically enjoyed the refined, superb, but perverse game he was playing, toying with his friends' curiosity, when finally Pignon, as if it were the most "natural" thing in the world, said to Pablo, "Shall we go up now?"

And up they went. At last. The wait was forgotten, and they were all delirious with enthusiasm. To quote Hélène:

> Picasso went from one canvas to another, the little ones and the big ones, taking them out, setting them up on the easel over the last one, taking them away, turning them over, putting up others. And no one said a word. It lasted for two hours, two long hours. Our legs were falling off, we could hardly stand, the pigeons were coming out of our ears. But there were *Las Meninas.* We had won.
>
> That's what I was thinking: we had won. I thought we, not he.

Exhausted with pleasure, the friends he had teased for almost two whole days had no words to express their delight. His implacable eye gazing at them, Don Pablo was thinking that, while it is sometimes difficult to tame painting, it is much easier and more amusing to toy with people. With them, he could do as he pleased.

Shown on several occasions—specifically, at the Galerie Louise Leiris in 1959, the Tate Gallery in London in 1960, and in Japan in 1964—the cycle of *Las Meninas* and the canvases done while they were being painted, *The Pigeons,* three landscapes, and the portrait of Jacqueline done December 3 were all presented by Picasso to the museum bearing his name in Barcelona, as a tribute to his friend Jaime Sabartés, who had died on February 13, 1968. In 1957, the Louise Leiris Gallery sold seventy Picassos for a total of 400 million francs, or almost six million francs apiece (over $17,000 apiece, at the exchange rate of the time). As Pablo used to say, "Dealing with Kahnweiler is like hitting the jackpot every day."

XXIII

ICARUS,
THE PICADOR,
AND THE DÉJEUNERS
(1958–1960)

"DO YOU THINK I AM DEAD?"
"DO YOU THINK I AM A MINISTER?"

THESE TELEGRAMS, EXCHANGED BETWEEN PICASSO AND ANDRÉ MAL-raux, General de Gaulle's Minister for Cultural Affairs, in 1965, reflect the strange relationship between the men who had practically not seen each other in twenty years. One had become an inflexible Gaullist, imbued with the importance of representing the General and the State, while the other had gone Communist—enough to create a chasm between them.

To Malraux, history counted more than anything. His purely bookish culture was concerned less with the present than "the vast past" which "reveals two constants of mankind: instincts and the questioning of the world." In Picasso, Chagall, Rouault, Braque, Matisse, he saw the history of art carried forward, for in his eyes the history of art was art plus history.

If he was to wait almost thirty years to write the "reportage" of his visit to Picasso a few months after the painter's death, it was because to him time destroyed the measly little daily banality and transcended action into epic. And because Jacqueline Picasso phoned him in September 1973 to ask him in his own kind of terms ("Do it for France!") to help get the State to accept Picasso's legacy of his own collection of old pictures. Forthwith, he was off to Mougins.

When the Spanish war, a turning point in Malraux's life, broke out in 1936, Picasso was fifty-five, and his work already part of the history of art; he was both symbol and institution. This was why the Spanish leaders asked him to do *Guernica.* The relations between the painter and writer, while distant, had been cordial, but now events would change things. Picasso, a part of the history of art, entered history outright with *Guernica,* and he was on the same side as

Malraux: what had been psychological and aesthetic analysis now took on emotional impact. They did not see that much more of each other ("I never belonged to his court," Malraux was to say of Pablo), but they now had closer links: helping the Spanish people, fighting for liberty. In the eyes of the International Brigade volunteers, Picasso was part of that people, and it was only natural for him to plan to illustrate *Man's Hope,* by the leader of the España Escadrille, even though it never came to pass.

Toward Picasso, Malraux never hid his hostility. In joining the Communists, the painter had resigned from history; he no longer belonged to destiny. As a painter who was friends with both said, "they felt themselves equals before eternity," and neither would take a step toward the other—yet it is not hard to imagine how Malraux would have extolled Picasso, had he died while the other was in office. For then Pablo would have become part of history and destiny. Reading the eulogies he gave Braque and Le Corbusier lets us in on what that recovery operation would have sounded like.

To him, "Do you think I'm a minister?" was a joke in keeping with his describing his place in the government as that of Mallarmé's cat "who-played-at-being-a-cat." But it scarcely explains his unbelievable attitude toward three problems he refused to face: Picasso's plan to leave a bequest to the State, the two great retrospectives held at the Grand and Petit Palais, and the matter of the Rue des Grands-Augustins studio. France had "other problems . . ."

Malraux and the Fifth Republic gave Picasso no commission. The Minister had given some thought to making *The Reaper* a monument to Baudelaire, or rather as he himself put it "to *The Flowers of Evil,*" at the prow of Île St.-Louis. But the ill-fated Opéra ceiling commission went to Chagall—the painter Pablo most detested (and it was mutual).

On the other hand, UNESCO had him decorate a wall of a hundred square meters in the main hall, known as the Delegates' Lounge, of its building in the heart of Paris. George Salles, honorary director of French Museums, and one of those who did the most to "normalize" relations between Picasso and the State, dubbed this huge composition, made up of several dozen panels each two meters square, *The Fall of Icarus.* Pablo just referred to it as "the UNESCO painting."

At first, he turned it down: "I'm no longer twenty. I can't do it." The Secretary General of UNESCO insisted, shrewdly pointing out how Picasso would be honoring the building, and, less subtly, stressing the other contemporaries involved, Miró, Henry Moore, Arp, Calder. Georges Salles went to La Californie as the final convincer, and Pablo looked at the mock-up of the building and gave in. The fee was not outside his considerations: the money was tax-free.

Picasso reminded his visitor that the Vallauris Temple of Peace was still unopened. Was this delay the result of the discord between the Communist municipality and the Paris government? Salles promised to look into the matter.

The UNESCO room was not easy to decorate in style. Its complex architecture, with columns and a catwalk going all the way across it, did not bother him—for he never went to look at it; nor was he ever to see the whole of his work installed there. Indeed, he did not return to Paris after Spring 1955, except for the ultra-secret trip to the American Hospital at Neuilly for his stomach-ulcer operation in November 1966. That was done in closed ambulance, from Mougins and back.

As usual, he did very numerous overall and detail drawings, in lead pencil, grease pencil, India ink, and color crayons. The first gouache study is dated December 6, 1957, while the final state of the maquette has several dates on it, January 18–29, 1958. So, day by day, and sometimes hour by hour, it is possible to follow the genesis of this largest, and most disconcerting, work done by the seventy-six-year-old Picasso.

From the softened gray-green December gouache to the final January color maquette, many changes took place in the original aim of the work; indeed, it is hard to see any relation between the beginning and the end of the preparatory studies. The December gouache shows the inside of a studio lighted by a skylight; a large vertical canvas shows swimmers at the edge of a pool or on the spring-board. Painted at La Californie in the summer of 1956, it is *The Springboard*. These characters are not unlike the ones he did at the same period with bits of wood. To the left, on an easel, a horizontal picture presents a woman reclining, decomposed in the Cubist manner; she spills over the borders of the picture, which can only mentally "contain" her. At the extreme right, a brownish-gray silhouette of the painter holding palette and brushes can be made out, allusive reminder of Velázquez' *Las Meninas*.

All these elements refer to earlier Picassos. Gaëtan Picon, who wrote a remarkable study on the genesis of *The Fall of Icarus*,* says that "each element, as both cause and effect, is part of a set of self-references containing its own principle of regeneration." The "painting within a painting," he says, was nothing new for Picasso, either: Picon discovered the root idea of the first version of the UNESCO work in a series of very schematic drawings done on April 18, 1956, which include the horizontal picture of the reclining figure and the vertical one that perhaps has the painter reflected in it.

On December 15, 1957, Picasso began the preparatory drawings in a large-size sketchbook finished January 4. It has several variants of the December 6 gouache, detail studies, especially of the reclining woman, who goes through a series of transformations, from the basic geometrical schema, by way of simplifications often used by Picasso, into a mere sign. Then he returned to the theme of the studio, returning again to the bather who, from being geometrical, becomes Matissian. On the right, the painter's silhouette was becoming more precise.

January 4, the first pad finished, he started another. As always when preoccupied with a job, he was *inside* his work, absorbed in it. The mock-up of the UNESCO lounge was on a large table in one of the ground-floor rooms of La Californie. One of the building's architects, Bernard Zehrfuss, would come by from time to time to see how Picasso was getting along, but the painter could still not say what the end result would be. Zehrfuss, naturally, was in a hurry, but not so Picasso, and the architect was never any the wiser for his visits.

The second sketchpad has more studies for the studio. The nude woman is no

* Gaëtan Picon, *La Chute d'Icare de Pablo Picasso* (Pablo Picasso's *Fall of Icarus*), Geneva, 1971.

longer in the picture, but lying voluptuously on a divan. The painter at the right
becomes taller and thinner, and seems about to vanish. The vertical picture of
Bathers has now become square.

This new composition was the basis for the two India-ink, pencil, and wash
studies of January 6, 1958. In the second, the painter, holding palette and brushes,
comes back into his own.

Now Pablo turned to color problems. On January 7, the painter gave way to a
vertical potted plant. The same day, the composition was suddenly simplified by
broad flat surfaces of bright green, yellow, blue, and red, the forms turning into
silhouettes of themselves, projections of a progressively more and more phantas-
mal reality. The picture is replaced by an image that combines children's drawing,
Matissian allusion, geometrical rigor, and arabesque.

The diver, alone, arms spread, on his board, was replaced in the third January
7 version by a silhouetted bust, the shadow of the painter, which in version No. 4
of the same day grew immeasurably, questioning the empty canvas, while the
nude woman, an odalisque outlined in water-green, stretched languorously. The
next day, swimmer and divers were back and the odalisque reduced to shapeless
magma.

Visibly, Picasso was wondering where his subject was taking him, as he
followed it through the meanders of the inventiveness in which, as he puts it,
painting made him do what it wanted. What turns and twists, switches of styles
and techniques and variations of forms, in this *mise-en-scène* of something that
kept evading him until, suddenly, he changed it all.

What did the UNESCO heads expect? What he himself expected of the struggle
he was engaged in: an act of painting. They, and he, worried, but for opposite
reasons, which they kept to themselves. Since the first space flights, outer space
had fascinated him; he kept up with the Sputniks in the press and on television:
they had become a part of his life, which he talked about as of an intimate.

One day, when he was with friends at the Nice Airport, someone shouted,
"Quick! Quick! Sputnik!" Picasso, like the others, ran out; they all peered up into
the sky, pointing, "There! There it is!" Everyone saw the Sputnik in its orbit and
heard its characteristic *beep-beep*. Pablo was tremendously excited, all evening
talking of nothing else, the promise opened up by moonships. Life on the moon.
Men living there. Were there painters among them? And going on to describe
the pictures they must paint, galleries and museums that showed them, dealers
who sold them, collectors who bought . . .

The "UNESCO painting" was transformed: the studio, reclining nude, painter,
and diver themes were all dropped, their variants having kept him busy for forty-
three days. On January 18, he started over from scratch. He had found his subject and was at the same time experimenting with a new technique: he drew or
painted each element of the composition on a little paper rectangle which he then
placed over the overall schema, moving them around, switching colors, and so on.

When Picasso finished his final maquette in color crayons, having put it together from January 18 to 29 like a jigsaw puzzle, he tried to find a large enough
room in Cannes in which he might execute the final work, but there was none

that would do. So he decided to work as he had for the successive sketches, on plywood panels that could later be assembled as indicated at UNESCO.

It was exhausting work, for each of the panels had to be painted on the floor, then moved so as to form the puzzle piece by piece, without ever seeing it overall. Jacqueline and his secretary, Miguel, helped him with the task, and he finally looked on it as a game: "I did the best I could," he would say.

By now, UNESCO was worried, having been rebuffed in all its attempts to find out what the work would be, and certain news reports contributed to the concern. How could Picasso, the writers wondered aloud, do one panel after another without seeing the whole? How come he had shown no one his sketches, or let anyone see the work in progress?

At first, Pablo ignored these attacks, but then they started to bother him. He, too, took to worrying: no longer was he immune to criticism, or scornful of it, as once he had been. It bothered him to read that he was toying with people, not working seriously, playing "solitaire" with the huge UNESCO assemblage. So he decided to unveil it in the Vallauris public schoolyard, with a delegation from the international organization in attendance, to receive the work from his hands.

Thus, the little town on March 29, 1958, held a celebration such as there had not been in a long time for Picasso, but the UNESCO representatives were thrown. The composition, of course, hardly benefited from being seen out of doors in the stark Mediterranean light, and they were at a loss for words, despite Pablo's friends, who kept assuring them volubly that this was an authentic masterpiece. Yet it did not ring true. Nor did the UNESCO people like the noisy propaganda of the Communists, who, once again, could not hide their embarrassment at this new work that, somehow, would have to be explained to "the masses."

When Georges Salles, in his inaugural speech, dubbed it *The Fall of Icarus,* great sighs of relief were heard: now it made some kind of sense. The atmosphere cleared and spirits were buoyed up. In the evening, with everyone gone, Picasso returned to Vallauris to look at his work. As Pignon described it:

> It was a very fine moment. There were just watchmen and the young potter handling the spots. Plus a symbol: a small potted olive tree. And, suddenly, all the true colors became apparent in total silence, including a certain green at the bottom which, in daylight, no one had been able to see . . .

The night was mild, the sky wondrously starry; Pablo, Jacqueline, and a few friends watched Georges Salles's Icarus fall quartered into the sea, the bathers remaining impassive in the sun. Who could say what differentiated a masterpiece from the sketchy daubing of a tired old great painter? No one.

Probably for the first time in his life, in this schoolyard, before ten or so people from whom he could not anticipate the slightest speck of truth, Picasso felt alone, terribly, tragically alone. In a loneliness that could only grow greater. Until it became despair.

The heads of UNESCO held a dinner in a large Champs-Élysées restaurant for the architects and artists of the new building, to thank them for what they had done, and the sole subject of conversation was of course *The Fall of Icarus.* Not

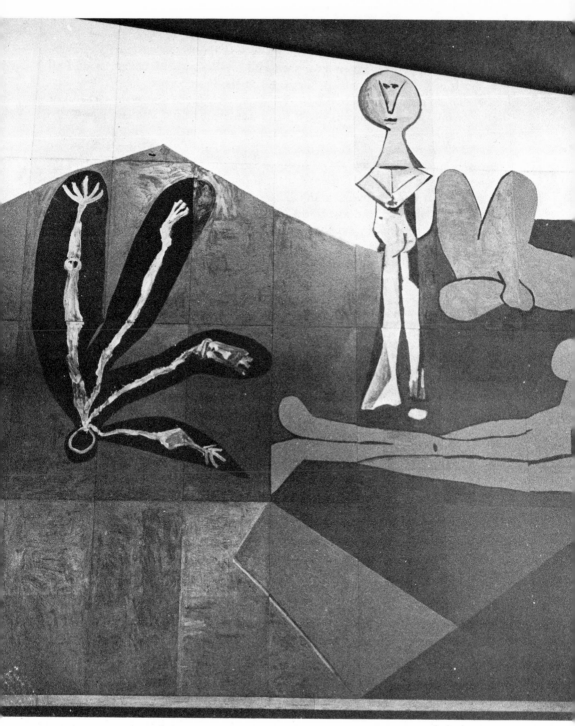

"The Fall of Icarus" mural 1958, Palais de l'UNESCO, Paris
(ROGER-VIOLLET)

all favorable, although the great painting looked impressive in the hall, where it fitted in perfectly. Without ever seeing them, Picasso had gotten around all the shoals of the questionable architecture and the location not easy to "live in."

He did not attend. At dessert time, Dr. Luther H. Evans, Secretary General of UNESCO, instead of raising his glass in the anticipated toast, merely banged the table, exclaiming, "That's it! It exists! And we're the ones who did it!"

But he was not one of the devotees of *Icarus*. Turning to Georges Salles, he somewhat mockingly added, "And now our friend in all sincerity will explain his friend Picasso's masterpiece to us!" The former museum head was somewhat taken aback. It was an obvious trap—but how to get out of it?

It was Le Corbusier who rose to the occasion, saying, "I want to say simply this —and you can trust in my experience and judgment—Picasso's panel is a masterpiece, and like all masterpieces it cannot be explained. What matter what we think of it today? Its beauty will be apparent ten years from now." And he moved that a congratulatory telegram signed by all present be wired to Cannes; which was done.

Life at La Californie was moving ahead. The children grew, the menagerie changed and multiplied, new sculptures adorned the garden: ceramic enlargements of fauns, women bathers cut out of cardboard, bronzes.

Days on end he would "draw" with his scissors, then folding his cutouts, marking rounded or flat folds; once he had finished, he gave the figure to a specialized workshop to reproduce in metal sheeting of varying thicknesses. If the metal shone too much, he would paint it, either with a solid coat of white or striped with colors, sometimes stressing the features or some detail in grease pencil.

In September 1958, after the grape-harvest bullfight at Arles, Picasso, Jacqueline, and their troupe were guests of Douglas Cooper's at his Château de Castille. Someone in the crowd mentioned the Château de Vauvenargues, near Aix-en-Provence, a magnificent if slightly forbidding structure flanked by enormous towers in a superb landscape. "You ought to go look at it," Cooper assured him. "It's for sale, and is a wonderful place."

The next day, the Picassos and Pignons were in Aix to see the show at the Pavillon Vendôme, where the Cuttoli Collection, including some of his finest works, was on display, and he suggested taking Cooper's advice and going on to Vauvenargues.

From Aix, one went up a little winding road up the Montagne Ste.-Victoire through admirable landscapes the more wonderful to Picasso because Cézanne had painted them. Turn after twisting turn, then suddenly: the château. "Magnificent!" he exclaimed.

Douglas was right: it was a very fine château, impressive but austere, atop a rocky tor amid pines, cypresses, and holm oaks. With round towers on either side, it was ringed by fourteenth-century fortifications; in 1644, the entrance facade had had a porch and a fine door with bossages and frontons added, creating a majestic character. Beneath it, a terrace.

It had been the family estate of the de Clapiers, including Luc de Clapiers,

Marquis de Vauvenargues, whose famous *Réflexions et maximes* were a standard part of seventeenth-century French literature. Though hating the place and its people, he had left it his title, which impressed Pablo less than its almost Spanish majestic appearance, and above all, the Cézannian countryside, so clear and orderly, harmonious and austere. Smitten with it, he made arrangements to go through it soon thereafter, confirming that its huge rooms would make superb studios, and moreover that everything he had collected and deposited everywhere throughout a lifetime would fit into it without trouble. All that was missing was a heating system.

Jacqueline shivered at the idea of living there, but he had already mentally acquired it, and answered her one timid objection with, "You forget that I am Spanish and love sadness." However, he agreed not to sell La Californie—which he had never intended to do.

He studied the château's history from the original Dame Béatrix of 1247 to one M. Touche, who owned it now. In the north tower, beneath a stone altar, reposed the body of St. Severin, a gift of Pope Pius VII to Cardinal d'Isoard, archbishop of Aix, whose successors remained in possession of it—to the gleeful delight of Picasso as well as some journalists titillated by the idea of a saint's remains in the château of a Communist! Some even maintained that buying the castle made Picasso the Marquis of Vauvenargues, which of course was untrue, despite what several biographers have alleged.

However, one day he did phone Kahnweiler, to say, "I've bought the Montagne Ste.-Victoire."

The dealer, knowing he owned several fine Cézannes, replied, "Good. Which one?"

"The original," Pablo beamed back.

And truly, it was in a Cézanne landscape, at the foot of Ste.-Victoire so often painted by him in his final years, that the château stood. And through the good offices of Maître Louis David, *notaire* at Arles, Pablo had now bought it for sixty million francs (about $120,000 at the time), with some twenty-five millions (or $50,000) of work to be done, one-third for central heating alone.

The improvements and installation took almost a year; endless crates were stored at the château, but never opened; on the other hand, hundreds of Pablo's paintings from all the periods soon adorned the walls. He was able to see again and show visitors the collection of Courbets, Cézannes, Matisses, Modiglianis, Derains, Renoirs, Braques, Corots, Douanier Rousseaus, and others he had ceaselessly accumulated. In May 1958, alerted by Douglas Cooper, he bought six Degas monotypes at the London Lefevre Gallery show, displaying them proudly to visitors and thirteen years later basing a series of famous engravings on them.

Pablo's enemies presented him as a "murderer of painting," but nothing could better show his devotion to classic pictorial tradition than the collection he made and never ceased to increase and dote upon.

One day he dragged a guest, the British critic John Richardson, into a little side room to show him several things that had arrived from one of his storages: two or three small Courbets, a Gauguin landscape, Vuillard's *The Lullaby*, a

Chardin, some Corots, and a magnificent Le Nain, one of the best in his collection, a *Horsemen's Halt.* There were also fifty-odd Picasso plates, never seen before, that he showed Richardson, adding, "I have lots more plates I've never bothered to have pulled."

All the bronze animals from La Californie were also moved to Vauvenargues. Yet, as in his earlier abodes, the furnishing remained fragmentary, except for a superb ultramodern bathroom that Pablo decorated with fancy-free musical fauns and nymphs at their voluptuous play in luxuriant greenery.

Jacqueline detested Vauvenargues. She was as ill at ease out in the harsh sun-drenched Provençal countryside as she was inside the château. Making the best of a bad bargain, she shopped for antique Provençal-style furniture for the huge rooms that upset her so, but it was Pablo who selected the enormous black Henri II buffet for the dining room. For months it fascinated him, and he did several paintings of it, the first on February 18, 1959, after which he individually drew all the details of its cornices, colonnettes, sculptures, and so on. The largest of the paintings, *The Vauvenargues Buffet* or *The Dining Room,* begun on March 23, 1959, was to be finished only on January 23, 1960, at La Californie, after he worked at it on several occasions. The Dalmatian Perro, present in the earlier versions, appears now with a little girl perched on a chair to the left of the buffet, the bust of a woman on a pedestal being to the right.

So the Vauvenargues period starts in February 1959 and goes to April 20, 1961, when he ceased working there. In those two years he was not in constant residence at the château, but stayed there frequently, always insisting Jacqueline go with him—although at first she tried to hold out for remaining at La Californie.

The Vauvenargues period is characterized by a return, not to Spain, as has been said, but to a kind of Hispanicism. Not only the austerity and nobility of the place but also a kind of nostalgic loneliness were reflected in this. Nearing eighty, he had apparently scarcely changed. But only apparently . . . Was he not beginning to sense a slowdown, a darkening of mood, which he would have to fight off so as to elude that fatal inactivity that comes before the end?

His friends had noted changes in his behavior and life-style: he did not go to the beach (although he would return to it after eighty), and even passed up many bullfights. He was quick to anger, and his once-Rabelaisian eroticism was turning morbid: he indulged in heavily obvious off-color stories. True, younger and younger women, ever more delectable, were at his beck and call, and this brought on a few painful scenes with Jacqueline.

During his early stays at Vauvenargues, he was at loose ends, finding it hard to adjust to the château despite his great affection for it, to the landscape, and perhaps also the presence of Cézanne. He told Cocteau (who visited him with Mme. Weisweiler), his nephew Vilato, and Duncan how dispirited he felt. After several paintings, he confided to one friend, "I'm just getting my hand in. I haven't done anything yet."

But back at La Californie all he thought of was returning to Vauvenargues. As he told Hélène Parmelin, "You know where you live, you live in Paris, you have a house and know where you are. I'm not anywhere, don't know where I live, you can't imagine how awful that is."

At Vauvenargues, he started using enamel paint, a first step toward the return to color which, after the austerity of the early months of becoming used to the new home, was to reach such proportions in years to come. Ripolin, enamel paint, both fluid and thick, gave brighter lacquered tones, but also ran in broad bleeding swatches, which, left as they were in the paintings, put off some collectors who felt they were just a sign of carelessness.

The pads went on accumulating. Tens and dozens of them piled up in the studio, for he could often fill a whole one in a single day. They included studies for Dominguín's toreador outfit (sixteen on August 5, 1959, and more the following days), scenes of bullfighting that gradually turn into a struggle between man and centaur, then groups of centaurs, studies of women washing their feet which were to serve for a series of paintings with fleshy, robust, angular nudes, in February. More bullfights. Nudes, women's heads, everything his eye could see and his hand put down.

All of April 1960 was devoted to drawings of nudes, some fifty-odd done in a few days in an unbelievable variety of techniques and styles, interrupted only on April 12 for the astonishing painting of the *Woman Beneath the Lamp*, reading a book in the cone of light projected by the electric bulb, while the rest of the room is split between broad planes of gray or dark-red shadows. He was to return to the same theme, notably in a 1962 linoleum cut, *Still Life Beneath the Lamp.*

The first drawings inspired by Manet's famous *Déjeuner sur l'herbe* were done on August 10 and 11, 1959, at Vauvenargues. That autumn, Pablo went back to linocuts, a technique he had essayed in 1954. He had always wanted a process which, retaining its craft quality, allowed him to express himself with restraint, whence his interest in lithography, etching, aquatint, or ceramics; but he deplored the limitations of the proofs and their high cost. When he discovered linoleum cutting at the shop of a Vallauris craftsman named Arnera, he was immediately won over. Arnera had inherited the technique from his father, and used it mainly for posters, which in fact was how Pablo originally came to him.

The "long distance" lithograph work he had been doing with Mourlot exasperated Pablo because he had to wait so long for first proofs. He liked having everything at hand, and working with Arnera allowed him quick results. He was familiar with relief engraving, having done some woodcuts back at the turn of the century. His first linoleum cut, *The Squab* (1939), was to appear much later in a deluxe edition of *Quarante Dessins de Picasso en marge de Buffon* (Forty Picasso Drawings to Go with Buffon).

One day he summoned Arnera to La Californie to show him a new technique he had developed, which might revolutionize linoleum cutting: all the colors on a single block. The idea was to work the linoleum with a gouge and then print it in the selected color, say, an ocher, in as many copies as planned. This gave a ground which would appear as lighter drawing when a darker color, say, a brown, was overprinted on it from the cut block. After that first run, the dominant color became the brown, against which the subjects stood out in ocher, coming through where the surface had been gouged out. The engraver then had only to go back to the block and take out those parts that were to remain dark brown; printed in black, this third state of the linocut sharpened the characters and gave them their final shape. Later, he was to vary the tones, using whites, greens, and blues.

Female nudes, bullfights, portraits of Jacqueline, Bacchanalia, variants of the *Déjeuner sur l'herbe,* guitar players, interiors, still lifes, all composed a parallel ballet to what Don Pablo was doing in painting and drawing. The matter forced the artist into more deeply pronounced rhythms, or more definitely broken ones, contrasting with the play of mass-forms which they balanced.

The series of Bacchanalia, done toward the end of 1959, like the paintings for the Antibes Museum, commingled musical fauns, leaping nymphs, bathers and dancers, goats, bulls, and Dionysiac sarabands at the seashore or before rolling hills. The colors were brilliant: ochers, blacks, whites, blues, greens; stark yet lush, all movement and harmony. Some figures were a mere arabesque: admirably stylized, they required no color to be as elliptical as signs.

Picasso dropped linoleum toward the end of 1967. The new process had forced him to rethink his themes and change his touch, the substitution of one technique for another always being evidenced in him by the substitution of one spirit, one expression, one style for another.

Le Déjeuner sur l'herbe is *The Painter and His Model* out of doors. He had been concerned with this theme for several years, as some August 1954 drawings show. He greatly admired Manet, and the big Jeu de Paume painting, which had been the scandal of the 1863 Salon, appealed to him by its double daring, on the purely pictorial level as well as the moral: with the stark-naked lady and the other in her chemise, wading in the stream before two fully clad gentlemen, Manet was thumbing his nose at propriety and common morals.

That *Luncheon on the Grass,* or all of the Déjeuners, would keep Pablo busy for more than two years, August 1959 to December 1961: twenty-seven paintings and 138 drawings begun at Vauvenargues and finished at Mougins, with a few interludes in the medieval château. This dialogue with Manet, often interrupted and characterized by so many variations, coincided with Picasso's eightieth birthday.

To think that he lived with Manet for two and a half years, while his intimacy with Delacroix and Velázquez had lasted only three or four months! What could the painter of *Olympia* have in common with the creator of *Les Demoiselles d'Avignon?* The nineteenth century. Pablo had started from it, and battened on its accomplishments; he had begun painting at a time when Manet was master to all the youth, much more than Cézanne or Van Gogh, whose influence was not felt till much later. Manet was heir to the creators of the nineteenth century as well as those who had gone before, heir to Velázquez and the Spaniards of the Golden Century, yet also the first of the moderns, the first of the great scandalizers of living art. He defied all tradition; he was the liberator; in all this akin to Picasso, who was also like him in that neither of them set

"Déjeuner sur l'herbe, after Manet" March 4–July 30, 1960, private collection (Louise Leiris Gallery— Paris)

out to be a revolutionary. They became such because others, penned within their own scleroses, their systematizations, their blindnesses, made them so. Reprovingly and horrifiedly.

Manet in doing the *Déjeuner sur l'herbe* had given much thought to Giorgione, whom he brought up to date, restructuring and revitalizing the theme of his *Concert in the Fields* with the deliberately "modern" character of his 1863 painting. No longer an allegorical scene, it was now a study of manners; the Venetian master's nude women, fleshly though they were, were museum nymphs, while Manet's were stripped-down strumpets, who had shed their clothes with no view to playing the pipes of Pan or making pretty talk with gentlemen.

He began by interrogating the characters, one after the other, taking them aside, giving them a life of their own, out of context. He varied their relationships, placing them closer together, further apart, thereby also varying their plastic proportions; little by little, they departed from the original, from Manet. They took on their own personality, changed their manner, their dress, and so on. Some details appeared, only to disappear, and new themes engrafted themselves on the earlier.

The figures, isolated at first, became part of nature. In the canvases of February 27 and 28, 1960, the volumes set up and took position; the characters of the Manet picture, the naked woman looking toward the spectator, the man talking to her whom Douglas Cooper dubbed the "Big Talker," his companion, and the other woman dipping into the stream. They were getting acquainted.

One of the figures that most interested Picasso was the bather in the background: leaning forward, naked, washing her feet or lacing her shoes, she was to be found in several drawings or paintings in 1943–1944, and was the subject of a whole series of studies in February 1960. In Fall and Winter 1959–1960, several linoleum cuts dealt with the Déjeuners.

On March 3, the protagonists of the scene, Big Talker, who is an "artist type," the two nude women, and the fellow smoking, half hidden by a tree, became part of a luxuriant abundance of forestry letting through broad puddles of blue sky, the whole not unlike the clustering of a medieval tapestry. Links began to set up among the figures, allowing anticipation of greater intimacy between the Talker and the naked women, whose distortions were especially daring.

That March 3 canvas has a second date, that of its completion: August 20, 1960. For five months, he came back to it again and again, making it a synthesis of the Manet painting, Cézanne and Courbet bathing women, Renoir's opulent nymphs, and Matisse's languid-odalisques, of the relationships of volumes in naturalism and the play of light in Impressionism. The woman dipping into the water and washing, moreover, is out of Degas. Bathing, summer, outdoors, rest, and nakedness in the landscape are all nineteenth-century contributions, and Don Pablo took them wherever he could. "He who does not imitate, does not invent," writes Alain.

On April 19, 1961, after a nine-month hiatus, he painted two pictures, one of which is curiously naïve in its "artistic" softness, the other much more elaborate. The woman in the foreground had become a big spot of pink flesh with summarily sketched characteristics, while the Talker was wearing a surprising long red robe. He is exclusively concerned with his speechifying, as Picasso is exclusively with the plastic relationships he is creating—for our painter too is a kind of storyteller. Was his ambition not always "to say"? *

On June 17, the dialogue with Manet's characters began again.

He painted a canvas in blues and greens, showing his feel, doubtless born of his contacts with the Provençal countryside, for the cool, flourishing landscape, as well as color. The Talker is holding forth, the smoker coming forward to take part in the conversation, the nude woman listens, hand under her chin, and the bather in the background goes on washing by herself.

On the twenty-eighth, another version, very quickly painted in circular or "macaroni" strokes, stressing the great green masses of the branches. The Talker is coming alive, the naked woman still listening, but her body has lengthened and her head shrunk till it is merely a miniature profile. The smoker and bather are still there.

June 20, Pablo did eight line drawings in a row on a first pad, redistributing the characters, who on the twenty-second were to be covered with varicolored confetti. Then, many more line or color-crayon drawings, of the two women in a variety of positions. A second pad could barely contain the studies done on July 8 and 9.

In the June drawings, and those in early July, he tried as much as possible to vary the physical looks and positions of the characters, as well as the composition as a whole. The Talker is naked, a third woman, also nude, joins the first two; she listens, then, doubtless uninterested in the talk, lies on her stomach on the grass and starts to read a book. A bearded, hirsute man takes her place. Then she reappears. A frugal meal is on the ground. The Talker has undergone changes: bearded, then beardless, he continues to speak seriously, with eye wide open. Pablo began a third pad, used on July 10, 11, and 24.

In the July 16 canvas, the reading woman, who had gone to the rear of the scene to be quiet, disappears. The one listening has become huge, a veritable anthropomorphic monster, her bent head with the immense eyes seeming to threaten the Talker, who quickly diminishes and seems to be cautiously retreating into the half-light.

Another rearrangement of the figures, done very summarily with color crayons, takes up eight drawings of July 26. With unbelievable dexterity, Picasso, juggling lines and bright color spots, makes sport of the theme, which changes several times until, in the painting of July 27, it becomes an antique pastorale. The Talker has become a kind of divine, or a bearded philosopher, whose bright-yellow peplum clashes with the harmony of greens, blues, and dark grays created by the broad belts of shadow and light in a flat space.

Between July 30 and August 10, 1961, he painted six big vertical canvases of a phantasmagorical character. The Talker is talking to the young woman in the

---

* In *Picasso Plain*, Hélène Parmelin had quoted him: "I want to SAY a nude . . . To SAY breast, SAY foot, SAY hand, belly. If I can find the way to SAY it, that's enough . . ."

heart of a beautiful night decor of black and green-gray with blue and light-green reflections, while in the background the bather is still at her ablutions. This mystery-laden confrontation, in which the listening woman takes on fantastic aspects of prodigious poetic and plastic inventiveness, also has an impressive dramatic intensity. While in the other canvases of the series this scene had no hidden meaning, here something seems to be going on; anecdote makes way for action.

Obviously, he did not do only Déjeuners for two and a half years. On January 30, 1960, he took inspiration from Rembrandt's *Bathsheba* to "say nude" in his way, which turned the young woman into a pink goldbeater's skin, parts of which seem gradually to be deflating. She is stretched on a water-green chair, a servant in large black cape at her feet.

He was also cutting out sheet iron, doing ceramics, drawing endless bullfight sketches in velvety black with the spots of grisaille and pitch duplicating the ballet of man and beast; then, starting June 5, 1960, no more bullfighting, but the life of the picador.

It had begun on July 11, 1959, and when the Galerie Louise Leiris presented the suite in November 1960 it would be called *Romancero of the Picador.* The slightly clumsy fellow is the scapegoat of the bullfights; with his broad *castoreño* held in place by a jugular strap, his thick leggings and his pike, he is the graceless supernumerary, the plebeian window dressing for the aristocratic virtuoso who is the torero. If anything goes wrong, if there is a mistake or anything phony, the picador is the one who gets hissed and hooted. Perched on his horse, using his *garrocha* more or less dexterously, he can scarcely defend himself and is forever held to be guilty on principle.

Even when having fun, he is awkward and self-conscious. At the whorehouse, when the madam trots out her fanciest fillies, he does not get turned on much. He looks. The girls display their luscious breasts for him, wiggle their rumps, dance nude to the accompaniment of castanets, and he applauds without ever becoming aroused. Is he impotent? Why doesn't he ever take off his hat and leggings, or even drop his pike? Sometimes he fingers a cigarillo that he calmly puffs at.

So Picasso surrounds him with a ballet of deadly winks, globular bosoms with brown nipples, hairy armpits, rounded bellies, appetizing hips, skirts, mantillas, obscene gestures. Sweat makes the girls' long black hair stick to their temples as they dance in the musky odor of their bodies. Castanets click, the guitar accompanies the wild gyrations of the women, urged on with clapping of hands and beating of feet. Impassive, the picador looks on. As he would at the bull. Watchful, worried. While in a corner Celestina the horrible smirks.

On June 11, in the brothel he has wandered into again, the dance of the stark-naked whore before him becomes delirious. She is so suggestive that the madam, enchanted, claps and claps; even the picador seems to be coming to life. Is he about to lose control? No. Yet, this time the wild-eyed girl, running with sweat, is dancing for him alone, presenting for his delectation her heavy breasts and the bushy bundle of her crotch. The picador hangs on to his *garrocha* a little harder. Eleven years later, Pablo was to return to the theme of the impassive voyeur in his series on Monsieur Degas among the whores. Those etchings are akin to these misadventures of the picador, with the same kind of sad disillusionment.

The Catalans visiting La Californie were reforging links between Barcelona and Picasso. The publisher Gustavo Gili and his wife, Juan Vidal Ventosa, the dealer Juan Gaspar, whose wife, Elvira, had been Malraux's secretary during the Civil War, his cousin and associate Miguel, Dr. Jacint Reventos, the son of Cinto Reventos Borday, known as Cinto Reventos II. His father and his uncle Ramón Reventos were among Pablo's oldest friends. The writer Josep Palau, who had devoted works to Pablo, Fenosa, who had now become accepted and established, Clavé, who was to move to Cap-St.-Pierre near St.-Tropez in 1965 and be a faithful caller. And especially Pallarés, keeper of the Picassian flame in his Via Layetana apartment, who in 1969 would see to it that a street in Horta was named for Don Pablo.

Antoni Tápies, who had been raised on Surrealism and was a friend of Fin and Xavier Vilato, Pablo's two painter nephews, was nevertheless introduced to Picasso by Dr. Jacint Reventos. He had at one time made copies of some Picassos, but his later development toward earthy, matterist painting of an elemental sobriety that could accommodate symbolic content of protest or accusation, the strangling of Spain, repression, prisons, arrests and tortures, was to move him away from the old master. Yet he visited him several times in Cannes. For if, in painting, Pablo was the hero of a revolution long accomplished, to him and other younger artists of Iberia he remained the first famous Spaniard to have come out against the Fascist régime and proclaimed his allegiance to democratic freedoms.

But all the attention he was receiving from Catalans was by way of prelude to his return to Barcelona—not in person, impossible as long as Franco was there—but through two key projects: the decorating of the Colegio de los Arquitectos, and the Picasso Museum in Calle de Montcada.

The College of Architects of Catalonia and the Balearics stood aggressively modern in glass and steel across from the Barcelona Cathedral, much to the dismay of impenitent *passéistes*. But when they heard that the creator of it, Xavier Busquets, had asked Picasso to decorate the walls, all hell broke loose. The city government paid no heed, nor did the Archbishop of Barcelona, who had already blessed its walls. Carl Nesjar, with his sandblasting technique, inside and out, cut right into the concrete walls the frisky scenes of Catalonian folklore that Pablo had drawn with his aerial grace and expressive schematicism sometimes mistaken for nonchalance. The sardana, the Giants, the "Xiquets de Valls," and bullfights mingled with sarabands of dancing and piping fauns inscribing their entrancing ballets like so many monumental graffiti. In order to recapture certain local traditions, Picasso asked Busquets to bring the film he shot on Catalonia's street festivals and show it to him at La Californie.

In 1962, the first Catalan book on Picasso appeared: *Vides de Picasso* by Josep Palau. The same year, the Vallés floods having caused terrible damage, the painter immediately contributed a painting to be sold for the benefit of the victims; unfortunately, the minimum price he himself had set, 250,000 francs (about 3,200,000 pesetas, or $50,000), was not bid, and since the City was not willing to purchase the work, Pablo took it back and himself sent a financial contribution to the fund for the victims.

The virtually annual exhibitions organized by the Sala Gaspar since 1956 had contributed much to making him generally known. Each opening was an event, and the works shown were bought up at top prices.

As usual, Picasso asked to have many photographs of the decorations of the College of Architects sent to him. Catalan friends coming to La Californie kept him abreast of public reactions; Barcelona, as ever, was dear to his heart. Thousands daily saw his monumental graffiti. While not the best Picasso, their choreographic shorthand suggested the very earliest origins of Iberian art.

Looking at photographs of his pictures shown here and there around the world, he was heard to muse, "If only a machine could record what I think while I'm painting!"

Four hundred thousand attended the exhibit that Penrose set up at the Tate in the summer of 1960, more than twice the Paris attendance five years before. But Pablo merely shrugged: "To me, exhibitions don't make any sense." What did, then? "Well, you see, I just have to get it out of me," he said one day to friends, in explaining that because of having had to go from Vauvenargues to Cannes that morning, he had not done any work since the day before: he was more obsessed than ever by his work, fuming when neglecting it, eager to get back to it.

In a faded blue sailor shirt, or bare-chested (for he was very proud of his muscular build), in one of the wildly checked pairs of trousers that Sapone made him, he would receive guests much more rapidly than in the past, scarcely listening to them, impatient to be done. Except, of course, when it was a question of work, discussing pulling his etchings with the Crommelinck brothers, lithographs with Mourlot, book problems with Charles Feld, the head of Éditions du Cercle d'Art, or Gustavo Gili, his Barcelona publisher, or the proofs of the monumental Zervos catalog that Dora Vallier brought him.

Picasso was literally enthralled by that undertaking; the correction of the proofs, which he did very carefully, elicited many comments, recollections, and when sometimes he discovered forgotten works, he would cry out with delight, explaining, placing them in context, and doing little sketches in the margins to make his points. When, later, he worked with Pierre Daix on the catalog of his Blue and Rose periods, he discovered the portrait of "la Madeleine," his Bateau-Lavoir mistress before Fernande. He also showed him a portrait of Casagemas at his death, done in 1901, never shown and unknown; Jacqueline had been told to photograph it.

While Paris ignored him, London showed sixteen first-rate Blue Period paintings, magnificent Cubist and "classicist" works, expressionistic still lifes and portraits of women from the Twenties and Thirties, the studies for *Guernica,* the *Parade* curtain (lent by Jean Cassou, who had bought it for the Musée d'Art

moderne from an Italian marquis), the classical Olgas, the undulating rounded
Marie-Thérèses, screaming, sobbing Dora Maars, pacified Françoises and majestic
Jacquelines, and *Las Meninas:* sixty-two years of challenges, confidences, angers,
spirit and flesh, invention and reflection. Penrose had accentuated the surrealistic
side of Picasso's oeuvre, avoiding the "committed" things, except for *The Charnel
House:* the result was a serene, "humanistic" aspect of the painter, as against the
Paris 1955 show, which had stressed his expressionistic character. .

He had seen the show on television, not his own set yet, but at friends'. He
had himself selected the recent things to be included in it. But he was wont to
say, "My old pictures don't interest me any more. I'm much more curious
about the ones I haven't painted yet." And, often, "That's what ought to be
painted . . . What needs painting is . . ." But how? "To be able to paint
everything *as it is,* without leaving anything out. Impossible, isn't it?"

When the Louise Leiris showed his Déjeuners, friends phoned to tell him
how well the new series was being received. He answered, "I'm still at it. I can't
stop." He was still doing more Déjeuners, fast, offhandedly, as he graphically
showed with a twist of the wrist.

Yet, what despair and what joy in his oft-repeated "I can't do anything other
than what I *am* doing."

The years 1960–1961 also were marked by a further decline in his rating with
young avant-gardists: now only the outdated, outdistanced idol of a vanished
world, he was no longer a creative force but a subject for gossip columnists,
pictured as clown rather than painter. His show at the Louise Leiris seemed
more a ritual than an event.

The rediscovery of Marcel Duchamp and his message, that is, the expressive values of an art of behavior, struck a rude blow against Picasso. From
American Neo-Dadaists to French "new realists," the reversal of values quickly
took effect. To these new generations the Great Disturber's "ready-mades," so
long ignored, became totems of a new religion of the object which, tied in with
the revelation of technological civilization and the lore of cities, seriously jolted
Picassian concern with the joy of painting. The virtuoso of *doing* was supplanted
by the moralist of *knowing,* in this youthful view.

This development increased the loneliness that Picasso had imposed on himself, with the unexpected result of turning him, so long an iconoclast and
destroyer, into the defender of painting, of the easel picture, against the provoking new iconoclasts. Picasso the man, dropping his terrorist's mask, became
a kind of preserver of tradition, a benevolent grandfather of the kind Penrose
had presented at the Tate. Had he not prefaced the show by saying Picasso's
oeuvre was born of understanding and love of humanity, aiming at emotional
intensification and spiritual uplift?

This sensitive, humanistic interpretation of Picassoism was to be the final in-
carnation of the Minotaur, no longer frightening to anyone, but most thoughtful
of his subject. He wanted to be admired, liked, respected, for himself alone.

In September 1960, Serge Lifar came to see Pablo. They had met in the Diaghilev period, Lifar in his heyday having been the star dancer of the Ballets

Russes. He had a picture Pablo had done of him and his partner Khoer at Monte Carlo in 1925, and it was Picasso, with Coco Chanel, who had first noted Lifar's talent at the time of *Le Train bleu* and urged Diaghilev to take him on. Now he wanted an illustration for an album of his ballets about to be published, and Pablo dashed off a color-crayon drawing of Icarus flying up toward the sun (a reference to a 1935 ballet of Lifar's) and a portrait.

Two years later, back as ballet master of the Paris Opéra, in August 1962, Lifar asked Picasso to do a drop curtain for his *Afternoon of a Faun,* and Pablo sketched a horned faun chasing a frightened nymph. Georges Auric, director of the Opéra (who composed the score for *Le Mystère Picasso*), however, turned it down—unsuitable for a respectable official theater. But it was made up and used in 1965 for a ballet performance in Toulouse that opened a "Picasso and the Theater" exhibit.

On the other hand, Picasso's setting for Lifar's *Icarus,* a gouache dated August 28, 1962, was accepted without demur; the backdrop depicted a pink Icarus with green wings overcome by a bright yellow sun, as in the UNESCO painting, falling into the sea to the horror of arm-waving spectators. Pablo also agreed to let Lifar use his 1960 Icarus soaring as drop curtain for the ballet.

These concluded Picasso's contributions to theater.

One day Picasso had asked Sabartés what he intended to do with his collection of Picassos and books. Jaime said he had been thinking of a Picasso Museum at Málaga. Pablo replied that, though born there, he felt closer to Barcelona. How about a Picasso Museum there? And Sabartés knew that even so offhand a remark amounted to a command. He started laying the groundwork.

To his surprise, Sabartés met little opposition from local officials, though on a higher level, in Madrid, there was more antagonism. Civil War wounds and grudges remained, and all the political and aesthetic accusations against Don Pablo cropped up in Jaime's interviews with high government officials. It took all the skill and wisdom of Pablo's Catalan friends, Juan Ainaud de Lasarte, director of the Barcelona Museums, the mayor, and several others with influence, to bring it off. Finally, General Franco himself had to give approval, and did— thus effecting a small political "coup" he thought helped his régime.

Sabartés had assured the Barcelona municipality that Picasso would endow the museum with a significant contribution of work. Since 1953 the city had owned the superb Berenguer de Aguilar mansion, on Calle de Montcada, one of a group of remarkable fourteenth- and fifteenth-century upper-bourgeois residences. Sabartés selected it for the museum, and Alcalde José de Porcioles agreed, as did Picasso, who was sent many photographs of the building, but the main credit for finalizing everything belonged to Juan de Lasarte. He commuted back and forth to Cannes to keep Picasso abreast of all the developments.

The collection of Picassos in Barcelona's Museum of Modern Art was impressive, as was the gift Sabartés made, and Pablo's Catalan friends promised to help. The painter himself kept saying he would "do something." His country now had come to him, the city of his youth and his painting debut calling home the prodigal. When he got the mayor's official telegram confirming the existence of the museum, he was deeply moved, but, turning to Jacqueline, sarcastically quipped, "Do you think I'm going to answer?" He had ignored it when, a few months earlier, also at Sabartés' initiative, Málaga had put a plaque on the house where he was born.

But Barcelona was another matter: as a first step, he asked that everything the Vilatos had of his, in their Paseo de Gracia apartment, paintings and drawings, be photographed and shown him. His huge and virtually invalided sister Lola, still lively and spirited, however, had for years guarded a treasure the true value of which she never imagined. She seemed to be living outside of time with a highly personal, somewhat disconcerting view of things. After her death, there was to be little change; only when Picasso actually made his gift in 1970 were the canvases taken down and cleaned, the endless folders of drawings, water-colors, gouaches, and other media inventoried, and the school notebooks, albums, and sketchpads sorted.

Fifteen canvases that had never been exhibited and another fifteen never be-fore shown in France were his gift to Marseilles in the summer of 1959: all periods were represented, although the selection was deliberately limited to fifty-eight works, and it was a clear, balanced, measured overview, the first ever as-sembled in France for knowledge rather than shock.

This collection, presented by Douglas Cooper, showed the "classicism" of Picasso, even in his most "daring" works—time having dimmed their scandalous-ness. Pablo appeared in it closer to the history of art than to living painting, more significant to historians than current critics, to say nothing of young paint-ers, who in return meant little to him. Did that surprise or disappoint him?

"No," he once told Dora Vallier, "there is nothing extraordinary in that. Young and old painters are bashful with each other. When I was young, I very much wanted to meet Renoir, but I never dared go to call on him. Besides, he didn't enjoy seeing young painters . . .

"Anyway, a show of mine is of no interest. People know what to expect."

Who first revived the idea of an Apollinaire monument? The City of Paris was not about to agree to the abstract iron construction Picasso had once elab-orated; the painter's worldwide reputation cut little ice with a notoriously artisti-cally retrogressive and ferociously anti-Communist City Council. True, neither the poet's widow nor certain of his friends wanted Pablo's monument, but he had offered it gratis to the city, and that was something. There was another monument planned, done by Zadkine in 1937, which had nearly been erected.

The City Councilman for the St.-Germain-des-Prés district, Jean Marin, got Apollinaire's name given to a street—or rather part of the street known as Rue de l'Abbaye—at the foot of the church hard by the lodging, still maintained unchanged, in which Guillaume had died. After which, he undertook to make his fellow councillors agree to using a Picasso work. The one decided on was a *Head of Dora Maar* (1941). Despite some objections, it was voted to set this tribute to the poet up in the small Square de la Charité, at the corner of Rue St.-Guillaume and Boulevard St.-Germain. Later, however, the garden of St.-Germain-des-Prés, outside the church, was found more appropriate.

Monument to Guillaume Apollinaire by Picasso,
Square Saint-Germain-des-Prés, Paris

The statue was unveiled on June 5, 1959. Picasso, obviously, did not attend, but mutual friends such as Jean Cocteau, André Salmon, André Billy, "Baron" Mollet, as well as numerous more recent admirers, surrounded the "pretty red-head" (the poet's widow) who unveiled the bust. "Honoring Apollinaire is also to honor Picasso, whom he compared to a pearl," said Cocteau in his talk. And thus, thanks to the poet of hapless love, the one of Picasso's mistresses whom he made suffer the most and most maltreated in his paintings has her bust displayed in Paris.

One month later to the day, July 5, Picasso and Jacqueline were at a bullfight in Arles, where Dominguín was appearing, and with them was Jean Cocteau, whose seventieth birthday it was. The torero, after the fight, solemnly presented the bull's ears and tail to him as a birthday tribute. At dinner that evening, Cocteau suggested that Picasso and Jacqueline, along with Dominguín and his wife, Lucia Bosè, appear briefly in the film he was due to shoot in September, *The Testament of Orpheus.* He was going to act in it himself and had already asked Mme. Weisweiler, Jean Marais, Maria Casarés, Yul Brynner, Maître Henry Torrès, Brigitte Bardot, Françoise Sagan, and Marlene Dietrich, among others, to join him. "You understand," he told Picasso, "I can't afford average actors."

The Picassos and the Dominguíns went along with the idea, and participated in the underground scene of the death of the poet (that is, Cocteau's own). When he saw the film, Pablo was struck by the pained look on Jacqueline's face. He found the experience wonderfully entertaining, and told Cocteau, "Your film will go its own way. Like my pictures, I start them and then they paint themselves. They have their own way. Your film won't obey you . . ."

Which is what happened. *The Testament of Orpheus,* though a commercial flop, was triumphant in its disobedience and freedom.

Picasso had become friendly with the American photographer David Douglas Duncan, who, between assignments, had come knocking at the door of La Californie in 1956. By miracle he had gotten in, and gotten to see the master, who, in his bathtub, waved welcome to him, naked. That, at least, is how he tells the story. The truth is that Duncan phoned, said he had been a friend of Robert Capa, for whom Picasso had great affection and who had died the year before in Indochina. After a bit of thought, Pablo told him to come on over. From then on, he was a fixture.

Duncan claimed to have spent more time at Picasso's than anywhere else, including his own home, in the past twenty-five years, and out of the innumerable pictures he took of Pablo, that fine tireless actor, that clown of genius in a circus with an ever-changing cast of children, wives, women, friends, animals, guests, parasites, jesters, he fashioned a book in 1958, *The Small World of Pablo Picasso.*

Picasso led him into a room filled only with canvases. Lying on the floor or leaning against the walls were paintings in heavy gilt frames wrapped in paper at the corners, indistinguishable in the gloom. Then he opened a window, and there, to Duncan's amazement, was the "Picasso collection": Cézannes, Corots, a Courbet, a Breton landscape by Gauguin, a Vuillard, Braques, Matisses, Grises,

Picasso and Mme. Weisweiler during the filming of
"Testament of Orpheus" by Jean Cocteau, 1959
(KEYSTONE)

some ten-odd Renoirs ("Corot discovered morning and Renoir young girls," Pablo said), a Van Dongen, a small Ingres, the Modigliani, Douanier Rousseau, and two famous Le Nains. Impossible to estimate their number, since the large paintings hid other smaller ones, but surely upward of a hundred.

Jacqueline came in with some friends. Some of the best things were set out on display. Pablo told stories as Duncan snapped pictures. Picasso grinned, "They're worth millions." Then, doing a little cleaning up, he came across some gouaches by Max Jacob, superb Laurens collages, some Derains, a Max Ernst, a Balthus, some Dalis. There were also sculptures, stored in another room, Laurenses again, Manolos, Gonzalezes, Lipchitzes, and all those Fenosas Pablo had bought up. To say nothing of the collection of African masks and artifacts, others of which were stored in Switzerland.

In Paris, dealers and brokers had often tried to sell him pictures. One time, it was a Cézanne, but before the man even finished unwrapping it he pointed out it had been retouched, and the man beat a hasty retreat. Another, a few months later, was brought in by a young man who said it had been found in Cézanne's studio and his family always deemed it authentic, from the *Card Players* period. It was fake, and Pablo turned it down, saying, "Cézanne was the only master I ever had; you can imagine how well I know his work." Then, as if his competence had been challenged, he added, "After all, I *am* the curator of the Prado."

Duncan was in for more surprises, though. A few months after that visit to Vauvenargues, Pablo suggested he visit one of the ground-floor rooms at La Californie before lunch. Again he took him into a dark room, and once the light was turned on, the same sight was before him, an amazing number of paintings of all shapes and sizes, standing against the wall according to size: "Picasso's Picassos."

No one was ever allowed in that room. Seemingly endlessly, Pablo, Jacqueline, and Duncan turned canvases around, carrying many into the nearby parlor, which, large as it was, was soon overrun with them. Duncan thought there must be a couple of hundred, but Picasso specified there were three hundred of them. Years later, still dazzled by what he had seen, Duncan wrote:

> . . . I remember that I said almost nothing. But Picasso nodded and welcomed each revealed painting as if he were witnessing the return home of a long wandering child . . .
>
> For three hours, in that sunstreaked room, I saw Pablo Picasso's life laid bare . . .

The canvases had come from Rue La Boétie, after Sabartés moved them out of there, and from Rue des Grands-Augustins; others had for years been in storage or in bank vaults. Pell-mell, there were paintings from his youth in Barcelona, the Blue and Rose Periods, Cubism, the neoclassical era, portraits of Olga, Marie-Thérèse, charming Maya, tragic, tearful faces of Dora Maar. Some were over half a century old, like that amazing *Flight into Egypt,* painted when he was fourteen, Barcelona street scenes, the dramatically "black Fauve" portrait of his father, over which Pablo wondered out loud how he had ever been able to paint it.

Picasso peeks at Picasso   Mougins
(RENÉ BURRI—MAGNUM)

Each picture was the subject for a remark by Picasso, an anecdote, a recollection. His whole life was passing before the old man's eyes. Then, he got up from his armchair, and even though there were still many works they had not seen, he had all the others put back in their places, and closed the blinds, the window, and the door himself. After which, the three of them went to lunch. Duncan asked the master whether he might photograph all those canvases they had just been looking at.

He recalls that at that very moment Picasso was whistling a Mexican military march, and, without turning around, for he was giving his arm to Jacqueline, or missing a single note of the chorus, he raised his right index finger and answered, "Fine, but only in color."

During the meal, he said there was another room at La Californie with as many pictures as they had just seen, and two others still at Vauvenargues. Duncan asked how many pictures there were in all, but all Pablo would say was, "All you want." (Later, he was to specify to him, eight thousand.)

Over a period of a year, the photographer made about five hundred negatives, covering all the older works at La Californie, most of which had never been exhibited and were completely unknown. Several of them surprised the Picasso experts when they were printed in *Picasso's Picassos:* his production in certain periods had to be reevaluated in the light of these discoveries.

Don Pablo sometimes came unexpectedly on the scene when Duncan was at work, and would jokingly say, "I'll only watch for a moment—I must keep ahead of you!" But when the American asked to photograph very recent paintings, for instance the portraits of Jacqueline, Pablo resolutely refused permission. "No!" he said. "They're not finished! You might take something away!"

Duncan was reminded by this reaction of those of Arabian or South American jungle tribes; they, like Picasso, had the same fear of and opposition to the photographic lens which, capturing an individual's double, might, they believed, steal away his soul. Pablo protected his paintings until they left him; after that, they would be on their own.

An old friend, Marcel Duhamel, editor of the famous French *"Série noire"* of detective/suspense novels, had a little house in Antibes, where one day the Pignons, Jacqueline, and Pablo dropped in on him and his wife. Going through the house, the windows of which faced the sea, Picasso stopped to lean over a second-story bedroom balcony, and taking in the view, said, "After all, for a painter, living here would be ideal: one blue line and the painting would be done."

It was obviously a joke, but more than that it expressed the artist's direct identification with things. The landscape—or rather seascape—he was seeing, and which the others were looking at as well, was indeed nothing but one blue line, separating sky and water. That's what painting was: the essential. But who would have settled for that, except Picasso?

THE PAINTER
AND HIS MODEL
(1961–1965)

A FTER A DRIVE TO VALLAURIS ON MARCH 2, 1961, MR. AND MRS. Ruiz Blasco returned in high spirits to La Californie and poured champagne for their domestic staff, the chauffeur Janot, and the amazed Piedmontese gardener and his wife. Picasso had just married Jacqueline and given her his name. The ceremony had been of the simplest, performed in his office by the mayor of the little town, M. Derigon, a friend of long standing. Maître Antebi, Pablo's *notaire* in Cannes, and his wife, had been the witnesses. Even Paulo had not been informed; he read about it in the press.

La Californie was threatened more and more by the building-up of the surrounding area, high-rises cropping up among the palm and orange trees. Vauvenargues was out of the question, since it depressed Jacqueline so: it would serve only as a stopover to and from bullfights, or a place to display its stock of art work. While retaining La Californie, so cluttered with statuary and pictures that moving out would hardly have been feasible, Picasso now had bought a magnificent estate on a hilltop, near Mougins, three kilometers northwest of Vallauris: Notre-Dame-de-Vie (Our Lady of Life).

He knew Mougins well, having spent the summers of 1936, 1937, and 1938 there with Dora Maar and the Éluards, at the Hôtel Vaste Horizon, a name that might have applied as well to his new home, which he had first visited some years earlier, when the British beer Guinnesses occupied it. An olive grove in front and a screen of cypresses behind enclosed Notre-Dame-de-Vie as it overlooked a magnificent panorama of villas and mansions surrounded by greenery dominated by the towers of the château of Les Broussailles. The tiled roofs of the village dwellings of Mougins were layers of brick, ocher, and faded old rose, the Bay of Cannes in the distance, the mountains of the Estérel beyond. A seventeenth-century chapel, lending its name to the property, perched behind an elevation near the old disused cemetery.

The rooms of the house, large and bright, like those in all his other homes, though here even more, would become so many studios. On the main floor a large arched hall, level with the terrace where meals were taken in fair weather, was to hold several sculptures sent up from Cannes and quickly joined by painted metal cutouts and large ceramic pieces. Despite the size of the house, there would soon not be enough room, and Picasso would have a wing added to the rear. The engraving shop for the Crommelinck brothers was set up in the village of Mougins.

Below Notre-Dame-de-Vie stood the *Man with the Sheep,* Picasso's identification.

Such was the sumptuous, disorderly, and preserved kingdom in which he was to spend his final years, the Jacqueline years, working there as he never had anywhere else. To his very last day. The discreet, industrious queen bee who was his second legal wife would firmly rule the man, the painter, and his world. As the years went by, she would gradually reduce the number of intimates until they formed the fawning, intriguing clique that smothered Pablo in adulation but never fooled him. Don Pablo no longer needed the outside world: he had Jacqueline. And TV.

Under the tender watchful eye of this woman, passionately admired by so many and equally violently detested by others, who had succeeded in establishing herself with him, despite public humiliations and private offenses, who had both the honor and responsibility of being wife to the least human of men and most benevolent of monsters, Don Pablo lived the twelve years that separated him from the death he constantly thought about. Twelve years of mad, ceaseless labors in which he, *capable of anything,* joyously and desperately plunged into painting, improvising the most unbelievable of metamorphoses. Continual creation determines the creative individual's freedom: if he did too much, was it not because too much, to him, was much better than too little? His mistake was perhaps to show *everything,* but was that not necessary when he was saying everything?

"The key to everything that happens is here," he said one day, pointing to his forehead. "Before it comes out of the pen or brush, the key is to have it at one's fingertips, entirely, without losing any of it." And he rubbed his fingertips against his thumb as if assuring himself of their mysterious power.

His continual creation kept him from thinking, obviated analysis. Since painting made him do what it wished, that would be pointless. One had to hear him wax ecstatic over his delight in externalizing life. "Wild, what painting makes me do, isn't it?" he would say as he went back and forth before his canvases in the large studio at Notre-Dame-de-Vie. He moved them around, commented on them, content with his prestigious privileges and his chorus of ecstatic courtiers, joining in the specifically Picassian liturgy. Transcribed by the hagiographer on duty, their adulation often sounded ridiculous (with a ridiculousness Picasso delighted in and at times "put on"). Yet, in reality, it was not without a kind of pathetic grandeur. Could he still ask himself or his intimates what in the past he so often had whispered?—"Will it hold up?"

"I haven't said what I had to say—and there's not much time left," might be the slogan of those last twelve years. His need to *say,* never fulfilled, was now an obsession, as he turned more and more away from the world and others, even from the problems that had so concerned him in the past. His main strength lay in his power of concentration, his forgetfulness of all else, when before a picture he was working on. He surely felt that, while at the picture, he could not die; it would protect him from the ineluctable. Or if he had to die one day, let it be while in the act.

He exposed himself one last time to the crowds—on October 28–29, 1961, to celebrate his eightieth birthday. It was a pitiful spectacle, grotesque and naïve. Preceded by two motorcycle cops, in a white Cadillac he toured through the cheering Vallauris mob, en route to receive the tributes of the Party, the potters' union, the people's democracies, local folk groups, Luis-Miguel Domínguín, Jacques Duclos, the pianist Sviatoslav Richter, novelist Hervé Bazin, the Spanish film director Juan Bardem, M. Henry Seyrig, director of the Museums of France, representing Minister André Malraux, and the ambassador of Ghana.

Before some thirty paintings of various periods shown at the Nerolium (which usually housed the jasmine, orange, and orange-blossom crops), in his black leather outfit ("Not really leather," Sapone says, "I cut it from a piece of unknown material I found in the Abruzzi"), he thoughtfully commented, "Those things have gone far away from me but I find them looking fine." When someone said both the man and his work retained their youthfulness, he quipped, "Maybe we ape each other."

This was the last show of his work he was to see, the last time his living gaze confronted those whose reflections over nearly seventy years of uninterrupted creation he had captured in his paintings. Just another moment and Jacqueline would take him by the arm, with the peremptory tenderness of powerful women, to guide him to the haven he was never again to leave except on rare occasions such as to La Californie, trips to the dentist in Cannes, brief sessions at the Madoura pottery, or a few drives in the car, with Jacqueline or the chauffeur at the wheel. Sometimes he went to the movies in Cannes, but more and more he preferred TV, on which, with Arias and a few friends, he was fascinated by the wrestling matches.

He liked to go to Nice Airport to meet people, or see them off, and one day he said to one of them, "People ask me what contribution I've made. Well, without Cubism, this airport would not have looked like this!"

Few outside events were to disturb the industrious existence of the alert old man: in 1962, he received the Lenin Peace Prize; in 1963, the deaths of Braque and Cocteau upset him, but he refused to make any statements or to open his door to anyone. He worked actively at helping the City of Barcelona get his museum ready. He paid more attention to the Cuban missile crisis in October 1962 (terribly alarmed by it) than to the many shows of his work around the world or the numerous books devoted to him. But, on the other hand, he carefully followed the work of reproducing his drawing pads, passionately interested especially in the superb *Picasso aujourd'hui* (Picasso Today), published by the

Éditions du Cercle d'Art in 1969; Charles Feld included in it four hundred drawings done between March 27, 1966, and March 15, 1968.

Picasso was also meeting with some extreme opposition, though it was not art critics or painters who waxed most antagonistic. The novelist Jean Dutourd was to characterize Picasso as a "sort of absolutely wild, delirious senile imbecile, drawing things with a stuttering line and extremely vulgar colors . . ." This kind of attack, of course having nothing to do with criticism, generally emanated from right-wing columnists or polemicists who sprinkled in their anti-Communist or anti-Semitic vitriol, shamelessly reviving the kind of accusations that had flourished in the press during the occupation.

"One has to dare to be vulgar," he said, and he was. He did "dirty," muddy painting, with smashed-down flats, rhythms corrupted by juices running out, parts in grisaille deliberately sloppy, daubed, with splashings, oozings—he had no control, was not erecting anything, was just running over.

We need not tarry long over the final works in which bullfights were increasingly present: he showed the various aspects of the corrida in the *tachiste* spirit of the washes of the 1957–1959 period, against a ground of pink faience. But henceforth heads were his favorites; there again, he was content to repeat on the plaques the form and color variations of painting, lithography, drawing, or even linoleum cutting. One series of seven plaques in 1964 was stamped in a plaster matrix supermolded over an original linoleum engraving intended for transfer to paper.

Later, he was to do round plates in white faience, and rectangular or square plaques that presented baroque color variations on the human face such as he was doing in paintings at the same time. In the Paris retrospective of 1966, the ceramics would stand out as his least interesting work.

The first of the series of *Woman with Dog* (Jacqueline and Kabul) are dated November 13, 21, and November 23–December 14. One, started December 13 and finished the next January 10, reflects his gifts for *mise-en-scène*. The theme was to recur for several months. It is contemporaneous with a number of heads, including several of warriors out of "The Rape of the Sabines," alongside several of the studies for that work.

With Picasso, it is hard to say where figures, compositions, ideas, or themes come from. From the outside, of course, but also from his daily life. *Mougins Landscape,* an admirable symphony of cold blues and whites, painted December 26, 1962, grew out of a drive in the snow of the nearby hills a little earlier, with Jacqueline. They were almost lost, as they skidded on the frozen road, and the tale of it grew to an epic in the telling.

At the same time he did a dutifully realistic portrait of Jacqueline's daughter, Cathy, with her willful little sharp-profiled head, teasingly dedicated "to my foster-daughter."

This relaxation did not last long. On January 9, 1963, Pablo began a vertical composition that he finished on February 7. Trampling a woman and her child, intermingled and shrieking with pain and terror, two fighters, one mounted, the other on foot, the latter taller than his adversary and horse combined, clash with ferocious determination. Titled *Rape of the Sabine Women, after David,* it is now in the Boston Museum of Fine Arts.

Despite the reference to David and the "antique" setting, the subject and picture were but a pretext for the condemnation of war, on a universal plane. David, after Poussin, had also rearranged history, and now Picasso reshuffled its data, changed its meaning, and varied the movements of the narrative. He confronted past and present in the same accusation, a denunciation into which he threw all of his octogenarian heart and soul. "No one will be able to say this didn't take doing," he said.

Massacres and warriors took up the winter months; the painter did all kinds of faces and images, but always ended up *siding with* the weak, the innocent, the vanquished, the wounded; the center of the *Rape of the Sabine Women— Massacre of the Innocents* of December 4, 5, and 8 is a tragically foreshortened figure in grisaille of a pitifully smiling victim being trampled under the hooves of the horses. For he cannot but record the strength, exalt the violence of the warriors. As in the cruel encounters in the arena, he is for matador and bull at the same time.

These heads of warriors, simultaneous with or following the Sabine rapes, grew so in number because of the theme that was announced for the 1963 Salon de Mai, the only group show which Picasso regularly entered. Labeled "Around the *Entry of the Crusaders into Constantinople,*" it was a tribute to Delacroix, the centennial of whose death was being celebrated that year.

Some artsts rebelled at the *pompier* or corny concept of returning to an assigned subject. Picasso, on the other hand, told his friend Pignon, "I've never been afraid of subjects . . . It's rubbish to think of cutting out the subject . . . Even if the canvas is green, well, the subject is green."

Later, he told Hélène Parmelin, "A warrior, naturally, if he has no helmet and no horse and no head, he's much easier to do. But for my part, at that point he simply doesn't interest me. At that point he might just as well be a chap getting on a train. What interests me in a warrior is the warrior." And he did so many warriors he jokingly said his studio was overflowing with them: "It's never been like this. It's the most difficult thing I've ever done."

Leading him to comment, "I don't know how much good that is, it's possibly appalling. But in any case I'm doing it, I'm doing thousands . . ."

All the varied helmeted heads he did that winter were to lead to a return to another favorite theme, now coming back in new dimensions: The Painter and His Model, beginning with a drawing of February 10, 1963. On March 13–14, he was doing his own version of the Dresden Museum's *Rembrandt and Saskia,* the joyously chaotic composition embodying all the elements of that superb work, the painter's exuberant joy, plumed hat on his head and sword at his side, as he raises the flask of wine in tribute to the woman on his lap. Pablo was to experiment in this Painter and Model series, sometimes showing the painter set apart.

The theme of Watcher and Watched gave him pause throughout that whole

year and beyond. Once it got hold of him, he "broke loose," says Hélène Parmelin, ". . . he painted like a madman." Probably with such frenzy as never
before, she adds.

A few years before, he had told Françoise Gilot, as she relates it in her book:

> "I paint the way some people write their autobiography. The paintings, finished or
> not, are the pages of my journal, and as such they are valid. The future will choose
> the pages it prefers. It's not up to me to make the choice. . . . I'm like a river that
> rolls on, dragging with it the trees that grow too close to its banks or dead calves one
> might have thrown into it or any kind of microbes that develop in it."

Picasso became the Watcher of his Painter and His Model as he had been the
Talker in the Déjeuners. Right off, he went to the heart of the matter, and from
the earliest paintings of March 1963 the confrontation between painter and
young woman took on its expressive significance: it was less a question of showing the artist painting than of dramatizing the process itself as Clouzot had done
in his film. Each picture is a link in the chain, one moment of the work in
progress; it already suggests the one to come which in turn will have something
of the preceding one, and so on.

Yet, painting continues to surprise and delight him. For all that he has accomplished, and all the position he holds, it remains his one way to get still further
ahead. And for the first time in a long time, his painting is showing some
sentiment. The Watcher-Watchee confrontation is almost without movement.
Nothing happens between them—except painting. This is the first—and last—
"abstract" set by the man who always put down and ridiculed abstractionism.
Now we know why. From April–May on, painter and model fill the whole frame.
But are they really its subject? Are their reality, their personality not completely
submerged by the interpretation Picasso gives of them? Having always wanted
to bring the viewer into his creative experience, his discoveries, his exaltation, to
be understood by one and all, he now is concerned exclusively, not with himself,
but with his dialectics. Perhaps because, having been alone in life, alone in the
century, he is alone too in painting, in his idea of painting.

Meanwhile, worriedly, he was following the almost daily reports of the illness
that was soon to carry away his friend Braque. The one who, with him, and even
against him, was so fully a painter. Which pained him as he was pained by Gris,
Léger, Bonnard, and Matisse.

Would the museum the City of Barcelona planned for its most famous adopted
son be named after him? Madrid was hesitant, for some felt this was a provocation. But work was going ahead and the opening was scheduled for 1963. As a
result of a stroke, Sabartés could no longer handle details of the "Picasso Museum." But his old friend did not let him down: he could no longer walk up
to his apartment in Rue de la Convention, so Pablo bought him one in an elevator
building at 124 Boulevard Auguste-Blanqui (in the Faubourg-St.-Jacques neighborhood, where he had lived a few years before), and he moved in in February
1962, with his young Catalan housekeeper-companion, Pilar Solano.

At Mougins, Picasso had before his eyes the models of the museum, and on

Juan Ainaud de Lasarte's frequent visits they discussed how the rooms should be laid out, lighted, where panels and display cases should be, the hanging of the works, of all of which he had photographs. As soon as Sabartés was able to get about sufficiently again, he went to Barcelona, where he was overjoyed to find that he had been named Honorary Curator of the Calle de Montcada museum.

"Now we're both in the same business," Pablo told him, referring to his own title of Curator of the Prado. "Only you can go to your museum, and I can't."

Now sick and impoverished, Fernande Olivier lived alone in a small apartment in Neuilly, sad among her misfortunes and memories, which always included the little Spaniard with the fiery glance she had met going for water in the Bateau-Lavoir, loved unwisely, and poorly understood. They had never seen each other again since their split, and the only souvenir she had of him was a little heart-shaped mirror.

Alice Derain, the painter's widow, had been helping Fernande financially, and in 1958 she asked Pablo for ten thousand francs ($2,000), which he gave for the medical care Fernande needed. But all the poor woman had to live on was an old-age pension, and a short time later Alice Derain asked the Braques to try to get Picasso to send her a regular amount. It would mean so little to him.

On a trip to Cannes, with Claude and Denise Laurens, the Braques took it up with him. Picasso agreed, sat down, put on his glasses, and took out his checkbook. Then, suddenly turning to Braque, before speechless young Laurens, he demanded, "Why shouldn't you be the one to help her?" And closed the checkbook, pocketed it, got up, and went out.

Only several years later, at Jacqueline's insistence, did he finally agree to send a stipend to Fernande. It was just one more check to be written in his name at the end of each month—along with the ones to Paulo, the domestic help, people he owed obligations to, and the requests he honored—by his banker, Max Pellequer. For it had turned out some people sold to autograph collectors the ones he himself signed at more than their face value!

Pablo's miserliness was well known. When Brassaï apologized for giving some examples of it in his book, Picasso told him that was all right: better to be known as a piker than as an easy mark. He was endlessly being dunned, yet, without being asked, he was capable on impulse of performing the *beau geste*—usually masking it behind total rudeness.

Valentine Hugo fondly remembered the afternoon in July 1935 when she was sobbing in the *Cahiers d'Art* shop, telling her friends the Zervoses that she was about to be evicted and all her possessions seized. Pablo happened in, overheard her, and the conversation went on to something else. But as he was leaving, he casually said to her, "Drop in at Rue La Boétie tomorrow. I want to show you something." She went, and, as she told it:

"It was the worst time of his life. Olga had left him and taken Paulo. His apartment was unbelievably messy and dirty. No one had cleaned up for months. No sooner did I get in than he said, 'I've been very much impressed with what you've been painting recently. I'd like to buy some of it. How much?'

"He took out his checkbook and looked around for a place to write on. Not finding any, he pushed away everything that was on that corner of the mantel, and there on the marble top he wrote a check, without even waiting for me to name a sum, and signed it. I asked him when he would come by my place to pick out what he wanted, and he said he'd phone in a few days. He never came."

Valentine Hugo died in 1967.

While such gestures might have become rare, he still gave money or pictures to good causes his friends were interested in, especially children's camps. Gone were the days when, as Françoise Gilot said in her book, he used to drag with him a huge sum in "an old red-leather trunk from Hermès . . . so that he'd always 'have the price of a package of cigarettes,' as he put it." She relates that he often counted the money in it, and since he was always making mistakes, it never came out the same and he went into a tizzy. Now he no longer ever had any money about him; he did not need anything for cigarettes, as he had quit smoking. And Jacqueline handled all petty details for him.

It was March 10, 1963, when the Barcelona museum opened its doors—or rather left them ajar, for there was no official opening. The governor of Catalonia and the mayor and all other notables prudently ignored it. Only three hundred invitations had been (discreetly) sent out—and even Sabartés was absent, in protest against what was going on and the fact that there was no sign saying "Picasso Museum" on the building. Public gossip had it that the Minister of the Interior had refused to authorize use of Pablo's name, although the Information and Tourism ministers were for it.

There was no greeting from the artist, whom the newspaper La Vanguardia referred to as "our illustrious countryman." He had always known how unlikely Sabartés' undertaking was and had been informed of every obstacle along its way. He would probably have been sorry if it had been accepted without demur. For he liked the idea of being a sort of "official" opposition; if he took to the idea of the museum and agreed to make a donation of works to it, including the Las Meninas series, a nonpareil gift, it was because he was proud of being honored while remaining faithful to himself. Barcelona and Picasso could defy the Franco régime no more flagrantly than with this museum.

The Crommelinck brothers, sons of the Belgian playwright Fernand Crommelynck, had set up an engraving workshop in Paris. They were wonderful technicians, and Pablo had fullest confidence in them, having met Aldo as an apprentice at Lacourière's in 1947–1948. In the interval, he and his brother Piero had frequently come to Cannes, whenever Picasso called on them for a new rash of graphics.

Suddenly, in October 1963, he decided to go back to engraving: call to arms. It started on the fourteenth by an etching with drypoint and burin, The Embrace, reviving a theme of his youth. The next day, he did it in etching alone, and on the twentieth in etching and burin, varying the style, which became more linear with Neo-Cubist structuring of masses; on the twenty-third, he did two aquatints.

On October 31, Picasso started on another favorite theme, The Painter at Work, a first etching in which the artist is portraying a fat bearded man on the canvas, while his female model looks on, all of them nude. In the Sculptor's

"The Painter and His Model" March 29–April 1, 1963, private collection

(GIRAUDON)

Studio, a complementary theme, was a second etching done the same day: nude collectors gaze in surprise and curiosity at an abstract sculpture set on its stand, as the equally nude model, seated seductively in an armchair, seems to be appealing to them: "Don't I look much better than that horror?"

One of the most striking paintings of the Painter and His Model series is dated June 10–12, 1963. The Watcher and the woman fill the canvas, the easel, seen from the side, as a sort of ideal frontier separating the two elongated characters. He, bearded, his body reduced to deliberately sketchy proportions, is painting, but his wide-open eye is fixed on the spectator rather than the model, seen from the front in one of the most extraordinary nudes Picasso ever did.

As this theme was being developed, the Painter himself dwindled in importance: what Picasso was doing was an interpretation of painting, and then suddenly its opposite. He was inventing a dialectics of diversity, multiplicity, antagonism, causing one to toy with the other, both subject and object. Could all this not be in danger of proving empty, a mistaken kind of exercise? Just a monotonous verbiage put forth by his irresistible urge *to say?*

He was soon to confess to Pignon:

> "But the worst thing of all is that [one] has never finished. There is never a moment when you can say 'I've done a good day's work and tomorrow is Sunday.' As soon as you stop you have to start again. . . . You can never write the words THE END."

That was how the old man crazy with painting, as Hokusai had said he was with drawing, justified the superabundant flow—paintings, drawings, engravings
• —of his final output. We are given fair warning: the amazing octogenarian paints constantly only because he cannot help it, his good health carrying him along like a mountain torrent.

The death of Braque, which he knew was imminent, on August 31, 1963, caused him deep suffering. A year earlier, for his eightieth birthday, he had sent him on May 13, 1962, *Braque's Breakfast,* a cup of coffee with a lump of sugar, a piece of zwieback, and a teaspoon on the saucer, all in painted ceramics. And engraved in his own hand, "For your 80th birthday. Picasso."

The funeral made him furious when he saw it on TV. The ridiculous pompousness, orchestrated by Malraux at the foot of the Louvre column facing St.-Germain-l'Auxerrois, with soldiers holding torches aloft around the hearse, the tricolor-draped coffin, crepe-enclosed drums, and the "Funeral March for a Hero" being mutedly played, all turned his stomach. As it did that of many of Braque's other friends. And no less disgusting was the warding-off of the people of Paris, kept far back behind police barriers and cordons of cops. The Minister's unbelievable speech completed Pablo's irritation. What would Braque have made of such funereal buffoonery, he who was so simple, so opposed to official honors, so foreign to verbiage? Pablo answered this Gaullish ghoulism by inviting Marcelle Braque to Notre-Dame-de-Vie. She arrived in mourning veils, almost obese, walking painfully, her beautiful blue eyes swimming in tears. And they went over their old memories, the whole past coming back.

Of all the great adventurers of the turn of the century, Pablo alone remained. "Braque dominated his powers; I just let myself go," was the way Pablo put it.

In November 1963 he took up lithography again, perhaps because Mourlot had been to see him a few months earlier with the dummy of Volume IV of his *Picasso lithographe* (Picasso Lithographer). Not only did he inspect each plate of the book with interest, but after drawing the cover he also did an unscheduled frontispiece on the theme of The Painter and His Model.

These nine heads were to be his last significant lithography. Later all he did was a few isolated items to answer special requests, such as the one for the special issue of the magazine *Derrière le miroir* (Behind the Mirror), published by Galerie Maeght as a tribute to Braque in 1964. He drew a nude, and above it in his saberlike handwriting he inscribed:

> Braque, you said to me one day, a long time ago, on meeting me as I was walking with a girl of what is known as classical beauty, whom I had found very pretty, "In love, you have still not gotten far enough from the masters." At any rate, I can still say to you today, "I love you." You see I still cannot get far enough.

Prices of Picassos were continuously going up. In New York, November 20, 1958, *Mother and Child* of the Blue Period, begun at $50,000, was bid up to more than $150,000, the most any of his works had brought to that date. A year later, a gouache of the same period, *Harlequin Family,* brought 12,000 pounds sterling in London. In May 1959, the 1905 *Beautiful Dutch Girl* topped even *Mother and Child,* going for 55,000 pounds (about $155,000), for a medium-sized work. In six months, Picasso had gone up another five thousand!

In December 1961, at the auction of the Jean Davray collections, the Nice bookseller Henri Matarasso paid 3,100 new francs (about $650) for a letter by Vauvenargues to give to his friend Pablo. After all, he felt, it *did* rightfully belong to the château's new owner. He also bid in, but for a customer, Éluard's copy of André Salmon's *Manuscrit trouvé dans un chapeau* (Manuscript Found in a Hat), illustrated with fifty-five drawings by Picasso. Pablo had inscribed it to him and put in the date of March 2, 1947.

At the Somerset Maugham sale, April 10, 1962, a "double Picasso," a cardboard on which in 1901 he had painted a *Woman Sitting in a Garden,* and five years later on the other side a *Death of Harlequin,* was acquired in London by Paul Mellon for 80,000 pounds (about $225,000). A few days later, on April 23 at Nice, a charcoal of the Barcelona period brought 35,000 new francs (something over $7,000).

Another jump came at the Lefèvre auction in Paris on November 16, 1966: *Red Head of a Woman* (gouache, 1906–1907) sold for 285,000 francs (about $57,000), and *A Demoiselle d'Avignon,* a study for the famous masterpiece, 350,000 francs (over $70,000), both going to the Paris Musée national d'Art moderne.

These were normal increases, but in December 1967 their climb was to be marked by a highly theatrical development. The Grand Council of the Canton of Basel (Switzerland) by an overwhelming majority voted for six million Swiss francs (approximately two million dollars) to be made available for the purchase of two "classical" Picassos, *Two Brothers* (1905) and *Seated Harlequin* (1923). They belonged to the collection of Peter Staechlin, whose father, Rudolf, had been a ranking collector. The collection had been turned into a foundation in 1931, with the proviso that none of it could be sold, except in case of absolute necessity.

Such a necessity arose in 1967, twenty years after the father died. A company the son controlled, Globe Air, was on the brink of bankruptcy as a result of a disastrous crash, and he desperately needed refinancing for it. An American collector offered to provide the funds plus a profit, in exchange for the two paintings, and the foundation left the decision up to him: if he accepted, Switzerland would lose two Picasso masterpieces. Franz Meyer, head of the Basel museum, did everything he could to avoid this, and Peter Staechlin was willing to take a lesser amount from the city, if it was Basel that put up the money so he could avoid bankruptcy.

The city voted six million francs, and an industrialist pledged an additional amount, but Swiss law provides for a referendum on any governmental action, if a petition of at least a thousand signatures calls for it. A service-station owner in Basel circulated such a petition and got two thousand names on it. The election was held on the first Sunday in December; on the Saturday the museum organized a street fair, raising two hundred thousand francs toward what was still needed.

The service-station man had gone overboard in his propaganda, decrying the lack of enough hospitals, old people's homes, and parking garages, when so much was being spent on two hunks of canvas. Let Basel's 180 millionaires pay for them! was his slogan.

The people took offense at him, and the tally was 32,000 for the purchase and 27,000 against. Meyer phoned Mougins to say the paintings were staying in Basel. Delighted, Don Pablo made the city a gift of four more to go with them, saying, "This is the first time in art history that the people have been allowed to speak their minds on a question of art and culture."

On October 11, 1963, he was at Vallauris with Jacqueline when he was informed of Cocteau's death; the Picassos had just lunched with friends and talked about the dying poet. For Pablo, this was the end of a friendship of more than forty years, not without its eclipses, but which Jean's boundless admiration for the painter had, even at the most difficult times, turned into a honeymoon. That "frivolous prince" needed Picasso's affection, and someone was to tell the latter that shortly before his death Cocteau had lamented, "I love him, but he doesn't like me." Pablo had said some very harsh things about Cocteau, using him at times as whipping boy, at others as buffoon; he hated the poet's mastery of language that he used for charm, and he wrote off as the incurable exhibitionism of an aging homosexual his flair for showmanship and the entourage of handsome youths whom he made into the angels of his chapels and the demons of Santo Sospir, what Picasso called that monumental "tattooing" in deplorable taste. For Jean, a very gifted sketch artist, was not much of a muralist, and Pablo made pitiless fun of that part of his work.

Cocteau doubtless masochistically delighted in Pablo's cruelty, his mocking of the paintings as he detailed their mediocrities or compromises with unsparing commentaries. He gloried in Pablo's "meanness," because it was so much more satisfactory than indifference: the barbs were part of his crown of thorns. He had always written Pablo two or three times a week, and the day after Cocteau died the last letter, scribbled two days earlier, was delivered.

Whenever they met, they fell demonstratively on each other's necks—which had led Cocteau to observe, "I love Picasso's displays of tenderness; one always wonders what they are meant to cover up."

At the end of December Pablo selected the works to be shown at the Louise Leiris starting January 15, 1964. Included were sixty-eight paintings done between December 13, 1961, and January 17, 1963: a thirteen-month period that with typical Picassian diversity covered variations of The Rape of the Sabines and The Painter and His Model, with a number of related studies of male or female heads, plus some landscapes. Female figures and still lifes, such as those of the threatening dog and cat of October 1962, completed the group.

Picasso had learned from Clouzot: the way the camera had recorded the painting of the *Beach at La Garoupe,* and the way the sequence had been assembled so as to make it integral to the overall film, gave him food for much thought. And as a result he introduced filmic "sequentialism" into his work: that is, try to see everything, get everything down so as to have a total out of which to choose the key moments, or in his case the paintings to be shown. With the rest (the outtakes, as it were), the film went on—but toward a different end.

Picassian improvisation was at its zenith: Pablo the hurried trier-out no longer had time to select; as narrator, he did not structure his language much, letting the incidents and awkwardness of the moment inform the medium. So that the painter-talker, as well as a number of listeners—that is to say, watchers— just gave up, a natural result of the speech disconcerting or boring them.

The whole collection of paintings and drawings on The Artist and His Model, or at least those seen at the Galerie Louise Leiris or in Hélène Parmelin's book of that title (published in France in 1965), give a curious feeling of potpourri. He was recapping his media and inventorying his abilities, painting out of his memories, which pushed him forward rather than carrying him back. And the usual question of "What's new with Picasso?" seems to evoke the answer, "His whole past."

The studio now was full of heads, replacing the women with cats. Heads of all colors and types, many of them marked with a yellow Z—heads that, mixed up and dense as they might be, all shared a common characteristic: they wore his favorite striped blue sailor shirt. And in reply to a phone call, the Crommelincks came in, like dancers in a ballet of Picasso the engraver. Together or separately, Aldo and Piero did the "copper dance," named after the "copper path."

He started etching with *In the Studio* on February 7, 1964, complemented the next day by *The Painter and His Model,* and then stopped, to touch no more copper till summer; the boys went back to Paris.

On a large drawing of May 26, the Smoker in the striped sailor shirt non-chalantly replaced the Painter alongside the curvaceous model, Picasso, as so often with him, mixing themes and characters. If they fit together, they stay; if not, they separate.

Summers and winters now were alike, all devoted to work alone, albeit still interrupted for corridas, such as the one at Fréjus in 1965, Hélène Parmelin's "corrida of the dead horse," or those at Arles or Nîmes, no longer the riotous events they once were, now quiet, if not even solemn. Sometimes Pablo went with Jacqueline and the driver alone, and came back that way. When the matador dedicated the bull to him before the fight, and afterward presented him with the ears and tail, he would stand up and thank him. Later, he would say, "Nice, wasn't it?" and head back to Mougins and his interrupted work.

The Smokers continued in oils, and in colored crayons, for several months. Early in August, the Crommelincks were back; August 19–September 8, Pablo did a series of Smokers in striped sailor shirts in colored aquatint. Also in aquatint, during the next winter and the spring of 1965, ten engravings for Pierre Reverdy's *Sable mouvant* (Quicksand), to be published the following year by Louis Broder.

All of his characters slipped easily from copper to paper, and he was indeed on such intimate terms with the members of his human comedy that one day, pointing to a little horse in his painter's studio, he said, "He likes doing a little sculpture once in a while." Sometimes the painting Pablo was doing appeared in his engravings, not as one of his own but as a work of the painter in his composition. And he would observe critically, "That's not all that bad," or else, "He didn't really try very hard today."

In this way, Picasso lived in his painting the day-by-day unfolding of his own existence; Jacqueline was always at his side, so naturally she was in the great majority of the pictures, drawings, or engravings, but there are also the domestics, friends, visitors, pets. Often recognizable, but sometimes also reinvented and metamorphosed. But the main character ever and always is Picasso. Who could doubt it?

Could he become fashionable again? After the return to realism of the Sixties and the rehabilitation of Marcel Duchamp, young painting had undergone a new switch. The years 1964–1965 were the pivotal years in a development that opposed the "new realism" of Pierre Restany and Yves Klein to the "new figurativeness," which, though rather mediocre on the whole, frankly faced up to the problem of narrative modernity. In introducing the "Narrative Figurativeness in Contemporary Art" show in Paris, October 1965, the critic Gérald Gassiot-Talabot saw as among the forebears of this return to realism the Picasso of *War* and *Peace,* the bullfights, and the *Dream and Lie of Franco,* which he said used "the methods of the comic strip." He also based himself on several statements by Picasso that Françoise Gilot had reported in her book.

In the final analysis, he was not greatly to influence the advocates of "narrative figurativeness," which seems now to have been a kind of catchall; what they learned from Picasso quickly sank beneath systematization, idle chatter, and mediocrity.

"Picasso is back among us with his daring, his humor, his flair for metamorphosis and juggling, his jokes and his unforgettable outcries," wrote Michel Ragon,* whose "Picasso is fading away" in 1950 had caused a scandal and provoked indignant protests when the Malagueño's glory was at its height. The time of condemnations without appeal was past, as was that of dithyrambs. The analytical exegesis by the British critic John Berger appeared as an attempt to understand the man and his work, its main merit being that it was personal. *The Success and Failure of Picasso,* published in London in 1965, went against currently accepted ideas; while irritating at times, it broke with the depressing monotony of the laudatory tomes, generally as mediocre as they were extravagant.

It brought out something too often forgotten: the master of Mougins was a man. Had he not asked Claude Roy to remember that? He could make mistakes, and be disagreed with, he might also lose some of his powers, and allowance might be made for his age—then eighty-four—however amazing his vitality remained. Berger attributed the untouchable character of Picasso's art to the dictatorship of the Communist Party over painting after World War II. It had indeed made it an offense to criticize, or even question, the "comrade of genius." The strange part was that the first protests against him came from within the Party, leading to the malaise that would result in there being questions raised about Picasso first in relation to socialist realism and then in relation to his commitment. After Budapest, and his public stand, he ceased being idolized, although he did still retain the comrades' respect—as traditionally due to old folks.

His life was so well organized that all he heard from the outside was compliments, flattery, and the glow of incense. Perhaps this kept him from finding too trying the "convict's life," as he called the existence of hard work without which he could not get along. But he actually cared little for the elegies. The only opinion that mattered finally was his own. The Picasso cult in Mougins was not unlike that of de Gaulle at the Élysée at the time, both bowing to an omniscient, invulnerable "sacred cow." As the years went by, the resemblance would grow even greater. Picasso at Mougins with his "family" was much like de Gaulle retired to Colombey with his entourage.

The two legends, Gaullian and Picassian, shared the same basis: the myth of the hero.

Each year Pablo sent a visiting card to the Salon de Mai, of which his friend Pignon was a committee member. In 1964, it had been a *Woman with Cat,* now in 1965 *One Canvas of Twelve, or Twelve Canvases in One,* an assemblage of nine heads and three nudes, baroque and colored, taken from the several

---

* "Picasso 1964," *Jardin des Arts* (Paris), May 1964.

recent series as well as *The Sculptor's Family, The Gardener's Family,* and *The Man of Letters.*

The "one canvas of twelve [parts]" came as a surprise, although there was no mystery about it. One morning, in the studio at Mougins, he had set several paintings up, and then with Pignon had assembled a dozen of them into a jigsaw that looked so good that it gave the feeling they had been intended for showing in this way, which they were. He might have done as much with twenty or thirty, for Picasso's ease and naturalness could be infinitely extended.

Meanwhile, big exhibits were being held around the world, museums and collections were acquiring Picassos, and their prices kept increasing. "Picasso and the Theatre" was a different kind of show: organized at the Musée des Augustins of Toulouse in 1965 by the curator Denis Milhau, it was one of the most original ever assembled, for not only had Pablo done much work for the theater, but his entire artistic conception was dramatization within a theatrical space in which decor and characters are used as on the stage. Time was used dramatically, too, if one considered some of the recent series, especially that of the Déjeuners: these were episodes in a story, with continuity of a sort, main characters, supporting roles, suspense, and switches in setting and point of view. Picasso's feel for theatrical costuming had also always been very pronounced, and his many actors often changed clothing, as he himself did. He had frequently shown himself in various disguises, Sabartés as a nobleman or monk, several people in Cocteau's Harlequin costume; and Paulo as a child had been both Pierrot and Harlequin. Jacqueline was to be Lola of Valencia (after Manet), a plumed equestrienne or a queen of Spain, and many more avatars.

As Jean Cassou wrote in his preface to the Toulouse exhibition catalog, "Picasso's genius is perpetually on stage, for its own benefit . . . A master of form, of deformation and transformation, he is also a demiurge of dramaturgy." And Milhau went further with "Whatever he got from life he put into the theater, and whatever he took from the theater showed up in the ensemble of his oeuvre."

It was a very lush exhibit, accompanied by ballets under the choreographic direction of Serge Lifar and the young Spanish dancer Rafael de Córdova, staged in the Théâtre du Capitole in Picasso sets and costumes.

Early in October 1964, Picasso had received a roll of reproductions of one of his paintings done by a publisher named Spitzer, a canvas called *The Painter,* of March 30, 1963, a pictorial commentary on The Painter and His Model. The bearded fellow beneath his wide hat, attentive to his easel, was gotten up in the typical outfit of the "artiste" that Pablo made fun of and referred to as "Poor Man." Or else Rembrandt.

Pablo unrolled the reproductions one after the other—there were some thirty in all—and quietly set about painting them in gouache and India ink. This was not the first time he played this game, not only on reproductions or posters, but also on photographs. Even photographs that were not of pictures set him to doing this, as when Douglas Duncan gave him some enlargements of photographs of Pallarés leaving to return to Spain after his regular visit to La Californie, and he immediately began embellishing them. One of them, showing Pallarés patting the face of his laughing friend, became a humorous Bacchic scene of two betogaed Romans crowned with laurels, as Pallarés with a broad gesture raised his cup of nectar.

From October 10 to October 24, Pablo recostumed, modified, and repainted all of Spitzer's reproductions. He was delighted with these "Picassos on Picasso," and for all their variations, a harmony of blue-gray, white, black, and solid blue lent unity to the thirty-odd versions of the same face. "I could do thousands of them," Pablo said. "It's marvelous to work like this, from a painter who's already there. Basically the most terrible thing of all for a painter is a blank canvas."

Day by day and hour by hour, paintings and drawings followed one another, in a veritable tidal wave. A virtual automatism made the themes proliferate, within each theme variants, and within the variants themselves spurts of humor, fantasy, anger, or challenge. Along with his own gifts, he was also exploiting the Matissian inheritance with a vengeance, as it expressed itself in the free-flowing arabesque, the distribution of light that swallowed form, and the kind of hedonism that reflected perhaps the old man's final conversion to life on the Riviera—another way of paying tribute to Matisse.

Suddenly, there was an earthquake in his painting. First the landscapes felt it, then the nudes, people, faces. In March and April some thirty-five canvases deal with variations of the artist and his model. A small one of April 3 shows at the left a side view of the painter's torso, his left hand holding palette and brushes, the right painting on a canvas placed vertically before him the model whom we do not see. This bald, bearded, serious-looking painter is practically an old man. What is he so assiduously painting? Don Pablo was not to leave us long in the dark: on the canvas that is the counterpart to this, a nude, laughing woman, thighs folded under her, head and shoulders covered with a sort of bridal veil, sits hieratically on the corner of a yellow and red couch, a slightly lewd idol quickly sketched in with broad geometrical sweeps of white and gray, and dirty greens and roses to stress her anatomical lures. Next to her, a virgin canvas stands on an easel.

Is this some new symbol of the painter's feeling of powerlessness to capture reality? The model is one thing, the canvas another, and they are not necessarily destined to meet. The painter is pitiful, in his devoted effort to capture the reality evading him. He and it are engaged in endless combat, which Picasso translates step by step, since there is no other way than to say what is happening. He varies the words, the meanings of sentences, uses different vocabularies, for painting is not an art of confidences or effusions, not intended to express states of the soul—as the "artistes" Pablo mocks try to do—or portray beauty—as they also do—but "to make us see," as Éluard said. Inside of insight.

The painter now was painting Painting.

Pablo's paintbrush grinds, kneads, tortures, caricatures its expressionism; with its at times grating, at others amusing baroque verve, transforms faces into bloated masks and attitudes, gestures, behavior into a festival of contortions, distortions, grimaces, and tomfoolery. *Man and Nude Woman, The Sleepers, Woman at the Seashore, Watermelon Eaters,* or *Guitar Player,* all done in April 1965, seem to illustrate a statement he made one day: "To try the impossible, we are all obligated." But so vehement an impossible had never been reached by anyone else: each picture is like a curse word or a pair of slaps. And each reflects the painter's mood; as he said, "What we do is like a thermometer. You use it to determine your weather."

In the greatest secrecy, he had come to Paris for a stomach-ulcer operation. Sneaked in and out of the American Hospital at Neuilly by ambulance, his presence was known to only a few intimates. Dr. Hepp, who operated on him on November 18, kept his identity secret, a bit of legerdemain for which Pablo was deeply grateful to him. "They cut me open like a chicken," he said. Of course, there were news leaks; his presence in a Paris hospital was rumored, and reporters and columnists ran down a number of leads, in vain. He was well protected.

Back at Our Lady of Life, now more than ever deserving of its name, he looked over his paintings lined up in all the rooms where he had left them, and said, "What's going to happen now?"

XXV

DON PABLO
IN ALL
HIS GLORY
(1965–1970)

I N THE SPRING OF 1965, THERE WAS A BOMBSHELL AT NOTRE-DAME-DE-
Vie. *Life with Picasso,* published the year before in English, now appeared
in its French edition, albeit with a few elisions.

The work of Françoise Gilot and the American art critic Carlton Lake,
who had interviewed Pablo several times in his capacity as contributor to *The
Christian Science Monitor, The New Yorker,* and *The Atlantic Monthly,* it
threw Jacqueline into a panic, since she could not keep it from her husband.
The Picasso "court" used every kind of pressure to try to bar publication of
the French edition, and then took action to have it seized in bookstores—but
to no avail.

As early as February 18, in *Les Lettres françaises,* Pierre Daix had led the
attack with:

> Twelve years after leaving Picasso, Françoise Gilot has given vent to a spitefulness
> and venom that spare neither the dead—Éluard especially, and Nush—nor the close—
> Olga Picasso, Dora Maar, Sabartés—in a hodgepodge of gossip and intimate con-
> fidences.
>
> . . . this embittered busybody, concerned exclusively with what she considers the
> failure of her own life, [paints] in the same colors those she was given the opportunity
> to frequent . . .

Which was not very gentlemanly.

Fervent as ever, Hélène Parmelin rushed to Pablo's defense, against a press
that tried to strike at his heart, while he, not having read the book or ever in-
tending to, was more sad than hurt. Having always lived as a public figure, he
did not expect to be immune to attack, yet he could not hold back the protest

movement his friends put on, which tended to earn him more ridicule than the book. However ill-served by Françoise's malicious though often amusing—if not necessarily "Picassian"—anecdotes, Pablo as man and painter was beyond their reach, whereas his friends' campaign on behalf of his lawsuit, meant to win the support of the largest possible number of painters, sculptors, and celebrities, combined pity and clumsiness, casting him in the role of victim—which he never was.

Following her break with Pablo, Françoise Gilot had gone with her children to the apartment he had bought for her in Rue Gay-Lussac, taking, by her own statement, only one picture by her mate of ten years, the *Flower-Woman* painted in 1946, which is one of the tenderest portraits he did of her. She married a young painter, Luc Simon, and they had a daughter, Aurelia, after which they split up. For vacations, Claude and Paloma had gone to La Californie, but as they grew older they spent their summers with English friends of hers at Cambridge. She was painting, and reported that after she left Pablo gallery doors were closed to her, as they later were to her husband, one of the reasons for her divorce from Simon.

For the summer of 1964, she wanted to send Claude and Paloma to stay with their father at Mougins, and according to what was agreed upon at their separation she called his lawyer to have him advise Picasso of the plan. Pablo answered that the dates she selected were not convenient, but offered no alternates. So she decided to take the children to Mougins herself; she dropped them a few hundred yards from the gate of Notre-Dame-de-Vie, and they went up and identified themselves on the intercom, only to be told by an anonymous voice that "Monsieur is not here." They returned to her, sad and convinced that he was inside.

The next summer, Claude, now eighteen, borrowed his mother's car and drove his sister down to Mougins, where once again the same voice turned them away with the same words. So they decided to seek their father out in person, going to the bullfight at Fréjus, which they knew he would attend. He was with Jacqueline, her daughter Cathy, and a group of friends, and all Claude could do was wave from a distance to his father, who evinced no interest in his presence.

Now there was that book. Parmelin, like a Pasionaria on the barricades, headed the irate protesters around the master. But was the book so awful? Françoise's part (disappointed love and getting even) and Lake's (exegesis of the painter and his work) were easily recognizable. Did they show him up so badly, as his courtiers claimed? Truth to tell, Françoise's delayed denunciation, if ill-intentioned, was nevertheless full of original material about Picasso's behavior, his ideas on painting, his life-style, and his way with women and friends. The court decree rejecting the request to have the book seized made much more telling points against him than Françoise had, and justified his being irked at those who had gotten him to sue.

For weeks, he sulked; in a fit of depression, Jacqueline took to her bed; and the entourage bit its lips. As Françoise had written, it was not easy to be Picasso, and even less so to live with him. She quoted him:

"Nobody has any real importance for me. As far as I'm concerned, other people are like those little grains of dust floating in the sunlight. It takes only a push of the broom and out they go."

"For me, there are only two kinds of women—goddesses and doormats."

Even if "arranged" by her—or made up, as his devotees insisted—these words had the true ring of Picasso.

The man Françoise portrayed was of course not the one the usual fawners wrote about—Party hacks or ladies turned on by the "Picasso business." Yet the Party faithful, already upset that he was allowed to practice an art condemned in all others, could not but be surprised at reading of his dragging his mistress into a church to make her swear she would "love him forever," or of his delight at finding that Françoise's grandmother was including him in her prayers.

But very few artists under the age of forty joined in the protest against *Life with Picasso*. Not many younger people felt concerned by all this, which kept him "in the public eye," albeit unflatteringly. The young artists discovering him in 1965–1966 were not only those associated with "New Figurativeness" who held him to be the pioneer of the realistic image; the "new realists" admired him, too, for opposite reasons, sometimes unrecognized: he had been one of the first to use trash and undistinguished materials in a picture. His early works with plaster or sand right on the canvas and his first collage with oilcloth in 1911–1912, the fragments of pasted newspaper in 1913, Cubist assemblages of 1914, the sackcloth *Guitar* of 1926, were forerunners of their Neo-Dadaist experiments and heralds of the recent forays designated as nihilworks, *arte povera,* or art in process, which called for direct contact and physical spectator participation. Besides, was not Cubism the first of the conceptual arts?

At the same time, he showed that profoundly personal art, growing out of the drama, anguish, all the feelings any man could experience in facing the modern world, was still possible. Against the "collectivism" of so many, the attempts to integrate art into the urban complex, the drive toward a global art tied in with architecture and environment, he asserted his individualism. Truly, he was the last great feudalist of painting and thus maintained a continuity of the behavior that had characterized so many painters of his generation. A whole aspect of his dramatic art, his obsessions, angers, revolts that continually surfaced in the diary of his work, was tied in directly with that individualism which he never gave up. He turned the artist into the protester he himself had always been, protesting against himself, others, painting, the outside world. With greater or lesser urgency in his final works.

Jacqueline was worried, telling visitors she was literally "terrified" by his painting. His wild expressionism had never been more aggressive, all in impasto furrows plowing the canvas with sine-wave tracings, crushing the color in thick big blobs spread by quick brushes that wiped, swept, or streaked the forms. And within these magmas in which the thick diggings of arabesque knotted and unknotted, disjointed bodies crashed together; arms, legs, heads, and genitals mixed and merged, as in headlong congress or clash; women, fauns, pipe players, smokers, musketeers, painters, nudes, and others, wallowed—with grotesque, repulsive bloated faces, eyes haggard, cheeks invaded by whiskers—their limbs deformed, haunches elephantine, thighs or feet monstrous, bellies swollen, boutonniere clitorises and dangling phalluses.

One ·day, the painter in the studio was replaced by a musketeer, and from then on the latter's fellows forcibly entered the Picasso world with their handlebar mustaches, ruffs, rapiers, and doublets. The musketeer sat before the easel and started to paint the model, after which it was the pipe player's turn to play at being artist, until the painter returned, followed by the ever-more-greedy watermelon eaters. Meantime, the circus had made an appearance, because Pablo had become enchanted with a TV show called *"La Piste aux étoiles"* (Stars in the Ring), and there were equestriennes, clowns, gymnasts, acrobats, and midgets.

Another day, he thought up a process which, when printed, brought out a white line against black ground, a sort of "dark manner" he used several times; these successive experiments came together in what he called the "extraction" of the portrait of Angela Rosengart, done on October 30, 1966. He was continually renewing himself, innovating, as the proofs poured off the presses.

On a sheet 75 centimeters by 56½ (30 inches by 22½), on September 3, 1967, he penciled three female figures in a delicacy of line that left all its fullness to the ocher color of the background. Only the one in the middle had a head more detailed than the others, outlined in blacks, stressed with shadows; at their feet crouched a man, and the profane trinity seemed to be like a fleeting echo of *Les Demoiselles d'Avignon*. The man perhaps is Picasso himself, shown in double side-view.

He had authorized staging of *Desire Caught by the Tail* by a young theatrical troupe run by the writer Jean-Jacques Lebel and director Alain Ziou. It had previously been given at Lausanne and Les Baux by a Swiss student troupe. To everyone's amazement, the mayor of St.-Tropez, where the play was to be given, banned it, and the show had to be moved to Gassin, where it was played on an invitation-only basis, with stripper Rita Renoir a knockout as its star. Lebel and Ziou merely followed in detail the author's stage directions, but they seemed so imaginative that the audience thought the producers had shown great inventiveness of their own: Picasso had in fact invented vocabulary and stage business twenty years ahead of their time, harbingers of the "happenings" that were to follow. When Act IV ends with

> (Great silence for a few minutes, during which, in the prompter's box, over a big fire and in a big pan, potatoes are seen, heard, and smelled frying in boiling oil; more and more, the smoke of the fried potatoes fills the hall to the point of complete suffocation.)

he is reflecting and ridiculing the petrified, literarily inspired theater of the between-the-two-world-wars period. Silence plays a great part in his play; Picasso uses it several times, and one of the characters is indeed named Silence. He answers "Will you please keep still," when Big Foot says, ". . . take Silence's suit off and put him naked into the soup which, by the way, is beginning to get cold at a mad rate." Here again Pablo is a forerunner of today's avant-garde theater, in which words signify much less than action, which is intended to decondition the spectator, wrest him out of his passiveness and fixedness, and allow him to make his own montage of events as he does in daily life, itself a sort of permanent collage of successive and/or simultaneous visions.

Fernande Olivier died in her small apartment in Neuilly, and on the cold February morning a little more than fifty years after the meeting in the Bateau-Lavoir that was to determine the future course of her life, Alice Derain, who had been the one to look after her at the end, was almost alone in following her cortège to the cemetery. Just a few days before, looking at a picture of Pablo in a tuxedo at the Cannes Film Festival of 1956 with Jacqueline, Fernande had commented laughingly, "To think that in the old days he wouldn't for anything in the world put on a white shirt and starched collar!"

For some time, several friends or devotees of Picasso had wanted to have a great Parisian retrospective of his work, the last one having been held at the Decorative Arts Museum in 1955. Since then, there had been large ones around the globe, and the "Picasso and the Theatre" show at Toulouse had proved that, with a little tact and some solid friendly support, one might get Pablo to lend some of the many works from his own private collection.

Malraux's presence at the head of the Ministry of Cultural Affairs and the prestige policy he was sponsoring seemed to create a climate favorable to organizing such a retrospective as a tribute to Picasso on his eighty-fifth birthday in 1966. Yet, no one knew what the Minister would do, considering how he felt about Picasso, to all the rest of the world the greatest of living painters. The question of whether Pablo would eventually make a significant donation to the State Museums, details to be worked out, had been broached to the painter by a close friend, and his answer was, "Well, if I were asked, I don't say I'd refuse . . ."

Who could approach the Minister on the subject and how? It fell to Gaëtan Picon, then director of Arts and Letters in the Ministry, a friend of Malraux's and a writer about his work. Malraux said that "with Picasso, nothing can be accomplished"; at the last minute he would refuse, he would raise every kind of obstacle, and his principal enjoyment was to "booby-trap" those who solicited him, for whatever purpose. That was the term his staff heard from Malraux every time anyone mentioned Picasso. The octogenarian, ensconced in his lonely position as feudal lord of painting, bothered Malraux, who had not seen him for several years. No dialogue seemed possible between them, no ground for understanding.

"The trouble was that they considered themselves equals before eternity," as a mutual painter friend put it. Which might make the first step? Not Pablo. So Malraux? But he was a Minister, a minister of de Gaulle, the man of history, which meant not just any plain old Minister—so he did not act just any old way.

Besides, there were those Communists around Picasso, and his recent stands that were all against Gaullism. Some of those close to him were against a show that might make Pablo more or less indebted to, if not indeed the accomplice of, a government at the time so virulently anti-Communist. If the show did take place, would it not provoke Party demonstrations in Paris?

To Malraux, all this added up to "booby traps," which could only end unfavorably for him and the régime. Yet, many urged him to take a chance on it: a well-organized exhibition, which Picasso supported, might lead to negotiations toward that gift of works. But Malraux still did not trust the mercurial painter's "I don't say I'd refuse . . ."

When someone advised him to go quietly to Notre-Dame-de-Vie to lay the groundwork with Picasso himself, Malraux replied, "You're mad! He'd leave me standing at the gate, sending word that someone was coming to open. And I'd wait there for hours while they tipped off *L'Humanité!*"

The Minister would take no chances, while as a man he was also paradoxically inclined to break away before any blows were struck. Fleeting, unstable, worried, given to audacious steps that were not followed up, good ideas that went nowhere, visionary intuitions and disconcerting cop-outs, a mobility of thought that did not rule out indecision or sudden switches, complicated by failures of memory, his inability to communicate directly with those working with him or to buckle down to the administrative routine of the ministry ("That's what we have civil servants for"), and his relative lack of interest in people, "those wretched little piles of secrets," all of this scarcely made Malraux the man to carry off undertakings that required sustained effort.

When Picon and one of his close associates, Blaise Gautier (later to be head of the National Center for Contemporary Art), conveyed to him that there was a moral obligation to celebrate the painter's eighty-fifth birthday with a Paris retrospective, Malraux of course knew it was France's job to take charge, but he countered with "Of course, you're doing this on your own initiative." Thereby clearing himself in case, as he considered certain, Pablo sprang so many "booby traps" that the plan fell through. He let them go ahead, while assuring them, "You'll see what'll happen!"

When later in *La Tête d'obsidienne* he was to make several mentions of this retrospective, "which I had had organized," he was novelizing, not reporting.

Picasso did at first refuse, but later, in January 1966, he accepted, when Jean Leymarie was put in charge, and he told him, "You'd have been better off never knowing me. You're going to have the worst problems."

"We made big decisions at night," Jacqueline was to say later. "Pablo worked late, and then we'd go into the kitchen to grab a bite, and that was when he'd make up his mind. I asked him about the exhibition, and he said no. An hour later, as we were going to bed, he said, 'If you insist, go ahead and do it, but don't expect me to get involved.' That was just after Leymarie was named."

The two had been friends since 1944, when André Chamson had asked this young museum employee, who was giving his daughter philosophy lessons, to handle three radio broadcasts with Picasso. The painter let him come and interview him for four hours, and the shows were a great success. Delighted, Picasso invited Leymarie to come back to see him and showed him paintings and especially sculptures no one else had ever seen. When Leymarie became curator of the Grenoble Museum, he was able to acquire four of them, at a minimum price. His contacts with Picasso followed his career as a government employee. When his acquaintance Malraux became Minister, Leymarie was a professor at the University of Geneva, and Malraux made every effort to get him back to Paris in an important position: commissioner-general of the Picasso exhibition at the Grand Palais was a first step. The opening of the show was to coincide with the unveiling of the first part of the renovated building.

At Easter 1966, two months after being confirmed in the job, Leymarie left for Mougins. The original plan was to show a hundred rankingly significant paintings of all the periods, and Leymarie drew up a list with Picasso. Malraux, still wanting to keep his name away from the inevitable failure, refused to sign the requests to foreign museums to lend their holdings, which his position called for him to do. Picon made the requests instead.

The museums of the United States, at the time very hostile to de Gaulle's foreign policy, almost universally said no. So Leymarie crossed the Atlantic to see those in charge in person, especially his friend Alfred Barr, Jr., first Director of the Museum of Modern Art of New York. He agreed to lend seven paintings, including the famous *Night Fishing at Antibes,* which Leymarie especially wanted, and the indispensable *Demoiselles d'Avignon.* On the other hand, *Guernica,* which Picasso had left in trust at the museum, was fragile and in need of some restoration, which Picasso had not agreed to; so, since it had already been shown at the Paris exhibition of 1955, it was not lent this time.

After the United States, Leymarie, who through the good services of Penrose had been able to get five paintings from London's Tate, went off to the USSR. His official mission was to bring back some Cézannes that the French museums had lent to the Russians. After a week of negotiations, Comrade Furtseva, Commissar of Culture, agreed to the loan of several youthful and Cubist works. Even more readily, Prague's National Gallery lent its key Cubist paintings. The great Dutch museums, the Picasso Museum of Barcelona, the museums at Liège, Stockholm, Basel, and elsewhere, all joined in helping fill the list.

Barr's example had "thawed" most of the other Americans: the Chicago Art Institute, the Guggenheim, the Metropolitan, Boston, Philadelphia, Cleveland, Hartford's Wadsworth Atheneum, and so on. The original hundred had long since been exceeded and the show was turning out to be much greater than had ever been anticipated.

As the loans grew more important, Leymarie thought of a real coup: to include Picasso's virtually unknown sculpture. That was not possible in the Grand Palais, but the Petit Palais, just across the way, would be ideal. The commissioner-general crossed Avenue Winston-Churchill to offer the master's bronzes, assemblages, and metal cutouts to the curatrix, Mlle. Cacan. She almost fainted with horror. Daughter of a traditionalist painter, she respected classical beauty and was not far from considering Picasso a hoax and a devotee of the devil. But how could she refuse? She transmitted Leymarie's request to the Paris Municipality, which controls the Petit Palais. And it was accepted. Leymarie went off to announce the good news to Malraux and Picasso.

Here was a good chance to try to get the two of them together again. After all, Pablo had once said to him, "Malraux is a real somebody!" If he came to Mougins now, would he be welcome? Picasso bored into his visitor with his terrible black eyes, saying, "I'd be delighted to see Malraux. He can eat in the kitchen with us like everyone else." Of course, it was out of the question to transmit such an invitation to the Minister in charge of Cultural Affairs, who would have ignored it anyway.

Malraux was appalled by the way the show was developing: "He thought I was crazy," Leymarie says today. There were to be 284 paintings in the Grand Palais, with the drawings and sculpture at the Petit. The latter were the big revelation of the exhibit, since most of the statuary had never left his studio—a total of 186 pieces (bronze, wood, cutout and painted metal, and sundry materials), dated from 1901 to 1963.

Picasso was delighted with the commissioner's activity; "Picasso always wanted to know how far one could go," says Leymarie, remembering that time of accomplishments and surprises. Such as the day he went with Don Pablo to select a painting at La Californie: September 28, 1966, the day André Breton died. Picasso talked about his old friend and then, when they got to the old place in Cannes, he opened a drawer and took out a packet of letters that he showed Leymarie. Written by Breton, they had been bought by Picasso: they were addressed to a woman, and the Surrealist leader had spilled his semen on them.

The retrospective was greeted in different ways. Much less centered, as the Decorative Arts Museum show had been, on one aspect of the Picassian universe, it was capable of satisfying almost everyone by offering each his or her own special Picasso: realist, expressionist, Cubist, classical, baroque, painter, sculptor, ceramicist, designer, engraver. The vastness of his production precluded any deciphering by press and public much more interested in the personality of its creator.

Once-horrified crowds now pushed their way into the two Palais on the Champs-Élysées: factory workers brought in busloads by Communist municipality charters uninhibitedly admired the "workers' friend," coincidentally also the greatest painter of the capitalist West whose works were bid for by Texas millionaires, while Soviet men and women went to see them in the Czar's onetime palaces. Schoolchildren were also brought in to admire—and at the same time find out why teachers or parents scoffing or frowning at their scribblings sometimes exclaimed, "Bah! a regular Picasso!"

On October 25, 1966, Pablo Picasso was eighty-five. The whole world joined in wishing him a happy birthday. But nothing happened in Vallauris, as it had five years before. Friends on the Riviera who called were told, "Monsieur is not in."

That evening, Madeleine and Antoni Clavé dropped by Notre-Dame-de-Vie with a set of little people sculpted and painted by a sailor at St.-Tropez. They meant to leave the gift for Picasso, without disturbing him, when, as they were about to go away, a car came up the road: Pablo and Jacqueline, after having hidden out all day, were coming home. They all embraced, exchanging greetings and congratulations, and Pablo invited them in.

The house was empty. "Is there anything to eat?" he asked Jacqueline. Fortunately, Félix the restaurateur at Cannes had sent up some oysters in a basket, and there was some ham and a few good bottles of wine. They sat down in the kitchen, ate, and invited the domestics in to drink a toast. That was how Pablo Picasso's eighty-fifth birthday ended. As he said to Clavé, "You know, I wasn't expecting anyone, so there was nothing in the house."

No one expected him to be there on the morning of November 19, when André Malraux presided at the opening of the exhibition, as one newspaper put it, "the revolutionary of literature [hailing] the revolutionary of painting." The Minister described the painter's work as "the greatest undertaking of destruction and creation of forms of our time, perhaps of all time."

Picasso did not attend these retrospective exhibitions any more than he had previous ones, nor would Jacqueline. "She would not have dared," said one of their intimates. After her husband's death, she was to go quietly to Avignon, where an eyebrow-raising collection of recent paintings was on show in the summer of 1973, then in September to the annual L'Humanité outing at La Courneuve, where the Party paid tribute to its most illustrious member.

Many friends phoned to tell Pablo of the crowds who attended and their (somewhat subdued) enthusiasm. Except for two or three, such as Kahnweiler, to whom shows like this were consecrations, he did not take the calls. While distant from such "triumphs," he was in fact quite present, since he had supervised everything—and Leymarie was not for a moment taken in by Pablo's feigned indifference, as he kept abreast of every detail. Nor was Pablo unaware of Leymarie's seeing through him, and that allowed him to carry off the task Malraux had been so sure was impossible.

November 19, for Picasso, was a workday like any other. His table was overflowing with photos he had requested from Paris, showing the rooms, the hanging of the pictures, the works themselves. Plus piles of letters and telegrams from all around the world. After lunch, he pushed it all aside, to inscribe two of the invitation cards to Jacqueline.

That evening he was in bed by midnight (he had been retiring much earlier recently than in the past), and that was where Hélène Parmelin, who had come down on the crack Mistral train to bring late reports to him, found him. With him in the bedroom, Jacqueline and Mme. Hepp, his surgeon's wife, listened to Hélène's news. Her words amused him, as did her fervent attention to every word he ever said, however insignificant. "As soon as I open my mouth, she rushes to a corner and takes out her little pad," he told a friend. And, of course, she did try, in books and articles, to be the faithful chronicler of everything he said. She helped keep enthusiasm alive in the isolated old man, as she brought her red-hot tale of the triumph, which he well knew was nothing but a very official show of esteem. "What will you say about the next one?" he chaffed, as she waxed enthusiastic over how Paris had been "turned upside down" by the retrospective.

A few days later, Jean Leymarie came down to make his own report on how things had gone. Jacqueline was indisposed, so he and Pablo dined opposite each other in the kitchen, "like Cézanne's card players," Picasso said, grinning. Later that evening, when they got around to problems of art, he was to say, "It's hard to inject a bit of absolute into the frog pond."

Several Parisian galleries took the occasion of the retrospective show to put on their own tributes to Picasso. And the comments on the big show were varied: in painting, there were regrets that the last room was rather incoherent and seemingly hurried, the weaknesses being the more apparent because all the rest was of such a high level. The sculptures created the biggest shock of all, causing Pierre Restany, for example, to ask whether Picasso was not mainly a sculptor, thus echoing Gonzalez' judgment of a few years before, that he was "a man of form." And Restany added, "The Picassian plastic itinerary is all dazzling fantasy, inventive extravaganza, rigorous control of volumes."

The French press as a whole was strangely embarrassed by the Picasso retrospective. Obviously, Jean Cassou, Bernard Dorival, André Chastel, Jean Leymarie, Hélène Parmelin, or Gaëtan Picon could be expected to express only fervent reverence or respectful analysis. The questions they might ask, some of which were fundamental—as Gaëtan Picon's on the contrast between the baroque turbulence of the most recent paintings with their studied negligence and the balance and density of the Cubist works, the conciseness of a neoclassical portrait against some other example of noisy ostentatiousness, the fabulous grandeur of the *Bathers,* the dramatic eloquence of *Guernica*—were raised with some hesitation, even some uneasiness, as if Don Pablo's terrible eye were fixed on their criticism, hemming it in.

The same was true of the critics to whom the whole of Picasso lay in his monstrous, terrifying, "cursed" aspect, in the "ugliness" of so many works. Referring to the true or apocryphal anecdote of Manolo before one of the Cubist paintings saying to Pablo, "How would you like it if your parents came to meet you at the Barcelona station looking like that?" Françoise Giroud wrote in *L'Express:* "What Manolo said to Picasso sixty years ago is what thousands of Frenchmen will think once they get inside the Grand Palais."

Could it be that, in sixty years, the French had really not developed in their appreciation and understanding of contemporary art? John Canaday of *The New York Times,* who perhaps had not read the French papers, thought otherwise, for, seeing the long lines outside the two Palais, he wrote, "French culture has, indeed, exploded." Yet he wondered whether people were actually looking at the pictures, since those truly interested were pushed around by a mob that "makes the New York subway rider look like an 18th-century courtier."

The circumspect English were full of questions. What sort of artist could this painter be, whom Nigel Gosling in *The Observer* compared to a triumphal pirate returning from many fruitful forays, with a wealth of booty? Humor keeping its place, John Russel in *The Sunday Times* had a (not very convincing) piece, entitled "The Perpetual Present." And Norbert Lynton compared the three-way Paris show to "a sort of deluge." Denys Sutton in *The Financial Times* wondered aloud whether Picasso's facility was not a handicap to him: lauding his constant inventiveness, his frenzy of discovery, the dizzying awareness of his fantastic imagination, he compared him to a Pirandello character in search of one style one day, and another on another. He saw him as a master of the theatrical gesture, "the true magician."

Werner Spies of the *Frankfurter Allgemeine Zeitung,* who was to write a capital work on Picasso's sculpture, found the works at the Petit Palais of course the most fascinating, the touchstone of the whole oeuvre. He was indifferent to the recent paintings, but a month later paid tribute to "the genius of remembrance" that Picasso was to him, memory in his art abolishing time.

In Italy, Guido Piovene in *La Stampa* wrote that "He seems to live in a time longer and greater than our own" and spoke of the "ceaseless figured autobiography of the painter and sculptor" that "never went in a realistic direction. The object before him is reinvented in a lightninglike manner." He said that to Picasso everything turned into his art, with no differentiation between the acts of thinking or feeling and their translation into his work. Piovene claimed that, looking at the works of young artists, he rarely found any that seemed born outside the ambit of Picasso, the "Buddha who has everything in his belly."

The Spanish press stressed two aspects: the vitality of the artist "who followed his destiny, resisting convenience and seduction" (Juan Cortés, *La Vanguardia Española*) and the magnitude of the tribute paid him. It was a good chance to remind the world that Don Pablo was a Spaniard and had his own museum in Barcelona. On January 20, 1967, in that city two hundred students and many intellectuals took part in a "free meeting" in tribute to Picasso. The demonstration, illegal because it was organized by the students' union (banned as were all unions), heard one of the organizers say, "We want to pay tribute not only to the painter, but also to the old democrat who all his life fought for his country's freedom, not yet achieved."

His eighty-fifth birthday saw many exhibitions of his work around the world. In the United States, those at the Los Angeles County Museum, and the Dallas Museum and Fort Worth Art Center Museum—the last two, organized by Douglas Cooper, depriving Paris of several significant works—were especially good. In Lucerne he was at the Rosengart Gallery, in Basel at the Galerie Beyeler, and the Sala Gaspar in Barcelona. Twenty-five 1963–1965 canvases were shown at the Manès in Prague, his first major exhibit in a Socialist country. The Pushkin Art Museum of Moscow showed over two hundred graphic works, drawings, etchings, lithographs, and so on, mainly coming from the Galerie Louise Leiris, Picasso himself, and numerous private collections, including that of Ilya Ehrenburg, establishing him as a master of drawing; the last time his work had been shown in the USSR, exactly ten years before, it had caused much controversy and discussion; this was no longer the case, but if most of those viewing it were still put off by his "distortions," that did not keep them from standing in line hours on end in the bitter cold outside the museum.

In Mougins, he was enjoying his triumph. By working. There was still talk of a gift he might eventually make, but no significant negotiations were taking place. No one, it seemed, dared approach him on the subject, and the idea dragged out and finally came apart.

It was the same way with Malraux's decision to make Pablo a high dignitary of the Legion of Honor. Since Braque was a Commander of the Order, Pablo was to be made a Grand Officer, the next higher rank. But such a distinction could not be given a foreigner who had not risen step by step in the Order, without special dispensation by the President. The decree was drawn up, and de Gaulle signed it. Malraux wrote Picasso to inform him of the honor, but it was now months since the matter had first been broached, and Pablo declined. "I am deeply touched," he told Leymarie, "but my business is painting."

Likewise, he would have agreed to the gift if a quick decision had been reached. He was not one for waiting and stalling. "I'll give you whatever you want, if you have a place to put it," he told Leymarie when the latter was named curator-in-chief of the Museum of Modern Art. The old Luxembourg Museum, no longer housing the Senate, was available to be taken over again by the Ministry of Cultural Affairs. "It's free, take it," he urged Leymarie. He would have filled it in short order.

It did not happen. Pablo loved that quarter which had been the home of so much of his youth, and would have loved to be in his own museum there. Another idea was to acquire the Rue des Grands-Augustins apartment and turn it into a Picasso museum, but there were almost insurmountable difficulties in getting up to it and fixing it up; yet, he would have truly appreciated such a gesture by the government.

Why did all these successive plans fall through? Who was to blame? Beyond Malraux, some of the higher-ups in the national museum organization were not enthusiastic over the idea of a Picasso museum. They would not have objected to his Blue or Rose or "classical" periods, but those disjointed women, with their double profiles, their layered eyes, legs at their shoulders and crotches gaping, were not for them!

For some years, the owners of the Rue des Grands-Augustins building (no less than the Association of Process Servers of the Department of the Seine) had been trying to take back his apartment, since he had not lived or worked there since 1955. Terrified of having to move everything out of those studios, and sentimentally attached to the house and its "attic," in which he had painted *Guernica* and spent the occupation, he called on his influential friends: he would have liked to hold onto his successive homes the way he kept his women on the string . . . In fact, that was where the idea of buying the building and turning it into his museum had originated.

André Malraux assured him he need not worry, and assigned a staff member to watch over it; while the latter was on vacation, the Process Servers moved for an eviction notice. The court, of course, cognizant only of the applicable law, ruled M. Pablo Ruiz Picasso would have to move; no appeal possible.

The Minister, informed by Picasso's friends, evasively apologized. He had done nothing and had no intention of involving his Ministry in keeping the studio for its famous tenant. "If it can be done, well and good," he had told one of his assistants, who expected precise instructions. But Malraux was disconcertingly contradictory, ambiguous, and vague in this affair, which concerned not him but the State itself. When he was asked what he might do about it, while the press was printing reports of a possible Picasso bequest, the Minister haughtily replied, "France asks favors of no one."

In Malraux's view, Pablo was not part of France's destiny. Gaullist destiny, that is. His idea of a "Gaullist artist" was clearly shown in an exchange between him and the General in *Les Chênes qu'on abat* (Felled Oaks), his report of his visit to Colombey, December 11, 1969: "An artist who defends you," he had told de Gaulle, and that obviously did not apply to Picasso; it did, Malraux said, to "Braque and Le Corbusier yesterday, Chagall and Balthus today. And they are not alone." His attitude therefore arose not only from his character, but also from political considerations—of the basest kind.

The deplorable Grands-Augustins business deeply depressed Pablo. "Sad, isn't it?" he said to Brassaï (as the photographer was to relate in *Le Figaro,* October 8, 1971). "But how can you fight when the owners are all process servers? All the process servers of France and Navarre united . . . Nobody tried to help me keep that studio in which I had worked for over twenty years! Every trace of the half-century I spent in Paris is now totally, finally eliminated . . ."

At eighty-five, Pablo had, he said, but one thought: to work. Jacqueline has been accused of isolating him, but her health was fragile, making it harder for her to cope with the problem of being his wife. The hardest part—for her more than him—was his children by Françoise. Since her book appeared, he would not allow the latter's name to be mentioned, or that of the children, though they were in no way responsible. Paloma told an interviewer how she tried in vain to see him several times, until on the last day of her vacation at Vallauris the Notre-Dame-de-Vie intercom finally said to come in.

"Jacqueline received me kindly. My father was in his usual mood. The meeting, at first, was strained. I was flushed," she said.

"I spent two hours with them, without trying to get any explanations. Finally, Papa asked, 'When are you leaving?'

" 'Today.'

" 'Good. Then it's time for you to be off. I was very happy to see you.' "

That was all. On her way back, she kicked herself for not having asked why his attitude had changed so. There had been only small talk with her indifferent, distant parent, once so wonderful and affectionate a playmate to her brother and her—doing several fine portraits of them—now only in a hurry to see her go.

True, Paloma added, "this little man creates about him a fascination that conquers and subjugates. No one can stand up to him as an equal."

She never saw him again. Nor did Claude, who became a photographer and traveled a great deal. By official decree in 1961, with the painter's permission, they were authorized to have the name of Ruiz Picasso and receive a monthly allowance, as did Maya, who had married a naval officer and was now Mme. Widmayer.

Under Pablo's fingers, drawings and engravings kept coming out like leaves of a diary as abundant as it was varied. Erotic themes were more and more in evidence. A few weeks after the end of the big Paris retrospective, the Louise Leiris Gallery exhibited ninety of his drawings that he had selected from his recent output. Watercolors, pencil drawings and color crayons, pen and ink, charcoal, wash with India ink, all were used. While the public had been going to his show, he had been turning out more work. The themes merged, mythology and circus, burlesque or off-color subjects, always with the Watcher all lusting eyes for the desirable exciting, almond-eyed, firm-breasted woman, twisting, tempting, or giving herself, her pretty hands with polished nails spreading the lips of her vulva, gaping buttonhole in her curly fleece.

This eroticism was still for a while to be mild. In these drawings of his everyone is either making love, just has, or is about to; that is clear from the looks, positions, gestures, mimicries: no problem is involved. It is like a symphony of desire, and he gives us nothing but the strong beats. He is not yet reminiscent of de Sade, but rather of Choderlos de Laclos: the voyeurism is veiled, sometimes furtive, bathed in mystery, and while the ladies may crudely reveal their clitorises, it is done with the charming mischievousness of Fragonard's hoydens. They are not concerned with the lubricious sprites who flit about them, brandishing their burnished blades.

Such scenes are still filled with Mediterranean vivacity and grace, in the vein of the beach play of 1925–1930, Ovid's *Metamorphoses,* and the Antibes Museum's *Joy of Living.* "Only when painting is not painting does it become an outrage against morality," as Picasso said. And in these scenes he is more interested in the act of saying than what he is saying. Don Pablo's license makes no bones of the kind of exploits the near-nonagenarian is still capable of; he is happy to say so, to have us share in his satisfaction.

Between March 16 and October 5, 1968, Picasso did a large number of engravings, including several never printed; 375 of them were shown at the Louise Leiris the next December to February. His voyeurism was gradually changing, getting heavier, more rasping and perverse, before blossoming into an especially spectacular erotic sequence. This priapic epic is a triumph, the hardworking member bearing witness to the unconquerable Picassian virility; it would be a little while yet before the latter waned and quieted, making way for the receptacle of regrets: the buttonhole-clitoris with the ladies appealingly spreading the lips in such highly promising poses. For the voyeur's pleasure, the eye never ceases its lookout.

The Minotaur grown old becomes more lonely: on February 13, 1968, Sabartés, never completely recovered from his stroke, succumbed to uremic poisoning. They had talked on the phone almost daily, and Pablo had instructed Paulo to make sure that the chum of his youth had everything he needed. Every time he came back from Mougins, he brought Jaime a package from the "Old Man." Now, there was only one of the early contemporaries left: Manuel Pallarés.

Don Pablo sent Sabartés a print of every one of his engravings, inscribed and dated; after his death, he did not stop, but the *P* and *S* of *Para Sabartés* now changed into elegant scrolls of arabesques made up of often complicated rhythms, as if, in spending time over these graphic games, he were keeping alive his affectionate thoughts of his old friend.

His engraving had now become Faust's alchemy; he had never kept the Crommelincks so busy. He worked so madly they could not keep up, they said; every day, doing new work, adding to it, superimposing, varying techniques on the same plate. "He dreamed up new processes without abandoning the traditional ways, which he used just as masterfully," says Aldo Crommelinck. "If some plates have several states, it does not mean that Picasso was correcting a detail; he just wanted to go further with what was already there, give it more scope and depth, make the theme he treated say as much as possible."

They called it his "logbook." Others make notes or sketches in or on a pad, but Picasso would take a plate and go at it with drypoint or burin—as if the restless, tireless old man needed this aggression, this penetration of matter to be able to continue *to say*.

Once Pablo had done the adventures of the picador; now it was the musketeer. He, too, had the worst troubles, following naked women at night while their madam sneered at him, forcing another of his victims to undress and show him her resplendent beauty as he watched with one of his mates also wrapped in a cape, carrying rapier and plumed hat. Then on horseback, wheeling in the wind and fog, and fighting. A woman, dressed in a simple wasp-waisted shift, comes in, her hand on a child's head. But what is hideous Celestina doing there in the corner? A profile sneaks in at the very edge of the plate: the Voyeur. We will be seeing much more of him.

The musketeer is off on his horse again. He carries away the nude woman. The ever-present bawd trots out another beauty. The musketeer goes into the brothel.

He fights again; with a broad sweep of his hat salutes a magnificent nude creature; paints a very erotic scene. And back to the whorehouse: the pretties rush to greet him. He has several rather frisky friends with him, including a monk who does not seem to approve. The Voyeur's profile now has a beard and mustache. Two musketeers duel, rapier in hand.

Naked women. Whorehouse. Celestina. The musketeer's friends. Embraces. And so on for plate after plate after plate. Pages and pages and pages. Stories without continuity, but not without suspense, bringing in from time to time unexpected people or events. Yet the leitmotiv remains the relations between the naked woman and the musketeer, to whom a thousand things happen between two embraces which, try as the belle might, never seem to come to a climax . . .

"What was important to him," say the Crommelincks, "was the engraved metal, which was end and originality in itself, quite apart from the means it gave him to increase his oeuvre. Even if only one proof were pulled, as Picasso said, he would remain attached to that medium of expression."

The intensive work the eighty-seven-year-old was demanding of himself and

his collaborators, the problems it raised, the new processes he tried out, the mixture of genres, styles, formats, and techniques, the prodigious inventiveness of
his narration, full of reprises, flashbacks, unexpected episodes, surprises—however great the weariness or nervous tension, all was done in finest good humor.
True, the misadventures of the musketeer were the kind that make one sad; the
film of his exploits was essentially comical with wild, baroque humor, lively,
dashing, happy, inimitably picaresque in tone. No repetitions or repentance; or
afterthoughts, either, or ulterior motives; everything out in the open, for all to
see.

Out of the past, only one, whose engraved work he knew by heart, obsessed
him, and he talked about him ceaselessly: Rembrandt.

No doubt about it, the Dutch master dominated the last years of the master
of Mougins. The musketeers are right out of him: "They came to Pablo when he'd
gone back to studying Rembrandt," Jacqueline told Malraux, who erroneously
saw them as an outgrowth of *Las Meninas*. Musketeers, reiters, swordsmen,
toreros, masques, or actors proliferated until the end, and it was among them
that Pablo was to die. They were symbolic of insolence, virility, fantasy; they
carried women off and violated them, fought each other, sped off on their horses
with their capes to the wind. A world separated those swashbucklers, whom he
turned into furious ideograms, from the serene studio dialogues, The Painter and
His Model, the Déjeuners under the cool branches and undergrowth.

A painter dressed in seventeenth-century-artist style, Rembrandt perhaps, came
close to a naked woman at the start of September 1968: they were close together,
then next to each other, then she was on top of him. He was dressed, but out of
his gaping breeches his taut member surged; their respective positions on the
bed where they lay were such that the most intimate portion of her body was
right over his face, as she delighted in this stroke of luck. A voyeur peeking
through the half-opened curtain followed developments attentively.

Touches; caresses; each seemed to be evaluating the other's potential before
beginning the engagement.

On September 2, the painter made up his mind: the lady was fulfilled; her
body was so wracked by the climaxes her partner's fervor created in her that it
was hard to tell whether he was entering her in the front or the rear. The size
of his pulsating piston explains the extreme character of her orgasms.

Easy to understand what they saw in each other. Now, in a few engravings that
hide nothing, their stormy intercourse goes on. It happened so fast the painter
did not even have time to put down his palette and brushes or take off his tam-o'-
shanter. Their bodies meet and melt together in fiery fornications like those of
rutting beasts, she all naked, caressed, twisted, turned upside down in the disorderly sheets, no longer knowing where best to apply her lips or labia, while
the painter wallows atop her and she lets herself go to the overwhelming sensa-
tions she is getting from the way nature so generously endowed him. The
voyeur, still behind his curtain, cannot hide his satisfaction at such a show, of
which not a drop escapes him. And the party goes on between woman and

painter on the torn-apart bed: a man hiding beneath it is lucky not to get crushed.

Here is how I conquer women, giving them full satisfaction, Picasso seems to be saying, adding to the autobiographical diary of his oeuvre these notations of triumphant virility (the most erotic of the plates were not shown at the Louise Leiris). Anatomically well endowed, having ample subjects in his sultan's harem, his endurance was famous, and he never refrained from telling of his exploits, each intimate detail made public. He was never one to blench at any means needed to win the ultimate goal, or the circumstances or partners carried off hussarlike with his weapon at the ready. No need to recount the many tales that were being told of Pablo's amatory prowess, some of which originated with him; they proved not only his violent and urgent taste for women, all women, but also the amazing power he so long retained to be able to give body to his desire and its urgency. Identified by the extravagant presents he usually gave them, with few exceptions his partners remained more discreet than he; no fault of his that some later took pen in hand.

Don Pablo's human comedy started with a line as fine as a hair, or a spot of heavy black ink, and went on in other lines no less supple and continuous, or somewhat more or less heavy, spots, spread about and graduated. With shadows, grays, dashes of light, contrasts, velvety or sooty blacks. Sometimes he would stop—not for long. Just to answer the phone or see a friend, Clavé coming in from Cap St.-Pierre near St.-Tropez, Guttoso from Milan, Miró from Paris or Mallorca, where he now was living. Josette Gris came to lunch every Wednesday, kissing Pablo and saying, doubtless with some loss of memory, "We've loved each other for over forty years."

One morning, Peinado came in. It was an off-day and Miguel, the secretary, whispered to him, "Make it short." He and Pablo hugged each other and Peinado noted that Picasso was very happy he came, but anxious to see him go, as if time were running out.

"I have to be very strict with visitors," Pablo told a friend the next day. "Yesterday, I had to be strict with one because I'm also strict with myself. The bell has tolled for me too. I have to work . . . ," adding in a hollow voice, "I have to keep going."

Yet he was still able jokingly to say, "When I rest is when I get tired. Some people drink Pernod all day; my Pernod is my work."

Time was haunting Pablo, and Jacqueline made herself the mistress of it, quickly understanding that what he needed most was peace, to work in, and seeing that he got it. One day when Brassaï was visiting with his wife, he asked Jacqueline to show him her latest photographs of his work, some of the early ones having been quite remarkable. "I haven't done any for years," she assured him. "I haven't time to. I'm entirely in the service of my master."

The photographer, who out of friendship and admiration had been recorder of Picasso's work, had begun sculpting; he had chiseled some pebbles found on the beach and brought a sack of them to show Pablo, who commented facetiously, "Everybody's a sculptor nowadays." Brassaï took his women and heads out one by one; it was getting warm. "Everybody's a sculptor nowadays," he repeated, holding a female form in his hands, a tiny sea goddess with little breasts and a triangular sex organ. "You know, I really like women, Brassaï . . . ," was the most he ever expressed by way of opinion.

What he had against Claude and Paloma was that they reminded him of "that woman who had done him so much harm," to quote Jacqueline, whose life had become submerged in her husband's. She had now taken over for Sabartés, though more attractively, and more tactfully, for she did not send visitors away impolitely but discouraged them by encouraging them to phone—calls that he never answered, or when he occasionally did, only to suggest they call back another time. It turned quite a few of them off.

Notre-Dame-de-Vie by now was a veritable jungle of pictures and statues. Canvases piled up, pushed one another aside, overlapped, while Pablo slipped among them like a cat, on the picture side or the stretcher side. When Malraux visited Mougins after the painter's death, he was to note a card on which he had inscribed: "If you think your picture is not a failure, go back to the studio, and you'll see what a failure it is."

"One day when he had to go out, he left that for a friend," Jacqueline explained. "Then he said he had kept it for himself because it was such good advice."

More work and more, all the old warriors, and some bullfights, and Jacquelines, mainly Jacquelines. "When it was going well," Miguel was to relate, "he would come out of the studio delighted, shouting 'Jacqueline, they're coming! More are coming!'" Supers for the huge travesty that was to cover the walls of the Palace of the Popes in Avignon.

Submerged by the moving creatures beneath his fingers, he would ask, "What will painting do when I'm no longer here? It'll have to run me over. It won't be able to pass me by, no, sir!"

Taking two or three art books off the table, and leafing through them, he would make a face at the bad quality of the reproductions. Having visited few museums during his lifetime, he had seen few of the works "au naturel." He quickly reviewed Titian, Rembrandt, Rubens, Goya, Delacroix; then jumped back to Egypt, Greece, the Cyclades. And murmured, "In the final analysis, I imitated everybody but myself."

A young painter had come away from Mougins one time completely despairing, because Picasso had said to him, "All the time you have to try to do somebody else's kind of work. That's harder, and generally you can't do it . . . It always fails. But so does your work when you do it your own way."

Picasso was quite happy to hear that the dealer Alex Maguy, whom he had known before the war when, still a couturier, he was already a collector, had bought several of the principal paintings of the Cuttoli collection. The unusually vibrant, voluble, enthusiastic, and clever little man amused him, and he needed to be amused, something Jacqueline was not always happy about. "If people bored him," she said, "he'd cut up, playing toreador . . ." And Braque had said, "Can you imagine me clowning like that poor Pablo? Painting, of course, is a circus, too . . . " But not for him, going back to his Studios and Plows, while Picasso had fun.

Pablo did the poster for a show of seven major contemporary paintings held in Maguy's gallery in 1962. When the dealer broached it to him, he said, "Jacqueline, take him for a walk in the garden." When they got back, he had drawn a large bister-and-black head, and said, "This is your portrait. My gift to you." That was the poster.

"I never went to Kahnweiler's but I know everything he has. I've never been to your place, but know everything you have," he told the ex-couturier. On several occasions he made trades with him, this being how Picasso came to own one of the most moving of Van Gogh's youthful paintings, *The Weaver*. He wanted to trade for a Toulouse-Lautrec of Maguy's, but nothing came of that.

There was talk again of a Picasso museum. An American jazz promoter and art collector, Norman Granz, thought he knew how to arouse public opinion to it and move the officials: he bought space in *L'Express* on October 27, 1970, to publish an open letter to President Georges Pompidou, calling for the creation of the Picasso museum that France simply had to have. He got twenty-seven letters in response, including two in protest; he had expected an avalanche of them, and gave up the fight.

According to Granz, Pablo had been agreeable to the idea, but was not ready to contribute anything until he saw how the plan worked out. Word came from Pompidou's office that the project was under consideration, but no details as to where, how, or by whom. There was some talk that it might be part of the contemporary art complex of the future Beaubourg Center.

In January 1970, Pablo had his three nephews and his niece formally instructed by his Barcelona *notario* Noguera de Guzman that they were to report to Mougins, to discuss their uncle's intention to turn over to the Calle de Montcada museum all the works their mother, Señora Vilato, had preserved, that is, everything that had been in their home since their earliest childhood. His relatives were not especially happy to lose this inheritance which might eventually have had quite considerable value, but his decision was final. By way of consolation, each of them was given one of his paintings.

Two of the nephews, Pablin and Jaime Vilato Ruiz, lived in Barcelona (as did their sister, Lolita, while the third brother, Xavier, a painter, lived in Paris; Fin, also a painter, had died in 1968). Pablo put them in charge of supervising the transfer of the works, under the terms of a grant he signed at Mougins on February 23, one of the most fabulous ever made to a museum.

It included eighty-two oils on canvas, twenty-one on other bases, 681 drawings, pastels, or watercolors on paper, seventeen notebooks or sketchpads, four books with drawings in the margins, and five assorted objects. Among the paintings, fourteen were painted on the backs of others, and 504 drawings had others on their reverse side. The pads were made up of a total of 580 pages with drawings on both sides of the sheet. In addition, there were some paintings by his youthful friends, Pallarés, Julio Gonzalez, Carlos Casagemas, Junyer, and others.

To house all this, the City of Barcelona bought a mansion abutting the one the museum was in: this had belonged to Baron de Castellet and was a fine fourteenth-century building that was part of the series of Gothic structures on Calle de Montcada, with their typical inner courtyards and gallerias with small columns connected by ogival arches.

Everything in the bequest was moved to Calle de Montcada, where the works were inventoried by Juan Ainaud de Lasarte and the museum's curatrix Rosa María Subirana, restored, and photographed. Meanwhile, repair work was done next door to get it ready for exhibition. Once more the Mougins émigré was defying his country's oppressive régime; his presence would be heavy in the city of his youth, center of the resistance to Franco as it had always been the focal point of wrath and rebellion.

The director of the museums of Barcelona made the trip to Mougins to bring Don Pablo photographs of all the works he had donated. It was a bright sunny day, and the painter was at the door waiting for him. He was happy; everything was now as it should be—or not quite, for Claude had had a court order served on him from Grasse, demanding recognition of paternity. Once more Pablo's private life was to be spread in broad daylight, commented on in the papers, as they accused Jacqueline of having kept apart the painter and his children by Françoise. Some said he was completely under her thumb.

Pablo was feeling bitter, deeply hurt by his son's action. "I was not the one who became estranged from Claude," he told his lawyer, Maître Roland Dumas. "He was the one who moved away from me. How could he forget all the tenderness I, and my wife too, always showed him?"

Ainaud de Lasarte's visit cheered him up, although Jacqueline remained very depressed by the suit and the new airing of their private lives. Hundreds of photos were placed on the table by Lasarte, and now Pablo's face changed entirely: gone were the worry and anger of recent days. Here was the past revived in Pablo's adolescent academic paintings that had brought him his first recognition, self-portraits, those of Don José, Doña María, Aunt Pepa, Lola in her radiant youthful beauty, the La Coruña and Madrid paintings, views of the port, Impressionist skies, corners of old Barcelona painted on a thumb box. There were bullfights and cabaret dancers, the friends of Els Quatre Gats, Bohemianism, high hopes, the first Blue canvases, rustic scenes from Horta . . .

Picasso asked his visitor questions about how certain neighborhoods had changed, whether an old friend whose face he saw was still alive. "This," he said in looking at one shot, "was the day my mother absolutely insisted I go to church with her." Then he took another out of the pile: "My father went through this street every day on his way from home to La Lonja. This one and no other street, ever . . ."

Ainaud de Lasarte took the opportunity to ask Picasso to come to Barcelona. "In a beard and wig?" the painter joked. But then, "You can't invite a Spaniard to come to Spain." His mind was made up: he would never go back as long as the régime stayed in power. What if Franco died? He shrugged. "He'll be replaced by another general who may be even stupider."

The youthful works should thus be in Barcelona, but what of the endless canvases at Mougins, La Californie, Vauvenargues, and perhaps elsewhere? There was talk of four or five thousand, not to mention drawings, sketchpads, and such. One day, going into a room where paintings were stacked against the walls back to back, Jacqueline had exclaimed, "*Mon Dieu,* the Valley of the Dead!"

Meanwhile, Claude had lost his suit. The court at Grasse ruled that it could not accede to his petition, since when he was born, Pablo was not divorced from Olga but only legally separated. When their father died, neither he nor Paloma would even be officially informed.

XXVI

"A SLIGHTLY
FABULOUS CHARACTER . . ."
(1971–1973)

ICASSO INVADED THE PALACE OF THE POPES AT AVIGNON AT THE head of a column of more than a hundred men, followed by about thirty women, two dwarfs, two Harlequins and a Pierrot, a certain number of children. several bouquets of flowers, and some fruit.

The communiqué to this effect "for immediate release" dated May 1, 1970, was signed by the Andalusian Spanish poet Rafael Alberti, who had met Pablo a few years before World War II, at Charles Dullin's Théâtre de l'Atelier, in Montmartre, where the actor-manager was staging *Rosalinde,* a Jules Supervielle adaptation of *As You Like It.*

Now, thirty-five years after that first encounter, the "Wandering Spaniard," as Alberti called himself, was saluting his fellow exile from Franco Spain, as the latter led his strange cortège in a triumphal entry into Clement VI's huge chapel and the other halls of the forbidding but majestic edifice overlooking the Rhône. A second communiqué followed, the same day:

> Just as the first column was invading the Palace of the Popes, a second column, no less daring or determined, led by the same Picasso, seized the Palace's sacristy and set up quarters in it. It was made up of a more mixed and less disciplined lot, some eighty-six in number . . .

The assault had its inception in October 1969 on the terrace adjoining the Mougins studio: Picasso was showing his friends his most recent paintings. Yvonne and Christian Zervos were among those present, and all were speechless before the powerful expressiveness of the figures that flashed before their eyes like the frames of a speeded-up movie. Time had suddenly been abolished by the plethora of inventiveness they had seen unreeling. Yvonne immediately thought of Avignon, where in 1947 she had put on a first great art exhibit away from Paris, intended as decentralization. She could just see his Musketeers, Smokers, and Nudes on the walls of Clement's chapel.

When she discussed it with Jean Vilar, who staged the theatrical presentations there, he was immediately enthusiastic; all that remained was to convince the State and the Historical Monuments Service, who had to agree, the city government, always favorable to anything like this, and—a different kind of problem—Pablo himself.

When all else was set, the Zervoses returned to Mougins to photograph the paintings for the next volume of their *catalogue raisonné*. Pablo supervised the operation, with his usual watchful look as he put a finger up to his left temple. Alberti was also there, with his wife and daughters. "We were fascinated and the absolute silence was interrupted only by comments from Picasso or the comings and goings of Jacqueline," as she brought assorted drinks for the various guests, Alberti wrote,* and for Pablo filipendula tea (of which he was taking several cups a day on doctor's orders).

Waiting for the psychological moment (and seconded by Jacqueline), Yvonne Zervos got him to agree on the Avignon exhibition. As usual, he demurred at first, but after gauging what was intended by her, whom he liked very much, he stated he "would not say no." Finally, after endless questions about which pictures would be selected, how and where they would be hung, and the like, he promised anything she wanted. Delighted, Yvonne jumped up and kissed him, as he exclaimed, "I might fill up the whole Palace. The Popes just better watch their step."

A few days later, Vilar and the mayor of Avignon came to Mougins to present their formal thanks. The friendly atmosphere of the whole thing was quite different from what the official retrospective at Paris had been, and those in charge of the Avignon Festival as well as the city government were of his political stripe, which sat very well with Picasso.

For Avignon he selected sixty-five paintings and forty-five drawings of the January 1969–February 1970 period, but Yvonne Zervos never lived to see the striking collection, having died of cancer January 20, 1970. Her husband carried on for her, but he also was too ill to attend the opening. Friends and notables called on him instead at the Hôtel de l'Europe, paying tribute to his late wife as well as him. Christian Zervos survived her by only eight months, dying in turn of a heart attack on September 12, in their Paris apartment on Rue de Bac.

A prodigious clamor of shapes and colors, a shooting gallery of a thousand heads, arms, legs, bellies, genitals invaded the pontifical Palace at Avignon: painting unleashed in broad brushstrokes laid on like whiplashes or slaps, the most insolent of inventiveness, and the most romantic as well, for endless tales, whose outcomes we would never know, were suggested in the shocking or racy improvisations . . .

This was the great Picassian panoply. Nothing in common with the half-didactic, half-synthetic retrospectives previously put on; here the river untamed by history flowed freely with all its refuse, its flotsam and jetsam, beating against the walls, assaulting the crowds, and spilling out beyond the Palace. A year of his daily work, a year of Don Pablo's life: Jean Vilar in his presentation re-

---

* Rafael Alberti, *Picasso en Avignon* (Picasso at Avignon), Paris, 1971.

marks did not omit the fact that the opening was being held on May Day, the Celebration of Labor. Respecting neither night nor day, Sundays nor holidays, Pablo's unbelievable vitality in work remained a challenge to time itself.

Simultaneism, all that was left of Cubism in its creator's works, was in full swing. Each character was multiplied out through what it was, what it represented, what connotations it evoked. Not only because of their physical aspects, in which they could be seen from several angles at once, but because the anatomical arbitrariness gave birth to all kinds of visions, in series or parallel. This arbitrariness is situated in an extraordinarily playful context; the characters, nude or clothed, alone, in couples or in groups, live with an intense, warm, lusty, delectable life . . .

The series of Kisses is a brilliant illustration of this. Fifteen faces of men and women, mouth to mouth, distorted, drawn out, or swollen. Popping eyes, greedy lips, red, full or pinched, moist or shy, insolent mustaches, hands that grasp the opposing rump or breasts . . . A whole repertoire of sweet puckers, labial suckers, meldings of noses and eyes, she and he conjoined, their ample salivation allowing us to divine the rest which the picture does not show—the height of the embrace, the paroxysm of desire, the wild passion that turns the couple into a single magma of lovers devouring, consuming one another, each swallowing the other through the oral aperture, that sexual receptacle in its own right.

But Avignon was not Kisses alone; there were also Pipe Smokers, Smoker with Love, Smoker and Child, Squatting Women, Nude Men and Women, Women with Bird, Couples, Busts of Men, Heads of Men, Seated Men, Man with Beard, Man with Laurels, Painter and Child, Painter and Model, Harlequin, Pierrot and Harlequin, Man in Helmet, Man with Sword, Man with Sword and Flower, and on and on—to say nothing of the black or color crayon drawings, the washes, charcoals, and inks displayed in the sacristy of the Popes, whose walls carried scenes that the most diabolical of deacons would never have dared dream in his tormented nights.

Avignon drew crowds; Barcelona's work went on; and Málaga was holding a minifestival for its "glorious son." Don José's ungrateful child seemed quite to have forgotten his native city; but it now had hopes that, in exchange, it might inherit his library. Avignon was a lesson less in painting than in liberty. Were not liberty, improvisation of hand and word criteria of aesthetic judgment? And would they withstand the passage of time as well as do patient research and depth of probing? He had asked himself a few years before, "Will it hold up?"

Now he was almost ninety: still parading, the multicolored musketeers with rapiers or muskets; still reclining, the beautiful pink and blond nude women with alluring contortions, the couples coupling, or who having just done so now appear in the shape of an enormous phallus; still pushing and shoving, the Harlequins, the Painters, the men lasciviously holding on their laps girls with large flabby breasts and plenty of bush in the proper spots, the apes, the whores . . . and everywhere and always coming back, imposing itself, offering itself, the vulva, fringed with lightly curling down, the gaping earmark of the whole ballet . . .

Now to Mougins came Albert Skira, reminding him that it was forty years since, as an unknown still putative publisher, he had asked him to illustrate Ovid's *Metamorphoses*. "So, for your ninetieth birthday, I want to do an album called *Picasso's Metamorphoses.*" And he asked the painter himself to select an author. Pablo named Jean Leymarie.

This was no longer a time for gossip and keyhole peeking, but a time for summing up, and none was more equipped than he to do that for the subject's life and work—or rather to afford the works themselves, through their endless manifestations, an opportunity to recount the existence of one whose unparalleled fertility had already covered more than thirty thousand days. The director of the Musée d'Art moderne felt all he could contribute was a simple introduction, and when the book came out in 1971 it was called *Picasso, métamorphoses et unité* (Metamorphoses and Unity of Picasso).

There were all the memories that came back. With each friend Pablo spoke to, new stories would pop up; each object found in his studio, each painting, drawing, book was food for thought or anecdote. Going through a copy of Douglas Cooper's *Picasso Théâtre* with Brassaï, and seeing a picture of Erik Satie, he was reminded of the composer with his goatee and ever-present umbrella, penniless and walking in from Arcueil, where he lived in a tiny apartment no one had ever seen. One day, when the Princesse de Polignac had made him a donation of a thousand francs, he had ceremoniously informed her, "My poor lady, your thousand francs did not fall on deaf ears . . ." And Pablo burst out laughing.

Then a quick good-bye, and back to work. Someone had just phoned, and Miguel once more had said, "The master is not in" (or asleep, or working).

"If I saw every person who asked to see me for just ten minutes, it would take till midnight every day," Picasso said. "It's the same for the mail; I can't read it all . . . I wouldn't have a minute left."

Jacqueline and Don Miguel took care of his secretarial chores, and when someone tried to tell him how Dubuffet handled his, he commented, "Dubuffet doesn't like me! Anyway, Paulhan created him!"

In Madrid, Luis González de Robles, director of the Museum of Contemporary Art that was being built, pointed a finger to a spot on the plan for the huge building: in the center was a large room, the heart of the complex, the place of honor, and in it the daring director planned one day to set up a work whose name was on every tongue: "In the heart of Spain, the heart of Madrid, *Guernica* will be a beacon for the whole world to see!" said Señor de Robles.

A few months earlier, Picasso's Barcelona *notario*, Señor Noguera de Guzman, had met with representatives of the New York Museum of Modern Art, and had let it be understood that the painter, who still owned the painting on deposit with that museum, might not oppose its return to Spain. The Spanish authorities, apparently, were suddenly turning liberal: everything that had to do with the Civil War was now a matter of history, above and beyond hatred and controversy!

Before permitting Señor de Robles to make his plan public, the National Director of Fine Arts, Señor Florentino Peréz, had respectfully sought the opinion of Franco, and the Caudillo had warmly concurred that the work belonged in Madrid. Generally speaking, Spain alleged to be most concerned for the welfare of its illustrious nationals living abroad (never referred to as "exiles")—in the case of Picasso, who had been so generous to the Barcelona Museum, the concern was more than warranted.

On December 3, 1970, a *sumariossimo* (most sumary) court-martial in Burgos, judging sixteen members of the Basque autonomist ETA movement, condemned six to death and gave the others terms totaling more than seven hundred years in prison. Demonstrations followed in Barcelona (three thousand people denouncing the régime), Madrid (with shouts of "Liberty" answering those of "Murderer Franco"), Paris, Lyons, Brussels, Rome, London, and throughout Europe and the world.

Not one Spaniard living abroad failed to share the revulsion of his compatriots, and all free people, at the régime's tyranny. Three hundred Catalan artists and intellectuals locked themselves into the Monastery of Montserrat, above Barcelona, a high place of the spiritual resistance to Franco. Painters such as Miró and Tápies, writers Ana María Mature and Terenci Noix, Dean of the College of Architects José María Farges, the architect Oriol Bohigas, academics, men of letters, vaudeville artistes, painters, musicians, poets, and many religious joined in thus expressing their indignation. They were to leave only after three days, when the police threatened to raid the monastery, so as to avoid its being damaged. Their exit took the shape of an amazingly dignified and quietly courageous cortège between two rows of cops armed with submachine guns, while the bells tolled for Spain . . .

The voluntary recluses of Montserrat published a manifesto denouncing the death penalty and demanding amnesty for all political prisoners. The Burgos Six awaited their fate.

Friday, December 18, was to be a great day in Barcelona: the magnificent Picasso gift to the museum was to be unveiled. But the painter had Señor Noguera de Guzman read a letter to the Montserrat protesters, and then send it to the City Council and Museum Director Juan Ainaud de Lasarte, asking that no ceremony be held and his friends not attend the Calle de Montcada show that day. He prevailed: there was no formal unveiling, and the posters for the *Donativo Pablo Picasso 1970* were not posted on city walls.

While Rafael Alberti, from Rome, was writing of the Burgos Six as "nails in Franco's coffin," Picasso with one stroke blasted Spain's hopes concerning *Guernica:* he signed an agreement with the Museum of Modern Art of New York leaving the masterwork there subject to conditions the Museum still does not feel authorized to disclose.

On January 2, in response to worldwide protest, but more especially, it was said, pressure from the Pope, Franco commuted the six death sentences.

Picasso had always been friendly and well disposed toward the photographer Lucien Clergue, whom Cocteau had introduced to him. A native of Arles, Clergue had done beautiful photographs of nude women in the water, shoulders and breasts dripping, dead birds half-devoured or buried in the sands of the Camargue, bullfights, and Pablo himself. He was also the manager of Manitas de Plata, the famous untutored guitarist, whose flamencos, fandangos, and malagueñas moved Picasso beyond words.

Clergue asked the painter to cooperate in a plan he had already discussed with the director of the Reattu Museum at Arles: a Summer 1971 show of his recent works. Arles had figured in Picasso's life, the city having feted him when he attended its many wild corridas, and in 1957 he had generously lent thirty-eight of his best works to a show of his drawings at the museum.

Picasso was not unreceptive, and on a warm afternoon in March Clergue brought the museum director, Jean-Maurice Rouquette, an archaeologist by training, to see him. The two, taking turns at being persuasive, ambitious, and cordial, left without a firm promise—but without a rejection, either.

Two months later, on the evening of May 24, Rouquette's phone rang at Arles. Picasso was on the wire, asking him to come to Mougins at once: "There's good news for you . . ." He was there the next day, even hotter than March had been, and the portly Provençal was perspiring—less with the heat than over the "good news" awaiting him. Pablo came right to the point: "I didn't bring you here for nothing. I have a good idea for your exhibit." And out came three cartons of drawings, bulging with pregnant promise.

As the overwhelmed Rouquette soaked handkerchief after handkerchief wiping his forehead, Pablo paraded the pictures: heads, nudes, couples, musketeers, painters, pianists, Harlequins, Pierrots, clowns, guitarists, and so on, all done in the past few months. "See what I've done for your show," he exulted.

How to choose among the hundreds of drawings? Picasso himself undertook to make the selection, with Jacqueline, and after much thought decided on fifty-seven pieces done between December 31, 1970, and February 4, 1971. Most were done on both sides of white or tinted cardboards, with ink, pencil, and wash mixing together, as well as at times colored chalks. On the back of one, dated February 3, 1971, and showing a painter at his easel, Pablo had written "Somewhat Matisse," for he did indeed look not unlike his late great painter friend.

Running through the whole batch, Picasso added nonchalantly to Rouquette that he would make a present of them to the Reattu Museum, "if that's what you would like."

Thus did the museum at Arles, set in the former priory of the Order of Malta, overlooking the Rhône in the pure light of river and sky, come in the summer of 1971, when Pablo Picasso was turning ninety, to welcome a selection of drawings that most great museums would have bid their weight in gold for. When the curator left Mougins with his booty, after having warmly thanked the painter, Pablo merely clapped him on the back and said, "Well, there's a good day's work!"

A new flare-up of engravings began in January 1970 to continue into May, with the next to start in February 1971. He was working so hard at the engravings that he scared even himself. "The other night," he told a friend, "I read that the price of copper in London, or somewhere, had gone down. So I got hold of Crommelinck and woke him—because the way I consume it . . . !"

He was drawing woman, women, Woman, Women—always and forever, plump, tempting, available, the painter recording and the voyeur watching.

Dancing, arms behind her neck, lying down, her breasts tense, mouth moist, thighs spread . . . Inviting the man, but strangely he was reluctant to accept the invitations . . . No more couples, nor copulations for such a long time now in his drawings and plates. There were women swooning with passion because passion kept them waiting and drove them crazy with unfulfilled desires . . . But neither musketeer, nor painter, nor any of the Johns seemed ready to indulge, despite the pressing offers of the ladies . . . So they had to give one another satisfaction, which seemed fantastically to upset the painter, who distorted them, disjointed them, stretched out their limbs, crushed them, broke them, rolled and unrolled them in heavy complicated body movements, as in the etching of March 5, 1971 . . .

Darkly or shiningly beautiful, yet always enigmatic, there was Jacqueline—the legitimized Sphinx, part of his great age and his approaching posthumous existence, who watched vigilantly over the obsessive formulations of desire bathing that erotic sequence of Spring 1971: there when needed, as needed, but outside the oeuvre of which she once occupied the principal place. And this absence is surprising, as if Jacqueline had suddenly ceased to be a part of his universe, as if the master had repudiated her . . . or she herself had put a distance between her and the closing solitude.

A strange phenomenon which has called forth many interpretations, it is best left to be the enigma it is.

One day in May 1971, he told Brassaï he wanted to show him something and, as the photographer tells it, "He disappeared into his cave and brought me back a sumptuously framed Degas monotype, a slave in a whorehouse. *'The Madam's Birthday,* a masterpiece, don't you think? Well, you see, I've based a series of etchings on it that I'm working on right now . . .'"

Picasso had eleven brothel monotypes by Degas, six of which he had bought from the London Lefevre Gallery in April–May 1958; he loved them and showed them to his visitors often, saying that Degas "never did better work."

Besides his penchant for the subjects—was not *Les Demoiselles d'Avignon* a whorehouse scene?—Pablo appreciated the "love of craft" aspect of Degas's work, for he can be said to have invented the monotype, having known nothing of its technique before experimenting with it in the shop of the copperplate printer who printed his engravings.

What concerned Degas was to get true attitudes and gestures; his eye was a recording instrument, and it would be quite a trick to detect his presence in those scenes that are neither risqué nor low-down, without the slightest eroticism. Nor any trace of enjoyment, either, for the ladies in question are monstrous matrons lacking the slightest allure, confoundingly vulgar in the way they toss their repulsive endowments at you.

Only, *The Madam's Birthday* is a ceremonial, almost sacred.

Is there a voyeur or a seer here? Hard to say. The lament of impotence runs through these joyless, spiceless episodes, whose sadly mechanical liturgy awakens in Degas neither desire nor pity. In Picasso, it's something else again: thirteen years after he got those six monotypes, the etchings based on them (March–June 1971) show us Degas, wearing his suit jacket, hands behind his back, watching the extraordinary metamorphoses Picasso's inventiveness puts the whorehouse scenes through. He is there, watching, showing no emotion whatever before this debauch of nudities which, turning Picassian, have become veritable disjointed, deformed female monsters. Outrageously made up, breasts superpendulous, buttocks brazen, displaying themselves in stag-party poses, the ladies are no longer waiting for the customer, but luring him on: their vulvas yawn with impatience in their settings.

Monsieur Degas watches, and can't get over it. The girls can't expect much from him. As he leans against a wall, his eye takes it all in; Picasso's lays bare the obscene carnival, the low-down fete in which everything is too much, from the outsize female anatomies to the vulgar exhibitionism of their poses.

Monsieur Degas draws. Once. He then sits (*Degas Seated,* March 15, 1971), gets up (*Degas Standing,* same date), but then stops sitting or drawing: he is just there.

Streaked with scars or lacerated with arabesques, the ladies of the evening find no takers—which is probably what makes them nervous. Their faces, profiles and full faces combined or conjoined, are repulsive to look at, and they have deformed fingers at the ends of their fatty little rubber arms. These often stray to their genitals, caressing them, opening the labia, twisting the fuzz, spreading the thighs as wide as possible so as to display the most of that sinister orifice, obsessive in the emptiness through which pleasure comes, no longer anything like the "rose and black jewel" dear to Baudelaire.

Monsieur Degas, being modest, looks away.

Is his round eye amazed at seeing the women turned so brutally repulsive? Or at what Picasso is doing to them? This nightmare display does more than arouse the Malagueño's sadistic cruelty; it provokes his ire. Love, now, has been reduced to that: creatures with gaping cracks whose love-for-money Saturnalia, on the madam's birthday, have been transformed into filial put-ons. Corseted, made up, powdered, perfumed, and flowered, the demoiselles rub so closely and effectively against the boss-idol that she dissolves into a shapeless magma—after which they pleasure one another, this being their last resort, for want of custom.

The unexhibited plates held the same leitmotiv: the obsession of the vulva, the impotence of the man. This twin preoccupation began getting desperate or frantic, as evidenced by the violence of the drypoint, the dark depth of the blacks. A seismograph of man, his anguish, his anger, his regrets, Picasso's line is incomparably strong; the ideas that screw hauntingly into the old man suddenly emerge from the shadows, his dark being reveals what is attacking it and leading it on, laying bare his phantasms in the loneliness to which the weaknesses of age have finally condemned him beside a beautiful young woman equally open to temptation.

He showed some friends the erotic scenes he had just cut. Without acrimoniousness. But with a kind of weariness many of his visitors notice, as he hides it with jokes or anecdotes the sycophants pathetically laugh at. Parading the ladies of the house at their sex play, he might comment, as he did before one especially daring graphic:

"When I see a friend, my first impulse is to put my hand in my pocket to offer him a cigarette, as in olden days. But I know we don't smoke anymore. Even though age makes us give up certain things, the desire stays on. The same with love. We may not make it anymore, but the desire's there. We put our hands in our pockets."

Some of the deliberately obscene plates were never even to leave Mougins, and Jacqueline asked him not to show them to his friends.

Every day some show of his work was announcd somewhere in the world, papers and magazines talked about him, doing articles on his life, his health, his wife, his relations with Spain. Books appeared about his oeuvre. He was more and more detached, seeing fewer and fewer visitors. He took some phone calls and enjoyed them, joking about his coming "centennial," next October 25, when he would reach ninety. But only to say he would accept nothing, take part in nothing, see no one. He was more bitter than ever about the way officialdom treated him; losing his Rue des Grands-Augustins studio was a heartbreak like the death of a loved one.

He is not easy to understand, and can be difficult if not revolting. One day, on the point of writing a condolence note to a friend whose wife had died, he simply decided not to: "He'll have to understand I live as I paint." That is, in full freedom, indifferent to others, wildly, cruelly egocentric. Now that he no longer had *l'amour,* what good was friendship? He liked to quote his father, "I like my friends best when they are leaving," and said to Brassaï, "All that interests me is creating.".

More troubles with the law: now he wanted to add a floor to his studio at Notre-Dame-de-Vie, to have a workplace that looked out on the Bay of Cannes and the Estérel, but his request was denied. Mougins had wanted to grant it, hoping he would switch some of his generosity from his former "hometown" of Vallauris to his present place of residence, but when the architect of the *département* vetoed his request, their hopes went glimmering. And Picasso fumed that no one in Paris came to his defense.

In February 1971, Don Pablo gave the New York Museum of Modern Art a metal sculpture done in 1912: *Guitar,* which had been shown at the Petit Palais retrospective of 1966; and a year later gave it the large 1930 *Wire Construction* that had been intended for the Apollinaire monument; it too had been part of the Petit Palais show.

"Picasso—Know Him?" was the title that, taking over where officialdom fell down, the French Association of Art and Experiment, Construction and Humanism, in conjunction with France 2000, gave to a show it organized in the buildings of the Halles de Baltard, about to be demolished. An audiovisual presentation of his oeuvre, it used ten screens in a semicircle to display his works before the eyes of a fascinated audience. Children were delighted and clapped their hands at the strange and violent kaleidoscope. And perhaps that was now the best way to display him: eternally young in his fabulous continuous creation. Picasso presented to the masses in this exploded space, entirely occupied and transcended by his genius, was the real one; this technique that allowed all the antagonistic or complementary aspects of an object to be seen at the same time was actually just the principle of Cubism set into motion.

The breakdown of *Guernica* that Resnais had attempted in his film here became actual fact. Sartre had once said that the movement that disintegrated that tragic page was the jerky, explosive movement of a bombing, whose effects sent the houses it hit flying in all directions, while the inhabitants fled, torn by strafing. Picasso's pulverized style on the Halles's multiple screens took on truly epic proportions.

On April 23, 1971, the Galerie Louise Leiris unveiled a fantastic and disconcerting show of 194 drawings, done in black, ink or wash, or colored chalks and crayons on cardboard, between December 15, 1969, and January 12, 1971, among hundreds of others.

More sprightly than ever, wearing a mackinaw and checked trousers, Picasso, with Jacqueline and lawyer Dumas, the latter headed for Paris, appeared at Nice Airport. Immediately, word got around, and the crowd surrounded him. By some mysterious method, reporters and photographers were there in just a few minutes: the chances of seeing the master were so infrequent . . . Smiling, he told them, "If I'd known you would be here, I'd have dressed more decently."

One reporter asked whether there was any truth to the report in a Spanish paper that he was going to attend a bullfight in Mallorca on June 10, to which Pablo categorically replied:

"Periodically, they say I'm coming there. It's untrue. For bullfights or vernissages, I·won't ever go to Spain, at least so long as my native country is under the domination of the Franco régime.

"Besides, I am overburdened with work. I don't have a single second to spare, and can't think of anything else. Every night I stay in the studio until very late."

That was true. He often worked late at night, but also all day, for Spring 1971, especially the month of March, was very fruitful. April slowed a bit, while May and June saw more engravings again; and unlike other years, he was painting and drawing copiously as he continued the graphics.

Early in April, while doing his "erotica," he painted a series of heads violently constructed with broad hasty brushstrokes, so roughly improvised that at times he failed to cover all of the canvas. The barbaric cacophonies seem so slapdash and haphazard as often to be upsetting or off-putting; his brush hand seemed to be wandering loosely, while in the engravings he still showed his incomparable sure-handedness. Nothing rushed on the copperplate; there seemed to be no haste to be done here as with the paintings: he was rather working in depth, from proofs and counterproofs, giving blanket coverage of the subject, overlooking nothing. No improvisation, but a patient exploration of his theme, following one idea through a whole series of plates—whereas in the paintings each canvas, even if part of a "sequence," remains autonomous.

Was he about to become part of order, of history? For his ninetieth birthday, the French government finally decided to devote the Louvre's Grand Gallery to eight Picassos belonging to the national museums. The selection was left to Jean Leymarie, who created a "symbolic" presentation of the painter, strangely bypassing everything that was subversive, audacious, or challenging in his work, that is, the creative period of Cubism and the paper paste-ups. The greatest pictorial revolution of the twentieth century was absent from the walls of the Louvre where its maker was being celebrated! That was not the least paradox of this official tribute.

In order to make room for Picasso, several eighteenth-century French works, occupying the "tribune of honor" in the Grand Gallery, were removed for ten days, and admission to the Louvre and other French museums showing Picassos was free. The President of the Republic, M. Georges Pompidou, unveiled the exhibition, saying that Picasso was "a volcano . . . Whether he is painting a woman's face or a Harlequin, there is always the same explosion of youthfulness."

But the Louvre showed no eruptions of the Picasso volcano, preferring his quiet periods.

Paris' elected officials named him an "honorary citizen," opting for this nod rather than a monument.

While the Louvre show was being unveiled, Don Pablo was home in bed at Mougins, reading the papers and his mail, resting after the night's work. He was pushing ahead, regardless of official or other tributes to his "centennial." The time of popular demonstrations was over, and he did not have happy memories of his eightieth birthday's festivities.

The new Minister for Cultural Affairs, Jacques Duhamel, had written him about what the government was doing; and Pablo knew that equally prestigious celebrations around the world marked his birthday and the unbelievable vitality of an oeuvre that dominated a whole century. While young artists queried by newspapers recognized its importance, they added that it offered them nothing. Julio Le Parc saw it as "one of the myths useful to the dominant ideology." Benrath called it "a sumptuous decadence." "The Greek inheritance ended with Picasso, who tops off the massacre. Duchamp is much more relevant at the moment," said Télémaque.

Martial Raysse declared that "Picasso confused creation with the pleasure of painting. Duchamp and Mondrian were the ones who persevered on the path of invention."

Before the works exposed in the Grand Gallery, M. Pompidou had paid tribute to Kahnweiler, who said, "From the very start, from the *Demoiselles d'Avignon,* I knew that paintings such as these must one day end in the Louvre." This was the exact truth; the onetime Rue Vignon dealer was the only one who had fully appreciated Picasso's genius, without reserve, the first time he laid eyes on his work—sixty-four years before.

When the President of the Republic was leaving the Louvre, a reporter asked whether he thought a Picasso museum might be created. "I would be happy to see such a museum," M. Pompidou replied; immediately adding "but what would we fill it with?"

Notre-Dame-de-Vie was continually surrounded by sightseers, and since the neighboring land was being subdivided, Picasso had to swear out a warrant to keep the work being done from totally blocking access to his home by its principal approach road. The matter was settled out of court, but the situation remained awkward.

For Pablo's ninetieth birthday, Vallauris set up a podium on the square facing the *Man with the Sheep,* but the painter, who had promised to come with Jacqueline to see the singing and dancing staged there, did not make it. All day, his arrival was anticipated, in vain. His home remained shuttered and the phone was turned off. Roland Leroy, sent specially from Paris with a Communist Party delegation, was turned away.

On the morning of October 25, 1971, workers and students of the underground Spanish Communist Party distributed leaflets on the streets of Madrid, reading "Picasso, whom the Republic named Curator of the Prado . . . and who will be able to return to Spain only with democracy, admirably portrayed the collective terror of Fascism." At eight o'clock that same evening, a tribute to Picasso was to take place at the Faculty of Biology, the art critic Carlos Areal scheduled to lecture. For the first time since the Civil War, the government had instructed teachers and students throughout the peninsula to celebrate Picasso. Schoolchildren were encouraged to write him congratulatory cards, asking him "to come back home to visit"!

A few minutes before the lecture was to start, the Minister of the Interior banned it. A thousand students had gathered outside the college. The same shouts of "Picasso! Freedom!" that had greeted Éluard's talk in Barcelona thirty-five years before arose from the crowd. Standing on a café table, the critic José Moreno Galvan began to speak, explaining why the painter had stayed outside the country and joined the Communist Party. The police demanded the students leave immediately.

"Let us go peacefully," Moreno Galvan urged, "toward Avenida Complutence and proclaim that henceforth it be known as Avenida Pablo Picasso!"

But they did not disperse fast enough, and the police charged, slugging the students and arresting five of them along with Moreno Galvan, who was jailed in the Carabanchel to await trial for obstructing public order.

The performers at a famous Madrid flamenco cabaret had decided that on that evening their show would honor Picasso, all their songs to be taped and sent him as a birthday present. The police seized the recorder; the painter Eusebio Sempere arrived on the scene to tell of the Franco forces beating the students outside the Faculty, and was immediately hauled off to jail.

The City of Málaga organized a celebration for the man born ninety years before in the big house on Plaza de la Merced. It was decided that a statue by sculptor Berrocal would be put up in his honor and a painting by his father,

Don José, formally presented to the painter by a delegation from the city. At La Coruña, a literary evening marked the occasion. In Barcelona, a dinner of honor was given by the weekly *Mundo,* with the mayor presiding, and a congratulatory telegram was sent to Picasso, terming him "Outstanding Spaniard of 1971."

Morena Galvan and Sempere were still in prison.

On October 28, the Paris Musée national d'Art moderne opened a show of twenty-five key works from Picasso's earliest days and the first Cubist period on loan from Leningrad's Hermitage and Moscow's Pushkin museums. That double-barreled show dwarfed the presentation of eight canvases at the Louvre, which mercifully closed three days later: it presented the major works of the great formal innovator Picasso had been when he created Cubism and opened the way to the principal pictorial revolution of the twentieth century, which had engendered all of modern art.

While the Blue and Rose Periods were represented by canvases as famous as the *Two Saltimbanques* (1901), *Old Jew* (1903), and *Little Girl with Ball* (1905), the no-less-famous *Nude with Drapery* contemporaneous with *Les Demoiselles d'Avignon,* a key work of the "Negro" period, the *Fruit Dish with Pears,* the sculptural *Farm Woman* with its rough impressive volumes squared off as if by hatchet strokes, *Queen Isabeau* and *Lady with Fan* (both 1909) affirmed the great formal constants of Cubism, along with several still lifes of 1912–1913. All of these deserved to be in the Louvre.

Like any good Spaniard, he would eschew leaving a will. When Dominguín wondered whether he ought not to give up bullfighting, Pablo said, "Luis-Miguel, you might get killed by a bull. But what better could you expect? And what could I want more than to drop dead while painting? When a man knows how to do something, he ceases being a man if he stops doing it. That's why, Luis-Miguel, you have to go back into the bullring, and die the best death possible."

Pablo never left his bullring.

Some visitors noted he seemed sad, depressed, or worried, while others insisted he was still "in top shape." There were not many, mainly because his wife tried to give him as much quiet as possible. Without interruptions, he could concentrate on his work. Ever superstitious, he felt that painting protected him; pictures were his amulets, exorcising the ineluctable.

On November 5, 1971, a right-wing mob calling themselves "Los Guerrilleros de Cristo Rey" destroyed twenty-four of the "Vollard Suite" plates in a Madrid gallery. A few days later a small exhibition hall in Barcelona, which was named Picasso Studio—having only his name, but none of his works on display—was burned down by an anti-Marxist group, as was the Cinc d'Oros bookstore, which had works on Picasso and Neruda in its windows.

The booksellers' association protested, but the goal was achieved—books on Picasso were withdrawn from display and the various tributes scheduled in one place or another canceled or banned, to "protect public order." So were a series of lectures planned by Josep Palau.

The latter had authored a play, depicting scenes of the life and work of Pablo, which was given for three months, October 1971–January 1972, in a small room of an eccentric Barcelona cabaret, La Cova del Drac. Using only three actors, and admirably staged, it was immensely evocative and met with huge success; the censors had cut only one line, dealing with the bombing of Guernica, one of the uncompromising high points of the presentation.

As long as it was played only in this out-of-the-way place, to few people at high prices and late at night, away from the workers' districts, it met with no objection. But when it was announced that it would be performed for general audiences at the Poliorama on the Ramblas, that was another story. Three hours before curtain time, on direct orders from Madrid, the show was closed—without explanation or possibility of appeal. The tour through Catalonia and several cities elsewhere in Spain had to be dropped. Palau's text, on the eve of publication, had two essential parts cut out: everything that referred to the martyr town of Guernica, and the sequence on *War* and *Peace* at Vallauris. The publishers protested the censorship, but got nowhere.

The Louise Leiris Gallery, on December 1, 1972, presented 172 caustic, humorous, parodic, violent drawings; then, on January 24, 1973, another show of the engraved erotic series, notably those inspired by the Degas monotypes. The latest etching was dated March 25, 1972, the most recent drawing August 18, but he had continued working after that.

In everything displayed, or just about, there was the same emblem: female genitalia. They were the obsessive constant of the sequences done in his final years: the escutcheon, the earmark of his old age. At sales, his prints and drawings were bringing higher and higher prices: a pen-and-ink portrait of Dora Maar done in 1941 was to fetch 25,000 francs (over $5,000) in Paris on June 10, 1972; on June 28, a pencil *Nude* of 1903–1904, one of the most sought-after periods, since the works from it are rare, reached 138,000 francs (almost $28,000).

Picasso prints had generally gone up about 50 percent in three years, and would rise even more after his death. High prices were also reached by the sculptures: almost 450,000 Swiss francs (some $105,000) at Geneva, June 12, 1970, for the *Jester's Head* done in 1905. The paintings were climbing just as fast: on October 25, 1972, *The Drawing Lesson* was sold in New York for $280,000, while on November 13 in Paris 360,000 francs ($72,000) was paid for the 1962 canvas, *Woman with Afghan Hound*. A month before he died, March 11, 1973, *Young Girl in Green* (Málaga, 1897) brought 155,000 francs (over $31,000).

In the work he was still doing, a monumental head filled a whole sheet of paper on June 30, 1972: it is troubling through the panicky expression the face done in green color crayons reflects, its eyes staring wide, its features drawn, its mouth bitter, with skinny, drooping, and poorly shaved jowls. Some have called it a self-portrait, and certain features lend credence to this: the fixed, terrified stare seems to see death approaching.

Pablo walked about the huge rooms of Notre-Dame-de-Vie, looked out the big bay windows at the landscape there. Spoke to Jacqueline and friends sitting on the large divan in the vestibule that he called "the station platform," one of the rare pieces of furniture not covered with junk. Petted the dogs. Watched television of an evening.

His robust body had settled and seemed shrunken. Sapone says that in the last months Picasso seemed smaller and smaller to him. Detached as he was from others and the world, so attached was he to his work; often feeling great weariness, but then suddenly catching fire with inventive verve that kept him before a canvas or over a copperplate for hours on end.

Don Pablo was thinking of death, and knew it was thinking of him. He had told Jacqueline and Maître Antebi what to do in case of his demise; but neither asked any questions, knowing that what he did not volunteer was what he did not want to talk about.

Getting up as usual around eleven-thirty or noon, he would go out on the balcony in his robe, and Miguel, saying it was a fine day, would ask whether he had slept well. "Yes," he would reply. "Another day. One more day to the good."

There was no talk of anyone but Picasso at Notre-Dame-de-Vie. Everything was for and about him. Jacqueline was the vestal of today, not the curatrix of the past. If there were none of the children about, it was that they were occupied elsewhere: Maya was married, Claude doing photography in New York, Paloma designing jewelry. Only Paulo came to Mougins once in a while; he was living with an *amie* in Paris and had kept Boisgeloup. His wife, Émilienne, from whom he was separated, and their two children lived very penuriously at Golfe-Juan. Though Picasso adored his grandchildren, Pablito and Marina, he had not seen them in several years and had done nothing to help them: he said that was Paulo's business, not his. (Marina, now a teacher of handicapped children, says her father sent her mother very inadequate support money.)

In January 1973 he agreed to have his recent works shown at the Avignon Palace of the Popes, as had been done three years earlier. Now it became known that he had very secretly come with Jacqueline to see that show and been delighted with the presentation, the dimensions his work took on in the great chapel. For the second exhibition, promising to be even more sensational than the first, he was sending 201 paintings done September 25, 1970–March 1, 1972. Since that date he had kept going with the same themes, in a torrent of life that often reduced human nature to its sexuality in the most animal form. It rang with the wild desire of one who did not hesitate to proclaim, "Each day I do worse"—and delighted in it as if it were his daily drug. His stimulant. His exorcism, as well.

Painting kept him busy all through that winter and the spring of 1973, despite a bad case of grippe that several times kept him in bed for a few days; it did not worry his doctors, who knew his constitution. He also drew a great deal, and as if to check on the dexterity of his fingers he made sketches before the television set, with the sound turned off. The solitude around him seemed intended more to avoid indiscreet reports about life at Notre-Dame-de-Vie than to ward off hypothetical intruders. Whether Pablo wanted this isolation or put up with it matters little, for the main character in this last period of his life was no longer he, but Jacqueline: Jacqueline and painting, and Picasso was not dupe to one or the other.

One outsider described it as an "awful old age": Pablo the aged sovereign flanked by an enigmatic Mme. de Maintenon who never answered the obvious questions that made people wonder. He was working, or so everyone was told. He was working when walking—less and less frequently—in the garden with her. Working when reading newspapers, or seeing a friend. Working also when he slept, got up, or ate. He claimed to be working all the time.

Paulo dropped in at the beginning of March. Rumors were rife a fortnight later that Picasso was ill. One weekly even wrote that he had been admitted to the American Hospital at Neuilly. Several friends phoned Mougins, and Jacqueline reassured them. Pablo had had that grippe during the winter, but was fine now. He was working.

Sunday, April 8, a bulletin on television at 3:00 P.M. announced the death of Pablo Picasso, that morning at eleven-forty.

Crowds of journalists stormed the closed gates at Mougins. A busload of cops arrived to keep the gapers in check, while the old Piedmontese gardener wept behind the fence and said into a proffered microphone: "Every day he walked in the garden. Only yesterday I saw him. I took some anemones and pansies up to him late in the day, because he liked them best. This morning, my wife came out crying: 'Master Picasso is dead.'"

There had been no hint of so sudden an outcome in the days immediately preceding: Pablo had been out driving with Jacqueline just two or three days before. Saturday night, on the eve of his death, he had had his *notaire* Maître Antebi and his wife to dinner. He seemed tired. And he had a bad night after that; he had started gasping for breath. Jacqueline immediately called the family physician, who gave him a sedative shot, and phoned a Parisian cardiologist. When the latter got there, the painter had fallen sleep; he was muttering a sentence from time to time, as if dreaming aloud. All could see the end was near, especially Jacqueline, who foresaw nothing but loneliness ahead.

Her face ravaged by sleeplessness, she stared at the man in bed, with whom one of the most amazing of all human destinies was coming to an end. After a bit, exhausted, she went out. As she related, "Five minutes later, I felt someone behind me in the corridor. I turned, and understood. I did not even hear the doctor say, 'He is dead.'"

The last painting Picasso was working on—having gone back to it several times over a period of weeks—was a *Man with a Sword*.

A short time later, Miguel went to the front gate to tell the persons attracted by the vehicular traffic, and the local reporters standing by, that Pablo Picasso had died of a heart attack as a result of pulmonary edema.

His relatives were the first alerted: son Paulo, Vilato and the Barcelona nephews and nieces, who were requested not to come. Then the spiritual family: Kahnweiler and the Leirises, Mayor Derigon of Vallauris, Maître Antebi, the

Pignons, and the Party. Arias the barber came in to give the body its farewell trim, as Jacqueline covered Pablo with a great black cape.

A few hours later Paulo was there, and came out of Notre-Dame-de-Vie with Maître Antebi to go to the City Hall and record the death with M. Pellegrin, first magistrate of Mougins. As at Vallauris, the latter had flags lowered to half-staff. By this time, all the wire services and radio and TV stations of the world had carried the news.

A light rain began to fall. Cocteau's great friend, Mme. Weisweiler, alighted from a car with her daughter, carrying a bouquet from her garden at St.-Jean-Cap-Ferrat, "flowers from Málaga," as she called them, while at the other end of Spain, the plaque on the house in which Picasso was born had been covered with crepe. Condolences poured in from everywhere.

Young couples, women, children hung bouquets on the gate of the estate, or placed them at the bottom of the wall. The poet Rafael Alberti spoke for the people of Spain:

> The honor of knowing him and loving him was reserved to the people. Picasso had come from them as had the high priest of Hita, as had Cervantes, Lope de Vega, Quevedo, Goya, Machado, García Lorca, his lungs alive with the breath of creation.
> And toward our people he will return . . .

In Madrid, José Moreno Galvan, who had been sentenced to two years in prison for linking Picasso with liberty at a banned meeting the evening of his ninetieth birthday, was not allowed to give a lecture about the late great man, but the Cortes did publish a resolution stating that "while Pablo Ruiz Picasso was never friendly to the régime . . . Spain has lost a genius." The Minister of National Education, the very one who had banned the meeting on October 25, 1971, set his flag at half-mast, and sent a telegram to the family "in the name of Spain," expressing sincerest condolences.

Most newspapers and magazines of the peninsula observed the occasion with extensive illustrated coverage. But Luis Apostus, assistant editor of the conservative Catholic *Ya,* alone dared write about *Guernica* that the painting symbolic of that painful event "has passed into the history of Spain. It does not belong to either of the two sides, even though its creator may have been a militant member of one of them."

What bothered Spaniards most was that France seemed to want to "lay claim" to Picasso. An untactful statement by the novelist Maurice Druon, now Minister for Cultural Affairs, to the effect that "France became the frame in which his aspiration flowered, no doubt because it was where the air of freedom could be breathed," gave some substance to that concern.

The period during which Picasso had lived in France, the first half of the twentieth century, was the one during which geographical and political limits disappeared and artists, breaking out of the narrow outdated frame of city and nation, joined the world. France and Paris in the final analysis played only a secondary part in the spread of a work of art or its creator's reputation, now situated on a planetary scale.

In this evolutionary context, the death of Picasso could have but one logical result: his prices would shoot up, as evidenced in the first sales following the event. In a parallel movement, it was just as logical that the society of cultural consumption should move to gather him in: as early as Fall 1973, Malraux, after being invited to Mougins by Jacqueline, started a book about him.

After Picasso's death, the artists who had been close to him—and they were so few in the last part of his existence—refused to voice a judgment on his art; some of his intimates, usually so verbose, kept still. Alone among those who had known him well, Beaudin made a statement: "From now on, for centuries to come, there will only be great painters." But L'Humanité, which had asked him for the opinion, thought better of it and left it unpublished. Two days after Picasso died, his body was taken to Vauvenargues and placed in the chapel where St. Severin lies. It was five o'clock of a snowy morning; the demesne of Notre-Dame-de-Vie, guarded by gendarmes accompanied by patrolling police dogs, was isolated from the world. Only Luis-Miguel Dominguín had been seen to go by, while a pickup truck brought a wreath of roses, "Tribute from the City of Má-laga."

Comrade Furtseva, Commissar of Culture of the USSR, had sent a telegram of condolences to Roland Leroy, "cultural" member of the Central Committee of the French Communist Party, who went to Vallauris to pay tribute to the deceased but was turned away from the house. The Young Communist Circle of La Celle-St. Cloud was renamed for Pablo Picasso.

Salvador Dali delivered himself of a statement:

> Picasso, who did not have the time to paint, at breakneck speed accomplished painting experiments that would have taken place anyway. But they would have required five hundred or a thousand years. He was the catalyst for everything that was to take place in the history of art. One understands that at such a rate he should not have had time to do more than drafts of his paintings . . .
>
> His excuse was that manually he had very little dexterity. All his sketches were full of spots and corrections. Which did not keep him from admiring finish . . .
>
> Picasso was a genius because he understood everything before anyone else. If the Spanish government wishes to honor him, it will put his picture on its thousand-peseta bills.

At the foot of the stairway leading to the main entrance to the Château of Vauvenargues, on that terrace where Pablo had spent such long hours contemplating "Cézanne's view" of Ste.-Victoire Mountain sharp against the sky, a grave was dug. There Picasso would be laid to rest.

Jacqueline in a long dark cape, her mother and her daughter, Paulo, Miguel the secretary were at the interment. The snow had fallen all night on the Provence countryside. A delegation from the city council of Vauvenargues, at Jacqueline's invitation, was also present. Picasso had sent a negative reply when the mayor had asked for a reproduction of one of his works signed by him to hang in the school; there had been problems when a request had been made for permission to use water from a spring that was on his property. So one might wonder why Pablo was buried at Vauvenargues, which he had not visited in years, and, if he had not so decreed, who made the decision. Jacqueline, it seems, wanted him buried on the Mougins estate, but communal statutes forbid private burial less than thirty-five meters outside the limits of population centers, so Vauvenargues was selected because it stood isolated.

A large 1934 statue that had recently been cast, of a woman holding a vase in her hand, was placed on the tomb. A Spaniard who had climbed a nearby hillock holding the flag of the Spanish Republic unfurled it for a few photographers, who snapped shots showing the tricolor of the former régime flying above Vauvenargues, symbolic of the life and death of Pablo Picasso.

Marie-Thérèse Walter, who had gone to Vauvenargues, was not allowed in; a gendarme and the gardener came out to tell her that inside the château "they were suffering so much that they could not receive her." Maya, Claude, and Paloma were also kept away, and went to the village cemetery to place the flowers they had brought for their father's grave. Jacqueline was trying to keep for her own the dead man who for so long had belonged to the entire world.

"On the lawn the black-bronze *Figure with a Vase*," wrote André Malraux in *Picasso's Mask,* "a guardian spirit, had one arm stretched out—parallel to the ground and against the noonday clouds—to present its offering."

A few days after the funeral, Picasso's son Paulo saw his wife and children, Pablito and Marina, at Golfe-Juan; there was a stormy discussion, obviously involving money; the next day Pablito was found unconscious, having swallowed a containerful of potassium-chloride bleach. He died three months later in a hospital at Antibes, his mother having been forced several times to make it known that she could not pay hospital costs or afford the numerous operations and grafts necessary to try to save him. Shortly before he died, an anonymous Parisian collector had written the young man, offering him a job so that his life might henceforth be "worthy of his grandfather's renown."

Scarcely a month after Picasso's death, his children born out of wedlock, Maya Widmayer and Claude and Paloma Ruiz Picasso, the latter two unmarried, petitioned for appointment of a judicial administrator to draw up a complete inventory of the painter's estate, with competent expert guidance. This was the first step in a long and complex legal fight, since Picasso had left no will or other instructions, except about the donation to the Louvre of a certain number of paintings from his private collection, which was carried out promptly by Jacqueline and Paulo Picasso.

Pablo had foreseen what the settling of his estate would be like, telling a friend, "It will be worse than anyone imagines."

Recognized as "natural children" of the painter by a court decree at Grasse, March 12, 1974, Claude and Paloma, as well as Maya, were thereafter entitled to share their father's legacy with Paulo.

"Bring him the kid with the topper," Picasso had said, the winter before he died, when Paul Puaux, director of the Avignon Festival, had come to Mougins to plan his exhibition there. Jacqueline had brought in an amazing portrait in bister monochrome of a young boy painting, with a slight smile on his lips and a huge hat on his head. The gesture of the hand holding the brush seemed as if

*Marie-Thérèse Walter, at home in Menton in front of
a photograph of Picasso, January 1974*

(LUC JOUBERT)

snapped by a candid camera just as the color was to be apposed on the canvas.

The Young Painter was used as a poster for the Avignon exhibit. An admirable work, of great tenderness, it contrasted with most of the recently dashed-off paintings, which were hurried and disjointed. It is dated April 14, 1972. That day, Picasso did four canvases on the same theme. Contrary to his usual custom, Picasso did not date or sign any of the pictures displayed; he was was not defying time; he was denying it.

The opening, attended by a distraught Paulo, Kahnweiler, and a number of Pablo's friends, took place May 23. The chaotic character of the overall show was disconcerting, like "circus music," as André Masson said. Sexual obsession was present almost everywhere in each of the replicated themes, The Couple, Embraces, and Kisses; to the end, Pablo had remained high priest of the un-leashing of physical love in its cynical, cruel animality. Genitals were now just a sign, a stenographic convention around which the furious bed-sheet encounters swirled with the outpourings of the senses in anarchic ebb and flow. This orgy of painting in estrus had come from the hands of a nonagenarian plunged into the inhuman loneliness of lost virility.

With Picasso dead, the Avignon show was less well received than usual; the customary fawners were silent. "No one can escape the horror of growing old," wrote André Fermigier, "and it is truly moving to see how this man unto his very last days continued his pursuit of the unknown masterpiece, his attempt to get back to his youth in Spain, the women he had loved, his fine torero's outfit." And the London *Sunday Telegraph*'s critic wondered whether the public was interested in anything but the living legend.

Douglas Cooper turned especially violent, urging that this be compared to the final Braques, the final Rembrandts, and averring that Picasso's work had ended ten years earlier, except for the graphics. When a magazine wrote that admirers had been enthusiastic over the paintings, he demanded to know what admirers they had talked to. He had looked long at the pictures, he said, and they were nothing but the incoherent scribblings of a frenetic old man in the antechamber of death . . .

If anything is worse than death, it is the very loss of the means that justify life. Voyeurism, at this stage, became the landing of despair; through his fan-tastic creative drive, Picasso was able to use theatrical tricks, makeup and cos-tuming, in order to survive. He became in turn Musketeer and Toreador, Man with Bird, Flute Player, Man with Vest, Man with Sword, Musician. But where an old, discouraged Rembrandt still found strength enough to laugh before the mirror, there was now nothing but indifference on these clowns' faces; for there was no remission: the show was over, and all these Picassos, all one and the same lone character, slipped imperceptibly away toward a tragic Punch and Judy show . . . Or perhaps, as Fermigier had said, toward raucous, rebellious Spain, the Spain of piebald, piercing *ferias,* bullfights, dances, songs, color, clangor, the Spain of the free happy life Pablo once had known. Toward youth, toward lost love, lost happiness. Now the circle was closing. Never had so fascinating, at once laughable and pathetic, a show been staged at Avignon: when Jacqueline came to visit, she was not able long to put up with the looks she got.

The day of the opening, May 23, 1973, Marie Cuttoli died at Antibes; she was ninety-four.

The Corpse (or *The Entombment*) (1901) from the collection of Edward G. Robinson, was sold by Sotheby in London in July 1973 for the equivalent of $55,000. In October, *Young Man with Bouquet* (1906) brought $720,000 in New York. Two months later, December 5, at Sotheby's in London, *Seated Woman* (1909), one of the capital works of analytical Cubism, broke all records —for the time being—at 340,000 pounds sterling, or roughly $800,000.

The collection of thirty-seven paintings by old masters and contemporary painters left to the French national museums by Picasso presented some problems of display: as has been several times pointed out in print, they are of varying degrees of excellence but by the terms of the donation may not be dispersed; his African sculptures, the witnesses of the first great pictorial revolution of the century, it is expected, will finally go to the Museum of Man. The Château of Vauvenargues may, if Jacqueline has her way, be turned into a "Pablo Picasso House," where near his grave would be on display the works he left as of April 8, 1973. But there is also some discussion of a special museum in Paris.

On February 28, 1974, a man who was held to be deranged used a bomb of red paint to write in capital letters KILL ALL LIES on *Guernica*, exhibited at the New York Museum of Modern Art. The next day, in the fosses of Montjuich, at Barcelona, a young anarchist accused without proof of murder, Salvador Puig Antich, was garroted to death on orders of Francisco Franco.

Over this Goyaesque scene, how can one not see the anger- and anguish-filled gaze of the man who painted *Guernica*, in the name not only of painting but of truth? That gaze still peers out at us with a barely endurable intensity. What can we answer to the question which, on all of his tragic faces, and his own as well, comes burning from the lips about to part? In his lifetime, Picasso asked before his paintings, "Will it hold up?" Dead, his oeuvre continues to live in the perpetual present of creation and goes right on disturbing it.

CHRONOLOGY

1881 October 25: Pablo Ruiz Picasso, son of painter-art teacher José Ruiz Blasco, born at Málaga, Spain.

1882 May 13: Georges Braque born at Argenteuil, France.

1884 June 25: Daniel-Henry Kahnweiler born at Mannheim, Germany. December 15: Lola, Pablo's sister, born at Málaga.

1891 September: family moves to La Coruña.

1895 September: move to Barcelona; enters La Lonja, School of Fine Arts.

1896 April: his *First Communion* shown at Barcelona's Third Fine Arts Exhibition. June/July: family moves to 3 Calle de la Merced; takes studio at 4 Calle de la Plata.

1897 June 12: Els Quatre Gats opens in Barcelona. Shown at the General Fine Arts Exhibition in Madrid, his *Science and Charity* gets honorable mention, then gold medal at Málaga Provincial Exhibition. Fall: to Madrid; enters San Fernando Academy, staying until June 1898.

1898 June: visits Pallarés at Horta, until February 1899.

1899 March/April: first meeting with Jaime Sabartés.

1900 February 1: his portraits exhibited at Els Quatre Gats. May 1: Universal Exposition in Paris, featuring Centennial and Decennial of Contemporary Art, includes *Final Moments*. Fall: leaves for Paris with Casagemas; moves into 49 Rue Gabrielle; meets Catalan dealer Manach. December: return to Barcelona; short stay at Málaga.

1901 Mid-January: to Madrid again. March 10: first issue of *Arte Joven*. April: return to Barcelona. April–May: exhibits at Fine Arts Show in Béziers. June: pastels shown at Sala Parés, Barcelona; goes back to Paris. June 24: Picasso show opens at Vollard Gallery, to favorable Fagus review in *La Revue Blanche;* meets Max Jacob.

1902 Mid-January: return to Barcelona. April 1–15: show at Berthe Weill's. June: group show at same gallery. October: return to Paris, this time with Sebastián Junyer-Vidal. Joint show, with Girieud, Launay, and Pichot, opens at Berthe Weill's (to January 1903). Lives at Hôtel du Maroc, Rue de Seine, then with Max Jacob on Boulevard Voltaire.

1903 Return to Barcelona; studio on Calle Riera de San Juan.

1904 January/February: moves studio to Calle del Comercio. April: Leaves again for Paris, settling at Bateau-Lavoir (to 1909). October 24–November 24: in group show at Berthe Weill's.

1905 Meets Apollinaire, Salmon, Wilhelm Uhde, Gertrude and Leo Stein. Takes up with Fernande Olivier. February 26–March 6: exhibits at Galerie Serrurier, with Gérardin and Trachsel. April: Apollinaire's first Picasso article in the *Revue immoraliste.* Summer: trip to Schoorl, Holland.

1906 Winter: Vollard buys several recent Picassos. March: meets Matisse at the Steins'. May–August: at Gosol with Fernande Olivier.

1907 February 22: Kahnweiler opens his Paris gallery on Rue Vignon. Spring–Summer: paints *Les Demoiselles d'Avignon.* Fall: meets Kahnweiler, on a visit to the Bateau-Lavoir.

1908 March: exhibits portrait and pastel at Toulouse. Meets Russian collector Serge Shchukine. Summer: in La Rue-aux-Bois, outside Paris. November: Braque, rejected by the Salon d'Automne, exhibits at Kahnweiler's; Rousseau banquet held at Pablo's Bateau-Lavoir studio.

1909 First Picasso show in Germany, at Thannhauser Gallery, Munich. Summer: second trip to Horta, this time with Fernande. Fall: moves to 11 Boulevard de Clichy.

1910 Summer: at Cadaqués with Fernande and the Derains; brief hops to Barcelona.

1911 Max Jacob's *Saint Matorel* appears, with Picasso illustrations. April: first Picasso show in New York, at Photo-Secession Gallery. April–June: Cubist room at Salon des Indépendants, without Picasso. Summer: at Céret, with Fernande, the Braques, and Kahnweiler. September 11: is indicted in case of Iberian heads stolen from the Louvre. October–November: Cubist room at the Salon d'Automne, without Picasso.

1912 February: show at Dalmau Gallery, Barcelona. Spring: break with Fernande Olivier; Éva Gouel (Marcelle Humbert) becomes his mistress. Juan Gris paints *Homage to Picasso;* first London Picasso show at Stafford Gallery. March–May: large Cubist participation at Salon des Indépendants, but still no Picasso. Marcel Duchamp paints final version of *Nude Descending a Staircase.* May: with Éva, to Avignon and Céret, joining Braques at Sorgues, June 12. September: return to Paris; move into 202 Boulevard Raspail. Fall: second German show at Thannhauser's. December 18: signs letter-agreement with Kahnweiler.

1913 February 17: Armory Show opens in New York City. Mid-March: return to Céret. Spring: with Éva, moves to 5 *bis* Rue Schoelcher. Late April: to Barcelona for his father's funeral. May: Apollinaire's *Alcools* published, frontispiece by Picasso. Shown at Moderne Galerie, Munich, Neue Galerie, Berlin, Rheinische Kunstsalon, Cologne, and Sezession Galerie, Berlin. June 20: at Céret, with Éva, Max Jacob, Braque, and Gris. July 20: back to Paris with Éva. Summer: his serious illness is covered by the press.

1914 March 2: *Peau de l'Ours* auction in Paris, Picasso's *Acrobats* bringing 11,500 francs. July: with Éva at Avignon, the Braques at Sorgues. August 2: start of World War I. Working at Avignon, 14 Rue St.-Bernard.

1915 February 18: godfather for Max Jacob's baptism. December: Edgar Varèse introduces Cocteau to Pablo. December 14: Éva dies.

1916 February/March: moves to 22 Rue Victor-Hugo, Montrouge. May: Cocteau brings him together with Diaghilev. August: agrees to do *Parade* with Cocteau and Satie. November 19–December 5: in exhibit organized by Cocteau at Salle

Huyghens, Montparnasse. December 31: is one of organizers of banquet for Apollinaire at Palais d'Orléans.

1917 February 17: to Rome with Cocteau, to work on Ballets Russes, where he meets Olga Khoklova, his future wife. End April: returns to Paris. May 18: première of *Parade,* Théâtre du Châtelet, Paris. June: in Barcelona, with Olga, to November. July 12: is feted by Catalan friends at Barcelona banquet. November 10: attends *Parade* opening in Barcelona. Returns to Montrouge with Olga.

1918 January 23–February 15: Picasso-Matisse show at Galerie Paul Guillaume, Paris. April/May: with Olga, moves into Hôtel Lutétia, Paris. May 2: witness at Apollinaire's wedding. July 12: marries Olga at Russian church and Mairie of Sixth Arrondissement. July–September: guests of Mme. Errazuriz at Biarritz. November 9: Apollinaire dies.

1919 April/May: Joan Miró calls on him in Paris. Summer: with Olga at St.-Raphaël.

1920 February 22: Kahnweiler back to Paris after wartime exile. May 15: première of *Pulcinella* at Paris Opéra, sets and costumes by Picasso. Summer: with Olga at Juan-les-Pins. September: Kahnweiler's Galerie Simon opens, 29 *bis* Rue d'Astorg.

1921 First Maurice Raynal Picasso monograph published in Munich (appears in Paris a year later). February 4: birth of son Paul (Paulo), in Paris. May 22: première of *Cuadro flamenco,* sets and costumes by Picasso, in Paris (then London). May 30: alien-property sale of Uhde collection. June 1: first Kahnweiler alien-property sale. Summer: with Olga and Paulo at Fontainebleau.

1922 Illustrates Cocteau's *Le Secret professionnel* and Reverdy's *Cravates de chanvre.* June: paints backdrop for Diaghilev's *Afternoon of a Faun.* Summer: with Olga and Paulo at Dinard. December 20: Cocteau's *Antigone* opens at Théâtre de l'Atelier, set by Picasso. Rejects André Breton's invitation to serve on committee for a Revolutionary Salon.

1923 May 19: first major interview: "Picasso Speaks," *The Arts,* New York City. July 6: Dada soirée: "Picasso dead on the field of honor." Summer: mother, Doña María, visits with them at Cap d'Antibes.

1924 April: show at Paul Rosenberg Gallery, Paris. June 18: première of *Mercure,* drop curtain, sets, and costumes by Picasso. June 20: première of *Le Train bleu,* drop curtain by Picasso. Most of the Surrealists join in "Tribute to Picasso" in the press. Summer: at Juan-les-Pins, with Olga and Paulo.

1925 March–April: Monte Carlo, with Olga and Paulo. Couturier-collector Jacques Doucet buys *Les Demoiselles d'Avignon* for 25,000 francs. Summer: Juan-les-Pins, with Olga and Paulo. November: first Surrealist exhibition at Galerie Pierre, Picasso participating.

1926 January: Christian Zervos launches *Cahiers d'Art,* beginning long friendly association. Temporarily "joins" Surrealists. Summer: Juan-les-Pins, with Olga and Paulo. October: visit to Barcelona. October 19: *La Publicidad* publishes "Conversation with Picasso," uncomplimentary statement causing break with Cocteau.

1927 January 11: meets Marie-Thérèse Walter. July: show at Paul Rosenberg's, Paris. Summer: Cannes, with Olga and Paulo. October: 1906 gouache *Harlequin Family* sold for 52,500 francs.

1928 Summer: Dinard with Olga and Paulo; also secretly with Marie-Thérèse. November 27: Tériade publishes "Visit with Picasso" in *L'Intransigeant*.

1929 Spring: Salvador Dali makes first visit. Summer: Dinard. Museum of Modern Art founded, New York City.

1930 March: Aragon's *La Peinture au défi* prefaces collage show at Galerie Goëmans, Paris. René Gimpel buys Blue Period *Blind Man* for Toledo Museum, 110,000 francs. Marie-Thérèse moves to nearby 44 Rue La Boétie.

1931 January–May: "Abstractions of Picasso" at Valentine Gallery, New York City; "Thirty Years of Pablo Picasso," Alex. Reid & Lefevre, London. Summer: Juan-les-Pins. 13 etchings, 67 drawings for Balzac's *Le Chef-d'oeuvre inconnu.*

1932 January 16: joins in protest against Aragon's indictment for inciting military to disobedience. June: retrospective at Georges Petit's, Paris, and Kunsthaus, Zurich. Buys Château de Boisgeloup. Zervos begins publishing monumental *catalogue raisonné.* October: City of Barcelona buys part of Luis Plandiura collection, including early Picassos.

1933 Does sculptures, assisted by Julio Gonzalez, Paris and Boisgeloup. May 25: first issue of Tériade-Skira *Minotaure,* with Breton study of Picasso's sculpture. August 18–25: Barcelona, with Olga and Paulo.

1934 August–September: Spain with Olga and Paulo (San Sebastian, Burgos, Madrid, Toledo, Saragossa, final brief stop in Barcelona). Winter: Lengthy Zervos interviews, for 1935 *Cahiers d'Art.*

1935 Spring: *papiers collés* show at Galerie Pierre, introduction by Tzara. June–July: Olga leaves him, taking Paulo; divorce proceedings started, but dropped. July 13: invites Sabartés to come live with him. October 5: María de la Concepción (Maya), his daughter, born to Marie-Thérèse. Start of friendship with Éluard. November 13: Sabartés arrives to join him at Rue La Boétie. First Marie Cuttoli drapes woven from Picasso subjects.

1936 January/February: meets Dora Maar. February 17: Éluard talk on Picasso, Barcelona. February 18: Picasso show opens at Sala Esteva, later to Madrid and Bilbao. March 31: show of 1931–1933 works opens at Paul Rosenberg's. March 25–May 14: Juan-les-Pins with Marie-Thérèse and Maya, prior to their settling at Le Tremblay-sur-Mauldre. July 14–23: Romain Rolland's *14 Juillet,* Alhambra, Paris, Picasso drop curtain. July 18: start of Spanish Civil War. Summer: Mougins, with the Ramiés and Éluard. *Minotaur Running* tapestry woven at Gobelins. Fall–Winter: often with Marie-Thérèse at Le Tremblay (until 1940).

1937 Moves to 7 Rue des Grands-Augustins; engraves *Dream and Lie of Franco.* Dora Maar gets Sabartés to move out. April 26: bombing of Guernica. May: begins *Guernica,* for Spanish Pavilion, Paris World's Fair (June–October). June: France buys *Still Life with Pitcher,* 56,500 francs; national museums spurn it after he urges replacement with something worthier. Break with Sabartés. July 18: anti-Franco statement printed in *Springfield* (Mass.) *Republican* on anniversary of Civil War. "Masters of Independent Art," Petit Palais, Paris, 32 Picassos. Summer: Mougins, with Dora and Éluards. Mid-September: Paris. October: Switzerland, sees Paul Klee. December 18: *New York Times* prints his call to American Artists' Congress, urging aid for Spain.

1938   April: reconciliation with Sabartés. Summer: Mougins; visits Matisse in Nice. October: Brassaï photo-story in his studio for *Life*. Switzerland with Zervoses. December: in bed several weeks with severe sciatica attack.

1939   January 13: mother dies in Barcelona. Multiple shows throughout world: 6 in New York, others London, Chicago, Los Angeles, Paul Rosenberg Paris gallery. Early July: Antibes, in apartment lent by Man Ray. July 22: Ambroise Vollard dies; to Paris from Antibes for funeral. Summer: "Picasso: Forty Years of His Art," Museum of Modern Art, New York, then at Art Institute, Chicago (1940). August 25: Paris with Dora, two days after Nazi-Soviet Non-Aggression Pact. September 1: with Dora, Sabartés and *amie,* and Kazbek, motors to Royan, where Marie-Thérèse and Maya already on vacation; juggles two-household situation. September 3: start of World War II; shortly quick trip to Paris with Sabartés. During "phony war" (to following spring), French soldiers billeted at Boisgeloup destroy or mutilate his sculptures.

1940   Early January: takes apartment in Royan, apart from both women. February 5–29: trip to Paris. Mid-March: to Paris again, with Dora, until Germans arrive. April 19: show at Yvonne Zervos' M.A.I. Gallery, Paris. May 16: with Dora, return to Royan. June 12: Kahnweiler leaves Paris, fleeing Nazis. August 15: with Sabartés, leaves Royan for Paris; Marie-Thérèse and Maya follow shortly, move into Boulevard Henri-IV. Fall: in his presence, Germans inventory his works in Paris bank vaults. To 1944: many exhibits in United States during war, number of books about him appear.

1941   January 14–17: writes *Desire Caught by the Tail.*

1942   February: with Kahnweiler in hiding in provinces, his sister-in-law, Louise Leiris, takes over the gallery. June 6: Vlaminck violently attacks Picasso in *Comoedia,* answered following week by André Lhote; number of artists protest Vlaminck attack. Fall: 31 etchings for Buffon's *Histoire naturelle.*

1943   May: meets Françoise Gilot. Anti-Semitic restrictions increase; Max Jacob forced to don yellow star; some "collaborators" call Picasso a Jew. Entertains his friends at restaurant Le Catalan; Gestapo visits his studio. August 11: with Cocteau, attends Soutine's Jewish funeral.

1944   March 5: Max Jacob dies at Drancy detention camp. March 19: private staging of *Desire* at Leirises'. June 6: Anglo-American troops land in Normandy. August 19: start of Paris uprising; takes refuge at Marie-Thérèse's. August 25: Liberation of Paris; returns to studio, which becomes a "Resistance" focal point and favorite GI attraction. October 5: joins French Communist Party. October 7: Salon d'Automne de la Libération opens, with 74 Picassos. Demonstrations against his work at Salon. October 24: *New Masses,* New York, publishes statement on why he became Communist (fuller version in *L'Humanité,* Paris, October 29–30). November 2: takes part in memorial to Resistance dead at Père-Lachaise Cemetery. Winter: Françoise works in his studio.

1945   March 4: *New Masses* publishes Jerome Seckler interview, "Picasso Explains." Mid-March: Joins Françoise at Golfe-Juan; visit to Matisse. May: first (Resistance-born) Salon de Mai. May 11: André Malraux visits him. June 15: Picasso drop curtain for *Rendezvous* at Ballets Roland Petit. Recent work shown at Galerie Louis Carré. Summer: to Cap d'Antibes with Dora Maar; temporary break with Françoise. November 2: sets up shop at Mourlot's, to do first of 200 lithographs there (to April 1949).

1946 June: second show at Galerie Louis Carré; "Picasso: Fifty Years of His Art," Museum of Modern Art, New York. July–August: Ménerbes with Françoise, then living together at Golfe-Juan. July 26: first visit to Ramiés' Galerie Madoura. September: starts working at Antibes Museum; visits Matisse.

1947 January–August: 50 lithographs done at Mourlot's; illustrates Ramon Reventos' *Dos Contes*. May 15: son, Claude, born to Françoise Gilot. Summer: Golfe-Juan, with Françoise and Claude. Starts working at Madoura works, Vallauris. Gives 11 paintings to Musée d'Art moderne, Paris. Sets for Pierre Blanchar's Paris production of *Oedipus Rex*.

1948 March: completes lithographs for Reverdy's *Chants des Morts;* 41 etchings for *Twenty Poems* by Góngora. Extensive ceramics. August 24: awarded Medal of French Gratitude. August 25: leaves for World Peace Congress at Wroclaw, fortnight in Poland. September 2: awarded commander's cross in Order of Polish Resurgence, by President of Poland. October: moves to La Galloise, Vallauris. November: Maison de la Pensée française, Paris, shows 149 Picasso ceramics.

1949 February/March: Aragon selects future *Dove of Peace*. 30 engravings for Mérimée's *Carmen*. April 19: daughter, Paloma, born to Françoise. July: 64 oils at Maison de la Pensée française.

1950 32 etchings for Aimé Césaire's *Corps perdu,* 9 lithographs for Tristan Tzara's *De mémoire d'homme*. February: named honorary citizen of Vallauris. August 6: *Man with the Sheep* unveiled on main square of Vallauris. November: awarded Lenin Peace Prize; attends World Peace Congress at Sheffield.

1951 Buys apartments at 7 Rue Gay-Lussac, Paris. January 15: begins *Massacre in Korea*. May: shown at Salon de Mai, *Massacre* gets cold reception from Communist press. Summer: Braque visits at Vallauris. October 11: Éluard talk on Picasso, London.

1952 Spring: Françoise Gilot's work exhibited at Kahnweiler's. April 28: starts preparing *War* and *Peace* for Vallauris chapel (completed later in year). Writes *Les Quatre Petites Filles*. November 18: Paul Éluard dies; attends funeral.

1953 March 12: *Les Lettres françaises* publishes his portrait of Stalin, upon latter's death, to scandalized reactions. April 9: Aragon publicly apologizes for Stalin portrait. Major exhibits at Lyons and Milan, latter moving to Rome, where Cocteau makes opening address. Luciano Emmer shoots film on Picasso. August–September: visits Lazermes at Perpignan with Maya; project for Temple of Peace at Fontfrede. Late in year, Françoise leaves him. Sets for *Chant funèbre pour Ignacio Sánchez Mejías,* French production of Lorca play. New Year's Eve party at Vallauris with Lazermes and others.

1954 Spring: meets Sylvette David and does several portraits of her. June: "Picasso 1900–1914, 1950–1954" at Maison de la Pensée française; Mme. Keller-Shchoukine loses court fight to regain works confiscated from her father by Soviets in 1917. July: visit to Perpignan. Summer: feted by Vallauris potters; to

Perpignan again, with Maya; considers settling thereabouts; Jacqueline Roque follows him there. August: to Paris with Jacqueline. Major show at São Paulo, Brazil. November 3: Matisse dies. December 13: begins *Women of Algiers.*

1955 February 11: Olga dies at Cannes. May: last visit to Perpignan and its bullfights. June–October: great official retrospective at Paris Musée des Arts décoratifs; another at Munich Haus der Kunst. Summer: Clouzot films *Le Mystère Picasso.* Buys La Californie, overlooking Cannes, main residence until 1961. October 20: Cocteau inducted into Académie française, wearing sword with Picasso-designed handle. October 23: Begins *Studios.*

1956 Shows at Rheinisches Museum, Cologne, and Kunsthalle, Hamburg. October 6–19: first post-Civil War show at Sala Gaspar, Barcelona. October 25: Madoura potters fete his 75th birthday; major exhibition in Moscow. November 22: joins 9 other Communist artists and intellectuals challenging Budapest events.

1957 Fascinated by Sputniks. May 22–September 8: "Picasso 75th Anniversary Exhibition," New York Museum of Modern Art, moving to Chicago, then Philadelphia (1958). Summer: exhibit at Reattu Museum, Arles. August 17: begins series of *Las Meninas.* UNESCO commissions mural for its Paris building. October 30–November 29: second show at Sala Gaspar, Barcelona. December 6–16: first studies for UNESCO composition. Show of 1956–1957 paintings at Galerie Louise Leiris.

1958 March 29: first viewing of UNESCO painting at Vallauris. June: paintings for Vallauris chapel finished. September: decides to buy Château de Vauvenargues. *Las Meninas* shown at Galerie Louise Leiris. November 20: Blue Period *Mother and Child* brings $150,000 in New York.

1959 February: begins to work at Vauvenargues. May: *Dutch Girl,* 1905, sold in London for £55,000. June 5: monument to Apollinaire inaugurated at St.-Germain-des-Prés. 26 aquatints, one etching for *La Tauromaquia,* by José Delgado (Pepe Illo). Summer: show at Musée Contini, Marseilles. August 10–11: first drawings for *Déjeuner sur l'herbe,* after Manet. Appears in Cocteau's *Testament of Orpheus.* Begins linoleum cuts.

1960 Spring: paints Déjeuners. October 15: starts cartoons for decoration of Barcelona College of Architects. November–December: 30 previously unshown oils at Sala Gaspar.

1961 March 2: marries Jacqueline Roque at Vallauris. June: moves to Notre-Dame-de-Vie, Mougins. Exhibit at UCLA Art Gallery, Los Angeles. October 28–29: eightieth birthday celebrated at Vallauris. December: 45 linocuts at Louise Leiris'.

1962 24 lithographs for Cocteau's *Picasso 1916–1961.* April 10: 1906 *Death of Harlequin* (1901 *Seated Woman* on back) brings £80,000 in Somerset Maugham sale, London. Awarded Lenin Peace Prize. May 14–September 18: "80th Birthday Exhibition—Picasso—The Museum Collection—Present and Future," Museum of Modern Art, New York.

1963 March 10: Picasso Museum opens, Barcelona. Paints *The Painter and His Model.* Show at Rosengart Gallery, Lucerne. August 31: Braque dies. Start of engraving teamwork with Crommelinck brothers, Mougins. October 11: Cocteau dies.

1964 January: work of past two years at Galerie Louise Leiris. Major shows, Toronto, Montreal, Tokyo, Nagoya, Kyoto.

1965 January: London Tate Gallery buys *Dance*. Summer: "Picasso and the Theatre" at Toulouse Museum. August: first public performance of *Desire* at Gassin, southern France. November 18: ulcer operation, American Hospital, Neuilly.

1966 January: Jean Leymarie named commissioner-general for planned fall retrospective in Paris. Exhibition at Helena Rubinstein Pavilion, Tel-Aviv Museum. October 25: many shows worldwide for 85th birthday. November 19: André Malraux, Minister for Cultural Affairs, inaugurates double retrospective at Grand and Petit Palais, Paris. November 26: 1906/1907 gouache *Head of Woman in Red* sold in Paris for 280,000 new francs ($56,000) and a *Demoiselle d'Avignon* for 350,000 ($70,000).

1967 January 20: 200 Catalan students and intellectuals in tribute to Picasso, despite Franco opposition. Declines French Legion of Honor. "Picasso and Concrete" at Galerie Jeanne Bucher, Paris. Evicted from Rue des Grands-Augustins studio. December: public referendum sustains purchase of two Picassos by Basel Museum.

1968 February 13: Sabartés dies. New edition of Fernand Crommelynck's *Le Cocu magnifique,* with 12 Picasso etchings and aquatints. December: 347 graphics shown at Louise Leiris'.

1969 *El Entierro del Conde de Orgaz* published in Barcelona, with one burin and 12 etchings and drypoints.

1970 January: gives Picasso Museum, Barcelona, all of his works kept by his family. May 12: Bateau-Lavoir destroyed by fire. May–October: major show at Avignon's Palace of the Popes. September 12: Christian Zervos dies. Gobelins weave *Women at Their Toilet*. October 29: Granz open letter urging creation of a Picasso museum. December 18: asks that no ceremony mark unveiling of his gift at the museum in the Calle de Montcada, Barcelona. Signs agreement with New York Museum of Modern Art about safeguarding of *Guernica*.

1971 February: gives 1912 *Guitar* to Museum of Modern Art, New York. April 23: 194 drawings at the Louise Leiris. May 25: gives 57 drawings to Arles's Reattu Museum, shown the following summer. Edition of F. de Rojas' *La Celestina,* with 66 Picasso engravings. October 25: 90th birthday; 8 canvases unveiled by French President in Grand Gallery of Louvre; Communist-sponsored celebrations at Vallauris and Paris; Franco police break up Barcelona "Tribute to Picasso," arresting several demonstrators. Named honorary citizen of Paris. Worldwide observances. October 28: 25 Soviet-owned paintings shown at Paris Musée national d'Art moderne. Lucien Clergue's film shown on French TV. November 5: extreme-right activists smash 24 "Vollard Suite" plates in a Madrid gallery.

1972 April–June: major exhibition at Tel-Aviv. Gives New York Museum of Modern Art the study for an Apollinaire monument done 30 years before. *The Drawing Lesson* sold in New York for $275,000. November 13: 1962 *Woman with Afghan Hound* brings 360,000 francs (approximately $70,000) in Paris. December 10: major show of 172 recent black-and-white and color drawings at the Louise Leiris.

1973 January: 156 recent graphics at Louise Leiris. April 1: his first (1904) etching,

The Frugal Meal, sold at Versailles for 88,000 francs. April 8: Picasso dies at Mougins. Buried April 10 at Vauvenargues, followed by grandson Pablito's attempted suicide, lingering three months before succumbing. May–September: exhibition at Avignon, Palace of the Popes. 1910 *Nude* bought by Ailsa Bruce Mellon Foundation for National Gallery, Washington, at reputed $1,000,000. July: 1901 *Death* sold in London for equivalent of $55,000. September: Jacqueline sees Malraux at Mougins and shows him through Vauvenargues. October: 1906 *Young Man with Bouquet* brings $720,000 in New York. November: 100 prints (1930–1937) at Galerie Guiot, Paris. December 5: 1909 *Seated Woman* goes for £340,000 ($800,000), London. December: "A Picasso Collection" (belonging to Marie-Thérèse Walter) shown at Krugier Gallery, Geneva.

1974 French government accepts Picasso bequest (including works by Le Nain, Chardin, Corot, Renoir, Braque, Miró, Gris, Degas, and others), although some attributions are questioned. February 28: a deranged painter discolors *Guernica* in New York. March: the three children by Marie-Thérèse and Françoise are recognized as legal heirs to their father's estate. April 9: 1910 *Woman with Mandolin* brings £273,000 (about $600,000) in London. October: Spanish government appoints committee of lawyers to investigate repatriation of *Guernica*. October–December: 67 watercolors, drawings, and gouaches (1897–1972) at Sala Gaspar, Barcelona.

1975 Barcelona decides to buy third Calle de Montcada mansion, adjoining first two, to accommodate all of youthful works, have room for eventual bequests, and install an information center. January 25: Michel Guy, French Secretary of State for Culture, announces creation of Picasso Museum in the Salé Building, Paris, by agreement with Jacqueline; the heirs lodge protest, since inventory has not been completed or legacies determined; Jacqueline states formally through her lawyer that she has not "made the slightest commitment concerning future gifts." March 27: Paris City Council confirms creation of the Picasso Museum. November 20: Francisco Franco dies. December 1: in reply to a printed suggestion that *Guernica* be returned to Spain, William Rubin, Director of Painting and Sculpture, Museum of Modern Art, writes to *The New York Times*: "Picasso made crystal-clear on a number of occasions through the years, indeed confirmed to me in person not long before his death, that 'Guernica' should be sent to Spain only when a genuine Spanish republic has been restored."

1977 Picasso estate reported finally valued at $240 million, with inheritance agreed upon among his widow Jacqueline, his children Maya, Claude, and Paloma, and the estate of his late son Paulo.

A SELECTIVE
BIBLIOGRAPHY

(*Translator's Note:* Any attempt at an exhaustive Picasso Bibliography would require a volume almost as large as the present book itself. This list covers the principal works referred to by the author, plus a few titles offering additional details, especially as available to American readers.)

ALBERTI, RAFAEL. *Los Ocho Nombres de Picasso y No digo más que lo que no digo (1966–1970)*. Barcelona: Ed. Kairós, 1970.

———. *Picasso en Avignon*. Paris: Éditions du Cercle d'Art, 1971. (Translated from the Spanish by Georges Franck; French and Spanish texts.)

APOLLINAIRE, GUILLAUME. "Les Commencements du cubisme." *Le Temps*, Paris, Oct. 14, 1912.

———. *Les Peintres cubistes*. Paris: Figuière, 1913. *The Cubist Painters*. New York: Wittenborn, Schultz, 1944. (Translated by Lionel Abel; 2nd rev. ed., 1949. Bibliographical notes on Apollinaire and Cubism.)

———. *Le Poète assassiné*. Paris: L'Édition, 1916; Gallimard, 1937. *The Poet Assassinated*. New York: Broom, 1923. (Translated by Matthew Josephson.) Holt, Rinehart, & Winston, 1968. (Translated by Ron Padgett.)

ARAGON, LOUIS. *La Peinture au défi*. Paris: Corti, 1930.

ARTS, THE. See: De Zayas, Marius.

BARON, JACQUES. *L'An I du surréalisme*. Paris: Denoël, 1969.

BARR, ALFRED H., JR. *Picasso: 50 Years of His Art*. New York: Museum of Modern Art, 1946.

BAZIN, GERMAIN. See: Huyghe, René.

BEATON, CECIL. *The Happy Years*. London: Weidenfeld & Nicolson, 1972. As: *Memoirs of the 40's*. New York: McGraw-Hill, 1972.

BERGER, JOHN. *The Success and Failure of Picasso*. Harmondsworth and Baltimore: Penguin, 1965.

BLUNT, ANTHONY, and POOL, PHOEBE. *Picasso, The Formative Years*. Greenwich, Conn.: New York Graphic Society, 1962.

BOECK, WILHELM, and SABARTÉS, JAIME. *Picasso*. New York: Abrams, 1955.

BOLLIGER, HANS. See: Geiser, Bernhard; Leonhard, Kurt.

BOUDAILLE, GEORGES. *Carnet de La Californie*. Paris: Éditions du Cercle d'Art, 1960. *Picasso Sketchbook*. New York: Abrams, 1960.

———, and DOMINGUÍN, LUIS MIGUEL. *Toros y toreros*. New York: Abrams, 1961. (Translated by Edouard Roditi; English and Spanish texts.)

———. See: Daix, Pierre.

BRASSAÏ [JULES HALASZ or GYULA HALÁSZ]. *Conversations avec Picasso*. Paris: Gallimard, 1964. *Picasso and Company*. Garden City, N.Y.: Doubleday, 1966. (Translated by Francis Price; preface by Henry Miller; introduction by Roland Penrose.)

———. See: Kahnweiler, Daniel Henry.

BRETON, ANDRÉ. *Le Surréalisme et la peinture*. Paris: Nouvelle Revue française, 1928; New York: Brentano's, 1945 (new and enlarged edition). See also: Révolution surréaliste, La.

CABANNE, PIERRE. *L'Épopée du cubisme*. Paris: La Table Ronde, 1963.

CAHIERS D'ART. Paris. Special issues: Picasso, 3-5, 1932; 7-10, 1935; "Guernica," 4-5, 1937; Picasso, 3-10, 1938; 15-19, 1940–1944; "Guernica," 1947; Picasso, 1, 1948. See: Jacob, Max; Zervos, Christian.

CAMÓN AZNAR, JOSÉ. *Picasso y el cubismo*. Madrid: Espasa-Calpe, 1956.

CARASSO, ROBERTA. "The Published French and Spanish Writings of Pablo Picasso, with English Translations." Unpublished M.A. thesis, Hunter College, New York City. In Library of Museum of Modern Art, New York City.

CASSOU, JEAN. *Picasso*. Paris and New York: Hyperion Press, 1940. (Translated by Mary Chamot.)

———, ed. *Le Pillage par les Allemands des oeuvres d'art et des bibliothèques appartenant à des juifs en France*. Paris: Éditions du Centre, 1947.

CASTLEMAN, RIVA. See: Rubin, William.

CHICAGO, ART ISTITUTE OF. *Picasso in Chicago*. Chicago: Art Institute, 1968.

CIRLOT, JUAN-EDUARDO. *Picasso: Birth of a Genius*. New York: Praeger, 1972. (Foreword by Juan Ainaud de Lasarte.)

COCTEAU, JEAN. *Ode à Picasso*. Paris: Bernouard, 1919.

———. *Picasso*. Paris: Stock, 1923.

———. *Le Rappel à l'ordre*. Paris: Stock, 1926. *A Call to Order*. London: Faber & Gwyer, 1927; New York: Henry Holt & Co., 1927. (Translated by Rollo H. Myers.)

———. "Angel Wuthercut," translated by Harold J. Salemson, in: *The European Caravan*, Samuel Putnam, ed. New York: Brewer, Warren & Putnam, 1931.

———. *La Corrida du premier mai*. Paris: Grasset, 1957.

———. *Picasso 1916–1961*. Paris, 1962.

———. *Entre Picasso et Radiguet* (presented by André Fraigneau). Paris: Hermann, 1967.

———. *My Contemoparies* (translated, edited, and introduced by Margaret Crosland). Philadelphia: Chilton, 1968.

———. *Professional Secrets*, an autobiography drawn from his lifetime writings, by Robert Phelps; translation by Richard Howard. New York: Farrar, Straus & Giroux, 1970.

COOPER, DOUGLAS DUNCAN. *Le Carnet catalan*. Paris: Berggruen, 1958.

———. *Pablo Picasso, "Les Déjeuners."* Paris: Éditions du Cercle d'Art, 1962.

———. *Picasso théâtre*. Paris: Éditions du Cercle d'Art, 1967. *Picasso Theatre*. New York: Abrams, 1968.

CRÉMIEUX, FRANCIS. See: Kahnweiler, Daniel Henry.

DAIX, PIERRE. *Picasso*. Paris, Somogy, 1964. *Picasso*. New York: Praeger, 1965.

———, and BOUDAILLE, GEORGES. *Picasso 1900–1906: Catalogue raisonné de l'oeuvre peint.* Neuchâtel: Ides et Calendes, 1966. *Picasso: The Blue and Rose Periods.* Greenwich, Conn.: New York Graphic Society, 1967 (compiled with the collaboration of Joan Rosselet).

DALI, SALVADOR. See: Parinaud, André.

DANZ, LOUIS. *Personal Revolution and Picasso.* New York: Longmans, Green, 1941; Haskell House, 1974.

DE ZAYAS, MARIUS, Interviewed by. "Picasso Speaks." *The Arts,* New York, May 1923.

DOMINGUÍN, LUIS MIGUEL. See: Boudaille, Georges.

DOR DE LA SOUCHÈRE, ROMUALD. *Picasso in Antibes.* London: Lund, Humphries, 1960. (Translated by W. J. Strachan.)

DOCUMENTS (magazine). "Hommage à Picasso," special Picasso issue. Vol. 2, No. 3, Paris, 1930.

DUBOIS, ANDRÉ-LOUIS. *Sous le signe de l'amitié.* Paris, Plon, 1972.

DUNCAN, DAVID DOUGLAS. *The Private World of Pablo Picasso.* New York: Harper, 1958.

————. *Picasso's Picassos.* New York: Harper & Row, 1961; revised, abridged edition, Ballantine, 1968.

ÉLUARD, PAUL. *À Pablo Picasso.* Geneva and Paris: Éditions des Trois Collines, 1944. *Pablo Picasso.* New York: Philosophical Library, 1947. (Translated by Joseph T. Shipley.)

————. See: Sabartés, Jaime.

FERMIGIER, ADRÉ. *Picasso.* Paris: Le Livre de poche, 1969.

GEISER, BERNHARD. *Picasso, peintre-graveur,* 2 vols. I. Berne: Chez l'auteur, 1933; II. Berne: Kornfelt et Klipstein, 1955.

————. *L'OEuvre gravé de Picasso.* Lausanne: Guilde du livre, 1955. (Translated by Gustave Roud; documentation by Hans Bolliger.)

GILOT, FRANÇOISE, and LAKE, CARLTON. *Life with Picasso.* New York: McGraw-Hill, 1964. *Vivre avec Picasso.* Paris: Calmann-Lévy, 1965.

GEORGES-MICHEL, MICHEL. *De Renoir à Picasso: Les Peintres que j'ai connus.* Paris: Fayard, 1954. *From Renoir to Picasso: Artists I Have Known.* London: Gollancz, 1957. (Translated by Dorothy and Randolph Weaver.)

GIMPEL, RENÉ. *Journal d'un collectionneur.* Paris. Calmann-Lévy, 1963. (Preface by Jean Guéhenno.) *Diary of an Art Dealer.* New York: Farrar, Straus & Giroux, 1966. (Translated by John Rosenberg; introduction by Sir Herbert Read.)

GOLDING, JOHN. See: Penrose, Roland.

HUYGHE, RENÉ, ed. (in collaboration with Germain Bazin). *Histoire de l'art contemporain.* Paris: Alcan, 1935; New York: Arno (reprint), 1968.

JACOB, MAX. "Souvenirs sur Picasso," *Cahiers d'Art,* Paris, 6, 1927.

————. *Chronique des temps héroïques.* Paris, 1956.

JANIS, HARRIET and SIDNEY. *Picasso: The Recent Years, 1939–1946.* Garden City, N.Y.: Doubleday, 1946.

JUNG, CARL G. "Picasso" [psychoanalyzed]. *Neue Zürcher Zeitung,* Zurich, Switzerland, 13, 1932.

JOHNSON, ELAINE L. See: Rubin, William.

KAHNWEILER, DANIEL-HENRY. *Der Weg zum Kubismus*. Munich: Delphin-Verlag, 1920 [under pseudonym of Daniel Henry]. *The Rise of Cubism*. New York: Wittenborn, Schultz, 1949. (Translated by Henry Aronson.)

————. *Juan Gris*. Paris, 1946. *Gris, His Life and Work*. New York: Curt Valentin, 1947; Abrams, 1969. (Translated by Douglas Cooper.)

————. *Les Sculptures de Picasso:* Paris: Éditions du Chêne, 1948. (Photos by Brassaï.) *The Sculptures of Picasso*. London: R. Phillips, 1949. (Translated by A. D. B. Sylvester.)

————. *Confessions esthétiques*. Paris: Gallimard, 1963.

————. See: Raymond, Marcel.

————, with CRÉMIEUX, FRANCIS. *Mes galeries et mes peintres*. Paris: Gallimard, 1961. *My Galleries and Painters*. London: Thames and Hudson, and New York: Viking Press, 1971. (Translated by Helen Weaver; introduction by John Russell.)

LAKE, CARLTON. See: Gilot, Françoise.

LARREA, JUAN. *Guernica* (with photographs by Dora Maar). New York: Curt Valentin, 1947. (Translated by Alexander H. Krappe, and edited by Walter Pach; introduction by Alfred H. Barr, Jr.)

LA SOUCHÈRE, ROMUALD DOR DE. See: Dor de La Souchère, Romuald.

LAUDE, JEAN. *La Peinture française (1905–1914) et "l'art nègre."* 2 vols. Paris: Klincksieck, 1968.

LÉAUTAUD, PAUL. See: Olivier, Fernande.

LEONHARD, KURT, and BOLLIGER, HANS. *Picasso: Recent Etchings, Lithographs, and Linoleum Cuts*. New York: Abrams, 1967. (Translated by Norbert Guterman.)

LEYMARIE, JEAN. *Picasso, métamorphoses et unité*. Geneva: Skira, 1971. *Picasso: The Artist of the Century*. London: Macmillan, 1972. (Designed and edited by Albert Skira; translated by James Emmons.)

LIFE (magazine). "Picasso," special double issue. Vol. 65, No. 26. New York, December 27, 1968.

MAAR, DORA. See: Larrea, Juan.

MALRAUX, ANDRÉ. *La Tête d'obsidienne*. Paris: Gallimard, 1974. *Picasso's Mask*. New York: Holt, Rinehart and Winston, 1976. (Translated and annotated by June Guicharnaud with Jacques Guicharnaud.)

MARINELLO, JUAN. *Picasso, sin tiempo*. Havana: Ucar, García y cia, 1942.

MOURLOT, FERNAND. *Picasso lithographe*. Monte Carlo: A. Sauret, 1949 (preface by Jaime Sabartés, translated from the Spanish by Geneviève Laporte). *Picasso Lithographs*. Boston: Boston Book and Art Publisher, 1970. (Translated by John Didry.)

NOUVELLE CRITIQUE, LA (magazine). Special issue, Paris, November 1961.

O'HIGGINS, PATRICK. *Madame*. New York: Viking Press, 1971.

OLIVIER, FERNANDE. *Picasso et ses amis*. Paris: Stock, 1933 (abridged from her articles in *Le Mercure de France*, 1931). (Preface by Paul Léautaud.) *Picasso and His Friends*. London: Heineman, 1964; New York: Appleton-Century, 1965. (Translated by Jane Miller.)

PALAU I FABRE, JOSEP. *Picasso en Cataluña*. Barcelona: Ediciones Polígrafa, 1967.

————. *Vides de Picasso*. Barcelona: Gràfica Bachs, 1962.

PARINAUD, ANDRÉ. *Comment on devient Dali: Les Aveux inavouables de Salvador Dali.*

Paris: Robert Laffont, 1973. *The Unspeakable Confessions of Salvador Dali.* New York: Wm. Morrow & Co., 1976. (Translated by Harold J. Salemson.)

PARMELIN, HÉLÈNE. *Picasso sur la place.* Paris: Julliard, 1959. *Picasso Plain.* London: Secker & Warburg; New York: St. Martin's Press, 1963. (Translated by Humphrey Hare.)

————. *Secrets d'alcôve d'un atelier.* 3 vols. Paris: Éditions du Cercle d'Art, 1964, 1965, 1966. *Picasso: The Artist and His Model.* New York: Abrams, 1965. *Picasso: Women, Cannes and Mougins, 1954–1963.* Paris: Éd. du Cercle d'Art, 1964. (Translated by Humphrey Hare; introductory comments by Milton S. Fox.) *Picasso at Notre Dame de Vie.* New York: Abrams, 1966.

————. *Picasso dit . . .* Paris: Gonthier, 1966. *Picasso Says . . .* London: Allen & Unwin, 1969. (Translated by Christine Trollope.)

PELLICER, ALEJANDRO CIRICI. *Picasso antes de Picasso.* Barcelona: Iberia, 1946. *Picasso avant Picasso.* Geneva: P. Cailler, 1950. (Translated from the Spanish by Marguerite de Floris and Ventura Gosol.)

PENROSE, ROLAND. *Portrait of Picasso.* New York: Museum of Modern Art, 1956 (revised and enlarged edition, 1971).

————. *Picasso: His Life and Work.* London: Victor Gollancz, 1958; New York: Schocken, 1962 (reprinted 1966).

————. *The Eye of Picasso.* New York: New American Library, with UNESCO, 1967.

————. *The Sculpture of Picasso.* New York: Museum of Modern Art, 1967. (Chronology by Alicia Legg.)

————, and GOLDING, JOHN, eds. *Picasso in Retrospect.* New York: Praeger, 1973.

PICASSO, PABLO. *Le Carnet catalan.* See: Cooper, Douglas Duncan.

————. *Carnet de La Californie.* See: Boudaille, Georges.

————. *Le Désir attrapé par la queue.* Translated by Bernard Frechtman, as: *Desire.* New York: Philosophical Library, 1948; and by Herma Briffault as: "Desire Trapped by the Tail," in: *New World Writing* (Second Mentor Selection). New York: New American Library, November 1952.

————. *Writings by.* See: Carasso, Roberta; Transition Forty-Nine.

PICON, GAËTAN. *La Chute d'Icare de Pablo Picasso.* Geneva, 1971.

POOL, PHOEBE. See: Blunt, Anthony.

RAYMOND, MARCEL. *De Baudelaire au surréalisme.* Paris: R.-A. Corrêa, 1933. *From Baudelaire to Surrealism.* New York: Wittenborn, Schultz, 1950; London: Methuen, 1970. (Appendix: "Mallarmé and Painting," by Daniel Henry Kahnweiler.)

RAYNAL, MAURICE. *Picasso, Biographical and Critical Studies.* Geneva: Skira, 1953. (Translated by James Emmons.)

————. *Anthologie de la peinture française de 1906 à nos jours.* Paris: Éditions Montaigne, 1927. *Modern French Painters.* New York: Brentano's, 1928.

REALISMO (magazine). Special Picasso issue, Rome, March–April 1953.

REVERDY, PIERRE. *Pablo Picasso.* Paris: Nouvelle Revue française, 1924.

RÉVOLUTION SURRÉALISTE, LA (magazine). "Le Surréalisme et la peinture" by André Breton, July 1925.

RICHARDSON, JOHN. *Pablo Picasso, Watercolours and Gouaches.* London: Barrie & Rockcliff, 1964.

RILKE, RAINER MARIA. "Elegy No. 5" in *Duineser Elegien.* Leipzig: Insel-Verlag, 1923. *Duino Elegies,* translated by J. B. Leishman and Stephen Spender. New York: W. W. Norton, 1939.

ROLLAND, ANDRÉE. *Picasso et Royan, aux jours de la guerre et de l'occupation.* Royan: Imprimerie Nouvelle, 1967.

ROY, CLAUDE. *Picasso: La Guerre et la Paix.* Paris: Éditions du Cercle d'Art, 1954.

RUBIN, WILLIAM. *Picasso in the Collection of the Museum of Modern Art.* New York and Greenwich, Conn.: Museum of Modern Art–New York Graphic Society, 1972. (Additional texts by Elaine L. Johnson and Riva Castleman.)

SABARTÉS, JAIME. *Picasso. Portraits et souvenirs.* Paris: Louis Carré et Maximilien Vox, 1946. *Picasso, An Intimate Portrait.* New York: Prentice-Hall, 1948. (Translated by Angel Flores.)

———. *Picasso: Documents iconographiques.* Geneva: P. Cailler, 1954. (Translated from the Spanish by Félia Leal and Alfred Rosset.)

———. *Picasso, "Les Ménines" et la vie.* Paris: Éditions du Cercle d'Art, 1958. (Translated by Alfred Rosset.) As: Pablo Picasso. *Variations on Velazquez' Painting "The Maids of Honor" and Other Recent Works* (with a personal reflection by Jaime Sabartés). New York: Abrams, 1959.

———. *A los toreros avec Picasso.* Monte Carlo: André Sauret, 1961. *Picasso: Toreros.* New York: Braziller, 1961.

———. See: Boeck, Wilhelm.

———, ÉLUARD, PAUL, and SIMA, MICHEL. *Picasso à Antibes.* Paris: R. Drouin, 1948. (Photos by Michel Sima, with commentary by Paul Éluard, and introduction by Jaime Sabartés.)

SACHS, MAURICE. *The Decade of Illusion, 1918–1928.* New York: Knopf, 1933. (Translated by Gwladys Matthews Sachs.) *La Décade de l'illusion.* Paris: Gallimard, 1950.

———. *Au temps du Boeuf sur le toit.* Paris: Nouvelle Revue critique, 1939 (reissued 1949). (Foreword by André Fraigneau.)

———. *Le Sabbat.* Paris: Corrêa, 1946. *Day of Wrath.* London: Barker, 1953. (Translated by Robin King.) As: *Witches' Sabbath.* New York: Stein & Day, 1964. (Translated by Richard Howard.)

SALMON, ANDRÉ. *Histoire anecdotique du cubisme.* Paris, 1912.

———. *La Négresse du Sacré-coeur.* Paris: Nouvelle Revue française, 1920. *The Black Venus.* New York: Macaulay, 1929. (Translated by Slater Brown.)

SIMA, MICHEL. See: Sabartés, Jaime.

SPIES, WERNER. *Picasso, das plastische Werk.* Stuttgart: Verlag Gerd Hatje, 1971. *Picasso Sculpture.* London: Thames and Hudson, 1972. (Translated by J. Maxwell Brownjohn.)

STAROBINSKI, JEAN. *Portrait de l'artiste en saltimbanque.* Geneva: Skira, 1970.

STEIN, GERTRUDE. *The Autobiography of Alice B. Toklas.* New York: Harcourt, Brace, 1933.

———. *Everybody's Autobiography.* New York: Random House, 1937.

———. *Picasso.* Paris: Floury, 1938; New York: Scribners, and London: Botsford, 1939; Boston: Beacon, 1959.

————. *Gertrude Stein on Picasso.* New York: Liveright, 1970. (Edited by Edward Burns; afterword by Leon Katz and Edward Burns; published in cooperation with the Museum of Modern Art.)

STRAVINSKY, IGOR. *Chroniques de ma vie.* 2 vols. Paris: Denoël et Steele, 1935. *Chronicle of My Life.* London: Gollancz, 1936.

TOKLAS, ALICE B. See: Stein, Gertrude.

TRANSITION FORTY-NINE (magazine). Pablo Picasso: "Poems." Pp. 14-17, No. 5, 1949, Paris.

UHDE, WILHELM. *Picasso et la tradition française.* Paris: Éditions des Quatre Chemins, 1928. *Picasso and the French Tradition.* Paris: 4 Chemins, and New York: Weyhe, 1929.

VALLENTIN, ANTONINA. *Pablo Picasso.* Paris: Club des éditeurs, 1957. *Picasso.* New York: Doubleday, 1963.

VERVE (magazine). Special Picasso issue. Paris, 1935.

VOLLARD, AMBROISE. *Recollections of a Picture Dealer.* London: Constable; Boston: Little, Brown, 1936. (Translated by Violet M. Macdonald from the original manuscript; first publication in any language.) *Souvenirs d'un marchand de tableaux.* Paris: Albin Michel, 1937 (reprinted, 1948).

WARNOD, JEANINE. *Washboat Days.* New York: Grossman, 1972. (Translated by Carol Green.)

WEILL, BERTHE. *Pan! dans l'oeil! (ou Trente ans dans les coulisses de la peinture contemporaine, 1900–1930).* Paris: Lipschutz, 1933.

ZAYAS, MARIUS DE. See: De Zayas, Marius.

ZERVOS, CHRISTIAN. *Pablo Picasso, OEuvres.* Paris: Cahiers d'Art, 1932–1974.

————. "Conversation avec Picasso." *Cahiers d'Art,* Paris, 10, 1935.

INDEX

(Titles of works of art that are not fol-
lowed by the artist's name are by Picasso)